DOUBTING THOMAS?

Praises for
DOUBTING THOMAS?

"In this honest and thorough examination of Thomas Jefferson's public and private life, authors Beliles and Newcombe make a strong and persuasive case that in his critical younger years—when he drafted the Declaration of Independence and the Virginia bill for religious freedom—Jefferson was a practicing orthodox Christian. Painstakingly researched and written, the authors refute those scholars who would superimpose Jefferson's later doubts about core Christian doctrines in support of their views that religion must be separated from politics. To the contrary, as Beliles and Newcombe ably contend, Jefferson's contribution to the Declaration and the Virginia statute for religious freedom evidences the work of a Christian statesman whatever his personal belief may have been about the redemptive work of Christ at the cross. Any one who wants to know Jefferson's real contribution to religious liberty ought to read this book."

—**Herb Titus,** Founding Dean, College of Law and Government,
Regent University (1986-1993)

"The Bible's first book, Genesis, is devoted to recounting the lives of Israel's founding fathers. Any healthy nation and robust culture remembers its founders with fond admiration. Willfully corroding the history of its founders is a sign of a culture's impending extinction. To our enormous appreciation, Beliles and Newcombe compellingly correct our recollection of Thomas Jefferson. A grateful nation will thank them."

—**Rabbi Daniel Lapin**-American Alliance of Jews and Christians.

"*Doubting Thomas* is a must read book regarding one of the most frequently discussed and often misunderstood Founding Fathers of the American experiment. This book is a refreshing analysis of the faith journey of Thomas Jefferson, and the reader will find particularly helpful how the book puts Jefferson's evolving views of God and religion in historical context. A quote from the later years of Jefferson cannot be used to fully explain his views at earlier times and vice versa. What is critically important is the fact that at the time of Jefferson's life when he had the most direct impact on the founding of America and some of its organic documents, such as the Declaration of Independence and the Virginia Statute on Religious Freedom, Jefferson was a faithful churchman in the Anglican Church.

The Jefferson that groups like the ACLU often present is not the Jefferson of history. This book deals openly and honestly with one of America's key Founding Fathers. *Doubting Thomas* is no doubt be one of the most important books on the faith of Thomas Jefferson."

—**Mathew D. Staver**, *Founder and Chairman*, Liberty Counsel

"A must read regarding one of our most commonly misunderstood Founders: Thomas Jefferson. While Jefferson's life and writings are used to create the "wall of separation" between church and state, the historical truth is far more complicated. This book takes you on a fascinating journey into the mind and life of man whose ideas regarding government, faith, and liberty are still impacting our culture today. Thoroughly documented and well-written, I gladly endorse this fascinating examination of our Third President. An important book for our generation to better understand the Jeffersonian balance between God and government."

—**Attorney David C. Gibbs III**, President & General Counsel,
National Center for Life and Liberty

"Dr. Mark Beliles and Dr. Jerry Newcombe are preeminent researchers who have uncovered priceless treasures of America's heritage long buried beneath generations of complacency and ideological drift. Newcombe and Beliles' classic work, *Doubting Thomas*, is destined to be THE authoritative treatise on Jefferson's many faceted beliefs. They honestly portray Jefferson's journey of faith through its ever-evolving nuances during a time when the world was going through unprecedented political changes. Jefferson was a brilliant leader who had profound influence on America at its most formative period. By understanding Jefferson and his faith, we gain a clearer understanding of the foundations of our freedoms, and possibly discover keys to preserving them. I highly applaud and wholeheartedly recommend every American read Dr. Mark Beliles and Dr. Jerry Newcombe's book, *Doubting Thomas*."

—**William J. Federer**, Bestselling Author and Speaker

"Fascinating, well researched, and wonderfully nuanced, *Doubting Thomas* pulls back the curtain and exposes the myths about this brilliant and controversial man of fascinating faith who helped birth America, write the Declaration of Independence, and shape the way Americans think about Church and State. This is a must read for anyone who wants the *real* story of Thomas Jefferson."

—**Kirk Cameron**, Actor, Host

"Christian values influenced our government for the first 160 years of our nation's history until a misreading of Thomas Jefferson on the subject of the separation of church and state. That's why I'm pleased to recommend this new book, *Doubting Thomas?* which helps set the record straight. Although Thomas Jefferson was no evangelical Christian, he was certainly far from the ACLU's version of Jefferson portrayed today as this book so aptly demonstrates."

—**Dr Robert Jeffress**, Pastor, First Baptist Church, Dallas

"Once in a great while a book so thoroughly and even-handedly treats a controversial topic that combatants are silenced, the uninfc.med argument is banished and learning gratefully reigns. Such a book is *Doubting Thomas?* In its pages, unflagging scholarship escorts an authentically complex Thomas Jefferson to the fore. The authors allow truth to settle where it may and are unapologetic that myths flee and that scholarly malpractice is exposed before their work. We are grateful for their devotion to their craft."

—**Stephen Mansfield**, Ph.D., New York Times Best-selling Author

DOUBTING THOMAS?

*The Religious Life and Legacy
of Thomas Jefferson*

MARK A. BELILES *and*
JERRY NEWCOMBE

NEW YORK

DOUBTING THOMAS?
The Religious Life and Legacy of Thomas Jefferson

Published in New York, New York, by Morgan James Publishing. Morgan James and The Entrepreneurial Publisher are trademarks of Morgan James, LLC. www.MorganJamesPublishing.com

The Morgan James Speakers Group can bring authors to your live event. For more information or to book an event visit The Morgan James Speakers Group at www.TheMorganJamesSpeakersGroup.com.

A **free** eBook edition is available with the purchase of this print book.

CLEARLY PRINT YOUR NAME ABOVE IN UPPER CASE

Instructions to claim your free eBook edition:
1. Download the BitLit app for Android or iOS
2. Write your name in **UPPER CASE** on the line
3. Use the BitLit app to submit a photo
4. Download your eBook to any device

ISBN 978-1-63047-150-7 paperback
ISBN 978-1-63047-151-4 eBook
ISBN 978-1-63047-152-1 hardcover
Library of Congress Control Number:
2014933723

Cover Design by:
Rachel Lopez
www.r2cdesign.com

Interior Design by:
Bonnie Bushman
bonnie@caboodlegraphics.com

In an effort to support local communities, raise awareness and funds, Morgan James Publishing donates a percentage of all book sales for the life of each book to Habitat for Humanity Peninsula and Greater Williamsburg.

Get involved today, visit
www.MorganJamesBuilds.com

Habitat
for Humanity
Peninsula and
Greater Williamsburg
Building Partner

This book was made possible through a generous writing grant to the authors from the Max B. Tharpe Foundation, and it is dedicated to the memory of Max B. Tharpe (1920-2010).

Called "The Norman Rockwell of Photography," Max's desire was to glorify and please God by sharing the beauty of His creation through photography.

TABLE OF CONTENTS

Foreword

Dr. Garrett Ward Sheldon

This is a surprising and very important book. It changes our views of the religious life and attitudes of perhaps the most significant American Founder: Thomas Jefferson. As such, it commends a re-examination of our entire view of Early American Religion and Politics, past scholarship on those subjects, and the implications on our contemporary debates on Church and State.

The analysis and documentation in this volume show Jefferson as an appreciative and thoughtful student of and actor in Christianity who genuinely esteems many of the doctrines and persons associated with the Faith. His letters often show an affectionate and respectful regard for religious persons, including Catholic clergy, priests, nuns, and teachers; evangelical Protestant preachers, Calvinists and Anglicans. His sensitivity to their character and motives belies the common caricature of Jefferson as dismissive or contemptuous of religious believers. Mr. Beliles' other recent book, *Selected Religious Letters,* further confirms this positive and catholic approach of Jefferson.

I grew up and was trained with the common view of Jefferson as a secular sceptic, an Enlightenment Deist, indifferent or even hostile to organized religion, spirituality, the Church, and Christianity. We read over and over his derisive comments on "monkish ignorance," or Catholic "priestcraft"; that Calvinists were rigid, Jews "barbaric" and simple religious folk naive and ignorant. All the Liberal prejudices against faith projected onto America's premier Founder. Where did this mainstream academic attitude come from? The negative attitudes were certainly there in some of Jefferson's correspondence. But, like his equally extreme characterizations of political opponents, they were written to certain colleagues, at certain times, and so in a context that cannot be generalized. Beliles and Newcombe provide that context along with the balance of Jefferson's other, overwhelmingly positive views on religion and religious people, movements, denominations and beliefs.

Jefferson comes across in this vast wealth of material as a sensitive, intelligent, appreciative student of religious people, beliefs and institutions. He was an intelligent seeker after truth with a seriousness unseen today in public figures. His attitudes, well represented in this book's selections, shows the real breadth and depth of religious consciousness in eighteenth century America. We are grateful for the authors' careful and serious corrective of this major figure in American history and thought. This scholarship finally places religion in its proper and prominent place in Jefferson's mind and life; and in America.

—**Dr. Garrett Ward Sheldon**
The John Morton Beaty Professor of Politics,
University of Virginia College at Wise
Author, *The Political Philosophy of Thomas Jefferson*
(Johns Hopkins University Press).
Co-editor, *Religion and Political Culture in Jefferson's Virginia*
(Rowman and Littlefield Press).

PREFACE

Dr. Peter A. Lillback

Thomas Jefferson is an omnipotent American icon of liberty. He, along with a few others, has an indisputable place in the American pantheon of Founders whose life and words have shaped the destiny of the United States. His words, "the wall of separation between church and state" from a private letter to the Baptists in Danbury, Connecticut, have been essentially read into the First Amendment by Supreme Court decisions, whether one agrees with them or not.

Bur for all this American certainty about the significance of Thomas Jefferson for what George Washington called "the American experiment in the Republican form of government," there is great dispute about the worldview and religious beliefs of Jefferson. Was he St. Thomas Jefferson, or, would he be better described as Doubting Thomas Jefferson? If he was an icon of liberty, was he an icon of faith as well?

The options are boldly asserted by scholars and citizens alike on either side of the fault lines of faith that divide contemporary American life. To most on the secularist bank of the cultural rift, Jefferson was a freethinking rationalist who deeply longed for the removal of the overt expressions of faith from public life. As a doubting deist, the church and the Scriptures belonged in the private sphere of life, where they could do no harm, not in the public arena of law and government. But those who stand opposed to the secular view often assert that Jefferson's life manifested a sincere faith in Christian truth. He worshiped as President in, of all places, a public church service held in the Supreme Court's chambers in the US Capitol Building. His faith, if not fully orthodox, extolled Jesus' ethics and celebrated divine providence.

But whose view is right? The problem for those who investigate the question is to let Thomas Jefferson speak for himself. It has been all too easy to rely on secondary sources, both past and present to make one's case. A far more daunting challenge is to dig into Jefferson's voluminous writings and let his own words and his own actions speak for themselves. When this is done, the person who emerges may not fit neatly into the well worn images crafted by a long dispute over a hero that all sides wish to identify with their partisan views.

So it is with gratitude to Mark Beliles and Jerry Newcombe that I commend to you their study, *Doubting Thomas?* These authors present a careful investigation of our American hero of liberty that should be taken seriously by reader and researcher alike due to their careful analysis of original sources and cogent construction of pertinent data. Their conclusion emerges from the sources left to us by Jefferson himself. The accuracy and nuance that are found here make for a compelling case that Jefferson was a complex personality and thinker whose beliefs cannot be expressed by pat answers, knee-jerk reactions or facile explanations. Instead, the Jefferson that emerges is a multifaceted figure whose thinking grows, develops, changes, and yet all the while simultaneously holds together disparate commitments as he moves through various stages of his life.

Please read, reflect, learn and be instructed. Jefferson may well have doubted, moved and changed over time, but there is no doubt that his intellectual journey was informed by faith all along the way.

—**Dr. Peter A. Lillback**
President, Westminster Theological Seminary
President, The Providence Forum
Author with Jerry Newcombe of *George Washington's Sacred Fire*

INTRODUCTION

This book deals with a well-worn subject. The faith—or the lack thereof—of Thomas Jefferson. While much ink has already been spilled over this subject, the truth is there are some little known facts we hope to bring to light in this fresh study.

Our Personal Note

We want to make a confession of our personal beliefs about Thomas Jefferson right from the start. Neither of us wants to make Jefferson into something he was not. We do not hold the opinion that by the end of his life he would be able to give the kind of evidence for authentic faith that we would seek today of members of our congregations. We know that most evangelicals who have read biographies of Jefferson to this date probably would have the same feeling. So we honestly do not have a goal of making him one of us.

However we believe only part of the story has been told and this book presents evidence—new evidence—that most have not heard about. Although our standards lead us to think of him late in life as a closet Unitarian more than a confirmed believer, it is entirely possible that he was a committed Christian in the first half of his life. And we have to acknowledge that the pastor of his local Episcopal Church in the last seven years of his life accepted him as a member in good standing (as did Jefferson's previous pastors). These men knew him by his life without knowing his private writings.

All of this leads us to believe that Jefferson is also misunderstood and his early views all too often misrepresented which usually makes him repugnant to many Christians. The quotes that are most often repeated today are in fact things that people in his lifetime never heard from him. They were found later as unsent letters or else were sent to a few people in confidence with the understanding that they would never be published. In other words, Jefferson never attacked orthodox Christian beliefs in public—*never.*

But Christians today have an impression of him as being disrespectful of their faith. We think this is unfair to Jefferson. Scripture tells us to not bear false witness and encourages us to be respectful of others and their reputation. A Christian should be dedicated to truth whatever it may show. This has motivated us to write this book so that both Christian and secular readers will appreciate Jefferson or criticize him for what he actually did or said in the context of the time and culture in which he lived. Then at least, they will be able to accept him for what he really was—a complicated person who sincerely thought himself to be a true Christian.

Sources Used in This Book

The disputes that commonly occur today concerning Jefferson and his religious actions and beliefs often emerge because people make use of quotations that are selective, out of context, or incomplete. Perhaps on rare occasions, this is due to personal agendas or motivations to prove a preconceived perception. But more often it simply is due to the fact that many of the primary sources have only recently become available and indeed many are still not in print.

The common approach to studies on Jefferson and religion has been quote-oriented (Examples include books by Charles Sanford and Stephen Vicchio and those by Eugene Sheridan, David Barton, Warren Throckmorton and Michael Coulter).[1] Dickinson Adams and Ruth Lester went further and provided a few dozen full letters in the appendix of their edited volume of Jefferson's digest of the philosophy and morals of Jesus (erroneously but more popularly known as "The Jefferson Bible").[2]

Meanwhile, at the end of 2013 the co-author of this book Mark Beliles edited a new volume entitled *The Selected Religious Letters and Papers of Thomas Jefferson*

---

1   See Charles Sanford, *The Religious Life of Thomas Jefferson* (Charlottesville, Va.: University Press of Virginia, 1984); Stephen J. Vicchio, *Jefferson's Religion* (Eugene, Oregon: WIPF and STOCK Publishers, 2007); Edwin Gaustad, *Sworn On the Altar of God: A Religious Biography of Thomas Jefferson* (Grand Rapids, Mich.: Wm. B. Eerdmans Publishers, 1996); Eugene R. Sheridan, *Jefferson and Religion* (Chapel Hill: The University of North Carolina Press, 2002); David Barton, *The Jefferson Lies* (Nashville: Thomas Nelson Publishers, 2012); Warren Throckmorton and Michael Coulter, *Getting Jefferson Right*, (Grove City, PA: Salem Grove Press, 2012).

2   Dickinson Adams and Ruth W. Lester, eds., *Jefferson's Extracts From the Gospels* (Princeton: Princeton University Press, 1983).

that provides the ability to see most of the rest of Jefferson's religious papers.[3] To our knowledge, no book on Jefferson has included half of the religious letters and documents that are found in it. Drawing on these new sources, we have made this new analysis of Jefferson's religious life and legacy. The picture is much more nuanced than the average portrait often drawn of a uniformly skeptical Jefferson.

The Ongoing Debate on Jefferson's Religion

Co-author Mark Beliles has lived in Jefferson's hometown of Charlottesville for over 30 years and has personally gathered many diverse scholars in two symposiums on this theme held at the University of Virginia and sponsored by the Virginia Foundation for the Humanities. These included such well-known scholars such as Martin Marty, Alan Heimert, Charles S. Sanford, James Smylie, James H. Hutson, Alf J. Mapp, Thomas Buckley, Daniel L. Dreisbach, David L. Holmes, Richard D. Brown, Robert O'Neil, Ralph Ketcham, A. James Reichley, David B. Mattern, Garrett Ward Sheldon, and Monticello's chief historian Douglas L. Wilson.

Through this experience Beliles is aware that some scholars will want more lengthy quotations in context than this book, designed for a general audience, can provide. Therefore, Beliles provides more material in his other concurrent books, *Free As the Air* and *Playful in His Closet* that may satisfy those questions.

The most recent example of debate among some contemporary scholars is found in the March 2014 issue of *Church History* magazine in an article by Arthur Scherr, entitled "Thomas Jefferson Versus the Historians: Christianity, Atheistic Morality, and the Afterlife." One of his concerns is the perception that some claim Jefferson was basically a devout Christian throughout his life. The reader will not find that claim in our book. But responses of other scholars toward Scherr's article show that the debate on Jefferson and religion is not as settled a science as some might think. And none of them have seen new material from recently published letters of Jefferson that are discussed in this book.

Why This Study Matters

In addition to scholarly questions of the modern image of Jefferson on religion in public life, co-author Jerry Newcombe notes that through the years, as a producer

---

3   Other small collections of Jefferson's religious papers are found in books on the theme of church and state. Examples are *Thomas Jefferson and the Wall of Separation Between Church and State* (New York: New York University Press, 2002) by Daniel L. Dreisbach. These are helpful, but limited in scope. More is found in *Jefferson & Madison on Separation of Church and State* (Fort Lee: Barricade Books, 2004) by Lenni Brenner but still missing many important letters.

for Coral Ridge Ministries (now Truth in Action Ministries), he has covered so many stories related to discrimination against Christians because of the flawed perspective of separation of church and state. Today's "separation of church and state" is often defined as separation of religion and state. It's often defined in such ways as to essentially mean "state-sanctioned atheism"—something very different from what the founders advocated. Groups like the ACLU actively promote the "state-sanctioned atheism" version of the separation of church and state.

And so, a few years ago, Jerry interviewed an African-American woman who was kicked off a public bus in the pouring rain in the Pacific Northwest. Even though she was pregnant, she had to walk home in the driving rain. She said by the time she got home, she felt like a drowned rat. Why was she kicked off the bus? Because she was telling another passenger (who was interested) about her church. The bus driver said in effect, "You can't talk about God [because it is city property]. Get off the bus!"

Jerry remembers another story where a girl got an F on a history paper she wrote in her public high school. Initially she had permission to write about Jesus of Nazareth, but then the teacher changed her mind and disallowed it—while permitting other students to write about subjects related to other religions or the occult. And this discrimination was done because of the supposed separation of church and state.

One time in the 1990s a federal judge in Texas said to students at a graduation celebration (that was actually sponsored by a group of ministers) that if any of them prayed in the name of Jesus at that service, he would have them arrested and thrown in jail for a minimum of 6 months. The judge said, "Anyone who violates this order, no kidding, is going to wish that he or she had died as a child when this Court gets through with it."[4] Somehow we don't think this is what the founders intended—certainly not Thomas Jefferson or James Madison. Yet Jefferson is the person most often cited for the reasoning of many modern secularist advocates.

What did Thomas Jefferson himself really believe about God and the Bible? And more importantly what were his policies and actions when it comes to religion and its relation to government and education? Various groups strongly assert what they think he would have said about issues of faith and public policy. But we think there is more nuance to it and that complexity is important for us to understand. To this goal we offer this our contribution.

---

4   Judge Samuel Kent, US District Judge, Southern District of Texas, TRO Hearing held on May 5, 1995 in the case of *Doe v. Santa Fe Indep. Sch. Dist.*, 933 F.Supp. 647 (S.D. Tex. 1996).

PART I

THE RELIGIOUS LIFE OF THOMAS JEFFERSON

We the Subscribers agree to pray on the 25th day of December in the present year 1777 & so on the 25th day of December annually in every year after till we shall notify the contrary in writing to the Wardens for our Congregation, the sums affixed to our respective names, to such person or persons as by a majority of our Congregation, to be called together by the wardens for that purpose, shall from time to time be appointed to the office of clerk for the said Congregation to assist the reverend Charles Clay in performing divine service whenever he shall attend at Charlottesville for that purpose.

Th. Jefferson thirty shillings.
Jn.° Harvie twenty shillings
Randolph Jefferson ten shillings
Peter Marks Five Shillings

Jefferson's 1777 document to raise funds for the Calvinistical Reformed Church in Charlottesville led by Rev. Charles Clay. See pp. 22-25 for details. Jefferson supported Rev. Clay's ministry in part because the minister was such a strong patriot. This book contains two of Rev. Clay's sermons in print for the first time. See Appendices 4 and 5. (Courtesy of the Library of Congress).

INTRODUCTION TO
THE RELIGIOUS LIFE OF
THOMAS JEFFERSON

"…divest yourself of all bias…"[1] —Thomas Jefferson, 1787

To say that controversy surrounds the faith of Thomas Jefferson (or the lack thereof) is quite an understatement. There are potential land mines. However, co-author Mark Beliles, a pastor in Charlottesville (Jefferson's home town) has spent much of his adult career studying Jefferson and his faith. He has discovered little known facts that demonstrate that our third president was much more active as a professing Christian than is commonly understood. Moreover, Dr. Beliles has come to the conclusion: Jefferson's religion is revealed most accurately when not only his letters but also his relationships and activities with religious communities are studied together.

Thomas Jefferson built his own home near Charlottesville, Virginia and called it Monticello, meaning "little mountain" in Italian. Its architectural beauty is

---

1   "From Thomas Jefferson to Peter Carr, with Enclosure, 10 August 1787," Founders Online, National Archives (http://founders.archives.gov/documents/Jefferson/01-12-02-0021, ver. 2013-06-26). Source: *The Papers of Thomas Jefferson*, vol. 12, *7 August 1787–31 March 1788*, ed. Julian P. Boyd (Princeton: Princeton University Press, 1955), 14–19. Subsequent citations will be the letter and simply www.founders.archives.gov

obvious to the half million tourists that visit it each year. Without prompting by the tour guides, however, most visitors would never notice the mistake made in the plan for the huge clock he had installed in his home. His clock required more space for the running cannon ball weights to descend properly than the room was designed to handle. Therefore, he had to cut a hole in the floor in two corners of the room for the clock to work. There were markers for every day of the week on the wall and only those who look carefully would notice that the marker for the last day of the week does not appear because it is in the basement. But only those in Jefferson's family or more intimate friends might be taken downstairs to see the marker for Saturday. Jefferson, a master architect, had to borrow from space beneath the floor.

Jefferson's religious life was also built upon the foundation of the religious culture of Central Virginia. Like the seventh day of Jefferson's clock at Monticello, the facts for understanding his religious life are beneath the surface and not easily accessed. They are found in part in the messy and scattered fragments of history left among the Piedmont religious communities at the time. They generally are not found on the Internet. Although there has been much research concerning Jefferson and religion, a variety of scholars have noted that there has yet to be written a sufficient account of the historical context. The local religious culture of the Central Virginia Piedmont, found beneath the surface of the readily-available writings and literature about Jefferson (and his friend and colleague James Madison) is not readily seen by many historians, yet it provides the largely forgotten foundation for much of what transpired in his life. Mark Beliles' Ph.D. dissertation, *Free As the Air: Churches and Politics in Jefferson's Virginia, 1736-1836*, is a recommended resource for studying this cultural context.[2]

Sadly, Jefferson's biographers tend to ignore the local and regional religious history (which was fervently evangelical), while exaggerating his few years in France and selective quotes later in life. This practice exaggerates the time of his life when he held more of a Unitarian position on the Trinity and the Person of Christ, and this has greatly shaped his modern image. Likewise the tendency of many religiously inclined historians, both liberal and conservative, have made the same historical errors as their secular colleagues when it comes to Jefferson. They have adopted a view of Jefferson that lacks the essential historical context of his religious community.

However, many respected scholars have begun to refute long-standing beliefs that exaggerate the role of Deism and secular Enlightenment thought

---

2   See back of this book for link for more information on Beliles' dissertation.

in colonial America and the belief that America's Christian culture was only of minor significance to the Revolution. There are many variations of Deism, and its definitions vary among scholars; but the assumption of irreligion or Deism in some form has been the norm of modern historians.[3] In the book by James H. Hutson, Chief of the Manuscript Division of the Library of Congress entitled *Religion and the Founding of the American Republic*, he states that for a long time the founders were considered as "nominally Christian" and "committed to the agenda of the Enlightenment." But Hutson provocatively asserts and effectively demonstrates that, according to recent authorities, "this view is wrong."[4] Indeed, said Harvard professor Perry Miller, in America "European deism [and] rationalism…was never so widespread as liberal historians, or those fascinated by Jefferson, have imagined."[5]

In an excellent study of colonial society, Patricia Bonomi wrote that the modern historians' hypothesis of "an eighteenth century of 'Enlightenment' skepticism coming between a 'Puritan' seventeenth century and an 'evangelical' nineteenth century simply does not add up."[6] She concluded that colonial society had "a far more vital religious culture than that portrayed by conventional historiography," and that for the colonies in general "no less than some 60 percent of the adult white population attended church regularly between 1700 and 1776."[7]

Historian Rhys Isaac made invaluable contributions to understanding the vitality of religion in Jefferson's Virginia in his work *The Transformation of Virginia 1740-1790*. Harvard historian Alan Heimert has also asserted that, "America's

---

3   For representative examples of modern scholars, see the writings of Merrill Peterson, Dumas Malone, David Little, Paul Conkin, Peter Onuf, Alf Mapp, Cushing Strout, Eugene Sheridan, Charles Sanford, Edwin Gaustad, Harry Ammon, Dickinson Adams, Jan Lewis, William Lee Miller, Martin Marty, Gordon Wood, Irving Brant, James Eckenrode, Thomas J. Curry, Thomas Buckley, Leo Pfeffer, Robert Alley, Robert Rutland, Jon Butler, Mark Noll, Nathan Hatch, George Marsden. Of these scholars, Marty, Lewis, Buckley, Butler, Noll, Hatch and Marsden will argue (somewhat sympathetically) that the Deism and Enlightenment that was dominant in the founding era was overcome by evangelicalism in subsequent generations.

4   James H. Hutson, *Religion and the Founding of the American Republic* (Washington, D.C.: Library of Congress, 1998), 19. This excellent book, written to accompany an exhibit by the Library of Congress, is perhaps the best short history of the role of religion in American public life. It challenges long held assumptions and brings out much material that has been ignored elsewhere.

5   Perry Miller, *Nature's Nation* (Cambridge, Mass.: Harvard-Belknap, 1967), 110.

6   Patricia U. Bonomi, *Under the Cope of Heaven: Religion, Society, and Politics in Colonial America* (New York: Oxford University Press, 1986), 220.

7   Bonomi, 220.

true Age of Reason unfolded...more as a reaffirmation of evangelical principle than as repudiation."[8]

Holes in Jefferson's Floor

In this book, the reader will take a tour of Jefferson's basement by probing into local historical connections with Jefferson that few have ever examined. In this work references in about 1000 of Jefferson's letters and documents will serve as "holes in the floor" (i.e., clues), signaling a need to go down below and find out more than is commonly found in the standard literature. Wherever Jefferson mentions a clergyman or church or religious event, we will dig down beneath the surface of conventional historiography and gather some facts that will perhaps offer a new perspective of the religious beliefs of Jefferson and a more accurate context for understanding the policies that he championed.

This book will include significant new material that has not been included in any other works of Jefferson's religious life. To our knowledge, none of the single volume books written specifically on the topic of Jefferson and religion have examined this new material. In this book, the reader will be provided with the most complete and comprehensive treatment of Jefferson's faith—exceeding material presented in any other biography or monograph perhaps by at least twenty times. And it especially fills in data in the periods of his life prior to 1813. Most modern books draw their quotes and information from 1813 until his death in 1826 and try to say it represented his whole life. Clearly, during that last phase, Jefferson skews toward a Unitarian and unorthodox perspective on some key Christian doctrines. Yet, ironically, even at that time in his life, he was still generous toward Trinitarian Christian causes and active in Trinitarian worship services. Of the biographies of Jefferson available, the average number of clergymen or churches listed that he interacted with is between 10 and 15. Of these about half are from a Unitarian or unorthodox theological orientation. In contrast, this study will mention over 200 clergymen or churches with whom Jefferson interacted. When this major increase is included, the percentage of unorthodox correspondents is well under ten percent—a remarkable difference. There are many other religious letters that Jefferson received, from both critics and supporters, and from both evangelical Christians and Deists and skeptics. However if Jefferson did not reply they are usually left out of this study.

---

8   Alan Heimert, *Religion and the American Mind: From the Great Awakening to the Revolution* (Cambridge, Mass.: Harvard University Press, 1966), 538. Rhys Isaac, *The Transformation of Virginia 1740-1790* (Chapel Hill: University of North Carolina Press, 1982).

Previous Studies of Jefferson

The disputes that occur today concerning Jefferson and his religious actions and beliefs occur mainly because people make use of quotations that are selective or out of context. Perhaps on rare occasions this is due to personal agendas or motivations to prove a preconceived perception. In most cases, it is because scholars and writers tend to quote each other. So once the narrative of Jefferson the lifelong skeptic was written, it has been very hard to accept any evidence for Jefferson in a different way.

Indeed, Jefferson's life provides plenty of ammunition for both secularists/atheists and, surprisingly, evangelical Christians, and for both those advocating religion in public life and those advocating exclusion of all interaction between religion and government. More often than not, historians coming from these diverging viewpoints have not made an exhaustive analysis of all the religious material available.

Some of the problem is that the complete papers and correspondence of Jefferson are not available to this day. To our knowledge, the only real religious biography of Jefferson ever written was Edwin Gaustad's *Sworn On The Altar of God*. But when Gaustad wrote his book in 1996, *The Papers of Thomas Jefferson* (Princeton University Press) were only available up to 1793, so Gaustad's ability to fully evaluate the primary sources was much more limited than today. Thankfully, in this regard, much progress has been made in just the last 15 years with the publication of new volumes of Jefferson's presidential years and also of his retirement.

Also published for the first time in 1997 were *Jefferson's Memorandum Books* (i.e., Account Books).[9] These books are another vital primary source that document what he spent money on, people he knew, places he visited, that sometimes do not show up in his letters. Often fiscal actions speak louder than that what a person may profess. Through this source one finds that Jefferson was a very generous giver to a variety of Christian causes, the majority of which were orthodox. Account books also prove the existence of relationships that sometimes do not have surviving letters to those persons. Unfortunately, few biographers have used this source.[10] The account books are very helpful for giving a sense of a religious life, not just a collection of writings.

---

9   James A. Bear Jr., & Lucia C. Stanton, eds., *Jefferson's Memorandum Books: Accounts, with Legal Records and Miscellany, 1767-1826*, 2 vols. (Princeton: Princeton University Press, 1997).

10   One exception is William E. Curtis, *The True Thomas Jefferson* (Philadelphia: J. B. Lippincott Co., 1901), 339.

Furthermore, other letters became available in 2013 through the National Archives' web-based source called Founders Online. There is still much to be finished in this regard, but without a doubt, a great deal more is known today than any historian had access to before 1996.[11]

The Arrangement of the Chapters

A common problem in every topical work on Jefferson's religion is the mixing of quotes from different time periods. Often when talking about the first part of Jefferson's life, biographers mix quotes from perhaps 40 or 50 years later without bothering to tell the reader (unless they are willing to sift through the endnotes). One of the main failures of biographers and commentators is to assert that one or several quotes or actions of Jefferson at one point in his long life best represents him.

This book will attempt to show that Jefferson is very complex, changing his views, doing contradictory things, and saying things that were not technically true or accurate about himself. First will be a presentation of most of the religious facts about Jefferson in the form of five chronological chapters, so that the reader is able to see Jefferson in the context of that time. It is vital to understand the differences between Jefferson's religious opinions and activities in five distinct major stages of his life. Each of these phases is marked by a new kind of quote or action not seen previously:

1. 1763-1787, mainly orthodox statements and involvement in Trinitarian churches,
2. 1788-1802, starts with a letter in which he says he did not comprehend the Trinity,
3. 1803-1812, starts with a syllabus that organizes the moral teachings of Jesus,
4. 1813-1819, starts with a letter rejecting the Trinity and the reliability of Scripture.
5. 1820-1826, starts with his recommitment to his local Episcopal church (when it finally reopened in Charlottesville).

---

11 Now over 16,000 of Jefferson's letters can be read for the first time without having to find a major library with the printed volumes. As of early 2014 there are still 16 years of letters to be added between April 1803 and early 1809 and again from spring of 1816 to 1826, but it is a major breakthrough in accessibility. For the remainder of our book, if we cite any of these sources, we will cite www.founders.archives.gov.

These phases of his religious life are not absolute. There are some gradual tendencies and hints that can be seen virtually throughout his life, and all phases have some quotations and actions that contradict the general description assigned to that phase. After the five chronological chapters that comprise Part 1, then follows a topical or thematic approach that will bring together some of the same quotes from many time periods; but the readers will also be able to cross-check the chronological context of them if they wish. Part 2 focuses on his religious legacy presented through a chapter on each of the three most significant accomplishments Jefferson identified in an epitaph he drafted for himself (i.e., writing the Declaration of Independence and the Virginia Statute for Religious Freedom and founding the University of Virginia). Then four other major issues about Jefferson are discussed in Part 3 that are often misunderstood. They will deal with Jefferson and the clergy, Jefferson and the Bible, Jefferson and orthodoxy, and Jefferson and the separation of church and state.

The previously unseen materials together with the analysis in this book calls into question the status quo view that Jefferson throughout most of his life was largely not connected to church and inclined to criticize traditional Christian doctrines, the Bible, priests/ministers, and religion in public life. It will show that the same quotations by Jefferson from a small and limited amount of evidence from mainly one period of his life has created a false impression. Whatever degree of private doubts and unbelief he may have personally held (especially by the end of his life), whenever it was available to him, Thomas Jefferson was a lifelong committed churchman. In this study all the complexity and nuance in his long spiritual journey will be evident because it contains virtually all of Jefferson's significant religious comments.

Reliable vs. Less Reliable Sources

Almost no secondary sources are used in the chronological chapters. And the approach taken in this study is to only include in the main account of Jefferson's religious life documents and actions that he clearly and consciously expressed to others. If a letter was never sent then it is only mentioned in passing in the main narrative. Whatever his motivation, it is only obvious that a letter he chose deliberately not to send is less reliable for drawing conclusions than one he did send. In private letters he sent late in life Jefferson himself sometimes asked the recipient to not make known because he did not give those letters the care required for public debate and it could stir up a hornet's nest. But also he acknowledged that his mind was not as sharp at his age, and so he asked for some latitude in judgment for letters in that last phase in his life.

If a document he drafted was done in a collaborative committee process or was signed by him into law without freedom to amend it, then it is less emphasized unless he seemed to make comments elsewhere about it that indicate some of his views. However, the three thematic chapters in Part II dealing with the topics Jefferson was most proud of will inevitably draw on sources that were collaborative in nature: the Declaration of Independence, the Virginia Statute, and the writings surrounding the establishment of the University of Virginia. All three had Jefferson as the driving force and leading author, but all were done with a group of others involved.

Unsent letters or private notes are evaluated only after the main narrative in this book. The same is done with notes he compiled without comment. If notes written by Jefferson about some other source are without any commentary from him—suggesting that he agrees or disagrees with those quotes—then they are only briefly mentioned in the main narrative. Just because he quoted at length from believers and unbelievers in some of his school books does not show what he himself believed what he copied. Examples are his literary commonplace book in 1765 and his "Notes on Religion" in 1776.[12] The same is true of his extracts of the Gospels, but they are treated more fully in a later chapter, due to their constant reprinting and distribution under the title of *The Jefferson Bible* (a title he did not use). Unless there are comments he provided that he agreed or not, these sources are unreliable for us to draw conclusions. Yet, sad to say, there is a tendency among some commentators to identify Jefferson's religion almost solely from these sources.

Our editorial method gives only minor mention in the primary narrative to any quotes that Jefferson copied without comment. Some quotes indicate unorthodoxy and the other orthodoxy in beliefs, so neither side can definitively claim this is what Jefferson himself did or did not believe. It would be completely baseless to choose one to adopt without the other; but, alas, this is often done by Jefferson's modern biographers. Edwin Gaustad, whose work is otherwise relatively good, makes an entire chapter just on the Literary Commonplace Notes, something he does not

---

12   "Notes and Proceedings on Discontinuing the Establishment of the Church of England," www.founders.archives.gov. The title for these notes varies in the collections of Jefferson's writings. Joseph Leicester Ford's collection, *The Writings of Thomas Jefferson*, uses the general "Notes on Religion," which is how we mention them in our text. Boyd presents them in the form of nine documents. Since none of them are dated or ordered in the original, there is no certainty of how they should be read. Paul Leicester Ford, ed., *The Writings of Thomas Jefferson*, 12 vols., (New York: G. P. Putnam's Sons, 1904-05), II:101ff.

do for other notes. Likewise, Eugene Sheridan gives over half of his monograph on Jefferson's religious life to focusing on these notes and the Gospel extracts (the so-called "Jefferson Bible"). Both are unfortunate amplifications of minor events and questionable sources. These works of Jefferson are important to analyze but only after more certain things are studied.

All of the aforementioned indirect evidence will not be ignored, but will be included only **after** all the direct evidence gives the most trustworthy picture. This will be discussed at the end of the chronological narrative and also in relevant thematic chapters. Then the reader may make informed conclusions as to whether the extra information truly represents Jefferson or not. Other primary sources that are second-hand accounts in which others say Jefferson said or did something will be used only when clearly identified as such, and only in the thematic chapters where it can be discussed fully. By the way, just because it is labeled as "less reliable" doesn't mean it did not happen. It simply can't be proven either way to be his own views and therefore is less reliable for making confident conclusions. It is best if perceptions are first formed by what is incontrovertible evidence, rather than let the other information influence it in one direction or the other.

The overall point of this is that it is best to not to be too hasty in drawing conclusions about the faith of Thomas Jefferson or the lack thereof. This book will apply what Liberty University professor and author Dr. Gary Habermas has called "the minimalist facts approach" (for another discipline[13]). If we err in this fresh evaluation of Jefferson's faith, we choose to err on the side of caution.

Jefferson's Advice

Perhaps Jefferson' advice to his nephew Peter Carr in a letter Jefferson wrote in 1787, regarding God and faith, can be applied to studying Jefferson himself. Jefferson wrote:

> ...divest yourself of all bias;...Question with boldness even the existence of a God;...Read the bible;...Examine therefore candidly what evidence there is of his having been inspired...Read the new testament. It is the history of a person called Jesus;...Keep in your eye...those who say:

- He was begotten by God,
- born of a virgin,

---

13   Dr. Gary Habermas is one of the foremost authorities alive on the subject of the historical Jesus and His resurrection.

- *suspended and reversed the laws of nature at will,*
- *and ascended bodily into heaven;*

(And those who say:)

- *He was a man of illegitimate birth,*
- *of a benevolent heart, enthusiastic mind,*
- *who set out without pretensions to divinity,*
- *ended in believing them…*

If the reader did this in the study of Jefferson's own religion, perhaps Jefferson's letter could be adapted in this following way:

Divest yourself of all bias;…Question with boldness even the predominance of assertions that Jefferson was not a Christian;…Read this book; It strives to be the most complete religious history of a person called Thomas Jefferson;… Examine therefore candidly what evidence there is of him having heterodox views or doubts of the Bible. Read his own words. They are the firsthand source to understand a person called Thomas Jefferson;…Keep in your eye… those who say:

- *He was a Christian,*
- *member and leading figure of Trinitarian churches,*
- *regular at worship, Bible reading and prayer,*
- *friend and supporter of many pastors and ministries,*
- *and advocate of non-coercive religious expression in public life.*
(And those who say:)
- *He was a rationalist Deist from an early age,*
- *of a skeptical heart, secular Enlightenment mind,*
- *who set out as an opponent to most clergy and religion in public life,*
- *ended as a Unitarian admirer of Jesus' words with no church affiliation.*

If the reader takes this open-minded approach, he will be likely be surprised by the result.

CHAPTER 1

THOMAS JEFFERSON'S RELIGIOUS LIFE, 1767-1787

"We . . . [are] desirous of encouraging and supporting the Calvinistical Reformed Church, and of deriving to our selves, through the ministry of its teachers, the benefits of Gospel knowledge and . . . for explaining the holy scriptures . . . in our town of Charlottesville; . . . ." —Thomas Jefferson, 1777 [1]

The religious life of Thomas Jefferson is complicated. Upon close examination, five phases of his adult life seem to appear—the first being from 1767 through 1787. The first 21 years of Jefferson's independent adult life from 1767-1787 show almost nothing but orthodox Christian beliefs and practice.

Jefferson's upbringing was in the context of the Anglican tradition in Virginia. Jefferson's parents were members of the Church and had Jefferson baptized as an infant. So Jefferson's adult religious life begins already as a member of the Fredericksville Parish in Albemarle County.[2] While in school and college Jefferson copied quotes of famous writers (i.e., in his Literary Commonplace Book) as part of his assignments, but

---

1   "Subscription to Support a Clergyman in Charlottesville, [February 1777]," www.founders. archives.gov.

2   Dumas Malone, *Jefferson the Virginian* (Boston, Mass.: Little, Brown and Co., 1948), 42-45.

these are unreliable for making definitive judgments about his personal beliefs. The best opportunity one has to discover Jefferson's freely-held beliefs as an adult really begins in 1767, once he returns from his college studies in Williamsburg.

Jefferson's Early Adult Years, 1767-1776

Jefferson returned to Albemarle County from Williamsburg and began practicing law in 1767. He also joined the vestry of Fredericksville Parish, which made him part of the lay-leadership of the church that was still served at that time by Rev. James Maury, whose school Jefferson had attended before college. The Anglican Church required that any vestryman enter the office by taking an oath to "conform to the doctrine and discipline of the Church of England."[3] The Fredericksville Parish Vestry Book has Jefferson's name listed under those words in that year. Thus, at this stage in his life he took an oath claiming belief in all the basics of the historic Christian faith, i.e., belief in the Trinity, the Deity of Jesus, that He died for sinners, that He rose again from the dead, that the Bible is God's Word, etc.

Some might think that Jefferson joining the vestry was simply building his resume, but where is the evidence for that? Certainly church attendance and donations were still legally required, but time serving on the vestry and even additional time as warden and doing various projects for the Church were voluntary choices of Jefferson. From these extra commitments isn't it more likely that these indicate that Jefferson did so sincerely in service to God? The Vestry Book shows that he attended at least two vestry meetings every year and six in 1768 alone. In 1769 it shows him also serving as warden and helping to choose the land for a new church building. The parish tax was not voluntary, but Jefferson's investment of time as vestryman and warden was above the common duty of a typical Anglican member, attending many meetings and giving time for various needs of the vestry.[4]

As an Anglican Churchman, Jefferson also made efforts to help other clergymen than just his own pastor. In a letter of August 18, 1768, Jefferson appealed to a Presbyterian elder from adjacent Augusta county named William Preston for his "...suffrage [i.e., vote] in favor of...the Revd James [Maury] Fontaine who

---

3   Rosalie Davis, ed., *Fredericksville Parish Vestry Book, 1742-1787* (Manchester, Mo.: self-published, 1978), 86-96.

4   William Meade, *Old Churches, Ministers and Families of Virginia*, 2 vols., (Philadelphia, 1857), I:191. William Meade wrote: "Even Mr. Jefferson and Wythe . . . took their parts in the duties of vestrymen. . . ." Writing three decades after Jefferson's death, Meade also made unfounded comments on Jefferson's disbelief and other motives, which we discuss in a later chapter.

offers himself as a candidate for the place of Chaplain to the House of Burgesses."[5] Meanwhile, Fredericksville Parish minister James Maury died and the vestry, including Jefferson, began looking for replacements to recommend to the bishop. Jefferson wrote several letters at this time in this regard. A man known to Jefferson was Rev. James Ogilvie, who visited the area and met Jefferson sometime prior to March 1770.[6] Jefferson tried to get him the position in a nearby parish.[7]

Jefferson himself was elected to the House of Burgesses and then went to Williamsburg frequently over the next several years. While there he worshiped at the Bruton Parish until the capital was moved to Richmond in 1779.[8] The significance of all this is that, at this point in his life, Thomas Jefferson was an active churchman, even an active lay-leader within the Church—and, was an earnest friend of orthodox Trinitarian ministers.

Jefferson moved south across the Rivanna River into the first completed section of his home, Monticello, on November 26, 1770. This move put him in the jurisdiction of a new parish and Jefferson, according to biographer Edwin Gaustad, "was also elected vestryman."[9] Bishop William Meade also confirms his place on the vestry, and Jefferson appears in the St. Anne's vestry minutes serving the parish. Rev. Charles Clay was its minister, who was unusual, being an evangelical Anglican. Evangelicals emphasize the authority of the Bible and the necessity of a personal conversion known as the "new birth." Only between three and eight percent of the Anglican clergy in Virginia was evangelical, but in the Anglican parishes of the Central Virginia Piedmont region, it was the norm (especially in St. Anne's in Albemarle and in St. Thomas in nearby Orange county).

Historian Harry S. Stout of Yale observes that the "most accurate guide we... have to what people actually heard are the handwritten sermon notes that ministers carried with them into the pulpit."[10] Significantly, fifty handwritten sermons by Clay from this period have been preserved. These were donated to the Virginia Historical Society in 1992 by Clay's descendants. Since having not been published and thus unavailable for two centuries, they have been overlooked in virtually

---

5   Letter to William Preston, August 18, 1768, www.founders.archives.gov.

6   This was according to Jefferson's letter a year later.

7   Letter to James Ogilvie, October 1770 (but now missing), and also *Letter to James Ogilvie*, February 20, 1771, www.founders.archives.gov.

8   Letter to John Bracken, August 2, 1811, www.founders.archives.gov.

9   Edwin Gaustad, *Sworn On the Altar of God: A Religious Biography of Thomas Jefferson* (Grand Rapids, Mich.: Wm. B. Eerdmans Publishers, 1996), 22.

10   Harry S. Stout, *The New England Soul: Preaching and Religious Culture in Colonial New England* (New York: Oxford University Press, 1986), 4-5.

all studies on Virginia's religious culture and Clay's famous parishioner, Thomas Jefferson.[11] Clay's messages are especially enlightening because, as Bishop William Meade said in his early history of the Episcopal Church in Virginia, they were "sound, energetic and *evangelical beyond the character of the times*."[12] For the first time ever, we have published two of those sermons. (They appear in the Appendix of this book.)

Rev. Clay and Jefferson became lifelong friends and neighbors for over 50 years and exchanged dozens of letters until 1819 when Clay died. No one outside of Jefferson's family corresponded with Jefferson longer than they did. Jefferson's letter to Clay in 1815 said he had spoken with Clay about religion more "than to any other person." So any biography of Jefferson's religion must have Clay as a prominent feature of it. Yet sadly, very few modern treatments do so.[13] A couple letters from Clay late in Jefferson's life will offer a new way of interpreting Jefferson's late unorthodoxy that has never been presented in any other biography.

A sense of Jefferson's personal religious life at this time also begins to be seen through some of his private actions and letters. Jefferson purchased a classic religious book in 1770, called *Pilgrim's Progress* by John Bunyan.[14] This bestselling 17th century allegory promotes spiritual discipline and is the source of common phrases, such as "Vanity Fair" or "Slough of Despond." Eventually Jefferson's library included a collection of many subjects including religious literature by various non-Christian faiths, atheists, and more. Some of the heterodox additions to his collection are discussed later in this study, but his purchases at this time seem consistent with letters Jefferson wrote to Robert Skipwith. In a August 3, 1771 letter, Jefferson urged his friend to "…exercise…the moral feelings" and cultivate "…a habit of thinking and acting virtuously…" In other letters Jefferson also asked his friend to

---

11   Fifty of Clay's sermons are found in the Clay Family Papers (Mss 1c5795a), Virginia Historical Society, Richmond, Virginia. Mark Beliles catalogued and analyzed these and assigned a numbering system and titles based on the first line of text or other data, for easy recognition. There are nine folders of sermons in the Clay Family Papers collection, plus Clay's "Account Book," which covers the years 1773-1818, and a subscription list that includes the name of "Thomas Jefferson." For more on Clay, see Gundersen, *The Anglican Ministry in Virginia*, 163.

12   Meade, *Old Churches, Ministers and Families of Virginia*, 2:49 (emphasis added). Meade, an evangelical, emphasized in his historical work others who were of similar persuasion. Meade's praise of Clay confirms his uncommon ministry.

13   Some writers on Jefferson's religion who have neglected Rev. Clay are Eugene Sheridan, Charles Sanford, and Dickinson Adams and Ruth Lester.

14   Account book, [c. March 1], 1770. Mark A. Beliles, ed., *The Selected Religious Letters and Papers of Thomas Jefferson* (Charlottesville, VA: America Publications, 2013), 27. "For *Pilgrim's Progress*."

"...offer prayers for me ..." and claims: "I pay [sic] continual devotions."[15] These actions and letters suggest a sincere person of faith. And when Jefferson decided to marry Martha Wayles Skelton, he chose an Anglican wedding that was conducted at the family plantation in Charles City County east of Richmond on January 1, 1772, by Rev William Coutts—a friend of Martha's family.[16]

Up until 1774, the Jeffersons worshiped at Clear Mount Church but then switched to the new Forge Church (both served by Rev. Clay). The Forge Church was chosen by Jefferson and fellow-Burgess[17] John Walker as the location for a 1774 special Fast Day service they requested on July 23. In a letter they sent "to the Inhabitants of the Parish of Saint Anne," they asked for "...prayers and a sermon suited to the occasion by the reverend Mr. Clay at the new church."[18] This Fast Day was observed earlier on June 1 in Williamsburg in order to coincide with the closing of the port of Boston on that day by the British. Jefferson wrote much later in his autobiography that he was the one who initiated a resolution "Designating a Day of Fasting, Humiliation, and Prayer" that was adopted by the House of Burgesses on May 24.[19]

The Public Fast day was necessary due to political conflict between the American colonies and England over taxation on tea and other products. The Boston Tea Party in Massachusetts led to a response by the King to blockade their harbor. A year later the first shots were fired and the American Revolution was in full motion.

Jefferson's Account book shows him giving money to Bruton Parish church in Williamsburg.[20] It was then from a worshiper and supporter of the church that the Resolution suggested a special service be held there on June 1..."to implore the divine interposition ..." regarding their national crisis.[21] But Jefferson was not satisfied with only calling for prayer and fasting on the part of the Burgesses,

---

15   Letter to Robert Skipwith, August 3, 1771, www.founders.archives.gov.

16   Account book, January 1, 1772. Beliles, *The Selected Religious Letters and Papers of Thomas Jefferson*, 30. Gave Revd. W. Coutts. Also Account book, January 2, 1772. Gave Revd. Mr. Davies [Davis] marriage fee. Also Account book, May 26, 1772. Pd. Revd. Wm. Coutts.

17   Jefferson was a member of the House of Burgesses (1769-1779), Virginia's colonial body of representatives. Note that it was no longer called the House of Burgesses after 1776.

18   Letter to the Inhabitants of St. Anne's Parish, June 1774, www.founders.archives.gov.

19   Jefferson's *Autobiography*, January 6, 1821. *Writings of Thomas Jefferson*, 1:3

20   Account book, May 23, 1774. Beliles, *The Selected Religious Letters and Papers of Thomas Jefferson*, 31. Gave the Sexton 1/3. [Bruton Parish].

21   Resolution for a "Day of Fasting, Humiliation, and Prayer," May 24, 1774, www.founders. archives.gov.

thus, his request for another service back in Albemarle on July 23. That Christian worship service featured a sermon by Rev. Clay based on 2 Chronicles 7:14 that promises God will heal a land when His people humble themselves to pray and turn from their sin. In Jefferson's autobiography, he said that a large crowd attended and that the day was like "…a shock of electricity, arousing every man …" to resist the tyranny of Britain.[22]

About half a year later in March 1775, Jefferson attended the Second Virginia Convention in Richmond, where he was elected one of Virginia's delegates to the Continental Congress. A notable event occurred at that gathering. One Virginia delegate named Patrick Henry made a speech that called the colony's leaders to begin to prepare for war, with his closing appeal to "give me liberty or give me death!" The convention met in St. John's Episcopal Church in Richmond, and the church's minister at the time was Rev. Miles Selden, who was at the convention and with whom Jefferson almost certainly became acquainted.

Jefferson was then in Philadelphia for the Second Continental Congress for about a month beginning in June 1775. At the Congress, Jefferson helped in the drafting of the "Declaration of the Causes and Necessity of Taking Up Arms," which included religious references. His initial draft cited God and religious freedom and "those powers which our creator hath given us." His draft also indicated a belief in a God who responded to prayer to intervene in human affairs, for it said "we devoutly implore the assistance of Almighty God to…dispose his majesty, his ministers, & parliament to reconciliation with us…"[23]

Jefferson's expressions of faith in public documents and acts were not the only indication of his faith in 1775. While in Philadelphia, there is also evidence that he attended church, as was his custom for most of his life (when available). His account book for July 14 says that he "…put in church box at German Church."[24] This church that he supported was apparently the German Lutheran Church in that city, led by Rev. Henry M. Muhlenberg (but also could have been the German Reformed church). Jefferson attended and donated again in October. This may have been the first time he worshiped at a different denomination than the one in which he was raised, and shows the willingness that Jefferson had to support

---

22   Jefferson's *Autobiography*, January 6, 1821. *Writings of Thomas Jefferson*, 1:3
23   Declaration of the Causes and Necessity of Taking Up Arms, June 1775, www.founders. archives.gov.
24   Account book, July 14, 1775. Beliles, *The Selected Religious Letters and Papers of Thomas Jefferson*, 32. Put in church box at German Church. And Account book, October 22, 1775. Put into German Church box.

various expressions of Christian faith even though many of the colonies still had laws limiting religious freedom. Jefferson had an unusual openness in an era when interdenominational persecution was still common.

1776 was a watershed year for both political and religious freedom. Jefferson was again in Philadelphia at Congress beginning May 14. He also wrote a preliminary draft of a constitution for Virginia on June 13 that said: "All persons shall have full and free liberty of religious opinion; nor shall any be compelled to frequent or maintain any religious institution."[25] It represented his first expression on this topic.

But his intellectual talents were also drawn on by the Congress to draft a Declaration of Independence.[26] His original language touched on religion when it mentioned "…the laws of nature and of nature's God" and "…We hold these truths to be sacred and undeniable, that all men are created equal." Jefferson's phrase "the laws of nature and of nature's God," was clearly defined by *Blackstone's Commentaries* as meaning the unwritten law of God in creation and the revealed law of God in the Bible. This is dealt with in greater depth in a later chapter.[27] Other references to God such as "endowed by their Creator" and "the Supreme Judge" and "the protection of divine providence" were added during the collaborative process by others in Congress before the final document was adopted but Jefferson never expressed any dissent with these phrases.

Providence terminology was used by his own pastor and orthodox theologians for many years, and was not known distinctly as an Enlightenment or Deist language. Jefferson wrote of God's providential help in private letters as well. To Richard Henry Lee, Jefferson reported on the military front: "Our camps recruit slowly, amazing slowly. God knows in what it will end. The finger of providence has as yet saved us by retarding the arrival of Ld. Howe's recruits."[28]

---

25   Proposed Constitution for Virginia, June 13, 1776, www.founders.archives.gov.

26   Draft of Declaration of Independence, June 1776, www.founders.archives.gov.

27   Louisiana State University professor Ellis Sandoz writes that Jefferson's language: ". . . harmonizes with the Christian religious and Whig political consensus that prevailed in the country at the time; . . . (and with) traditional Christian natural law and rights going back to Aquinas…" Similar language was used by the Protestant John Calvin, John Locke and others. See Sandoz, *A Government of Laws*, 190-191. Jefferson defined the law of nature in 1793 as: "the moral Law to which man has been subjected by his creator," Opinion on the Treaties with France, 28 April 1793, www.founders.archives.gov. Also see Gary Amos, *Defending the Declaration* (Charlottesville, Va.: Providence Press, The Providence Foundation, 1994), and see John Whitehead, *An American Dream* (Westchester, Ill.: Crossway Books, 1987).

28   Letter to Richard Henry Lee, July 29, 1776, www.founders.archives.gov.

While in Congress, Jefferson also served on a committee to propose a national seal for authenticating official documents. Jefferson proposed on August 20 they use an image of "…the Israelites: rays from a pillar of fire in the cloud, expressive of the divine presence, and command, reaching to Moses who stands on the shore and, extending his hand over the sea, causes it to overwhelm Pharaoh. Motto: Rebellion to tyrants is obedience to God." Jefferson biographer Dumas Malone says that Jefferson had the motto "put on his own seal later, and made it a personal slogan throughout life."[29]

About this same time, his account book shows his ongoing relationships with Anglican clergymen. In Philadelphia he came to know Rev. Jacob Duché of Christ Church who also served as chaplain for the Continental Congress. In fact, Jefferson enclosed a copy of a new form of prayer suggested by Duché in a letter to John Page.[30] This form of prayer in his possession implies also Jefferson's attendance at Christ Church, while residing in Philadelphia.

Jefferson returned home briefly from Philadelphia before going to Williamsburg on October 6 for two months of service in the General Assembly in order to revise various laws. In the course of this work during the final months of 1776, Jefferson personally compiled nine documents that reflected very orthodox beliefs.[31] He may have agreed with these beliefs, but like his earlier literary commonplace college notes, it cannot be proven because he made no comments on them.[32]

In the capital of Williamsburg on October 11, he joined the committee on religion in the legislature and began meeting with many dissenting clergymen. A Dissenter was one who was not part of the government-favored denomination (i.e. Anglicans) and who wished the laws to be revised in favor of religious freedom

29   Jefferson also embraced Ben Franklin's proposal for the seal and rewrote it as follows: "Pharoah . . . passing thro' the divided waters of the Red sea in pursuit of the Israelites: rays from a pillar of fire in the cloud, expressive of the divine presence and command, reaching to Moses who stands on the shore and, extending his hand his over the sea, causes it to overwhelm Pharaoh. Motto: Rebellion to tyrants is obedience to God." It was proposed to Congress on August 20 but tabled. Julian Boyd, ed., *The Papers of Thomas Jefferson* (Princeton, NJ: Princeton University Press), 1:495. Henry Randall writes that "had his wishes been consulted, the symbol borne on our national seal would have contained our public profession of Christianity as a nation." For more on this motto, see Malone, *Jefferson the Virginian* (Boston, Mass.: Little, Brown and Co., 1948), 226. On the opposite side of the seal, Jefferson proposed recognizing the Anglo-Saxon founders of Britain who were pagans at the time.

30   Letter to John Page, August 5, 1776, www.founders.archives.gov.

31   "Notes on Religion" otherwise called "Notes and Proceedings on Discontinuing the Establishment of the Church of England," 1776, www.founders.archives.gov.

32   Since neither can be proven to be Jefferson's own beliefs, they will only be examined after the more reliable documents are presented first.

for all denominations equally. Rev. John Todd, the moderator of the Hanover Presbytery, led the Presbyterian effort to bring in petitions that fall.[33] Since petitions and declarations written by these dissenters are found in Jefferson's papers, it is likely that Jefferson obtained these through meeting them while at the assembly.[34] One petition was drafted by a local Charlottesville Presbyterian minister named William Irvin, sometime before the end of October, titled "Petition of Dissenters in Albemarle and Amherst Counties." Rev. Irvin sent the petition to his "friend" Jefferson and included a personal letter.[35]

Another petition dated October 16, 1776 and signed by over 10,000 people was put in Jefferson's hands by Baptist Rev. Jeremiah Moore and other clergy leaders. Baptist ministers who lobbied Jefferson and the legislature included Rev. John Waller, Rev. Elijah Craig of Orange, and Rev. John Leland of nearby Louisa, who had presented Jefferson a "Declaration of the Virginia Association of Baptists."[36] It is worth noting that these orthodox Christian leaders sought out Jefferson, not vice-versa, and they found a reliable friend for their cause.

In late 1776, the state legislature finally suspended the law that required dissenters to support the state church, and launched a total voluntary system in its place. Denominationalism had been strong in European culture for several centuries, but in America, due especially to the Great Awakening, it was waning – at least in the frontier areas such as Jefferson's home county. And as diverse denominations were gaining acceptance, so there began a new era. Once free from England's control the Americans began shifting toward a society having no state-established churches where all citizens were required to worship or at least financially pay taxes to support one particular denomination.

Jefferson in the Revolutionary Period, 1777-1783

Concrete indications of Jefferson's own religious beliefs began to be clear in the early months of 1777, as he took voluntary initiatives to support a new church in his town. The legislature had created a new Anglican parish eastward in Fluvanna

---

33   Robert P. Davis, *Virginia Presbyterians in American Life: Hanover Presbytery 1755-1980*, (Richmond, Va.: Hanover Presbytery, 1982), 50.

34   Editors of Jefferson's papers make this assumption in their editorial notes, even though there is no hard evidence other than the fact that the letter or item is in Jefferson's possession. We assume the same.

35   Rev. William Irvin to Jefferson, pre-November 1776, www.founders.archives.gov. Also see "Petition of Dissenters in Albemarle and Amherst Counties," November 1, 1776, www. founders.archives.gov.

36   According to Baptist historians, the chief author of the Baptist Declaration was Rev. John Leland.

County, carved out of St. Anne's Parish at the end of 1776, and this required a new vestry to be chosen for each. Jefferson, along with Wilson Cary and William Oglesby, were re-appointed to their vestry in February 1777, but all three refused to serve while a lawsuit was pending.[37] Perhaps due to this legal mess, or perhaps simply due to a spiritual movement in the culture away from denominationalism, many of the vestry followed Jefferson's lead to propose an entirely new independent congregation in February 1777.

Jefferson drafted a document entitled a "Subscription to Support a Clergyman in Charlottesville," and a companion document called a "Subscription to Support a Clerk of the Congregation in Charlottesville." Actually Jefferson drafted another document first that organized what was called the Protestant Episcopal Church, but it did not have good response, so the document cited above was then circulated for signatures and voluntary pledges of money to create a fund for a "Calvinistical Reformed Church" in the new era of non-state churches. A subscription was the new way of indicating membership in a church (and involved paying money of support), and in 1777 Jefferson wasn't a mere bystander in this. In the *Papers of Thomas Jefferson*, the editors say that it was Jefferson himself who "organized" this new congregation.[38] Indeed, Jefferson's name appears first among the voluntary subscribers, and his financial pledge is the largest amount. Under his signature followed many of St. Anne's former members and vestrymen, including a veritable who's who of leading families of Charlottesville.

Because of its historic importance, most of the February 1777 document is shown as follows. Keep in mind as you read this that it was Thomas Jefferson himself who wrote it:

Subscription to Support a Clergyman in Charlottesville

Whereas by a late act of General assembly freedom of Religious opinion and worship is restored to all, and it is left to the member of each religious society to employ such teachers as they think fit for their own spiritual comfort and instruction, and to maintain the same by their free and

---

37   *Vestry Book of Saint Anne's Parish, 1772-1785* (February 1777), 10.

38   See editorial notes, "Subscription to Support a Clergyman in Charlottesville," February 1777, and "Testimonial for Rev. Charles Clay," August 15, 1779, www.founders.archives.gov. Two subscriptions were used to raise the support of a clergyman. The first one called the church the "Protestant Episcopal Church." It was soon changed. "Calvinistical Reformed Church" is used in this book. Late in life Jefferson said he was a "lifelong" Episcopalian, so although he became part of this independent congregation at this point, he apparently never renounced his membership in the Episcopal Church.

voluntary contributions. We the subscribers, professing the most Catholic [i.e., universal] affection for other religious sectaries who happen to differ from us in points of conscience, yet desirous of encouraging and supporting the Calvinistical Reformed Church, and of deriving to our selves, through the ministry of its teachers, the benefits of Gospel knowledge and religious improvement; and at the same time of supporting those, who, having been at considerable expense in qualifying themselves by regular education for explaining the holy scriptures, have dedicated their time and labour to the service of the said church; and moreover approving highly the political conduct of the Revd. Charles Clay, who, early rejecting the tyrant and tyranny of Britain, proved his religion genuine by its harmony with the liberties of mankind, and, conforming his public prayers to the spirit and the injured rights of his country, ever addressed the God of battles for victory to our arms, while others impiously prayed that our enemies might vanquish and overcome us: do hereby oblige ourselves our heirs executors and administrators to pay to the said Charles Clay of Albemarle his executors or administrators the several sums affixed to our respective names...; In consideration whereof we expect that the said Charles Clay shall perform divine service and preach a sermon in the town of Charlottesville on every 4th Saturday till the end of the next session of general Assembly and after that on every 4th Sunday or oftener if a regular rotation with the other churches which shall have put themselves under his care will admit a more frequent attendance. And we further mutually agree with each other that we will meet at Charlottesville on the 1st day of March in the present year and on (_____)[39] in every year following so long as we continue our subscriptions and there make choice by ballot of three Wardens to collect our said subscriptions to take care of such books and vestments as shall be provided for the use of our church to call meetings of our Congregation when necessary and to transmit such other business relating to our said Congregation as we shall hereafter confide to them.[40]

Jefferson was the first and most generous benefactor to this up-and-coming church he called "our congregation." The companion document at the same time, "Subscription to Support a Clerk of the Congregation in Charlottesville," reads: "We

---

39   On occasion, we have used (_____) to indicate that the original is illegible or missing.

40   "Subscription to Support a Clergyman in Charlottesville, [February 1777]," www.founders. archives.gov.

the Subscribers agree to pay on the 25th day of December in the present year 1777 and so on the 25th day of December annually in every year after till we shall notify the contrary in writing to the Wardens for our Congregation, the sums affixed to our respective names, to such person or persons as by a majority of our Congregation, to be called together by the wardens for that purpose, shall from time to time be appointed to the office of clerk for the said Congregation, to assist the reverend Charles Clay in (____) performing divine service whenever he shall attend at Charlottesville for that purpose."[41] On that document Jefferson's name is followed by John Harvie, Randolph Jefferson, and Peter Marks.

The fact that Jefferson voluntarily helped create and support a "Calvinistical Reformed" congregation that he cited as "our church" and whose pastor was Charles Clay, is one of the strongest indicators of the faith and religious preferences of Jefferson at this time in his life. (See for yourself an example of Rev. Clay's preaching with a sermon reproduced in the Appendix that Jefferson helped support financially.) Since Rev. Clay was one of the few overtly evangelical Anglican preachers in Virginia this suggests that Jefferson's own faith was proximate to this as well.[42] This congregation apparently met in the Charlottesville courthouse from 1777 through at least 1782, and one of Clay's handwritten sermons had a notation identifying that location. It is possible the church lasted beyond 1782, but that is less clear.

The 50 handwritten sermons by Clay that survive in the Virginia Historical Society collection bear Clay's notations indicating 76 delivery dates before 1777 and 47 delivery dates during the six years (1777-1782) of this new congregation. Plus there are 17 undated sermons. From 1777 onward, after Clay resigned from St. Anne's and the parish was defunct, all sermons from 1777 and 1782 cannot be indications of his ministry in that parish.[43] St. Anne's Parish remained without a resident priest from then onward for over 40 years.

---

41   "Subscription to Support a Clerk of the Congregation in Charlottesville, [February 1777]," www.founders.archives.gov.

42   You can see two of Rev. Clay's sermons for yourself in the Appendix. These were unavailable to the general public while in the private family possession for two centuries until Mark Beliles began writing about them in 1996. Other than Beliles' dissertation, it is the only time (to our knowledge) to be in print.

43   Elizabeth C. Langhorne, *A History of Christ Church, Glendower* (Albemarle County, Va.: Christ Church, 1957), 6. On page 19 the St. Anne's vestry book shows that Clay certainly had quit as its minister as of December 22, 1780 because it speaks of him as "the *late* Rev'd Mr. Clay." But other historical sketches say he stopped preaching for them after 1777 when he switched to the Calvinistical Reformed Church. See Frances M. Walker, *The Early Episcopal Church in the Amherst-Nelson Area* (Lynchburg, Va.: J. P. Bell Co. Inc., 1964), 51.

On March 9, 1778, an account book entry says, "Paid Mr. Clay for Rand[olph] Jefferson...for P[hillip] Mazzei...[and] for myself." The editors of the *Papers of Thomas Jefferson* note that "these payments are in accordance with the subscription of Feb. 1777 by TJ and other Albemarle County citizens to provide an annual contribution to the Rev. Charles Clay."[44] Since St. Anne's Parish was not operational, this payment was clearly for the Calvinistical Reformed Church, whose founding document of February 1777 is correctly cited by these editors (i.e., James A. Bear, Jr. and Lucia C. Stanton). Jefferson would help other friends pay for Clay at times, such as when in 1778 he "Paid Mr. Clay for T[homas] Garth."[45] Jefferson was determined to ensure Rev. Clay had the financial means to continue his ministry.[46]

Subscription is often only thought of today as something for magazines or other services that already exist, so it is worth some comment here. Jefferson's account book mentions him subscribing to churches and publishing books and other projects many times throughout his life. Especially at this point, since churches in Virginia were no longer tax-supported, the use of subscriptions emerged. It was a way for members to declare in advance how much they planned to tithe or donate and thus give a church an idea of a budget for the year. Some churches would have families pay for use of a pew ahead of time that served the same purpose. Private schools operated by subscription as did large publishing projects for Bibles and other literature. As will be seen Jefferson subscribed to all of these things and thus invested the capital for various ministries to develop their projects.

The account book also shows Jefferson donating "to the Timber ridge academy" in November 1777.[47] This donation was to what normally was known as Liberty Hall Academy located near Timber Ridge in present Rockbridge County. What is significant with this entry is that it was a Presbyterian founded and controlled institution that Jefferson was supporting. Its head was Rev. William Graham from Princeton. It shows for the first time no qualms on Jefferson's part about personally investing in the efforts of dissenters, particularly Presbyterian educators.

There was also someone named Holmes who occasionally preached in the parish during these years (also known as a patriot).

44   Account book, March 9, 1778. Beliles, *The Selected Religious Letters and Papers of Thomas Jefferson*, 37. Pd. Mr. Clay for Rand[olph] Jefferson...for Mazzei...Pd. ditto for myself.

45   Account book, August 18, 1778. Beliles, *The Selected Religious Letters and Papers of Thomas Jefferson*, 37. Also October 19, 1778. For Clay.

46   Account book, April 28, 1779. Beliles, *The Selected Religious Letters and Papers of Thomas Jefferson*), 39. Pd. Revd. Chas. Clay for P. Mazzei's subscription to him the 2nd year.

47   Account book, November 11, 1777. Beliles, *The Selected Religious Letters and Papers of Thomas Jefferson*, 37. Gave to Timber Ridge Academy.

(This academy eventually became known as Washington and Lee University in Lexington. Graham also was a supporter of religious freedom.)

Whenever Jefferson was residing in Williamsburg to do legislative business, he apparently was involved with the Bruton Parish Church still led by Rev. John Bracken. His account book reveals little things, such as when he "Paid for hearing organ at church" a year later in June 1778.[48] Although this is minor evidence, he said later in his life that he was a lifelong member of the Episcopal Church, and it certainly would have aroused some reaction if he avoided church there or later in Richmond—especially when he was the governor. Since there was never a single comment in any Virginia clergyman's writings, nor in any Virginia newspaper, indicating Jefferson's absence at church or of communion, it makes it very likely that he maintained attendance. Nothing at this time would have suggested to anyone that Jefferson was anything but orthodox (straight in his views) and orthopraxic (straight in his practice) in his faith. Therefore, it gives a different context than modern commentators suggest for his work on revising the state's religious laws.

A general revision of all laws in Virginia was necessary once America was independent of England. Virginia's leaders needed to decide how much of the English legal system they would keep as is, and what they would modify to more accurately represent them as independent Virginia Americans. Jefferson and his old law teacher George Wythe and a few others worked on the project but Jefferson especially took responsibility for the religious laws. After a couple years of work Jefferson became governor on June 1, 1779 and other finished the task of submitting the package of revised laws to the legislature. John Harvie, a fellow member of the Calvinistical Reformed Church in Charlottesville, was given the task of formally submitting to the legislature the bills to revise the religious laws on June 12.[49] Church-state historian Daniel Dreisbach, professor at American University, is correct when he writes of Jefferson that being "chair of the Virginia

---

48   Account book, June 2, 1778, James A. Bear, Jr. and Lucia C. Stanton, eds., *Jefferson's Memorandum Books: Accounts, with Legal Records and Miscellany, 1767-1826* (Princeton: Princeton University Press, 1997), 465. For hearing organ at church [Bruton Parish].

49   Harvie was appointed by the legislature to a committee, along with George Mason and Jerman Baker, to prepare two bills: one for religious freedom and the other for saving the property of the formerly-established church. See Hamilton James Eckenrode, *Separation of Church and State in Virginia: A Study in the Development of the Revolution* (Richmond, Va.: Davis Bottom, 1910), 56. See also Edward Frank Humphrey, *Nationalism and Religion in America, 1774-1789* (Boston: Chipman Law Publishing Co., 1924), 388. For more on the struggle for religious freedom in Virginia see: Thomas Buckley, *Church and State in Revolutionary Virginia, 1776-1787* (Charlottesville, Va.: University Press of Virginia, 1977).

Committee of Revisors, he was chief architect" of the set of religious bills that were "apparently framed by Jefferson."[50]

The bills on religion were first presented to the legislature as a package with consecutive numbering.[51] When one considers all these bills as a package, instead of just the bill for religious freedom isolated from the others, it certainly shows that Jefferson was not trying to remove all religion from public life nor to undermine religion. Quite frankly, if Jefferson had only written #82 (what we know as the Virginia Statute for Religious Freedom), that alone was interpreted by the evangelical dissenting churches in the state to have been a very pro-Christian act on his part, but their awareness of the package of bills certainly cemented their positive view of him. This is seen in detail in a later chapter.

Bill #83 was for "Saving the Property of the Church Heretofore by Law Established" thus protecting the now disestablished Anglican Church from lawsuits. Bill #84, "A Bill for Punishing Disturbers of Religious Worship and Sabbath Breakers," eventually passed in 1786, along with #82 on Religious Freedom. Bill #85 authorized the governor to issue proclamations of Public Days of Prayer, but it also included penalties for ministers who failed to observe the day! And Bill #86 "for Annulling marriages Prohibited by the Levitical Law" was deliberately based on the Bible. Many years later Jefferson said of this bill: "...early in our revolution the legislature of Virginia thought it necessary that their code of laws should be revised, and made homogeneous with their new situation. this task was committed to mr. Wythe, mr. Pendleton and myself, among others, the law regulating marriages came under consideration. We thought it most orthodox and correct to copy into our bill the very words of the Levitical law."[52] This paints a different picture than the common one of today where Jefferson seeks to keep religion separate from civil law.[53]

Few modern scholars mention these bills as being equally identified with Jefferson, perhaps because it doesn't fit the secular motivation paradigm that they

---

50   Daniel Dreisbach, *Thomas Jefferson and the Wall of Separation of Church and State* (New York: New York University Press, 2002), 59, 187.

51   Bills Reported by the Committee of Revisors, 1779, [see Bills 82-87], www.founders. archives.gov. See the excellent analysis by Daniel Dreisbach in *A New Perspective on Jefferson's Views on Church-State Relations* in The American Journal of Legal History (Temple University School of Law, April 1991), Volume XXXV, Number 2, 172-204.

52   Letter to Frances Adrian Van der Kemp, February 9, 1818. Beliles, *The Selected Religious Letters and Papers of Thomas Jefferson*, 285.

53   See Jefferson's Thoughts on Lotteries, January 20, 1826. www.founders.archives.gov. He talks about lotteries being used to build churches as a good thing.

assign to Jefferson with Bill #82 for religious freedom. But since the whole package of religious bills were mainly Jefferson's work over the previous two years it is without scholarly basis to give Jefferson credit for the one bill on religious freedom but not for the others. In any event, Bills #83 through #86 are essential to form a balanced view of what separation of church and state meant at that time. In light of these other bills in the package, the words of Bill #82 on religious freedom become more understandable in their intent. The original draft in 1777 reads in part:

> ...Almighty God hath created the mind free, and manifested his supreme will that free it shall remain by making it altogether insusceptible of restraint; that all attempts to influence it by temporal punishments, or burthens, or by civil incapacitations...are a departure from the plan of the holy author of our religion, who being Lord both of body and mind, yet chose not to propagate it by coercions on either, as was in his Almighty power to do...

> ...that to compel a man to furnish contributions of money for the propagation of opinions which he disbelieves and abhors, is sinful and tyrannical; that even the forcing him to support this or that teacher of his own religious persuasion, is depriving him of the comfortable liberty of giving his contributions to the particular pastor whose morals he would make his pattern, and whose powers he feels most persuasive to righteousness...

> ...We the General Assembly of Virginia do enact that no man shall be compelled to frequent or support any religious worship, place, or ministry whatsoever, nor shall be enforced, restrained, molested, or burthened in his body or goods, nor shall otherwise suffer, on account of his religious opinions or belief, but that all men shall be free to profess, and by argument to maintain, their opinions in matters of religion, and that the same shall in no wise diminish, enlarge, or affect their civil capacities...[54]

Religion was to neither "diminish" nor "enlarge" a person's civil capacities and government was to be excluded from controlling it in any way. It should be

---

54   Thomas Jefferson, Virginia Statute for Establishing Religious Freedom, 1777 / 1786, in Bruce Frohnen, ed., *The American Republic: Primary Sources* (Indianapolis: Liberty Fund, 2002), 330-331.

noted that although the example of Jesus was indirectly cited as the model for this act, nonetheless, Jefferson said in his *Autobiography* (1821) about a half century later that

> …its protection of opinion was meant to be universal…an amendment was proposed by inserting the word "Jesus Christ" so that it should read "A departure from the plan of Jesus Christ, the holy author of our religion;" the insertion was rejected by a great majority, in proof that they meant to comprehend within the mantle of its protection the Jew and the Gentile, the Christian and Mahometan, the Hindoo and Infidel of every denomination."[55]

This was certainly true and commendable—that everyone, regardless of their religious persuasion, would find religious freedom. The leading dissenting clergy agreed with this idea. That this bill was presented together with bills punishing Sabbath breakers and authorizing the governor to proclaim public days of prayer, clearly shows that it meant only to prevent the coercion of specific beliefs and did not restrict non-denominational expressions of the majority faith in public life. And as with the marriage law, Jefferson was not universally trying to keep the Bible out of the law.

In fact, the power for the government to proclaim public days of prayer in Bill #85 was applied by Jefferson while Governor of Virginia later in 1779. On November 11, Governor Jefferson issued a "Proclamation for a Public Day of Thanksgiving and Prayer." The official document began: "By his Excellency Thomas Jefferson, Esq. Governour or Chief Magistrate of the commonwealth of Virginia; Proclamation…Impressed with a grateful sense of the goodness of Almighty God, in… manifesting in multiplied instances his divine care…" and then it quoted at length from a proclamation made by the Continental Congress (from October 20, 1779), which stated in part:

> …he hath diffused the glorious light of the gospel, whereby, through the merits of our gracious Redeemer, we may become the heirs of his eternal glory…that he would grant to his church the plentiful effusions of divine grace, and pour out his holy spirit on all ministers of the gospel; that he would bless and prosper the means of education, and spread the light of

---

55   Jefferson's *Autobiography*, January 6, 1821, in Andrew A. Lipscomb and Albert Ellery Bergh, eds., *The Writings of Thomas Jefferson*, 20 vols. (Washington, D.C.: The Thomas Jefferson Memorial Association, 1904-05), 1:67.

Christian knowledge through the remotest corners of the earth…that he would in mercy look down upon us, pardon our sins and receive us into his favor, and finally, that he would establish the independence of these United States upon the basis of religion and virtue.[56]

After these overt Christian statements from Congress (using the words "Christian," "Redeemer," "church," "gospel") that Jefferson included in his proclamation, Jefferson then with his own words in the closing paragraph said: "…I do therefore by authority from the General Assembly issue this my proclamation, hereby appointing…a day of thanksgiving and prayer to Almighty God, earnestly recommending to all the good people of this commonwealth, to set apart the said day for those purposes" and for "the several Ministers of religion to meet their respective societies thereon, to assist them in their prayers, [and] edify them with their discourses."[57]

Besides these public actions, while governor, Jefferson's personal faith was evident through his continuing support of Rev. Clay and the Calvinistical Reformed Church. On August 15, 1779, he recorded in his account book that he "Paid Rev. Charles Clay in consideration of parochial [i.e., church-related] services."[58] And on the same day, Jefferson drafted a public Testimonial for Rev. Charles Clay which said: "The reverend Charles Clay has been many years rector of this parish, and has been particularly known to me…[H]is deportment has been exemplary…"[59]

This testimonial seems to indicate that Clay's role in St. Anne's parish was never going to be an option for him again, so this document gave Clay help if he sought other opportunities. But Clay continued to minister in Charlottesville for at least three more years. Jefferson's endorsement letter mentioned that besides his religious work, Clay also was politically active. He was a magistrate on the Albemarle County Court from 1771-1783, and his political leadership prompted contemporary historian Hugh Blair Grigsby to assert that Clay's merit was even greater than that of Presbyterian Samuel Davies.[60]

---

56   "Proclamation for a Public Day of Thanksgiving and Prayer," November 11, 1779, www.founders.archives.gov.

57   Ibid.

58   Account book, August 15, 1779. Beliles, *The Selected Religious Letters and Papers of Thomas Jefferson*, 39. Pd. Revd. Charles Clay in consideration of parochial services.

59   Testimonial for Rev. Charles Clay, August 15, 1779, www.founders.archives.gov.

60   Hugh Blair Grigsby, *The History of the Virginia Federal Convention of 1788*, 2 volumes (Richmond, Va.: Virginia Historical Society, 1891), I:255-258.

Jefferson's friendly relationship with orthodox Christian clergy was not limited to his own pastor. The main leader of Presbyterian clergy in Virginia, Rev. Samuel Stanhope Smith, wrote to Jefferson in March and April 1779, proposing "a coalition of the principal religious sects" to provide nonsectarian religious instruction in the public schools. Smith then offered his "influence on one of the parties," saying "my utmost exertions shall be at your service."[61] Smith was head of Hampden-Sydney College and apparently already knew Jefferson from earlier lobbying, hence, his freedom to propose an alliance for the purpose of pushing religious freedom in the legislature.

Smith began to rise in political influence earlier in April 1777 when he drafted a "Remonstrance Against a General Assessment" for the Hanover Presbytery. But before Smith was able to organize this interdenominational Christian "coalition" in opposition to a state church, he was called back to the College of New Jersey (Princeton) in 1779 (retaining some ministry in Virginia up to 1782).[62] It is important to notice that Jefferson wrote to Rev. Smith in early April 1779. This letter is missing today, but Smith's reply on April 19 mentions it approvingly.[63] Later when Jefferson was president, he also made a donation to Rev. Smith and the College at Princeton, of which he served as president.

Smith's protégé was Rev. John Todd of Louisa County, who continued Smith's effort when he moved away. Jefferson had probably met Todd in October 1776 and now communicated again. He sent a letter to Todd at this time, and although what Jefferson expressed in it cannot be known, because this letter is also missing, still it shows another example of Jefferson reaching out to work together with Presbyterians.[64] Then on August 16, 1779, Rev. Todd replied to Jefferson, which implies much of what Jefferson had said:

> I thank you for the favour you have done me in inclosing me the bill for establishing religious freedom. I had not seen it before—....Now I have a peculiar pleasure, sir, in finding that we are blessed with men, some men at

61 From Rev. Samuel Stanhope Smith to Jefferson, March and April 19, 1779, www.founders. archives.gov. It indicates a letter from Jefferson to Smith that is now missing.

62 Fred Hood, *Reformed America: The Middle and Southern States, 1783-1837* (University of Alabama Press, 1980), 7-26.

63 The editors of the Papers of Thomas Jefferson say that Smith's April 19 letter was "manifestly a reply to TJ's (missing) answer to Smith's letter." "To Thomas Jefferson from Samuel Stanhope Smith, 19 April 1779," www.founders.archives.gov.

64 Letter to Rev. John Todd, August 1779 (now missing but cited in reply of Todd to Jefferson, August 16, 1779), www.founders.archives.gov.

and near the helm with clear heads and honest hearts, zealous to bring to light and secure to all good men their rights without partiality. I guess at the author of the bill [i.e., Jefferson] and I love and esteem the man.

These opening sentences show the enthusiastic support of Presbyterians, like the Baptists, for Jefferson at this point in his life. They certainly show their appreciation of his efforts to disestablish the state-church in Virginia, so that all denominations would be on an equal footing. Rev. Todd continues:

> …the experience of all the Churches Since *Constantine*, shew the absurdity of Establishments. *Virtue and pure religion* do better without earthly emoluments than with…Wishing Success to the bill, and the certain Security of our Rights on so large and righteous a foundation, and that you may, Sir, long live to fill up the most important places in the State, and be blessed with every kind of happiness…[65]

Todd says that history proves the linkage of church and state beginning in fourth century Europe was a mistake. He even is willing to give Roman Catholics religious freedom, even though this was a radical measure at that time. Christian dissenters drove the tolerance and freedom movement in Virginia.

Jefferson's account book also shows that he paid "for the year" to the sexton of Bruton Parish in Williamsburg on September 30, 1779, which indicates a relationship with the church while he was now serving and residing as governor in that city.[66] Also Jefferson served on the board of the College of William and Mary, led at that time by its president, Rev. James Madison (not to be confused with the fourth president of the country, who was also a friend of Jefferson's). Jefferson's correspondence multiplied from this point onward with Rev. James Madison, with a minimal degree of religious content in over 40 letters over subsequent decades.[67] Rev. Madison would also later come and stay a week at a time with Jefferson at Monticello.

All this correspondence and notes in his account books show a comfortable relationship between Jefferson and Anglican, Presbyterian and Baptist clergy

---

65   From Rev. John Todd to Thomas Jefferson, August 16, 1779, www.founders.archives.gov.

66   Account book, September 30, 1779, Bear and Stanton, *Jefferson's Memorandum Books*, 487. To Michael McCarty, sexton for the year [at Bruton].

67   Letter to Rev. James Madison and Rev. Robert Andrews, March 31, 1781, www.founders. archives.gov. Madison had sent a letter to Jefferson on July 26, 1778.

at this point. In April 1780, the capital of Virginia was moved from Williamsburg to Richmond for security reasons, and while Jefferson was there he almost certainly worshiped in St. John's Church led by Rev. Miles Selden.

Jefferson finished his term as governor in June 1781 and then wrote his only book *Notes on Virginia*. It condemned coercion in religion and said:

> The legitimate powers of government extend to such acts only as are injurious to others. But it does me no injury for my neighbour to say there are twenty gods, or no God. It neither picks my pocket nor breaks my leg…; And can the liberties of a nation be thought secure when we have removed their only firm basis, a conviction in the minds of the people that these liberties are of the gift of God? That they are not to be violated but with his wrath? Indeed I tremble for my country when I reflect that God is just…[68]

Jefferson's belief in a God who acts in human history to punish injustice is certainly far from a perceived Deist way of thinking.

In 1782, it becomes apparent that a change occurs in Jefferson's home church. On June 29, Jefferson records in his account book that he subscribed to a new minister: "M[atthew] Maury annually to preach at Charlottesvlle."[69] This seems to indicate that Rev. Clay had ceased (or was intending soon to cease) his ministry as pastor of the Calvinistical Reformed Church. Indeed by the next year, Clay clearly had departed from the area. Without a minister, the Calvinistical Reformed Church ceased to exist at this point, so Jefferson makes a commitment to a new minister and a new church.

Since the Episcopal St. Anne's Parish still was inactive, which Jefferson had previously been a member of before starting the Calvinistical church, Jefferson renewed his involvement in the neighboring Fredericksville Episcopal parish, where he had been a member prior to 1769. Charlottesville was the closest location where the neighboring parish held services, using the courthouse. Jefferson continued to support and correspond with Rev. Maury for the next 25 years or so. Jefferson financially supported either Clay or Maury for over 30 years.

---

68   Jefferson's *Notes On the State of Virginia*, 1782, www.founders.archives.gov. (1787 in English).

69   Account book, June 29, 1782. Beliles, *The Selected Religious Letters and Papers of Thomas Jefferson*, 43. Subscribed…to Mr. M. Maury annually to preach at Charlsville.

The independent Calvinistical Reformed Church apparently disbanded as the war wound down because of financial hardships and the absence of major financial supporters. (Members such as Fillippo Mazzei and John Harvie both moved away permanently around 1780, and Jefferson went to France in 1784 for about six years). The loss of financial support led to the close of the church, which perhaps has led many biographers to overlook its significance.

The birth of another child and then death of both that child and Jefferson's wife in 1782, due to complications of child birth, were the most significant disappointments of Jefferson's life. Jefferson's account book on September 6, 1782, shows that he obtained Rev. Maury's services for the funeral.[70] His daughter Mary said this loss produced in her father a fragile state of mind, and others in Jefferson's family wrote of their concern for his emotional wellbeing at this time.[71]

And shortly after this loss and in the midst of the grieving period in his life, he went to France in 1784 and was separated from his religious roots back in Virginia. It perhaps would explain religious questions that began to emerge in his correspondence about six years later.

After Christmas 1782, Jefferson traveled to Philadelphia to serve in Congress, and despite his loss and grieving, at that time he continued to attend church, as was his custom. His account book says he "…paid at church" on March 31, 1783. This most likely was in the Episcopal Christ Church led now by Rev. William White.[72]

Sometime in May or June of 1783, Jefferson composed a draft of a Constitution for Virginia that included a reference to the "Sovereign Disposer of all Human Events" and also some clauses protecting religious freedom. In his draft, he wrote: "…The General assembly shall not have the power to…abridge the civil rights of any person on account of his religious belief; to restrain him from professing and supporting that belief, or to compel him to contributions, other than those he shall himself have stipulated…"[73]

Jefferson also discussed faith in a private letter to his daughter Martha on December 11, 1783, writing from Annapolis where Congress had moved. He said:

---

70 Account book, September 6, 1782, Bear and Stanton, *Jefferson's Memorandum Books,* 522. For M. Maury.

71 Randolph, *The Domestic Life of Thomas Jefferson,* 63.

72 Account book, March 31, 1783. Beliles, *The Selected Religious Letters and Papers of Thomas Jefferson,* 44. Pd at church [in Philadelphia]. Rev. White was also a fellow-officer with Jefferson in the American Philosophical Society along with several other clergymen.

73 Draft of Constitution for Virginia, May-June, 1783.

I hope you will have good sense enough to disregard those foolish predictions that the world is to be an end soon. The almighty has never made known to any body at what time he created it, nor will he tell any body when he means to put an end to it, if ever he means to do it. As to preparations for that event, the best way is for you to be always prepared for it…If ever you are about to…do anything wrong…You will feel something within you which will tell you it is wrong…: this is your conscience, and be sure to obey it. Our maker has given us all, this faithful internal Monitor, and if you always obey it, you will always be prepared for the end of the world: or for a much more certain event which is death…[74]

On the last day of 1783, Jefferson wrote a letter that told of his recent meeting with Presbyterian Rev. John Witherspoon of Princeton to ask his help in finding a tutor for Charlottesville.[75] This indicates a relative comfort with Presbyterian religious approaches to education at this point. He later wrote four other letters to Rev. Witherspoon along these lines in 1792.

Jefferson traveled to New England in mid-1784 and records in his account book that he "…paid a visit to the president of Yale College, Ezra Stiles."[76] Stiles was a clergyman at the head of this Congregationalist college. A couple days later on June 10, Jefferson followed up with a letter to Rev. Stiles saying: "…I had the pleasure of seeing you in New Haven…After repeating to you assurances of the pleasure with which I shall render any services in my power to the institution over which you so worthily preside, as well as to yourself personally, I have the honor to subscribe myself with the most perfect esteem & respect."[77] Stiles sent a friendly reply on June 21 and again on July 7, asking for Jefferson's extra help in fundraising for the college but Jefferson replied that it would not be possible while he was in France.[78] Jefferson was clearly friendly with Baptist, Presbyterian, and now Congregationalist clergymen (and they with him) in this period of his life.

---

74   Letter to Martha Jefferson, December 11, 1783, www.founders.archives.gov.

75   Letter to Wilson Cary Nicholas, December 31, 1783, www.founders.archives.gov. Jefferson said: "Just before I left Albemarle a proposition was started for establishing there a grammar school….on my part I was to enquire for a tutor. To this I have not been inattentive. I enquired at Princetown of Dr. Witherspoon. But he informed me that…no such person could of course be had there."

76   Account book, June 8, 1784, Bear and Stanton, *Jefferson's Memorandum Books,* 552. Pd. at Newhaven for 2oz bark. [Visit to Yale and Stiles].

77   Letter to Rev. Ezra Stiles, June 10, 1784, www.founders.archives.gov.

78   Letter to Rev. Ezra Stiles, July 17, 1784, www.founders.archives.gov.

Jefferson in France, 1784-1787

On July 5, 1784, Jefferson had sailed for France to serve as our government's representative there. On August 26, Jefferson enrolled his daughter Martha in a Bernadine Catholic convent school called Abbey Royale de Panthemont, led by Abbess Marie-Catherine Bethisy de Mezieres.[79] This school required attendance at daily chapel and doctrinal classes but did not require personal belief of its students.[80] So Jefferson had comfort with Catholic religious education at this point and even gave extra in "charity," but his Protestant family and friends back home would later criticize him for it.

At the very end of 1784, Jefferson sent a letter to his friend, lawyer James Madison (the later president), who was pushing for religious freedom in the Virginia legislature. Madison informed Jefferson that the Episcopal clergy were now advocating for legal incorporation status for their Church. Although sounding benign in modern times, it was new for Virginia churches and sounded to most dissenters as a way to gain a special relationship with government once again. To most dissenters this was terrifying for their experience had proven that one denomination having a favored relationship with the government resulted in much persecution, imprisonment, fines and discrimination. Jefferson knew of this responded that "...the Episcopalians have again shewn their teeth and fangs..."[81] Other than his *Notes on Virginia*, 1782, this was the first critical statement that Jefferson ever expressed about clergy in America. Most comments before then were about power-hungry priests in European history. Despite growing friendships with a handful of Catholic priests in France, Jefferson also wrote in a letter to Abigail Adams that he wished the French had a "better religion" than the Catholic expression he was seeing.[82] This was not an opinion limited to Jefferson. Other founders made similar comments after going to Europe.

In a letter to Marquis de Chastellux on September 2, 1785, Jefferson defended (even though he was not responsible for) the Virginia Constitution's prohibition of clergy in public office: "The clergy are excluded, because, if admitted into the

---

79   Account book, August 26, 1784. Beliles, *The Selected Religious Letters and Papers of Thomas Jefferson*, 46. Pd. at the Abbaie de Panthemont for Patsy – charity. Also see Account book, May 2, 1785. Pd. at Panthemont for Patsy.

80   Some biographers incorrectly claim that because religious belief was not required to be enrolled, that therefore non-Catholics were not exposed to the chapel and religious instruction.

81   Letter to James Madison, December 8, 1784 www.founders.archives.gov, (This is not the clergyman of the same name.)

82   Letter to Abigail Adams, June 21, 1785, www.founders.archives.gov.

legislature at all, the probability is that they would form its majority. For they are dispersed through every county in the state, they have influence with the people, and great opportunities of persuading them to elect them into the legislature. This body, tho shattered, is still formidable;...(and) merit a proscription from meddling with government."[83] Jefferson would reverse this opinion fifteen years later - when he sensed this danger no longer existed.[84] A modified version of Jefferson's original *Statute for Religious Freedom*, along with the *Statute to Punish Sabbath Breakers* finally passed in early 1786. Jefferson also mentioned "the Almighty" in a 1786 letter to George Wythe that also said: "Our act for freedom of religion is extremely applauded," and Jefferson said this was in contrast with France where "people are yet loaded with misery by kings, nobles and priests."[85]

Jefferson visited London, England for six weeks in the spring of 1786 to confer with America's envoy to that country—John Adams. While there Jefferson apparently for the first time went to a Unitarian church on March 12 that was frequented by John Adams.[86] This Unitarian church was led by Rev. Richard Price in Hackney, with whom Jefferson had just recently corresponded. This first exposure to Unitarianism, supported warmly by his colleague John Adams, seemed to sow a seed that would later grow in significant ways.

After returning to Paris, Jefferson wrote in a May 4 letter to his old college friend John Page, who now was a member of the Virginia legislature, "I...seek my religion out of the dictates of my own reason, and feelings of my own heart."[87] And to Jean Nicholas de' Meunier on June 26, he spoke of "an overruling providence...; a God of justice will...manifest his attention to the things of this world...; by diffusing light and liberality;...[there is no] blind fatality."[88] Jefferson's idea of Enlightenment here was in the light diffused by God, not by unaided reason. And Jefferson still believed in a God who intervened in issues of justice, not an aloof deistic God.

He corresponded with various French priests, but most of his interaction was not religious in nature. In a much later letter (1816) from Jefferson to Baptist

---

83   Letter to Marquis de Chastellux, September 2, 1785, www.founders.archives.gov.

84   Letter to Rev. Jeremiah Moore, August 14, 1800, www.founders.archives.gov.

85   Letter to George Wythe, August 13, 1786, www.founders.archives.gov.

86   Account book, March 12, 1786, Bear and Stanton, *Jefferson's Memorandum Books*, 613. Price's Church. The first openly Unitarian church in England had begun in 1774.

87   Letter to John Page, May 4, 1786, www.founders.archives.gov.

88   Letter to Jean Nicholas de Meunier, June 26, 1786 (also one on June 22), www.founders. archives.gov.

minister James Fishback, an important comment on this time period occurred. Jefferson pointed out that Fishback had published an account that "…mr Jefferson, it is said, declared that when he was in Paris, atheism was the common table-talk of the French bishops." Jefferson corrected this saying:

> I protest to you, Sir, that I never made such a declaration; and that as far as my knowledge of that order of clergy enabled me to judge, it would have been entirely untrue…The importance of religion to society has too many founded supports to need aid from imputations so entirely unfounded. I am persuaded of the innocence with which you have introduced this matter of report: but being myself quoted by name, and in print too, as the author of such a calumny on a respectable order of prelates, I owe to them, as well as to myself, to declare that no such declaration, or expression, was ever uttered by me.[89]

In public Jefferson was always conscientious to be respectful of religious beliefs of others, including all clergy. This was very important to him. However in private, especially later in life, he expressed to a few individuals more critical views. This was true on many topics, not just religion.

In 1787, his account book said that he "Paid at Mont Calvaire" on July 2.[90] This Catholic monastery, now known as Mont Valerien in Paris, became what he called his "hermitage," where he often stayed in the autumns of 1787 and 1788. A few months later, he wrote to Abigail Adams of the: "The Hermits of Mont Calvaire with whom I go and stay sometimes, and am favoured by them."[91] Silence was required except for mealtimes. Although it was possible that he simply lodged there, it is plausible that he also attended services and used it for spiritual contemplation and prayer as well since that is the reason most people went there. His payment was for his lodging of course but also indirectly supported the religious work of the Catholic monastery.

---

89   Letter to Rev. James Fishback, September 19, 1816. Beliles, *The Selected Religious Letters and Papers of Thomas Jefferson*, 273

90   Account book, July 2, 1787. Beliles, *The Selected Religious Letters and Papers of Thomas Jefferson*, 47. at Mont Calvaire [monastery].

91   Letter to Abigail Adams, February 2, 1788, www.founders.archives.gov. Editors of the Papers of Jefferson make this note: "The hermits of Mont Calvaire (also known as Mont Valérian), located near the village of Suresnes, France,…offered accommodations to paying guests. Jefferson visited them often while living in Paris."

Probably one of the most misquoted letters of Jefferson was written in 1787. On August 10, Jefferson wrote to his 18-year-old nephew, Peter Carr. Carr and other children of Jefferson's wife's sister looked to him for guidance in life and education after their father, Dabney Carr, died young. Since Peter was now an adult enrolled at the College of William and Mary, Jefferson writes to him about religion and starts by asserting that a Creator "made us" and that we were "endowed with a sense of right and wrong…or conscience" to ponder spiritual matters. Then Jefferson confidently asserted that: "If you find reason to believe there is a God… [and] that Jesus was also a God, you will be comforted by a belief of his aid and love;…Reason is…given you by heaven."[92] With this obvious presupposition that a Creator exists and that heaven gives each one a conscience and reason, Jefferson then tells Carr that to honestly consider religion he should:

> …divest yourself of all bias;…Question with boldness even the existence of a God;…Read the bible;…It is said that the writer of that book was inspired. Examine therefore candidly what evidence there is of his having been inspired. The pretension is entitled to your inquiry, because millions believe it;…Read the new testament. It is the history of a person called Jesus.[93]

Jefferson then presented to Carr comparative statements of both faith and skepticism. He said:

> Keep in your eye the opposite pretensions [i.e., claims] of those who say: 1. He was begotten by God, born of a virgin, suspended and reversed the laws of nature at will, and ascended bodily into heaven, and 2. He was a man of illegitimate birth, of a benevolent heart, enthusiastic mind, who set out without pretensions [i.e., claims] to divinity, ended in believing them…judge their pretensions by your own reason, and not by the reason of those ecclesiastics.[94]

Note that Jefferson had already indicated his belief in a creator, so we know He was not favoring atheism. But often today apologists for Jefferson being a skeptic

---

92   Letter to Peter Carr, August 10, 1787, www.founders.archives.gov.

93   Ibid.

94   Ibid.

will lift the quotes from only one side of the list and suggest that it most represents Jefferson's views. But there is really no basis whatsoever for this claim. Jefferson makes virtually no comment to favor either side. The gist of the letter to Peter Carr is *to think for yourself, do your own research, and draw your own conclusions.* Since Jefferson up to this time had been constantly attending churches and voluntarily supporting his local clergyman and Reformed or Episcopal Church, if there is anything up to this moment that would be more plausible that he believed, it would appear to be the side of the list that mentions Jesus being "…begotten by God, born of a virgin, suspended and reversed the laws of nature at will, and ascended bodily into heaven…"[95] Those were the statements of the creeds in the churches he voluntarily attended and funded. Up to this moment, after looking over the first 21 years of Jefferson's adult life (1767-1787), a single definitive sign of unbelief or of disagreement with an orthodox article of faith cannot be found.

---

95   Ibid.

CHAPTER 2

THOMAS JEFFERSON'S RELIGIOUS LIFE, 1788-1802

"The difficulty of reconciling the ideas of Unity and Trinity, have, from a very early part of my life, excluded me from the office of sponsorship [of a child in baptism]...Accept therefore Sir this conscientious excuse..."
—Thomas Jefferson, 1788[1]

The reason the beginning of the second phase of Jefferson's religious life starts at this point is mainly because of one particular letter from that time, where he questioned the Christian doctrine of the Trinity. The first significant evidence of a change in beliefs was revealed in a reply Jefferson made to Justin P. P. Derieux on July 25, 1788. Derieux, a neighbor of Jefferson's in Albemarle, had asked Jefferson to be a sponsor for his child in baptism—i.e., a godfather. Jefferson declined, saying:

...The person who becomes sponsor for a child, according to the ritual of the church in which I was educated, makes a solemn profession, before God and the world, of faith in articles, which I had never sense enough

---

1   Letter to Justin P. P. Derieux, July 25, 1788, www.founders.archives.gov.

to comprehend, and it has always appeared to me that comprehension must precede assent. The difficulty of reconciling the ideas of Unity and Trinity, have, from a very early part of my life, excluded me from the office of sponsorship...; the church requires—faith. Accept therefore Sir this conscientious excuse...[2]

This letter has been used by biographers without careful analysis. They have said therefore that Jefferson never assented to church beliefs as an adult. But it was already seen that in the first 21 years of Jefferson's adult life, he had been an active member and vestryman of the Anglican Church requiring assent to its doctrines, including the Trinity. His name was listed in the Vestry Book under the oath of assent to its doctrines for all to see. And virtually every biographer says that he baptized his children in the Church, which required similar affirmations. And in addition to that he led the effort to start the Calvinistical Reformed Church and voluntarily funded its pastor and his uncommon evangelical preaching.

So when Jefferson now says that "from a very early part of my life," he never had sense enough to comprehend and reconcile the ideas of Unity and Trinity, and therefore never had faith in the church's articles, it creates a dilemma. It can indicate one of two possibilities: (1) This long-held inward dissonance was true but never strong enough that he tangibly acted upon it; or (2) He has developed dissonance recently but perhaps exaggerated its length in an effort to excuse himself to Derieux. It's also possible that he was just plain inconsistent. One thing is certain: a new era of questioning his beliefs was real now. Although he would privately but clearly reject some articles of faith by 1813, Jefferson was only willing to say at this point that he was unsure of his beliefs. He was now pondering these things sincerely and did not want to be a hypocrite. As will be seen, his questions eventually led him to think incorrectly that the Trinity was not a part of the original Christian revelation but rather a later corruption.

The Unitarian clergyman in London, Rev. Richard Price, wrote several times to Jefferson at this time. His letter on October 26, 1788, spoke of the problems with "Popery...Mahometans ...Pagans...and of many Protestants...[and asked] Would not Society be better without Such religions? Is Atheism less pernicious than Demonism?...Plutarch, it is well known, has observd very justly that it is better not to believe in a God than to believe him to be a capricious and malevolent being."[3]

---

2   Letter to Justin P. P. Derieux, July 25, 1788, www.founders.archives.gov.

3   Letter from Rev. Richard Price, October 26, 1788, www.founders.archives.gov.

Jefferson replied to Price on January 8, 1789: "…Atheism and demonism:…[I] see nothing but the latter in the being worshipped by many who think themselves Christians…"[4] It is important to read this comment on demonism in context. Jefferson was specifically talking about French Catholicism in specific response to that focus in Price's letter. And even while doing so, he still commended some Catholic clergy, retreated at a Catholic monastery, and kept his children enrolled in the Catholic school there.[5]

As Jefferson began commenting on the political instability in France, he frequently mentioned in various letters in late 1788 and 1789 about the "…priests and nobles combining together against the people …" and that "The clergy and nobility, as clergy and nobility eternally will, are opposed to giving…representation [to the people] as may dismount them from their back."[6] Almost every reference to "clergy" in this period is in regard to the Catholic French clergy, and it would be incorrect to apply them as general comments on all clergy in Christianity. Protestant clergymen made the same judgments about the French and medieval clergy and sometimes even more harshly than did Jefferson.

The first clear evidence of Jefferson's thoughts opening to unorthodox religious opinions is seen at this point when he again wrote to Rev. Richard Price in London on July 12, 1789, asking: "…Is there any good thing on the subject of the Socinian doctrine?…I would thank you to recommend such a work to me."[7] Socinianism was a kind of Unitarianism. Price replied to Jefferson on August 3 and included two pamphlets: "Sermons on the Christian Doctrine," and "Two Schemes of a Trinity considered."[8] Now Jefferson was doing more than confessing incomprehension of the Trinity; he was studying heterodox opinions on it.

When Jefferson returned home from France in December 1789, he soon became aware of a Virginia religious revival if he was not already that was impacting the Presbyterian college of Hampden Sidney.[9] He still found his St. Anne's Parish

---

4   Letter to Rev. Richard Price, January 8, 1789, www.founders.archives.gov.

5   Account book entry for April 20, 1789: "Pd. at Panthemont in full." For Panthemont Catholic School. Beliles, *The Selected Religious Letters and Papers of Thomas Jefferson*, 52.

6   Letter to George Washington, November 4, 1788; Letter to W. Carmichael, December 25, 1788, www.founders.archives.gov.

7   Letter to Rev. Richard Price, July 12, 1789, www.founders.archives.gov.

8   Letter from Rev. Richard Price, August 3, 1789, www.founders.archives.gov.

9   Carlos Allen, "The Great Revival in Virginia, 1783-1812" (Unpublished master's thesis, University of Virginia, 1948), 89-91, 96. For more in-depth research that provides some insight into the religious communities of Virginia, see Mark A. Beliles, *Churches and Politics in Jefferson's Virginia* (Ph.D. Dissertation, published in electronic format by America

to be missing any clergyman and largely defunct, so he continued what he had begun shortly before going to France—he joined the services in the courthouse of Charlottesville led by Episcopal minister Rev. Matthew Maury of the adjacent Fredericksville Parish. That parish was also no longer functioning formally and thus unable to support Maury, so in fact Maury operated more as an independent (as Clay had done) through donations of supporters such as Jefferson.

Jefferson wrote to Rev. Maury on January 8, 1790, asking for information on a Bible and pledging to support Rev. Maury's school: "I recollect you have… Grabe's septuagint [i.e., Old Testament in Greek] in 10. vols. Not knowing where, when, and by whom it was printed, I have been unable to ask for it in Europe, which I had wished to do. I will thank you to inform me of these circumstances that I may be enabled to have the edition procured for me by the first occasion in Europe."[10] Jefferson reading the Bible in Greek showed that he was a serious student of the Scriptures.

Six weeks later Jefferson noted on February 23 in his account book that he "Paid Mr. Maury marriage fee."[11] This was for performing the wedding of his daughter Martha to Thomas Mann Randolph at Monticello. A Trinitarian marriage service was held in Monticello. Even if Jefferson was beginning to doubt some of the orthodox creeds, it was now easier for him to participate in worship because the more complex and detailed Athanasian Creed had been removed from the Episcopal service in 1785 in favor of the simpler Apostles' Creed and Nicene Creed.[12] More about the 4th century St. Athanasius and the highly-detailed Trinitarian creed named after him is explained in a later chapter, but now it is enough to know that without this change, it is possible that Jefferson may have discontinued participating in Episcopal worship when he returned to America, but he does not. No attacks later during the presidential campaign claimed that he did not attend church or refrained from taking communion.

Publications, 2000). Also see works of Rhys Isaacs, Thomas Buckley, Daniel Dreisbach, and John Ragosta.

10   Letter to Rev. Matthew Maury, January 8, 1790, www.founders.archives.gov.

11   Account book, February 23, 1790. For M. Maury. Beliles, *The Selected Religious Letters and Papers of Thomas Jefferson*, 56.

12   Of course, the structure of both the Apostles' Creed and the Nicene Creed is Trinitarian: In essence, they say: I believe in God the Father (etc.), in God the Son (etc.) and in God the Spirit (etc.) The Nicene Creed in particular is even more explicitly Trinitarian, saying of Jesus that He is "God from God, light from light, true God from true God, begotten, not made, one in being with the Father…" The Athanasian Creed was more detailed and complex.

Rev. Charles Clay, who had been Jefferson's earlier pastor both in St. Anne's Parish and in the independent Calvinistical Reformed Church that Jefferson helped found, had ended up settling in Bedford County while Jefferson was in France. He apparently resumed a relationship with the Episcopal Church in Virginia to serve as a priest both formally and later informally.[13] This minister was also very active in politics and in 1788 was elected by his area to be a delegate to the Virginia Constitutional Convention. There he came down on the side of opposition to the proposed U.S. Constitution because it lacked a Bill of Rights to secure "the great principles of civil and religious liberty."[14] After it passed and the new U.S. government was being formed, Rev. Clay then stood for election as a congressman to represent his district.

Jefferson hears of this and writes Rev. Clay on January 27, 1790: "I understand you are a candidate for…Congress;…I am sure I shall be contented with such a representative as you will make;…Wishing you every prosperity in this… undertaking;…your friend & servant."[15] Jefferson certainly did not have any qualms with this clergyman running for federal office, even though the Virginia constitution still prohibited state offices from being held by ministers. This general endorsement did not help Clay win the election, however, and when Clay sought even more direct help two years later Jefferson declined saying it was "due to … considerations respecting myself only, and not you to whom I am happy in every occasion of testifying my esteem."[16] Indeed Jefferson continued to correspond and dine with Clay frequently over the next 25 more years.

Jefferson made religious references and spoke of his belief in prayer in a public letter to the Citizens of Albemarle on February 12: "In the holy cause of freedom…heaven has rewarded us…that it may flow through all times…is my

---

13   Katharine L. Brown, *Hills of the Lord: Background of the Episcopal Church in Southwestern Virginia 1738-1938* (Roanoke, Va.: Diocese of Southwestern Virginia, 1979), 134-136. Before settling permanently in Bedford, Clay also traveled and preached in Chesterfield County and was active in the state Episcopal conventions in 1785 and 1786, representing Manchester Parish. Clay served on a committee concerning altering the *Book of Common Prayer*. He and Bishop Madison opposed it. When he moved to Bedford, he served part-time in Russell and Lynchburg Episcopal Parishes until his death.

14   Grigsby, *The History of the Virginia Federal Convention of 1788*, I:344. Clay also spoke against Congress having the power to tax and to call forth the militia.

15   Letter to Rev. Charles Clay, January 27, 1790, www.founders.archives.gov.

16   Letter to Rev. Charles Clay, 11 September, 1792, www.founders.archives.gov. Clay had written him asked for support on August 8, 1792. Clay did not win his elections for Congress.

fervent prayer to heaven."[17] In April he sent a letter back to France to some of his close Catholic friends there – Abbes Arnoux and Chalut. He closed it saying: "That heaven may bless you with long years of life and health, is the fervent prayer of him [i.e., Jefferson]."[18]

Serving As Secretary of State

When appointed by President Washington to be Secretary of State, Jefferson moved to New York City and was there from March 21-August 31 in 1790. Rev. Ezra Stiles, President of the Congregational Yale College in New Haven, wrote Jefferson expressing his desire for him to become the next president.[19] Jefferson and fellow-politician James Madison made a trip to New England and New York between May 17 and June 19 in 1791 and attended churches during that trip. For instance, they worshiped in the First Congregational Church in Bennington, Vermont, (led by Rev. Job Swift) along with Vermont's governor, Moses Robinson.[20] Rev. William Linn was pastor of a Presbyterian church in New York, who praised Jefferson on July 18 as: "among its [i.e., America's] greatest ornaments."[21] Jefferson replied saying: "...my thanks for the copy of the sermon you were so good as to send me, which I have perused with very great pleasure."[22] Jefferson was still a person enjoying a warm relationship with clergy of the northern states at this point, from Congregational and Presbyterian traditions.

In his book, *Religion and the American Mind,* Harvard historian Alan Heimert observes that there "...were many preachers—many more than historians allow—who avidly and vocally supported the Republican party'" and many "found their way into state legislatures...[and] mingled the two careers, generally with their people's understanding that Republican politics was an appropriate channel for the expression and achievement of Evangelical goals."[23] It is worth clarifying here that

17   Letter to the Citizens of Albemarle, February 12, 1790, www.founders.archives.gov.

18   Letter to Abbes Arnoux and Chalut, April 5, 1790, www.founders.archives.gov.

19   Letter from Ezra Stiles, August 27, 1790, www.founders.archives.gov.

20   Account book, June 1791. Beliles, *The Selected Religious Letters and Papers of Thomas Jefferson,* 58. Later, Jefferson affirmed his belief in Christianity in a letter to Moses Robinson in 1801, www.founders.archives.gov.

21   Letter from Rev. William Linn, July 18, 1791, www.founders.archives.gov.

22   Letter to Rev. William Linn, July 31, 1791, www.founders.archives.gov.

23   Alan Heimert, *Religion and The American Mind: From the Great Awakening to the Revolution* (Cambridge, Mass.: Harvard University Press, 1966), 534-536, 538, 541. Reichley affirms that "the support the Evangelicals gave the Republicans contributed importantly to Jefferson's triumph in 1800." James A. Reichley, *Religion in American Public Life* (Washington, D.C.: The Brookings Institution, 1985), 181.

the "Republican party" that Jefferson helped lead was not the same as the modern party by that name. But the earlier party began to emerge due to the opposition that grew up to the Federalist party that defined presidents Washington and Adams. Jefferson and Madison became the beneficiaries of the emerging new party (that was also called the Democrats or Democratic Republicans, but was likewise not the same as the modern Democrat party).

Early in 1791 Jefferson wrote a letter to his son-in-law Thomas Mann Randolph. In it Jefferson rejoiced in the birth of a new family member and quoted a verse from the book of Psalms from the Bible in doing so: "I congratulate you sincerely, my dear Sir, on the birth of the little daughter. 'Happy the man, in the scripture phrase, who hath his quiver full of them.'"[24] Jefferson then went home for a visit between September 3 and October 21, 1791. A letter to Maury mentioned a donation to his home church on October 25: "to Revd. Matthew Maury 75.5 Dollars."[25] (Keep in mind with such donations, which will be seen throughout the book, that to approximate what that would mean in today's dollars, we need to multiply by over 20 times.) More money was given on November 4, 1792, to "Revd. Matthew Maury."[26] Some of these expenditures were for church work and some for school fees of Jefferson's dependents.

Back in Philadelphia, Jefferson also writes to Presbyterian Rev. John Witherspoon, as he did a decade earlier to request him to provide a teacher for a school in the Charlottesville area "in hopes that your seminary, or your acquaintance may furnish some person, whom you could recommend as fitted to the object..."[27] And Jefferson sent an earlier (January 12) letter to Rev. Witherspoon to recommend a student for enrollment in his seminary at Princeton, and another on June 3 and July 29 asking for teachers to come.[28] To Rev. Needler Robinson, Episcopal minister in Chesterfield County, Virginia, Jefferson sent a letter, saying that he "inclosed to Mr. Baker for you a letter from Dr. Witherspoon."[29]

---

24 Letter to Thomas Mann Randolph, February 24, 1791, www.founders.archives.gov.

25 Letter to Rev. Matthew Maury, October 25, 1791, www.founders.archives.gov. Also see Account book entry for M. Maury. (Note: Jefferson would simply use a single letter D in his account book to refer to Dollars. We have chosen to spell it out for the clarity of the reader.)

26 Letter to Matthew Maury, October 10, 1791, www.founders.archives.gov. Also see entries for Maury in Account book, for the same day, and later in October and November of 1792. Beliles, *The Selected Religious Letters and Papers of Thomas Jefferson*, 58.

27 Letter to Rev. John Witherspoon, March 12, 1792, www.founders.archives.gov.

28 Letters to Rev. John Witherspoon, January 12, June 3 and July 29, 1792, www.founders. archives.gov.

29 "From Thomas Jefferson to Needler Robinson, 9 September 1792," www.founders.archives.gov.

His account book also reveals that Jefferson "Paid. Mr. B[___]et a subscription for missionaries" near the end of 1792.[30] This support of missionaries is interesting because it begins to emerge in various correspondence at this time between Jefferson and Rev. Samuel Miller. Miller was a Presbyterian minister who Jefferson may have met earlier when he was in New York.[31]

When Jefferson ends his term as Secretary of State and returns home, he again is found supporting his pastor Rev. Matthew Maury. The account book said on June 21, 1794: "Paid. Revd. Matthew Maury,"[32] and in 1795 an entry for May 4 said: "Paid Revd. M. Maury on account of my subscription for 1793."[33] Jefferson apparently discovered his failure, from two years earlier, to support his home church while he was living in New York.

In contrast to these friendly clergy relationships in 1794 Jefferson mentioned in a letter to Pennsylvania politician, Tench Coxe, that "…priests…have been so long deluging with human blood…"[34] The context of this is mainly referring to state-church clergy in European history, no different from what dissident Protestant clergy often said. It was not an anti-clerical statement but an anti-tyranny statement.

Serving As Vice-President

Presbyterian Rev. William Linn of New York wrote Vice-President Jefferson, now residing in Philadelphia much of the time, on May 25, 1797, on the subject of missions to Indians and included a pamphlet from the New York Missionary Society.[35] Linn was one of the directors of the Society that sent its first missionary

---

30   Account book, November 27, 1792. Beliles, *The Selected Religious Letters and Papers of Thomas Jefferson*, 60. Subscription for missionaries.

31   Letter to Rev. Samuel Miller, September 3, 1793, www.founders.archives.gov. Editors of *The Papers of Thomas Jefferson* note: "Samuel Miller (1769–1850) had been ordained as a Presbyterian clergyman in New York City earlier this year and officiated in that city until 1813, after which he served on the faculty of Princeton Theological Seminary until his death. The discourse Miller had sent TJ was his first publication, *A Sermon, Preached in New-York, July 4th, 1793. Being the Anniversary of the Independence of America: at the request of the Tammany Society, or Columbian Order* (New York, 1793), which among other things criticized slavery and defended the French Revolution."

32   Account book, June 21, 1794. Bear and Stanton, 917. For M. Maury.

33   Account book, May 4, 1795. Beliles, *The Selected Religious Letters and Papers of Thomas Jefferson*, 61. For M. Maury. This was noted to be a tardy payment for his 1793 subscription as his local minister.

34   Letter to Tench Coxe, May 1, 1794, www.founders.archives.gov.

35   Letter from Rev. William Linn, May 25, 1797, www.founders.archives.gov. In William Linn's letter the editors of *The Papers of Thomas Jefferson* say the enclosed circular was the printed address of the newly established Missionary Society that was distributed "To all them that love our Lord Jesus Christ in sincerity." (The Address and Constitution of the

to the Chickasaws two years later in 1799. The editors of *The Papers of Thomas Jefferson* note that Jefferson and Linn often "…corresponded about their common interest in the American Indian tribes and their languages." On February 5, 1798 Jefferson told Linn: "I should be very glad to [_____]…one of my [_____]… for the use of (your missionaries)."[36] Although some words are illegible in the letter so that it is not clear what specifically he offered them, the main point is that he wanted to help their missionary work. And with previous donations to religious missionaries and later for Bible distribution to "the heathen" (their term for an unevangelized people group, but in this context, Indians), this cannot be dismissed as merely a secular motive.

Jefferson was back home in 1797 for the last half of the year and obtained Rev. Maury to conduct the Episcopal wedding for his daughter Mary [called Polly] and John Wayles Eppes in October.[37] The account book on December 5, says: "pay my subscription to end of this year…for Mr. Maury."[38] It does the same in 1799. These voluntary gifts continued to show his commitment to the Episcopal Church.

He returned to Philadelphia and there met Rev. Joseph Priestley, a Unitarian clergyman who had emigrated from England in 1794 to Northumberland, Pennsylvania and was a guest preacher in the area. Jefferson heard some of Priestley's sermons at that time.[39] Much later in 1822, Jefferson said: "there was a respectable congregation of that sect, with a meeting-house and regular service which I attended, and in which Doctor [Joseph] Priestley officiated to numerous audiences."[40] If Jefferson's comment a quarter of a century later is true, then it is the second time where Jefferson attended an unorthodox church service. The first was in England as a guest of John Adams but now he does

New-York Missionary Society, 1796). Letter to Rev. William Linn, June 3, 1797, www. founders.archives.gov. Nothing religiously significant was in the letter.

36   Letter from Rev. William Linn, February 8, 1798 and April 4, 1798, and Letter to Rev. William Linn, February 5, 1798, www.founders.archives.gov. The words "your missionaries" was inserted by the editors of *The Papers of Thomas Jefferson*. But it is clearly what was meant. The editors note: "Writing on 2 Apr. 1798 to Linn, one of the directors of the New York Missionary Society, TJ made his blank form available to the fledgling organization, which began its evangelical work with one minister sent to the Chickasaws in 1799. The directors' instructions to missionaries that year referred obliquely to TJ's word list."

37   Account book, October 13, 1797. Beliles, *The Selected Religious Letters and Papers of Thomas Jefferson*, 62. For M. Maury.

38   Account book, December 5, 1797. Beliles, *The Selected Religious Letters and Papers of Thomas Jefferson*, 62. For M. Maury.

39   Joseph Priestley to Thomas Belsham, March 14, 1797.

40   Letter to Rev. Benjamin Waterhouse, July 19, 1822, Dickinson Adams and Ruth W. Lester, eds., *Jefferson's Extracts From the Gospels* (Princeton, N.J.: Princeton University Press, 1983), 406.

so as a personal choice. Jefferson also around this time purchased Priestley's *History of the Corruptions of Christianity.*[41] There is no contemporary reference to Jefferson attending Priestley's church in any of his letters or account book entries, yet he later claims he attended his church at that time. So for us to accept this statement at face value requires us to also assume he likely attended churches in other times of his life, since he later said he was a *lifelong* member of the Episcopal Church and is proven to have donated to it consistently and generously.[42] Jefferson's mention of worshiping with Priestley requires the scholar to assume church attendance throughout his life, unless proven otherwise. (The main exception to this may well be when he is in France from 1784-1789, and Protestant worship was not available to him.)

On February 5, 1798, Jefferson wrote some *Notes on Newspaper Articles,* which spoke of Jesus as "Saviour." This term describes a redemptive mission. Jefferson also used this term or "Christ" in other letters; but in this 1798 case, like his earlier commonplace notes and other "Notes on Religion" cited previously, it is impossible to say if it definitely expressed his own personal beliefs here, since Jefferson made no comment on the notes.

A few weeks later in February 1798, Jefferson "Paid…subscription for a hot press bible," published by Thompson and Small.[43] A hot press Bible refers to a new way they printed the holy book. A contemporary ad said that publishers John Thompson and Abraham Small believed it "to be the most beautiful production of its nature, hitherto seen." To subscribe meant to make a pledge ahead of time to the publishers so that the capital was there to accomplish the project. But more significant was the fact that Jefferson approved his name to be listed publicly in the volume as a subscriber or advance investor. He also subscribed and thus approved his name to be printed later in two other biblical works.[44]

Jefferson wrote a letter on April 11, 1798, to a Moravian [i.e. United Brethren] minister John G. E. Heckewelder of Bethlehem, Pennsylvania, who was a missionary

---

41   As we will see in a later chapter, the essence of Priestley's thesis in that book is that God revealed Himself in Christianity, but very early on in the church, there was a corruption in the transmission of that revelation. (The problem with his thesis is just how early he believed that corruption began.)

42   Letter to Rev. Benjamin Rice, August 10, 1823. Jefferson Collection, College of William and Mary.

43   Account book, February 26, 1798. Beliles, *The Selected Religious Letters and Papers of Thomas Jefferson,* 62. Subscription for a hot press bible. A second payment for it is found in the Account book at January 5, 1799. The second payment was $10 which is about $250 today.

44   These were in 1805 for *The History of our Blessed Lord and Saviour Jesus Christ* and in 1807 for the Scott Bible.

to Indian towns in that state and Ohio. They exchanged several letters regarding Indian missions.[45] And later as president Jefferson endorsed treaties that funded the work of United Brethren missionaries to the Indians. Jefferson's occasional generosity to Christian missions to the Indians was such that New York Presbyterian Rev. Samuel Miller felt comfortable to seek Jefferson's support for same (March 4, 1800). No response by Jefferson to Miller's request is found, either way.

In November, 1798, while Jefferson was back home, he anonymously drafted the *Kentucky Resolutions*. Kentucky was still part of Virginia at that point. His resolution revealed Jefferson's Christian idea of man, which is that all men are sinners in need of restraint and essentially argued the need for decentralized (i.e., state and local) authority over religious policy.[46] He argued that security for religious freedom lies in the Constitutional principle of federalism rather than of secularism.[47] Along this line of reasoning Jefferson also wrote to Elbridge Gerry of Massachusetts on January 26, 1799, saying "I am for freedom of religion, and against all maneuvers to bring about a legal ascendency of one sect over another."[48]

In contrast to his friendly relations with his local clergy, Jefferson made his first criticism of northeastern clergymen in a letter to James Madison, dated March 2, 1798, when he said that the New England states "are so priest-ridden, that nothing is to be expected from them, but the most bigoted passive obedience."[49] State-churches still existed in New England and therefore priests still had favored status with government. But in contrast to this was Virginia which is illustrated by Jefferson's reference to Albemarle County Baptist pastor William "Baptist Billy" Woods who Jefferson mentions in a letter on December 21, 1799: "our election [for Virginia House of Delegates] was yesterday. Woods carried it..."[50] Woods,

---

45   Letter to Rev. John G. E. Heckewelder, April 11, 1798; Heckewelder sent two replies in April. And two years later see a letter from Rev. John Heckewelder, February 24, 1800, www.founders.archives.gov.

46   The fundamental Biblical premise of men being sinners and prone to evil is why America's founders emphasized the need for government in the first place. Madison said in Federalist Papers (#51) that "if men were angels no government would be necessary." The same premise applies to their concern with controlling those who wield government authority. John Adams and other founders also expressed this idea. Jefferson similarly wrote in the Kentucky Resolutions saying: "In questions of power, then, let no more be heard of confidence in man, but bind him down from mischief by the chains of the Constitution."

47   Kentucky Resolutions, November 16, 1798, www.founders.archives.gov.

48   Letter to Elbridge Gerry, January 26, 1799, www.founders.archives.gov.

49   Letter to James Madison, March 2, 1798, www.founders.archives.gov. [not the clergyman]

50   Letter to John Wayles Eppes, December 21, 1799, www.founders.archives.gov.

who corresponded and met with Jefferson on occasion, relinquished his ministerial license because the Virginia constitution barred clergymen from being elected to the assembly.[51] Eight months later, Jefferson told Baptist clergyman Jeremiah Moore that he no longer supported this restriction.[52]

Campaign Attacks From Northeastern Clergy

The Federalist-aligned northern clergy, such as Congregationalists Rev. Timothy Dwight in Connecticut and Rev. Jedidiah Morse of Boston, began to question the faith of the presidential candidate Jefferson. Not a single clergyman in Virginia or any city south of New York ever opposed Jefferson on religious grounds while he was alive. Jefferson wrote to his friend, Bishop James Madison of Virginia at this time saying: "...Morse...& his ecclesiastical and monarchical associates have been making such a hue and cry."[53] Bishop Madison replied giving his endorsement of Priestley as a philosopher and sharply criticized these Congregationalist leaders and especially Rev. Morse as "a blockhead."[54]

Sometime that spring of 1800, the Presbyterian of New York, Rev. William Linn, with whom Jefferson had previously corresponded in a friendly way seven times, wrote an essay attacking Jefferson's religious beliefs titled: "Serious Considerations on the Election of a President."[55] Using Jefferson's *Notes on the State of Virginia*, he argued against Jefferson's election, asserting "his disbelief of the Holy Scriptures... his rejection of the Christian Religion and open profession of Deism." This was the second time the term "Deism" was used of Jefferson.

There is nothing in Jefferson's public writings to this point that would substantiate that charge, and in light of the previous friendly private correspondence

---

51   According to Baptist historian John Turpin, "at the urgent solicitation of Thos. Jefferson he [Woods] ...became a candidate for the Legislature. . . ." John B. Turpin, *A Brief History of the Albemarle Baptist Association* (Richmond, Va.: Virginia Baptist Historical Society, 1891), 31. See also Mary Rawlings, *The Albemarle of Other Days* (Charlottesville, Va.: Michie Co., 1925), 100. Rev. Jacob Watts replaced him at the Albemarle Baptist Church, however Woods gave a farewell sermon in 1810 before moving to Kentucky. The 1797 letter of Woods to Jefferson is now missing, but another survives from 1805.

52   Letter to Rev. Jeremiah Moore, August 14, 1800, www.founders.archives.gov.

53   Letter to Rev. James Madison, January 31, 1800, www.founders.archives.gov.

54   Rev. Madison to Jefferson, February 11, 1800, www.founders.archives.gov.

55   Jefferson himself received a copy of Rev. Linn's attack entitled *Serious Considerations* in a letter from George Harrison Smith on September 11. Smith said: "For my single self I believe . . . you have not that mean contempt of Religion you are said to have by your *enemies,* and as for what is contained in your writings I find nothing to establish that opinion with me. . . ." Letter from George Smith, September 11, 1800, www.founders. archives.gov.

between Jefferson and Rev. Linn, this attack makes a historian scratch his head. What happened? Unfortunately, there is no evidence that explains it. With all other things remaining equal, the only thing new in 1800 was the looming presidential election. Clergy in the northeast did not criticize Jefferson's faith until it was apparent that he would be the political opponent of that region's favorite son, John Adams.

The other opposition piece was "The Voice of Warning, to Christians, on the Ensuing Election of a President of the United States," by Rev. John M. Mason of New York (who claimed Jefferson was a "confirmed infidel").[56] A decade later Jefferson said: "I do not know Dr. Mason personally, but by character well. He is the most red hot federalist, famous, or rather infamous for the lying & slandering which he vomited from the pulpit, in the political harangues with which he polluted that place. I was honored with much of it. He is a man who can prove every thing if you will take his word for proof."[57] Such attacks on Jefferson were more commonly leveled by Congregationalists, "Rational Christians," Unitarians, and "Deists" of New England who supported the Federalists—the opposing party of Jeffersonian Republicans.[58]

Of course, as of the date of these pamphlets, Jefferson had only once expressed that he did not comprehend the Trinity, and did so totally private. He had never rejected Christianity or the Bible and had never said anything whatsoever about Deism, much less a profession of it. Jefferson's report to James Madison on these false charges said that "...the republican papers of Massachusets & Connecticut continue to be filled with the old stories of deism, atheism, antifederalism &c."[59] The editors of *The Papers of Thomas Jefferson* give these comments regarding this letter to Madison: "John Beckley, characterizing the piece as a virulent portrayal of TJ 'as an Atheist and Deist,' countered it with a series of four articles...[and] DeWitt Clinton responded with essays...published in New York in 1800 as 'A Vindication of Thomas Jefferson; Against the Charges Contained in a Pamphlet Entitled, 'Serious Considerations,' &c.'"

---

56   Ellis Sandoz, *Political Sermons of the American Founding Era, 1730-1805* (Indianapolis, Ind.: Liberty Press, 1991), 1448-1554. See also Malone, *Jefferson and the Ordeal of Liberty,* 522.

57   Letter to Rev. Joel Barlow, January 24, 1810, www.founders.archives.gov.

58   H. Shelton Smith, Robert T. Handy, and Lefferts A. Loetscher, eds., *American Christianity: An Historical Interpretation With Representative Documents,* 2 vols, (New York: Charles Scribner's Sons, 1960), I:486-487.

59   Letter to James Madison (not the clergyman), August 29, 1800, www.founders.archives.gov.

Uriah McGregory wrote Jefferson on July 19 to tell the negative things he heard Rev. Cotton Mather Smith of Sharon, Connecticut, say about Jefferson's financial dealings. Jefferson replied on August 13 saying:

from the moment that a portion of my fellow citizens [looked towards me] with a view to one of their highest offices, the floodgates of calumny have been opened upon me; not where I am personally known [i.e., in Virginia], where their slanders would be [instant]ly judged & suppressed, from a general sense of their falshood; but in the remote parts of the union, where the means of detection are not at hand,"[60]

At this same moment, Jefferson's evangelical allies corresponded with him. The Rev. Jeremiah Moore was a Baptist leader in Fairfax, Virginia, who apparently had delivered a petition to Jefferson over 15 years before. Moore wrote Jefferson on July 12, 1800, wondering if Jefferson still supported that clause in the Virginia constitution that prohibited clergy from holding elected office. Jefferson had not authored that particular clause but had supported it. On August 14 Jefferson replied, saying:

...after 17 years more of experience and reflection, I do not approve. It is the incapacitation of a clergyman from being elected. The clergy, by getting themselves established by law, & ingrafted into the machine of government, have been a very formidable engine against the civil and religious rights of man. They are still so in many countries & even in some of these United States;...It now appears that our means were effectual. The clergy here [in Virginia] seem to have relinquished all pretension to privilege and to stand on a footing with lawyers, physicians, etc. They ought therefore to possess the same rights.[61]

Two years later Rev. Moore started the first Baptist Church in Washington, D.C. and then one in Alexandria, Virginia, in 1803, and *The Papers of Thomas Jefferson* editors confirm that "He was one...to which TJ contributed $50 [on February 20] in 1805." Although the earlier connections to Baptists were known generally, it is only at this later period that there is documented proof that Jefferson knew Moore and John Leland personally.

---

60   Letter to Uriah McGregory, August 13, 1800, www.founders.archives.gov.
61   Letter to Rev. Jeremiah Moore, August 14, 1800, www.founders.archives.gov.

And Jefferson replied to his evangelical Presbyterian friend Dr. Benjamin Rush of Philadelphia on September 23, 1800, saying:

> ...I promised you a letter on Christianity...; I have a view of the subject which ought to displease neither the rational Christian nor Deists...; I do not know that it would reconcile...genus irritable vatum who are all in arms against me. Their hostility is on too interesting ground to be softened;...the clause of the constitution, which...covered...the freedom of religion, had given to the [northeastern Federalist] clergy a very favorite hope of obtaining an establishment of a particular form of Christianity thro' the U.S.;...especially the Episcopalians & Congregationalists. The returning good sense of our country threatens abortion to their hopes, & they believe that any position of power confided to me will be exerted in opposition to their schemes, and they believe rightly for I have sworn upon the altar of God, eternal hostility against every form of tyranny over the mind of man..."[62]

This was not a rejection of all clergy or of the Christian faith. Jefferson biographer Merrill Peterson stated it correctly when he wrote that "unlike the anti-clericalism of the Old World, his hatred of establishments and priesthoods did not involve him in hatred of religion. He wished for himself, for all his countrymen, not freedom from religion but freedom to pursue religion..."[63] This was also Jefferson's very first mention of Deists and it seemed to portray them objectively separate from himself, rather than identifying himself as being one. In fact, he never said he was one his whole life, not even in private letters later to his most trusted confidants to whom he was freely revealing his spiritual beliefs and identity, and where he would be expected to say he was a Deist if he really was one. But, incredibly, today many commentators say he was.

A Presbyterian clergyman in Baltimore, Rev. Samuel Knox, wrote a defense of Jefferson's faith at that time, entitled "A Vindication of the Religion of Mr. Jefferson." Jefferson would later offer him the first professorship at his University in Charlottesville. Knox was a strong opponent of Unitarian Joseph Priestley, and yet united in the Jeffersonian Republican cause.[64]

---

62   Letter to Benjamin Rush, September 23, 1800, www.founders.archives.gov.

63   Merrill Peterson, *Thomas Jefferson and the New Nation* (New York: Oxford University Press, 1970), 143.

64   A Jeffersonian Republican is a term for people supporting the political goals of Jefferson's party because of principles they shared in common.

Meanwhile, local clergy in Charlottesville and other parts of Virginia never knew Jefferson to be anything but a regular Episcopal church member. On November 24, 1800, he records in his account book that he gave "Revd. M[atthew] Maury for 15.Dollars [for] last year's subscription" to his home church.[65]

On November 27, 1800, Jefferson moved to Washington, D. C. where the new Capitol opened. In Margaret Bayard Smith's *First Forty Years of Washington Society,* she wrote:

> …During the first winter, Mr. Jefferson regularly attended service on the sabbath-day in the humble church. …The custom of preaching in the Hall of Representatives had not then been attempted, though after it was established Mr. Jefferson during his whole administration, was a most regular attendant.[66]

Dr. James Hutson of the Library of Congress notes that "Other anecdotes survive from that time consistent with [Smith's] report."[67] On December 4, 1800, Congress approved that the Capitol building be used for worship services. The minutes of the House that day stated: "The Speaker informed the House that the Chaplains [both House and Senate] had proposed, if agreeable to the House, to hold Divine service every Sunday in their Chamber."[68] Episcopal Bishop and Senate Chaplain John Claggett's letter of February 18, 1801, said that Jefferson "very constantly attended prayers every morning and…a course of Sermons which I have delivered in the Capitol."[69] On January 11, 1801, Jefferson heard a sermon of Episcopal Chaplain John Claggett.[70] These services in the Capitol were to continue until the 1880s. Hutson writes,

---

65 Account book, November 24, 1800. Beliles, *The Selected Religious Letters and Papers of Thomas Jefferson,* 78. For M. Maury (for previous year of 1799).

66 Margaret Bayard Smith, *First Forty Years of Washington Society* (London: T. Fisher Unwin, 1906), 13.

67 James H. Hutson, *Religion and the Founding of the American Republic* (Washington, D.C.: Library of Congress, 1998), 96.

68 Congressional Record for December 4, 1800. It was approved without a vote, so it seems that it was by discretion of the President pro Tempore of the Senate—which means Jefferson himself in that position.

69 Thomas Claggett to James Kemp, February 18, 1801, Maryland Diocesan Archives, Baltimore.

70 Jon Meacham, *Thomas Jefferson: The Art of Power,* (New York: Random House, 2012), 333.

Jefferson permitted executive branch employees under his direct control, members of the Marine Band, to participate in House church services...on Sundays, as they tried to help the congregation by providing instrumental accompaniment to its psalm singing;...[He also decided] to let executive branch buildings, the War Office and the Treasury, be used for church services. Episcopal services in the War Office [adjacent to the White House, and in]...the Treasury...a Baptist service.[71]

First Presbyterian Church meetings were also conducted by Rev. Ashbel Green and Rev. John Brackenridge and then Rev. Robert Elliott in the Capitol (and later in the public school, where Ford's Theatre is now). Jefferson wrote a letter to Rev. Stephen B. Balch on December 18, 1800, pastor of the West Street Presbyterian Church in Georgetown (on today's M Street), that included: "my contribution...I therefore inclose [$50]...which you will be so good as to apply to the object explained to me. I have the honor to be with great personal respect & esteem."[72] And his account book shows he gave Rev. Balch another donation of $75 in 1802.[73]

Jefferson also bought a new Bible at that time. In a letter to Henry Remsen on December 31, 1800, he said: "I see advertised...Scatcherd's pocket bible, bound in Marocco, it is an edition which I have long been wishing to get, to make part of a portable library which the course of my life has rendered convenient. Will you be so good as to get a copy for me and forward by post."[74]

Another clergyman wrote him in early January 1801 named Rev. Joseph Moss White. Rev. White was of the Sandemanian sect in Danbury, Connecticut, who supported Jefferson's church-state views. The famous Danbury letter on the "wall of separation of church and state" that Jefferson wrote about a year later was to Baptists there who held similar views. Rev. White enclosed in his letter to Jefferson two pamphlets[75] Jefferson replied to him with thanks on January 11, 1801, saying: "I shall with pleasure read the pamphlet you send me;...when these questions shall

---

71 Hutson, *Religion and the Founding of the American Republic*, 89. Christ Church also used a former tobacco warehouse on New Jersey Avenue (near D. Street, S. E.), but the War Office close to the President's residence was where Jefferson apparently worshipped most.

72 Letter to Rev. Stephen B. Balch, December 18, 1800, www.founders.archives.gov.

73 Account book, October 20, 1802. Beliles, *The Selected Religious Letters and Papers of Thomas Jefferson*, 103. For Balch. It is spelled Baulch in that entry.

74 Letter to Henry Remsen, December 31, 1800, www.founders.archives.gov.

75 Letter from Rev. Joseph Moss White, January 1, 1801, www.founders.archives.gov.

have passed away, I am in hopes my fellow citizens who have given ear to the calumnies, will be disposed to make a juster estimate of my character."[76]

About the same time a former Governor of Vermont, Moses Robinson, wrote Jefferson on March 3, 1801, speaking of "our Civil and Religious Rights" and rejoicing in a recent election victory.[77] Jefferson replied on March 23:

> ...The eastern States will be the last to come over, on account of the dominion of the clergy, who had got a smell of union between Church and State...; The Christian religion, when divested of the rags in which they have enveloped it, and brought to the original purity and simplicity of its benevolent institutor, is a religion of all others most friendly to liberty, science, and the freest expansion of the human mind.[78]

This was one of the first criticisms Jefferson ever made about clergy in America, but it was specifically about the "eastern States," meaning New England and New York, and about clergy there who were predominantly allied with the Federalists. Jefferson often did not provide specificity in his anti-clerical statements but this instance provides one of the few times he does so. But the context within most of his letters along with the other body of relationships with clergy is essential to correctly understand the narrow focus of his clerical criticism.[79] And even in this criticism, it is clear that Jefferson maintains a high view of Christianity itself as a main source of freedom in world history. Furthermore, in this letter Jefferson makes one of his first criticisms of "they" who corrupted original Christianity, and this meant the medieval clergy of Europe. Explanation of this trend in his thinking will come later.

On February 11, 1801, the House of Representatives finally determined on its 36th ballot that Jefferson would be the next president. (This was a political cliffhanger that lasted for weeks. Jefferson beat Adams handily. But Jefferson was tied with Aaron Burr; tied ballot after tied ballot created a logjam. When Jefferson finally

---

76   Letter to Rev. Joseph Moss White, January 11, 1801, www.founders.archives.gov.

77   "To Thomas Jefferson from Moses Robinson, 3 March 1801," www.founders.archives.gov.

78   Letter to Moses Robinson, March 23, 1801, www.founders.archives.gov.

79   Sadly very few modern scholars have studied the material offered in this book, and have relied on the same few circle of sources and commentary that had led to a view of a general anti-clericalism that is simply incorrect. To correct this misrepresentation, we have inserted in this book the descriptive words similar to his term here (words such as: "eastern," "northeastern," "northern," "Federalist," "medieval" or "Catholic"), so that the reader can accurately grasp the limited focus of his criticism. Our insertions are hopefully faithful to the context in each case.

won, Aaron Burr became his Vice President—this was obviously before presidents and vice-presidents ran on the same ticket.) Jefferson sent a message on February 20 to Congress accepting the call to the Presidency saying: "…whatsoever…it has pleased providence to place within the compass of my faculties, shall be called forth for the discharge of the duties confided to me."[80]

Jefferson Begins Serving As President

When Jefferson was sworn in as president on March 4, 1801, with his hand on the Bible, he also followed it with religious references in his public address. In his First Inaugural Address he said:

> …having banished from our land that religious intolerance under which mankind so long bled and suffered;…enlightened by a benign religion, professed, indeed and practiced in various forms…; acknowledging and adoring an overruling Providence, which…with all these blessings, what more is necessary to make us a happy and a prosperous people?

> …And may that Infinite Power which rules the destinies of the universe lead our councils to what is best, and give them a favorable issue for your peace and prosperity.[81]

It is noteworthy that in this speech, Jefferson not only spoke of religious freedom but of an enlightenment that came not from unaided reason, but from religion—in a country which was overwhelmingly Christian in profession. He spoke not of a disengaged Deist God, but of a Providence and a Power that overruled human affairs and guided councils of government. As Gregg Frazer shows in *The Religious Beliefs of America's Founders*, Jefferson certainly did not hold to a view of a disengaged god as Deists typically believed.[82]

The New Jerusalem Church of Baltimore, led by Rev. John Hargrove, wrote to congratulate the new president on that inauguration day, March 4, 1801.[83] Rev. Hargrove had been a Methodist but now was a Swedenborgian minister. Swedenborgians or "New Church" adherents held to a non-Trinitarianism more

---

80   Message to the House of Representatives, February 20, 1801, www.founders.archives.gov.

81   First Inaugural Address, March 4, 1801, www.founders.archives.gov.

82   Gregg Frazer, *The Religious Beliefs of America's Founders* (Lawrence, Kansas: University Press of Kansas, 2012), 162. Frazer defines Jefferson's faith as "theistic rationalism."

83   "To Thomas Jefferson from the New Jerusalem Church of Baltimore, 4 March 1801," www. founders.archives.gov.

similar to a new emerging Arminian[84] evangelical Restoration Movement, than the English skeptical variety of Unitarianism.[85] Jefferson replied on March 9.[86] Jefferson later the next year heard Rev. Hargrove preach in the Capitol and corresponded in 1807.

Having won the election, Jefferson privately expressed his frustration with the religious attacks in a letter to friend and former ambassador William Short on March 17, 1801, that "...in this transition the New England states are slowest because under the dominion of their priests who had begun to hope they could toll us on to an established church to be in union with the state..."[87] A few days later he wrote to Unitarian Rev. Joseph Priestley of: "...the times..., when ignorance put everything into the hands of power and priestcraft;...[they fear you will] render them useless by simplifying the Christian philosophy—the most sublime and benevolent, but most perverted system that ever shone on man..."[88]

And a few days later he said to his political ally in New England, Elbridge Gerry:

> ...[In] Your part of the Union...the temples of religion and justice, have all been prostituted there to toll us back to the times when we burnt witches ...; ...[the] priesthood...twist it's [i.e., Christianity's] texts till they cover the divine morality of it's author with mysteries, and require a priesthood to explain them.[89]

Later on July 21, 1801, he told a Connecticut ally, U.S. Attorney Pierpont Edwards that: "...[If] the nature of...government [were] a subordination of the civil to the ecclesiastical power, I [would] consider it as desperate for long years to come...; And there [the Federalist] clergy will always keep them if they can."[90]

---

84   Arminianism refers to that theological school within Christianity named after Jacob Arminius (1560-1609) from Holland. Arminianism opposes Calvinism and emphasizes the free will of human beings in matters of salvation.

85   This group believed that their founder, Emanuel Swedenborg from Sweden, had received special revelations from Jesus; essentially this group was a quasi-Christian cult.

86   Letter to Rev. John Hargrove and New Jerusalem Church, March 9, 1801, www.founders. archives.gov.

87   Letter to William Short, March 17, 1801, www.founders.archives.gov.

88   Letter to Rev. Joseph Priestley, March 21, 1801, www.founders.archives.gov.

89   Letter to Elbridge Gerry, March 29, 1801, www.founders.archives.gov.

90   Letter to Pierpont Edwards, July 21, 1801, www.founders.archives.gov.

Jefferson's assessment and concern at this time was unusually but understandably strong after the attacks he had personally suffered.[91]

While privately deploring the religious situation in the northeast, Jefferson was not opposing Christianity per se. He sent letters that also expressed his faith in God. To Benjamin Waring and citizens of Columbia, South Carolina, he said on March 23: "...I offer my sincere prayers to the Supreme Ruler of the Universe, that He may long preserve our country in freedom and prosperity..."[92]

Episcopal clergyman Rev. Mason Locke Weems, famous for his biography of Washington the year before (popular at the time, but now criticized), wrote Jefferson on June 6, 1801, to promote other religious publications such as sermons by Presbyterian Hugh Blair. Jefferson replied that although he had not read them: "...The publication of these [sermons] cannot therefore but be publicly useful:... wishing you sincerely therefore success in your undertaking."[93]

Jefferson did not just give lip service to clergymen and religion. He went further by also financially supporting clergy—most of whom were Trinitarian. His account book entry of June 9, 1801, records a "payment of $20 to the bearers, two foreign ecclesiastics," and then a specific reference to "Lora reverend mr."[94] Ten days later he noted a gift for two "mendicant friars." Jefferson as president used his influence also to help Roman Catholics residing in the new capital. The bishop of Baltimore, Rev. John Carroll, wrote to Jefferson on August 13, 1801, regarding a plan for a Catholic Church to be erected in Washington to which Jefferson replied on September 3 saying he had gladly recommended it to the District Commissioners.

Jefferson also corresponded with several Presbyterians at this time. On September 26, 1801, Jefferson wrote to General Samuel Smith of Baltimore recommending:

---

91   The acrimonious 1800 election is discussed fully in the later chapter on Jefferson and the clergy.

92   Letter to Benjamin Waring, Esq., and Columbia, South Carolina, Citizens, March 23, 1801, www.founders.archives.gov.

93   Letter from Rev. Mason Locke Weems, June 6, 1801 and Letter to Rev. Mason Locke Weems, June 12, 1801, www.founders.archives.gov. This idea of religion having public good is similar to a quote attributed to Jefferson saying that, "I have always said, and always will say, that the studious perusal of the sacred volume [i.e., the Bible] will make better citizens, better fathers, and better husbands." Remembered by Daniel Webster in his 1824 Monticello visit (Webster letter to Pease, June 15, 1852).

94   Account book, June 9, 1801. Beliles, *The Selected Religious Letters and Papers of Thomas Jefferson*, 88. For two foreign ecclesiastics or mendicant friars. And another entry for Lora.

...Mr. [John] Glendy a Presbyterian clergyman from Ireland, who settled two or three years ago at Staunton about 40 miles from this place,...[is] the most eloquent preacher of the living clergy whom I have heard. In this he is really great, and without disparaging any other, I may safely say he is unrivalled. ...he wishes to go to Baltimore...being desirous that I should say to you what I can with justice, I do it with great satisfaction persuaded you will be uncommonly pleased with such an acquisition to your city.[95]

Jefferson followed up a few days later, saying of Rev. Glendy that "...a man rarely sees as eloquent a preacher twice in his life."[96] It is hard to square today's common view of Jefferson the skeptic with the man who often recommended quality preaching, even from orthodox Trinitarian preachers. Then on December 5, Rev. John Glendy himself wrote to Jefferson, to express gratitude and say he was praying for him.[97] Besides the previous letters, Jefferson later told Delaware statesman Thomas McKean on March 3, 1805, that Glendy was "without exception the best preacher I ever heard."[98]

Jefferson said that he had previously heard Glendy preach and this would have occurred sometime within the three years prior to 1801 although there is no record of it. And in fact, just a month before this recommendation letter for Glendy, Jefferson's secretary Meriwether Lewis (later famous for the Lewis and Clark expedition) wrote to Jefferson from Staunton, Virginia, saying: "I was a few minutes since with Mr. Glendy: on Saturday last...he laments much that his indisposition [being sick] prevents his keeping the appointment he had made to preach in Charlottesville on Thursday next: he requested me to give you this information as early as possible."[99]

These letters are important evidence to understand Jefferson's religious life for it shows that Jefferson clearly heard preachers outside of his own Anglican/Episcopal tradition prior to going to Washington. Before looking at more of Jefferson's

---

95 Letter to General Samuel Smith, September 26, 1801, www.founders.archives.gov. Jefferson misspelled Glendy's name as Glendye in this letter but we corrected it.

96 Letter to General Samuel Smith, October 10, 1801, www.founders.archives.gov. Joseph A. Waddell, *Annals of Augusta County, Virginia, 1726-1871, 2d ed.* (Bridgewater, Va.: C. J. Carrier Co., 1958), 374. Waddell writes that Glendy at the "invitation of President Jefferson...delivered an address in the Capitol."

97 "To Thomas Jefferson from John Glendy, 5 December 1801," www.founders.archives.gov.

98 Letter to Thomas McKean, March 3, 1805. Beliles, *The Selected Religious Letters and Papers of Thomas Jefferson*, 134.

99 Meriwether Lewis to Jefferson, August 31, 1801, www.founders.archives.gov.

relationship with clergymen and religious groups while president in Washington, the previous reference to Glendy's preaching in Charlottesville induces us to understand more about the religious culture back in Jefferson's home of Central Virginia, something ignored by most Jefferson biographers.

The Second Great Awakening And The Restoration Movement

The Second Great Awakening first emerged in the Piedmont in the late 1780s but then, after sporadic revival activity in the 1790s, exploded again in a second wave about the turn of the century and was mainly expressed in the form of interdenominational camp meetings. The camp meeting was a uniquely American contribution to evangelicalism. In these popular open-air meetings, hundreds and even thousands of people would gather for five or six days to hear preaching from a variety of ministers, sometimes of various denominations.

In Virginia, this phase of the revival began among Baptists around 1800 (lasting through 1804). Presbyterians were less involved, but Rev. Drury Lacy and the Hanover Presbytery spoke of it approvingly in 1801 and 1802.[100] Methodist Bishop Francis Asbury preached in Jefferson's Albemarle County on September 8, 1800 and records in his journal that he "was divinely assisted." Itinerant evangelist Lorenzo Dow also preached in an Albemarle camp meeting in 1802. Significant revival came to Albemarle in 1802 and in the adjacent counties that today are identified as Orange and Madison. Its primary leader was Jefferson's old friend on the Anglican vestry but now a Methodist circuit rider – Rev. Henry Fry.[101] Rev. Fry organized some of these open-air camp meetings in the town of Milton, east of Charlottesville and very close to Monticello. In 1802, one of these lasted for a whole week, and fifty people were converted.[102]

Of special notice is the fact that during the camp meeting years, the highest number of new converts reported in the state of Virginia occurred in 1802, with

---

100   Robert P. Davis, et al., *Virginia Presbyterians in American Life: Hanover Presbytery, 1755-1980* (Richmond, Va.: Hanover Presbytery, 1982), 61.

101   Allen, "The Great Revival in Virginia, 1783-1812," 69-70, 103-104; and William Bennett, *Memorials of Methodism in Virginia* (Richmond, Va.: self-published, 1871), 489-490. Allen provides one of the few historical accounts of the Great Revival that adequately highlights events in Albemarle County and areas nearby and gives due attention to its leader Henry Fry. Bennett includes much local history which is, perhaps, due to the fact that he was the pastor of a Methodist church in Charlottesville for a while and had great access to local records and oral histories. See Edgar Woods, *Albemarle County in Virginia* (Charlottesville, Va.: Michie Co., 1901), 135.

102   Bennett, *Memorials of Methodism in Virginia*, 490-491.

Albemarle County second only to adjacent Augusta County in this regard.[103] In fact, between 1801 and 1806, there were more camp meetings in Albemarle County than in *any other single county in the entire Commonwealth of Virginia*.[104] Jefferson's home county saw a great deal of Virginia revivalism.

In the open-air "camp meetings," preachers of various denominations cooperated, taking turns preaching. Denominational titles, creeds, names, and distinctives were downplayed for the common identity of simply "Christians," and this eventually gave rise to what became known as the Restoration movement as the dominant trend in Jefferson's home county. In its effort for unity, part of this movement not only rejected creeds but also the concept of the Trinity, while still holding to a belief in the atonement and resurrection of Jesus. By requiring no creed, both Trinitarians and non-Trinitarians could be tolerated in their fellowship. The earliest group in Virginia in this movement was led by Rev. James O'Kelly. They were first known as Republican Methodists but soon simply changed their names to "Christian Churches."

One of these unorthodox Restorationist preachers, Rev. Thomas Stett Cavender, apparently had met with Jefferson in the summer of 1801 in Charlottesville and then again for "a few minutes…in the president's house" in Washington in October of 1801.[105] Cavender is an obscure person who seems to have been based in Albemarle or else made it a common place of ministry during his itinerating circuit. Jefferson in September 1801 records in his account book of being in Charlottesville and "paid contribution at a sermon."[106] Usually he would identify the church, so it is likely that this was a non-denominational gathering (camp meeting?) in the area and, being close in time to the meeting with Cavender (mentioned above), possibly a service led by him.

Rev. Cavender wrote several more times to Jefferson after this. Writing from adjacent Orange county, he told Jefferson in late 1802 that "I still continue Traveling and preaching the unitarian doctrine in opposition to the Trinitarian System and all other political and Ecclesiastical impositions whatever."[107] His letter written from Milton near Monticello on March 22, 1803 led to a donation of

---

103   Allen, "The Great Revival in Virginia, 1783-1812," 56-58.

104   Ibid., 89-91, 96.

105   Letter from Rev. Thomas Cavender, December 25, 1802, www.founders.archives.gov. This letter mentioned these earlier visits with Jefferson in 1801.

106   Account book, September 23, 1801. Beliles, *The Selected Religious Letters and Papers of Thomas Jefferson*, 92. "Contribution at a sermon." In Albemarle.

107   Letter from Rev. Thomas Cavender, December 25, 1802, www.founders.archives.gov.

$10 from Jefferson on that day for a medical need.[108] Cavendar is important for, although the Restoration movement had already been strong in the area for several years, he is the first locally-based clergyman holding non-Trinitarian views that now is documented having correspondence with Jefferson.[109]

Of course, when President Jefferson visited his home, he most likely would attend church there in the courthouse in services led by Episcopal/Independent Rev. Matthew Maury. Or he might possibly attend a Restoration gathering led by the previously-mentioned Rev. Cavender or some other independent preacher.

Jefferson's Relations With Clergy in the Capitol

President Jefferson corresponded with various Baptist groups at this time as well. On June 26, 1801, he received an "Address of the Delaware Baptist Association," which represented five churches in the area. Their Moderator, Rev. Joseph Flood, and Clerk, Rev. John Boggs, sent their congratulations.[110]

Jefferson replied to this Baptist group on July 2 in a letter that was printed later in the Wilmington, Delaware newspapers:

> ...I join you, fellow-citizens, in rendering the tribute of thankfulness to the Almighty ruler, who, in the order of his providence, hath willed that the human mind shall be free in this portion of the globe: that society shall here know that the limit of its rightful power is the enforcement of social conduct; while the right to question the religious principles producing that conduct is beyond their cognizance...I thank you, fellow-citizens, for your congratulations on my appointment to the chief magistracy, and for your affectionate supplications on my behalf, to that being, whose counsels are the best guide, & his favor the best protection under all our difficulties, and in whose holy keeping may our country ever remain.[111]

One of the most unusual of Presbyterian clergymen whom Jefferson came to know at this time as president was Rev. David Austin. He first wrote Jefferson on March 9 and then many more times in 1801. Austin informed Jefferson on June

---

108   Letter from Rev. Thomas Cavender, March 22, 1803; and Account book, March 22, 1803. Beliles, *The Selected Religious Letters and Papers of Thomas Jefferson*, 105. For Cavender.

109   If Cavender was not originally from the Albemarle area, he at least made it a frequent base of his itinerating ministry. Lorenzo Dow did the same about a decade later.

110   To Thomas Jefferson from the Delaware Baptist Association, 26 June 1801," www.founders. archives.gov.

111   Letter to the Delaware Baptist Association, July 2, 1801, www.founders.archives.gov.

17 that he hoped "to bring the different denominations of professing Christians, in the City, to a more united concurrence in the general principles of Christian unity, & eventually to cause a general assemblage at the City Hotel…"[112] On June 18, Austin asked Jefferson to arrange for him to preach a "discourse…[to] be delivered in the Capitol." Austin replied to a note from Jefferson on June 22, saying: "Mr. Austin …has the happiness to find that …The doors of the Capitol are cheerfully opened for the purposes of the 4th of July" and hoped that "the President should judge proper to move for a general display of the Civil & military powers, under his control on that day…"[113]

In his account book on June 25, 1801, Jefferson said he "Gave…25.Dollars towards fitting up a chapel for Mr. Austin."[114] This became known as "'Lady Washington's' chapel" at Eighth and E streets, N.W. Rev. Austin took this donation as a sign of support that led to three other letters to Jefferson within the week that included a request for a job. Indeed on July 4th Rev. Austin preached in the House of Representatives with Jefferson present and the sermon later appeared July 24th in a newspaper. Jefferson then wrote to Austin on July 14, 1801 and communicated his approval of a marriage among two of his servants and asked Austin to perform the wedding.[115] On July 17, Austin suggested that appointing a clergyman such as him to Jefferson's cabinet (in the Navy Department) would counter those who attacked the president on religious grounds. Austin said they "would never, more say, the President was not a friend to Zion, so long as he had a Chaplain in his counsels."[116]

A handful of other letters followed, and then on November 5, 1801, Jefferson's account book reveals that he "Gave Mr. Austin (charity)…$25."[117] After the turn of the year on January 4, 1802, Austin told Jefferson that he had taken "the place" of the pastor of the Presbyterian Church of Alexandria, Virginia.[118] Several more letters followed that still included appeals for Jefferson to appoint him to his government and claimed that it was God's will. So Jefferson finally responds with

---

112   "To Thomas Jefferson from David Austin, [17 June 1801]," www.founders.archives.gov.

113   "To Thomas Jefferson from David Austin, [22 June 1801]," www.founders.archives.gov. And although now missing there was a Note or Letter to David Austin, 21 June 1801.

114   Account book, June 25, 1801. Beliles, *The Selected Religious Letters and Papers of Thomas Jefferson*, 89. For a chapel for Mr. Austin.

115   "To David Austin, [14 July 1801]," www.founders.archives.gov.

116   "To Thomas Jefferson from David Austin, [17 July 1801]," www.founders.archives.gov.

117   Account book, November 5, 1801. Beliles, *The Selected Religious Letters and Papers of Thomas Jefferson*, 95. For Austin.

118   "To Thomas Jefferson from David Austin, [4 January 1802]," www.founders.archives.gov.

another letter to Rev. Austin on January 21, 1802, saying: "…Your talents as a divine I hold in due respect, but of their employment in a political line I must be allowed to judge for myself…Of the special communications to you of his will by the supreme being, I can have no evidence, and therefore must ascribe them to the false perceptions of your mind."[119] Seemingly unaffected by this, Austin sent Jefferson two copies of his collected sermons generally titled *The National Barley Cake,* and Jefferson's account book then shows on January 29, 1802, that he "Paid David Austin for 2. Pamphlets."[120] And the account book entry for May 1, 1802 said: "Gave Revd. D. Austin in charity…$20."[121]

Also in public messages at that time, Jefferson included religious expressions. In his *First Annual Message to Congress* on December 8, Jefferson said: "…While we devoutly return thanks to the beneficent Being who has been pleased to breathe into them the spirit of conciliation and forgiveness, we are bound with peculiar gratitude to be thankful to him…"[122] And in his reply to an address from the state of Vermont, Jefferson said: "I join in addressing Him whose Kingdom ruleth over all, to direct the administration of their affairs."[123] In these statements, again, Jefferson shows a belief in a God who is active in influencing human affairs, and to whom Jefferson prays.

In similar manner Jefferson made various addresses to Native American groups while president and always made reference to God in them. For example, on January 7, 1801, he told the Brothers and Friends of the Miamis, Powtewatamies,

---

119   Letter to Rev. David Austin, January 21, 1802, www.founders.archives.gov.

120   Account book, January 29, 1802. Beliles, *The Selected Religious Letters and Papers of Thomas Jefferson*, 100. For Austin.

121   Account book, May 1, 1802. Beliles, *The Selected Religious Letters and Papers of Thomas Jefferson*, 102. For Austin.

122   First Annual Message to Congress, December 8, 1801, www.founders.archives.gov. This continued in later annual messages to Congress: In 1802 ". . . circumstances which mark the goodness of that Being from whose favor they flow and the large measure of thankfulness we owe for His bounty. Another year has come around, and finds us still blessed with peace and friendship abroad; law, order, and religion at home . . . ; under the smiles of Providence. . . ." In 1803, Jefferson said: ". . . let us bow with gratitude to that kind Providence which, inspiring with wisdom and moderation our late legislative councils, . . . guarded us. . . ." In 1805, he said: ". . . the fatal fever which in latter times has occasionally visited our shores. Providence in His goodness gave it an early termination on this occasion and lessened the number of victims which have usually fallen before it." On November 8, 1808: "I carry with me the consolation of a firm persuasion that Heaven has in store for our beloved country long ages to come of prosperity and happiness." See all at http://avalon.law. yale.edu/subject_menus/sou.asp.

123   Letter to Amos Marsh and the State of Vermont, November 20, 1801, www.founders. archives.gov.

and Weeauks: "…I thank the Great Spirit who has conducted you to us…; [we are] Made by the same Great Spirit, and living in the same land with our brothers, the red men…"[124] On February 10, 1802, Jefferson said to the Brothers of the Delewar and Shawanee nations: "…I thank the Great Spirit that he has conducted you hither…; We are all created by the same Great Spirit…"[125] And later in November, he said to Brother Handsome Lake: "…you have been so far favored by the Divine Spirit…"[126] Jefferson also used religious language when writing to Mawlay Sulayman, Sultan of Morocco: "I pray God to have you, very great & good friend in his holy keeping."[127] Sulayman was the Muslim religious leader, as well as head of state of that country.

On December 28, 1801, James Jackson wrote Jefferson, saying that he stopped by to see him but "…found you were gone to Church in the Morning…" The editors of *The Papers of Thomas Jefferson* say of this that:

When the federal government moved to Washington, TJ began attending Sunday worship services at Christ Church, an Episcopalian parish founded

---

124   Letter to the Brothers and Friends of the Miamis, Powtewatamies and Weeauks, January 7, 1801, www.founders.archives.gov.

125   Letter to the Brothers of the Delewar and Shawanee Nations, February 10, 1802, www.founders.archives.gov.

126   Letter to Brother Handsome Lake, November 3, 1802, Barbara B. Oberg, ed., *The Papers of Thomas Jefferson*, (Princeton: Princeton University Press, 2012), vol. 38, 628. He did similarly in other messages later: Letter to the Brothers of the Choctaw Nation, December 17, 1803, said: " . . . we thank the Great Spirit who took care of you on the ocean, and brought you safe and in good health to the seat of our great Council; and we hope His care will accompany and protect you, on your journey and return home; and that He will preserve and prosper your nation. . . ." Letter to the Osage nation on July 16, 1804, said: ". . . The Great Spirit has given you strength; . . . may the Great Spirit look down upon us and cover us with the mantle of his love." Letter to the Chiefs of the Chickasaw nation on March 7, 1805, spoke of how the ". . . the Great Spirit has covered you with His protection. . . ." And on January 10, 1806, he said in his Letter to the Chiefs of the Cherokee Nation, ". . . I . . . pray to the Great Spirit who made us all . . . that He will conduct you safely to your homes. . . ." In his Letter to the Chiefs of the Osage nation on December 3, 1806: " . . . I thank the Master of life, who has preserved you . . . ; may the Great Spirit look down upon us and cover us with the mantle of His love." And in the December 30 Address to the Wolf and People of the Mandan nation: ". . . I thank the Great Spirit that he has protected you . . . ; I hope He will have you constantly in His safe keeping, and restore you in good health to your nations and families." Find all these messages at Andrew A. Lipscomb and Albert Ellery Bergh, eds. *The Writings of Thomas Jefferson*, 20 vols., (Washington, D.C.: The Thomas Jefferson Memorial Association, 1904-05), Vol. 16. [hereafter *Writings of Jefferson*].

127   Letter to Mawlay Sulayman, August 5, 1802. Oberg, *The Papers of Thomas Jefferson*, vol. 38, 162.

in Washington in 1795 that met in a converted tobacco house at what is now New Jersey Avenue and D Street. In 1807, the congregation moved to G Street to a newly constructed building designed by Benjamin Henry Latrobe, which had a pew reserved for the president. TJ was an admirer and supporter of its pastor, Reverend Andrew McCormick. He also chose to attend services held in the House of Representatives on occasion.[128]

These services in the Capitol at first were held in the Supreme Court chamber before the construction of the House of Representatives Chamber was completed. Although Jefferson quickly connected and established his membership and financially supported the Episcopal parish in Washington, the first record of his financial support did not appear in his account book until July 2, 1804, but it references commitments for previous years. Rev. McCormick became Jefferson's primary pastor during most of his two terms in Washington.

Some Evangelicals Urge Ending Presidential Fast Proclamations

A religious freedom ally in the Valley of Virginia, Archibald Stuart, wrote Jefferson on June 4, 1801, saying: "I expect in process of time to hear some censures on the administration from the clergy on the score of publick fast & days of thanksgiving—Would it be worth while to anticipate these Cavils by takeing some favorable opportunity to deny the authority of the Executive to direct such religious exercises?..."[129] Jefferson had yet to indicate that he would not proclaim a fast day as president, but this supporter already expected Jefferson's administration to refrain because of the federalism principle that Jefferson and the Democratic-Republicans had already articulated. As Governor of Virginia, Jefferson had no problem declaring a Day of Prayer, and this was acceptable to his supporters but some felt that as president, such a move would usurp authority belonging to the people and the states.

Although Jefferson agreed, he knew the political dangers of not calling for days of prayer and thanksgiving, as he wrote to Attorney General Levi Lincoln on August 26: "...From the clergy I expect no mercy. They crucified their Savior who preached that their kingdom was not of this world, and all who practice on that precept must expect the extreme of their wrath. The laws of the present day withhold their hands from blood. But lies and slander still remain to them."[130]

---

128   "To Thomas Jefferson from James Jackson, 28 December 1801," www.founders.archives.gov.

129   "To Thomas Jefferson from Archibald Stuart, 4 June 1801," www.founders.archives.gov.

130   Letter to Levi Lincoln, August 26, 1801, www.founders.archives.gov.

Again, it is obvious from all of the favorable relations with about 100 clergy that he had interacted with favorably up to this point that these comments of Jefferson are limited to those clergy aligned with the Federalist Party from New England (some of whom were Unitarians) and New York and none in Virginia and Washington.

Perhaps the most well-known religious event and correspondence in Jefferson's presidency took place at the turning of that year connected to this issue. It involves Jefferson's letter to the Danbury Baptist Association in Connecticut—a group of 26 churches in the western part of the state and eastern New York. They had supported Jefferson for president, and in their address, signed by Reverends Nehemiah Dodge, Ephraim Robbins, and Stephen S. Nelson, they acknowledged God's hand in raising him up, and then expressed their concern that their religious freedom could be threatened.[131] Jefferson, upon receiving it, informed his Attorney General Levi Lincoln on January 1, 1802 that:

> …The Baptist address, now enclosed, admits of a condemnation of the alliance between Church and State, under the authority of the Constitution. It furnishes an occasion, too, which I have long wished to find, of saying why I do not proclaim fastings and thanksgivings, as my predecessors did;…I know it will give great offense to the New England clergy [Federalists; certainly not the Baptists]; but the advocate of religious freedom is to expect neither peace nor forgiveness from them.[132]

Lincoln advised Jefferson on how to reply so as not to offend most New Englanders regarding their fasting and Thanksgiving traditions. Connecticut native Gideon Granger also advised Jefferson that a reply expressing opposition to national fast days would "delight the Dissenters" but would be "*felt* by a great Majority of New England."[133] Jefferson's reply to the Danbury Baptist Association on January 1, 1802 said in part:

> …Believing with you that religion is a matter which lies solely between man and his God, that he owes account to none other for his faith or his

---

131 Letter from Dodge, Robbins, Nelson and the Danbury Baptist Association, October 1801, www.founders.archives.gov.

132 Letter to Levi Lincoln, January 1, 1802, www.founders.archives.gov.

133 Letter to Gideon Granger, December 31, 1801 and Letter from Gideon Granger, January 1, 1802, www.founders.archives.gov.

worship, that the legitimate[134] powers of government reach actions only, and not opinions, I contemplate with sovereign reverence that act of the whole American people [i.e., the First Amendment to the Constitution] which declared that their Legislature should 'make no law respecting an establishment of religion, or prohibiting the free exercise thereof,' thus building a wall of separation between Church and State. Adhering to this expression of the supreme will of the nation in behalf of the rights of conscience...; I reciprocate your kind prayers for the protection and blessing of the Common Father and Creator of man, and tender you for yourselves and your religious association, assurances of my high respect and esteem.[135]

It is interesting to note that a sentence in Jefferson's first unsent draft of this letter was deleted because as he noted in the margin of the draft: "this paragraph was omitted on the suggestion that it might give uneasiness to some of our republican friends in the eastern states where the proclamation of thanksgivings &c by their Executive is an antient habit, & is respected." The sentence that was deleted came immediately after the phrase "separation between Church and State." It read:

Congress thus inhibited from acts respecting religion and the Executive authorised only to execute their acts, I have refrained from prescribing even occasional performances of devotion prescribed indeed legally where an Executive is the legal head of a national church, but subject here, as religious exercises only to the voluntary regulations and discipline of each respective sect.[136]

Jefferson had no problem proclaiming a fast day as governor of Virginia because that did not interfere with the prerogative of other states. And he had no problem as president in personally asking these citizens for their prayers. But he agreed with

---

134   The word "legitimate" is often incorrectly printed as "legislative." Daniel Dreisbach made this discovery and made an excellent revisal of it. See Daniel L. Dreisbach, *Thomas Jefferson and the Wall of Separation Between Church and State* (New York: New York University Press, 2001), 98,181n. Interestingly, "Legitimate" was the word also used by Rev. John Leland much earlier in 1790 when arguing for religious freedom in his Virginia. Leland carried this letter from Jefferson back to Danbury.

135   Letter to Danbury Baptist Association, January 1, 1802, www.founders.archives.gov.

136   Ibid. [but see the unsent draft]

them to refrain from officially proclaiming a public day of prayer as president. These Baptists were very pleased. The U. S. Supreme Court used this letter over a century and a half later to reframe church-state relations, which soon led to striking down school prayer and Bible reading. This formerly obscure letter is often quoted so it is given more discussion in a later chapter in this book.

When Jefferson received the Danbury letter he also received one from the predominantly Baptist Committee of the neighboring community of Cheshire, Massachusetts. The letter bore the names of five men (Brown, Mason, Richardson, Waterman, and Wells) that said: "we believe the Supreme Ruler of the Universe, who raises up men to achieve great events, has raised up a Jefferson at this critical day, to defend Republicanism, and to battle the arts of Aristocracy;...To that infinite Being who governs the Universe we ardently pray, that your life and health may long be preserved..."[137] Jefferson's reply to the Committee of Cheshire, Massachusetts, on January 1, 1802, said that he concurred with them that the most precious aspect of the Constitution was "the prohibition of religious tests."[138]

Two men representing Cheshire, Rev. John Leland and Rev. Darius Brown, met with Jefferson in person on January 1, 1802, at the President's House. Rev. Leland had likely met Jefferson previously in the 1770s and 1780s at which time Leland lived in adjacent Louisa, Virginia. He then moved back to his home state of Massachusetts in 1790 and worked for the Jeffersonian Republicans there.[139] In 1811, Leland was elected to a seat in the Massachusetts Legislature and served two terms, and while doing this he defended what he called "the proper line between church and state, religion and politics."[140] Now on January 1, 1802, Reverends Leland and Brown presented Jefferson with a 1,235 pound block of cheese transported all the way from Massachusetts as a gift from Baptists in Cheshire. There was an exchange of addresses by Leland and Jefferson. The "Mammoth

---

137   "To Thomas Jefferson from the Committee of Cheshire, Massachusetts, December 30, 1801, www.founders.archives.gov. [Some call it the Baptist Committee of Cheshire] Also date: January 1, 1802.

138   Letter to the Committee of Cheshire, Massachusetts, January 1, 1802, www.founders. archives.gov. Greene, 255. See also Hatch, 95-101.

139   Ketcham quoted in Robert S. Alley, *James Madison On Religious Liberty* (Buffalo, N.Y.: Prometheus Books, 1985), 186.

140   Heimert, *Religion and the American Mind*, 532-544. Heimert provides valuable information on religious communities and leaders that supported Jefferson, especially in New England and the middle states. In reality, Unitarian pulpits such as those in New England denounced Jefferson and the Republicans, just as much as the Congregationalists and Presbyterian denominations. Republicanism was not allied with Unitarianism but with evangelicalism. See also Robert M. Healey, *Jefferson on Religion in Public Education* (New Haven, Conn.: Yale University Press, 1962), 243-244.

Cheese," as it was called by the press, occupied the East Room of the President's House for at least two years. The cheese bore Jefferson's favorite motto: "Rebellion to tyrants is obedience to God." Leland spoke in the East Room of the White House these words: "We believe the Supreme Ruler of the universe, who raised up men to achieve great events, has raised up a JEFFERSON at this critical day to defend republicanism."[141]

Jefferson also had Leland preach in the church service in the Capitol. A political opponent in Congress who also was a Congregational minister, Rev. Manasseh Cutler, noted in a January 4 letter to a friend: "Last Sunday, Leland, the cheesemonger, a poor, ignorant, illiterate, clownish preacher was introduced as the preacher to both Houses of Congress, and a great number of gentlemen and ladies from I know not where. The President, contrary to all former practice, made one of the audience."[142] Cutler's confirmation that Jefferson attended is accompanied with a claim that it was his first time, but Cutler had just recently joined Congress so was not present during the previous session when others testified of Jefferson's frequent attendance.

In Jefferson's account book for January 4, 1802, it says: "Gave Revd. Mr. Leland bearer of the cheese of 1235 lb weight 200 Dollars."[143] Some suggest this was payment for the cheese, but there is no evidence to assume that. There is no reasonable basis to think the word "gave" used here by Jefferson is any different from the 50 or so other such times that Jefferson wrote he "gave" to other clergy he listed in his account book. It was a donation like all the others. The mention of Leland as the "bearer of the cheese" is only an identifier, like when he says "foreign ecclesiastics" or "mendicant friars" in previous donation notes. The money was not for the cheese, but for the bearer of it. Apparently Jefferson also had received some of Leland's writings and was reading them, for a couple weeks later he comments to a friend that Leland "…has written lately a pamphlet on our public affairs. His testimony of the sense of the country is the best which can be produced…"[144]

---

141   Bettie Woodson Weaver, *Thomas Jefferson and the Virginia Baptists* (Richmond, Va.: Virginia Baptist Historical Society, 1993), 7-8.

142   Letter from Manasseh Cutler to a friend, January 4, 1802.

143   Account book, January 4, 1802. Beliles, *The Selected Religious Letters and Papers of Thomas Jefferson*, 100. For Leland. Jefferson already made donations to many clergymen and churches, and his note above was no different than all the others. In fact, the term "payment" would likely have been used by Jefferson, as he did in other places, if that is what he meant. Jefferson also later gave $200 one year to his local Episcopal Church in Charlottesville (the equivalent of about $4,800 in today's dollars).

144   Letter to Pierre Samuel Du Pont de Nemours, January 18, 1802, www.founders.archives.gov. Leland was called a "plain country farmer" by Jefferson in this letter, but see editor's note.

Baptist friends clearly saw President Jefferson differently than the Congregationalists of New England. Another Baptist man, Daniel D'Oyley, wrote Jefferson on July 24, 1802. Jefferson replied on August 15, thanking him for a sermon by Baptist Rev. Richard Furman, and said:

> ...the restoration of the rights of conscience to two thirds of the citizens of Virginia in the beginning of the revolution, has merited to those who had agency in it, the everlasting hostility of such of the clergy as have a hankering after the union of church & state...[145]

Clergy of almost all denominations in Washington saw Jefferson as a worshiper and supporter of the Christian faith. On February 14, Rev. Cutler noted: "Mr. Gant[t] preached in the Hall. A very full Assembly. Mr. Jefferson present."[146] Rev. Edward Gantt was an Episcopal Senate Chaplain for most of Jefferson's first term as President (December 1801-November 1804 and again, December 1805-1806).[147] Jefferson's account book for February 9, 1802 says he "Gave...in favor [of] Revd. Mr. Eaden in charity" (spelled Eden in his account book entry of February 12) and on February 17, he gave "$30 to Reverend John Debois."[148] Rev. Debois was a Catholic priest in Frederick, Maryland. And on March 13, Jefferson "gave...25 Dollars charity for meeting house for blacks." It was given to the Methodist "Reverend Thomas Lucas."[149] On April 7, 1802, Jefferson "Gave...in favour of the Revd. Mr. [William] Parkinson towards a Baptist meeting house." Rev. Parkinson was also the chaplain in Congress at this time.[150] On April 9, Jefferson "Gave... in favor [of] The Revd. Doctor [Samuel S.] Smith towards rebuilding Princeton college 100 Dollars" (about $2400 in today's dollars).[151] Presbyterian Rev. Smith

---

145   Letter from Daniel D'Oyley, July 24, 1802 and Letter to Daniel D'Oyley, August 15, 1802. Oberg, *The Papers of Thomas Jefferson*, , vol. 38, 224. (also spelled Oylety)

146   Journal of Rev. Manasseh Cutler, February 8 and 14, 1802.

147   He also was a physician whose service to the President's household is evident in a November 20, 1802 Statement of Account with Edward Gantt and other letters. Oberg, *The Papers of Thomas Jefferson*, (Princeton: Princeton University Press, 2013), vol. 39, 48.

148   Account book, February 9 and 12, 1802. Beliles, *The Selected Religious Letters and Papers of Thomas Jefferson*, 101. For Eden. And another entry February 17 For Debois.

149   Account book, March 13, 1802. Beliles, *The Selected Religious Letters and Papers of Thomas Jefferson*, 101. For Lucas. And For "meeting house for blacks."

150   Account book, April 7, 1802. Beliles, *The Selected Religious Letters and Papers of Thomas Jefferson*, 101. For Baptist meetinghouse and Parkinson.

151   Account book, April 9, 1802. Beliles, *The Selected Religious Letters and Papers of Thomas Jefferson*, 101. For Princeton college and Smith. Jefferson and Smith corresponded in 1779.

was president of the College of New Jersey and the recent national Moderator of Presbyterians. His account book also says he "Gave…in favor [of] Revd. Mr. Baulch $75 in charity" according to an October 20 entry.[152] This was the Presbyterian pastor in Georgetown mentioned previously as receiving aid from Jefferson in December 1800. Little is known of some of these clergymen Jefferson was contributing to, but they serve to show Jefferson's numerous friendly connections to many clergy of various denominations and parties. About 90 percent of these were members of orthodox denominations.

On May 27, 1802, a Quaker from Delaware named William Canby wrote Jefferson and mentioned that he had "…attended with Dorothy Ripley, on her application for thy concurrence with her desire, to attempt the education of about 64 female black or colored Children…" Rev. Ripley was a British non-denominational/Quaker missionary. Editors of *The Papers of Thomas Jefferson* say that they went with Secretary of State James Madison to "the President's House, where they met with TJ on 5 May, with the goal of gaining TJ's approval…"[153] On page 67 of her memoir, entitled *Extraordinary Conversion*, Ripley recorded this meeting and reported that TJ wished her success…" She wrote that she said to Jefferson: "…I wish to have thy approbation before I move one step in the business [of abolitionism], understanding thou art a slave-holder. The President then rose from his seat, bowing his head and replying, 'You have my approbation, and I wish you success, but I am afraid you will find it an arduous task to undertake.' I said again, 'Then I have thy approbation,' to which he [i.e., Jefferson] rose and performed the same ceremony over, repeating nearly the same sentence he had already done…"[154] Rev. Ripley also lodged with the Madisons while in Washington. Ripley's vision for a school never materialized due to lack of funds, but she later preached in the Capitol with Jefferson in attendance on January 12, 1806. Rev. Dorothy Ripley (1767-1832) was the first woman to speak in the Capitol and gave an evangelical, camp meeting style sermon on the voice of God. She later became an associate of Lorenzo Dow—the most famous national evangelist of the era.

Opposition Congressman Rev. Cutler noted in his journal on December 12, 1802: "Attended worship in our Hall [i.e., House of Representatives]. Dr. Gant[t] preached, A.M. [morning service]; Mr. McCormick, P.M. [evening

---

152   Account book, October 20, 1802. Beliles, *The Selected Religious Letters and Papers of Thomas Jefferson*, 103. For Balch.

153   See editorial note. "From William Canby to Thomas Jefferson, 27 May 1802," Oberg *The Papers of Thomas Jefferson,*, vol. 37, 506.

154   *The Extraordinary Conversion and Religious Experience of Dorothy Ripley*, 1810.

service]. Meetings very thin, but the President, his two daughters, and a grand-son, attended in the morning." In his entry on December 26, Cutler said: "Attended at the Hall. A Mr. Hargrove, of Baltimore, a Swedenborgian, preached. Gave his creed in part; not very exceptionable. President attended, although a rainy day. In the afternoon, attended at the Treasury. Heard a newly-imported Scotchman [Presbyterian James Laurie]—pretty good speaker."[155] Jefferson obtained a copy of John Hargrove's sermon. His account book also shows him possessing a book called *Swedenborg on the Soul* that he orders to be bound for him. Cutler, although a critic of Jefferson, nonetheless shows in his diary Jefferson's faithfulness to worship and also endorsement by his presence of the use of the Capitol building for worship, and his comfort with various denominations. Recapping the same information as above, Rev. Cutler wrote in another letter, January 3, 1803, to Joseph Torrey, that

He [i.e., Jefferson] and his family have constantly attended public worship in the Hall [of the House of Representatives]. On the first Sabbath before the Chaplains were elected [i.e., December 12], and when few members had arrived, Dr. Gant[t] proposed, on Saturday, to preach the next day December 13, 1802, when the President, his daughter and grandson, and Mr. [Meriwether] Lewis, attended. On the third Sabbath [i.e., December 26], it was very rainy, but his ardent zeal brought him through the rain and on horseback to the Hall.[156]

Cutler also recorded that "…Mrs. Eppes [i.e., Jefferson's daughter Mary] and her sister [Martha], as well as the President, have constantly attended worship at the Capitol during this session." On New Year's Day 1803, Rev. Cutler reported visiting Jefferson and seeing the year-old Mammoth Cheese at the President's house, and again seeing the person who brought the cheese the year before, Baptist Rev. John Leland. Leland again preached in Congress on January 3, 1803, and Jefferson, his daughter, and Meriwether Lewis attended.[157] Note how a political opponent of Jefferson refers to his "ardent zeal" to attend Christian worship, despite inclement weather.

---

155   Journal of Manasseh Cutler, December 1802. William Parker Cutler, *Life, Journals and Correspondence of Rev. Manasseh Cutler, LL. D.* (Cincinnati: R. Clarke & Co., 1888).

156   Rev. Manasseh Cutler to Joseph Torrey, January 3, 1803. Repository: Northwestern University Library, Evanston, Illinois.

157   Journal of Manasseh Cutler, January 1803. Ibid.

Cutler's New England region and fellow-Congregational clergy strongly held suspicions of Jefferson's religious infidelity, yet here he ends up documenting a religious life of President Jefferson that few today believe is true. Cutler also did not believe Jefferson a religious man when he first arrived; but Jefferson, the supposed skeptic, was proving to be quite faithful as a churchman. By the end of this second phase of Jefferson's religious life, there has only been one statement saying he did not comprehend the Trinity and declining therefore to be a godfather, but yet an overwhelming amount of evidence that shows him to be regular in attendance and financial support of not only his own church, but many other Trinitarian congregations. Yes, he had also visited Priestley's church some times while in Philadelphia and had studied some Unitarian literature, but as of the end of 1802, he still remained orthopraxic, if not also orthodox, in belief.

CHAPTER 3

THOMAS JEFFERSON'S RELIGIOUS LIFE, 1803-1812

"...The question of his [Jesus] being a member of the Godhead...is foreign to the present view [the Syllabus of the Doctrines of Jesus], which is merely an estimate of the intrinsic merit of his doctrines...To the corruptions of Christianity I am indeed opposed; but not to the genuine precepts of Jesus himself. I am a Christian." —Thomas Jefferson, 1803 [1]

Now the third phase of Thomas Jefferson's religious life becomes noticeable because of a Syllabus and letters he writes in which he, nonetheless, identifies himself as a Christian, yet holding to a notion that some of the words of Jesus were corrupted in earlier times. But before discussing that, it is worth noting his giving and correspondence that year (1803) to many ministries.

On March 2, 1803, the account book shows: "Gave in charity to the Revd. Mr. chambers of Alexandria for his church...50 Dollars." This gift of about $1200 in today's dollars was to Rev. James Chambers who led the Independent Protestant

---

1   Syllabus of an Estimate of the Doctrines of Jesus Compared with Others, 1803. Mark A.
     Beliles, ed., *The Selected Religious Letters and Papers of Thomas Jefferson* (Charlottesville, VA:
     America Publications, 2013), 110. (Enclosed in a Letter to Benjamin Rush, April 21, 1803
     from which the last sentence is taken).

Episcopal Church of Alexandria, Virginia. Plus Jefferson's account book in 1803 said: "Gave Revd. Jacob Eyerman...charity."[2] He was a German preacher among Lutheran and Reformed congregations in northeastern Pennsylvania. But Jefferson also gave money "...in favor [of] Revd. Mr. Coffin for a college in Tenissee."[3] Charles Coffin was a Presbyterian professor of Greeneville College.

But one of the most interesting donations was in March 1803 while Jefferson was back home. The local courthouse in Charlottesville was rebuilt that year in brick (and to this day is the only standing building in town where Jefferson is known to have worshiped). But in this same year his account book records that he "Paid...for meeting House."[4] This was not a term used for an Episcopal church, so it seems to be associated with the other Protestants who used plain style buildings. Sometimes the term "union" or "free" was associated with meetinghouses and this was mainly due to the influence of the Restoration movement in Central Virginia that emphasized unity across denominations. It is interesting then to note that the day after Jefferson gave to the meetinghouse, his account book on March 22 also says he "Gave Cavendar in charity."[5] Rev. Thomas S. Cavender was, as already observed, a local Restorationist/non-Trinitarian minister.[6] Jefferson's donations to a local meetinghouse and the next day to Albemarle-based Rev. Cavender suggests that they were connected, and is the clearest indication that he was a friend and supporter, and perhaps a participant, with the Restoration movement in his area.

Missions and the Abridgement of Jesus' Morals "For...The Indians"

Presbyterian Rev. Samuel Miller of New York had previously urged Jefferson's support of missions in a February 1800 letter, and then wrote Jefferson more on this theme on June 10, 1802, saying: "I do myself the honor to transmit herewith a copy of the annual publication of our Missionary Society. The information which

2   Account book, November 5, 1803. For Eyerman. Beliles, *The Selected Religious Letters and Papers of Thomas Jefferson*, 117.

3   Account book, December 18, 1803. For Coffin. Beliles, *The Selected Religious Letters and Papers of Thomas Jefferson*, 118.

4   Account book, March 21, 1803. For meeting House. Beliles, *The Selected Religious Letters and Papers of Thomas Jefferson*, 104.

5   Account book, March 22, 1803. For Cavender in charity. Beliles, *The Selected Religious Letters and Papers of Thomas Jefferson*, 105. Cavender was based often in the Charlottesville area and perhaps a native. Cavender wrote again to Jefferson on November 17, 1804 from North Carolina.

6   Letter from Rev. Thomas Cavender, March 22, 1803. Beliles, *The Selected Religious Letters and Papers of Thomas Jefferson*, 104.

it contains respecting our exertions, & the result of them during the past year, may, perhaps, not be altogether uninteresting to you." Enclosed was: "A Sermon, Delivered Before the New York Missionary Society, at their Annual Meeting April 6th, 1802," and also Miller's publication of the report of the society.[7]

On March 3, 1803, Rev. John Bacon wrote to Jefferson. Bacon was a Massachusetts Congressman at this time but previously had been an itinerant Presbyterian minister after graduating from Princeton and then the minister of the Old South Church in Boston for a short time. Bacon had also corresponded with Jefferson a year earlier and then sent to Jefferson in February 1803 two letters from Rev. John Sergeant, a Congregationalist missionary from Massachusetts to the Mohican Indians in New Stockbridge in central New York State, who collected information from as far west as the Mississippi River. Jefferson forwarded these letters to Secretary of War Henry Dearborn on February 15. And Rev. Sergeant himself wrote Jefferson later in 1803 on June 25.[8] Jefferson appreciated keeping informed of the impact of missions to the Indians, but in his reply to Bacon on April 30 Jefferson also touched on religion stating that he wanted his government to "strengthen…religious freedom."[9]

Edward Dowse of Massachusetts was another person from New England who was interested in Indian missions. He had corresponded with Jefferson at least six times previously, beginning in the 1790s. Now on April 5, 1803, Dowse sent President Jefferson a copy of a sermon by Rev William Bennet of Scotland, "The Excellence of Christian Morality," and spoke about the importance of promoting the "extension of civilization and Christian knowledge among the Aborigines of North America." Dowse said that "it seemed to me to have a claim to your attention: at any rate, the idea, hath struck me that you will find it of use; and, perhaps, may see fit, to cause some copies of it to be reprinted, at your own charge, to distribute among our Indian Missionaries." Mr. Dowse apparently understood Jefferson's interest in Christian missions to the Native Americans in a way that many modern scholars have dismissed as irrelevant.

Jefferson replied to Dowse on April 19, 1803, saying: "…I now return the sermon you were so kind as to enclose me, having have perused it with attention;…

---

7   Letter from Samuel Miller, June 10, 1802, and Letter to Samuel Miller, June 13, 1802 www.founders.archives.gov.

8   Letter from Rev. John Bacon, March 3, 1803. Oberg, *The Papers of Thomas Jefferson*, vol 39, 622.

9   Letter to Rev. John Bacon, April 30, 1803. *The Works, vol. 9*, http://oll.libertyfund.org. *320*. Bacon also wrote Jefferson on April 11, 1803 . Beliles, *The Selected Religious Letters and Papers of Thomas Jefferson*, 107.

the morality of Jesus, as taught by himself, and freed from the corruptions of latter times, is far superior;...In a pamphlet lately published in Philadelphia by Dr. Priestley, he has treated, with more justice and skill than Mr. Bennet, a small portion of this subject..."[10] This is among the first times Jefferson perhaps alluded to alleged corruptions and the connection in this correspondence between Indian mission work and distilling a simple expression of the morality of Jesus that could be printed "to distribute among our Indian Missionaries" is important to note here. It soon leads to Jefferson's abridgement of the moral teachings of Jesus. And like the previous letter to John Bacon, Jefferson's letter to Dowse also leads to comments on of religious freedom.

In that same month, Jefferson replied to Unitarian Rev. Joseph Priestley: "...I received from you a copy of your comparative view of Socrates & Jesus;... In consequence of some conversation with Dr. Rush, in the year 1798-99, I had promised some day to write him a letter giving him my view of the Christian system. I have reflected often on it since, & even sketched the outlines in my own mind..."[11] Jefferson enclosed to him his "Syllabus of an Estimate of the Merit of the Doctrines of Jesus Compared with Those of Others" that deliberately avoided addressing the debate over Jesus' divinity. In fact, Jefferson said "the question of his being a member of the Godhead...is foreign to the present view, which is merely an estimate of the intrinsic merits of his doctrines."[12] Jefferson said that what he was trying to accomplish in the syllabus was simply to compare the philosophy of Jesus with other classical systems. But in the letter to Priestley, Jefferson also asserted that scripture texts had been corrupted over time and needed correction. Then for the first time in a letter to the Presbyterian layman Benjamin Rush on April 21, 1803, Jefferson seems to imply his belief that Jesus was not divine in the syllabus that he enclosed with it:

> ...In some of the delightful conversations with you, in the evenings of 1798-99...the Christian religion was sometimes our topic...; My views of it...are the result of a life in inquiry & reflection, and very different from that Anti-Christian system imputed to me by those who know nothing of my opinions. To the corruptions of Christianity I am indeed opposed;

---

10   Letter to Edward Dowse, April 19, 1803. Beliles, *The Selected Religious Letters and Papers of Thomas Jefferson*, 108.

11   Letter to Rev. Joseph Priestley, April 9, 1803. Beliles, *The Selected Religious Letters and Papers of Thomas Jefferson*, 106.

12   "Syllabus of an Estimate of the Merit of the Doctrines of Jesus, Compared with Those of Others", April 1803. Beliles, *The Selected Religious Letters and Papers of Thomas Jefferson*, 110.

but not to the genuine precepts of Jesus himself. I am a Christian, in the only sense he wished any one to be; sincerely attached to his doctrines, in preference to all others; ascribing to himself every human excellence; & believing he never claimed any other...[13]

This was the first time Jefferson clearly gives himself a religious identity. He says he is a Christian and that only his enemies describe him as "anti-Christian." In 1788 Jefferson had only stated that he did not comprehend the Trinity and therefore declined being a godfather. But he had not stated that he had made any definitive conclusions, and he never did anything to distance himself from traditional church life. Now Jefferson is more assertive privately about his theology, yet doing so as a self-identified Christian who attended and financially aided Trinitarian churches and ministries. But Jefferson appreciated that Rush was trustworthy to not let it become public where others would misrepresent it. The full Syllabus that Jefferson sent to Rush is in a later chapter on Jefferson and Orthodoxy. In the Syllabus Jefferson says Jesus' moral teachings were superior to all others in the world and he simply does not address theological controversies surrounding His professed divinity.

Jefferson also expressed his views in private letters to his daughters, in which he similarly says he is a Christian.[14] And to Secretary of War Henry Dearborn, Attorney General Levi Lincoln, and other trusted advisers.[15] Jefferson then sent another letter to Priestley on April 24, 1803, saying they likely differed on some points.[16] Priestley replied to question Jefferson's view that Jesus did not have a divine mission. He wrote: "...It is an opinion that I do not remember ever to have heard before..."[17] Rush also replied in a letter expressing some disagreement, saying:

---

13   Letter to Benjamin Rush, April 21, 1803. Beliles, *The Selected Religious Letters and Papers of Thomas Jefferson*, 109.

14   Letter to Martha Jefferson Randolph, April 23, 1803. *The Family Letters of Thomas Jefferson*, Edwin Morris Betts and James Adam Bear, Jr., eds. (Columbia, Missouri: University of Missouri Press, 1966) 243-244. Letter to Mary Jefferson Eppes, April 25, 1803. *The Family Letters*, 245.

15   Letter to Henry Dearborn, Levi Lincoln, and others, April 23, 1803. Beliles, *The Selected Religious Letters and Papers of Thomas Jefferson*, 113.

16   Letter to Rev. Joseph Priestley, April 24, 1803. Beliles, *The Selected Religious Letters and Papers of Thomas Jefferson*, 113.

17   Letter from Rev. Joseph Priestley, May 7, 1803. Beliles, *The Selected Religious Letters and Papers of Thomas Jefferson*, 115.

I have read your Creed with great attention, and was much pleased to find you are by no means so heterodox as you have been supposed to be by your enemies. I do not think with you in your account of the character and mission of the author of our Religion...In the mean while we will agree, to disagree...[18]

Jefferson's friends, one orthodox and one unorthodox, were certainly willing to challenge Jefferson's views yet remaining very respectful and keeping it completely private. Jefferson's former pastor Charles Clay later described Jefferson as being theologically "playful in the closet" but not as a person who intended to spread his private questions and assertions publicly. This seems to be how Priestley and Rush viewed Jefferson's intellectual religious discussions.

Congregationalist Rev. John Sergeant wrote again that summer to Jefferson on missions work among the Indians.[19] And on October 31, 1803, he presented a "Treaty with Kaskaskia and other Tribes," which provided federal funds for the construction of churches and salaries for Catholic priests and missionaries in the federal Illinois Territory. It said:

...whereas, The greater part of the said tribe have been baptised and received into the Catholic church to which they are much attached, the United States will give annually for seven years one hundred dollars towards the support of a priest of that religion, who will engage to perform for the said tribe the duties of his office...; And the United States will further give the sum of three hundred dollars to assist the said tribe in the erection of a church...[20]

Since a treaty was something under the president's authority, it reflects on Jefferson's thinking about the relationship of religion and government more so than legislation that originated in Congress. And using government money for supporting this work for Indians was apparently not a violation of separation of church and state to Jefferson because it did not violate the constitutionally-established authority given to states

---

18   Letter from Benjamin Rush, May 5, 1803. Beliles, *The Selected Religious Letters and Papers of Thomas Jefferson*, 114.

19   Letter from Rev. John Sergeant, June 25, 1803. Oberg, *The Papers of Thomas Jefferson*, vol 40.

20   "A Treaty with Kaskaskia and Other Tribes," October 31, 1803. http://digital.library.okstate.edu/kappler/vol2/treaties/kas0067.htm

in the area of religious exercises—since the Indians were under the jurisdiction of the federal territorial government.[21] And apparently at Jefferson's direction, Secretary of War Henry Dearborn in the summer of 1804 allocated $300 in federal funds (about $7,200 modern equivalent) to help another Presbyterian missionary - Rev. Gideon Blackburn, the Superintendent of the Indian School in the Cherokee Country in Tennessee.[22] Dearborn confirmed this aid as did Blackburn later in a letter to Jefferson saying that his "...Mission [had]...already obtained your patronage" when he later wrote Jefferson in 1807.[23] Here's a key to understanding Jefferson's policies on church-state matters: If it did not intrude on the jurisdiction of the states, then it was not per se unconstitutional.

About this time Rev. William Pryce, of the Protestant Episcopal Church in Wilmington, Delaware, wrote to Jefferson asking for his subscription for his very orthodox book about the life of Jesus, and Jefferson replied from Washington on October 15, 1803: "Your favor of the 10 is duly recieved, and I subscribe with great pleasure to the work you propose."[24] Monticello historians note that "Jefferson was one of the original subscribers to this work, and his name heads the list ([found in] vol. II, page 435)."[25] A few days after Jefferson began his second term in 1805, he acknowledged the receipt of Pryce's book and added no objection or comment on Pryce's decision to publish Jefferson name as a subscriber.[26] To be listed as a subscriber was a way of giving public support for it.

As shown earlier, Jefferson had started giving time to comparing moral teachings of philosophers This was not something common to most sitting presidents so

---

21   Since religion and education was likely to encourage peace, the war department paid for these.

22   Letter to Henry Dearborn, August 3, 1804. www.founders.archives.gov. Also see *TN Encyclopedia of History and Culture, online edition* (Knoxville, Tennessee: The University of Tennessee Press, 2002-2013), http://tennesseeencyclopedia.net/entry.php?rec=96 .

23   Letter from Henry Dearborn, August 23, 1804. www.founders.archives.gov. And letter from Rev. Gideon Blackburn, September 11, 1807. Beliles, *The Selected Religious Letters and Papers of Thomas Jefferson*, 155. Also see Jefferson letter to Elias Boudnot, June 13, 1805. www. founders.archives.gov. Apparently a proposal was made by Boudinot for the government to give War department funds to a missionary organization to manage. Dearborn and Jefferson declined to do that but apparently gave funds for such missions works through the war department's "regular agents."

24   Letter to Rev. William Pryce, October 15, 1803. Beliles, *The Selected Religious Letters and Papers of Thomas Jefferson*, 117.

25   "Thomas Jefferson and the Bible Publications He Owned," Thomas Jefferson Foundation, January 2007. http://www.monticello.org/library/exhibits/images/biblepublications.pdf.

26   Letter to Rev. William Pryce, March 13, 1805. Beliles, *The Selected Religious Letters and Papers of Thomas Jefferson*, 142.

itself is remarkable. It arose perhaps from his relationship with Joseph Priestley while living in Philadelphia and continued to this time. With this comparison of philosophy Jefferson also began thinking of a digest of the moral teachings of Jesus in conjunction with it. This digest is mentioned for the first time in a letter to Priestley on January 29, 1804. It was raised due to the confluence of interests not only with Priestley on philosophy but with various missions organizations that were seeking to serve Native Americans. The issue came to a head at that moment due to the Louisiana Purchase, America's largest single property acquisition that brought thousands of new tribal groups under American oversight. Henry Randall's biography of Jefferson, one of the earliest, written when his family and friends were still alive, states about his digest that he "conferred with friends on the expediency of having it published in the different Indian dialects as the most appropriate book for the Indians to be instructed to read in."[27]

Around February or March 1804, Jefferson compiled it himself and called it: *The Philosophy of Jesus of Nazareth Extracted From the Account of His Life and Doctrines as Given by Matthew, Mark, Luke & John; Being an Abridgement of the New Testament for the Use of the Indians Unembarrassed with Matters of Fact or Faith Beyond the Level of Their Comprehensions.*[28] This abridgement, clearly intended for the Indians, was not a biography of Jesus, only His "philosophy" as the title states. As such it left out most material found in the Gospels that did not fit the goal of compiling a "philosophy," but there is no evidence at this time of a motive to delete all of the miracles or evidences of Jesus' divinity. (It does contain some references to miracles.) But this (after a revision in 1820) was the beginning of what many popularly call today the "Jefferson Bible" – a title never used by Jefferson. Sadly, few today ever hear of the original missionary purpose Jefferson gave it.

Later that year while visiting his home, Jefferson wrote on August 8, 1804 to his evangelical friend Benjamin Rush, saying: "...I have also a little volume, a mere and faithful compilation which I shall some of these days ask you to read as containing the exemplification of what I advanced in a former letter as to the excellence of 'the Philosophy of Jesus of Nazareth.'"[29] When Rush heard of it, he

27   Henry S. Randall, *The Life of Thomas Jefferson*, 3 vols. (New York: Derby and Jackson, 1858), 453, n.1.

28   You can read this digest for yourself in Beliles, *The Selected Religious Letters and Papers of Thomas Jefferson*, 397-428. It's just selections from the Gospels of the teachings of Jesus.

29   Letter to Benjamin Rush, August 8, 1804. Beliles, *The Selected Religious Letters and Papers of Thomas Jefferson*, 126.

said that the death of Jesus on the cross needed to remain in it.[30] Although Jefferson was not attempting a biography, only a digest of Jesus' philosophy, still he decided to cease the project altogether. He never sent the extracts to anyone.

Jefferson's Louisiana Purchase sparked other correspondence on religious matters. As chief executive over the new federal Louisiana Territory Jefferson received a letter from the federally appointed Governor of Louisiana, William Claiborne, on June 15, 1804. It included a letter from Rev. Soeur Therese de St. Xavier Farjon, and 11 other Nuns of the Order of St. Ursula at New Orleans.[31] They requested that Jefferson make sure that the Catholic convent's property ownership be confirmed by Congress.[32] Jefferson replied on July 13:

> ... The principles of the constitution and government of the United States are a sure guarantee to you that it will be preserved to you sacred and inviolate, and that your institution will be permitted to govern itself according to it's own voluntary rules, without interference from the civil authority. Whatever diversity of shade may appear in the religious opinions of our fellow citizens, the charitable objects of your institution cannot be indifferent to any; and it's furtherance of the wholesome purposes of society by *training up it's younger members in the way they should go* cannot fail to ensure it the patronage of the government it is under. Be assured it will meet all the protection which my office can give it. I salute you, holy sisters, with friendship and respect.[33]

This is a remarkable letter that goes beyond simply assuring this Catholic convent that it has nothing to fear from the more Protestant-oriented American government. He paraphrases Proverbs 22:6 ("train up a child in the way he should go") and affirms this Christian educational ministry, and promises "patronage" of the U.S. government. Government aid for missions and Indians in federal

---

30   To Thomas Jefferson from Benjamin Rush, August 29, 1804. The Thomas Jefferson Papers Series 1, General Correspondence, 1651-1827, Library of Congress Manuscript Division.

31   Letter from William Claiborne, June 15, 1804. [Note: The letter from the Ursulines is found with Claiborne's letter and not separately on its own.] The Thomas Jefferson Papers Series 1, General Correspondence, 1651-1827, Library of Congress Manuscript Division.

32   Letter from Ursuline Nuns of New Orleans (Sister Therese Farjon, et al), April 23, 1804. Beliles, *The Selected Religious Letters and Papers of Thomas Jefferson*, 120.

33   Letter to Ursuline Nuns of New Orleans (Sister Therese Farjon, et al), July 13, 1804. Beliles, *The Selected Religious Letters and Papers of Thomas Jefferson*, 126. Also see their letter of March 21, 1804 (but received by Jefferson June 14). Italics added by authors for emphasis.

territories is again constitutionally permissible to Jefferson. His ruling principle in the religious issue was federalism not secularism. Federalism embodies the concept of independent jurisdictions of the national and state governments – neither of which may interfere in each other's unique responsibilities and authority.

It is worth noting here that a couple years later on May 20, 1806, Jefferson's account book said he "Gave…50 Dollars to the order of Governor Wilkinson or other acting governor of Louisiana for building a church there."[34] So in addition to supportive federal governmental words and policies for religious groups in the new federal territory, Jefferson also puts his personal resources into the same efforts. And although here it is not government money, he has no qualms with giving it to the Governor for distribution for church purposes.

Aiding Campmeeting Evangelists and Capitol Worship

The president went home on April 2, 1804 and entered another period of grieving as his twenty-five year old daughter, Mary (Polly), died on April 17, due to complications arising from giving birth to a child two months before. Jefferson turned to his home pastor Rev. Matthew Maury to conduct the funeral.[35] His other daughter Martha said she "found him with the Bible in his hands [seeking]… consolation in the Sacred Volume."[36] And in a letter to his boyhood friend and devout Christian, John Page, Jefferson quoted the Apostle Paul's argument that because of a belief in resurrection and eternal life, "We sorrow not then as others who have no hope."[37] This not only shows his use of the Bible, but notably his use of more than just the words of Jesus. Even more notably, he claims the assurance of faith in dealing with death—one of the great comforts of the believer.

As was mentioned earlier, Albemarle County was the Virginia epicenter of the camp meeting revivals of the Second Great Awakening. The most prolific of these camp meeting preachers was a man named Rev. Lorenzo Dow, the most famous of all evangelists in the early 19th century. He traveled throughout the nation and spoke to more people than any other preacher at that time. He came that

---

34   Account book, May 20, 1806. To Louisiana Governor Wilkinson. For "building a church there." Beliles, *The Selected Religious Letters and Papers of Thomas Jefferson*, 147.

35   Account book, April 25, 1804. For M. Maury. Beliles, *The Selected Religious Letters and Papers of Thomas Jefferson*, 121.

36   Sarah N. Randolph, *The Domestic Life of Thomas Jefferson* (Charlottesville, VA: University Press of Virginia, 1988), 300.

37   Letter to John Page, June 25, 1804. Beliles, *The Selected Religious Letters and Papers of Thomas Jefferson*, 124. He quoted Bible verse from 1 Thessalonians 4:13. This also cited by Edwin Gaustad, *Sworn On the Altar of God: A Religious Biography of Thomas Jefferson* (Grand Rapids, Mich.: W. B. Eerdmans Publishers, 1996), 142.

spring of 1804 to a gathering in the town of Milton near Monticello (where he had preached in 1802 also). Dow wrote in his journal that in "...Charlottesville near the President's seat in Albemarle County; I spoke to about four thousand people, and one of the President's daughters who was present, died a few days after."[38] This crowd was over ten times the size of Charlottesville and attracted every level of society together. Jefferson's daughter Mary, wife of Congressman John Wayles Eppes, and some of the Monticello enslaved community came to these meetings that lasted a week there at the base of Jefferson's mountain, but there is no evidence that the President attended (perhaps it ended just before he arrived from Washington). Dow's wild unorthodox style of preaching gave him the title of "Crazy Dow," but he was also an avid supporter of the president and his Democratic-Republican Party.

The chief organizer of these camp meeting revivals in Central Virginia was Methodist Rev. Henry Fry. Jefferson and Fry knew each other going back to serving together on the Anglican vestry and in the legislature in the 1760s.[39] But it was in this new season of grief that Jefferson's friendship with him becomes more evident because of a letter Jefferson wrote to Rev. Fry on May 21, 1804, saying: "...When I had the pleasure of seeing you at your own house you expressed a wish to see Priestley's *Corruptions of Christianity*. But the morning I passed you...meeting with mr. [Rev. Matthew] Maury in the road I was glad to leave them with him to be presented to you in my behalf..."[40] Obviously, Jefferson and Rev. Fry had met in his home and discussed religion recently, and it led to the topic of alleged corruptions of Christianity.

Rev. Fry replied on June 9, and Jefferson wrote again on June 17, speaking of "priestcraft and...kingcraft constituting a conspiracy of church and state against the civil and religious liberties of mankind."[41] When he condemned priestcraft and the conspiracy of church and state, his anti-clericalism here was obviously narrow, since Rev. Fry was himself a minister, political activist, and ally. The context shows that it was a reference to Europe's type of state government-established religious

---

38   Peggy Dow, *The Dealings of God, Man, and the Devil; as Exemplified in the Life, Experience, and Travels of Lorenzo Dow* (New York: Cornish, Lamport and Co., 1852), 87. Journal entry is number 653.

39   William Bennett, *Memorials of Methodism in Virginia* (Richmond, Va.: self-published, 1871), 413.

40   Letter to Rev. Henry Fry, May 21, 1804. Beliles, *The Selected Religious Letters and Papers of Thomas Jefferson*, 121.

41   Letter from Rev. Henry Fry, June 9, 1804 and Letter to Rev. Henry Fry, June 17, 1804. Ibid. Beliles, *The Selected Religious Letters and Papers of Thomas Jefferson*, 121.

system that Virginia had thrown off with the help of evangelical clergy allies like Rev. Fry who had served in the legislature on the Committee on Religion in 1785-1786 that passed the Virginia Statute for Religious Freedom. This critique of the state-church system was something that Jefferson and these revivalist preachers held in common. Modern commentators too often ignore or fail to understand who Fry was and the context of this statement.

Rev. Fry responded on February 26, 1805 by suggesting a more orthodox writer than Priestley for Jefferson's study of historical theology and the letter also introduced to Jefferson "The bearer Lorenzo Dow…" Dow apparently met the president and recorded in his journal later that he was "invited to preach in Congress-Hall before the House."[42] With Jefferson likely in attendance, he spoke from Proverbs 14:34 in the Bible: "Righteousness exalteth a nation; but sin is a shame to any people." Historian Jon Butler notes that after this Dow "regularly carried letters on his travels from political officials, especially Jeffersonian Republicans like James Madison."[43]

Correspondence of Jefferson with groups of Baptists from Delaware and Connecticut respectively has already been noted. Another group of Baptists wrote the President in late 1803 from the towns of Portsmouth and Norfolk in Virginia.[44] Then in January of 1804 Jefferson replied to them saying he believed in: "…the genuine spirit of their primitive Christianity, which so peculiarly inculcated the doctrines of peace, justice, and good will to all mankind."[45]

And it was also around this time that hard evidence of Jefferson's previously-mentioned membership in the Episcopal Church in Washington became clear

---

42 Lorenzo Dow, *The History of the Cosmopolite, or the four volumes of Lorenzo Dow's Journal* (Wheeling, Va.: Joshua Martin, 1848), 331. It is known for sure that he later preached in the Capitol in January 1813. If Dow did not personally meet Jefferson, it is certain Dow met Secretary of War Henry Dearborn on March 2, 1805 to give some documents to the President. See letter from Henry Dearborn to Jefferson, March 2, 1805 in which he mentions the "celebrated preacher." www.founders.archives.gov. The documents were regarding the Mississippi Territory according to a letter from Samuel Coburn to Lorenzo Dow, December 8, 1804, found in Thomas Jefferson Papers at the Library of Congress.

43 Jon Butler, *Awash in a Sea of Faith: Christianizing the American People* (Cambridge, Mass: Harvard University Press, 1990), 287.

44 Letter from Rev. Davis Biggs, John Foster and the Baptists of Portsmouth and Norfolk, Virginia, November 12, 1803. Beliles, *The Selected Religious Letters and Papers of Thomas Jefferson*, 117. [Note: The letter is incorrectly identified as being from Portsmouth, New Hampshire in the digital collection at the Library of Congress]

45 Letter to Rev. Davis Biggs, John Foster and the Baptists of Portsmouth and Norfolk, Virginia, January 20, 1804. Beliles, *The Selected Religious Letters and Papers of Thomas Jefferson*, 118. [This reply is not easy to connect to the one above because it not found under Portsmouth in the digital collection at the Library of Congress. It is also filed under "Briggs" instead of "Biggs."]

in his account book: "Drew check on bank in favor Revd. Mr. McCormic for 100 Dollars being my subscription to him for 1802. & 1803."[46] This amount is equivalent to about $2,400 today. Rev. Andrew T. McCormick was rector of the Episcopal parish of Washington. While Jefferson was in Washington, his account book also records that on October 7, 1804, he gave "Charity…at church."[47] It is not known what church this referred to. But Jefferson certainly continued regularly attending services led by the chaplains in the "Hall" or House of Representatives of the U.S. Capitol building.[48] On November 11, Reverend Manasseh Cutler, Massachusetts Congressman of the opposing Federalist party, noted in his journal: "Attended worship at our Hall [i.e., House of Representatives]. Mr. McCormick preached a very good sermon on Charity—the good Samaritan. Jefferson at the Hall in the morning." Then on December 2, Cutler said: "Attended worship at the Capitol. Mr. McCormick preached. Mr. Jefferson and his Secretary, Burril, attended."[49]

Attendance was not Jefferson's only role. On December 10 John Hollins wrote to Jefferson about coming with Rev. Glendy to Washington.[50] To this Jefferson replied with delight saying "I obtained the Speaker's order for reserving the desk of the H. of R. for mr. Glendy on Sunday next, where many of us will be glad to see him…I will expect him to dine with me…"[51] Jefferson then wrote to Senate chaplain McCormick, who, weekly alternating responsibilities with the House chaplain, jointly oversaw the services in the Capitol, to ask for Rev. John Glendy to preach there:

> The liberality which I have seen practiced by the gentlemen, chaplains of Congress, in admitting others of their profession who happen here occasionally to perform the Sabbath day functions in the chamber of the

---

46   Account book, July 2, 1804. Subscription for McCormick (for previous years of 1802 and 1803). Beliles, *The Selected Religious Letters and Papers of Thomas Jefferson*, 126.

47   Account book, October 7, 1804. Donation "at church" [in Washington]. Beliles, *The Selected Religious Letters and Papers of Thomas Jefferson*, 127.

48   James H. Hutson, *Religion and the Founding of the American Republic* (Washington, D.C.: Library of Congress, 1998), 96. Other references are found of Jefferson attending worship in the Capitol. In 1806 Catharine Mitchill records stepping on Jefferson's foot at the end of a House service.

49   Journal of Manasseh Cutler. Manasseh Cutler, *Life, Journal, and Correspondence*, 2 vols. (Cincinnati, Ohio: Robert Clarke and Co., 1888).

50   From John Hollins to Jefferson, December 10, 1804. www.founders.archives.gov.

51   Letter to John Hollins, December 12, 1804. www.founders.archives.gov.

H[ouse] of Representatives, induces me to ask that indulgence for the revd. Mr. Glendye, a Presbyterian clergyman from Baltimore who will be in this place next Sunday forenoon. Being acquainted with mr. Glendye, I can assure you that no person to whom that permission could be transferred, will be heard with more satisfaction than he would…could I be allowed so far to profit of your friendship as to ask your requesting this favor from mr. Lowry.[52]

"Lowry" as Jefferson spelled it above was Scotch Presbyterian Rev. James Laurie who was one of the chaplains in the House of Representatives from the end of 1804 to the end of 1806. That's why his permission was needed, along with McCormick's, for Glendy (whose name Jefferson also misspelled in this letter) to preach in the Capitol service (which he did on December 16). McCormick wrote back the same day that Laurie agreed to have Glendy speak, so Jefferson's desire for Presbyterian Rev. John Glendy to preach at the Capitol service came to fruition.[53] Congressman Cutler's journal noted this on December 16: "Attended in the Hall. A Mr. Glendy, now settled in Baltimore, preached… but his adulation offered to the President disgusting."[54]

After his sermon in the Capitol at the end of 1804, Jefferson received a letter from Glendy on February 28, 1805 to ask Jefferson's assistance (particularly a recommendation to Governor Thomas McKean) for a potential post as the pastor at First Presbyterian Church in Philadelphia. (Governor McKean, who had been a signer of the Declaration along with Jefferson, was a member of that church.) Such a request indicates that Presbyterian leaders there would respect Jefferson's request, which would not make sense if they thought Jefferson a Deist or enemy of the Christian faith. Indeed no church leaders in Philadelphia (like those in Virginia) where Jefferson resided for many years ever questioned or attacked Jefferson's faith. Jefferson replied a few days later saying: "I have this day written to Governor McKean, on the subject of it, so as to produce any dispositions & measures on

52   Letter to Rev. Andrew McCormick, December 12, 1804. Beliles, *The Selected Religious Letters and Papers of Thomas Jefferson*, 128.

53   Andrew McCormick to Thomas Jefferson, December 12, 1804. Beliles, *The Selected Religious Letters and Papers of Thomas Jefferson*, 129. Also see another letter from John Hollins, December 14, 1804. www.founders.archives.gov. He told Jefferson he could not come but Mr. Emmett would bring Glendy.

54   Cutler, *Life, Journal and Correspondence*.

his part which my indisposition can produce."[55] On that same day his letter to McKean said that Glendy was "without exception the best preacher I ever heard."[56]

Jefferson's account book also says on January 15, 1805: "Promised to give 50 Dollars [i.e., $1200 today] towards building a Presbyterian church on F. street."[57] This was the congregation led by Rev. James Laurie which met in the Capitol regularly at this point. Its own building was completed in 1807 on the site of what is now 1414 F. Street, N.W., just a block or so away from the White House. Laurie's Associate Reformed Presbyterian Church began after a split from First Presbyterian Church in 1802.[58]

Religious leaders in Washington, and those back home in Virginia, were well aware of Jefferson's active church life and support of religion, but northerners did not know of this (or ignored it for political reasons) and so there were still occasional attacks on his faith by clergy from the northeastern states. An example from sometime in 1804, was by Rev. Clement C. Moore of New York, who wrote "Observations Upon Certain Passages in Mr. Jefferson's Notes on Virginia which appear to have a tendency to subvert religion and establish a false philosophy." Jefferson ally DeWitt Clinton, who led the Republicans in New York, wrote to Jefferson a few years later to say that he was working hard to "…disassociate republicanism from deism" in the minds of many up north due to the false information spread by Linn, Moore, and others.[59] Jefferson replied to Clinton saying that perceptions of Deism were "…an unfounded falsehood…" and the idea that Jefferson wanted government to be without religion was "slander" which "…Th: J. has thought it best to leave to the scourge of public opinion."[60] But in reality pieces such as written by Moore in 1804 soon ceased being published after Jefferson's presidential re-election, and most of the country no longer believed it. Sadly, Jefferson's widespread support of various orthodox clergy and churches such as led by Laurie and Glendy is almost

---

55   Letter from Rev. John Glendy, February 28, 1805 and Letter to Rev. John Glendy, March 3, 1805. Beliles, *The Selected Religious Letters and Papers of Thomas Jefferson*, 131 and 133.

56   Letter to Thomas McKean, March 3, 1805. Beliles, *The Selected Religious Letters and Papers of Thomas Jefferson*, 134.

57   Account book, January 1805. For "building a Presbyterian church" in Washington. Beliles, *The Selected Religious Letters and Papers of Thomas Jefferson*, 129.

58   The pastor of First Presbyterian Church was Rev. John Brackenridge, who later became Senate chaplain in 1811.

59   DeWitt Clinton to Thomas Jefferson, May 16, 1807. The Thomas Jefferson Papers Series 1, General Correspondence, 1651-1827, Library of Congress Manuscript Division.

60   Letter to DeWitt Clinton, May 24, 1807. Beliles, *The Selected Religious Letters and Papers of Thomas Jefferson*, 154.

unknown today, and only the attacks by people such as Rev. Moore are recounted by modern biographers.

In the account book for February 20, 1805, it says Jefferson: "Gave Alexander Smith…for a Baptist church in Alexandria."[61] Smith was a member of First Baptist Church of Alexandria, Virginia, whose pastor was Rev. Jeremiah Moore, who had previously corresponded with Jefferson. Also in early 1805 Jefferson wrote to Matthew Carey to request some Greek and English New Testaments and a copy of the Benjamin Johnson-Robert Carr Bible. He also noted that he had received a French New Testament from Mr. Reibelt of Baltimore.[62] Jefferson at that time also "…subscribes with pleasure for a copy of Brown's dictionary of the bible which he proposes to print…"[63]

A Second Term as President

When inaugurated president for his second term on March 4, 1805, Jefferson again took the oath with his hand on a Bible, and offered the voluntary appeal for God's help which, like the presidential prayer proclamations, he certainly could have dropped this custom if he wished. Then in his Second Inaugural Address, he said: "…In matters of religion, I have considered that its free exercise is placed by the Constitution independent of the powers of the general [i.e., national] government. I have therefore undertaken on no occasion to prescribe the religious exercises suited to it; but have left them as the Constitution found them, under the direction and discipline of State or Church authorities acknowledged by the several religious societies."[64] Here he affirmed again his view that oversight of religion is a state power or a church power, not a national one. He continued by mentioning that a "Creator made them" and spoke of "religious liberty unassailed." Then Jefferson again refers to guidance and enlightenment not as coming from reason alone, but from God:

> I shall need, too, the favor of that Being in whose hands we are, who led our forefathers, as Israel of old, from their native land, and planted them

---

61   Account book, February 20, 1805. For a Baptist Church in Alexandria. Beliles, *The Selected Religious Letters and Papers of Thomas Jefferson*, 131.

62   Letter to Matthew Car[e]y, February 3, 1805. The Thomas Jefferson Papers Series 1, General Correspondence, 1651-1827, Library of Congress Manuscript Division.

63   Letter to Zakok Cramer, March 8, 1805. Beliles, *The Selected Religious Letters and Papers of Thomas Jefferson*, 142.

64   Second Inaugural Address, March 4, 1805. Beliles, *The Selected Religious Letters and Papers of Thomas Jefferson*, 140.

in a country flowing with all the necessaries and comforts of life; who has covered our infancy with his providence, and our riper years with his wisdom and power; and to whose goodness I ask you to join with me in supplication that He [God] will enlighten the minds of your servants, guide their councils, and prosper their measures.[65]

Jefferson biographer Alf J. Mapp says that with these words, Jefferson certainly "refuted the contention that his philosophy held enlightenment and religion to be irreconcilable enemies."[66]

An orthodox Calvinist pastor from New England wrote Jefferson a lengthy commendation on his inauguration day. Rev. Thomas Allen of the Pittsfield, Massachusetts Congregational Church was one of the rare leaders of that denomination who supported Jefferson and the Republicans. He disagreed with the attacks of some of his Congregationalist brethren of New England and was hopeful that with Jefferson's re-election it was finally going to end. Rev. Allen also said that in fact Deism was the basis of the Federalist's views, not Jefferson's party.[67] Jefferson replied a week later to thank Rev. Allen for the friendly letter and then said:

... with us character must be offered on the altar of public good. ....[and] after so much misrepresentation, to see my countrymen coming over daily to a sense of the injustice of a certain party towards me, is peculiarly gratifying & will sweeten the latest hours of retirement & life.[68]

On March 9, 1805 Albemarle Baptist preacher William Woods visited Washington and wrote Jefferson saying: "I must take the liberty to congratulate you on your reelection to that solemn and important [_____] as the Chief of so great a nation, and I hope Sir, that that God whose Dominion is over all may be your Guide, Counselor, and kind Preserver. Though I believe you have some enemies yet sure I am that many there are that implore the Divine hand to help

65   Ibid.

66   Alf J. Mapp, Jr., *Thomas Jefferson: A Strange Case of Mistaken Identity* (New York: Madison Books, 1987), 399." Also see William D. Gould, "Religious Opinions of Thomas Jefferson," *Mississippi Valley Historical Review* (Cedar Rapids, Iowa: 1933), XX: 191.

67   Letter from Rev. Thomas Allen, March 4, 1805. Beliles, *The Selected Religious Letters and Papers of Thomas Jefferson*, 134.

68   Letter to Rev. Thomas Allen, March 12, 1805. Beliles, *The Selected Religious Letters and Papers of Thomas Jefferson*, 142.

you."[69] It is known that he is yet another of the numerous ministers who personally met with Jefferson.

Besides being a member of Christ Episcopal Church in Washington, Jefferson on May 15, 1805 also "Subscribed towards building an Episcopal church in Washington 100 Dollars [about $2400 in today's dollars] payable in 3 Monthly installments beginning June 1."[70] When this building opened in 1807, pew No. 42 was reserved for Jefferson. This church is still standing at present at 622 G. Street, S. E. in Washington, D.C. Jefferson also "Drew on bank U.S. in favor [of] Revd. A. McCormic for 50 Dollars [for] one year's subscription."[71] But, as usual, Jefferson also supported other churches. On April 19, 1805, his account book says he "Gave…charity to…Methodist church in Alexandria [Virginia]."[72] Later on November 15, the account book says he "Paid Michael Nourse 50 Dollars towards building a church."[73] This was Rev. Laurie's F Street Presbyterian Church in Washington, D.C.

And on May 1, it says he "Subscribed 200 Dollars [i.e., $4800 today] to an academy at this place."[74] The editors of the account book say, "The movement to establish public elementary schools in Washington began in 1805 with the formation of the Permanent Institution for the Education of Youth; TJ was named president of its board of trustees. Although Jefferson replied that he would do what he could with limited time, in reality Robert Brent led the board. Two schools, the western academy near the President's House and the eastern academy near the Capitol, opened in 1806…"[75] For several years Jefferson did give help as the chief author of the first plan adopted for the city. The board hired two clergymen as

69　Letter from Rev. William Woods, March 9, 1805 and Letter to Rev. William Woods, March 9, 1805. The Thomas Jefferson Papers Series 1, General Correspondence, 1651-1827, Library of Congress Manuscript Division.

70　Account book, May 15, 1805. For "building an Episcopal church in Washington." Beliles, *The Selected Religious Letters and Papers of Thomas Jefferson*, 144.

71　Account book, June 3, 1805. For subscription for McCormick. Beliles, *The Selected Religious Letters and Papers of Thomas Jefferson*, 144.

72　Account book, April 19, 1805. For Methodist Church in Alexandria. Beliles, *The Selected Religious Letters and Papers of Thomas Jefferson*, 143.

73　Account book, November 15, 1805. For building a Church (to Nourse who represented Laurie's Presbyterian church). Beliles, *The Selected Religious Letters and Papers of Thomas Jefferson*, 144.

74　Account book, May 1, 1805. For Academy in Washington. (led by Elliott) Beliles, *The Selected Religious Letters and Papers of Thomas Jefferson*, 143.

75　Letter from Robert Brent, August 6, 1805 and Letter to Robert Brent, August 14, 1805. The Thomas Jefferson Papers Series 1, General Correspondence, 1651-1827, Library of Congress Manuscript Division.

its first teachers and began using the Bible and Isaac Watt's hymnals for teaching reading.[76] And on December 11, Jefferson "Inclosed to the Revd. Mr. [George Addison] Baxter 50 Dollars [for] my subscription to Washington academy....in Rockbridge."[77] This Presbyterian religious school later became known as Washington and Lee University in Lexington, Virginia. At the time, it was distinctively Christian. So Jefferson's support of Christian education is clear.

Jefferson attended a sermon by the non-denominational/Quaker Rev. Dorothy Ripley in early 1806 and his worship in the Capitol was also referenced by Catherine Mitchill in an April 1806 letter because of her embarrassment for stepping on the president's toes in the crowded room of worshipers (apparently a few months earlier).[78]

The idea of foreign missions was still new to most Americans when an appeal was made to Jefferson on February 24 by Reverend Doctor William Rogers and Rev. William Staughton on behalf of other clergymen in Philadelphia for his support of William Carey's mission in India. Rogers was a Baptist minister serving at that time as professor at the University of Pennsylvania, and Staughton was pastor of First Baptist Church of Philadelphia. Their appeal included a flier that described the mission more in-depth, and it asked for money to translate the Bible into seven languages. The letter was also signed by eleven other clergymen of Philadelphia:

> Ashbel Green, 2d Presbyterian Church
> J. Henry C. Helmuth, German Lutheran Church
> John Hey, Independent Church
> Joseph Pilmore, Episcopal Church of St. Paul's
> James Gray, Scotch Presbyterian Church
> George Potts, 4th Presbyterian Church
> William White, 2d Baptist Church
> Joseph Shaw, Associate Congregation
> Samuel Helfenstein, German Reformed Church

---

76 John C. Proctor, ed., *Washington Past and Present* (New York: Lewis Historical Publishing Co, 1930), 414-423. Jefferson personally was involved in granting two lots of land for the schoolhouses on October 27, 1806, and allowed churches to use them for worship as well. Isaac Watts from England was a prolific writer of Christian hymns. Rev. White later wrote to Jefferson on May 16, 1807, asking for a job as librarian of Congress. The Thomas Jefferson Papers Series 1, General Correspondence, 1651-1827, Library of Congress Manuscript Division.

77 Account book, December 5 and 11, 1805. For Baxter and subscription to Washington Academy. Beliles, *The Selected Religious Letters and Papers of Thomas Jefferson*, 145.

78 Hutson quotes Mitchell's letter to Margaret Miller dated April 8, 1806.

Jacob J. Janeway, 2d Presbyterian Church [co-pastor]
William Colbert, Methodist Episcopal Church of St. George [79]

It is important to see that this Who's Who of clergy from many denominations in Philadelphia had no reason to think their appeal to Jefferson would be useless. On the contrary, these Gospel ministers asserted that "the name of Jefferson will be long and with pleasure repeated" in regards to his benevolence for such things. But the idea of foreign missions for Protestants was still very new.[80] So on March 2, 1806, Jefferson replied with a letter in which he declined to donate because, as he explained to these clergymen, he preferred to support charitable programs closer to home with which he was familiar, were more accountable, and believed to be more likely to be successful. This was something he had already expressed a couple times to previous requests for aid outside of Washington or his home state.[81] The reader will also see consistently similar responses for the same reason later in Jefferson's life.

Similarly, a Committee of Missions of the Presbyterian Church in the United States sent an appeal for help of their missionary among the Indians by the name of Gideon Blackburn. This committee was led by Rev. Ashbel Green who had served as congressional chaplain and therefore was known to Jefferson already (Green was among the Philadelphia list of clergyman in the previous appeal also).[82] As noted previously, Jefferson had begun aiding Blackburn in 1804. Although no reply from Jefferson to this committee survives, Blackburn came to Monticello a year later to give a report and thank him for his support of his schools. Finding Jefferson not there on September 11, 1807, Rev. Gideon Blackburn left a written report and a request for more aid since indeed he had already received support from Jefferson's

---

79   Letter from Rev. Doctors William Rogers and William Staughton and Clergy of Philadelphia, February 24, 1806. Beliles, *The Selected Religious Letters and Papers of Thomas Jefferson*, 145.

80   The Haystack Prayer Meeting took place later in 1806 and is often spoken of as the birth of foreign missions in American Christian history. It is understandable why Jefferson was not yet for the concept. Virtually no one in America had yet to support it.

81   Letter to Rev. Doctors William Rogers and William Slaughter [Staughton], March 2, 1806. Beliles, *The Selected Religious Letters and Papers of Thomas Jefferson*, 146. Slaughter was a misspelling. The correct name was Staughton. Rogers was known for his sermon given at the request of the Constitutional Convention on July 4, 1787, in the Calvinistic Reformed Church of Philadelphia. Staughton later was chosen to preach a sermon before Congress in memory of Jefferson shortly after his death.

82   Letter from Rev. Ashbel Green and the Committee of Missions of the Presbyterian Church in the United States, March 13, 1806.

administration.[83] It is not clear if Jefferson had the government provide more aid, but clearly he had already been cooperating with Presbyterian missionaries.

An appeal from Wyandot Indians was sent to Jefferson via John George Jackson in late 1805 asking for land near Sandusky, Ohio be granted to them in part for "some missionaries." that served them. Another appeal was made by the Western Missionary Society of the Presbyterian denomination apparently for the same purpose.[84] Jefferson replied to Jackson on February 22, 1806 saying that Congress should deal with the request since it "…alone being competent to determine on the merits" of it. Jefferson also noted that since Ohio was now a state and not a federal territory the all important principle of federalism must be applied, saying that "… the incorporation of religious societies in the states being out of the constitutional notice of the general [i.e., national] government."[85]

Jefferson was asked for a donation to a church in Wickford, Rhode Island at that time but declined saying he could not afford to give beyond his area of residence, which he often did.[86] His account book entry for April 18, 1806 says: "Subscribed 50 Dollars towards Methodist church in Georgetown."[87] This church was in Georgetown, led by Rev. William Walters. Then on June 28, the account book said he paid: "…my subscription to the…Methodist meeting House."[88] A half year later on January 6, 1807, Jefferson "Subscribed to church Episcopal near Navy yard 50 Dollars."[89] And on October 6, Henry Ingle then informs Jefferson that pew 42 was reserved for him in the church.[90] But a month later on November 4, 1807,

83 Gideon Blackburn to Thomas Jefferson, September 11, 1807. Beliles, *The Selected Religious Letters and Papers of Thomas Jefferson*, 155. [Included with his letter are notes from a few Cherokee children.]

84 From Wyandot Chiefs, August 16, 1805. www.Founders.archives.gov. From Rev. John McPherrin & Western Missionary Society of the Presbyterian Church in America, October 5, 1805. www.Founders.archives.gov. From Rev. James Hughs and [Western?] Missionary Society, October 23, 1805. www.Founders.archives.gov.

85 Letter to John G. Jackson, February 22, 1806. www.founders.archives.gov.

86 Joseph Stanton, Jr., to Jefferson, March 26, 1806. www.founders.archives.gov. Letter to Joseph Stanton, Jr., March 28, 1806. www.founders.archives.gov.

87 Account book, April 18, 1806. For Methodist Church in Georgetown. Beliles, *The Selected Religious Letters and Papers of Thomas Jefferson*, 147.

88 Account book, June 28, 1806. For "Methodist meeting House." Beliles, *The Selected Religious Letters and Papers of Thomas Jefferson*, 149.

89 Account book, January 6, 1807. For Episcopal Church (near Navy Yard). Beliles, *The Selected Religious Letters and Papers of Thomas Jefferson*, 152.

90 Henry Ingle to Thomas Jefferson, October 6, 1807. Beliles, *The Selected Religious Letters and Papers of Thomas Jefferson*, 157.

Jefferson sends a letter to his Washington pastor, Rev. McCormick, notifying him of a change:

> I take this occasion of testifying the…satisfaction with which I have continued a member of your congregation [Christ Episcopal Church] from my first residence here till the removal of the church to its present distance. This circumstance solely occasioning my discontinuance of attendance….[91]

Although Jefferson had been a faithful supporter and attendee when the Episcopal services were in a government building near the President's mansion, he felt the new distance was just too far. Plus McCormick had just been elected to be the Senate chaplain again and would serve for the next and final year of Jefferson's term as President. Jefferson could enjoy his pastor's sermons during the last year in the Capitol without having to travel a further distance to the new Episcopal Church building. And on the same day Jefferson writes another to Ingle mentioning that "…the distance of the new building…obliging me to decline."[92] But still Jefferson gave "…[for Rev.] McCormac…100 [dollars]."[93] Yet despite this evidence, most modern commentators make the untenable claim that Jefferson was not part of any church.

Continuing Study of the Bible Along With Unorthodox Opinions

As this year of 1807 closed, Jefferson's account book on December 21 shows that he "Inclosed…for subscription to bible."[94] His signature is seen on the subscription document that survives.[95] And his name is on the list printed with other subscribers in the Bible itself. This was called Scott's Bible because it included commentary by the evangelical Anglican Rev. Thomas Scott. Also in this time period, Jefferson's personal overseer at Monticello, Edmund Bacon, who

---

91   Letter to Rev. Andrew McCormick, November 4, 1807. Beliles, *The Selected Religious Letters and Papers of Thomas Jefferson*, 158.

92   Letter to Henry Ingle, November 6, 1807. Beliles, *The Selected Religious Letters and Papers of Thomas Jefferson*, 158.

93   Account book, November 6, 1807. For McCormick. Beliles, *The Selected Religious Letters and Papers of Thomas Jefferson*, 158.

94   Account book, December 21, 1807. For Scott's Bible. Beliles, *The Selected Religious Letters and Papers of Thomas Jefferson* (Charlottesville, VA: America Publications, 2013), 165.

95   Scott Bible subscription document with Jefferson's signature. University of Virginia Library.

lived there for twenty years and began working in late 1806, spoke of often seeing Jefferson with his Bible. He wrote: "[There was] a large Bible which nearly always lay at the head of his sofa. Many and many a time I have gone into his room and found him reading that Bible."[96]

At the same time, further hints as to Jefferson's emerging doctrinal unorthodoxy occur in a November 18, 1807 reply to Universalist minister Rev. Ralph Eddowes of Philadelphia. Eddowes, who had been mentored earlier by Unitarian Rev. Joseph Priestley, had written to Jefferson and enclosed some Unitarian literature.[97] Jefferson replied to Eddowes and gave his "...thanks for the two pamphlets he has been so kind as to send him. He has read them with so much satisfaction that he has desired mr. Dobson to forward him the successive discourses as they shall come out, and also the new translation of the New Testament announced in page 22. This latter work is particularly interesting as he has always been persuaded that the different translations of that book have been warped in particular passages to the tenets of the church of which the translator has been a member..."[98] On February 6, 1809, his account book shows he paid for these "Unitarian pamphlets and a new Unitarian version [by Thomas Belsham] of William Newcome's translation of the New Testament."[99]

These titles and Jefferson's response are among the earliest examples of his own emerging interest in unorthodox doctrines while still being orthodox in practice. He also ordered an essay by William Austin about "the human nature of Jesus Christ" in July 1808.[100]

Jefferson's passion for study of Scripture continued to be evident in his letters to Bible translator Charles Thomson, a fellow patriot leader who served as the official Secretary of the Continental Congress. (Thomson was orthodox.) Jefferson writes him in early 1808 saying: "I see by the newspapers your translation of the Septuagint is now to be printed, and I write this to pray to

---

96 See *Jefferson At Monticello*, ed. James A. Bear, Jr. (Charlottesville, Va.: University Press of Virginia, 1967), 109.

97 Letter from Rev. Ralph Eddowes, November 14, 1807. Beliles, *The Selected Religious Letters and Papers of Thomas Jefferson*, 162.

98 Letter to Rev. Ralph Eddowes, November 18, 1807. Beliles, *The Selected Religious Letters and Papers of Thomas Jefferson*, 162.

99 Account book, February 6, 1809. For books (including some Unitarian pamphlets and New Testament). Bear and Stanton, 1240.

100 Letter to William Pelham, July 12, 1808. www.founders.archives.gov. Also see letter from William Pelham, July 20, 1808.

be admitted as a subscriber… God bless you and give you years and health…[101] On December 13 Thomson, sent Jefferson a copy of his translation of the Old Testament from the Greek—providing evidence once again that our third president was a serious student of the Bible.[102] Jefferson replied on Christmas day saying: "I have dipped into it at the few moments of leisure which my vocations permit, and I perceive that I shall use it with great satisfaction on my return home. I propose there, among my first emploiments, to give to the Septuagint an attentive perusal…"[103]

But Jefferson ordering Unitarian-oriented literature about the same time as the evangelical Scott Bible, and Thomson's Old Testament and corresponding equally warmly with orthodox and unorthodox religious leaders, and also attending and funding Trinitarian church services, makes it difficult to make absolute declarations about specifics of his beliefs at this time in his life. But his extended and repeated correspondence with Gospel ministers demonstrates his affinity and support for the Christian faith, and many clergy at this time still respected and praised Jefferson for it.

Corresponding With Many Religious Groups

At the end of 1807, a group of Quaker leaders wrote to Jefferson from their Yearly Meeting in Baltimore representing the Western Shore of Maryland, the adjacent parts of Pennsylvania and Virginia, and the State of Ohio. They commended Jefferson for avoiding war, aiding Indians, and stopping the slave trade.[104] In his reply to Mr. Thomas, Mr. Ellicott, Mr. Hopkins, and the Society of Friends, Jefferson said: "….I learn with satisfaction their approbation of the principles which have influenced the councils of the General Government….It was dictated by the principles of humanity, [and] the precepts of the gospel…." Jefferson also

---

101   Letter to Charles Thomson, January 11, 1808. Beliles, *The Selected Religious Letters and Papers of Thomas Jefferson*, 166.

102   Letter from Charles Thomson, December 13, 1808. The Thomas Jefferson Papers Series 1, General Correspondence, 1651-1827, Library of Congress Manuscript Division. . Note: the Septuagint was the Greek translation of the Old Testament, completed more than a century and a half before Christ. It was created because Alexander the Great (died 323 BC) made Greek the lingua franca of the Western world.

103   Letter to Charles Thomson, December 25, 1808. Beliles, *The Selected Religious Letters and Papers of Thomas Jefferson*, 180.

104   Letter from Thomas, Ellicott, Hopkins and the Yearly Meeting of the Society of Friends, November 9, 1807. Beliles, *The Selected Religious Letters and Papers of Thomas Jefferson*, 160. [Note: Although only Hopkins' name was on the letter, the other names appear on Jefferson's reply. Quakers would not call them clergymen but they were the equivalent.]

thanked them for helping "...to ameliorate the condition of the Indian natives...; ...preparatory to religious instruction..."[105]

Jefferson did not comment on the topic of slavery, his opposition for which they gave their "warmest approbations." But the topic of slavery came up again in a letter from about 30 leaders of "the Baptized Church of Christ" in Ohio and Kentucky written to Jefferson at the end of August. They called themselves the "Friends of Humanity" that had gathered at New Hope meeting house in Woodford County, Kentucky. The letter of commendation was sent by Rev. John Thomas (and Rev. John Winn). On November 18, 1807, Jefferson replied and again claimed that Christianity provided the basis of his administration:

> ...Among the most inestimable of our blessings, also, is that you so justly particularize, of liberty to worship our creator in the way we think most agreeable to his will; a liberty deemed in other countries incompatible with good government, and yet proved by our experience to be its best support...[106]

Another group of Baptist churches wrote to Jefferson with appreciation at this time on May 20, 1806 from "...the North Carolina Chowan Association, held at Salem, on Newbiggin Creek, in the District of Edenton, & State of North Carolina..."[107] Jefferson replied on June 24th "...with gratitude to the being under whose providence these blessings are held. we owe to him especial thanks for the right we enjoy to worship him, everyone in his own way..."[108]

Over a year later a sixth group of Baptists wrote to the President to commend him and wish for his party to continue in power since he was planning to not seek reelection. They were "...of the Appomattox Association within the County of

---

105   Letter to Messrs. Thomas, Ellicot and the Society of Friends, November 13, 1807. Beliles, *The Selected Religious Letters and Papers of Thomas Jefferson*, 161.

106   Letter to Captain John Thomas of the Baptist Church of New Hope, November 18, 1807. Beliles, *The Selected Religious Letters and Papers of Thomas Jefferson*, 163. [Rev. Thomas was apparently a Captain.]

107   Letter from George Outlaw, Lemuel Burkitt and the Baptist Churches of the North Carolina Chowan Association, May 20, 1806. Beliles, *The Selected Religious Letters and Papers of Thomas Jefferson*, 147.

108   Letter to George Outlaw, Lemuel Burkitt and the Baptist Churches of the North Carolina Chowan Association, June 24, 1806. Beliles, *The Selected Religious Letters and Papers of Thomas Jefferson*, 149.

Prince Edward & the Counties adjacent."[109] Jefferson replied to them with similar words on December 21, 1807.[110]

And a year after that Rev. William Tristoe and Rev. Thomas Buck wrote to Jefferson on behalf of a seventh group of Baptists, the Ketockton Baptist Association meeting in Loudoun County, Virginia. They reminded him of presenting their petition for religious freedom a quarter of a century earlier, saying "...We have not forgotten that, into your hand, our petition on this interesting subject was put."[111] Jefferson's reply was October 18, 1808:

> ...although your favor selected me as the organ of your petition to abolish the religious denomination of a privileged church, yet I was but one of the many who befriended its object, and am entitled but in common with them to a portion of that approbation which follows the fulfillment of a duty....a recollection of our former vassalage in religion and civil government will unite the zeal of every heart, and the energy of every hand, to preserve that independence in both, ...and I return your kind prayers by supplications to the same Almighty Being for your future welfare, and that of our beloved country.[112]

Baptist Rev. Jeremiah Moore wrote Jefferson on October 17, 1808, from Georgetown and stated that he "had the pleasure of Seeing you on Saturday Last" (October 10) and apparently gave Jefferson the previous letter from "the Katocton association."[113] Rev. Charles P. Polk had already arranged to have a meeting that same week with President Jefferson along with a committee of Baltimore Baptists.[114] Rev.

109   Letter from Rev. Abner Watkins and Rev. Bernard Todd of the Appomattox Baptist Association [VA], October 21, 1807. Beliles, *The Selected Religious Letters and Papers of Thomas Jefferson*, 157.

110   Letter to Rev. Watkins and Rev. Todd of the Appomattox Baptist Association, December 21, 1807. Beliles, *The Selected Religious Letters and Papers of Thomas Jefferson*, 164.

111   Letter from Rev. William Tristoe, Rev. Thomas Buck, and the Ketocton Baptist Association of Virginia, August 18, 1808. Beliles, *The Selected Religious Letters and Papers of Thomas Jefferson*, 170.

112   Letter to Tristoe, Buck and the Ketocton Baptist Association of Virginia, October 18, 1808. Beliles, *The Selected Religious Letters and Papers of Thomas Jefferson*, 175. Jeremiah Moore was the one who likely put the petition in Jefferson's hand in the 1770s.

113   Letter from Rev. Jeremiah Moore, October 17, 1808. Beliles, *The Selected Religious Letters and Papers of Thomas Jefferson*, 173.

114   Letter from Rev. Charles P. Polk, October 15, 1808. Beliles, *The Selected Religious Letters and Papers of Thomas Jefferson*, 172.

Obadiah Brown presented the letter from the Baltimore Baptist Association.[115] Rev. Brown was chaplain in the House of Representatives from October 1807 to May 1809, and thus, along with Senate chaplain Episcopalian Andrew McCormick, they were the main clergymen whom Jefferson heard preach in the Capitol services during the President's last year or so in Washington. Jefferson replied with similar language.[116] This was now the eighth such Baptist group he addressed.

About a week after this letter, Jefferson received a letter from another group of Baptists in Virginia, this time from Chesterfield County.[117] On November 21, 1808, Jefferson sent his reply to Rev. Robert Semple and the Six Baptist Associations of Chesterfield, Virginia, as follows: "…we have experienced the quiet as well as the comfort which results from leaving everyone to profess freely and openly those principles of religion which are the inductions of his own reason, and the serious convictions of his own inquiries…"[118] Jefferson sent another letter to Rev. Semple about six weeks later with "…real concern that my answer" did not get to them. He hoped they did not think he was "wanting in respect to…the Baptist associations of Chesterfield" and asked Rev. Semple to "do me the favor to deliver this my apology."[119] This letter indicates that these replies of the president were not just form letters done for political purposes. Jefferson really seems to care about his relationship with these Baptists, even though he was about to depart from political life.

But correspondence wasn't limited to Baptist groups. A Methodist congregation from Pittsburgh, Pennsylvania wrote him with appreciation.[120] Jefferson replied on December 9, 1808 to Rev. Robert McElhenny, John Wrenshall, Thomas Cooper, and the Society of the Methodist Episcopal Church at Pittsburgh that "… Our excellent Constitution…has not placed our religious rights under the

---

115   Letter from Rev. Obadiah Brown, Rev. John Welch and the Members of the Baltimore Baptist Association, October 15, 1808. Beliles, *The Selected Religious Letters and Papers of Thomas Jefferson*, 172.

116   Letter to Rev. Brown, Rev. Welch and the Members of the Baltimore Baptist Association, October 17, 1808. Beliles, *The Selected Religious Letters and Papers of Thomas Jefferson*, 174.

117   Letter from Rev. Robert Semple and the Six Baptist Associations of Chesterfield, Virginia, October 24, 1808. Beliles, *The Selected Religious Letters and Papers of Thomas Jefferson*, 176.

118   Letter to Rev. Robert Semple and the Six Baptist Associations of Chesterfield, Virginia, November 21, 1808. Beliles, *The Selected Religious Letters and Papers of Thomas Jefferson*, 178.

119   Letter to Rev. Robert Semple, January 7, 1809. Beliles, *The Selected Religious Letters and Papers of Thomas Jefferson*, 180.

120   Letter from Rev. Robert McElhenny, John Wrenshall, Thomas Cooper and the Methodist Episcopal Church at Pittsburgh, November 20, 1808. Beliles, *The Selected Religious Letters and Papers of Thomas Jefferson*, 177.

power of any public functionary..."[121] Then on January 19, 1809, Rev. Richard Douglas, Isaiah Bolles, and the Society of the Methodist Episcopal Church at New London, Connecticut wrote to the President. Jefferson replied to the church on February 4, saying:

> ...No provision in our Constitution ought to be dearer to man than that which protects the rights of conscience against the enterprises of the civil authority. It has not left the religion of its citizens under the power of its public functionaries ...To me no information could be more welcome than that the minutes of the several religious societies should prove, of late, larger additions than have been usual to their several associations...[122]

Church and State Policy Defined Further

In addition to all these letters from friendly Presbyterians, Quakers, Baptists, and Methodists, there was one very important letter from one of the foremost leaders of the Presbyterians in the nation at that time that clarified Jefferson's church and state policy even more sharply.

Earlier in 1806, Rev. Samuel Miller served as the national moderator of the Presbyterian General Assembly. He had long been a political supporter of Jefferson and had often corresponded with Jefferson on missions, etc, beginning as early as 1792. Jefferson thanked Miller in February 29, 1804, for a book and said he "... shall with pleasure avail himself of his first leisure to read it. He salutes him with respect & friendship." A similar reply from Jefferson on May 13, 1805 gave thanks for "the pamphlet he has been so kind as to send him, which he has perused, as he does whatever comes from his pen, with great pleasure. He salutes mr. Miller with esteem and respect."[123]

But now in 1808, Rev. Miller wrote to the President on the topic of presidential prayer proclamations. He knew Jefferson felt it violated the prerogative of the states, but clergy in his city suggested that Jefferson could "recommend" national days of prayer without requiring its observance and thus avoid violating Jefferson's understanding of the Constitution. Now he wrote to the President saying in part:

---

121   Letter to Rev. Robert McElhenny, John Wrenshall, Thomas Cooper and the Methodist Episcopal Church at Pittsburgh, December 9, 1808. Beliles, *The Selected Religious Letters and Papers of Thomas Jefferson*, 179.

122   Letter to the Society of the Methodist Episcopal Church at New London, Connecticut, February 4, 1809. Beliles, *The Selected Religious Letters and Papers of Thomas Jefferson*, 183.

123   Letter to Rev. Samuel Miller, February 29, 1804, and Letter to Rev. Samuel Miller, May 13, 1805. Beliles, *The Selected Religious Letters and Papers of Thomas Jefferson*, 143.

I hope You will pardon the liberty which I take in addressing You on a subject of considerable delicacy. Several of my Clerical brethren, and other friends of Religion, in this city, deeply affected with the present aspect of our public affairs, have lately expressed an earnest wish that we might be called upon, as a nation, to observe a day of Fasting, Humiliation and Prayer. The object of this letter is frankly to ask, whether such an application to you would be agreeable or otherwise....Allow me, Sir, further to observe, that while I should be much gratified at your viewing this subject with a favorable eye, both as a warm friend of the proposed Solemnity, and as a cordial well-wisher to your happy administration; yet if it would be, on the whole, more agreeable to your wishes that no such application, as that alluded to, should be made, I shall consider it as my duty to oppose, and endeavor to prevent it. I have only to add, that, in making this communication, I act without the suggestion, and without the knowledge of any other person. I have the honor to be, Sir, with very great respect, Your sincere friend & humble Servant.[124]

Miller, being a supporter, perceived a conflict that could occur (if they sent him their advice and he rejected it) and wanted to help the president avoid more bad press in the Federalist-dominated New England religious world. Jefferson's reply to Rev. Samuel Miller on January 23, 1808 again declined to support proclamations by the Chief Executive, but he explained (as Miller had suspected he would) that it solely was due to his view that it violates the states' and individual citizen's prerogative (i.e., federalism):

...I consider the government of the United States as interdicted by the Constitution from intermeddling with religious institutions, their doctrines, discipline, or exercises. This results not only from the provision that no law shall be made respecting the establishment, or free exercise, of religion [i.e., the First Amendment], but from that also which reserves to the states the powers not delegated to the United States [i.e., the Tenth Amendment]. Certainly no power to prescribe any religious exercise or to assume authority in religious discipline has been delegated to the general [i.e., national] government. It must then rest with the states as far as it can be in any human authority. But it is only proposed that I

---

124 Letter from Rev. Samuel Miller, January 18, 1808. Beliles, *The Selected Religious Letters and Papers of Thomas Jefferson*, 166.

should recommend, not prescribe a day of fasting and prayer. That is, that I should indirectly assume to the U. S. an authority over religious exercises which the Constitution has directly precluded them from.

...I am aware that the practice of my predecessors may be quoted. But I have ever believed that the example of state executives led to the assumption of that authority by the general government, without due examination, which would have discovered that what might be a right in a state government, was a violation of that right when assumed by another [i.e., national government]. Be that as it may, everyone must act according to the dictates of his own reason, & mine tells me that civil powers alone have been given to the President of the U.S. and no authority to direct the religious exercises of his constituents;...and I pray you to accept the assurances of my high esteem & respect.[125]

Rev. Miller apparently convinced his colleagues to make no appeal to the president on this front, and this highest of Presbyterians in the nation remained a supporter while Jefferson was alive. This letter is discussed more in a later chapter.

Toward the end of 1809, Jefferson's practice of federal financial assistance of a Catholic missionary to the Indians was evident in a letter from Rev. Gabriel Richard who asked Jefferson to inform President Madison of the money promised him from the government.[126] Jefferson forwarded it to Madison saying: "The inclosed letter is from Father Richard, the Director of a school at Detroit."[127] Jefferson forwarded to Madison another letter from Rev. Richard two years later, saying: "...you will see exactly how far he had a right to expect the government would go in aid of his establishment."[128] Clearly this shows more of Jefferson's idea that government may help religion in the federal territories, even if not in the states.

---

125   Letter to Rev. Samuel Miller, January 23, 1808. Beliles, *The Selected Religious Letters and Papers of Thomas Jefferson*, 167.

126   Letter from Rev. Gabriel Richard, September 9, 1809. Rev. Richard sent almost the exact same letter as a follow-up on November 9, 1809 and another on February 9, 1811. The Thomas Jefferson Papers Series 1, General Correspondence, 1651-1827, Library of Congress Manuscript Division.

127   Letter to James Madison, December 7, 1809, www.founders.archives.gov. See also his Memoranda to James Madison, March 4, 1809. Beliles, *The Selected Religious Letters and Papers of Thomas Jefferson*, 185. And then a Letter to James Madison, April 11, 1811, www. founders.archives.gov.

128   Letter to James Madison, April 7, 1811. www.founders.archives.gov.

Another example was in Jefferson's dealings with Rev. John Cunow of the Society of the United Brethren [i.e., Moravians] for propagating the Gospel among the Heathen. The federal government, with Jefferson's approval, had been supporting their missions to the Indians. Rev. Cunow was introduced to Jefferson by George Logan in December 1808 and Cunow gave the president a letter. In regard to this Jefferson wrote to Logan saying: "Your favor of the 8th. by mr Cunow was duly recieved & I now return you the letter it covered. mr Cunow's object was so perfectly within our own views that it was readily obtained, & I am in hopes he has left us with a more correct opinion of the dispositions of the administration than his fraternity [i.e. the Moravians] has generally manifested."[129]

Religious Language in Official Correspondence

Regardless of Jefferson's policy that restrained him from declaring national days of prayer, Jefferson had no qualms in using religious language in public documents such as on January 10, 1808, in his reply to the North Carolina Legislature, saying: "...I supplicate the Being in whose hands we all are, to preserve our country in freedom and independence, and to bestow on yourselves the blessings of His favor."[130] To the New York Society of Tammany on February 29, 1808, he wrote: "...I supplicate a protecting Providence to watch over your own and our country's freedom and welfare."[131] And to the Delegates of the Democratic Republicans of Philadelphia on May 25, he said: "...I supplicate the care of Providence over the well-being of yourselves and our beloved country."[132] On February 16, 1809, his letter to the General Assembly of Virginia said: "...that the supreme Ruler of the universe may have our country under His special care, will be among the latest of my prayers."[133] On the same day he said to the citizens of Wilmington, "...I...offer to Heaven my constant prayers for the preservation of our republic..."[134] On February 24 Jefferson mentioned "...religious rights;...under the favor of Heaven..." in his

---

129 Letter to George Logan, December 27, 1808. www.founders.archives.gov. Also see letter from Logan on December 8, 1808 and letter from Rev. John Cunow and Society of the United Brethren for propagating the Gospel among the Heathen, December 17, 1808.

130 Letter to North Carolina Legislature, January 10, 1808. Lipscomb and Bergh, eds. *The Writings of Thomas Jefferson*, Vol. , 11, 299.

131 Letter to the New York Society of Tammany, February 29, 1808. Ibid., 301.

132 Letter to the Delegates of the Democratic Republicans of Philadelphia, May 25, 1808. Ibid., 303.

133 Ibid., 333.

134 Letter to the Citizens of Wilmington [Delaware], February 16, 1809. Ibid., 335.

letter to the Republicans of Niagara.[135] And on the same day, in his reply to an Address from the Republican Young Men of New London, Connecticut, he said: "…I join in supplications to that Almighty Being, who has heretofore guarded our councils, still to continue His gracious benedictions towards our country, and that yourselves may be under the protection of His divine favor."[136] And on March 2 his letter to the Tammany Society of Washington said: "…your prayers…I sincerely supplicate Heaven…"[137]

Even at the beginning of his retirement Jefferson continued to receive thank you letters for his service to his country. He replied with religious language to Stephen Cross and the Republicans of Essex County, Massachusetts on March 28, 1809, saying: "…I sincerely supplicate that overruling Providence which governs the destinies of men and nations; to dispense His choicest blessings on yourselves and our beloved country."[138] The next day he said: "…I pray Heaven to keep you under its holy favor," in his reply to the Friends of the Administration of the United States in Bristol County, Rhode Island.[139] And two days later to the Democratic Republican Delegates from the Townships of Washington County, Pennsylvania, he said: "…by the favor of Heaven;…my prayers will ever be offered for your welfare and happiness."[140]

These letters do not seem to fit the idea of a president seeking to maintain a secular public life.

Back to Private Life in Albemarle County

Now that Jefferson was back home, his local connections became more of a focus in his letters. On March 19, 1809, the main local Baptist church with which Jefferson had been friendly for decades sent him a congratulatory welcome home letter. This was now the tenth letter to Jefferson from a friendly group of Baptists. But this one was different. Albemarle Baptist Church began in 1773 in what is now Charlottesville, but in 1801 it moved to the Buckmountain area of the county. The

---

135   Letter to the Republicans of Niagara, February 24, 1809. Ibid., 343.

136   Letter to the Republican Young Men of New London (Connecticut), February 24, 1809. Ibid., 339.

137   Letter to the Tammany Society of Washington, March 2, 1809, Ibid., 346.

138   Letter to the Republicans of Essex County, Massachusetts [and to Stephen Cross], March 28, 1809, www.founders.archives.gov.

139   Letter to the Friends of the Administration of the United States in Bristol County, Rhode Island, March 29, 1809, www.founders.archives.gov.

140   Letter to the Democratic Republican Delegates from Washington County, Pennsylvania, March 31, 1809, www.founders.archives.gov.

pastor for most of those years was Rev. William Woods who had stepped out of the pulpit while serving in the legislature. The church's letter expressed to Jefferson their pleasure with his public service and prayed:

> ....May your Days be many and Comfortable, in a word (may we say) we wish you health, wealth, and prosperity through life, and in the world to come life everlasting.[141]

Jefferson replied on April 13 to the members of the Baptist Church of Buck Mountain in Albemarle as follows:

> ...I thank you, my friends and neighbors, for your kind congratulations on my return to my native home, and on the opportunities it will give me of enjoying, amidst your affections, the comforts of retirement and rest. Your approbation of my conduct is the more valued as you have best known me, and is an ample reward for any services I may have rendered. We have acted together from the origin to the end of a memorable Revolution, and we have contributed, each in the line allotted us, our endeavors to render its issue a permanent blessing to our country...[142]

This response by Jefferson to these evangelicals in his home area says that they had worked together and that they "have best known me." Indeed it appears that most of the public today do not understand Jefferson the way Christians in his time knew him – especially those south of New York.

A year before Jefferson returned home, his local Episcopal pastor died. With Matthew Maury's death, there was now no resident Episcopal priest for either St. Anne's Parish or the adjacent Fredericksville Parish, thus no regular Episcopal church services available in Charlottesville or the entire county of Albemarle from this date for the next decade. So attending an Episcopal church regularly as he did in Washington was impossible at this time for Jefferson. Therefore, very few references to subscribing financially to a church regularly appear in his account book for another ten years.

---

141   Letter from George Twyman and the Albemarle Buckmountain Baptist Church, March 19, 1809. Beliles, *The Selected Religious Letters and Papers of Thomas Jefferson*, 185.

142   "Thomas Jefferson to George Twyman and the Albemarle Buckmountain Baptist Church, 13 April 1809," www.founders.archives.gov.

Also notable is that not only was there no Episcopal church now in Charlottesville, but no others of the traditional denominations either. All their pastors had either died or were incapacitated in some way, and no replacements had emerged as of yet. So a historian would find but few references to Jefferson attending church in Charlottesville between 1809 and 1819, but neither would they find references in that era in the diaries of *any* Episcopalians, Presbyterians, Baptists, and Methodists who lived in that town!

But occasional guest preachers of these denominations would pass through from time to time. Captain Edmund Bacon, the overseer of Monticello for 17 years, recalled that despite the lack of regular ministers in the main denominations, during his overseer tenure from 1806 until 1822, "Mr. Jefferson never debarred himself from hearing any preacher that came along."[143]

Jefferson's personal beliefs were expressed in a very limited way at this time in correspondence with several people. One was a Quaker named Thomas Leiper but with whom Jefferson had only discussed secular subjects previously. Now Jefferson replied to his letter about endtime prophecies and world affairs:

….as to myself, my religious reading has long been confined to the moral branch of religion, which is the same in all religions; while in that branch which consists of dogmas, all differ, all have a different set. The former instructs us how to live well and worthily in society; the latter are made to interest our minds in the support of the teachers who inculcate them. Hence for one sermon on a moral subject, you hear ten on the dogmas of the sect. However, religion is not the subject for you & me. Neither of us knows the religious opinions of the other. That is a matter between our maker & ourselves….[144]

Jefferson also exchanged letters with a Presbyterian layman named James Fishback. Fishback was a neighbor in Kentucky of Andrew Tribble—the first pastor of the Baptists in Albemarle before migrating west. Fishback wrote to Jefferson on June 5, 1809, and enclosed a pamphlet entitled "A new and candid investigation of the question, is revelation true?" He asked for Jefferson's feedback on the pamphlet, which opposed natural religion in favor of revelation and Christian principles for the good of the nation. Jefferson replied to Fishback in agreement on September 27,

---

143   Bear, Jr., ed., *Jefferson At Monticello*, 74-75.
144   Letter to Thomas Leiper, January 21, 1809. www.founders.archives.gov.

...the interests of society require the observation of those moral precepts only in which all religions agree...The practice of morality being necessary for the well-being of society, he has taken care to impress its precepts so indelibly on our hearts that they shall not be effaced by the subtleties of our brain. We all agree in the obligation of the moral precepts of Jesus, and nowhere will they be found delivered in greater purity than in his discourses...[145]

These were modest comments compared to more critical thoughts about religious controversies in an unsent version to Fishback that will be discussed in a later chapter. On January 7, 1810, William Baldwin wrote to Jefferson, and he responded with a letter having nothing religious in it. However, an unsent draft of it contained some of his religious thoughts, which will be examined later.

The Presbyterian clergyman who had responded with a defense of Jefferson in 1800 now sent a letter to Jefferson on January 22, 1810. Rev. Samuel Knox of Baltimore informed Jefferson of his earlier pamphlet entitled, "A Vindication of the Religion of Mr. Jefferson."[146] Jefferson replied on February 12 saying:

... The preservation of the holy fire is confided to us by the world, and the sparks which will emanate from it will ever serve to rekindle it in other quarters of the globe, numinibus secundis [i.e., by the favor of the powers above]. ...I retain a remembrance of the pamphlet you mention...[147]

William Woodward wrote on April 27 that he had sent "as you requested the last part of Scott's Bible."[148] This Bible was the first American edition, printed in five volumes over the years 1805-1809. Jefferson had subscribed to this and was now receiving the final volume. It was the Bible Jefferson mainly used for the rest of his life and has his signature prominent on the front page. If someone asked Jefferson what was his Bible this is what he would have shown to them,

---

145   Letter to Rev. James Fishback, September 27, 1809, www.founders.archives.gov.

146   Letter from Rev. Samuel Knox, January 22, 1810. Beliles, *The Selected Religious Letters and Papers of Thomas Jefferson*, 190.

147   Letter to Rev. Samuel Knox, February 12, 1810, www.founders.archives.gov.

148   Letter from William Woodward, April 27, 1810. www.founders.archives.gov. Also see Jefferson Letter to William Woodward, December 21, 1806.

and it included all 66 books that are in a typical Bible.[149] Truly, this was the real "Jefferson Bible."

Rev. Robert Elliott, pastor of First Presbyterian Church in Washington and House chaplain when Jefferson was president, had also been hired to teach school there. His church used the school building close to the President's House as a place of worship when not using the Capitol building itself. He now writes to Jefferson on March 6, 1811, offering his "prayers for your Happiness both here and hereafter" and asking for his subscription to a proposed volume of Elliott's sermons:

> I take the liberty of sending the enclosed for your signature—If not presumptuous, (with permission) would wish to dedicate them to you—as these now selected for publication with many others were preached in your presence & during your administration. [150]

Clearly most orthodox clergy who knew Jefferson still knew him only to be a supporter of Christianity and were proud to be associated with him. Jefferson replied affirmatively to the subscription on March 17, saying:

> …I shall be glad to see in print discourses which I heard delivered with much satisfaction [in the church services in the Capitol]…; my particular thanks are due to you…To those of your society [i.e., Presbyterians] we owe an acknowlegement of the zeal they have generally manifested for the republican principles of our government;…[but there are some] professors of religion who admit none to be Christians who are not so in their way… [and] those in whose religious code no chapter is to be found on the duties of a citizen to his country…[151]

A local Presbyterian minister was called upon by Jefferson at this point to perform the funeral of his sister, Martha Jefferson Carr, in the Monticello graveyard.[152] Rev. Charles Wingfield seems to have been an Anglican minister

---

149 Today both his family Bible handed down from his father and then this Bible he purchased are housed at the University of Virginia library. The table of contents show 66 books in the Scott's Bible and the earlier Bible included the Apocrypha common to the earlier King James Versions.

150 "Rev. Robert Elliott to Thomas Jefferson, 6 March 1811," www.founders.archives.gov.

151 "Thomas Jefferson to Rev. Robert Elliott, 17 March 1811," www.founders.archives.gov.

152 Letter to Rev. Charles Wingfield, September 8, 1811, www.founders.archives.gov.

earlier in life, but was ordained a Presbyterian in 1808, and he also served in local government as a magistrate and sheriff. Three other letters were exchanged between them that month. Occasional gifts to other unidentified clergy also appear in the account books in 1811: "Gave the Revd. Mr. Osgood in charity 10 Dollars."[153] This was one of Jefferson's smallest donation amounts, yet is the equivalent of about $250 today. It along with all the other donations seen over the years to dozens and dozens of clergy and churches, reveals a generous supporter of Christianity that should not be overlooked.

Rev. Hugh White was another local minister who wrote to Jefferson on April 16, 1812. He was a neighbor of Jefferson with land in Charlottesville and Milton next to Monticello. He had been a Scottish Presbyterian minister until that year when he was ordained a Swedenborgian clergyman, meaning a Christian with non-Trinitarian heterodox theological views. This again shows the kind of theological dominance of these unorthodox movements that still claimed the Christian label in Jefferson's hometown. Rev. White sent Jefferson one of his pamphlets to read, and Jefferson replied on April 25, 1812, saying:

…The questions this presents are certainly difficult, and mr White has done what alone can be done, he has presented ingenious views of them. Th:J. has long ago abandoned them as insoluble by understandings limited as ours are…[154]

Another nationally-prominent clergyman moved into the area at this time. He was Rev. Lorenzo Dow. As seen previously, he had led a huge camp meeting near Monticello in 1804 and then apparently had met Jefferson in Washington in 1805 (when he delivered Rev. Fry's letter and preached in the Capitol) and was the nation's foremost itinerant evangelist of the time. Although he was constantly traveling throughout America, it is interesting to note that in 1812, this non-denominational camp meeting preacher settled briefly in Buckingham County, adjacent to Albemarle and also filled the pulpit temporarily for Preddy's Creek Baptist Church in Albemarle County and served as an assistant to its pastor, John Goss.[155] So for a time, he was weekly in Jefferson's home county.

153   Account book, April 15, 1811. For Osgood. Beliles, *The Selected Religious Letters and Papers of Thomas Jefferson*, 196.

154   Letter from Rev. Hugh White, April 16, 1812 and Letter to Rev. Hugh White, April 25, 1812, www.founders.archives.gov.

155   W. L. Mundy, *A Brief Historical Sketch* (Charlottesville, Va.: Delivered before the Albemarle Baptist Association in 1921). This sketch is cited in Preddy's Creek's records.

It is not known if Dow interacted with Jefferson directly while in the area, but Dow wrote on August 21, 1812 an influential political pamphlet in support of Jefferson, Madison, and Democratic-Republican principles.[156] Dow's pamphlet was called "Analects Upon Natural, Social, and Moral Philosophy," and it grounded all human rights upon "the great and universal 'Law of nature.'" Dow wrote boldly about the politics of church and state, saying that:

> Jefferson, seeing the evil of law religion [i.e., state government-established, coercive religion], etc, had those barbarous laws…repealed…which compelled every man in the parish, be his sentiment what it might, to give his quota…for the Church Priest;…These things procured the epithet "infidel" for a mark of distinguishment;…From those circumstances arose the prejudice of the clergy of different societies who would be fond of a law religion, as the ground of their animosity and ambition against him…[157]

This perspective held by America's most prominent evangelist about Jefferson as being falsely portrayed as an infidel is how evangelical people in most of America viewed him by this point in his life. Indeed, Dow had traveled throughout the country and preached to more people than anyone in his generation, but he especially expressed the religious and political views that dominated Jefferson's Central Virginia Piedmont region that Dow now called home. There is no evidence of anyone there from his region, in his lifetime, among those who personally knew him longest and best, that thought of Jefferson as anything but a sincere believer and friend of all religious institutions on an equal basis. (However, the vast majority of them would not necessarily have been aware of his growing Unitarian and univeralist views expressed in private.)

---

156 Gayle Marshall, *Preddy's Creek Baptist Church, 1781-1981* (Albemarle County, Va.: Published by the church, 1981), 185, 251. See also Dow, *The History of the Cosmopolite.*

157 Analects Upon Natural, Social, and Moral Philosophy, August 21, 1812; in Dow, *The History of the Cosmopolite*, 345. Dow also said that, "James Madison, believing in universal rights of conscience, . . . also rejected the bills to incorporate the Baptists in the Mississippi Territory, and the Church of England at Alexandria—[because] the principle, once admitted by Congress, might be plead as a precedent, and it would be uncertain where the evil would end!"

CHAPTER 4

THOMAS JEFFERSON'S RELIGIOUS LIFE, 1813-1820

"We should all then, like the Quakers, live without an order of priests, moralize for ourselves, follow the oracle of conscience, and say nothing about what no man can understand, nor therefore believe....[i.e.,] in the Platonic mysticism that three are one and one is three..." —Thomas Jefferson, 1814 [1]

The fourth phase of Jefferson's religious life commences in 1813 when he expresses for the first time his clear rejection of Trinitarian doctrine. He does it in a private letter to John Adams. But to understand it correctly it is essential to first look at the local religious landscape.

The Context of Charlottesville's Religious Culture

In Jefferson's Central Virginia Piedmont, James O'Kelly's Christian Churches (first known as Republican Methodists) emerged first in the 1790s—the earliest Restoration movement in America—and then came followers of Kentucky camp-meeting leader Presbyterian Barton W. Stone at the turn of the century.[2]

---

1   Letter to John Adams, August 22, 1813, www.founders.archives.gov.

2   David L. Goetz, "The Gallery: Zealous, Eccentric Leaders," in *Christian History Magazine* (Carol Stream, Ill.: *Christianity Today*, 1995).

Stone's followers also become very strong in Jefferson's area. A similar movement emerged in New England led by former Congregationalist Elias Smith and in Pennsylvania led by former Presbyterian Alexander Campbell. Campbell's churches eventually became known as the Disciples of Christ, and Albemarle and Orange Counties (where Jefferson grew up and then lived) eventually became one of Campbell's strongest areas in Virginia. In 1810 O'Kelly's group met at the Pine Stake Church in Orange County and decided to henceforth call themselves the "Independent Christian Baptist Church." And a year later in 1811 the northern and southern Restoration movements met together in Orange County adjacent to Jefferson's Albemarle and created the national "Christian Connection." Elias Smith was at that meeting and became its national spokesman. He then preached about 30 times in the Piedmont and valley of Virginia and published news of the national movement in his *Herald of Gospel Liberty* newspaper.[3]

The most important thing to note is that all these leaders were non-Trinitarian, anti-creedal, and anti-Calvinist, and they were the dominant religious influence in Jefferson's part of Virginia.[4] The next year, 1812, Elias Smith published his New Testament Dictionary containing his Unitarian beliefs. It said: "In all the glorious things said of Christ, there is no mention of his divinity, his being God-man, his incarnation, the human and divine nature, the human soul of Christ, his being God the Creator, and yet the Son of the Creator; these things are the inventions of men, and ought to be rejected."[5] Thomas H. Olbricht, in *Christian Connexion and Unitarian Relations 1800-1844*, explains the movement as "a Biblically oriented anti-Calvinism" and adds:

> Because of anti-Calvinism, however, one is not to suppose that the early members of the Christian Connexion felt a kindred spirit with the Arminian Congregationalists. The gap between the two was a wide one, for the Christians emphasized revivalism, experiential conversion, baptism by immersion and had an uneducated ministry...The Christians are a sort of Unitarian Methodist, having the theology of the elder [i.e., European] Unitarians without their culture, and the heat and fervor, the camp-

---

3   MacClenny, *The Life of Rev. James O'Kelly*, 158-159. See also Michael G. Kenny, *The Perfect Law of Liberty: Elias Smith and the Providential History of America* (Washington, D.C.: Smithsonian Institution Press, 1994), 25, 188, 294. Smith is likely to have included Charlottesville in the itinerary but nothing specifically mentions it.

4   Hatch, *Democratization of American Christianity*, 163.

5   Kenny, *The Perfect Law of Liberty*, 93.

meeting usages, and emotional feelings of the Methodists, without their ecclesiastical system of opinions.[6]

All of these groups preferred just calling themselves "Christians" and felt very different from the New England rationalist Unitarians (identified above as the "Arminian Congregationalists"), even though both rejected the Trinity.

A major reason no traditional church denominations existed in the second decade of the 19th century in Charlottesville was because their members went to these new non-denominational gatherings. Since Jefferson was living there at the time, it is likely that he became aware of these trends if he was not already. Indeed some of Jefferson's first overt expressions of unorthodox religious opinions now emerged, but they were no different from what most of the evangelical clergy in his area were already saying. In fact, the writings of some religious leaders in the Piedmont at this time were far more harsh (against certain doctrines, clergy, etc.) than any of Jefferson's writings. Jefferson's religion for the rest of his life cannot be properly understood apart from this context of non-denominational, non-creedal, non-Trinitarian and anti-Calvinist, anti-clerical movement that he now found predominant in his home town. Many in the movement were strongly anti-Trinitarian, but the highest value was unity and this meant they attempted (but failed) to be inclusive of both views by requiring adherence to no one view.

The fact that Jefferson did not speak clearly against the Trinity until these churches were prevalent is often overlooked by most biographers and erases the entire context for understanding him accurately. One of the few to mention it at all is Edwin Gaustad's biography of Jefferson which says that his statements about this time have "language remarkably similar to that of [Alexander] Campbell."[7] Campbell said that he wanted to save "the Holy Scriptures from the perplexities of the commentators and system-makers of the dark ages" and therefore (similar to Jefferson), published his own edition of the New Testament in 1826 to correct the perceived textual flaws and corruptions. And Gaustad noted that "…Barton Stone could have…provided a most suitable preface" to Jefferson's abridgement of the New Testament.[8]

---

6   Thomas H. Olbricht, "Christian Connexion and Unitarian Relations 1800-1844," in *Restoration Quarterly* (Abilene, TX, Restoration Quarterly Corporation, 1966), Vol. 9, No. 3.

7   Gaustad, *Sworn On the Altar of God*, 145.

8   Ibid, 214.

Letters to Unitarian John Adams and Quaker William Canby

Benjamin Rush died on April 19, 1813, and Jefferson then asks his son for his April 1803 letters to be returned. The reason he asks is that other letters had just been published in England in 1812 in *Lindsey's Memoirs* without Jefferson's permission (Rev. Theophilus Lindsey was a Unitarian in England). Richard Rush returned the letters to Jefferson as asked, and Jefferson's follow-up to Richard Rush explained that:

> These will probably soon find their way into the newspapers, and the whole kennel of priests will open upon me. My letter to Dr Rush, written more in detail than that to Dr Priestley would much enlarge the field of their declamations...[9]

Jefferson received four letters from John Adams that summer on religious topics. Adams' letters specifically rejected the Trinity and much of orthodoxy, and Jefferson finally responds in agreement.[10] Now on August 22, 1813, Jefferson wrote plainly to John Adams, but yet still wishes it to remain private. Jefferson wrote: "…It is too late in the day for men of sincerity to pretend they believe in the Platonic mysticism that three are one and one is three, and yet, that the one is not three, and the three not one."[11] This is the very first time Jefferson overtly said this. Plato's name is used negatively by Jefferson as a rejection of the historic Christian doctrine of the Trinity. As will be seen, Jefferson bought into the Joseph Priestley myth that the Trinity was not revealed in early Christianity, but was rather a later corruption.

Jefferson continues his letter to Adams:

> But this constitutes the craft, the power, and profits of the priests. …We should all then, like the quakers, live without an order of priests, moralise for ourselves, follow the oracle of conscience, and say nothing about what no man can understand, not therefore believe; for I suppose belief to be the assent of the mind to an intelligible proposition… I have read his [i.e., Priestley's] *Corruptions of Christianity*, and *Early Opinions of Jesus*, over and

---

9   Letter to Richard Rush, June 17, 1813. Beliles, *The Selected Religious Letters and Papers of Thomas Jefferson*, 203.

10   Letters from John Adams, June 28, July 16, July 18, 1813. Beliles, *The Selected Religious Letters and Papers of Thomas Jefferson*, 204-208.

11   Letter to John Adams, August 22, 1813, www.founders.archives.gov.

over again; and I rest on them, and on Middleton's writings, especially his *Letters from Rome*, and *To Waterland*, as the basis of my own faith...[12]

One of Jefferson's Quaker friends from Delaware named William Canby wrote to Jefferson on August 27, 1813. They had corresponded in 1802, 1803, and 1808 on religion, and Canby had come earlier with the non-denominational/Quaker-allied Rev. Dorothy Ripley to a meeting with the President. But here Canby especially urges Jefferson to pursue a deeper relationship with God. Jefferson, confident in Canby's Quaker rejection of creeds and even professional clergy, replied on September 18, saying:

> ...An eloquent preacher of your religious society, Richard Motte, in a discourse of much emotion and pathos, is said to have exclaimed aloud to his congregation, that he did not believe there was a Quaker, Presbyterian, Methodist or Baptist in heaven, having paused to give his hearers time to stare and to wonder. He added, that in heaven, God knew no distinctions, but considered all good men as his children, and as brethren of the same family. I believe, with the Quaker preacher, that he who steadily observes those moral precepts in which all religions concur, will never be questioned at the gates of heaven, as to the dogmas in which they all differ. That on entering there, all these are left behind us, and the Aristides and Catos, the Penns and Tillotsons, Presbyterians and Baptists, will find themselves united in all principles which are in concert with the reason of the supreme mind. ...Of all the systems of morality, ancient or modern, which have come under my observation, none appear to me so pure as that of Jesus....[Some,] usurping the judgment seat of God, denounce as his enemies all who cannot perceive the Geometrical logic of Euclid in the demonstrations of St. Athanasius, that three are one, and one is three; and yet that the one is not three nor the three one. In all essential points you and I are of the same religion; and I am too old to go into inquiries and changes as to the unessential.[13]

---

12   Ibid.

13   Letter to William Canby, September 18, 1813, www.founders.archives.gov. Aristides (530-468 BC) was a Greek statesman. Cato the Younger (95-46 BC) was a Roman. William Penn was the 17th century Quaker leader, who founded Pennsylvania—a haven for non-conformists. Tillotson was the Archbishop of Canterbury who lived 1630-1694. Thus, here is a mixture of ancient pagans (Greek and Roman) and relatively recent Christians.

St. Athanasius was the fourth century church father who led the effort against heresies regarding the nature of Christ, and for whom an historic creed is named. When Jefferson includes pagans with Christians as going to heaven, he strays into the error of Universalism similar to Elias Smith and a few Restorationists who rejected the need of Christ's atoning death for men to be restored to fellowship with God. This private letter to Canby would eventually be published in American newspapers and cause Jefferson concern.

On October 12, 1813 Jefferson wrote to John Adams and included a copy of the Syllabus of Jesus' morals, i.e., the document that he had written in 1803 for Benjamin Rush. Here Jefferson also spoke about the 1804 compilation of verses from the Gospels, but he never shared it with anyone. Jefferson wrote:

> ...I now send you, according to your request a copy of the Syllabus... It was the reformation of this 'wretched depravity' of morals which Jesus undertook. In extracting the pure principles which he taught, we should have to strip off the artificial vestments in which they have been muffled by priests, who have travestied them into various forms, as instruments of riches and power to them...We must reduce our volume to the simple evangelists, select, even from them, the very words only of Jesus, paring off the Amphibologisms [i.e., phrases that can be interpreted in different ways] into which they have been led by forgetting often, or not understanding, what had fallen from him, by giving their own misconceptions as his dicta, and expressing unintelligibly for others what they had not understood themselves. There will be found remaining the most sublime and benevolent code of morals which has ever been offered to man. I have performed this operation [in 1804] for my own use, by cutting verse by verse out of the printed book, and arranging, the matter which is evidently his, and which is as easily distinguishable as diamonds in a dunghill. The result is an 8 vo. [i.e., Octavo format] of 46. pages of pure and unsophisticated doctrines, such as were professed and acted on by the *unlettered* apostles, the Apostolic fathers, and the Christians of the 1st. century;....

Jefferson continues: "We must leave therefore to others, younger and more learned than we are, to prepare this euthanasia for Platonic Christianity, and it's restoration to the primitive simplicity of it's founder...."[14] Jefferson also says in this

---

14   Letter to John Adams, October 12, 1813, www.founders.archives.gov.

letter for the first time that his abridgement of the words of Jesus was something he personally used, ten years after first doing it "for the use of the Indians" (in his own words in the subtitle). Jefferson uses the term "Platonic" for a form of Christianity that he felt emerged in Europe due to a mixture of Christianity with the thought of the Greek philosopher Plato who lived a few centuries before Christ. This letter is discussed more fully in the chapter on the Bible.

Adams replied with a blatant critique of scripture texts that led to Jefferson's reply on January 24, 1814, in which Jefferson agreed with Adams in expressing his mistrust of scripture texts passed down over time.[15]

> ...Where get we the ten commandments? The book...itself tells us they were written by the finger of God on tables of stone...; But the whole history of these books is so defective and doubtful that it seems vain to attempt minute enquiry into it; and such tricks have plaid with their text, and with the texts of other books relating to them, that we have a right, from that cause, to entertain much doubt what parts of them are genuine. In the New Testament there is internal evidence that parts of it have proceeded from an extraordinary man; and that other parts are of the fabric of very inferior minds. It is as easy to separate those parts, as to pick diamonds from dunghills.[16]

Jefferson spoke to Adams of concentrating on the Gospels in this letter while still quoting and using the Psalms. He was not rejecting everything else in the Bible. This is illuminated further when Jefferson on January 31, 1814, wrote in his account book: "Inclosed to Samuel Greenhow an order...for 50 Dollars for the Bible society of Virginia [$1200 equivalent today]."[17] Indeed, as correspondence with Greenhow shows, Jefferson's $50 made him a "member for life" of the Virginia Bible Society.[18] This society was started in 1813 mainly through the leadership of Presbyterian Rev. John Holt Rice to distribute Bibles "...to the poor of our country, and to the Heathen [i.e., the Indians]."[19] Jefferson wrote to Greenhow:

---

15   Letter to John Adams, January 24, 1814, www.founders.archives.gov.

16   Letter to John Adams, January 24, 1814, www.founders.archives.gov.

17   Account book, January 1814. For "the Bible Society of Virginia." Beliles, *The Selected Religious Letters and Papers of Thomas Jefferson*, 223.

18   Letter to Samuel Greenhow [of the Virginia Bible Society], January 31, 1814, www.founders.archives.gov. See fully in chapter eight on the Bible.

19   Ibid.

...Your letter on the subject of the [Virginia] Bible Society arrived here while I was on a journey to Bedford,... I therefore enclose you cheerfully... fifty dollars, for the purposes of the [Virginia Bible] society, sincerely agreeing with you that there never was a more pure and sublime system of morality delivered to man than is to be found in the four evangelists...[20]

Greenhow in turn wrote to Jefferson again saying that he was:

...gratified, that my Application has been successful as to it's Object, because that Success assures me that you approve our Association...[21]

Despite some private reservations about the reliability of the Scripture texts and references to the "dunghill," it is important to remember that at that very moment, Jefferson, nonetheless, believed in the benefit of knowing the whole Bible and supported its distribution. That in fact was all that the public knew of him at this point, and the other speculations and opinions to John Adams and other friends was in confidence that it would stay private.

Private Criticism of Some Clergy; Friendship With Others

Another letter was sent by Adams to Jefferson in early March 1814 that said some Bible texts and basic doctrines of Christianity could not be true, and asserted that they were corruptions by early European church leaders. Jefferson replied on July 5, 1814 saying: "...The [early European] Christian priesthood, finding the doctrines of Christ levelled to every understanding, and too plain to need explanation, saw in the mysticism of Plato, materials with which they might build up an artificial system, which might, from its indistinctness, admit everlasting controversy, give employment for their order, and introduce it to profit, power and pre-eminence..."[22]

The context of his criticism shows again it to be narrowly focused on early European priests. It's interesting also that while making strong critiques of Scripture, nonetheless Jefferson uses the term "Christ" (i.e., Messiah) for Jesus in this letter. This signifies perhaps that Jefferson held to a view of Jesus that was

---

20   Letter to Samuel Greenhow [of the Virginia Bible Society], January 31, 1814, www.founders.archives.gov.

21   Letter from Samuel Greenhow and the Bible Society of Virginia, February 4, 1814. Beliles, *The Selected Religious Letters and Papers of Thomas Jefferson* (Charlottesville, VA: America Publications, 2013), 223.

22   Letter to John Adams, July 5, 1814, www.founders.archives.gov.

more than mere human but difficult to label. Meanwhile, he blames the rise of Plato's mysticism for the doctrine of the Trinity. He sees Trinitarian priests as intentionally creating a complicated scheme for their own power and profit—as opposed to sincere people discerning that the Trinity is something revealed in the Bible.

Similarly on December 6, 1813 Jefferson wrote to Alexander von Humboldt, Prussian geographer (who traveled to Latin America), saying the "…History [of Europe with state-established churches], I believe, furnishes no example of a priest-ridden people maintaining a free civil government. This marks the lowest grade of ignorance of which their civil as well as religious leaders will always avail themselves for their own purposes."[23] Many Protestants at that time in America would agree with this observation.

A New York political and business leader Horatio G. Spafford had previously corresponded with Jefferson and informed him that "…to destroy Thomas Jefferson, is the summum bonum of the ecclesiastic junta of New-England…" So Spafford asked Jefferson to tell him his beliefs about Christ and the Bible so that he could defend Jefferson properly. So now on March 17, 1814, Jefferson wrote: "…In every country and in every age, the priest has been hostile to liberty. He is always in alliance with the despot, abetting his abuses in return for protection to his own. It is easier to acquire wealth and power by this combination than by deserving them, and to effect this, they have perverted the purest religion ever preached to man into mystery and jargon…"[24]

Once again it is clear that by saying "every country and in every age" Jefferson is referring mainly to Europe's history of Catholic priests having political power. But, of course it is also true that abuse by Protestant priests against dissident Christians was also experienced often in post-Reformation Europe.

In late 1813 Jefferson also wrote John Adams, saying "…The law for religious freedom…[in Virginia has] put down the aristocracy of the clergy and restored to the citizen the freedom of the mind."[25] This shows that Jefferson no longer viewed clergy in Virginia in the same way he viewed those in New England, where state-favored denominations still existed. In fact, Jefferson only once in his entire life had mentioned a critical remark about Episcopal clergy in Virginia, and in his lifetime not a single Virginia clergyman (that we're aware of) ever criticized

---

23   Letter to Alexander von Humboldt, December 6, 1813, www.founders.archives.gov.

24   Letter to Horatio G. Spafford, March 17, 1814, www.founders.archives.gov. (Years later, Spafford's son wrote the famous hymn, "It is Well with My Soul.")

25   Letter to John Adams, October 28, 1813, www.founders.archives.gov.

or questioned Jefferson's religion. Unfortunately, Jefferson's criticism of state-established and law-religion (as Lorenzo Dow had described them) clergy quotes are used over and over by modern commentators without the contextualized narrow focus and other counterbalancing facts, and thus perpetuate a distorted image of Jefferson's anti-clericalism.

Jefferson wrote to Philadelphia bookseller Nicholas G. Dufief on April 19, 1814, with concern over a case up north where the sale of a book was being prosecuted:

> ...I am really mortified to be told that, in the United States of America...a question about the sale of a book can be carried before the civil magistrate. Is this then our freedom of religion? ...Is a priest to be our inquisitor, or shall a layman, simple as ourselves, set up his reason as the rule for what we are to read, and what we must believe? ...If [this] book be false in its facts, disprove them; if false in its reasoning, refute it. But, for God's sake, let us freely hear both sides, if we choose;...[26]

Since Virginia's law on religious freedom was adopted, such incidents almost never occurred.

Jefferson wrote again to a northern Unitarian layman, Thomas Law, on June 13, 1814, saying: "... I have observed, indeed, generally, that while in Protestant countries the defections from the Platonic Christianity of the priests is to Deism, in Catholic countries they are to Atheism..."[27] This is one of only three references to Deism Jefferson made and is something he is critical of and the destination of the apostate "Platonic" (i.e., Trinitarian) Christians he strongly criticized, and not likely to identify with himself. It is explained more in the later chapter on orthodoxy.

One of Jefferson's Catholic clergy friends who certainly was not an atheist was a Portuguese diplomat who began to come and frequently stay with Jefferson at Monticello. Rev. José Francisco Correa da Serra (1750-1823) was ordained as a Catholic priest in 1775 but became more famous as a botanist, geologist, and natural scientist, and was the founder of the Academy of Science in Lisbon. He came to the U.S. in 1812 and resided in Washington, 1816-1820, as Portugal's ambassador. Correa was "a staunch defender of his [Catholic] faith... (and) an active liturgist, having performed baptism on the children of Thomas

---

26   Letter to Nicholas G. Dufief, April 19, 1814, www.founders.archives.gov.
27   Letter to Thomas Law, June 13, 1814, www.founders.archives.gov.

Cooper."[28] Correa made eight lengthy visits at Monticello up until 1820, and one room at Monticello came to be known as "Abbe Correa's room." Unfortunately, as with Rev. Clay, little on religion is found in their letters because they could discuss that topic better in person.[29]

One item in their letters that touched on religion arose concerning a project for a new non-denominational Christian school of higher learning beginning in Charlottesville called the Albemarle Academy. Its Board of Trustees met on March 25, 1814, and Jefferson was a member of the Board, for which he drafted his Plan for Albemarle Academy that included three "Professional Schools," one of which was "Theology and Ecclesiastical History." On September 7, Jefferson wrote to his nephew Peter Carr and enclosed this plan.[30] Jefferson shared this information with several people, and Unitarian scientist Thomas Cooper wrote Jefferson on September 22 that having a professional school of Theology was not a good idea. But a week later Catholic Rev. José Correa da Serra disagreed with Cooper and advised that a divinity professor would be good to have.[31]

Presbyterian Rev. Samuel Knox had previously proposed a plan for public institutions of higher learning that avoided establishing a divinity school in order to maintain a nondenominational character. Jefferson sided with Knox and Cooper. Jefferson wrote to Cooper that: "I agree with yours of the 22d, that a professorship of Theology should have no place in our institution. But we cannot always do what is absolutely best. Those with whom we act, entertaining different views, have the power and the right of carrying them into practice...."[32] It could be argued that if he were able to, Jefferson would eliminate some things that he could not do in a collaborative board process but at the same time it could be argued that Jefferson was open to a theology professorship, and other religious elements because he was more pragmatic in the way he approached issues of church and state than many modern secularists portray him to be.

---

28   *The Portuguese American*, 1992 (Article in files of Monticello). Although Correa was at Monticello often between 1813 and 1820, there was no Catholic church in the area for another 50 years.

29   In 1819 Jefferson wrote to William Short that "it will add much to the happiness of my recovery to be able to receive Correa and yourself. . . ." Letter to William Short, October 31, 1819. Beliles, *The Selected Religious Letters and Papers of Thomas Jefferson*, 300.

30   "Thomas Jefferson to Peter Carr, September 7, 1814," www.founders.archives.gov.

31   Letter from Rev. Jose' Francesco Correa da Serra, after September 30, 1814. Beliles, *The Selected Religious Letters and Papers of Thomas Jefferson*, 249.

32   Letter to Thomas Cooper, October 7, 1814. The Thomas Jefferson Papers Series 1, General Correspondence, 1651-1827, Library of Congress Manuscript Division.

Rev. Clay and Others Ask Questions About His Beliefs

Jefferson continued in his own private study of religion. In August 1814 Jefferson wrote to Mr. Dufief asking: "...of him to procure and send him a copy of [Edward] Evanson's Dissonance of the four Evangelists."[33] Evanson, a Unitarian minister, rejected most of the books of the New Testament as forgeries, and of the four Gospels he accepted only the Gospel of Luke.

A Methodist layman in Virginia named Miles King (and later a minister) wrote Thomas Jefferson about his religion on August 20, 1814, and Jefferson replied on September 26:

> ...our reason...is the only oracle which God has given us to determine between what really comes from him...; Our particular principles of religion are a subject of accountability to our God alone. I enquire after no man's and trouble none with mine; nor is it given to us in this life to know whether yours or mine, our friend's or our foe's, are exactly the right.... that you and I may there [in heaven] meet and embrace is my earnest prayer...[34]

This letter's affirmation of reason is well known but often overlooked is that it is based on the premise that reason is an endowment from God.

It was at this time that Jefferson's earlier private letter to William Canby (subscribing to universalism) was published (slightly modified) without Jefferson's permission in a Delaware newspaper on November 1, 1814. It was then picked up and reprinted in newspapers in Virginia and New York. This began to raise questions about Jefferson's faith among more than just his political opponents. Despite the Canby letter in the news, attacks on his faith still never happened by any clergymen in Virginia or anywhere south of New York in Jefferson's entire lifetime. But one of the most important inquiries came on December 20, 1814 from his former pastor, the evangelical Rev. Charles Clay. He said:

> Reflecting on an expression of yours relative to an Idea Sometimes entertained by you of Compressing the Moral doctrines taught by Jesus

---

33   Letter to Nicholas Dufief, August 21, 1814. Beliles, *The Selected Religious Letters and Papers of Thomas Jefferson*, 227.

34   Letter to [Rev.] Miles King, September 26, 1814, Beliles, *The Selected Religious Letters and Papers of Thomas Jefferson*, 248. See later correspondence linking God and reason in Letter to William Carver, November 25, 1823. www.founders.archives.gov.

of Nazareth in the Gospels, divested of all other Matters into a small and regular system of the purest morality ever taught to Mankind…however laudable may be your Views and meritorious your intentions in such a nice and critical (delicate) undertaking, I cannot help entertaining doubts and fears for the final issue, how it may effect your future character and reputation on the page of history as a Patriot, legislator and sound Philosopher.

…I feel sensibly for the final event, should you be induced to permit yourself to send forth such a piece to the public, lest they might not Sufficiently appreciate your good intentions, but ascribe it to views as inimical to the Christian religion in particular, and eventually to all religion from divine Authority, which I am persuaded you Can have no intention of doing.

…My fears are, that should your performance not exactly meet the approbation of the public, (both now and hereafter), that your Name will be degraded from the Venerable council of true, genuine, Useful Philosophy; & Condemned to be Ranked with the wild Sophisters of Jacobinsm [i.e., French underground secretive revolutionaries]…Masonry…Illuminism, etc; which…future Historians will most assuredly denominate by some opprobrious epithet, as the Maniacs of Philosophy &c. And it certainly may be expected that the whole of your numerous Enemies on the Northern and eastern parts of the U.S…should the performance not exactly Coincide with their Ideas and meet their entire approbation, even in the Minutiae of diction (which it is highly probable it would not) they would greedily seize the Occasion, and raise the hue and Cry after you…[35]

Jefferson's letter in the papers may have become known to Rev. Clay, for in this letter to Jefferson he warned against publishing anything because people would misjudge "your good intentions" and "ascribe it to Views as inimical to the christian Religion in particular,& eventually to all Religion from divine Authority,—which I am persuaded you Can have no intention of doing." To paraphrase: Jefferson, I know you as a Christian, active in the church, but the masses out there might not think so, if you publish some of these things.

35   Rev. Charles Clay to Jefferson, December 20, 1814. Beliles, *The Selected Religious Letters and Papers of Thomas Jefferson*, 250.

About a month later, on January 29, 1815, Jefferson replies to the warning of his evangelical friend Rev. Clay:

> Of publishing a book on religion, my dear Sir, I never had an idea. …
> Probably you have heard me say I had taken the four Evangelists, had cut
> out from them every text they had recorded of the moral precepts of Jesus,
> and arranged them in a certain order….and the idea of its publication may
> have suggested itself as an inference of your own mind. I not only write
> nothing on religion, but rarely permit myself to speak on it, and never but
> in a reasonable society.
>
> I have probably said more to you [on religion] than to any other
> person, because we have had more hours of conversation in *duetto* in our
> meetings at the Forest [i.e., Jefferson's retreat in Bedford where Clay was a
> neighbor]. I abuse the [northern and eastern, as identified by Clay's letter]
> priests, indeed, who have so much abused the pure and holy doctrines of
> their Master…and [replaced it with] artificial structures…[36]

In this important letter, Jefferson identified Clay as his confidant on religious subjects "more than to any other person." This orthodox evangelical minister knew Jefferson to be a faithful supporter and communicant of the Church, and this context led him to believe Jefferson's intentions for his private speculations as nothing of serious concern. But Clay warned that "future Historians will most assuredly…[create]…Some opprobrious epithet" for Jefferson if his private thoughts were published. It turns out in history that Clay's fears came true. He's now almost universally described as a Deist, skeptic, atheist or other terms, even though Jefferson never used those terms to describe himself. Jefferson's one time pastor and longtime friend also never thought of Jefferson as anything other than a sincere believer.

But Rev. Clay no longer had concerns after hearing that Jefferson was not planning to publish anything. His reply to Jefferson on February 8 said:

> I am pleased to find you viewed my letter in the light it was intended, A
> Real Concern for your present peace & future Reputation alone dictated
> it, & Strongly impressed my mind to draw your attention to the probable

---

36   Letter to Rev. Charles Clay, January 29, 1815. Beliles, *The Selected Religious Letters and Papers of Thomas Jefferson*, 251. This is discussed further in our chapter on Jefferson and Orthodoxy.

Consequences Should your ultimate Views have been publication in the brokn form of fragments [in Jefferson's abridgement for the use of the Indians] & which must have been connected perhaps by some observations, or explanations, to preserve a concatenation of Ideas. In these lay the difficulties & dangers I was apprehensive of; & although everyone may, & everyone has an undoubted Right to amuse himself sometimes, & even be playful in his Closet on any Subject, yet an Idea Suggested itself, most possibly it might not be for yourself only the time was Spent, & from hence the inference of probable publication naturally occurred. I sincerely will your name may Remain in the Annals of America as [highly respected]...& if anything has escaped from me that would imply the Contrary, my Dear Sir Correct it, & make it Speak better things.[37]

It is clear to Rev. Clay that Jefferson's abridgement (again, popularly known today as "the Jefferson Bible") and other private letters were nothing more than him being "playful in his Closet" and affirmed that anyone has the "Right to amuse himself sometimes" with speculations on religious topics. Of course, church members today may do this in private with friends, or perhaps express questionable views while learning about it during a theology course, but evangelical clergy would not excoriate them for it. They realize that they are in a learning process, which is how Rev. Clay interpreted his former parishioner.

This interpretation of Jefferson's good intentions by his pastor, the man who Jefferson said he spoke with more than anyone else on religion, is one of the most important to consider. It provides a viewpoint missing today in modern Jefferson historiography. Unfortunately, today Jefferson is not treated fairly for his private speculations. Even modern clergy have embraced the uninformed view of the northerners and reject Jefferson because they fail to understand him as did his pastor Rev. Clay. More critical views seem to become more justified if Jefferson's private unsent views (revealed a century or more later) are taken into account, but the question remains if that is indeed fair to do. (A purposefully unsent draft does not have the same standing as a letter that is sent.)

Jefferson and Rev. Clay also exchanged more letters at that time, and on August 25 Jefferson invited Clay to come over for a visit at his home at Poplar Forest.[38]

---

37   Rev. Charles Clay to Jefferson, February 8, 1815. Beliles, *The Selected Religious Letters and Papers of Thomas Jefferson*, 252.

38   Letter to Rev. Charles Clay, August 25, 1815. J. Jefferson Looney, ed., *The Papers of Thomas Jefferson*, Retirement Series (Princeton, N.J.: Princeton University Press), vol. 8, 685.

Little religious content is in the letters since they discussed those things in person. It is unfortunate that Clay and Jefferson's religious discussions were almost all verbal and not written. A letter to Clay on April 25, 1816, said: "I return the 10 first volumes and will be glad of the next 10."[39] The editors of *Jefferson's Papers* cannot identify what literature this referred to that Jefferson borrowed from Rev. Clay but coming subsequent to the previous letter, it seems that Clay may have recommended some of his religious books for Jefferson's further study. Jefferson wrote to Clay on November 18 that "tomorrow, weather permitting, will pay you a morning visit."[40]

Jefferson's Attendance at Preaching in Charlottesville

That year Jefferson purchases and has bound various books, including "the Book of Common Prayer,…the power of religion on the mind by Lindlay Murray; [Lawrence] Sterne's sermons" and later "Religious Pamphlets, Sermons 22, Pamphlets: Ethics 9, Unitarian 3."[41] So here he obtains both orthodox and unorthodox literature but Unitarian literature is no more than ten percent of the total. Joseph Milligan replied on May 6 to Jefferson and confirmed that Jefferson bought "Thompsons Four Gospels" which was the newly published book by Charles Thomson: "A Synopsis of the Four Evangelists: or, a Regular History of the Conception, Birth, Doctrine, Miracles, Death, Resurrection, and Ascension of Jesus Christ, in the Words of the Evangelists."[42]

Jefferson's familiarity with the liturgy of the Episcopal Church is evident in a letter to Albert Gallatin on October 16, 1815[43] This was a paraphrase of "The order for Evening Prayer" in *The Book of Common Prayer*, which Jefferson had just recently purchased a new copy. Jefferson's family Bible and prayer book is deposited in the University of Virginia library today.

Jefferson's favorite preacher, Presbyterian Rev. John Glendy, stopped by Monticello a few weeks earlier on September 28, 1815 and found Jefferson absent

---

39   Letter to Rev. Charles Clay, April 25, 1816. Beliles, *The Selected Religious Letters and Papers of Thomas Jefferson*, 269.

40   Letter to Rev. Charles Clay, November 18, 1816. The Thomas Jefferson Papers Series 1, General Correspondence, 1651-1827, Library of Congress Manuscript Division.

41   Letter to Joseph Milligan, March 28, 1815 and July 31, 1815. Looney, *The Papers of Thomas Jefferson*, Retirement Series, vol. 8, 386 and 628.

42   Letter from Joseph Milligan, May 6, 1815. Looney, *The Papers of Thomas Jefferson*, Retirement Series, vol. 8, 471.

43   Letter to Albert Gallatin, October 16, 1815. Looney, *The Papers of Thomas Jefferson*, Retirement Series, vol. 9, 94.

so he left a letter that day saying he had dinner the previous day at Montpelier with President Madison and Secretary of State James Monroe. Glendy then wrote: "I am on my way to Staunton, and purpose returning to Baltimore by the way of Charlottesville—were I to Occupy the bench [i.e., pulpit] in the CourtHouse of this town, as an itinerant preacher on Sunday week, the 8th day of October next, pray, could I have the honor of your sitting under my ministry on the Occasion? If you could promise me a Congregation on that day (and that the stated pastor would not be jealous) I would pledge myself to deliver a discourse at that period." Unfortunately, it did not happen due to bad weather as Jefferson described on October 22:

> …the change in the weather was a great disappointment; and the morning itself so threatening as to deter all distant persons from coming. I set out from home myself at 11. aclock in expectation momently of rain; but before I reached Charlottesville, it cleared away. You had left the place about an hour. About twelve aclock many came, all indeed who were near enough to get there in time after the weather cleared up. The loss of the pleasure of hearing you is the more regretted, as it can rarely if ever be expected to be renewed.[44]

A few years later a similar story is reported in 1818 by Monticello overseer Edmund Bacon:

> There was a Mr. Hiter, a Baptist preacher, that used to preach occasionally at the Charlottesville Courthouse…Mr. Jefferson nearly always went to hear him when he came around. I remember his being there one day in particular. His servant came with him and brought a seat—a kind of campstool— upon which he sat…After the sermon there was a proposition to pass around the hat and raise money to buy the preacher a horse. Mr. Jefferson did not wait for the hat. I saw him…take out a handful of silver. I don't know how much. He then walked across the Courthouse to Mr. Hiter and gave it into his hand.[45]

---

44   Letter to Rev. John Glendy, October 22, 1815. Beliles, *The Selected Religious Letters and Papers of Thomas Jefferson*, 254.

45   James A. Bear, Jr., ed., *Jefferson at Monticello* (Charlottesville, Va.: University Press of Virginia, 1967), 74-75. This story never seems to be remembered by modern evangelicals like the one told of when Benjamin Franklin was moved by the preaching of George Whitefield to give a donation.

Rev. William Y. Hiter, who preached over 4,000 sermons in thirteen years as a traveling evangelist, occasionally preached in Charlottesville, and later became pastor of Goldmine Baptist Church in Louisa (John Leland's old church). It is also worth noting that Hiter preached at the Albemarle Buck Mountain Baptist Church as early as 1810 after Rev. Woods left for Kentucky. It is also interesting that Bacon mentioned Jefferson having a "campstool" because this was something that those who participated in "camp meetings" used. This anecdote also helps us to realize that although attendance at church and financial gifts may not appear in Jefferson's account books at this time, it occurred nonetheless through itinerating preachers. But worship being erratic in Charlottesville at the time, due to a lack of resident denominational pastors, precluded the typical way of Jefferson recording it.

Previously it was noted that there were no settled pastors locally at this time in Charlottesville where Jefferson could attend church (not Episcopal, Presbyterian, Methodist, or Baptist). But here is evidence that Jefferson not only attended various religious meetings he heard about, he also actively arranged for some itinerants to preach in services in the courthouse. Even though the weather hindered that particular meeting with Glendy (to Jefferson's great disappointment), it furnishes the image of Jefferson as an active Christian sponsoring the preaching of orthodox clergymen. This aspect of Jefferson's life is never mentioned in any modern biography. The picture of Thomas Jefferson on October 8, 1815 waiting longingly at the Charlottesville courthouse for a Presbyterian preacher to arrive is simply nonexistent in the modern public consciousness. Virtually all that is ever reported today is the letters to Unitarians in this phase of Jefferson's life. The absence of such facts (and the earlier Calvinistical Reformed Church) in modern biographies of Jefferson creates a false impression that needs correcting in Jeffersonian scholarship.

Correspondence With Northern Clergy

Some northern clergy were strong supporters of Jefferson. In New York, a layman named Peter H. Wendover of the Dutch Reformed Church, who was a Democratic-Republican Congressman, sent a sermon from a New York pastor to Jefferson on January 30, 1815 entitled *A Scriptural View of the Character, Causes, and Ends of the Present War* (the War of 1812) by Rev. Alexander McLeod of the First Reformed Presbyterian Church.[46]

Rev. McLeod was a friendly clergy ally of Jefferson. Jefferson replied to Wendover on March 13, telling him:

---

46   Letter from Peter Wendover, January 30, 1815. Looney, *The Papers of Thomas Jefferson, Retirement Series*, vol. 8, 228.

Th: Jefferson presents his compliments to Mr [Peter] Wendover and his thanks for the volume of mr [Alexander] Mcleod's discourses which he has been so kind as to send him. He has seen with great satisfaction the able proofs adduced by the eloquent author from Scriptural sources, in justification of a war so palpably supported by reason, he supposes indeed that true religion and well informed reason will ever be in unison in the hands of candid interpretation and that in the impassioned endeavors to place these two great authorities at variance, on so important a question, the Eastern clergy have not deserved well either of their religion or their country. He renders deserved honor to [Rev.] mr Mcleod for the piety and patriotism of his discourses, and salutes mr Wendover with respect and esteem.[47]

The *Papers of Thomas Jefferson* include a longer unsent version of this letter that will be discussed later.

At this same time Jefferson received a letter from a northern Unitarian Rev. Benjamin Waterhouse, a pastor of First Parish Church in Portland, Maine. On October 13, Jefferson replied to Rev. Benjamin Waterhouse with discussion of New England clergy:

…I have read with pleasure the orations of Mr. [John] Holmes & Mr. [Benjamin] Austin [i.e., Unitarians in New England, who were opponents of];…the reverenced leaders of the Hartford nation [i.e., Connecticut]; the religious and political tyranny of those in power;… this Sodom and Gomorrah of parsons [include: David] Osgood, [Elijah] Parish & [John] Gardiner [of Massachusetts].[48]

Jefferson wrote in late 1815 to Thomas Ritchie, a journalist in Richmond, Virginia. Jefferson's letter referenced a pamphlet by northern minister Lyman Beecher that Unitarian Rev. Benjamin Waterhouse had sent him regarding a plan to train more ministers for places in the south such as Virginia. Jefferson was not opposed to more religions per se, but was concerned with an invasion

---

47   Letter to Peter H. Wendover, March 13, 1815. Beliles, *The Selected Religious Letters and Papers of Thomas Jefferson*, 253. Note Jefferson's use of the term "Eastern Clergy," which being east of New York means New England.

48   Letter to Rev. Benjamin Waterhouse, October 13, 1815. Beliles, *The Selected Religious Letters and Papers of Thomas Jefferson*, 255.

"...of New England religion and politics" i.e., more law-religion instead of the transdenominational religious culture that Jefferson admired.[49]

With this letter Jefferson included the following message that he felt would be best if Ritchie would perhaps publish it, but not with Jefferson's name on it. The message follows:

> ...You judge truly that I am not afraid of the [northern Federalist] priests. They have tried upon me all their various batteries, of pious whining, hypocritical canting, lying & slandering, without being able to give me one moment of pain...

Jefferson was not troubled by the attacks against him from those New England clergy, whom he dismissed as religious hypocrites. And yet he was friendly to many northern clergy. Again, his anti-clericalism was nuanced and specific for certain clergy.

Another Unitarian, Rev. Noah Worcester, of Massachusetts wrote him and enclosed pamphlets against war on October 18, 1815.[50] Jefferson replied with comments regarding war on January 29, 1816.[51]

To John Adams he wrote on April 8 of "...Atheism...It was a numerous school in the Catholic countries, while the infidelity of the Protestant took generally the form of theism."[52] An earlier letter by Jefferson used the word "deism" in place of theism, so it's apparently interchangeable in Jefferson's thinking.[53]

Jefferson the Avowed Christian Plans to Revise the Extracts

After Joseph Milligan sent Jefferson a copy of Charles Thomson's *Synopsis of the Four Evangelists*, Thomson sent another copy himself so Jefferson replied to Thomson on January 9, 1816 saying,

> ...I, too, have made a wee-little book from the same materials, which I call *the Philosophy of Jesus* [1804 version]; it is a paradigma of his

49   Letter to Thomas Ritchie, January 21, 1816. Beliles, *The Selected Religious Letters and Papers of Thomas Jefferson*, 264.

50   Letter from Rev. Noah Worcester, October 18, 1815. Looney, *The Papers of Thomas Jefferson*, Retirement Series, 9:104.

51   Letter to Rev. Noah Worcester, January 29, 1816. Ibid, 9:410.

52   Letter to John Adams, April 8, 1816. Beliles, *The Selected Religious Letters and Papers of Thomas Jefferson*, 265.

53   Modern definitions are much more complex and nuanced as we discuss in a later chapter.

doctrines, made by cutting the texts out of the book, and arranging them on the pages of a blank book, in a certain order of time or subject. A more beautiful or precious morsel of ethics I have never seen. It is a document in proof that I am a real Christian, that is to say, a disciple of the doctrines of Jesus, very different from the Platonists, who call me infidel and themselves Christians and preachers of the gospel, while they draw all their characteristic dogmas from what its author never said nor saw. They have compounded from the heathen mysteries a system beyond the comprehension of man, of which the great reformer [i.e., Jesus] of the vicious ethics and deism of the Jews, were he to return on earth, would not recognize one feature...If I had time I would add to my little book the Greek, Latin and French texts, in columns side by side...[54]

In this letter Jefferson refers to the 1804 abridgement and says a similar statement that he made to Rush in 1803, that he was a Christian, while defining it without reference to creedal statements. But, of course, he views many core Christian doctrines, like the Trinity, as being the work of "the Platonists." He also uses the word "deism" to describe the religion of the Jews. Furthermore, he gives us the first inklings of a later version of his extracts—one that includes not just verses from the King James Bible, but side by side verses in these other languages (including the original Greek).

On January 20, 1816, Jefferson wrote to Peter Wilson (who apparently had urged support of Bible translations in languages of Indians), saying:

...I think, therefore, the pious missionaries who shall go to the several tribes to instruct them in the Christian religion will have to learn a language for every tribe they go to; nay, more, that they will have to create a new language for every one, that is to say, to add to theirs new words for the new ideas they will have to communicate. Law, medicine, chemistry, mathematics, every science has a language of its own, and divinity not less than others. Their barren vocabularies cannot be vehicles for ideas of the fall of man, his redemption, the triune composition of the Godhead, and other mystical doctrines considered by most Christians of the present date

---

54   Letter to Charles Thomson, January 9, 1816. Beliles, *The Selected Religious Letters and Papers of Thomas Jefferson*, 259.

as essential elements of faith. The enterprise is therefore arduous, but the more inviting perhaps to missionary zeal...[55]

This comment on the difficulty of communicating all of the doctrines of the Christian faith, was in line with his reason over a decade earlier for compiling his *Philosophy of Jesus...an Abridgement of the New Testament for the Use of the Indians.* His reason for the 1804 compilation was in its subtitle saying it was "for the Use of the Indians." Now this letter to Wilson repeats the reasoning of that purpose that was not stated as clearly, anywhere else. And worth noting is his list of orthodox "mystical" doctrines in a non-critical way.

A Congregational clergyman who was a missionary for the Bible Society of Massachusetts and also a teacher in Maine was Rev. Amos Jones Cook. He wrote Jefferson in December 1815; and Jefferson sent a reply on January 21, 1816, in which he quoted extensively from Ecclesiastes 2:3-13.[56] Jefferson obviously still read the Bible (including the Old Testament) and quoted it approvingly. Another example of Jefferson using the Old Testament was in his letter to Mary Briggs on April 17, 1816. It is noteworthy also that in it, Jefferson calls a passage from the Old Testament "inspired." He encouraged her from Psalm 37:25 saying: "Be strong in the assurance given by an inspired pen, 'I have been young, and now I am old; and yet never saw I the righteous forsaken, or his seed begging their bread': and if the prayers of an old man can be of any avail, you shall ever have mine most ardently."[57]

With this in mind, it is interesting to see the content of his correspondence at this time with Francis Van der Kemp, another northerner. This Mennonite immigrant, being oriented now more in the unorthodox camp, wrote Jefferson on March 24 and reported a conversation with his friend John Adams: "...He had then lately received from you a Syllabus, exhibiting your view on a most momentus subject...."[58] He asked Jefferson if he could therefore have a copy of the Syllabus and to share it with friends in England.

---

55   Letter to Peter Wilson, January 20, 1816. Beliles, *The Selected Religious Letters and Papers of Thomas Jefferson*, 262.

56   Letter to Rev. Amos Jones Cook, January 21, 1816. Beliles, *The Selected Religious Letters and Papers of Thomas Jefferson*, 263.

57   Letter to Mary Briggs, April 17, 1816. Beliles, *The Selected Religious Letters and Papers of Thomas Jefferson*, 267.

58   Letter from Francis Van der Kemp, March 24, 1816. Looney, *The Papers of Thomas Jefferson, Retirement Series*, 9:595.

On April 25, 1816, Jefferson replied to Van der Kemp with the permission and told him of his other work in 1804, saying, "...after writing the Syllabus, I made, for my own satisfaction, an *Extract from the Evangelists* of the texts of his morals, selecting those only whose style and spirit proved them genuine, and his own: and they are as distinguishable from the matter in which they are imbedded as diamonds in dunghills. A more precious morsel of ethics was never seen. It was too hastily done however, being the work of one or two evenings only, while I lived at Washington, overwhelmed with other business: and it is my intention to go over it again at more leisure."[59] Jefferson continues to Van der Kemp about his plan to upgrade his digest of Jesus' moral teachings,

> This shall be the work of the ensuing winter. I gave it [the 1804 version] the title of "The Philosophy of Jesus extracted from the texts of the Evangelists;"...the world, I say, will at length see the immortal merit of this first of human Sages...I ask one only condition, that no possibility shall be admitted of my name being even intimated with the publication.[60]

Although the "ensuing winter" was his plan, it was at least 1819 before the "Extract" was done but it was never sent to anyone. (For the sake of identification, we assign 1820 as the date for the second version.) On July 30, Jefferson wrote back to him again saying: "...I rarely waste time in reading on theological subjects, as mangled by our Pseudo-Christians...; no man ever had a distinct idea of the trinity. It is the mere Abracadabra of the mountebanks [i.e., charlatans] calling themselves the priests of Jesus."[61]

Reaffirmation of His Christian Identity (Although Noncreedal)

On May 16, 1816, Charles Thomson replied to Jefferson saying he was glad to hear of his extracts of the Gospels and proof that he was a "real Christian, that is, a disciple of the doctrines of Jesus." Thomson also told him of his habit every morning and sometimes at night of reading religious literature.[62] Through

---

59 Letter to Francis Van der Kemp, April 25, 1816. Beliles, *The Selected Religious Letters and Papers of Thomas Jefferson*, 267.

60 Ibid.

61 Letter to Francis Van der Kemp, July 30, 1816. Beliles, *The Selected Religious Letters and Papers of Thomas Jefferson*, 271.

62 Letter from Charles Thomson, May 16, 1816. Beliles, *The Selected Religious Letters and Papers of Thomas Jefferson*, 269.

Thomson, a dedicated Christian, others heard this news of Jefferson reportedly being a Christian and wrote to Jefferson with the assumption that this marked a change. On August 6, 1816, Jefferson replied to one of these, a Washington author Margaret Bayard Smith (also known as Mrs. Samuel Harrison Smith), saying:

> …I recognize the same motives of goodness in the solicitude you express on the rumor supposed to proceed from a letter of mine to Charles Thomson, on the subject of the Christian religion. It is true that, in writing to the translator of the Bible and Testament, that subject was mentioned; but equally so that no adherence to any particular mode of Christianity was there expressed, nor any change of opinions suggested. A change from what? The priests indeed have heretofore thought proper to ascribe to me religious, or rather anti-religious sentiments, of their own fabric, but such as soothed their resentments against the act of Virginia for establishing religious freedom. They wished him to be thought atheist, deist, or devil, who could advocate freedom from their religious dictations.[63]

To understand that last sentence, the reader has to realize that he speaks of himself in the third person. Jefferson identified at this time with Christianity in general but no "particular mode" of it. Note also that Jefferson puts "deist" and "atheist" in the same category of "devil," certainly none of which he felt was true of himself. Priests here can be only referring to northerners.

Jefferson continues (to Mrs. Smith),

> But I have ever thought religion a concern purely between our God and our consciences, for which we were accountable to him, and not to the priests. I never told my own religion, nor scrutinized that of another. I never attempted to make a convert, nor wished to change another's creed. I have ever judged of the religion of others by their lives, and by this test, my dear Madam, I have been satisfied yours must be an excellent one, to have produced a life of such exemplary virtue and correctness. For it is in our lives, and not from our words, that our religion must be read. By the same

---

63   Letter to Margaret Bayard Smith, August 6, 1816. Beliles, *The Selected Religious Letters and Papers of Thomas Jefferson*, 272.

test the world must judge me. But this does not satisfy the priesthood. They must have a positive, a declared assent to all their interested absurdities...[64]

The New Testament certainly prioritizes deeds over words when it says, faith without works is dead (James 2:26) and that true religion is not mere talk but actions (1 John 3:18). In saying that he "never told my own religion," he had done so with a variety of individuals in private, but he seemed to define what he meant by this statement in this letter by adding that he "never attempted to make a convert" to his views (similar to his letter to Rev. King in 1814).

To Philadelphia publisher Matthew Carey on November 11, Jefferson wrote:

... On the dogmas of religion as distinguished from moral principles, all mankind, from the beginning of the world to this day, have been quarrelling, fighting, burning and torturing one another, for abstractions unintelligible to themselves and to all others, and absolutely beyond the comprehension of the human mind.[65]

The next day he wrote former Pennsylvania Senator George Logan, a Quaker and frequent correspondent, his general agreement with the need for religion and morals to influence national leaders.[66] He wrote also saying:

...Christianity itself [is] divided into its thousands also, who are disputing, anathematizing and, where the laws permit, burning and torturing one another for abstractions which no one of them understand, and which are indeed beyond the comprehension of the human mind;...[but] The sum of all religion as expressed by it's best preacher [i.e., Jesus], "fear God and love thy neighbor," [and] contains no mystery, needs no explanation.[67]

---

64   Ibid.

65   Letter to Matthew Carey, November 11, 1816. Beliles, *The Selected Religious Letters and Papers of Thomas Jefferson*, 276.

66   Letter from George Logan, October 16, 1816. Beliles, *The Selected Religious Letters and Papers of Thomas Jefferson*, 275.

67   Letter to George Logan, November 12, 1816. Beliles, *The Selected Religious Letters and Papers of Thomas Jefferson*, 276.

On December 25, 1816, Jefferson wrote Philadelphia religious publisher Joseph Delaplaine, saying: "my religion…is known to my God and myself alone."[68] As already seen, this only makes sense if one realizes what has come before. Jefferson's views were known to quite a few people with whom he was more intimate, and he attended church throughout his life. But Jefferson was now prone to give such answers to less intimate inquirers (see letter to King and to Mrs. Smith), to try and discourage discussion of his religion. This was true of both his heterodox beliefs as well as his recent statement that he was a Christian. He wished to avoid further communication on the subject with anyone.

To John Adams on January 11, 1817, Jefferson said:

The result of your fifty or sixty years of religious reading in the four words: "Be just and good," is that in which all our enquiries must end…; What all agree upon is probably right; what no two agree in most probably is wrong. One of our fan-coloring biographers, who paints small men as very great, inquired of me lately…My answer was "say nothing of my religion. It is known to my God and myself alone. Its evidence before the world is to be sought in my life. If that has been honest and dutiful to society, the religion which has regulated it cannot be a bad one.[69]

Clergy, Church and State Law, and Jesus as the Root of Rights

In Charlottesville, various clergy held public office at this time. Baptist Rev. John Goss was elected magistrate in 1816, and on May 5, 1817, Goss records in his diary of being with "…Jefferson and Madison, the former Presidents, and Monroe, the present President, together."[70] In this time period Rev. Goss and Baptist Rev. Benjamin Ficklin were reelected as magistrates, and Presbyterian Rev. Charles Wingfield was elected as sheriff.[71] Jefferson never makes any criticism of these local

---

68 Letter to Joseph Delaplaine, December 25, 1816. Dickinson Adams and Ruth W. Lester, eds., *Jefferson's Extracts From the Gospels* (Princeton, N.J.: Princeton University Press, 1983), 382.

69 Letter to John Adams, January 11, 1817. Beliles, *The Selected Religious Letters and Papers of Thomas Jefferson*, 277.

70 Garland Tyree, *Old Blue Run Baptist Church* (Orange, Va.: self-published, 1994), 68-69. Also see John Goss Diaries, 1800-1807, Accession #5737, Special Collections, University of Virginia Library, Charlottesville, Va.

71 Edgar Woods, *Albemarle County in Virginia* (Charlottesville, Va.: Michie Co., 1901), 192-193. Also see *Virginia Magazine of Genealogy*, Volume 26. See also *Magazine of Albemarle County History*, (1948-1949), 9:51. And see Mary Rawlings, *Antebellum Albemarle* (Charlottesville, Va.: Michie Co., 1935), 11.

evangelical clergymen being politically active and elected as leaders in government. In fact, these magistrates began enforcing the Sabbath laws more consistently than before in the years that followed, and yet there is no document of Jefferson that criticized this.[72] (Remember—back in the 1770s, he had a part in writing those very laws.) On that same day that Rev. Goss met with Jefferson, the latter wrote to John Adams with contrasting criticism of the behavior of clergy in New England that was finally changing:

> ...I join you therefore in sincere congratulations that this den of the priesthood [i.e., an official state Congregational church in Connecticut] is at length broken up, and that a protestant popedom is no longer to disgrace the American history and character. If by religion we are to understand sectarian dogmas, in which no two of them agree, then your exclamation on that hypothesis is just, "that this would be the best of all possible worlds, if there were no religion in it." But if the moral precepts, innate in man, and made a part of his physical constitution, as necessary for a social being, if the sublime doctrines of philanthropism [i.e., love of man] and deism [i.e., one God] taught us by Jesus of Nazareth, in which all agree, constitute true religion, then, without it, this would be, as you again say, "something not fit to be named even, indeed, a hell."[73]

Connecticut in 1817 was working on a new constitution that would finally in 1818 do away with a state-established, coercive law-religion. Adams and Jefferson had completely different experiences with religion and clergy in their respective states. Jefferson's state had already made these steps over 30 years earlier, but Adams's New England churches were far more resistant, and he therefore more pessimistic about change. To Jefferson a world without the teachings of Jesus would be "a hell." It should be noted that Jesus' teachings are described as "deism" here, meaning, as shown previously to be equivalent with monotheism and not to be confused with modern concepts of Deism.

Jefferson also clearly affirmed again at this time the religious basis of human rights. Dr. John Manners of New Jersey wrote Jefferson inquiring about the origin of American civil liberties and Jefferson replied: "...our right to life, liberty, the use

---

72   Indeed, in the 1770s, Jefferson had helped write the law to punish Sabbath-breakers. Bill #84 for Punishing Disturbers of Religious Worship and Sabbath Breakers, 1777. The bill passed in 1786.

73   Letter to John Adams, May 5, 1817. Beliles, *The Selected Religious Letters and Papers of Thomas Jefferson*, 280.

of our faculties, the pursuit of happiness, is not left to the feeble and sophistical investigations of reason, but is impressed on the sense of every man. We do not claim these under the charters of kings or legislators, but under the King of kings. If He [i.e., God] has made it a law in the nature of man to pursue his own happiness, He has left him free in the choice of place as well as mode..."[74] King of kings, of course, is a biblical phrase describing Jesus Christ.

Jefferson's home town and state, like Pennsylvania's, was also in great contrast to New York. He wrote politician Albert Gallatin on June 16, 1817, about a new law there saying:

> ... This act...contrasts singularly with a contemporary vote of the Pennsylvania legislature, who, on a proposition to make the belief in God a necessary qualification for office, rejected it by a great majority, although assuredly there was not a single atheist in their body. And you remember to have heard, that when the act for religious freedom was before the Virginia Assembly, a motion to insert the name of Jesus Christ before the phrase, "the author of our holy religion," which stood in the bill, was rejected, although that was the creed of a great majority of them. [75]

Jefferson wrote a letter in 1817 with references to God's providence to Harvard professor George Ticknor which said: "...The penance he [i.e., Napoleon Bonaparte] is now doing for all his atrocities must be soothing to every virtuous heart. It proves that we have a God in heaven. That he is just, and not careless of what passes in this world."[76]

Religion at the Beginning of Central College

The central focus of Jefferson's retirement years was the establishment of an institution of higher learning. It began with his service a few years earlier on the board of the Albemarle Academy, a private nondenominational Christian institution that was renamed the Central College. Now on July 28 the Board of Visitors of Central College met under the leadership of Jefferson and the minutes record that:

---

74   Letter to John Manners, June 12, 1817, Beliles, *The Selected Religious Letters and Papers of Thomas Jefferson*, 281. And Letter from John Manners, May 20, 1817, The Thomas Jefferson Papers Series 1, General Correspondence, 1651-1827, Library of Congress Manuscript Division.

75   Letter to Albert Gallatin, June 16, 1817. The Thomas Jefferson Papers Series 1, General Correspondence, 1651-1827, Library of Congress Manuscript Division.

76   Letter to George Ticknor, November 25, 1817. Ibid.

"It is agreed that application be made to Doctor [Rev. Samuel] Knox of Baltimore to accept the Professorship of Languages, Belles Lettres, Rhetoric, History and Geography."[77] This Rev. Knox was the Presbyterian minister who had corresponded with Jefferson earlier (and who had suggested the idea of a non-denominational college having no divinity professor). However, due to a miscommunication, Knox did not receive or respond to the offer in a timely fashion, so by the time he responded the private college became a public state university with a new protocol for hiring professors.

The second offer of a professorship was on September 1, 1817, when Jefferson wrote to Unitarian chemist Thomas Cooper:

> …Charlottesville is…free as air in religion and politics. Fanaticism and Philosophy have their equal scope, on the principle that *de gustibus non est disputandum* [i.e., In matters of taste, there can be no disputes] and I believe that a moral lecturer, on Sundays, would be as well attended, and paid, if he would add a rational prayer, as a brawling presbyterian or baptist. I have been thus particular, because I am very anxious you should come and give us the benefit of your aid in making this seminary the first in the Union, and drawing to it the youth of the other states…[78]

The board met on October 6, 1817, and the *Minutes of Central College* show that they approved the program in advance for the laying of the cornerstone of Central College (later known as University of Virginia). The minutes included a pre-approved prayer and Scripture reading as follows: "…May almighty God… bless this…College, the object of which institution, is to instill into the minds of Youth…the love of religion & virtue." The Scriptures that were preapproved in the Board's minutes to be read at the ceremony were:

> Thus saith the Lord God, behold I lay in Zion for a foundation a stone, a tried stone, a precious corner stone a sure foundation, — Judgment also will I lay to the line, and righteousness to the plummet [Isaiah 28:16-17]; for behold the Stone which I have laid before Joshua, upon one stone shall be seven eyes: behold I will engrave the engraving thereof saith the Lord of

---

77   Minutes of Central College, July 28, 1817. Beliles, *The Selected Religious Letters and Papers of Thomas Jefferson*, 283.

78   Letter to Thomas Cooper, September 1, 1817. The Thomas Jefferson Papers Series 1, General Correspondence, 1651-1827, Library of Congress Manuscript Division.

Host [Zechariah 3:9]; bless Ye the Lord, all ye servants of the Lord lift up you hands in the sanctuary and bless the Lord; the Lord that made heaven & earth bless thee out of Zion [Psalm 134:1-3].[79]

Episcopal Rev. William King of Staunton led this religious portion of the Masonic[80] ceremony in the presence of Jefferson, Madison, and Monroe who had approved it all.[81]

One day after the cornerstone ceremony, the board met and said: "On information that the Rev. Mr Knox formerly thought of for a Professor of Languages is withdrawn from business the order of 28th. July is resumed, and it is resolved to offer in the first place the Professorship of Chemistry &c to Doct Thomas Cooper..."[82] So when the public learned Cooper the Unitarian (and an aggressive one at that) was hired, and never knowing of the offer to Rev. Knox, this combination of events created an impression that unorthodoxy would be favored by the university. It became a public relations disaster with its evangelical supporters.

By the fall of 1818 Jefferson's private Central College was on its way toward becoming the state's University of Virginia (but not chartered as such until January 1819). On August 4, the commissioners for the university made their report for the legislature. This is treated more fully in a later chapter on the university, but below is a quote from this Report:

> ...It is supposed probable, that a building of somewhat more size in the middle of the grounds may be called for in time, in which may be rooms for religious worship, under such impartial regulations;... we have proposed no professor of divinity; and the rather as the proofs of the being of a God, ...will be within the province of the professor of ethics... Proceeding thus far without offence to the Constitution, we have thought it proper at this

---

79   Outline of Cornerstone Ceremonies, October 6, 1817, Beliles, *The Selected Religious Letters and Papers of Thomas Jefferson*, 283.

80   At that time, there were many practicing Christians involved in the Masons; anti-Christian views arising among some Masons was to come later.

81   Joseph A. Waddell, *Annals of Augusta County, Virginia, 1726-1871, 2d ed.* (Bridgewater, Va.: C. J. Carrier Co., 1958), 451.

82   Minutes of the Board of Visitors of Central College, October 7, 1817. The Thomas Jefferson Papers Series 1, General Correspondence, 1651-1827, Library of Congress Manuscript Division. See *Early History of Virginia as contained in the Letters of Thomas Jefferson and Joseph C. Cabell* (Richmond, Vir.: J.W. Randolph, 1856), 396-ff.

point to leave every sect to provide, as they think fittest, the means of further instruction in their own peculiar tenets.[83]

This report is significant in that it affirms the use of buildings for Christian worship and the teaching of the existence of God as being constitutional actions in this state university.

Evangelicals gave their support for its passage in the General Assembly and were very much interested in it as a non-denominational alternative to the Episcopal College of William and Mary. In October 1818, Rev John Holt Rice, Pastor of First Presbyterian Church in Richmond and the most influential person of that denomination in Virginia, visited the site of Jefferson's proposed University in Charlottesville and wrote approvingly: "The plan humbly suggested [for the university concerning religion] is to allow Jews, Catholics, Protestants, Episcopalians, Methodists, Baptists, any and all sects, if they shall choose to exercise the privilege, to endow professorships, and nominate their respective professors;...The students shall regularly attend divine worship; but in what form, should be left to the direction of parents; or, in failure of this, to the choice of the students."[84] In 1818, Rice started the *Virginia Evangelical and Literary Magazine*, and in 1819, was elected as the national moderator of the General Assembly of the Presbyterian Church. Rice's support of Jefferson's school was no small endorsement.

The Board of Visitors of Central College, of which Jefferson was the leading part, had extended its first invitation to hire a professor in 1817. As noted, that person was Presbyterian Rev. Samuel Knox of Maryland. Unfortunately, Knox did not accept at that time for reasons that are unclear (perhaps never having received it?), but he inquired over a year later on November 30, 1818. His recent application to Jefferson ended saying "...That it may please Divine Providence to spare your useful life, to see its' advantages realized by society is the sincere prayer of your greatly respectful and most obedient humble servant." To this Jefferson replied on December 11 to explain that hiring was no longer something that he

---

83   "Report of the Board of Commissioners for the University of Virginia to the Virginia General Assembly, August 4, 1818" (also known as the Rockfish Gap Report). Founders Online, National Archives (http://founders.archives.gov/documents/Madison/04-01-02-0289, ver. 2013-06-10).

84   William Maxwell, *Memoir of the Rev. John H. Rice* (Philadelphia: J. Whetham, 1835), 151-153.

was responsible for, now that the private Central College had been changed into the public University of Virginia.[85] Jefferson wrote:

> ... Its present situation then is such that...no new authorities yet exist who can act on any applications. As to myself, I give all the aid I can towards bringing it into existence, but, that done, age and declining health and strength will oblige me to leave to other characters the details of execution.[86]

First Conflict With Presbyterians

Presbyterian Rev. Conrad Speece passed through and preached in the Charlottesville courthouse in 1818 and felt the city was under Satan's control, and that's why he advocated for the new university to be established there. Rev. Benjamin Holt Rice settled in as the permanent pastor in 1822 with Rev. Francis Bowman as his assistant. Benjamin Rice also preached in the Episcopal church building near Keswick (unofficially known as Walker's Church), since it had no regular minister, and was well-received even by some of Jefferson's family members, such as granddaughter Ellen Coolidge who attended Rice's preaching and later wrote of how his messages moved her.[87] So Presbyterian and Episcopalian churches were the first to get reestablished in the area.

To orthodox Christians who only heard of the Unitarian Cooper's hiring and nothing of the failed attempt to get Rev. Knox, it appeared that the University of Virginia was going in the direction of Unitarianism as Harvard had recently done up north. It was then that Rev. John Holt Rice (brother of Benjamin Rice above), just weeks away from the vote in the legislature to charter the new university, began in his influential *Evangelical Magazine* to publicly call for the firing of Unitarian Thomas Cooper as a professor. If Presbyterians pulled their support the university would likely not succeed. Rice wrote on January 10, 1819: "A critical time in our state is approaching. Religion is to triumph before long or the pestilence of Socinianism [i.e., Unitarianism], will grow;...They fear a defeat [in

85   Letter from Rev. Samuel Knox, November 30, 1818 and Letter to Rev. Samuel Knox, December 11, 1818. Beliles, *The Selected Religious Letters and Papers of Thomas Jefferson*, 293.

86   Letter to Rev. Samuel Knox, December 11, 1818. Beliles, *The Selected Religious Letters and Papers of Thomas Jefferson*, 297.

87   Walker's Church [Grace Church today] got its name from Thomas Walker who gave the land for it. It was part of Fredericksville Parish where Jefferson served as a vestryman almost half a century earlier.

the legislature], and dread Presbyterians most of all. I have…[however] gone in among the Monticello-men, and assured them that…far from being opposed, we are ready to give all our aid in the establishment, support, and proper management of such an institution."[88]

The charter passed but Jefferson truly did not understand the uproar among Presbyterians, as a form of Unitarianism had been acceptable among evangelicals (Restorationists) in the Piedmont for years. Although Jefferson knew the board was not favoring Unitarianism, he couldn't see how it appeared to the evangelical public. So he began to attribute the criticism to a desire among Presbyterian clergymen to control the university for themselves. Jefferson was also embarrassed and angry at what he thought was a betrayal by Presbyterians who had supported the school so far. In the heat of the moment, Jefferson's first private letters against Virginia Presbyterians were written the following year in 1820. The only other time Jefferson made any statement critical of Christian leaders in Virginia was one reference to the Episcopalians in 1785—thirty-five years earlier! Almost all other of his anti-clergy remarks were about northerners ("Easterners") or Europeans. This criticism now of Virginia clergy by Jefferson was really unfounded and unfair, but thankfully his targets never knew of it since it was done in a few private letters.

First Criticism of Calvinism

To Samuel Wells and Gabriel Lilly, Jefferson wrote a letter in 1818 that used the term "primitive" in conjunction with Christianity, which was used almost interchangeably with Restorationist theology and Unitarianism. To Wells and Lilly he said:

> …I make you my acknowledgement for the sermon on the Unity of God, and am glad to see our countrymen looking that question in the face. It must end in a return to primitive Christianity, and the disbandment of the unintelligible Athanasian jargon of 3 being 1 and 1 being 3. This sermon is one of the strongest pieces against it. I observe you are about printing a work of [Thomas] Belsham's on the same subject, for which I wish to be a subscriber…[89]

---

88   Maxwell, *Memoir of the Rev. John H. Rice*, 154.

89   Letter to Samuel Wells and Gabriel Lilly, April 1, 1818. The Thomas Jefferson Papers Series 1, General Correspondence, 1651-1827, Library of Congress Manuscript Division.

On March 9, 1818, Jefferson's account book said he "Paid for a book."[90] The editors say it was a book by George Bethune English entitled *The Grounds of Christianity Examined by Comparing the New Testament with the Old*. It was not an orthodox work and earlier had led to the excommunication of Mr. English in Britain.

At that same time, another friend from New Hampshire, Republican congressman Salma Hale, sent Jefferson some Unitarian literature that was strongly anti-Calvinist. In reply, Jefferson makes his first statement that was critical of Calvinism, while also acknowledging Calvin along with Luther as reformers. This short complete letter is below:

> …The truth is that Calvinism has introduced into the Christian religion more new absurdities than it's leader had purged it of old ones. Our Saviour did not come into the world to save metaphysicians only. His doctrines are leveled to the simplest understandings and it is only by banishing Hierophantic [i.e., priestly] mysteries and Scholastic subtleties, which they have nick-named Christianity, and getting back to the plain and unsophisticated precepts of Christ, that we become *real* Christians. The half reformation of Luther and Calvin did something towards a restoration of his genuine doctrines; the present contest will, I hope, compleat what they began, and place us where the evangelists left us.[91]

He believes that the Reformation didn't go far enough in its return to basic Christianity, as he sees it. He hopes a more complete restoration is soon to come. This letter is interesting also because it again includes the usage of "our Saviour" and "Christ" to refer to Jesus. These terms implied that perhaps Jefferson believed Jesus to be more than just a moral teacher. The references are too slight to make any conclusions, but should not be ignored either.

In a letter to Matthew Carey, he said: "In a letter of Oct. 6 I requested the favor of you to send me Griesbach's Greek Testament, …and the New Testament in an improved version on the basis of Newcome's translation…" Johan Griesbach's New Testament was notable for its synthesis of Matthew, Mark and Luke into one synoptic gospel account and elimination of verses having no repetition in one of the

---

90   Account book, March 1818. For a book. (editors say it was *The Grounds of Christianity* by George Bethune English). Beliles, *The Selected Religious Letters and Papers of Thomas Jefferson*, 289.

91   Letter to Salma Hale, July 26, 1818. Beliles, *The Selected Religious Letters and Papers of Thomas Jefferson*, 292.

other gospels. The "improved version" of Newcome's New Testament was published by Unitarians and noted for leaving out most of 1 John 5:7 for its Trinitarian text. This is notable because Jefferson apparently was revising his original abridgement of the Gospels at that time.

On May 15, 1819, Jefferson replied to northern Unitarian clergyman Thomas B. Parker. Rev. Parker had sent a letter in April saying: "I have just published a small work against the doctrines of [John] Calvin and [Samuel] Hopkins and have taken the liberty to forward you a copy of it presuming you to be a friend to the great cause of truth." Jefferson replied saying:

> ...I thank you, Sir, for the pamphlet you have been so kind as to send me on the reveries, not to say insanities of Calvin and Hopkins...Were I to be the founder of a new sect, I would call them Apiarians [i.e. beekeepers], and, after the example of the bee, advise them to extract the honey of every sect. My fundamental principle would be the reverse of Calvin's, that we are to be saved by our good works which are within our power, and not by our faith which is not within our power.[92]

Jefferson, being more and more influenced by the Restorationist anti-creedal inter-denominational orientation, preferred to be connected to many varieties of Christianity, like a bee landing on many flowers, getting the best of the variety. Later in August, Jefferson replied to Parker who wished to publish Jefferson's letter. But Jefferson refused saying: "Nothing gives me more pain than to have letters, written in the carelessness & confidence of private correspondence, exposed to the public...At my time of life, tranquility is it's summa bonum. To preserve this, I wish to offend no man's opinion. Much less to take the maniac post of a religious controversialist."[93]

In Baltimore that year, 1819, Rev. William Ellery Channing gave a sermon on Unitarian Christianity, which was obtained by Jefferson. This sermon caused a reaction of condemnation by the Hanover Presbytery in Virginia.

Meanwhile a prominent Presbyterian minister in Philadelphia named Rev. Ezra Stiles Ely wrote to Jefferson on June 14. He became national moderator of

---

92   Letter from Rev. Thomas Parker, April 12, 1819 and Letter to Rev. Thomas B. Parker, May 15, 1819. Beliles, *The Selected Religious Letters and Papers of Thomas Jefferson*, 297.

93   Letter to Rev. Thomas Parker, August 2, 1819 and Letter from Rev. Thomas Parker, August 14, 1819. Beliles, *The Selected Religious Letters and Papers of Thomas Jefferson*, 299-300.

the Presbyterians some years afterward. In light of the emerging conflict with Presbyterians, it is included in part below:

> Permit a young Philosopher, to present a veteran with a copy of his "Conversations on the Science of the Human Mind." ....I am, dear Sir, a Presbyterian, a Calvinist, and a man of common sense: I can, therefore, respect and esteem a literary man, of distinguished talents, & usefulness to his country, however I may differ from him, even in important theological opinions.

Jefferson replied on June 25, saying:

> On looking over the summary of the contents of your book, it does not seem likely to bring into collision any of those sectarian differences which you suppose may exist between us...We probably differ on the dogmas of theology, the foundation of all sectarianism, and on which no two sects dream alike; for if they did they would then be of the same.
>
> You say you are a Calvinist. I am not. I am of a sect by myself, as far as I know... [Jesus] has told us only that God is good and perfect, but has not defined Him. I am, therefore, of His theology, believing that we have neither words nor ideas adequate to that definition. And if we could all, after his example, leave the subject as undefinable, we should all be of one sect, doers of good, and eschewers of evil. No doctrines of His lead to schism.[94]

Jefferson condemns ministers in the letter but it is obvious that Jefferson is not making a blanket statement, for Rev. Ely got his respect as did many others. One of the more notable statements in the letter was when Jefferson said that he is of "a sect by myself." This is often repeated by modern commentators whose paradigm for understanding Jefferson is separate from any organized church. But Jefferson is speaking at a time immediately before Rev. Frederick Hatch came to town to restart a permanent Episcopal congregation and in 1820 Jefferson resumed his lifelong membership in that orthodox Trinitarian church. It soon was an *obsolete* characterization of himself, but modern biographers fail to mention this fact.

---

94   Letter from Rev. Ezra Stiles Ely to Jefferson, June 14, 1819 and Letter to Rev. Ezra Stiles Ely, June 25, 1819. Beliles, *The Selected Religious Letters and Papers of Thomas Jefferson*, 298.

Actually the previous year, his account book showed on November 22, 1818, that he "Gave…20 Dollars my subscription to the Revd. [_____] for one year."[95] The account book editors say that the 1818 donation to an unnamed clergyman "was probably" Rev. John P. Bausman, but since the name in the entry was blank, it is possible that it was to support another minister, such as Baptist Rev. Hiter or rotating ministers in the Union meetinghouse. But by 1820, if not earlier, a permanent Episcopal pastor finally was in place. Regardless of how Unitarian some of his views may have been in this last phase of his life, Jefferson's account books then shows him recommitting to the support of orthodox churches regularly from then until his death in 1826.

Unreliable, Unedited, Private Criticism of Orthodoxy, Clergy

More significant letters were written to Unitarian Rev. John Brazer of Salem, Massachusetts when Jefferson affirmed his belief in: "…the doctrines of the earliest fathers;…To these original sources he must now, therefore, return, to recover the virgin purity of his religion."[96] Then about three months later he wrote again in response to Brazer's request to publish Jefferson's letter:

> Letters too which are written when in the carelessness and confidence of private correspondence, may have blots to be hit, which could have been filled up if meant to meet public criticism [_____] and to these considerations I am therefore in a period in the life of man when he should cease to trust himself on paper. The precise moment indeed may not be distinctly marked but when the body is sensibly decayed, we may well suspect that the mind is in some sympathies with it, when the coat is well-worn we ought to expect that the lining also is becoming thread bare. We are the last too ourselves in perceiving this wane of the understanding… Pardon me then, good Sir, if I wish the letter to remain as a private testimonial only of my respect…[97]

---

95 Account book, November 1818. Subscription "to the Revd. [_____]." Beliles, *The Selected Religious Letters and Papers of Thomas Jefferson*, 292.

96 Letter to Rev. John Brazer, August 24, 1819. The Thomas Jefferson Papers Series 1, General Correspondence, 1651-1827, Library of Congress Manuscript Division. Rev. Brazer wrote to Jefferson on July 15 and October 18, 1819. www.founders.archives.gov.

97 Letter to Rev. John Brazer, August 24, 1819. The Thomas Jefferson Papers Series 1, General Correspondence, 1651-1827, Library of Congress Manuscript Division. Also Letter to Rev. John Brazer, November 22, 1819. Beliles, *The Selected Religious Letters and Papers of Thomas Jefferson*, 303.

This appeal is important for the modern reader for it encourages us not to scrutinize Jefferson's private letters too much. He did not intend for them to meet public criticism which, if he did, he would have worked on them more. He also asks additional grace for any of his letters at this elderly stage of his life when his mental faculties were not at their best. Brazer apparently visited Jefferson later in the fall of 1825.

In light of Jefferson's appeal to Brazer, a letter at that time to his former secretary and diplomat William Short should be read. On October 31, 1819, Jefferson said:

> ... But the greatest of all the reformers of the depraved religion of His own country, was Jesus of Nazareth. Abstracting what is really His from the rubbish in which it is buried, easily distinguished by its lustre from the dross of His biographers, and as separable from that as the diamond from the dunghill, we have the outlines of a system of the most sublime morality which has ever fallen from the lips of man;...the rescuing it from the imputation of imposture, which has resulted from artificial systems, invented by ultra-Christian sects, unauthorized by a single word ever uttered by Him, is a most desirable object, and one to which Priestley has successfully devoted his labors and learning..."[98]

This letter to Short also has an *unsent* version that is discussed fully in the chapter later on Jefferson and orthodoxy.

About the same time that Jefferson was expressing his heterodox views in private with his closest confidants, he wrote to Unitarian Thomas Cooper to report on the status of the university and expressed criticism for Presbyterians for the first time in his life:

> ...I must explain to you the state of religious parties with us. About 1/3 of our state is Baptist, 1/3 Methodist, and of the remaining third two parts may be Presbyterian and one part Anglican. The Baptists are sound republicans and zealous supporters of their government. The Methodists are republican mostly, satisfied with their governmt. Medling with nothing out the concerns of their own calling and opposing nothing, these two sects are entirely friendly to our university, the anglicans are the same, the Presbyterian clergy alone (not their followers) remain bitterly federal and

---

98   Letter to William Short, October 31, 1819. Beliles, *The Selected Religious Letters and Papers of Thomas Jefferson*, 300.

malcontent with their government, they are violent, ambitious of power, and intolerant in politics as in religion and want nothing but license from the laws to kindle again the fires of their leader John Knox, and to give us a 2d blast from his trumpet. Having a little more monkish learning than the clergy of the other sects, they are jealous of the general diffusion of science, and therefore hostile to our Seminary ...[99]

Jefferson, feeling emotional about the situation he felt was unfair, goes overboard in accusations about the motives and intentions of the Presbyterians. Knox was the 16th century Reformer in Scotland who founded the Presbyterian Church and who had written a famous pamphlet titled *The First Blast of the Trumpet* in 1558. Jefferson apparently held distaste for him as he did of John Calvin.

On April 11, 1820, Jefferson expressed similar sentiments in writing to his Portuguese Catholic friend Abbe' Correa da Serra who had visited Jefferson recently. Now he was about to return to Europe to Jefferson's personal regret, but Jefferson reported:

...there exists indeed an opposition to it [i.e., the University of Virginia] by the friends of [the Anglican College of] William and Mary, which is not strong. the most restive is that of the priests of the different religious sects, who dread the advance of science as witches do the approach of daylight; and scowl on it the fatal harbinger announcing the subversion of the duperies on which they live. In this the Presbyterian clergy take the lead. The tocsin [i.e., warning bell] is sounded in all their pulpits, and the first alarm denounced is against the particular creed of Doctr. Cooper; and as impudently denounced as if they really knew what it is. But, of this we will talk when you see us at Monticello.[100]

Again Jefferson's condemnation of clergy is selective—certainly not inclusive of this Catholic clergyman to whom he was writing.[101]

---

99   Letter to Thomas Cooper, March 13, 1820. The Thomas Jefferson Papers Series 1, General
      Correspondence, 1651-1827, Library of Congress Manuscript Division.

100   Letter to Rev. Correa da Serra, April 11, 1820. Beliles, *The Selected Religious Letters and
      Papers of Thomas Jefferson*, 305.

101   Also see Letter to Ambrose Marechal, January 17, 1820. Beliles, *The Selected Religious Letters
      and Papers of Thomas Jefferson*, 304. As representative of the Pope at the French court,
      Jefferson said Dugnani became "an intimate acquaintance . . . of several years at Paris..."

About a month later Jefferson wrote to one of the university's board members Robert Taylor about "the hue and cry raised from the different pulpits on our appointment of Doctor Cooper, whom they charge with Unitarianism...."[102] Jefferson said therefore that the board of Visitors of the University had to finally let Cooper go.

Jefferson also wrote to his former secretary William Short a report on the opposition to the university similar to other letters:

> The Presbyterian clergy are loudest; the most intolerant of all sects, the most tyrannical and ambitious; ready at the word of the lawgiver, if such a word could be now obtained, to put the torch to the pile, and to rekindle in this virgin hemisphere, the flames in which their oracle Calvin consumed the poor Servetus, because he could not find in his Euclid the proposition which has demonstrated that three are one and one is three, nor subscribe to that of Calvin, that magistrates have a right to exterminate all heretics to Calvinistic Creed. They pant to re-establish, *by law*, that holy inquisition, which they can now only infuse into *public opinion*;...[103]

But also in this letter to Short Jefferson enclosed a copy of the 1803 Syllabus as requested and made some of his most troubling comments on Scripture:

> But while this syllabus is meant to place the character of Jesus in its true and high light, as no impostor Himself, but a great Reformer of the Hebrew code of religion, it is not to be understood that I am with Him [i.e., Jesus] in all His doctrines. I am a Materialist; he takes the side of Spiritualism; he preaches the efficacy of repentance towards forgiveness of sin; I require a counterpoise of good works to redeem it, etc., etc.

---

102 Letter to Robert Taylor, May 16, 1820. Beliles, *The Selected Religious Letters and Papers of Thomas Jefferson*, 309. Jefferson quoted from Cooper the following: "I regret the storm that has been raised on my account...Whatever my religious creed may be, and perhaps I do not exactly know it myself, it is a pleasure that my conduct has not brought, and is not likely to bring, discredit to my friends."

103 Letter to William Short, April 13, 1820, Beliles, *The Selected Religious Letters and Papers of Thomas Jefferson*, 306. Michael Servetus was a Unitarian preacher burned at the stake in Geneva.

Among the sayings and discourses imputed to Him by His biographers, I find many passages of fine imagination, correct morality, and of the most lovely benevolence; and others, again, of so much ignorance, so much absurdity, so much untruth, charlatanism and imposture, as to pronounce it impossible that such contradictions should have proceeded from the same Being. I separate, therefore, the gold from the dross; restore to Him the former, and leave the latter to the stupidity of some, and roguery of others of His disciples. Of this band of dupes and impostors, Paul was the great Coryphaeus [i.e., leader of the chorus], and first corruptor of the doctrines of Jesus. These palpable interpolations and falsifications of his doctrines led me to try to sift them apart. I found the work obvious and easy, and that his part composed the most beautiful morsel of morality which has been given to us by man. The syllabus is therefore of *his* doctrines, not *all* of *mine*. I read them as I do those of other ancient and modern moralists, with a mixture of approbation and dissent…[104]

Perhaps this means the new version of the Life and Morals of Jesus (the so-called Jefferson Bible of 1819—the one with columns in English, Greek, etc.) was also finished. Clearly to an orthodox believer, these are very troubling sentiments. His charges are discussed in the Appendix with an essay: Christian Answers to Jefferson's Objections to the New Testament.

In this letter, perhaps the most unorthodox of any he had sent, Jefferson speaks of the corruption of Jesus' teachings by followers as early as the Apostle Paul. But he went further and said even the true teachings of Jesus on "spiritualism" and repentance for forgiveness of sin was something he could not accept as true. Jefferson required "good works to redeem" man. It's one thing for Jefferson to say he disagreed with the alleged corruptions of Jesus' words, and it's brash to say he dissented from the Apostle Paul, but for Jefferson to have the arrogance to say that he dissented from Jesus Himself brings him to a new stage. By Jefferson's own earlier definition of a Christian being one who accepted all that Jesus taught, he no longer was a faithful disciple.

By this stage in his life, based on his own admission, Jefferson seemed to define himself out of the bounds of historic Christianity. Outwardly, he was faithful in church attendance (at a Trinitarian church) and also generous to Christian causes. Privately, he seemed to reject the core Christian doctrines, including the salvation Jesus gives to sinners who trust in Him.

---

104   Ibid, 306.

CHAPTER 5

THOMAS JEFFERSON'S RELIGIOUS LIFE, 1820-1826

"I think it as reasonable when our pastor builds a house, that each of his flock should give him an aid of a year's contribution. I enclose mine [for Episcopal Rev. Hatch]…" —Thomas Jefferson, 1821 [1]

The final phase of Jefferson's religious life begins when he rejoins the Trinitarian Episcopal Church in his home town. Jefferson rejoins it and funds its ministry from at least 1820 (but perhaps a year or two earlier) until dying in 1826. This makes for a continuing complexity in Jefferson's religious life because he was privately expressing serious doubts about key Christian doctrines.

Maintaining Private Agreement With Unitarianism

In the previous chapter, the first half of 1820 revealed some of Jefferson's most blatant statements of unorthodoxy and anger against major denominations in his state, mainly due to his misunderstanding of how they perceived the beginnings of the University of Virginia. But influences were at work to soften and modify some

---

1   Letter to Rev. Frederick Hatch, December 8, 1821. Mark A. Beliles, ed., *The Selected Religious Letters and Papers of Thomas Jefferson* (Charlottesville, VA: America Publications, 2013), 322.

of his feelings and perceptions. A follow-up letter to Short was sent on August 4, 1820 in which Jefferson slightly softened his previous letter saying:

> …My aim in that was, to justify the character of Jesus against the fictions of his pseudo-followers, which have exposed him to the inference of being an impostor… That Jesus did not mean to impose himself on mankind as the son of God, physically speaking, I have been convinced by the writings of men more learned than myself in that lore. But that he might conscientiously believe himself inspired from above, is very possible.[2]

Jefferson either accepted Jesus' inspiration and divine mission as Son of God, or at the very least, Jefferson thought it was "possible." Jefferson's modification shown in this letter is slight, but that along with some orthodox statements and actions that follow, are at least worth noting. In the previous letter, Jefferson also mentioned his "creed of materialism." Jefferson corresponded with John Adams in August and discussed materialism much more, saying: "…At what age of the Christian church this heresy of immaterialism, this masked atheism, crept in, I do not know. But a heresy it certainly is. Jesus taught nothing of it…"[3] So Jefferson's concept of Jesus as "son of God, physically speaking" apparently was a fine point that Jefferson did not want misinterpreted. His ideas concerning materialism ties in to his use of "physically," and the nuance of it all is challenging for the general reader.

At the end of October 1820 Jefferson wrote to John D. Wolf saying, "…altho' we are entitled to religious freedom by law, we are denied it by public opinion fanaticism being in fact stronger than law. Th:J. is one of those who fondly believes in the improvability of the condition of man, and anxiously prays for it."[4] Similar ideas were expressed a few days later in a reply to northern Unitarian Rev. Jared Sparks, saying:

> …I adhere to the principles of the first age; and consider all subsequent innovations as corruptions of his religion, having no foundation in what came from him. The metaphysical insanities of Athanasius, of Loyola,

---

2   Letter to William Short, August 4, 1820. Beliles, *The Selected Religious Letters and Papers of Thomas Jefferson*, 311.

3   Letter to John Adams, August 15, 1820. Beliles, *The Selected Religious Letters and Papers of Thomas Jefferson*, 315.

4   Letter to John D. Wolf, October 30, 1820. www.founders.archives.gov.

and of Calvin, are, to my understanding, mere relapses into polytheism, differing from paganism only by being more unintelligible…If the freedom of religion, guaranteed to us by law in theory, can ever rise in practice under the overbearing inquisition of public opinion, truth will prevail over fanaticism, and the genuine doctrines of Jesus, so long perverted by His pseudo priests, will again be restored to their original purity.[5]

Northern Unitarian Rev. Thomas Parker asked Jefferson about the effect of Virginia's religious freedom law adopted 35 years earlier, and Jefferson replied:

… the principle of perfect freedom in religion at length prevailed and we have not since found in experience that the zeal of either pastors or flocks has been damped by this reference to their own consciences; and the proposition of a general assessment, on which, before it was tried, were almost equally divided, would not now I think get one vote in ten.[6]

On February 27 Jefferson replied to Timothy Pickering thanking him for a copy of a discourse on Unitarianism by William Ellery Channing and speaking of the progress of such ideas: "…I have little doubt that the whole of our country will soon be rallied to the unity of the Creator, and, I hope, to the pure doctrines of Jesus also…"[7]

Meanwhile up north Rev. Thomas Whittemore was the minister of the First Universalist Society in Cambridge, Massachusetts. On June 5, 1822, Jefferson replied to him, rejoicing in Unitarian doctrine advancing up north and criticizing the fighting of one denomination against another. But Whittemore asked Jefferson to endorse his unorthodox catechism, to which Jefferson said:

I have never permitted myself to meditate a specified creed. These formulas have been the bane and ruin of the Christian church, its own fatal invention, which, through so many ages, made of Christendom a slaughter-house,

5   Letter to Rev. Jared Sparks, November 4, 1820. Beliles, *The Selected Religious Letters and Papers of Thomas Jefferson*, 318. Sparks had sent a pamphlet to Jefferson in his Letter from Jared Sparks, September 18, 1820, The Thomas Jefferson Papers Series 1, General Correspondence, 1651-1827, Library of Congress Manuscript Division.

6   Letter to Thomas Parker, January 30, 1821. Beliles, *The Selected Religious Letters and Papers of Thomas Jefferson*, 319.

7   Letter to Timothy Pickering, February 27, 1821. Beliles, *The Selected Religious Letters and Papers of Thomas Jefferson*, 319.

and at this day divides it into castes of inextinguishable hatred to one another. Witness the present internecine rage of all other sects against the Unitarian. The religions of antiquity had no particular formulas of creed. Those of the modern world none, except those of the religionists calling themselves Christians, and even among these the Quakers have none. And hence, alone, the harmony, the quiet, the brotherly affections, the exemplary and unschismatizing Society of the Friends, and I hope the Unitarians will follow their happy example. With these sentiments of the mischiefs of creeds and confessions of faith, I am sure you will excuse my not giving opinions on the items of any particular one...[8]

The Restoration churches called themselves by no other title than "Christians" and believed that creedalism, i.e. a requirement of assent to precise statements of doctrine, maintained unbiblical and unnecessary divisions in Christianity. It was not simply that they did not value creeds, but they thought them detrimental. Jefferson completely agreed with this critique and declined any affirmation even if he agreed with it (which seemed likely to Whittemore). He would not permit his views to be published for the public whether favorable to orthodox Christianity or to unorthodox theology.

While Jefferson declined making public affirmation of doctrines he did not refrain from making a summary privately as seen in a reply to Rev. Benjamin Waterhouse of Harvard University in Massachusetts. Waterhouse wrote Jefferson with news of the relationship between Calvinists and Unitarians in New England. On June 26, 1822, Jefferson replied to him with a summary of "the doctrines of Jesus" into three points:

> ... The doctrines of Jesus are simple, and tend all to the happiness of man.
> 1. That there is one only God, and he all perfect.
> 2. That there is a future state of rewards and punishments.
> 3. That to love God with all thy heart and thy neighbor as thyself; is the sum of religion.

These are the great points on which he endeavored to reform the religion of the Jews. But compare with these the demoralizing dogmas of Calvin.

---

8   Letter to Rev. Thomas Whittemore, June 5, 1822. Beliles, *The Selected Religious Letters and Papers of Thomas Jefferson*, 327.

1. That there are three Gods.
2. That good works, or the love of our neighbor, are nothing.
3. That faith is every thing, and the more incomprehensible the proposition, the more merit in its faith.
4. That reason in religion is of unlawful use.
5. That God, from the beginning, elected certain individuals to be saved, and certain others to be damned; and that no crimes of the former can damn them; no virtues of the latter save.[9]

Jefferson continued:

Now, which of these is the true and charitable Christian? He who believes and acts on the simple doctrines of Jesus? Or the impious dogmatists as Athanasius and Calvin? Verily I say these are the false shepherds foretold as to enter not by the door into the sheepfold, but to climb up some other way [i.e., John 10]. They are mere usurpers of the Christian name, teaching a counter-religion made up of the deliria of crazy imaginations, as foreign from Christianity as is that of Mahomet.

Although Jefferson expressed his three points of the doctrines of Jesus, he still (as in his previous reply to Whittemore) opposed Unitarians starting to make their own creedal or organized statements of faith:

….the genuine doctrine of one only God is reviving, and I trust that there is not a young man now living in the United States who will not die an Unitarian. But much I fear, that when this great truth shall be re-established, its votaries will fall into the fatal error of fabricating formulas of creed and confessions of faith, ….How much wiser are the Quakers, who, agreeing in the fundamental doctrines of the gospel, schismatize about no mysteries…Be this the wisdom of Unitarians.[10]

Church and state historian Thomas Buckley writes of Jefferson's faulty prediction that Unitarian views would ultimately dominate: "The sage of Monticello was never further from the mark. The Unitarianism of New England was not the wave of the

---

9   Letter to Rev. Benjamin Waterhouse, June 26, 1822. Beliles, *The Selected Religious Letters and Papers of Thomas Jefferson*, 329.

10   Ibid.

future for his Virginia or the South; or even the nation, for that matter. Rather, the faith and order of Evangelical Protestantism—identified first with Baptists, Methodists, and Presbyterians, and later with the Episcopalians and the Christian churches of Alexander Campbell—this evangelical religion came to dominate Virginia."[11] But some of these groups, especially Campbell's churches, were not really that different from Jefferson's beliefs about the Trinity and Scripture and such.

Waterhouse replied on July 8 asking to publish Jefferson's letter affirming Unitarian doctrine to which Jefferson declined. Jefferson spoke of his memory of respectable Unitarians in Philadelphia and how it seemed to be gaining respect everywhere, but said:

> … That doctrine has not yet been preached to us: but the breeze begins to be felt which precedes the storm;…I am in hopes that some of the disciples of your institution [i.e., Harvard] will become missionaries to us, of these doctrines truly evangelical, and open our eyes to what has been so long hidden from them. A bold and eloquent preacher would be nowhere listened to with more freedom than in this State…The preacher might be excluded by our hierophants [i.e., priests] from their churches and meeting-houses, but would be attended in the fields by whole acres of hearers and thinkers. Missionaries from Cambridge would soon be greeted with more welcome, than from the tritheistical school of Andover…[12]

Non-Trinitarian theology had certainly been preached in Central Virginia and Jefferson certainly knew, for example, of Rev. Thomas Cavender doing so twenty years earlier. So Jefferson must have meant the rationalistic brand of Unitarianism in New England, in contrast to the Restorationist brand of it already active locally. Waterhouse replied again on September 14 in a lengthy description of religion in the Boston area. To this Jefferson replied with surprise that Congregationalists and Unitarians in Boston could share pulpits and said: "… Here no clergyman of any sect ever pronounced the word Unitarian…."[13] This clarifies what Jefferson meant earlier. Non-Trinitarian theology was certainly popular in Jefferson's area, but there

---

11   Thomas Buckley, "Establishing an Evangelical Culture: Religion and Politics in Jeffersonian Virginia" (paper presented at a symposium at the University of Virginia, January 19-20, 1996), 2-3.

12   Letter to Rev. Benjamin Waterhouse, July 19, 1822. Beliles, *The Selected Religious Letters and Papers of Thomas Jefferson*, 333.

13   Letter from Rev. Benjamin Waterhouse, September 14, 1822, The Thomas Jefferson Papers Series 1, General Correspondence, 1651-1827, Library of Congress Manuscript Division.

was no such thing as a "Unitarian" church or preacher. In fact, there would not be one for well over a century.

The southern/western brand of this belief was seen in a letter from Ohio Restorationist/Non-Trinitarian (and former Methodist) minister Rev. James Smith to Jefferson.[14] Smith lived to the west where the country was growing fast, and perhaps this made Jefferson feel confident that the future belonged to Unitarianism. Jefferson replied to Rev. Smith saying:

> The pure and simple unity of the Creator of the universe, is now all but ascendant in the eastern States; it is dawning in the west, and advancing towards the south; and I confidently expect that the present generation will see Unitarianism become the general religion of the United States...I write with freedom, because, while I claim a right to believe in one God, if so my reason tells me, I yield as freely to others that of believing in three. Both religions, I find, make honest men, and that is the only point society has any right to look to...And with the assurance of all my good will to Unitarian and Trinitarian, to Whig and Tory, accept for yourself that of my entire respect.[15]

The American Unitarian Association began a few years later—but in reality it was at the pinnacle of its influence, and it began to decline from that point forward. Rev. Waterhouse of Massachusetts replied again on February 8 to Jefferson to help him understand New England Congregationalism better. He explained to Jefferson that both Calvinists and Unitarians were Congregationalists and that Presbyterian churches had no influence in their state, so Jefferson's accusations of Presbyterian there were misplaced.[16]

Meanwhile, John Adams had written a letter months before that was supportive of Calvinists and wished Jefferson to become one. Jefferson replied:

Letter to Rev. Benjamin Waterhouse, October 15, 1822. Beliles, *The Selected Religious Letters and Papers of Thomas Jefferson*, 335.

14   Letter from Rev. James Smith, November 4, 1822. Beliles, *The Selected Religious Letters and Papers of Thomas Jefferson*, 339.

15   Letter to Rev. James Smith, December 8, 1822. Beliles, *The Selected Religious Letters and Papers of Thomas Jefferson*, 340.

16   Letter from Rev. Benjamin Waterhouse, February 8, 1823. Beliles, *The Selected Religious Letters and Papers of Thomas Jefferson*, 341.

...I can never join Calvin in addressing *his God*. He was indeed an Atheist, which I can never be; or rather his religion was Daemonism. If ever man worshipped a false god, he did. The being described in his 5. points is not the God whom you and I acknolege and adore, the Creator and benevolent governor of the world; but a daemon of malignant spirit. It would be more pardonable to believe in no God at all, than to blaspheme him by the atrocious attributes of Calvin.[17]

Then the chief author of the Declaration of Independence who said that rights come from our Creator provides evidence for that Creator in His creation. He continues:

...I hold (without appeal to revelation) that when we take a view of the Universe, in its parts general or particular, it is impossible for the human mind not to percieve and feel a conviction of design, consummate skill, and indefinite power in every atom of it's composition...So irresistible are these evidences of an intelligent and powerful Agent that, of the infinite numbers of men who have existed thro' all time, they have believed, in the proportion of a million at least to Unit, in the hypothesis of an eternal pre-existence of a creator, rather than in that of a self-existent Universe. Surely this unanimous sentiment renders this more probable than that of the few in the other hypothesis...Jesus tells us that "God is a spirit." 4. John 24 [John 4:24]...and his doctrine of the Cosmogony [i.e. origins] of the world is very clearly laid down in the 3 first verses of the 1st. chapter of John..."in the beginning God existed, and reason (or mind) was with God, and that mind was God. This was in the beginning with God. All things were created by it, and without it was made not one thing which was made."[18]

Jefferson showed that he read the Bible extensively but then continued his criticism of Trinitarian theology:

---

17   Letter to John Adams, April 11, 1823. Beliles, *The Selected Religious Letters and Papers of Thomas Jefferson*, 343.

18   Ibid.

And the day will come when the mystical generation of Jesus, by the supreme being as his father in the womb of a virgin will be classed with the fable of the generation of Minerva in the brain of Jupiter...[19]

Despite these troubling statements rejecting the virgin birth and the misreading of John's Gospel Jefferson argued that even without the aid of revelation anyone should be able to believe in God's existence by looking at the intelligent design of the universe. Yet all of this was completely private thoughts between friends.

Peace With Presbyterians, Rejoining the Episcopal Church

Unitarians were not the only northern clergy in correspondence with Jefferson. He exchanged letters several times between 1819 and 1821 with a friendly Lutheran pastor of St. Matthews Church in New York City named Rev. Frederick Christian Schaeffer. An earlier letter discussed ideas on solving issues of poverty in the city, but then Rev. Schaeffer sent Jefferson a sermon he preached at the laying of the church's cornerstone in 1821. Jefferson replied saying he read it: "... with the pleasure it always gives him to see among all religious sects that spirit of toleration and brotherly affection which our weaknesses & wants so urgently & mutually call for..."[20]

Three different Jefferson letters in 1820 had criticized Presbyterians, the latest being a letter to Thomas Cooper where he expressed hope that Presbyterian opposition to the university would fade.[21] The leader of the opposition was the previously-mentioned Rev. John Holt Rice who lobbied the legislature on behalf of the university before leading the charge to get Cooper dismissed. Once Cooper was gone, in October, 1820, Rice made a donation of a book that included a letter to Jefferson expressing support for the university: "May it become an honour and a blessing to our native state, and a model for the literary establishments of others."[22] This was important, coming from the most influential religious figure in Virginia at the time.

---

19   Ibid.

20   Letter to Rev. Frederick C. Schaeffer, November 28, 1821. www.founders.archives.gov. Also see two letters from Rev. Schaeffer December 30, 1819 and November 19, 1821 along with Jefferson's previous reply January 7, 1820. All are found at www.founders.archives.gov.

21   Letter to Thomas Cooper, August 14, 1820. Beliles, *The Selected Religious Letters and Papers of Thomas Jefferson*, 314.

22   Letter from Rev. John Holt Rice, October 30, 1820. Beliles, *The Selected Religious Letters and Papers of Thomas Jefferson*, 317.

For the sake of the university, it was good that the strong condemnation Jefferson made of Presbyterians in some of his letters remained completely private and never known to them. Now at the very end of 1820, Jefferson puts the emotional disappointment behind him and replied to Rev. John Holt Rice with gratitude for his gift and then appealed for continuing support of the creation of the University of Virginia: "...I return you thanks for the donation and also for the friendly interest you are pleased to express for its success...I hope it will be recommended and conducted us to merit the continuation of your friendly dispositions toward it."[23] In light of his deep disappointment in the loss of Cooper, this was also a gracious effort by Jefferson.[24]

Despite the heterodoxy of private beliefs of Jefferson and the strong words towards Presbyterians, when an Episcopal clergyman finally settled in town to restart the church (having no minister since 1809), Jefferson is quick to recommit to it. Apparently the Episcopal Rev. John Bausman did not stay in the area permanently in 1818 as people hoped; however Jefferson's account book on February 25, 1820, said: "I subscribe 20 Dollars a year to the Revd. Mr. [Frederick] Hatch."[25] Rev. Hatch had been rector of a church in North Carolina and then Maryland, before coming to officiate in the Fredericksville Parish.

As was shown earlier, this subscription or pledge meant that Jefferson was an active member again in the Episcopal Church in Charlottesville. Jefferson began attending Christ Church regularly, bringing his prayer book with him to its services in the "union" frame meetinghouse.[26] As he resumed attendance, there is no evidence that Jefferson refused taking Holy Communion or reciting the liturgy of the Episcopal Church. This would include the regular practice of rising as a congregation and reciting the written Apostles' Creed hanging on the church wall. It is also worth noting that shortly after Jefferson's death in 1826, Jefferson's grandson, Thomas Jefferson Randolph, later a rector of the University of Virginia, wrote of his time while living with Jefferson, from 1815 to his death:

---

23   Letter to Rev. John Holt Rice, December 29, 1820. Beliles, *The Selected Religious Letters and Papers of Thomas Jefferson*, 318.

24   Account book, April 15, 1820. To J. H. Rice for subscription for book. The entry says: "Drew . . . 33.D. [$33.00] in favor of . . . Revd. John H. Rice for my subscription for 6. Copies of *Smith's hist. of Virga.*" Beliles, *The Selected Religious Letters and Papers of Thomas Jefferson*, 308.

25   Account book, February 25, 1820. Subscription for Hatch. Beliles, *The Selected Religious Letters and Papers of Thomas Jefferson*, 305. Also see page 317.

26   The prayer book at the library is the one that Jefferson's father used. Jefferson signed his name under his father's. Jefferson also bought another newer version of the Book of Common Prayer in later years.

I was more intimate with him than any man…His private apartments were open to me at all times, I saw him under all circumstances… He was regular in his attendance on church, taking his prayer book with him…[27]

Ironically, in some ways it appears that 1820 turns out to be the pinnacle of Jefferson's unorthodoxy. His writings do not show any major retreat from those views before he died, but clearly at this time he reasserted an orthopraxy – a regularity of participation and funding of traditional Trinitarian worship. This gave him access for the first time in a dozen years to an orthodox pastor and congregation with biblical liturgy, fellowship and influence.

The new minister of the Christ Episcopal Church in Charlottesville also conducted a school which had Jefferson's support. Jefferson's account book for March 13 states (in reference to his grandsons): "Entered Ben and Lewis with Mr. Hatch and gave him an order on B. Peyton for 50 Dollars being half a year's tuition fees."[28] In Rev. Hatch's Christian school the Bible was used as a textbook in class. Hatch reported on the progress of his grandsons' education saying that one of them completed a "…revision of his Greek & Latin Grammar, [and] has read about two books in the N Testament…"[29] A Christian classical education continued to be endorsed by Jefferson as it was throughout all his life.

Several letters also show Hatch to have more than merely a pastoral role, and he enjoyed a deepening friendship. Jefferson sent a letter to Rev. Hatch on January 8, 1823, to invite him to dinner at Monticello.[30] Another letter later in the year similarly said: "Th: Jefferson asks the favor of mr Hatch to dine at Monticello tomorrow (Saturday)."[31] Hatch was included in a special event very dear to Jefferson in 1824: "Th: Jefferson asks the favor of mr Hatch to dine at Monticello with Genl La

---

27 Henry S. Randall, *The Life of Thomas Jefferson*, 3 vols. (New York: Derby and Jackson, 1858), vol 3, 555. Also see William Henry Foote, *Sketches of Virginia, Historical and Biographical* (Philadelphia: William S. Martien, 1850).

28 Account book, March 13, 1821. For Hatch's school. There are annual payments to Hatch's school that are separate from donations to Hatch's ministry and the church. Beliles, *The Selected Religious Letters and Papers of Thomas Jefferson*, 321.

29 Letter from Rev. Frederick Hatch, December 19, 1823. The Thomas Jefferson Papers Series 1, General Correspondence, 1651-1827, Library of Congress Manuscript Division.

30 Letter to Rev. Frederick Hatch, February 8, 1823. The Thomas Jefferson Papers Series 1, General Correspondence, 1651-1827, Library of Congress Manuscript Division.

31 Letter to Rev. Frederick Hatch, September 26, 1823. The Thomas Jefferson Papers Series 1, General Correspondence, 1651-1827, Library of Congress Manuscript Division.

Fayette today Tuesday."[32] In early 1822, Rev. Hatch wrote that he could not accept an invitation to dine with Jefferson due to a wedding, but said: "He regrets this the more on account of the long suspension of that friendly intercourse from wh[ich] he has already derived no little satisfaction, & which he will improve the earliest opport[unit]y to renew..."[33] Another time Hatch wrote that: "...I had intended visiting you today but circumstances prevented." And Hatch asked Jefferson: "... will you do me the favor to make my house your Head quarters as a relief from the fatigues incident to a crowd, & take a family dinner with us."[34]

Unfortunately, almost nothing religious shows up in their correspondence since they could do that in person when dining at Monticello or in other meetings. But a few letters hint at such discussions when they shared literature on that topic. On September 9, 1821, Jefferson replied to Rev. Hatch saying: "I thank you, dear sir, for the volume of the LXX [i.e., the Greek translation of the Old Testament, known as the Septuagint] sent me..."[35] The Septuagint is named after 70 Hebrew-Greek scholars who finished their translation in the mid-second century before Christ. But one letter that is worthy of noting was from Hatch to Jefferson on May 1, 1824 which said: "...the Pamphlet which I now return...has been read by me with pleasure. Most of the sentiments contain'd in it are perfectly congenial with my own, tho' from others I am constrain'd to dissent. The introductory remarks to the sermon are truly excellent & eloquent; ..."[36] Here Jefferson's pastor let it be known that some views were not theologically right, but does not elaborate in the letter. They possibly discussed it more in detail in person. This exchange is important, for it shows that Hatch was not ignorant of any heterodoxy in Jefferson nor was he deliberately ignoring it just to maintain Jefferson's aid in other ways. Yet Hatch raises no serious concern that would call Jefferson's membership into question and indeed performed Jefferson's burial service a couple years later. He

---

32   Letter to Rev. Frederick Hatch, November 9, 1824. The Thomas Jefferson Papers Series 1, General Correspondence, 1651-1827, Library of Congress Manuscript Division. Another was sent two days later due to weather delaying the first. Letter to Rev. Frederick Hatch, November 11, 1824. www.founders.archives.gov.

33   Letter from Rev. Frederick Hatch, January 23, 1822. Beliles, *The Selected Religious Letters and Papers of Thomas Jefferson*, 323.

34   Hatch to Jefferson, March 3, 1824. Beliles, *The Selected Religious Letters and Papers of Thomas Jefferson*, 359.

35   Letter to Rev. Frederick Hatch, September 9, 1821. Beliles, *The Selected Religious Letters and Papers of Thomas Jefferson*, 321.

36   Hatch to Jefferson, May 1, 1824. Beliles, *The Selected Religious Letters and Papers of Thomas Jefferson*, 361.

apparently interpreted Jefferson's religious opinions in the same way as Rev. Clay had done previously.

Donations for Hatch and the Episcopal Church appeared each year in Jefferson's account book until his death (only a few are mentioned in this book). One example is on October 2, 1821, it said: "Gave…20 Dollars…for my subscription to Mr. Hatch for the current year."[37] In 1824 an entry in Jefferson's account book says he: "Gave Mr. Hatch…for 20 Dollars annual subscription."[38] Plus, besides annual donations for Hatch's ministry, Jefferson once wrote in 1821: "Inclosed to Revd. Mr. Hatch 20 Dollars as an Aid in building his house."[39] This latter donation for his house was explained in more detail by a letter from Jefferson to Rev. Hatch that day:

Dear Sir, In the antient Feudal times of our good old forefathers when the Seigneur married his daughter, or knighted his son, it was the usage for his vassals to give him a year's rent extra in the name of an *Aid*. I think it as reasonable when our pastor builds a house, that each of his flock should give him an aid of a year's contribution. I enclose mine…[40]

Jefferson's acknowledgement here that Hatch was "our pastor," and that he was a part of Hatch's Episcopal "flock," is more evidence that Jefferson was an official member and an enthusiastic one at that—with extra donations, invitations to the pastor to dinner at Monticello, and the like. It is intellectually irresponsible for modern biographers to say Jefferson was not part of a church when Jefferson clearly testified that he was.

Hatch told Jefferson in January 1822 that a clergyman "who has been already mentioned to you will do himself the pleasure to wait on you in a few days." It is not clear who the unnamed clergyman is that was going to visit. Apparently, many clergy would do so when in the area. In May Jefferson's letter to Hatch explains that he knew the Episcopal Church convention was bringing over a

37   Account book, October 2, 1821. Subscription for Hatch. Beliles, *The Selected Religious Letters and Papers of Thomas Jefferson*, 321.

38   Account book, February 12, 1824. Subscription for Hatch. Beliles, *The Selected Religious Letters and Papers of Thomas Jefferson*, 359.

39   Account book, December 8, 1821. For Hatch's house. Beliles, *The Selected Religious Letters and Papers of Thomas Jefferson*, 322.

40   Letter to Rev. Frederick Hatch, December 8, 1821. Beliles, *The Selected Religious Letters and Papers of Thomas Jefferson*, 322. Also see http://www.monticello.org/site/research-and-collections/frederick-hatch - _note-7.

thousand clergy to town, and Jefferson wanted to help Rev. Hatch to cover any extra expenses so he gave 20 dollars. Jefferson also added that he would not be in town:

> … I should have gladly profited of that occasion of manifesting my respect to that body, with some of whose members I may probably be acquainted, but it seems…my place is considered as among the curiosities of the neighborhood, and that it will probably be visited as much by most of the attendants. I have neither strength nor spirits to encounter such a stream of strangers from day to day, and must therefore avoid it…[41]

Jefferson does not skip town because of animosity or conflict with Episcopal clergymen in Virginia, but because of the anticipated crush of visits from them. Clergy from various denominations respected Jefferson and sought to visit him. Sometimes they went through Jefferson's pastor Rev. Hatch to secure a meeting with him. Hatch wrote Jefferson on April 22, 1824, as follows: "Dear Sir, The Rev. Mr [William?] McMahon from Alabama, an intelligent gentleman, with two of his friends, Ministers of the Methodist Church;…has express'd to me a wish to call for a few minutes at Monticello to see its grounds & make his respects to yourself. I could do no less than to name him to you, & to express to you by the occasion my best wishes & prayers for your present & eternal [___]. Very respect & affect'y."[42] The general stereotype today that clergy and Jefferson did not get along is obviously exaggerated and erroneous.

Charlottesville Religious Developments

Sometime in 1822, South Plains Presbyterian Church in Keswick, Virginia, near Charlottesville and Monticello finally obtained a resident minister named Francis Bowman, a native of Vermont and a Princeton graduate. Another pastor helping him was Rev. Benjamin Holt Rice, brother of John Holt Rice of Richmond. Rev. Bowman became a friend of Jefferson who worked with him on the local committee to establish a public library (1823). Baptists had also started meeting in town so now Charlottesville had regular Episcopal, Presbyterian, and Baptist

---

41   Letter to Rev. Frederick Hatch, May 12, 1822. Beliles, *The Selected Religious Letters and Papers of Thomas Jefferson*, 326. Also see Account Book, May 12, 1822. Beliles, *The Selected Religious Letters and Papers of Thomas Jefferson*, 326.

42   Hatch to Jefferson, April 22, 1824. Beliles, *The Selected Religious Letters and Papers of Thomas Jefferson*, 359.

congregations operating locally again, all sharing space in the Union meetinghouse or the courthouse.

Jefferson in 1822 criticized the religious revivalism he heard about and yet praised the Union services in his town saying:

> ... In our Richmond there is much fanaticism, but chiefly among the women. They have their night meetings and praying parties, where, attended by their priests, and sometimes by a hen-pecked husband, they pour forth the effusions of their love to Jesus, in terms as amatory and carnal, as their modesty would permit them to use to a mere earthly lover. In our village of Charlottesville, there is a good degree of religion, with a small spice only of fanaticism. We have four sects, but without either church or meeting-house. [Note: The Union meetinghouse had just been demolished]. The court-house is the common temple, one Sunday in the month to each. Here, Episcopalian and Presbyterian, Methodist and Baptist, meet together, join in hymning their Maker, listen with attention and devotion to each others' preachers, and all mix in society with perfect harmony.[43]

Indeed all the traditional evangelical churches in town were growing. The Union meetinghouse in Charlottesville had just been bought by Sarah Gilmer about this time, who gave it to the Episcopalians. They then tore it down to begin building a new structure (Christ Church) on the site – where a third church building sits to this day. Because of this, all the Union services had to be moved to the Albemarle County Courthouse.[44]

Jefferson loved attending all the church services and despite mistrust of some Scripture, Jefferson wrote to Jacob Engelbrecht at that time saying he knew of "... nothing more moral, more sublime, more worthy of your preservation than David's description of the good man, in his 15th Psalm..."[45] In this letter, Jefferson quotes

---

43   Letter to Thomas Cooper, November 2, 1822. Beliles, *The Selected Religious Letters and Papers of Thomas Jefferson*, 337.

44   Jennie Grayson, "Old Christ Church," in *Magazine of Albemarle County History*, (1947-1948), VIII: 27-37. Originally printed in *The Parish Register*, 1918-1923.

45   Letter to Jacob Engelbrecht, February 25, 1824. Beliles, *The Selected Religious Letters and Papers of Thomas Jefferson*, 360.

the whole psalm. This letter was in response to one from Engelbrecht requesting a letter on "anything moral, religious or political."[46]

A letter from Rev. Hatch on February 22, 1824 has very interesting information about the local church history in Charlottesville and Jefferson's own connection to it all. It shows the effort for a new Union meetinghouse to be erected, which Jefferson wished to happen. Remember that the first Union meetinghouse was bought by the Episcopalians and torn down in 1822. Instead of just building their own exclusive building, much discussion had occurred about building a nicer Union building. But Hatch's letter to Jefferson shows that it was thwarted, with the result being Rev. Hatch turned toward building an Episcopal place of worship:

> Our plans for a Church [i.e., a new Union church building], which it was thought promis'd well, have all fail'd. The meeting (of the citizens)... appointed a Committee to select a site for...a Free Church...[with] Trustees consisting of six, in which body each of the four denominations existing among us sh[oul]d be entitled to a single representative...elected by the subscribers.

Rev. Hatch then laments that the attempt for a non-denominational meeting house in Charlottesville failed. He continues:

> In consequence of the unpopularity of the propos'd subscription & the assurances of its failure...I have determin'd to build a Church...The public sentiment is with us & with the blessing of He'ven we shall succeed...Only do not say to me "relinquish the plan." My heart is very deeply engag'd in it, & for its success, I am willing to pledge a servitude of at least two long years of my life, shd it be thus far protracted & be found necessary. I will forward to you a plan of the building for your approbation as soon as it comes to hand, but would prefer receiving from you a draft...& I trust that the interest which you have taken in it will ever be remember'd as a subject of pleasing reflection...
> F W Hatch
> P.S. I have omitted to solicit your [i.e., Jefferson's] aid & countenance for my Church, which, with the explanation given, was the object of my letter – I know the plan does not meet your views – but when you consider

---

46   Letter from Jacob Engelbrecht, February 14, 1824. The Thomas Jefferson Papers Series 1, General Correspondence, 1651-1827, Library of Congress Manuscript Division.

how seldom it is that two families in a house can agree & how low – how very low our poor Church has fallen, I hope you will not think the present cause unworthy of your notice & approbation.[47]

Although it is apparent that Jefferson wanted the denominations to stay united in a building project, Hatch informs him it is no longer possible and asks Jefferson to support the Episcopal church in this new direction: "...For a plan of a Church that might be built for $2,500 [$60,000 today] we would be much oblig'd to you, & for your subscription..."[48] Five days later on March 8, 1824, Jefferson noted in his account book not only a gift to his Episcopal church for their building, but also for two other denominations: "I have subscribed to the building an Episcopalian church 200 Dollars, a Presbyterian 60, a Baptist 25."[49] In today's dollars these would be $4,800, $1,400 and $600. Jefferson would apparently have made one combined donation to a union building but now splits his donations into three parts.

A Mr. "Maury" was mentioned by Hatch as part of the building planning, and his son Jesse Maury, a teenager at the time, remembered what happened and later told the following:

Some gentlemen who were Presbyterians suggested getting subscriptions to build a hall that could be used by all denominations, or for general religious gatherings. The idea was well received, especially by Mr. Jefferson. A meeting was held to decide on the details; [and] "there the trouble began."... Mr. Jefferson and all the other prominent Episcopalians followed Mr. Hatch...Mr. Jefferson himself subscribed $300...[and served] on the building committee...[50]

---

47 Letter from Rev. Frederick Hatch, February 22, 1824. Beliles, *The Selected Religious Letters and Papers of Thomas Jefferson*, 359-360.

48 Hatch to Jefferson, March 3, 1824. Beliles, *The Selected Religious Letters and Papers of Thomas Jefferson*, 359.

49 Account book, 8, March 1824. For building Episcopalian, Presbyterian and Baptist churches. Beliles, *The Selected Religious Letters and Papers of Thomas Jefferson*, 362.

50 Jennie Grayson, "Old Christ Church," in *Magazine of Albemarle County History*, 8 (Charlottesville, Va.: Albemarle County Historical Society, 1947-48). Originally printed in *The Parish Register* 1918-1923, 27-37. Maury also said that it was Jefferson who was "... insisting that, contrary to the aristocratic custom of the time, the [pews] should be 'benches, without doors, and free so that people may be seated without regard to class or condition, pell mell, as they shall lie in death.'"

Jefferson's account book says on February 22, 1826 that he gave: "installment [for] Church," meaning the donation for building Christ Church.[51] The new church was completed before Jefferson's death and he probably worshiped in it but the formal consecration of the structure took place after his passing when the bishop came to town. The Trinitarian congregation of Hatch and Jefferson would regularly recite the Apostles' Creed which, with Jefferson's financial help, was displayed at the altar.

Of course, the creed included words about the Father, Son and Holy Ghost, and that after being crucified *"he rose again from the dead."* In that light it is interesting that on March 24, 1824, Jefferson wrote Federal Judge Augustus Woodward, saying: "...Indeed, Jesus Himself,...teaches expressly that the body is to rise in substance. In the Apostles' Creed, we all declare that we believe in the 'resurrection of the body.'"[52] Here Jefferson seems to affirm the teachings of Jesus on resurrection and references the Apostles' Creed that his church used each week, and when he says "we all declare," it appears he includes himself. If he did not participate in the liturgy, he would have written that "they all declare." At the very least, in this letter he declines to disassociate himself from the creed which affirmed the resurrection of Christ and also clearly states belief in God the Father, Son and Holy Ghost. A few months later Jefferson wrote to Major John Cartwright about Christianity allegedly not being part of the Common Law of England, mentioned God, and used the word "Christ" when referring to Jesus, thus implying again a view of him as more than simply human.[53]

All of this perhaps is evidence that Jefferson's views were moderating slightly now that he was worshiping in an orthodox congregation again. It is hard to say definitively because all private letters in his declining years should be considered with caution (as previously noted regarding some heterodox letters). But just as the nuanced Syllabus in 1803 led us to mark a transition point in Jefferson's life, his new commitment to his church along with these letters equally qualify to indicate this final phase.

---

51   Account book, February 22, 1826. "installment church." Beliles, *The Selected Religious Letters and Papers of Thomas Jefferson*, 375.

52   Letter to Augustus Woodward, March 24, 1824. Beliles, *The Selected Religious Letters and Papers of Thomas Jefferson*, 364.

53   Letter to John Cartwright, June 5, 1824. The Thomas Jefferson Papers Series 1, General Correspondence, 1651-1827, Library of Congress Manuscript Division.

Religious Policy at the University of Virginia

Besides Jefferson's personal development, religion was also being addressed by the Board of Visitors of the University of Virginia, led by Jefferson. They decided in their meeting of October 7, 1822 to do something to overcome the reluctance of evangelicals to send their students to it. People still mischaracterized the university as being unorthodox or non-religious so the board wanted to clarify that they were nothing more than non-denominational in their policies. They addressed their policy to not have a divinity professor saying:

> ...It was not, however, to be understood that instruction in religious opinion and duties was meant to be precluded by the public authorities, as indifferent to the interests of society. On the contrary, the relations which exist between man and his maker, and the duties resulting from those relations are the most interesting and important to every human being, and the most incumbent on his study and investigation.

Religion is the "most important" of subjects, but they want to make sure it is taught while keeping one denomination or theological viewpoint from gaining predominance over the others. Jefferson and the Board continue:

> A remedy however has been suggested of promising aspect...to give to the sectarian schools of divinity the full benefit the public provisions made for instruction in the other branches of science...[We invite them] to establish their religious schools on the confines of the University, ... Such establishments would offer the further and greater advantage of enabling the students of the University to attend religious exercises with the professor of their particular sect, either in the rooms of the building still to be erected [i.e., the Rotunda], and destined to that purpose under impartial regulations, as proposed in the same report of the commissioners, or in the lecturing room of such professor...Such an arrangement ...would fill the chasm now existing, on principles which would leave inviolate the constitutional freedom of religion, the most inalienable and sacred of all human rights...[54]

---

54   Report to the President and Directors of the Literary Fund, October 7, 1822. Beliles, *The Selected Religious Letters and Papers of Thomas Jefferson*, 334.

A few months earlier William Short wrote to Jefferson from Philadelphia inquiring about the university and said: "It is said here that a disposition hostile to the University is growing up in the State, principally from the increasing influence of the Presbyterian preachers."[55] Jefferson replied on October 19 (just shortly after the above policy was decided) saying:

> Our enemies are in the vicinage of Wm. & Mary, to whom are added the Presbyterian clergy. This is rather the most numerous of our present sects, and the most ambitious, the most intolerant & tyrannical of all our sects… Unitarianism has not yet reached us, but our citizens are ready to recieve reason from any quarter. …such would gather into their fold every *man* under the age of 40. *Female* fanaticism might hold out awhile longer.[56]

Jefferson's private opinions of women and older persons in matters of religion was certainly condescending. It was already noted that Jefferson and the leading Presbyterian in Virginia made efforts in late 1820 (after the job offer to professor Cooper was rescinded) to restore their partnership for the university but apparently there were still many others in opposition that stirred Jefferson's private harsh comments. Shortly after this, he explained the university's recent decision in a letter to Thomas Cooper, saying: "In our university you know there is no Professorship of Divinity. A handle has been made of this, to disseminate an idea that this is an institution, not merely of no religion, but against all religion." Jefferson explained that the board adopted "an idea that might silence this calumny" (i.e., slander) by inviting and "…encouraging the different religious sects" and giving them access to the university facilities and "…every other accommodation we can give them…."[57]

A few months later Jefferson's reply to Thomas Cooper provided additional commentary by Jefferson on the situation with clergy opposing the University. He said of priestcraft:

> …here their effort has been to represent ours as an anti-religious institution. We disarmed them of this calumny, however in our last report by inviting

---

55   Letter from William Short, July 2, 1822. Beliles, *The Selected Religious Letters and Papers of Thomas Jefferson*, 330.

56   Letter to William Short, October 19, 1822. Beliles, *The Selected Religious Letters and Papers of Thomas Jefferson*, 336. [Emphasis his]

57   Letter to Thomas Cooper, November 2, 1822. Beliles, *The Selected Religious Letters and Papers of Thomas Jefferson*, 337.

the different sects to establish their respective divinity schools on the margin of the grounds of the University…one sect, I think, may do it, but another, disdaining equality, ambitioning nothing less than a soaring ascendancy, will despise our invitation. They are hostile to all educn of which they have not the direction, and foresee that this instn, by enlightening the minds of the people and encouraging them to appeal to their own common sense is to dispel the fanaticism on which their power is built…[58]

The denominations really started considering this invitation, and one of the most interesting of letters from Pastor Hatch to Jefferson was to inform him of the interest that Episcopalians had in the university. Rev. Hatch gave a full report of the thoughts of Episcopal leaders in this regard:

By a letter which I have just receiv'd from one of the Trustees of our Theological school I am inform'd that a proposition has been made by a part of the Ep. Clergy of Maryland, to unite their influence & funds with ours of Virginia with a view to extending the influence & increasing the means of the establishment.

….I was well covinc'd at the last Convention that a very favorable disposition towards this place existed in the minds of the Clergy generally & the Trustees…I feel pretty confident that very little is wanting to cause the scale to preponderate in our favor, & I flatter myself that the Church & University will derive mutually essential benefits from this location…[59]

Episcopalians certainly did not seem deterred from associating their seminary with Jefferson's university. And Presbyterians were also looking seriously at doing the same in Charlottesville. At this time local Presbyterian minister Rev. Benjamin H. Rice, brother of Rev. John Holt Rice (who had led the Presbyterians to support the creation of the University of Virginia and then the subsequent protest of Cooper), sends a letter to Jefferson after having met him in person previously. He expresses the intentions of Presbyterians to start a seminary somewhere and that they were considering responding to the appeal that Jefferson and the Board of the University had made the previous year. The letter is here in part below:

---

58   Letter to Thomas Cooper, April 12, 1823. www.founders.archives.gov.
59   Letter from Rev. Frederick Hatch, July 1, 1823. Beliles, *The Selected Religious Letters and Papers of Thomas Jefferson*, 347.

...When I did myself the pleasure of calling on you it was my purpose not to solicit your to aid...But the approbation which you appeared to me to manifest of our designs has led to the hope that you may be willing to give some further token of your good will...I know that there are strong prejudices against the church of which I am a member and in whose behalf I plead, but Sir, like all other prejudices they are unsupported by reason...

Rice also mentions that "we have been suspected of desiring an establishment [i.e., a government-favored status]...This however is an unwarranted suspicion... We do not desire it & we never did desire it." These accusations against the Presbyterians are false, he notes. Historically, he said, Presbyterianism was the least likely to create an established church. Jefferson noted in 1776 that "the Presbyterian spirit is known to be congenial with friendly liberty..."[60] As King James I once said, "Presbytery agreeth with monarchy like God with the Devil."[61] Rev. Rice continues with Presbyterians' response to the University board's invitation:

...Our plan is, in relation to a Theological Seminary, to erect an institution and a president of all literary [institutions?] in which there shall be three professorships, one of Oriental languages, and of Ecclesiastical History and church polity, and one of didactic Theology. We wish to have it near some college...I herewith send a subscription paper which I must hope will be returned with your name. Your compliance with this request will greatly oblige a respectable body of Christians, but none more than the Agent of the Presbytery, Who is your servant, Respectfully, B. H. Rice[62]

Rev. Rice also added a postscript saying, "If my dear Sir, you should condescend to reply to this communication, please to send your answer to the care of Mr. Bowman, Charlottesville." This letter is very interesting because Rev. Rice was one of the pastors, along with Rev. Francis Bowman, of the new local Presbyterian Church. Rice invites Jefferson to make a donation to support the Presbyterian theological school. Since Jefferson's criticism of Presbyterians and Calvinism was not ever public—only via private letters—Rice probably never knew it but made

---

60   "Notes on Religion," 1776. Ibid, 383.

61   King James I quoted in Paul Carlson, *Our Presbyterian Heritage* (Elgin, IL: David C. Cook, 1973), 13.

62   Letter from Rev. Benjamin H. Rice, August 8, 1823. Beliles, *The Selected Religious Letters and Papers of Thomas Jefferson*, 348-349.

a defense of Presbyterians anyway. Benjamin H. Rice later became the national Moderator of the Presbyterians in 1829, as his brother, John Holt Rice had a decade earlier.

Does it seem logical that a Presbyterian leader of his caliber would ever have invited Jefferson to support a Calvinistic Presbyterian ministry if there was any real knowledge in the public of Jefferson's unorthodoxy or of Jefferson's condemnation of Virginia churches and clergy? The reality is that Jefferson's unorthodox persona spread today by modern biographers, relying on unsent letters and documents, was simply unknown or not believed by Virginians. (They dismissed what they heard during the 1800 election as spurious and politically-motivated. And Jefferson's attendance and generous donations to churches was likely known to them.)

When Jefferson replies to Rice and declines Rice's financial appeal, he does so in a notable way—not by asserting independence or dissonance with orthodox Christianity, but doing almost the opposite by affirming his Episcopal membership. In his August 10, 1823 letter he writes:

> ...I have been from my infancy a member of the Episcopalian Church and to that I owe and make my contributions. Were I to go beyond that limit in favor of any other sectarian institution I should be equally bound to do so for every other, and their number is beyond the faculties of any individual...I trust that your candor will excuse my returning the enclosed paper without my subscription...[63]

Even though here Jefferson declined supporting the Presbyterian Church's theological school, he did so with respect, and just seven months later Jefferson gave a donation for the local Presbyterian church to erect their building. Jefferson was also comfortable enough with the local pastor, Rev. Francis Bowman, to invite him to officiate at a Monticello funeral the very next month after this letter.[64] Although some clergy had opposed Cooper as a professor at the university, still to this point in Jefferson's life, there had yet to be a single instance of any Virginia clergyman attacking or even questioning Jefferson's personal religious beliefs. The letters of Rev. Hatch and Rev. Rice on behalf of their respective denominations shows their continuing positive opinion of Jefferson.

63   Letter to Rev. Benjamin Rice, August 10, 1823. Beliles, *The Selected Religious Letters and Papers of Thomas Jefferson*, 349.

64   Account book, September 17, 1823. Beliles, *The Selected Religious Letters and Papers of Thomas Jefferson*, 349. And Letter to Rev. Francis Bowman, September 23, 1823. www.founders.archives.gov.

Meanwhile the Board of Visitors—including Jefferson, James Madison and James Monroe—continued their efforts to rebuild trust with their Christian constituents. Their "Regulations for the University" that Jefferson drafted on October 4, 1824 said: "...one of [the Rotunda's] large elliptical rooms on its middle floor shall be used for...religious worship [and]...the students of the University will be free, and expected to attend."[65] Although a collaborative process, Jefferson was a leading part of drafting this regulation and therefore it shows his affirmation of state facilities being used for religion, but a later more in-depth chapter on the university clarifies his guidelines for it.

Classes commenced at the University of Virginia in 1825, and the denominations still were using the courthouse in turn, so a natural question arose needing clarification when a couple of the local churches asked to use the Rotunda for their weekly worship services in similar fashion. Jefferson had already shown approval in Washington of government buildings being used for Christian worship and in the local Charlottesville courthouse for same, so people thought it would be true in the state university buildings. But Jefferson, in a letter to the University Proctor, Arthur Brockenbrough, clarifies that the university buildings should not be used for worship by non-students (i.e., local churches), although religious services for students were permitted and expected.[66]

Besides the application of religious freedom to the University's policies, he also advocated it for other nations. In replying to a gentleman from Greece he explained the common ideas of the American nation, saying: "I have stated that the constitutions of our several states vary more or less in some particulars. But there are certain principles in which all agree, and which all cherish as vitally essential to the protection of the life, liberty, property and safety of the citizen." Then Jefferson began listing the key principles of which number one was: "Freedom of religion, restricted only from acts of trespass on that of others." Then he added four more: "Freedom of person...Trial by jury...the Exclusive right of legislation and taxation in the Representatives of the people, [and] Freedom of the Press." Then Jefferson concluded his letter saying, "...we offer to heaven the warmest supplications for the restoration of your countrymen to the freedom and science of their ancestors..."[67]

---

65   Regulations for the University [of Virginia], October 4, 1824. Beliles, *The Selected Religious Letters and Papers of Thomas Jefferson*, 368.

66   Letter to the University Proctor, Arthur Brockenbrough, April 21, 1825. Beliles, *The Selected Religious Letters and Papers of Thomas Jefferson*, 373. Emphasis added.

67   Letter to Adamantios Coray, October 31, 1823. www.founders.archives.gov

Final Years of Jefferson's Religious Life

In his closing years Jefferson continued to express his religious faith in various letters. He replied to Richard Bruce regarding the mementous events of the American Revolution saying, "...as Providence intended that such events should take place, we should be thankful they were destined for our times and we chosen as instrunts for effecting them."[68]

In a letter to William Carver Jefferson described himself as "a devoted friend myself to freedom of religious enquiry and opinion, I am pleased to see others exercise the right without reproach or censure; and I respect their conclusions, however different from my own." Jefferson again linked reason and God:

"Then it is their own reason, not mine, nor that of any other, which has been given them by their Creator for the investigation of truth, and of the evidences even of those truths which are presented to us as revealed by himself. Fanaticism, it is true, is not sparing of her invectives against those who refuse blindly to follow her dictates in abandonment of their own reason. For the use of this reason however every one is responsible to the God who has planted it in his breast, as a light for his guidance, and that, by which alone, he will be judged."[69]

Besides his own university Jefferson's name had been given to another educational institution called Jefferson College. In reply to a literary society at that college Jefferson offered his: "...prayers for their success and exhortations to perseverance. The cultiv[atio]n of science is an act of religious duty to the Author of our being who gave us the talent of superior mind not to be hid under a bushel but to raise us to that eminence of intellect which may prepare us for the future state of blessedness which he destines to those who render themselves worthy of it."[70]

To P. B. Tindal Jefferson replied saying, "...I am pleased with every effort to restore the primitive and genuine doctrines of Jesus, and to overturn the corruptions which have been introduced solely to answer the worldly purposes of those who preach them."[71] And Lydia Sigourney, a strongly religious poet in Connecticut, wrote to Jefferson regarding the condition of Indians in 1824 and Jefferson replied saying that

---

68   Richard Bruce to Jefferson. February 17, 1823 and Jefferson's Letter to Richard Bruce, February 19, 1823. www.founders.archives.gov.

69   Letter from William Carver, November 25, 1823 and Jefferson Letter to William Carver, December 4, 1823. www.founders.archives.gov.

70   Letter to Ira Taylor, Benjamin Nourse, and John Tidball of the Franklin Literary Society of Jefferson College, March 8, 1824. www.founders.archives.gov.

71   Letter from P. B. Tindall, April 13, 1824 and Jefferson Letter to P. B. Tindall, April 20, 1824. www.founders.archives.gov.

he looked: "...to the dispensations of an all-wise and all-powerful providence to devise the means of effecting what is right..."[72]

In late December 1824 Jefferson received a letter and pamphlet from Congregationalist Rev. Benjamin Hale about an educational project up north, and Jefferson replied with approval.[73] Unitarian Rev. Waterhouse sent another letter to Jefferson at that same time.[74] Now Jefferson replied to this Unitarian clergyman: "[In the university] There remains therefore no place in which we can avail ourselves of the services of the revd. Mr. Bertrum as a teacher. I wish we could do it as a Preacher. I am anxious to see the doctrine of one God commenced in our State...I must therefore be contented to be an Unitarian by myself..."[75] This is the first time, just a year and a half shy of his death, that Jefferson actually called himself a Unitarian. It was still in a private letter so no one in the public knew it, and he remained an active member and donor of the Christ Episcopal Church, which was Trinitarian. Although it was the first time to use the Unitarian label for himself, he implied as much in a number of other letters since 1813 or arguably even 1803. Saying he was "by myself" obviously did not refer to church, for he most certainly had a congregation that he frequented, so he must have meant that Charlottesville lacked a self-described Unitarian church. There were Restoration "Christian" churches in Central Virginia with similar theological leanings, but none started in the town of Charlottesville itself (that would occur a few years after Jefferson's death with the founding of the first "Church of Christ" with connections to Alexander Campbell). Again, when modern commentators highlight this statement, they should also counterbalance it with his active Trinitarian church membership that is now made clear.

In the year before his death, Jefferson informed Thomas Jefferson Smith that he did not accept the book of Revelation as inspired by God, and he did so in a way that was very derogatory toward the content of the last book of the Bible. Meanwhile, he apparently did view the Psalms with high regard and said: "...Adore God. Reverence and cherish your parents. Love your neighbor as yourself, and your country more than yourself. Be just. Be true. Murmur not at the ways of Providence. So shall the life into which you have entered, be the portal to one of eternal and

---

72   Letter to Lydia H. H. Sigourney, July 18, 1824. www.founders.archives.gov.

73   Letter from Benjamin Hale, November 19, 1824 and Letter to Benjamin Hale, December 6, 1824. www.founders.archives.gov.

74   Letter from Rev. Benjamin Waterhouse, December 20, 1824. The Thomas Jefferson Papers Series 1, General Correspondence, 1651-1827, Library of Congress Manuscript Division.

75   Letter to Rev. Benjamin Waterhouse, January 8, 1825. Beliles, *The Selected Religious Letters and Papers of Thomas Jefferson*, 370.

ineffable bliss…"[76] Jefferson then enclosed a poem based on Psalm 15. In 1826 Jefferson declined an invitation to celebrate the approaching 50th anniversary of the Declaration of Independence and said that "…the few surviving signers of [that] memorable instrument…owe indeed peculiar thanks to Providence…"[77] When Jefferson died on July 4th, a great-granddaughter there reported that Jefferson quoted the Gospel of Luke ("Lord, now lettest thou thy servant depart in peace") and said as he was dying: "I now resign my soul, without fear, to my God."[78] Then Rev. Hatch performed the Episcopal burial service at Monticello.[79]

Summary of All Of Jefferson's Adult Years, 1762-1826

Before proceeding to the next section of this book that looks at the same material but in a more topical way, it is important to look back at what was discovered. In reading about a thousand letters to and from Jefferson that have religious information, plus about another 100 entries from his memorandum books, five religious phases of his adult life seemed to appear. The first phase spanned about 25 years and showed nothing that proves him to be anything but an orthodox believer. Then in 1788 a second phase emerged with a letter that said he did not comprehend the Trinity while maintaining involvement in orthodox churches. In 1803, a third phase seemed to appear when Jefferson clearly said "I am a Christian" but began expressing agreement with Joseph Priestley and a belief in the corruptions of the original Christian faith. The fourth phase began in 1813 with Jefferson's first clear rejection of the Trinity and other fundamental doctrines in private letters. In 1820 the final phase began with his recommitment to the Episcopal church even while identifying himself privately as a Unitarian in theology.

For 65 years as an adult, there is hard evidence of Thomas Jefferson being involved in church for at least 80 percent of the time (virtually 100 percent when it was available), and indirect evidence and eye-witness testimony of his attendance in other years. (Basically, when church was available to him, he was there.). Even

---

76   Letter to Thomas Jefferson Smith, February 21, 1825. Beliles, *The Selected Religious Letters and Papers of Thomas Jefferson*, 372. Almost the exact same words were in a previous letter to another namesake. See: Letter to Thomas Jefferson Grotjan, January 10, 1824. www. founders.archives.gov.

77   Letter to Jacob Taylor and the Corporation of the City of New York, June 8, 1826. www. founders.archives.gov.

78   Randall, *The Life of Thomas Jefferson*. Also see William Henry Foote, *Sketches of Virginia, Historical and Biographical* (Philadelphia: William S. Martien, 1850), 68.

79   Woods, *Albemarle County in Virginia*, 127. Jefferson's minister later went on to become a chaplain in Congress. Woods also has a humorous story about Rev. Hatch on pages 128-129.

in years lacking hard proof of attendance, there is still plenty of evidence of prayer and Bible study, etc.; plus he says in various times that he worshiped somewhere (i.e., in Philadelphia at Priestley's Unitarian church) when contemporary records are not found for it.

Plus, if he had not attended church in some periods, such as when he was governor (1779-1781) in Williamsburg (at Bruton Parish Church, where you can visit to this day and see where he sat) or in Richmond (at St. John's Episcopal Church), it would have likely generated some comment in the press or private letters. Since it did not, it seems likely that he attended worship at that time also. The periods when he was not attending any one church regularly were those where regular Episcopalian worship was not available to him—when he was in France and during the time after his presidency until a church was re-established near his home (1809-1819). (When it was re-established a few years before his death, he then attended and committed his financial resources to support the church.)

Jefferson never expressed an explicit heterodox belief for at least the first 40 of his adult years and perhaps 50. And even then his growing sympathy with Unitarianism was not expressed publicly, and he still worshiped in traditional orthodox churches.[80] But it is clear that Jefferson's religious beliefs were constantly developing and nuanced and easily misunderstood if taken out of context. Hopefully, these chronological chapters have helped to restore that context before attempting to analyze Jefferson's religious life in a topical thematic way.

---

80   Orthodox is a term defined by the core doctrines of historic Christianity, generally articulated in the Creeds.

PART II

THE TRUE RELIGIOUS LEGACY OF THOMAS JEFFERSON

Jefferson's 1804 letter to Methodist camp-meeting revivalist Rev. Henry Fry. The Piedmont area in Virginia where Thomas Jefferson and James Madison lived was a hotbed of evangelical revivalism during their lifetimes. They both were heroes to the evangelicals of Virginia for their fight for religious liberty (Courtesy of the Library of Congress).

INTRODUCTION TO THE TRUE RELIGIOUS LEGACY

"…on the faces of the Obelisk the following inscription, & not a word more— 'Here was buried Thomas Jefferson, Author of the Declaration of American Independence, of the Statute of Virginia for religious freedom, Father of the University of Virginia'—because by these…I wish most to be remembered."
—Thomas Jefferson[1]

To this point the religious life of Jefferson has been examined as it developed chronologically. There has been no attempt to make any conclusions or deal with any topics in-depth. The three-part true legacy of Jefferson which he suggested that he be remembered for on his own gravestone will be the focus of the next section of this book.

Visible Evidence of History

Shortly after Jefferson's death in 1826 the Christ Episcopal Church, built with donations and apparently architectural help from Jefferson, was dedicated by the bishop of Virginia. Although a newer sanctuary stands there today, a visitor can

---

1   Jefferson's undated memorandum on epitaph, Thomas Jefferson Papers, Library of Congress.

still see (in another part of the church) the original reredos, i.e., the writings on the back wall behind the altar (apparently there in Jefferson's time) that included the Ten Commandments, the Lord's Prayer, and the Apostles' Creed. And a few blocks away stands the courthouse where Jefferson worshiped most of his life. Earlier there he personally organized a Calvinistical Reformed congregation led by the evangelical Rev. Clay, and later shared Sundays approvingly with various denominations, and sometimes even arranged services there for a traveling preacher (such as Presbyterian John Glendy).

Also nearby in downtown Charlottesville today is First Church of Christ (i.e., the Christian Church) that began shortly after Jefferson's death by those who were part of the Restoration movement. It was non-creedal and accepted non-Trinitarians at first but eventually returned to Trinitarianism as did most such churches. But its building still stands in the city as a reminder of the once dominant mostly non-Trinitarian Restoration movement that had partially shaped Jefferson's views and many others in his lifetime.

When Jefferson was alive, a visitor to Monticello would have found forty percent of the artwork in his home dealing with the Bible in some way. He had at least 28 paintings pertaining to Christian or biblical characters in the hall, parlor and dining room.[2] That means that virtually on a daily basis, he surrounded himself with biblical themes. Unfortunately, the artwork that has been recovered and on display today are not as religious, but are of Enlightenment figures and the like in such distorted proportion as to create an impression that is different than what a person visiting Monticello would have formed in Jefferson's time.

And similarly the local religious history of Jefferson's Central Virginia Piedmont is now largely left out of most studies and discussions of Jefferson. This local religious history, uncovered through little noticed and just recently-published letters and papers of Jefferson, have served as clues for us—as many "holes in the floor" that have led us to go down beneath the surface of conventional biographies and discover new things about the religious life of Thomas Jefferson. Many positive relationships and activities with orthodox churches were revealed in this process.

The reality is that Jefferson was a hero to many evangelicals in his day. And in fact, when Jefferson died, Congress requested Rev. William Staughton, the Senate Chaplain and Baptist clergyman who had corresponded with Jefferson in 1806 (and

---

2   Transcription from Seymour Howard, "Thomas Jefferson's Art Gallery for Monticello" *The Art Bulletin* LIX(1977): 597-600. The original manuscript is at the Albert and Shirley Small Special Collections Library, University of Virginia, Accession #2958-b. Jesus was in thirteen of the paintings in the three public rooms.

president of what is now George Washington University), to preach a sermon to a joint session of the Senate and House. Jefferson was defended in this eulogy as a believer by an orthodox evangelical, not by a Unitarian, Deist or some heterodox or secular representative. This Christian image was the prevailing perspective of Jefferson at his death because of his public orthopraxy and strictly private heterodoxy.

Documents Less Reliable For Understanding Jefferson

Having completed the study of reliable sources to make an analysis of the phases of Jefferson's religious life, it is worth mentioning that some documents were briefly noted in the narrative but were not discussed fully. These, for various reasons, are deemed less reliable for making conclusions about Jefferson's religious beliefs, but will be discussed more now.

The first category of less reliable sources would relate to any documents or actions he was party to drafting or approving while serving in the Virginia legislature or in the Continental Congress. These documents often mention God and endorse various policies. But since they are done in a collaborative process, there are some parts he may have objected to but ended up supporting anyway. There is no way of knowing unless he specifically wrote a comment to that effect. To these are added actions while Jefferson served as Governor and as President. As chief executive he had more leeway, yet perhaps went along with some things out of mere convention or custom that he did not feel strongly enough opposed to stop it. He certainly showed himself willing to change precedent in regards to presidential prayer proclamations, yet he did not do so with others below. Does this indicate some degree of acceptance? It is possible, but one cannot know for sure:

1. 1769, Resolutions for an answer to Governor Bottetourt's Speech; Burgesses adopted Resolutions on May 8 that included references to "Prayers" and "Providence."
2. 1774, A Summary View of the Rights of British America which said: "The God who gave us life, gave us liberty at the same time."
3. 1774, Resolutions and Association of the Virginia Convention adopted in August,
4. 1775, Declaration of the Causes and Necessity of Taking Up Arms (other than his draft),
5. 1776, Declaration of Independence (additions to his draft),
6. 1780, grant of 8,000 acres to religious-oriented state college in Kentucky that was controlled by Presbyterians and had religious exercises,

7. 1780, state medal with reference to God,
8. 1783, Reply of Congress to General Washington,
9. 1784, Report for Western Territory included land for churches and Christian schools,
10. 1802, signed "An Act Concerning the District of Columbia" (tax exemption to churches),
11. 1802, signed (and again in 1803, and 1804) an Act that gave federal land to "the Society of the United Brethren for Propagating the Gospel Among the Heathen,"
12. 1804, signed a law providing chaplains in Congress,
13. 1806, signed "Act for Establishing the Gov't of the Armies" (it punished irreverent soldiers),
14. 1808, signed an "Act Appointing a Chaplain to Each Brigade of the Army."

Another category of sources less reliable for concluding anything about Jefferson's religious beliefs are the notes and letters that Jefferson never sent or showed to anyone ever in his life, and he made virtually no comments about their contents anywhere else (On several occasions he told people he had made an abridgement of the Gospels but did not specifically say anything about the choice of texts). These sources are listed below:

- 1760s, Literary Commonplace notes,[3]
- 1776, "Notes on Religion,"[4]
- 1801, Unsent Letter to Danbury Baptist Association,
- 1804, The *Philosophy of Jesus...for the Use of the Indians,*
- 1809, Unsent Letter to Rev. James Fishback,
- 1810, Unsent Letter to William Baldwin,
- 1815, Unsent Letter to Peter Wendover,
- 1819, Unsent Letter to William Short,
- 1820, The *Life and Morals of Jesus* (known today as *Jefferson Bible*).

---

3   Douglas Wilson, *Jefferson's Literary Commonplace Book* (Princeton, N.J.: Princeton University Press, 1989), 40-50.

4   Scholars have used "Notes on Religion" as one way to identify these documents. But another way is "Notes and Proceedings on Discontinuing the Establishment of the Church of England," 1776, www.founders.archives.gov.

Many of these documents will be addressed in the following chapters. Christians may be tempted to use some of these actions and documents as ammunition to prove Jefferson as a Christian or as favoring their viewpoint. Secularists and skeptics likewise may wish to use some other items from this list. Both are ill-advised.

Some of the items in the list were orthodox but some showed some unorthodoxy emerging in Jefferson's life. But with all of them this is the supreme fact: he did not send them. This should make the reader question that it accurately reflects Jefferson's mind. It certainly **may** be true to his beliefs, but he also may have felt what he wrote did not express himself in a way that he was happy with.

One thing is certain. It is not legitimate to quote from Jefferson's Literary Commonplace Notes (with quotes that were unorthodox) and not his "Notes on Religion" (with orthodox quotes), or to assert that one truly represents him and the other does not. The honest historian must either leave both out, or include both and say this represents a shift in his views, or else say that he was inconsistent. Neither is it valid to mention critical quotes about clergy and not show the positive relations with clergy, or to include Jefferson's rejection of Jesus' name in a law, but not show him identifying "the King of Kings" as his source for human rights.

Examining His Legacy

It is critical to understand that even if Jefferson personally did not embrace Christ, His atoning death for sinners, His resurrection, the Trinity, the inspiration of the Bible, etc., a Judeo-Christian worldview provided the overall framework for Jefferson's well-articulated ideas. When he contributed the most to his country, e.g., as chief author of the Declaration of Independence, as the author of the Virginia Statute for Religious Freedom, as the first Governor of Virginia, and as the third president of the United States, he was active in orthodox Trinitarian churches.

As journalist and author Rod Gragg asserts, the founding fathers—regardless of their own particular views on God, Christ, and faith—represented a people who were for the most part very committed to the Christian faith. Gragg, the author of the books, *Forged in Faith* and *By the Hand of Providence,* says: "Many of the founding fathers were Christians but the better question is, What is the worldview held by the founding father and held by the American people they represented? It was overwhelmingly a Judeo-Christian worldview; [the country] was Christian in great numbers, and it was also Protestant."[5]

---

5   Transcript of a television interview with Rod Gragg by Jerry Newcombe (Ft. Lauderdale: Truth in Action Ministries-TV, 2012).

That touches on one of the most important points of this book. That Jefferson's views on religious freedom and on God-given rights and higher education grew out of the Christian tradition. Without Christianity, there would be no Jefferson, even if Jefferson himself later rejected some tenets of the faith. The worldview of Jefferson led him to articulate principles that millions of people around the world cite to this day. If that worldview is lost, what will be the outcome for America going forward?

Jefferson felt he contributed an important legacy in the movement towards political and religious freedom in Virginia, and later in the founding of the University of Virginia. It is worth the time to now take another look at these topics Jefferson chose for his own epitaph, and examine how his religious beliefs may have influenced these three achievements—the Declaration of Independence, the Virginia Statute for Religious Freedom, and the University of Virginia.

CHAPTER 6

Non-Secular Government: God-Given Political Freedom in the Declaration of Independence

"Our right to life, liberty, the use of our faculties, the pursuit of happiness, is not left to the feeble and sophistical investigations of reason, but is impressed on the sense of every man. We do not claim these under the charters of kings or legislators, but under the King of kings." —Thomas Jefferson, 1817 [1]

E veryone would agree that one of Thomas Jefferson's finest moments was when he wrote our nation's birth certificate—the Declaration of Independence. He was so pleased with this achievement that he had it listed on his tomb as one of three great successes in a very accomplished life.

The Declaration of Independence explains why America exists. Most importantly, it says that human rights come from the Creator and are not to be taken away arbitrarily by the state (in this case, King George III).

The Declaration of Independence, mentions God four times:

---

1   Jefferson to John Manners, June 12, 1817. Mark A. Beliles, ed., *The Selected Religious Letters and Papers of Thomas Jefferson* (Charlottesville, VA: America Publications, 2013), 281.

- "[T]he Laws of Nature and of Nature's God…"
- "[A]ll Men are created equal, they are endowed by their Creator with certain unalienable Rights…"
- "[A]ppealing to the Supreme Judge of the World…"
- "[W]ith a firm Reliance on the Protection of Divine Providence…"[2]

The third phrase was added by the Congress and not written by Jefferson himself but the really important phrase is #2. This is not some tangential point, because it says that rights come from God. God-given rights are not up for debate. God and American ideas of government were linked by Jefferson here and in many other of his papers. Thus a nonsecular state is part of his true legacy.

The Declaration was a monumental achievement. But it's not as if it all flowed from the brain of the young Thomas Jefferson. Dr. Donald S. Lutz, professor of political science at the University of Houston and author of *The Origins of American Constitutionalism,* said "there was nothing new in the phrasing and ideas of the Declaration."[3] But indeed it was well put together.

Jefferson himself would agree that it wasn't original. Almost half a century after serving as chief author of the document, he said he was not "aiming at originality of principle or sentiment…[It] was intended to be an expression of the American mind, and to give to that expression the proper tone and spirit called for by the occasion."[4] The Declaration was indeed an excellent "expression of the American mind."

Law professor and author Gary Amos wrote a helpful book, *Defending The Declaration: How the Bible and Christianity Influenced the Writing of the Declaration of Independence.* He notes, "Jefferson's Declaration was a masterpiece of law, government, and rights. He tied together with few words hundreds of years of English political theory. The long shadows of the Magna Charta, the common law, Catholic and Calvinist resistance theories, the English Bill of Rights, and the Petition of Right are cast within its lines."[5]

---

2   Bruce Frohnen, ed., *The American Republic: Primary Sources* (Indianapolis: Liberty Fund, 2002), 189-191.

3   Donald S. Lutz, *The Origins of American Constitutionalism* (Baton Rouge: Louisiana State University Press, 1988), 121.

4   Letter to Henry Lee. May 8, 1825. www.founders.archives.gov.

5   Gary T. Amos, *Defending The Declaration: How the Bible and Christianity Influenced the Writing of the Declaration of Independence* (Charlottesville, Virginia: Providence Foundation Press, 1994), 33.

"The General Principles of Christianity"

Professor Amos points out how the Declaration was a product of the Christian tradition: "…every key term in the Declaration of Independence had its roots in the Bible, Christian theology, the Western Christian intellectual tradition, medieval Christianity, Christian political theory, and the Christian influence on the six-hundred-year development of the English common law."[6]

Christians today should know that the Declaration is not contrary to the Bible and Christianity. Rather, its design of ideas and terminology have many historical connections to the Bible and Christian theology.

When they were both older men, and no longer political rivals, John Adams and Thomas Jefferson began to correspond. They were two of the five men on the committee to produce a Declaration of Independence for the approval of the Continental Congress. Some of their correspondence is very helpful to understand their thinking.

One time, John Adams was ruminating on the overall thrust of American independence. Here's what he wrote to Jefferson in 1813: "The general Principles, on which the Fathers Achieved Independence, were the only Principles in which that beautiful Assembly of young Gentlemen could Unite, and these Principles only could be intended by them in their Address, or by me in my Answer. And what were these general Principles?"[7]

When Americans are asked today to identify the source of those general principles, it is common to hear answers along the lines of reason, of Enlightenment thinking, of "free-thought," and of skepticism. Is that what Adams said? No. He answered his own question: "I answer, the general Principles of Christianity, in which all those Sects were united: And the general Principles of English and American Liberty, in which all those young Men United, and which had United all Parties in America, in Majorities sufficient to assert and maintain her Independence."[8] It was Christian principles that united the thirteen colonies of America.

If that isn't politically incorrect enough, John Adams goes on to assert that Christianity, and not any other philosophy or religious system, gave birth to America's freedom:

---

6   Ibid., 3.

7   John Adams to Thomas Jefferson, June 28, 1813, Beliles, *The Selected Religious Letters and Papers of Thomas Jefferson*, 204.

8   Ibid.

Now I will avow, that I then believed, and now believe, that those general Principles of Christianity, are as eternal and immutable, as the Existence and Attributes of God; and that those Principles of Liberty, are as unalterable as human Nature and our terrestrial, mundane System. I could therefore safely say, consistently with all my then and present Information, that I believed they would never make Discoveries in contradiction to these general Principles.[9]

Jefferson didn't disagree with this idea. Note: It's safe to say that both Adams and Jefferson seemed to have adopted a Unitarian perspective of the Godhead before they died. Some today would try to use that fact to negate the importance of such a statement from Adams (or other positive statements on Christianity from him or Jefferson). But these were complex men, and John Adams' statement stands on its own.

When looking at the sources that were influential for Jefferson as he penned the Declaration of Independence, many instances of "the general principles of Christianity" appear.

God-Given Rights

The Declaration said that the Founders held "these truths." One truth they held in common was that America's rights come from God. Again, that's what the Declaration of Independence says. The Constitution is predicated on the Declaration. America's 1776 birth certificate explains why the nation exists. The Constitution then explains how our government is to work. The Constitution is signed in the Year of our Lord 1787 and the 12th year of the Declaration. No Declaration, no Constitution. Likewise, no birth of Jesus (reportedly 1787 years earlier), no Constitution.

When rights come from God, they are non-negotiable. Modern society has become disconnected from its original understanding of rights. This is because the culture has explicitly moved away from its Judeo-Christian influence. But, contrary to the historical revisionists, the founders of America understood their rights with great depth as to their origins. As Amos writes: "If we examine the component parts of the founders' concept of inalienable rights and trace those ideas into ancient history, we find that the Bible and the church had more influence on the formation of rights theories than did Greece, Rome, or the Renaissance."[10]

---

9   Ibid.

10   Amos, *Defending the Declaration*, 105.

Reliance on Mostly Christian Sources

The ideas in the Declaration of Independence were not Jefferson's, but the writing was. An important point, too, is that these were mainly Christian ideas.

In 1775, an assembly of 27 Presbyterian elders from Mecklenburg, North Carolina, led by Elder Ephraim Brevard (a man who had studied under John Witherspoon at Princeton) declared independence. This was a full year before the Continental Congress did. These men of Scotch-Irish origin sent their resolves to Great Britain. What is amazing is to see some of the similarities of their short declaration, dated May 20, 1775, from "the Crown of Great Britain" to what ended up in the Declaration of Independence. Said the Mecklenburg Presbyterians:

> That we do hereby declare ourselves a free and independent people; are, and of right ought to be a sovereign and self-governing association, under the control of no power, other than that of our God and the General Government of the Congress: To the maintainance of which Independence we solemnly pledge to each other our mutual co-operation, our Lives, our Fortunes, and our most Sacred Honor.[11]

More than a year later, Jefferson and the Continental Congress produced the Declaration of Independence, including the following portions:

> We, therefore, the representatives of the United States of America, in General Congress, assembled, appealing to the Supreme Judge of the world for the rectitude of our intentions...declare that these united colonies are, and of right ought to be free and independent states; that they are absolved from all allegiance to the British Crown...And for the support of this declaration, with a firm reliance on the protection of Divine Providence, we mutually pledge to each other our lives, our fortunes and our sacred honor.[12]

Clearly, Jefferson's verbiage in the Declaration of Independence is along the same lines as that of the Presbyterian elders who wrote their document a year before. It does not necessarily indicate that Jefferson directly drew from that source, but

---

11   "Mecklenburg County, Declaration of Independence," May 20, 1775. Raleigh (North Carolina) Register, April 30, 1819. Charles W. Eliot, LL.D., ed., *American Historical Documents 1000-1904* (New York: P.F. Collier & Son Company, The Harvard Classics, 1910), Vol. 43, 166.

12   Frohnen, *The American Republic*, 190-191.

it indisputably shows a common way of reasoning. That both Jefferson and these Presbyterians would write almost the same thing indicates a common worldview in America – a Christian worldview.

Independence From God?

Some secular-minded scholars like to imply that the Declaration of Independence was not only an assertion of independence from Great Britain, but also from God. But is that true? The great British historian, Paul Johnson, author of *A History of the American People,* penned this about the Declaration of Independence:

> There is no question that the Declaration of Independence was, to those who signed it, a religious as well as a secular act, and that the Revolutionary War had the approbation of divine providence. They had won it with God's blessing and, afterwards, they drew up their framework of government with God's blessing, just as in the 17th century the colonists had drawn up their Compacts and Charters and Orders and Instruments, with God peering over their shoulders.[13]

Key influential ideas Jefferson drew from in putting the document together are rooted in biblical concepts that will be examined more in the next section. But it seems to go beyond that. One could argue that its appeal "to the Supreme Judge of the world" and it's assertion of trust "in the protection of Divine Providence" did more than just declare independence from British rule, it simultaneously declared dependence upon God, the source of our rights.

"The Laws of Nature and of Nature's God"

Sometimes, some modern writers argue that Jefferson was speaking in a Deistic way when he used the phrase "the laws of nature and of nature's God." Is that true? Gary Amos provides a compelling critique to that canard. He points out that this phrase was in common usage by Christian sources, long before Thomas Jefferson employed it in the Declaration. He observes:

- "It was a legal phrase for God's law revealed through nature and His moral law revealed in the Bible."[14] [Psalm 19 provides a perfect example

---

13   Paul Johnson, *A History of the American People* (New York: HarperCollins Publishers, 1997), 204-205.

14   Amos, *Defending the Declaration,* 35.

of this. We see in the first part of the psalm that God speaks through His creation; then in part two we see that He also speaks in His revealed Word.]

- "James Otis relied upon the law of nature in his famous protest against the legality of the Stamp and Sugar Acts."[15]
- "The practice of appealing to the 'law of nature' was more than a hundred years old in the colonies. It was firmly established by Puritans coming to New England in the early 1600s."[16]
- "William Ames [Puritan writer, 1576-1633] said, for example, that 'the Law of Nature' was the same as 'that Law of God, which is naturally written in the heart of all men.'" [17]
- "The longer phrase 'law of nature or God' was used as early as the first decade of the 1300s in a debate between rival Catholic monastic orders."[18]
- "Sir Edward Coke (pronounced Cook)" wrote c. 1610 in *Calvin's Case*: "The law of nature is that which God at the time of creation of the nature of man infused into his heart, for his preservation, and direction..."[19]
- "Part of the Christian tradition was to speak of the 'law of nature' and the 'law of God' as two sides of the same coin." [20]
- "By using the distributive plural 'laws,' Jefferson distinguishes between two laws: the law of nature, and the law of God who is over nature."[21]
- "...the phrase 'laws of nature and nature's God' cannot be a product of deism or the Enlightenment because the term and the ideas embodied in it were in common use in the Christian common law and in Catholic and Protestant theology for centuries before 1776."[22]

It is therefore historically short-sighted and misinformed to say that "nature's God" refers to the god of Deism and the Enlightenment when terms existed before these new religious movements came into existence. And if it was distinctly non-

---

15   Ibid., 37.
16   Ibid.
17   Ibid., 38.
18   Ibid., 41.
19   Ibid., 43.
20   Ibid.
21   Ibid., 46.
22   Ibid., 74.

Christian Deistic terminology then most American citizens (and founding fathers, most of whom were committed Christians) never would have accepted it.

By referring to the phrase 'laws of nature and of nature's God,' Jefferson incorporates the moral law of the Bible into the founding document of our country.

John Locke (1632-1704)

Jefferson drew from sources deeply rooted in centuries of political writings from mostly Christian sources. Even when these sources are sometimes categorized as "Enlightenment thinkers," the fact of the matter is that usually the Founders cited writers representing a Christian strand of the Enlightenment that held a high view of the Bible. There was also an unbelieving strand, as typified by David Hume or Voltaire. The founders, including Jefferson, were far more influenced by the Christian thinkers, especially the Scottish stream, but also by Montesquieu, Locke and Blackstone.

For example, John Locke, the seventeenth century political writer from England, wrote the heavily influential *Two Treatises on Civil Government,* in which he used over 1500 references to the Bible. Modern editions used in universities today edit out most of these and thus Locke's sources of thought and presuppositions are removed from the modern reader's view.

Who ordained government? John Locke, the Christian political scientist who used the phrase "life, liberty, property," said it was God. Locke said: "God hath certainly appointed government to restrain the partiality and violence of men."[23] The essence of this concept is the essence of the American experiment as articulated in the Declaration of Independence: Our rights come from God, and not man.

Some people claim that John Locke was a Deist. But his use of the phrase "law of nature" to describe the natural part of God's revealed law and how it relates to the Bible, was clearly within the tradition of mainstream Christianity.

Locke also believed that men could be saved only by believing in Jesus Christ. For example, he wrote:

> Not that any to whom the gospel hath been preached shall be saved, without believing Jesus to be the Messiah; for all being sinners, and transgressors of the law, and so unjust, are all liable to condemnation, unless they believe,

---

23   John Locke, *Second Treatise of Civil Government,* 1690, in http://www.constitution.org/ jl/2ndtr02.htm

and so through grace are justified by God for this faith, which shall be accounted to them for righteousness.[24]

Furthermore, not only was Locke not a Deist, but he wrote a book of Christian apologetics—that is, a defense of the faith. The book is called *The Reasonableness of Christianity*. Co-author Jerry Newcombe knows a man who earned his Ph.D. at Yale University, Dr. Greg Forster, who told him that he had become a Christian by reading that book and Locke in his own words. He did not expect what he found when he read Locke for himself. Locke also wrote *A Commonplace Book to the Holy Bible* that contained thousands of Scripture passages he copied for his own use.

Meanwhile, Locke argued that Intuitive reason is 'a revelation from God to us by the voice of reason,' which causes us to know a truth which we had not known before. Some think incorrectly that Locke subjected divine revelation to human reasoning, but Locke connected faith and reason.

To understand Jefferson it is important to study Locke's ideas, especially those embodied in his *Second Treatise on Government* that are then echoed in the Declaration of Independence. For example, Locke writes about the "Law of Nature":

Thus the Law of Nature stands as an eternal rule to all men, legislators as well as others. The rules they make for other men's actions must...be conformable to the Law of Nature, i.e., to the will of God, of which that is a declaration, and the fundamental Law of Nature being the preservation of mankind, no human sanction can be good or valid against it.[25]

Note how such concepts are found in the Declaration. The law of nature stands outside of any one nation. It's up to nations to conform to the will of God and not vice versa. Government becomes invalid when it contradicts such higher laws. In some ways the essence of the Declaration of Independence is summed up in that very passage from Locke. Jefferson writes that it is the duty of nations to recognize the God-given rights of the people. When they don't, that government becomes tyrannical and is no longer legitimate. That's the revolutionary nature of the Declaration, and it was effectively expressed eighty years before by Christian political philosopher, John Locke. It is not surprising that Jefferson's motto that he

---

24   Amos, *Defending the Declaration*, 55.

25   John Locke, *The Second Treatise of Government: And, A Letter Concerning Toleration* (Courier Dover Publications, 1956), 62.

suggested be put on America's official seal was "Rebellion to Tyrants is Obedience to God."[26]

Sir William Blackstone (1723-1780)

In addition to Locke, one of the most influential writers who impacted Thomas Jefferson and the Declaration of Independence was Sir William Blackstone, the British jurist par excellence. Blackstone wrote four volumes of commentaries on the British law. These commentaries were studied by most of the founders and influential in their thinking, including Jefferson as he penned the Declaration.

Jefferson and numerous others of the Founding Fathers themselves declared that the law of nature was the will of God, and that it was binding upon all people, in all ages, in all geographic locations. All men have God's general revelation but need the Bible to know it most accurately.

The words of Blackstone are quite instructive. For example, he observed:

- "Those rights then which God and nature have established, and are therefore called natural rights, such as are life and liberty, need not the aid of human laws to be more effectually invested in every man than they are."[27]
- "But man was formed for society; and, as is demonstrated by the writers on this subject, is neither capable of living alone, nor indeed has the courage to do it."[28]

---

26   Letter to Edward Everett, February 24, 1823, The Thomas Jefferson Papers Series 1, General Correspondence, 1651-1827, Library of Congress Manuscript Division. Jefferson said that this motto came from one "of the regicides of Charles I." Charles tried to force English forms of worship on Scotland in 1637, and this action created a resistance movement among the Scottish people who signed a National Covenant in 1638 and supported the Long Parliament in 1640. Christian rebellion to tyrants was articulated clearly and Scripturally by Scottish clergyman Samuel Rutherford during the Westminster Assembly in 1643-1644, when he wrote Lex Rex, (meaning The law is king). The Scottish Covenanters who migrated later to the Virginia Piedmont became the tutors of Jefferson and Madison. The idea of resistance to evil-doers as obedience to God was also a strong French Huguenot theme found in Philippe du Plessis-Mornay's Defense of Liberty Against Tyrants, written in 1579. Rev. James Maury, one of Jefferson's tutors, was born of Huguenot parents, and also could have given Jefferson exposure to this motto.

27   Chief Justice Roy S. Moore, Our Legal Heritage (Montgomery, AL: The Administrative Office of Courts, June 2001), 27.

28   Ibid., 16.

- "If men were to live in a state of nature, unconnected with other individuals, there would be no occasion for any other laws, then the law of nature, and the law of God."[29]

What link is there between Blackstone and the phrase from the Declaration, "the laws of nature and of nature's God"? The answer is in Blackstone's *Commentaries* in a section called "Of the Nature of Laws in General." This goes beyond the laws of England, this applies to all countries on earth; it gets back to creation. Says Blackstone:

This will of his Maker is called the law of nature. For as God, when He created matter, and endued it with a principle of mobility, established certain rules for the perpetual direction of that motion; so, when He created man, and endued him with free will to conduct himself in all parts of life, He laid down certain immutable laws of human nature, whereby that free will is in some degree regulated and restrained, and gave him also the faculty of reason to discover the purport of those laws.[30]

Not only did God create physical laws in the universe, He also created moral laws that are just as binding and unchangeable. Furthermore, Blackstone says:

But as He is also a Being of infinite wisdom, He has laid down only such laws as were founded in those relations of justice, that existed in the nature of things antecedent to any positive precept. These are the eternal, immutable laws of good and evil, to which the Creator Himself in all his Dispensations conforms; and which He has enabled human reason to discover, so far as they are necessary for the conduct of human actions. Such among others, are these principles: that we should live honestly, should hurt nobody, and should render to everyone his due; to which three general precepts Justinian has reduced the whole doctrine of law...[31]

Blackstone is saying that the golden rule—which, by the way, first came from the lips of Jesus Christ (Matthew 7:12)—is the summary of God's moral law. Blackstone goes on to point out that our happiness is to be found in obeying

---

29   Ibid.

30   Sir William Blackstone, *Commentaries on the Laws of England, 4 Volumes*

31   Ibid.

God's law, "For he has so intimately connected, so inseparably interwoven the laws of eternal justice with the happiness of each individual, that the latter cannot be attained but by observing the former..."[32] There is a link, says Mr. Blackstone, between our happiness and our acting justly, according to God's law:

> In consequence of which mutual connection of justice and human felicity, he has not perplexed the law of nature with a multitude of abstracted rules and precepts, referring merely to the fitness or unfitness of things, as some have vainly surmised; but has graciously reduced the rule of obedience to this one paternal precept, "that man should pursue his own happiness." This is the foundation of what we call ethics, or natural law.[33]

Observe that the idea of the "pursuit of happiness"—words made famous by the Declaration of Independence—originally meant obedience to God, according to the influential Blackstone. Jefferson, like other founding fathers read and admired Blackstone's *Commentaries*. Today the pursuit of happiness is often thought in terms of freedom from God's law, not the freedom to obey it.

Jefferson certainly drew from the Virginia Constitution of 1776, which spoke of 'pursuing...happiness' as follows: '(A)ll men...have certain inherent rights, of which, (are) the enjoyment of life and liberty, with the means of acquiring and possessing property, and pursuing and obtaining happiness and safety."

These Christian ideas that had developed over centuries and were effectively expressed by men such as Lock and Blackstone truly were part of "the American mind" including Jefferson's.

The Irony of Thomas Jefferson Being the Chief Author

Isn't it fascinating that among the 56 men who signed the Declaration of Independence, Providence raised up Jefferson to be the chief writer of the document?

As seen in the first half of this book, at the time of his writing the Declaration of Independence, Jefferson appeared to have been an orthodox practicing Christian. Within several months of writing the bulk of that document, he publicly identified with and voluntarily financed evangelical and Calvinistic preaching and ministry. Statements questioning major Christian doctrines were not to flow from him until at least a dozen years later (and especially 1813 and onward)-and privately, at that...

---

32   Moore, *Our Legal Heritage*, 13.
33   Ibid., 13-14.

America's birth certificate was not some sort of sub-Christian or anti-Christian writing. Jefferson is a notable example of how a man can be influenced by Biblical ideas and Christian principles even if he did not leave a record of having ever had a personal encounter with God as Evangelicals typically emphasize.

The bottom line is this: The Declaration of Independence was not the fruit of anti-Christian deism or Enlightenment rationalism. The ideas in it were Christian and Jefferson was its chief architect.

Jefferson Statements and Actions Favoring Non-Secular Government

It is amazing that Thomas Jefferson is used today to promote a totally secular government, especially when you consider the following facts. Note: this incomplete list—much of which has been seen (and sourced) in previous chapters—shows a consistency throughout his life of approaching government in a non-secular manner, even through his own phases of partial doubt or unbelief:

1768 Jefferson said that "the place of Chaplain to the House of Burgesses... should be reserved..."

1774 Jefferson advocated a resolution "Designating a Day of Fasting, Humiliation, and Prayer" that was adopted by the House of Burgesses.

1776 While in Congress, Jefferson proposed a national seal with a Biblical image "...expressive of the divine presence, and...[the] Motto: Rebellion to tyrants is obedience to God."

1777 He prepared laws on religion in Virginia for "...for Punishing Disturbers of Religious Worship and Sabbath Breakers" (#84), and "... for Appointing Days of Public Fasting and Thanksgiving" (#85).

1777 He advocated a bill "...for Establishing General Courts" which required oaths and a prayer "so help me God" (#88).

1779 As Governor he issued a Proclamation for a Public Day of Thanksgiving and Prayer.

1800 Jefferson as leader of the U. S. Senate approved (at least tacitly) that the Capitol building be used for worship services. He personally attended many times during his years in Washington.

1800 When Jefferson was sworn in as president, he added the additional voluntary (and customary) appeal to God's aid at the end of the oath and then mentioned God in his First Inaugural Address.

1802   As President he arranged for Rev. John Leland to speak in the Executive Mansion and preach in the Capitol.

1803   He presented a Treaty with the Kaskaskia and other Indian Tribes, which provided federal funds for the construction of churches and salaries for Catholic priests and missionaries.

1803   He promised the Nuns of the Order of St. Ursula at New Orleans "the patronage of the government it is under. Be assured it will meet all the protection which my office can give it."

1804   He had $300 in federal funds given to help Presbyterian Rev. Gideon Blackburn build a school for the Cherokees in Tennessee.

1804   Jefferson wrote to the Senate chaplain "to ask that indulgence for the revd. Mr. Glendy, a Presbyterian clergyman" be given to preach in the Capitol."

1804   He signed an act that approved the payment of chaplains for the government.

1805   In his Second Inaugural Address, he said that "religious exercises," according to "the Constitution,…[are] under the direction and discipline of State or Church authorities …" and then he asked citizens "to join with me in supplication that He [God] will enlighten the minds of your servants, guide their councils…"

1806   He "Gave…50 Dollars to the order of Governor Wilkinson or other acting governor of Louisiana for building a church there."

1807   He said an accusation that he "wanted government to be without religion" was "a lie."

1807   He wrote that "the councils of the General Government in their decisions…[were drawn from] the…precepts of the gospel…"

1807   He wrote that "liberty to worship our creator…[is] deemed in other countries incompatible with good government, and yet proved by our experience to be its best support."

1808   He signed an Act Appointing A Chaplain to Each Brigade of the Army.

1817   He wrote: "Our right to life, liberty…is not left to the feeble and sophistical investigations of reason, but is impressed on the sense of every man. We do not claim these under the charters of kings or legislators, but under the King of kings." [the King of kings refers to Jesus Christ]

1822   He praised the use of the Albemarle County courthouse by churches and personally attended their services.

There were also dozens of official letters he sent as President with references to God and prayer. As noted previously, a few of the acts or statements listed above were done in a collaborative environment with a committee or as a customary activity and would not be definitive of his non-secular approach to government if they stood alone. But if Jefferson was part of a committee, and in his writings did not express his disapproval of what was done, then it at least has his tacit approval. Jefferson has a record of making his opinion know when he disagreed with something, so it is safe to include all these as his own. He did not express any dissent from these actions even later in life in his private correspondence.

The Non-Secular State University

Besides the actions above while serving directly in government, Jefferson's work at establishing a new state-funded and state-controlled university provides some explicit commentary by Jefferson on how it can be non-denominational yet non-secular at the same time. It was his pet project and, being a state tax-payer funded institution, is worth some extra time to see Jefferson's comments upon it.

In 1817 Jefferson and the board of Central College (which developed into the University of Virginia) approved the program in advance for the laying of the cornerstone that included prayer and Scripture reading by Episcopalian Rev. William King.

A year later the 1818 minutes of the board of visitors that Jefferson led stated more on the role of religion at the institution. The minutes, written by Jefferson, state that:

> In conformity with the principles of our Constitution, which places all sects of religion on an equal footing,…we have proposed no professor of divinity; and the rather as the proofs of the being of a God, the creator, preserver, and supreme ruler of the universe, the author of all the relations of morality, and of the laws and obligations these infer, will be within the province of the professor of ethics; to which adding the developments of these moral obligations, of those in which all sects agree, with a knowledge of the languages, Hebrew, Greek, and Latin, a basis will be formed common to all sects. Proceeding thus far without offence to the Constitution."[34]

---

34 "Report of the Board of Commissioners for the University of Virginia to the Virginia General Assembly, [August 4,] 1818," Founders Online, National Archives (http://founders.archives.gov/documents/Madison/04-01-02-0289, ver. 2013-06-10). Source: David B. Mattern, J. C. A. Stagg, Mary Parke Johnson, and Anne Mandeville Colony, eds.,

Jefferson specifically describes these religious provisions as being in line with the Constitution's principles. He may have primarily meant the Virginia state constitution but it admits a larger application. Exclusion of all religion was certainly not required, but equality of opportunity for all denominations was.

Then in the 1822 minutes, Jefferson and the board of the University of Virginia stated it even more strongly, just in case some misunderstood the previous arrangement. "It was not, however, to be understood that instruction in religious opinion and duties was meant to be precluded by the public authorities, as indifferent to the interests of society. On the contrary, the relations which exist between man and his Maker, and the duties resulting from those relations, are the most interesting and important to every human being, and the most incumbent on his study and investigation."[35]

Then the board said: "Such an arrangement would complete the circle of the useful sciences embraced by this institution, and would fill the chasm now existing, on principles which would leave inviolate the constitutional freedom of religion, the most inalienable and sacred of all human rights..."[36]

And just to go a step further in their Regulations for the University that Jefferson drafted on October 4, 1824, the board made it abundantly clear that in the central building of the University, called the Rotunda,: "...one of the large elliptical rooms on its middle floor shall be used for...religious worship [and]...the students of the University will be free, and expected to attend."[37]

The idea in the Declaration of Independence of a government that presupposed a Creator and religion as a source of rights continued in Jefferson's pet project of his old age (i.e., the University of Virginia)—even as his personal theology was clearly skewing in the Unitarian direction. God was part and parcel of the school, and religious content was valued supremely, as long as it was also non-denominational. Being a state institution it provides more evidence of his non-secular concept of government.

The Papers of James Madison, Retirement Series, vol. 1, *4 March 1817–31 January 1820* (Charlottesville: University of Virginia Press, 2009), 326–340.

35   Report to the President and Directors of the Literary Fund, October 7, 1822, Beliles, *The Selected Religious Letters and Papers of Thomas Jefferson*, 334.

36   Ibid.

37   Regulations for the University [of Virginia]. University of Virginia Board of Visitors Minutes, October 4–5, 1824, Beliles, *The Selected Religious Letters and Papers of Thomas Jefferson*, 368.

Conclusion

The attempt to drive out all expressions of religion, including Christianity, from the public square in Thomas Jefferson's name shows a deep misunderstanding both of Jefferson and of American history. It's time to set the record straight. Separation of the institution of the church from the institution of the state is something Jefferson believed in. Special status of one denomination could not be permitted, but that is far from the separation of God and the state, or the exclusion of general religious principles from expression in the public arena, including in the curriculum of higher education at state schools.

What has made America so great for more than two centuries? One reason is the fact that our nation recognizes that our rights come from God. Regardless of Jefferson's personal doubts, he articulated for all time a very Christian understanding that God is the source of our rights. This gave America a foundational view of government that was non-secular.

One of Jefferson's greatest legacies was the knowledge that God-given rights were the only secure basis for our rights. In his *Notes on the State of Virginia* (1781), Jefferson said, "God who gave us life gave us liberty. And can the liberties of a nation be thought secure when we have removed their only firm basis, a conviction in the minds of the people that these liberties are of the Gift of God? That they are not to be violated but with His wrath?"[38]

How different when a nation officially and in reality recognizes and protects God-given rights. Jefferson helped put America on that trajectory, and his true legacy on that point should not be denied because of political correctness or because of personal theological doubts he himself entertained as an older man.

Something very new emerged in the twentieth century – the modern secular state. Historian Paul Johnson said in his book, *Modern Times* that twentieth century godless states where atheistic ideas were put into action on a mass scale have proven to be the greatest killers of human beings in all history.[39] Millions have died as a result. In his book, *The Quest for God*, Paul Johnson elaborates further:

> The evil done in our times is beyond computation and almost beyond the imagination of our forebears. There is nothing in the previous history of the world to compare with the scale and intensity of destruction of the two world wars, with the indiscriminate slaughter of the bombing of European

---

38   Thomas Jefferson, "Notes on Virginia," 1781, http://etext.virginia.edu/toc/modeng/public/JefVirg.html.

39   Paul Johnson, *Modern Times* (New York: Harper and Row, Publishers, 1983), 729.

and Japanese cities—even before the use of the A-bomb—and with the colossal cruelty of the Nazi death-camps and Soviet Gulag. More than 150 million people have been killed by state violence in our century.[40]

In the twentieth century with its new secular states the word genocide was coined. Johnson adds, "...the two greatest institutional tyrannies of the century—indeed of all time—the Nazi Reich and the Soviet Union, were Godless constructs: modern paganism in the first case and openly proclaimed atheist materialism in the second. The death-camps and the slave-camps were products not of God but of anti-God."[41]

The United States has never approached that kind of abuse of government authority mainly due to the connection of God and government as articulated by Thomas Jefferson. If he had done nothing more than give us the brilliant first draft of the Declaration of Independence, his would have been a life worth living. Others around the world, even non-Christians, have found inspiration in its words. The brave Chinese dissidents who challenged China's tyrants in Tiananmen Square quoted Jefferson as they called for liberty in the land of Mao. No wonder that he instructed for it to be one of his three most important achievements to be memorialized on his tomb.

---

40   Paul Johnson, *The Quest for God: A Personal Pilgrimage* (New York: Harper Collins Publishers, 1996), 14.

41   Ibid., 15.

CHAPTER 7

NON-COERCIVE RELIGION: LIBERTY OF CONSCIENCE IN THE VIRGINIA STATUTE FOR RELIGIOUS FREEDOM

"...all men shall be free to profess, and by argument to maintain, their opinions in matters of Religion, and that the same shall in no wise diminish, enlarge or affect their civil capacities. —Thomas Jefferson, 1779 [1]

Regardless of how heterodox Thomas Jefferson's personal religious beliefs may have become at the end of his life, regardless of where he will ultimately spend eternity, regardless of whether or not he was a true Christian, Jefferson helped make a great contribution to humanity in paving the way for greater religious freedom. In this effort, he also received much aid from his friend and colleague, James Madison.

However, today's secularists are taking the work of Jefferson and Madison and using it to strip away religious freedom from believers (and ultimately everyone else,

---

1   Jefferson, Virginia Statute for Establishing Religious Freedom, 1777 / 1786, in Bruce Frohnen, ed., *The American Republic: Primary Sources* (Indianapolis: Liberty Fund, 2002), 330-331.

too). Many Jewish leaders and thinkers like Rabbi Daniel Lapin warn that Jews in America will lose their rights soon after the Christians lose theirs. Secularists are misreading both Jefferson and Madison—not only in terms of their writings but their actions.

One of the great contributions of Thomas Jefferson to the world is this: He gave religious freedom a major boost in America. This helped religious freedom blossom elsewhere as well as what began in America spread to other places. The most important aspect of the religious liberty championed by Jefferson is that it is rooted in a Christian theological base, and that it extends to all regardless of their beliefs.

As noted before, when Jefferson died, he listed his three most important accomplishments as he saw them. Writing the Virginia Statute for Religious Freedom was one of the three. It's no exaggeration to say that Thomas Jefferson has a lot to do with the religious freedom enjoyed today or that has been historically enjoyed.

Non-Denominationalism or Pure Secularism?

The battle over religious liberty is extremely important. It is stated elsewhere in this book that the separation of church and state that Jefferson advocated has now been twisted to mean the separation of God from the official public sphere, something that neither Jefferson nor virtually any other founder desired.

But there are "civil libertarians" today who will sue at the drop of a hat against any form of public expression of religion in our society. Actually, it seems they reserve their litigation against any *Christian* expression in the public arena. It's only the faith that gave birth to religious freedom in the first place that they reserve their animus against. Some may be well-intended for they wish to have people of minority faiths not to be offended. But discomfort from the expression of a majority faith was never the purpose of the Statute or of the First Amendment of the Constitution.

It is clear that Jefferson opposed national days of prayer or of thanksgiving because it was the prerogative of individual states, not the federal government. As Governor of Virginia, Jefferson did make such proclamations. Perhaps the most important message of this book is that many are misreading Jefferson (and Madison) in order to reach their conclusions. Jefferson and Madison believed in non-coercion, but not pure secularism.

The founders believed in a separation of the institution of the church from the institution of the state. That is not the same as the separation of God and state, which civil libertarians seem to believe in. Furthermore, the effect of repeated lawsuits from groups like the ACLU is to create state-sanctioned (or mandated) atheism.

The battle between which vision (theistic vs. secular foundation for government) shall prevail is one of the key battles of our time. The founders gave us freedom of religion while the ACLU and their colleagues are fighting for freedom from religion. They tried to remove all barriers to religious expression, but the ACLU argues for many barriers.

Freedom of religion provides freedom for all, including non-believers. Freedom from religion restricts freedom for those who do believe. Which view did Jefferson and Madison hold to? The evidence points to freedom of religion.

The Push For Religious Freedom Came From Christians

In April 1777, the General Association of Baptists met at Sandy Creek Meeting House, and "a law was drawn up in form, and reported, entitled 'An Act for the Establishment of Religious Freedom,' to be presented to the Legislature, with an earnest petition that it might be adopted as a law of the State."[2] This proposal, authored apparently by Rev. John Leland (who Jefferson hosted in Washington in 1802), "attracted the attention of several members of the Legislature, and especially of Mr. Jefferson and Mr. Madison, and had led to various private interviews between them," said historian Robert Howell. Howell said that Jefferson, using Leland's draft of a bill for religious freedom, 'had kindly undertaken to prepare the law; make it accord with their wishes;…and secure its adoption by the General Assembly as a law of the State.'" According to other Baptist accounts, Jefferson drew on this draft when he wrote the Statute for Religious Freedom.[3]

This suggests that evangelicals were not merely political supporters of Jefferson's campaign for religious liberty; rather, the impetus and, perhaps, actual content of the celebrated religious freedom bill emanated from evangelical sources. Historian

---

2   Robert B. Howell, *The Early Baptists of Virginia* (Philadelphia: The Bible and Publication Society, 1857), 164-165, 167-168. See also Edward Frank Humphrey, *Nationalism and Religion in America, 1774-1789* (Boston: Chipman Law Publishing Co., 1924), 382.

3   See also Charles F. James, *Documentary History of the Struggle for Religious Liberty in Virginia* (Lynchburg, Va.: J. P. Bell Co., 1900), 102-107. See also Joseph Martin Dawson, *Baptists and the American Republic* (Nashville, Tenn.: Broadman Press, 1956), 101. Howell's and James' accounts are often ignored by historians because the initial Baptist draft is not specifically mentioned in Jefferson's writings, yet neither was Leland's "Declaration of the Virginia Association of Baptists," cited above, although it (and petitions from other religious groups) is found among the *Papers of Thomas Jefferson*, 1:660-661.

J. G. A. Pocock asserted that "the 'Statute [for Religious Freedom]' was indebted to the revival [in Virginia] and allied with it."[4]

Jefferson in 1776 joined a committee in the Virginia legislature to revise the state's religious laws. He wrote sometime later in 1800 a "Memorandum" that included his reflections on his activity during the Revolution regarding religion. He said: "I proposed the demolition of the [Virginia] church establishment, and the freedom of religion. It could only be done by degrees; to wit, the Act of 1776, exempted dissenters from contributions to the church,...[and] the act for religious freedom in 1777."[5]

In fact when Jefferson returned to the General Assembly in Williamsburg on May 5, 1777, he, as a member of the new Calvinistical Reformed church worked to prepare bills to revise laws related to religion.[6] The Statute for Religious Freedom did not get passed until 1786 when it was shepherded through the Virginia legislature by James Madison, Jefferson's partner on these things, while Jefferson served as the U.S. ambassador to France (1784-1789.) Again, it was dissenting Christians who pushed for this bill after a brief period of division on the issue.[7] This was not some gift of atheists to the world, with dissenting Christians as happy recipients. This was a gift of Christians to the world, with everyone benefiting, including atheists and people of all faiths.

It was noted earlier that Baptists helped positively influence the bill. But they were not the only ones. J. G. A. Pocock, Johns Hopkins University Professor of History, said that the Statute for Religious Freedom is better understood in the context of a "Protestant Enlightenment," especially the Scottish Common Sense philosophy that Piedmont evangelicals believed was consistent with their Reformed Faith.[8] Professor of History at LaTrobe University in Australia Rhys Isaac goes further and writes that, "Thomas Jefferson's statute...was welcomed—

---

4   Merrill Peterson and Robert Vaughan, eds., *The Virginia Statute for Religious Freedom* (New York, NY: Cambridge University Press, 1988), 67. Pocock says: "Jefferson was allied with the sects against the establishment." Also see John Ragosta, *Wellspring of Liberty: How Virginia's Religious Dissenters Helped Win the American Revolution and Secured Religious Liberty* (Oxford University Press, 2010).

5   "Summary of Public Service, [after 2 September 1800]," www.founders.archives.gov.

6   See Chapter 1 for more information about the Subscription to Support a Clergyman, February 1777.

7   Some Presbyterians briefly supported the idea of a general religious assessment that would be divided up by the government for all major denominations. But the idea to get government out of the religion business completely is what most eventually supported.

8   Pocock, "Religious Freedom and the Desacralization of Politics: From the English Civil Wars to the Virginia Statute," Peterson and Vaughan, *The Virginia Statute for Religious Freedom*, 66.

indeed, had been keenly sought—by New Light (or)...born-again Christians. There was a basis for this alignment beyond the circumstantial combination to overthrow designs for Establishment."[9]

Ralph Ketchum, respected biographer of James Madison, has admitted that "a fresh approach is warranted in the light of new evidence" and that it is now "... unwarrantable to portray Madison as a Voltairian skeptic who championed...the expulsion of religion from the care of the state:...The very opposite inference is more tenable."[10]

Revising Religious Laws

In conjunction with that 1777 bill for religious freedom, Jefferson was involved in writing other bills to be presented as a package to the Virginia General Assembly.

One was a bill "...for a More General diffusion of Knowledge" (#79), another "...for Establishing Religious Freedom" (#82), another "...for Saving the Property of the Church Heretofore by Law Established" (#83), another "...for Punishing Disturbers of Religious Worship and Sabbath Breakers" (#84), another "...for Appointing Days of Public Fasting and Thanksgiving" (#85), another "...for Annulling Marriages Prohibited by the Levitical Law" (#86), and there were others such as a bill "...for Establishing General Courts" with required oaths and a prayer "so help me God" (#88).[11]

All these measures are Jefferson products. Professor Daniel Dreisbach is correct in asserting that Jefferson, "as chair of the Virginia Committee of Revisors,...was chief architect" of the set of religious bills that were "apparently framed by Jefferson."[12]

When one considers all these bills as a package, instead of just the bill for Establishing Religious Freedom (#82) isolated from the others, it certainly shows that Jefferson was not trying to remove all religion from public life, nor to undermine religion. A year later in 1778 Jefferson also proposed that "Pardon and privilege of clergy, shall henceforth be abolished," which was intended to create greater equality

---

9   See Isaac's essay in Peterson and Vaughan, *The Virginia Statute for Religious Freedom*, 139-169; "'The Rage of Malice of the Old Serpent Devil': The Dissenters and the Making and Remaking of the Virginia Statute for Religious Freedom."

10   Robert S. Alley, ed., *James Madison on Religious Liberty* (Buffalo: Prometheus, 1985), 192.

11   See Daniel L. Dreisbach, "A New Perspective on Jefferson's Views on Church/State Relations," *The American Journal of Legal History* (Philadelphia: Temple University School of Law, 1991), 35.

12   Daniel L. Dreisbach, *Thomas Jefferson and the Wall of Separation of Church and State* (New York: New York University Press, 2002), 59, 187.

of opportunity for all denominations and not just the Anglican Church. It was not anti-clergy but anti-privileges for only Anglican clergy.

When looking at all these bills, there is certainly not any strict wall of separation between church and state—especially any separation of religion and state. Instead, what is found is the goal to have religious freedom for all, while still remaining as a civil society under God. This becomes even more evident when looking at the remaining bills in the set that Jefferson personally had a leading role:

- Bill #83 - A "Bill for Saving the Property of the Church Heretofore by Law Established" said: "...the several tracts of Glebe land, the churches, and chapels,...shall be saved in all time to come to the members of the said English church, by whatever denomination they shall henceforth call themselves..." This protected the Anglican Church's property from lawsuits even though it was losing its favored state-established position. (Glebe refers to land granted to a cleric as part of his pay.)[13]

- Bill #84, a "Bill for Punishing Disturbers of Religious Worship and Sabbath Breakers," said: "...if any person shall of purpose, maliciously, or contemptuously, disquiet or disturb any congregation assembled..., then any Justice...shall commit him to prison, there to remain till the next court to be held for the same county; and...If any person on Sunday shall himself be found labouring at his own or any other trade or calling, or shall employ his apprentices, servants or slaves in labour,...he shall forfeit the sum of ten shillings for every such offence..."[14] This bill passed in 1786 along with #82 on Religious Freedom.

- Bill #85, a "Bill for Appointing Days of Public Fasting and Thanksgiving," said "...the power of appointing days of public fasting and humiliation, or thanksgiving, throughout this commonwealth, may in the recess of the General Assembly, be exercised by the Governor...Every minister of the gospel shall on each day so to be appointed, attend and perform divine service and preach a sermon, or discourse, suited to the occasion, in his

---

13   "83. A Bill for Saving the Property of the Church Heretofore by Law Established, June 18, 1779," Bills Reported by the Committee of Revisors, 1779, [see bills 82-87], www.founders. archives.gov.

14   "84. A Bill for Punishing Disturbers of Religious Worship and Sabbath Breakers, June 18, 1779," Bills Reported by the Committee of Revisors, 1779, [see bills 82-87], www.founders. archives.gov.

church, on pain of forfeiting fifty pounds for every failure, not having a reasonable excuse."[15]

- Bill #86, a "Bill Annulling Marriages Prohibited by the Levitical Law and Appointing the Mode of Solemnizing Lawful Marriage," said: "…marriages prohibited by the Levitical law shall be null; and persons marrying contrary to that prohibition, and cohabitating as man and wife, convicted thereof in the General Court, shall be amerced, from time to time, until they separate."[16] A rooting of marriage as defined by the Bible seems strange to the modern reader, but came under the category of Jefferson's package of proposed revisal of religious laws.

Bills 83 through 86 should never be forgotten, for all were proposed by Jefferson and form a balanced view of what separation of church and state meant at that time, i.e., not a totally secular society. In fact, the power to proclaim public days of prayer (on the state level) in bill 85 was applied by Jefferson while Governor of Virginia (even though apparently the bill authorizing it never was formally adopted). On November 11, 1779, Governor Jefferson issued a "Proclamation for a Public Day of Thanksgiving and Prayer." The official document began: "By his Excellency Thomas Jefferson, Esq. Governour or Chief Magistrate of the commonwealth of Virginia; Proclamation…Impressed with a grateful sense of the goodness of Almighty God, in… manifesting in multiplied instances his divine care…"[17] and then Jefferson chose to quote at length from the one announced by the Continental Congress, thus specifically declaring to Virginians that:

> "…he hath diffused the glorious light of the gospel, whereby, through the merits of our gracious Redeemer, we may become the heirs of his eternal glory…[and suggested prayer] that he would grant to his church the plentiful effusions of divine grace, and pour out his holy spirit on all ministers of the gospel; that he would bless and prosper the means of education, and spread the light of Christian knowledge through the remotest corners of the earth…that he would in mercy look down upon

---

15 "85. A Bill for Appointing Days of Public Fasting and Thanksgiving, June 18, 1779," Bills Reported by the Committee of Revisors, 1779, [see bills 82-87], www.founders.archives.gov.

16 "86. A Bill Annulling Marriages Prohibited by the Levitical Law, and Appointing the Mode of Solemnizing Lawful Marriage, June 18, 1779," Bills Reported by the Committee of Revisors, 1779, [see bills 82-87], www.founders.archives.gov.

17 "Proclamation Appointing a Day of Thanksgiving and Prayer, 11 November 1779," www.founders.archives.gov.

us, pardon our sins and receive us into his favor, and finally, that he would establish the independence of these United States upon the basis of religion and virtue."[18]

After these overt Christian statements from Congress that Jefferson included in his proclamation, he then, with his own words in the closing paragraph, said: "...I do therefore by authority from the General Assembly issue this my proclamation, hereby appointing...a day of thanksgiving and prayer to Almighty God, earnestly recommending to all the good people of this commonwealth, to set apart the said day for those purposes" and for "the several Ministers of religion to meet their respective societies thereon, to assist them in their prayers, [and] edify them with their discourses."[19] As was noted earlier, Jefferson chose not to declare days of thanksgiving and prayer when he was president, not because he opposed them per se, but because he thought this was a matter left up to the states, not the federal government.

"An Act For the Establishment of Religious Freedom"

Much of the impetus for the Virginia Statute for Religious Freedom came from Christian dissenters. James Madison's Baptist friend, the Reverend Elijah Craig of Orange County, was again sent by the General Association of Baptists to lobby the Virginia General Assembly in October 1778.[20] His Presbyterian friend and college classmate, Samuel Stanhope Smith, began to rise in political influence in April 1777 when he drafted a "Remonstrance Against a General Assessment" for the Hanover Presbytery. (A Presbytery is a group of ministers and elders who are the leaders of the Presbyterian churches in a particular area. Hanover represented most of Presbyterian churches in Virginia at that time.)

The idea of a general tax to support all the major denominations was put forth by some religious leaders as a replacement for the previous religious tax that exclusively went for the support of the Anglican Church. Although some thought this a good plan, leaders such as Rev. Smith opposed it for more complete removal of the state from any role in funding churches. Two months later, Smith drafted another petition opposing the maintenance of a state-established church and personally presented it to the legislature.

---

18   Ibid.

19   Ibid.

20   John E. Kleber, et al., eds., *The Kentucky Encyclopedia* (Lexington, KY: University Press of Kentucky, 1992), 238-239.

On June 12, 1779, the famous "Bill for Establishing Religious Freedom" was submitted to the General Assembly by none other than John Harvie, one of Jefferson's fellow members of the independent and Evangelical Calvinistical Reformed Church of Charlottesville.[21] This congregation represented a blend of Anglican and Presbyterian communities and beliefs. It also was evidence of a merger of political goals by some in these religious traditions. For example, Rev. Smith had written to Jefferson just a couple months earlier two letters in which he proposed "a *coalition* of the principal *religious* sects" to provide nondenominational instruction in the public schools. Smith then offered his "influence on one of the parties [i.e. Presbyterians]," saying "my utmost exertions shall be at your service."[22] Jefferson replied to Smith also but the letter today is missing.

Also, in 1779 Rev. James Madison (a cousin of U. S. President James Madison), president of the College of William and Mary, worked with Jefferson to do away with a Professor of Divinity in the school in order to create more of a non-denominational educational environment.[23] This was not the work of a "secular" coalition, but a religious one. It promoted a non-denominational vision, not a secular one. At times scholars use the term non-sectarian of Jefferson to mean non-religious or secular, but it should be understood as inclusive of religion yet in a non-denominational way.

Rev. Samuel Stanhope Smith, foremost leader of Presbyterians in Virginia as moderator of the Hanover Presbytery, wrote to Jefferson that he was against "a legal establishment" or a "public religion." He argued that "[i]f Christianity is of divine original it will support itself or forfeit its pretensions."[24] In 1778, Smith wrote to James Madison (the later president) that, "there seems to be a favourable opportunity to unite some of our religious parties, if their leaders were sufficiently catholic [i.e., universal]. I should be ready to concur in such a design." Smith then asked Madison to predict "what turn *religious politics* are likely to take in the legislature?"[25] Before

---

21 Harvie was appointed by the legislature to a committee to prepare two bills: one for religious freedom and the other for saving the property of the formerly-established church. Eckenrode, 56.

22 "To Thomas Jefferson from Samuel Stanhope Smith, [March? 1779]," www.founders. archives.gov.

23 Jefferson's *Notes on the State of Virginia*, Query 15, 1781, www.founders.archives.gov. It is difficult to claim this as a sign of Jefferson's anti-clericalism, since this clergyman was Jefferson's chief ally in this effort.

24 "To Thomas Jefferson from Samuel Stanhope Smith, April 19, 1779," www.founders. archives.gov.

25 "To James Madison from Samuel Stanhope Smith, 15 September 1778," Founders Online, National Archives (http://founders.archives.gov/documents/Madison).

Smith was able to organize an interdenominational Christian "...coalition..." in opposition to ecclesiastical establishment, he was called back to teach at the College of New Jersey (i.e., Princeton) in 1779. (Jefferson donated to Smith and Princeton in 1802).[26]

When Smith departed Virginia, Jefferson recruited the new moderator of the Hanover Presbytery, John Todd, as a key ally in the political struggle for passage of the "Bill for Establishing Religious Freedom." Jefferson had probably met Todd in October 1776, and now communicated again with Todd. He sends a letter to Todd at this time, and although this letter is missing and what Jefferson expressed cannot be known, it nonetheless indicates an initiative taken by him in pursuit of a partnership with the Presbyterians.[27] Then on August 16, 1776, Rev. Todd replies to Jefferson, which implies much of what Jefferson had said. Todd expressed his support for the bill, saying that "there is a wide difference between religion sinking and some of its miserable Clergy sinking;... *Virtue and pure religion* do better without earthly emoluments than with." Todd also expressed his "love and esteem" for Jefferson and his desire that he "long live to fill up the most important places in the State."[28] In 1780, the Hanover Presbytery met in Pastor James Waddell's home in Augusta County and asked one of his elders Zachariah Johnston (who was also a member of the House of Delegates at the time) to meet with Governor Jefferson and to present their petitions for religious freedom to the legislature.[29]

Although Presbyterians and Baptists primarily led the way in petitioning for the cause of religious freedom, many Methodists in the Albemarle area also signed petitions against an established church. This, Jefferson observed, was *unlike* most of the Methodists in the state, but typical of the freedom-loving communities of the Central Virginia Piedmont.[30] It was a Christian movement that produced the bill.

The Virginia Statute For Religious Freedom

It is important to study the wording of the Virginia Statute for Religious Freedom— the act itself—which Jefferson wrote in 1777 and that finally passed in 1786. The statute declares:

---

26   Hood, 7-26.

27   Letter to Rev. John Todd, August 1779, (now missing but cited in reply of Todd to Jefferson, "To Thomas Jefferson from Rev. John Todd, 16 August 1779," www.founders.archives.gov).

28   "To Thomas Jefferson from Rev. John Todd, 16 August 1779," www.founders.archives.gov.

29   Joseph A. Waddell, *Annals of Augusta County, Virginia, 1726-1871*, 2d ed. (Bridgewater, Va.: C. J. Carrier Co., 1958), 304.

30   Buckley, *Church and State in Revolutionary Virginia*, 29 n. 50.

An Act for establishing religious Freedom.
Whereas, Almighty God hath created the mind free;...[31]

Let's stop right there. There is a religious premise on which the bill is based. Remove the theistic base and the argument falls apart. Even though Jefferson did not draft these initial words, which were added by the legislature, he still supported them. Remember how in a different context Jefferson asked, "Can the liberties of a nation be secure when we have removed a conviction that *these liberties are the gift of God?*"[32]

The Statute continues:

...that all attempts to influence it by temporal punishments or burthens, or by civil incapacitations tend only to beget habits of hypocrisy and meanness, and are a departure from the plan of the holy author of our religion, who being Lord, both of body and mind yet chose not to propagate it by coercions on either, as was in his Almighty power to do, that the impious presumption of legislators and rulers, civil as well as ecclesiastical, who, being themselves but fallible and uninspired men have assumed dominion over the faith of others, setting up their own opinions and modes of thinking as the only true and infallible, and as such endeavouring to impose them on others, hath established and maintained false religions over the greatest part of the world and through all time;...[33]

It is obvious that the "holy author of our religion" couldn't be Allah or Mohammad, on the face of it. The lack of religious freedom in most countries where that faith has prevailed is a matter of historical and current record. Of course, Judaism does not believe that a human could be divine. In fact, Jesus was condemned to death by the Temple authorities because He claimed to be the Son

---

31   Bills Reported by the Committee of Revisors, 1779, [see bills 82-87], www.founders. archives.gov. Actually, Jefferson's initial draft did not begin with a reference to God but began as follows: "Well aware that the opinions and belief of men depend not on their own will, but follow involuntarily the evidence proposed in their minds. . . ." The General Assembly replaced this with the famous opening words it has today. But Jefferson never distanced himself from this modification. Also see Frohnen, 330-331.

32   Thomas Jefferson, *Notes on the State of Virginia* (Boston: David Carlisle, 1801, Eighth American Edition), 241. Emphasis added.

33   Frohnen, ed., *The American Republic*, 330-331. Emphasis is ours.

of God. Furthermore, where is the evidence that Jefferson in 1777 would refer to Hindu deities when writing these words? There is none, to our knowledge.[34]

All attempts to force people to believe in a certain way violate the spirit and example of "the holy author of our religion." Who is that? It is unquestionably Jesus, who Jefferson later said was the person worshiped by almost every member of the legislature. Church and state historian Thomas Buckley of Santa Clara University wrote that "The God described here is not deistical…rather Jefferson posited a Creator who is personally involved…The Statute is not neutral toward religion."[35]

The moral authorities for its arguments were cited as "Almighty God," "the Lord" and "our religion," meaning Christianity in a general sense. It labeled certain actions (i.e., coercion) to be "sinful," and affirmed that the state was "meant to encourage" the "principles of that religion." Being a member in a particular church, according to the statute, would certainly no longer be used to "enlarge" the "civil capacities" of a citizen, but neither would it force a person's political activity to "diminish." However, it should be noted that although Christianity was the religion cited as the foundation of this act, nonetheless, Jefferson said in his *Autobiography* (1821) that it was intended to be "universal" for although:

> …The bill for establishing religious freedom…declares that coercion is a departure from the plan of the holy author of our religion, an amendment was proposed by inserting the word "Jesus Christ" so that it should read "A departure from the plan of Jesus Christ, the holy author of our religion;" the insertion was rejected by a great majority, in proof that they meant to comprehend within the mantle of its protection the Jew and the Gentile, the Christian and Mahometan, the Hindoo and Infidel of every denomination."[36]

---

34   It would be theoretically possible to claim that this refers to Hindu Avatars (which as a concept is as close to the Christian view of incarnation as exists). But even there, there is a major distinction between the Christian view and the Hindu view. The Hindus do not in any way claim historical accuracy. For example, they do not claim that Krishna was a real human, born in this world as an historical figure. In contrast, Jesus is an historical figure. If Jesus didn't in reality rise from the dead in human history, then Christianity is bogus, and it ought to be frankly and explicitly abandoned. Jesus was born in Bethlehem, a real place. He died just outside Jerusalem. History and the details of Christ's life intersect in Christianity. Again, this tie to history is not found in Hinduism.

35   Peterson and Vaughan, *The Virginia Statute for Religious Freedom*, 87. See Buckley's essay in the volume.

36   Jefferson's *Autobiography*, January 6, 1821, Lipscomb and Bergh, 1:67.

This was certainly true and commendable—that everyone, regardless of their religious persuasion—would find religious freedom

Although less reliable for interpreting Jefferson's private faith, his "Notes on Religion" in 1776 spoke clearly of Jesus when he quoted Locke, saying: "our Savior chose not to propagate his religion by temporal punishments or civil incapacitation…"[37] The interesting thing about it is that the Statute declared that the state is not to interfere with the conscience. Even God Himself leaves that up to the individual. In 1817 Jefferson wrote (as previously noted) that they claimed their rights came from "…the King of kings."[38]

The statute continues:

> …that to compel a man to furnish contributions of money for the propagation of opinions which he disbelieves is sinful and tyrannical; that even the forcing him to support this or that teacher of his own religious persuasion is depriving him of the comfortable liberty of giving his contributions to the particular pastor, whose morals he would make his pattern, and whose powers he feels most persuasive to righteousness, and is withdrawing from the Ministry those temporary rewards, which, proceeding from an approbation of their personal conduct are an additional incitement to earnest and unremitting labours for the instruction of mankind;…[39]

Who speaks of sin? The Christian religion does. To force people to support something that violates their consciences is sin. Jefferson put his money where his mouth was. He did not think it was right for the Anglican Church of Virginia to force him to pay for it through his taxes. As has been thoroughly documented earlier, Jefferson contributed to many churches and many Christian causes. He did this even in his last few years, which was more of an unorthodox phase of his life. No one forced him to do this. Nor should they have, as his bill argues.

The statute goes on:

> …that our civil rights have no dependence on our religious opinions any more than our opinions in physics or geometry, that therefore the

---

37 Ford, *The Writings of Thomas Jefferson*, 2:101.

38 Jefferson to John Manners, June 12, 1817. Mark A. Beliles, ed., *The Selected Religious Letters and Papers of Thomas Jefferson* (Charlottesville, VA: America Publications, 2013), 281.

39 Frohnen, ed., *The American Republic*, 330-331. Emphasis ours.

proscribing any citizen as unworthy the public confidence, by laying upon him an incapacity of being called to offices of trust and emolument, unless he profess or renounce this or that religious opinion, is depriving him injuriously of those privileges and advantages, to which, in common with his fellow citizens, he has a natural right, that it tends only to corrupt the principles of that very Religion it is meant to encourage, by bribing with a monopoly of worldly honours and emoluments those who will externally profess and conform to it; that though indeed, these are criminal who do not withstand such temptation, yet neither are those innocent who lay the bait in their way; ...[40]

All have civil rights, regardless of our opinions on religion. No one should be viewed as a second class citizen for what he does or does not believe. Of course, in today's context, often some secular progressives are working hard to marginalize those who do believe. Meanwhile, Jefferson in this passage above is alluding to how true Christianity has been perverted through religious coercion, where people (whether they really believe or do not) get rewarded for pretending they do. This only leads to what Jefferson refers to in this act as "habits of hypocrisy."

The Statute further states:

...that to suffer the civil magistrate to intrude his powers into the field of opinion and to restrain the profession or propagation of principles on supposition of their ill tendency is a dangerous fallacy which at once destroys all religious liberty because he being of course judge of that tendency will make his opinions the rule of judgment and approve or condemn the sentiments of others only as they shall square with or differ from his own; that it is time enough for the rightful purposes of civil government, for its officers to interfere when principles break out into overt acts against peace and good order; ...[41]

Who authorizes the state (the "civil magistrate") to decide what is or what is not correct doctrine? What qualifies the magistrate to decide which doctrines and which religious practices are legitimate or not? Nothing, they should therefore not be rewarding or punishing religious behavior. (Nor should the state favor and

---

40   Ibid.
41   Ibid.

reward anti-Christian behavior, which is what they often engage in now, thanks to a massive misreading of Thomas Jefferson.)

Jefferson prepares to close:

> …and finally, that Truth is great, and will prevail if left to herself, that she is the proper and sufficient antagonist to error, and has nothing to fear from the conflict, unless by human interposition disarmed of her natural weapons free argument and debate, errors ceasing to be dangerous when it is permitted freely to contradict them: …[42]

This is a biblical concept. We are admonished to discern truth from error. Christianity and truth will prevail in the market place of ideas if given the chance. The statute concludes:

> Be it enacted by General Assembly that no man shall be compelled to frequent or support any religious worship, place, or ministry whatsoever, nor shall be enforced, restrained, molested, or burthened in his body or goods, nor shall otherwise suffer on account of his religious opinions or belief, but that all men shall be free to profess, and by argument to maintain, their opinions in matters of Religion, and that the same shall in no wise diminish, enlarge or affect their civil capacities. And though we well know that this Assembly elected by the people for the ordinary purposes of Legislation only, have no power to restrain the acts of succeeding Assemblies constituted with powers equal to our own, and that therefore to declare this act irrevocable would be of no effect in law; yet we are free to declare, and do declare that the rights hereby asserted, are of the natural rights of mankind, and that if any act shall be hereafter passed to repeal the present or to narrow its operation, such act will be an infringement of natural right.[43]

With this law being enacted, Baptists (and everyone else too) could be free to preach and not have to be approved by the state to do so. (The state generally shouldn't grant such freedoms anyway, nor should the ministers seek them, since it's up to God, not the state, to do the calling and ordaining.) With this statute of Jefferson and a similar one passed the year before (1785) by James Madison, the

---

42   Ibid.
43   Ibid.

two men were highly loved and regarded by the religious dissenters…the Baptists, the Presbyterians, the Methodists, etc.

The Library of Virginia notes this about the passage of the Bill: "Thomas Jefferson's eloquent statement of the principles of separation of church and state and of complete religious freedom was originally drafted in 1777 as the Bill for Establishing Religious Freedom. Although it was introduced in the General Assembly on June 12, 1779, it did not pass. James Madison, without whom it probably would never have been enacted, engineered its passage in the General Assembly in 1786 and thus shared with the state's dissenters the credit for detaching the state from the church in Virginia. And without TJ's work, and his laborious efforts and farsighted vision, the state might never have been detached in Virginia."[44]

The Mantle of Protection

Writings by lobbyists such as Baptist Rev. John Leland at the time of the passage of the Virginia Statute for religious freedom asserted that religious freedom should indeed be for all faiths, not just Christians. Jefferson was no different.

The premise of the Bill is twofold (and both are theological points): 1) God has created the mind free. 2) We deviate from the plan of "the holy author of our religion" when we coerce religion. Only Christianity teaches the notion that God allowed people to believe or disbelieve. They will give an account to Him for their thoughts and beliefs, but this account is not to be given to civil authorities.

To Jefferson and the legislature, it was obvious who that description referred to and to have said more might unnecessarily offend those whom it sought to protect. Despite the fact that the Virginia Statute arose from a Christian culture, no one disputes that the effect of the law is to provide "within the mantle of its protection" anyone and everyone, regardless of his religious or non-religious affiliation. But modern commentators try to make Jefferson's remembrance of this proposal a secret sign that he was not a Christian and was more aligned with atheism or unorthodoxy.[45] The facts already presented in this book show him to be arguably orthodox at the time of the statute's passage (written 1777, passed in 1786) and unorthodox later in life.

---

44 "Act for Establishing Religious Freedom, January 16, 1786," Virginia Memory: Library of Virginia. http://www.virginiamemory.com/online_classroom/shaping_the_constitution/doc/religious_freedom

45 See page 264 for comments in this regard on Christopher Hitchens.

Broad religious freedom and protections for all faiths can and does exist only in a society where the pure Christian gospel has paved the way. One exception to this notion can be found in the example of Japan. But part of that is because Japan chose to adopt Western ways. This was not something that they invented. Religious liberty springs from theological beliefs, not secular ones, and from Christian sources, not other religious sources, but other cultures can adopt the same principles they see worked well first in Christian ones.

There is no original religious freedom in those societies with a different worldview, than that derived from Judeo-Christian civilization. Broad religious tolerance and freedom of religion is not found in Hindu lands. Certainly not in Muslim lands. Author Dr. Paul Marshall of the Hudson Institute points out that even in "moderate Muslim" lands, there is wide acceptance of many aspects of Shariah law, such as the view that Muslims who fall away from the faith (for example, one who becomes a Christian) should be put to death.[46]

Broad religious freedom is not found in purely secular nations. In countries based on atheism (such as Communist lands) or practical atheism (such Nazi Germany), there is a total curbing of religious freedom (much less other freedoms). Only in a country with a largely Christian base (even if that foundation is waning) is religious freedom found. Virtually every one of the thirteen founding states had specific references to the Christian religion, Jesus Christ, and the Bible in their Constitutions and other documents. That culture produced the precious gift of religious freedom. It's appropriate indeed to thank Jesus, "the holy author of our religion," for it.

A Christian philosophical foundation was the basis on which Jefferson and Madison argued for religious freedom for all. Remove that Christian theological base, and you ultimately lose the freedom it affords. Ironically, the West is moving away from Christianity, and at the same time it is moving away from religious freedom, while other cultures are increasingly embracing it.

James Madison's "Memorial and Remonstrance"

As noted above, James Madison clearly played a pivotal role in getting the Virginia Statute passed. Madison was trained by a strong Presbyterian minister, Rev. John

---

46   Author Paul Marshall, a scholar with the Hudson Institute, said: "A survey done by the Pew Research Center in 2010 found that eighty-four percent of Egyptians were in favor of executing anybody who converted out of Islam; the figure in Jordan was eighty-six percent and these are countries we usually regard as moderate." Source: Transcript of a TV interview on location in DC of Paul Marshall by Jerry Newcombe (Ft. Lauderdale: Truth in Action Ministries-TV, 2011).

Witherspoon, the president of Princeton. John Eidsmoe, former professor of Constitutional Law and author of *Christianity and the Constitution,* points out that Witherspoon was a man who greatly multiplied his influence on America: "John Witherspoon is best described as the man who shaped the men who shaped America. Although he did not attend the [1787] Constitutional Convention, his influence was multiplied many times over by those who spoke as well as by what was said."[47] Eidsmoe says that when Madison graduated Princeton in his early twenties, he spent a year of further study there under Dr. Witherspoon's tutelage, translating portions of the Hebrew Bible into English.

Madison wrote *Memorial and Remonstrance Against Religious Assessments.* The purpose of this petition in 1785 was to rally opposition to a proposal for the government to subsidize all of the main denominations with tax dollars. Some Christians thought this was progress since it was tax dollars going no longer to only one denomination (as it had previously to the Anglican Church). The goal of Madison's essay was to eliminate all tax dollars going to any denominations and thus not force people to pay for something against their consciences. (Presbyterians wouldn't want to subsidize the Anglicans, and vice versa.) In examining the text itself, one finds—just as in the case of the Virginia Statute for Religious Freedom—that there is a Christian theological base for Madison's arguments. Madison wrote:

> Whilst we assert for ourselves a freedom to embrace, to profess and to observe the Religion which we believe to be of divine origin, we cannot deny an equal freedom to those whose minds have not yet yielded to the evidence which has convinced us. If this freedom be abused, it is an offence against God, not against man: To God, therefore, not to man, must an account of it be rendered.[48]

Again, just as Jefferson's bill had a theological base that he argued from, so does Madison's petition. But today's secular activists have attempted to remove that theological basis. Both Madison and Jefferson played pivotal roles in helping to unleash the church from the burden of formal control by the state.

---

47   John Eidsmoe, *Christianity and the Constitution* (Grand Rapids: Baker Book House, 1987), 81.

48   James Madison, "Memorial and Remonstrance Against Religious Assessments," 1785 in Frohnen, ed., *The American Republic,* 327-330.

Jefferson and Madison—
Clear Opponents of Coercion in Religion

Much of the criticism against Thomas Jefferson in his lifetime alleged that he was a secret atheist or enemy of religion.[49] But the problem is that his critics confused his clear goal to disestablish the state-church (which he and Madison were successful at in Virginia) with being anti-Christian or anti-religion.

History professor Merrill Peterson, who wrote numerous books on Jefferson, said that Jefferson: "…had no respect for the Established Church on any ground…"[50] But Peterson warns against misreading unbelief into Jefferson's disestablishmentarian views:

> Nothing could be more mistaken. As a philosopher has said, "The power and eloquence of Jefferson's writings on religious freedom is due largely to his evident religious devotion." Unlike the anti-clericalism of the Old World, his hatred of establishments and priesthoods did not involve him in hatred of religion. He wished for himself, for all his countrymen, not freedom from religion but freedom to pursue religion wherever reason and conscience led, and the more sensitive and upright the pursuit the more respect it won from him. He attempted to say as much but, of course, the onus of his public work and utterance was on the side of tearing down, so he must appear to many as a mere destroyer of religion. Yet he gave generous support to various churches throughout his life.[51]

This is significant coming from a leading Jefferson biographer. Peterson adds (in reference to Jefferson's generosity to help found Rev. Clay's church in 1777): "…his contribution—proved Jefferson's readiness to accept the consequences of his own principle: the voluntary support of churches and ministers."[52]

Anti-State-Established Church Vs. Anti-Church

The period in which Thomas Jefferson wrote the Declaration of Independence was a phase in his life in which he was a very clearly identified with Christianity. He was not anti-church, but anti-state-established church. And when saying he was

---

49   For example, see pp. 273ff in this book.

50   Merrill D. Peterson, *Thomas Jefferson and the New Nation: A Biography* (New York: Oxford University Press, 1970), 50.

51   Ibid., 143.

52   Ibid.

non-sectarian, it should be explained that this meant non-denominational, not anti-religious or secular.

And yet these things have been turned around, and now he's considered almost an outsider of the church—an opponent of Christianity and clergymen, a proponent of secularism—all claims that could not be further from the truth about the real Thomas Jefferson.

Thomas Jefferson was clearly a person working toward disestablishment. He was a disestablishmentarian because he clearly wanted all people—especially Christians, but really people of all faiths—to have an equal access to public life without limitations or favors based on their beliefs or nonbeliefs. So he was doing away with the idea of a coercive state church and state favors toward one denomination. But that itself is now used to make him out to be a secularist who would want no expression of faith in public life. He is used today in this incorrect way to limit the expression of religion in public life. But Jefferson made it very clear in the Statute for Religious Freedom that a person's religious convictions should neither enlarge nor diminish "his civil capacities."

That is what Jefferson wanted—that there would be neither advantages nor disadvantages based on what one believes. And yet, today, Thomas Jefferson's words are used to diminish the freedom of many Christians from being in public life by saying they are somehow disqualified. Coercion by the state is now employed in blocking any religious expression in public. In fact, the secular media have pretty much bought this concept in its entirety.[53] If there are people trying to express religious faith, say they're running for president or they're in the public square, they're often made out to be an extremist. Religious motivation is portrayed as an extreme thing, and used against Christians to diminish their bid for public service.[54]

These religious persons getting involved in his Jefferson's new Democratic Republican Party (forerunner to today's Democrat Party) would have been portrayed as dangerous by the modern media, or as religious extremists trying to bring faith into the public square. Jefferson and Madison, by today's standards, would have been held up to pillory because they based their arguments on God and encouraged clergy and religious persons considering elective offices.

The beliefs of Jefferson and Madison on religion and state throughout their lives for the most part reflected the dominant religious trends in the region—a hotbed of American revivalism. Instead of considering Jefferson to be unique and

53   David Limbaugh, *Persecution* (DC: Regnery, 2003), Chapter 10.
54   Todd Starnes, *God Less America* (Lake Mary, FL: Charisma, 2014).

standing outside of his religious culture, it would be more accurate to identify him as a fair representation of it.

In short, America owes its religious freedom to Bible-based reformation Christianity, and Thomas Jefferson and James Madison were indispensable in helping mediate that process. But freedom of religion must not be confused with freedom from religion, as so many are doing today. The future of freedom is at stake.

Conclusion

Jefferson's Virginia Statute for Religious Freedom is "...considered today to be one of the most influential documents in American history, it laid the foundation for the official acceptance of the principles of religious liberty and the separation of church and state that later were enshrined in the Bill of Rights."[55] This was a great achievement. But new religious discrimination is taking place today.

The witch hunt against all things Christian in public that is undertaken allegedly on Jefferson's and Madison's behalf should stop. It was never their intention in the first place. Remove the Christian underpinnings of the Virginia Statute for Religious Freedom or of the Memorial and Remonstrance Against Religious Assessments, and you remove their foundation. As modern culture and jurisprudence moves further away from our God-given rights, Americans are losing those formerly-cherished and diligently-protected religious rights.

Today, a valedictorian can thank any power or person or force he or she wants to—unless it's the G-word or worse, the J-word. One valedictorian actually had her microphone cut off in the middle of her speech because the authorities feared she was going to thank Jesus Christ for His help. That's government censorship of speech. Would Jefferson have been forced to edit the language in his Declaration of Independence and Virginia Statute for Religious Freedom with those overt references to God if he drafted it as a student in a modern public school?

In his Inaugural Address, John F. Kennedy said, "the same revolutionary beliefs for which our forebears fought are still at issue around the globe—the belief that the rights of man come not from the generosity of the state, but from the hand of God. We dare not forget today that we are the heirs of that first revolution."[56]

---

55   "January 16, 1786, On This Day: Legislative Moments in Virginia History," Virginia Historical Society. http://www.vahistorical.org/onthisday/11686.htm.

56   John F. Kennedy, Inaugural Address, January 20, 1961, in William J. Federer, *America's God and Country: Encyclopedia of Quotations* (St. Louis, MO: Amerisearch, 2000), 346.

Would Kennedy have been forced to edit this language if he drafted it as a student for a modern public school?

As we have seen, how contrary this anti-Christian intolerance is to the spirit of Thomas Jefferson and James Madison—who explicitly said that religion was not only to be tolerated, but to be freely exercised. Noted Constitutional attorney Herb Titus says:

> There is a rich Christian background charting a path from religious toleration to freedom of religion, culminating in 1776 with Article I, Section 16 of the Virginia Declaration of Rights. While Jefferson did not expressly anchor his statute for religious freedom in the language of the Virginia declaration, Madison did in his Remonstrance….There is a clear separation of church and state as a matter of civil jurisdiction based upon the law of the Creator separating those duties owed exclusively to God (enforceable only by reason and conviction) and those duties owed to the civil order (enforceable by force or violence). Jefferson's preamble refers to 'opinions' not just 'religious opinions.' Why? Because one's opinions about anything, religious or otherwise, are outside the jurisdiction of civil authorities. In short, thanks to Christianity, true freedom of religion is freedom for everyone not just for religious persons or persons with religious convictions. That is the telling point of Jefferson's statute and it is also the foundation upon which the First Amendment religion guarantees rest.[57]

Thomas Jefferson was among the first to call for religious freedom in his time so that religion would "neither enlarge nor diminish" the rights of citizens. After all, "Almighty God hath created the mind free…" Americans shed their blood to have that freedom. It is critical that a full restoration of that Jeffersonian principle be restored in this land.

---

57   For more details, see pp. 11-18 of the Friend of the Court brief remonstrating against the HHS Mandate. Conestoga Wood Specialties Corp., Et al. (Vienna, VA: William J. Olsen, PC, 2014). See http://wwwlawandfreedom.com.

CHAPTER 8

NON-DENOMINATIONAL EDUCATION: EQUAL OPPORTUNITY AT THE UNIVERSITY OF VIRGINIA

"...in favor of freedom of religion,...we have proposed no professor of divinity; ...the proofs of the being of a God, the creator, preserver, and supreme ruler of the universe,...will be within the province of the professor of ethics;... Proceeding thus far without offence to the Constitution, we...leave every sect to provide, as they think fittest, the means of further instruction in their own peculiar tenets." —Thomas Jefferson, 1818 [1]

T he third of the three things for which Jefferson wanted to be remembered was his founding of the University of Virginia. Today, some of those who argue for Thomas Jefferson the skeptic point to his founding of the

---

1   "Report of the Board of Commissioners for the University of Virginia to the Virginia General Assembly, August 4, 1818" (also known as the Rockfish Gap Report). Founders Online, National Archives (http://founders.archives.gov/documents/Madison/04-01-02-0289, ver. 2013-06-10). Source: David B. Mattern, J. C. A. Stagg, Mary Parke Johnson, and Anne Mandeville Colony, eds., *The Papers of James Madison*, Retirement Series, *4 March 1817–31 January 1820*, (Charlottesville: University of Virginia Press, 2009), 1:326–340.

university as an explicitly secular institution. Is that how Jefferson designed it to be? That question will be explored here.

A Review of Early Correspondence and Actions on Education

To properly comprehend Jefferson's plans for the University of Virginia it is helpful to review some of his educational endeavors earlier in life.

In addition to the numerous donations already cited that Jefferson gave to religious and Trinitarian schools, his account book shows him donating "to the Timber ridge academy" in November 1777.[2] This donation was to what normally was known as Liberty Hall Academy located near Timber Ridge in present Rockbridge County. This is another Presbyterian founded and controlled institution that Jefferson was supporting, and its head was Rev. William Graham from Princeton. It shows the earliest time that he personally invested in the efforts of Presbyterian educators. (This academy eventually became known as Washington and Lee University in Lexington. Graham, like many others who were the recipients of his financial gifts, also was a supporter of religious freedom.)

As we have already seen, in 1779, Rev. James Madison (the later bishop, not the later American president) was president of the College of William and Mary and worked with Jefferson in the drafting of a Bill regarding the College of William and Mary that abolished the Professor of divinity. This was to make it more of a non-denominational educational institution.[3] William and Mary was founded in the seventeenth century to train Anglican priests.

When revising Virginia's laws Jefferson drafted a "Bill [#79] for the More General Diffusion of Knowledge" which would have established a system of public education. It was proposed in 1779 and did not pass. But this bill is often cited by modern scholars as evidence that Jefferson opposed religion in the public arena. This theory is based on a comment he made a few years later in his *Notes on the State of Virginia* that history would be better for teaching reading in the elementary schools, "instead of putting the Bible and Testament into the hands of the children at an age when their judgments are not sufficiently matured for religious inquiries."[4] A careful reading of these words shows that Jefferson made no argument here for a

---

2   Account book, November 1777. For Baxter and Timber Ridge Academy. Beliles, *The Selected Religious Letters and Papers of Thomas Jefferson*, 37.

3   Jefferson's *Notes on the State of Virginia*, 1781-1782, Query 15, www.founders.archives.gov. Jefferson's comments concerning his hopes for the Indian school at the College were that: "The purposes of the . . . institution would be . . . instructing them in the principles of Christianity. . . . "

4   Jefferson's *Notes on the State of Virginia*, 1781-1782, Query 14 www.founders.archives.gov.

general exclusion of religion on the grounds it violated separation of church and state. He did not argue for the curriculum to never allow for "religious inquiries." Rather, his argument was for such inquiries to be addressed in the schools at "an age when their judgments are…sufficiently matured." He was arguing for age-appropriate religious content in the curriculum.[5]

On the last day of 1783, Jefferson wrote a letter to Albemarle County political leader, Wilson Cary Nicolas, in which Jefferson spoke of his meeting with Presbyterian Rev. John Witherspoon, the president of Princeton, to ask his help in finding a tutor for Charlottesville.[6] Dr. Witherspoon was a very devout Christian and a great patriot. He was one of the delegates (from New Jersey) at the same Continental Congress that produced the Declaration of Independence (with Jefferson as its chief author). Jefferson's attempt to enlist Witherspoon's help indicates a relative comfort with Presbyterian religious approaches to education at this point. Witherspoon replied, but his letter is now missing.

Jefferson also traveled to New England in mid-1784 and records in his account book that he paid a visit to the president of Yale College, Ezra Stiles. Stiles was a clergyman at the head of this Congregational college. Jefferson's account book also said that on June 8 he "Paid at Newhaven" which indicates his visit (and financial donation) in a church there, probably Stiles' congregation, but perhaps to the college.

A couple days later on June 10, 1784, Jefferson followed up with a letter to Rev. Stiles, saying: "…I had the pleasure of seeing you in New Haven…After repeating to you assurances of the pleasure with which I shall render any services in my power to the institution over which you so worthily preside, as well as to yourself personally, I have the honor to subscribe myself with the most perfect

---

5   Bill for the More General Diffusion of Knowledge, 1777," Bills Reported by the Committee
     of Revisors, 1779, [see bills 82-87], www.founders.archives.gov. Jefferson's 1779 *Bill* stated:
     "no religious reading, instruction, or exercise, shall be prescribed or practiced *inconsistent*
     with the tenets of any religious sect or denomination." Robert Healey comments: "To
     Jefferson the elimination of whatever was inconsistent with the tenets of any particular
     sect did not mean that religion itself was to be outlawed in public education. . . . Rather,
     [it] meant that those areas of religion upon which all sects agreed were certainly to be
     included…" Robert M. Healey, *Jefferson on Religion in Public Education* (New Haven,
     Conn.: Yale University Press, 1962), 208. Paul Rahe states: "neither [Jefferson] nor Madison
     ever supposed that the existence of a 'wall of separation between church and State' precluded
     governmental encouragement of belief in God." Paul A. Rahe, *Republics Ancient and
     Modern: Classical Republicanism and the American Revolution* (Chapel Hill, N.C.: University
     of North Carolina Press, 1992), 708.

6   "From Thomas Jefferson to Wilson Cary Nicholas, December 31, 1783," www.founders.
     archives.gov.

esteem & respect Sir Your most obedient & most humble servt."[7] Subscribe here is likely to mean he pledged to financially support Stiles and/or the college. Stiles sent a friendly reply on June 21 and again July 7, asking for Jefferson's extra help in fundraising for the college. Jefferson wrote a year later to Rev. Stiles on July 17, 1785, saying: "Colo. Humphreys having satisfied you that all attempts would be fruitless here [in France] to obtain money or other advantages for your college I need add nothing on that head. It is a method of supporting colleges of which they [i.e., Catholics in Europe] have no idea, tho' they practise it for the support of their lazy monkish institutions. I have the honour to be with the highest respect and esteem Sir Your most obedient & most humble servt."[8]

On August 26, 1784, he enrolled his daughter Martha in a Bernadine Catholic convent school called Abbey Royale de Panthemont led by Reverend Mother Louise-Therese and Abbess Marie-Catherine Bethisy de Mezieres. This school required attendance at daily chapel and doctrinal classes but did not require personal belief of its students in Catholic tenets of faith. So Jefferson was comfortable with Catholic religious education at this point, regardless of criticism later to come from Protestant family and friends back home. To his home pastor's brother, James Maury, Jr., in late 1786, Jefferson defended his decision to put his children in a Catholic school: "…my daughter is indeed in a convent, but in one where there are as many protestants as Catholics, where not a word is ever said to them on the subject of religion, and where they are as free in the profession and practice of their [Protestant] religion as they would be in their own country. It is a house of education only…"[9]

Similarly, half a year later in 1787, Jefferson claimed in a letter to his sister (Mary Bolling) that Polly (i.e., his daughter Mary, who arrived in Paris July 15) "is now in the same convent with her sister; it is a house of education altogether; There are in it as many Protestants as Catholics, and not a word is ever spoken to them on the subject of religion."[10] In both letters Jefferson says in regards to religion that "not a word is ever spoken." Since chapel and general religion classes were required, it is obvious that students were exposed to the Catholic religion but appears that Jefferson meant that a personal effort to convert a student to Catholic ecclesiastical beliefs never happened. Jefferson may have deliberately downplayed the situation to ease the concerns of Protestant friends back home, or else he was

---

7   "From Thomas Jefferson to Ezra Stiles, June 10, 1784," www.founders.archives.gov.

8   "From Thomas Jefferson to Ezra Stiles, July 17, 1785," www.founders.archives.gov.

9   "From Thomas Jefferson to James Maury, December 24, 1786," www.founders.archives.gov.

10   "From Thomas Jefferson to Mary Jefferson Bolling, July 23, 1787," www.founders.archives.gov.

sincerely misinformed. And an Irish priest there, Abbe Edgeworth, was such a strong influence in this regard that by mid-1788, Jefferson's oldest daughter Martha told her father of her desire to become a nun.[11]

After Jefferson returned to America and became Secretary of State in 1789, he wrote to Episcopal Rev. Maury on January 8, 1790 asking for information on a Bible and pledging to support Rev. Maury's school.[12] And again he wrote to Presbyterian Rev. John Witherspoon of Princeton, as he had a decade earlier, to request him to provide a teacher for a school in the Charlottesville area. Jefferson wrote on March 12, 1792: "The head of a school of considerable reputation in Virginia having occasion for an Assistant, I take the liberty of inclosing to you the letters I have received on that subject in hopes that your seminary, or your acquaintance may furnish some person, whom you could recommend as fitted to the object...giving me an opportunity, which is ever welcome, of assuring you of those sentiments of esteem & respect with which I am Dear Sir your most obedt. & most humble servt."[13] And Jefferson sent an earlier (January 12, 1792) letter to Rev. Witherspoon to recommend a student for enrollment in his seminary at Princeton, and another on June 3 and July 29 asking for teachers trained by Witherspoon to come to Virginia.

Not long after this, Jefferson wrote in 1794 about a "...splendid project... to arrange for the removal to America of the Calvinistic college of Geneva, Switzerland."[14] This letter to Wilson Nicholas of Charlottesville discussed this project, as he also did in one to Francois D'Ivernis, and in one to George Washington at that time. Although the college in question was certainly not as strong in its theology as it once was—during the days of the great Protestant Reformer John Calvin—nonetheless it was an institution clearly with some degree of religious influence that Jefferson favored bringing to Virginia.

A teacher named James Ogilvie wrote to Jefferson sometime prior to July 3, 1795. He worked as a teacher at this time of Fredericksburg Academy. He said: "...I had long suspected that whilst Religion Philosophy and the fine Arts were so deeply

---

11 Jefferson kept her in the school until they returned to America, but talked her out of that course of life.

12 "From Thomas Jefferson to the Rev. Matthew Maury, January 8, 1790," www.founders. archives.gov.

13 "From Thomas Jefferson to John Witherspoon, March 12, 1792," www.founders.archives. gov.

14 "From Thomas Jefferson to Wilson Cary Nicholas, November 23, 1794," www.founders. archives.gov. Also Dumas Malone, *Jefferson and the Ordeal of Liberty* (Boston, Mass.: Little, Brown and Co., 1962), 191-192. In 1780 Governor Jefferson already approved giving land for Presbyterian-controlled Transylvania University in Kentucky.

infected with the maladys which the injustice and oppression of Europe diffused so widely, education could hardly be so fortunate as to have escaped untainted…"[15] Later from 1805 to 1807, Ogilvie directed an academy at Milton on the outskirts of Charlottesville.

Comfort with Presbyterian, Congregational, Calvinist, and Catholic approaches to education were evident in Jefferson up to this point.

A Review of His Support of Christian Education While President

On October 5, 1801, a friend passed along a letter to Jefferson from "the Rev. Mr [Samuel] Knox a very Republican Minister and the Head of an academy in Frederick town [in Maryland]."[16] Knox was principal of the academy from 1797-1803 and 1823-1827. Jefferson knew of Knox for defending him during the election and had one of his essays on education. In 1799, Knox wrote an "Essay on the Best System of Liberal Education," in which he proposed a plan for a state university that would have no clergy as professors and no theological school, so as to prevent it from being controlled by or favoring one single denomination.

Knox's idea of essentially a non-denominational school would eventually become Jefferson's model for his University of Virginia. Rev. Knox's Christian proposal was in contrast with what was seen earlier in the American colleges where, for example, Harvard was founded to train Congregational ministers, as was Yale. The College of New Jersey (Princeton) was founded by Presbyterian elders to train Presbyterian clergymen. William and Mary's purpose was to educate the Anglican clergy, and so on.

On April 9, 1802, Jefferson "Gave…in favor [of] the Revd. Doctr. Smith towards rebuilding Princeton college 100 Dollars."[17] Presbyterian Rev. Samuel Stanhope Smith was president of the College of New Jersey (later called Princeton). He also had just served as the national Moderator of Presbyterians in 1799. On December 18, 1803, Jefferson's account book shows his entry saying: "Gave…in

---

15   "To Thomas Jefferson from James Ogilvie, [before July 3, 1795]," www.founders.archives. gov. This was not the same person as Rev. James Ogilvie who corresponded with Jefferson back in the 1770s in an effort to help him be appointed to an Anglican parish.

16   "To Thomas Jefferson from John Thomson Mason, [5 October 1801]," www.founders. archives.gov. And note the missing Letter from Rev. Samuel Knox, October 1801.

17   Account book, April 1802. For Smith and Princeton College. Beliles, *The Selected Religious Letters and Papers of Thomas Jefferson*, 101.

favr. Revd. Mr. Coffin for a college in Tenissee."[18] Charles Coffin was a Presbyterian professor of Greeneville College.

Jefferson corresponded in 1804 with the Nuns of the Order of St. Ursula at New Orleans regarding their Catholic school:

> ...the charitable objects of your institution cannot be indifferent to any; and it's furtherance of the wholesome purposes of society by training up it's younger members in the way they should go, cannot fail to ensure it the patronage of the government it is under. Be assured it will meet all the protection which my office can give it.[19]

As noted in an earlier chapter, this is a remarkable letter that quotes scripture, affirms this Christian educational ministry and promises the patronage of the U.S. government. Federal aid to a religious educational institution was acceptable to Thomas Jefferson. Most education was private, but government found ways to encourage the private sector in their task, and often those schools were Christian of one denomination or another.

Also while president in Washington, Jefferson "Subscribed 200 Dollars to an academy at this place."[20] "This place" being Washington, D.C. The Permanent Institution for the Education of Youth was formed in 1805 and Jefferson was named president of its board of trustees.[21] It is unclear how much time Jefferson could not give to it but he never expressed opposition to the board hiring two clergymen as its first teachers and the use of the Bible and Watt's hymnals for teaching reading.[22]

A Presbyterian minister, Rev. Gideon Blackburn, wrote Jefferson in 1807 and gratefully reminded him that the "...Mission [had]...already obtained your patronage."[23] This refers to an action in the summer of 1804 when Jefferson's

---

18   Account book, December 1803. For Coffin and College in Tennessee. Beliles, *The Selected Religious Letters and Papers of Thomas Jefferson*, 118.

19   Letter to Ursuline Nuns of New Orleans (Sister Therese Farjon), July 13, 1804. Beliles, *The Selected Religious Letters and Papers of Thomas Jefferson*, 126.

20   Account book, May 1805. For academy in Washington (led by Elliott). Beliles, *The Selected Religious Letters and Papers of Thomas Jefferson*, 143.

21   Ibid.

22   The board granted two lots for schoolhouses on October 27, 1806, and allowed churches to use them as well.

23   Gideon Blackburn to Thomas Jefferson, September 11, 1807. Beliles, *The Selected Religious Letters and Papers of Thomas Jefferson*, 155. [Included with Blackburn's letter are the notes from Cherokee children.]

administration allocated $300 in federal funds to help Blackburn build a Christian school for the Cherokees in Tennessee.[24]

During the time of his presidency, Thomas Jefferson consistently supported various forms of Christian education—as he did virtually all his adult life.

Post-Presidential Efforts of Jefferson to Promote Education

After Jefferson retired from the presidency and moved back to Monticello, he did not retire his efforts to promote education, including Christian education. The Presbyterian clergyman, Rev. Samuel Knox of Baltimore, who had responded with a defense of Jefferson's religion during the election of 1800, now sent a letter to Jefferson on January 22, 1810, regarding his latest educational work. Jefferson replied on February 12, 1810, saying:

> ...truth and reason are eternal. They have prevailed. And they will eternally prevail, however in times and places they may be overborne for a while by violence, military, civil, or ecclesiastical. The preservation of the holy fire is confided to us by the world, and the sparks which will emanate from it will ever serve to rekindle it in other quarters of the globe, *numinibus secundis* [i.e., by the favor of the powers above]. Amidst the immense mass of detraction which was published against me, when my fellow citizens proposed to entrust me with their concerns, and the efforts of more candid minds to expose their falsehood, I retain a remembrance of the pamphlet you mention...Wishing every good effect which may follow your undertaking, I tender you the assurances of my high esteem and respect.[25]

This relationship between Jefferson and Knox is important because Knox not only came up with the idea of a Christian but non-denominational state college, but he became the first person Jefferson and the board of the college invited to be a professor. And it is interesting to know that the model for public education that Knox proposed in an essay of 1799 was what Jefferson implemented later. (This was the plan mentioned above that eliminated a professor of divinity.) Thus, Rev. Knox provided the philosophical foundation for the University of Virginia.

Several years after the third president retired from the White House, a project for a new non-denominational Christian school of higher learning

---

24   *Tennessee Encyclopedia of History and Culture,*(Knoxville, Tennessee: University of Tennessee Press, 1998), http://tennesseeencyclopedia.net/entry.php?rec=96

25   "Thomas Jefferson to Samuel Knox, February 12, 1810," www.founders.archives.gov.

was begun in Charlottesville. This was what would ultimately become the University of Virginia. Minutes of the Albemarle Academy Board of Trustees on March 25, 1814, nominated Thomas Jefferson to the Board. There is no evidence that Jefferson attended this meeting but certainly appeared at the next meeting and subsequent ones. On September 7, Jefferson wrote to his nephew Peter Carr and enclosed his "draft of a Plan for Albemarle Academy," which included a professional school of "Theology and Ecclesiastical History."[26] This theology and church history school was obviously Christian in nature but not denominational. It clearly was not a secular school when conceived, and Jefferson corresponded with different friends for advice as they planned to change it to a state Central College.

In changing to a public tax-supported institution that was accountable to the legislature, a Unitarian professor of chemistry in Pennsylvania named Thomas Cooper advised school leaders to exclude religion. But on September 30, 1814, Jefferson received Catholic priest and diplomat José Correia da Serra's "Memorandum on Religious Education" that said that Cooper's suggestion was unwise and proposed rather that although no one should teach sectarian beliefs, there should be learned clergymen to teach on that theology "in which all sects agree."[27] This was similar to the approach of the Catholic school in France where Jefferson placed his children. It was also the same as Rev Samuel Knox's proposal 15 years earlier for American education.

Jefferson then wrote Cooper on October 7, 1814, saying:

> ...I agree...that a professorship of Theology should have no place in our institution. But we cannot always do what is absolutely best. Those with whom we act, entertaining different views, have the power and the right of carrying them into practice. Truth advances, and error recedes step by step only; and to do to our fellow men the most good in our power, we must lead where we can, follow where we cannot, and still go with them, watching always the favorable moment for helping them to another step.[28]

Jefferson truly felt that a professor of divinity was not wise in a state school, but implied that he might have to compromise. Like the Rev. Knox who first proposed

---

26   "Thomas Jefferson to Peter Carr, September 7, 1814," www.founders.archives.gov.

27   Letter from Rev. Jose' Francesco Correa da Serra, after September 30, 1814. Beliles, *The Selected Religious Letters and Papers of Thomas Jefferson*, 249.

28   Letter to Thomas Cooper, October 7, 1814, www.founders.archives.gov.

it, Jefferson wanted to avoid division between denominations over whose professor teaches the subject. In November 1814, Jefferson helped draft the "Bill to Create Central College and Amend the 1796 Public Schools Act" so that the private Albemarle Academy could legally become the public state Central College.

While non-creedal churches were dominating in numbers, the leading Presbyterians in the state were most influential in educational endeavors. Rev. John Holt Rice, Rev. Archibald Alexander, and Rev. Conrad Speece gave their support to Jefferson's bill to create a new university and lobbied the state legislature in 1816. They generated the popular support for its passage that year and the founding of the college.[29]

The new Central College Board of Visitors met on July 28, 1817. With Jefferson present, the minutes show that: "...it is agreed that application be made to Dr. [Rev. Samuel] Knox, of Baltimore, to accept the professorship of languages, belles-lettres, rhetoric, history and geography..."[30] An article on "The Establishment of the University" on Monticello's 2011 website refers to the "...hiring of the college's first professor, Dr. Samuel Knox..." Knox was a Presbyterian minister, but since this was not a theological professorship, the board felt comfortable with him, especially since the very concept of non-denominational state education with no divinity professors was first proposed by Knox some 20 years earlier. It is a noteworthy fact that this Presbyterian minister—known for publishing a tract against the religious beliefs of Unitarian Joseph Priestley.

Although he was offered the very first teaching position at Jefferson's college, which later became the University of Virginia, due to a miscommunication, Knox did not receive or respond to the offer in a timely fashion, so his teaching slot was finally offered to someone else. And then on September 1, 1817, Jefferson wrote to Unitarian Thomas Cooper to offer him the chemistry professorship. Jefferson also wrote:

> ...Charlottesville is...free as air in religion and politics. Fanaticism and Philosophy have their equal scope, on the principle that *de gustibus non est disputandum* [i.e., In matters of taste, there can be no disputes] and I believe that a moral lecturer, on Sundays, would be as well attended,

---

29   William Maxwell, *Memoir of the Rev. John H. Rice* (Philadelphia: J. Whetham, 1835), 121. Robert P. Davis, et al, *Virginia Presbyterians in American Life: Hanover Presbytery 1755-1980* (Richmond, Va.: Hanover Presbytery, 1982), 66, 72.

30   "Minutes of the Board of Visitors of the Central College, 28 July 1817," Founders Online, National Archives (http://founders.archives.gov/documents/Madison/04-01-02-0091, ver. 2013-06-10).

and paid, if he would add a rational prayer, as a brawling [quarrelling, dogmatic] presbyterian or baptist. I have been thus particular, because I am very anxious you should come and give us the benefit of your aid in making this seminary the first in the Union, and drawing to it the youth of the other states...[31]

Although Jefferson describes the evangelicals as a quarrelling stream within Christianity, he affirms that their characteristic of defending their beliefs was popular nonetheless.

Jefferson wrote to college board member Joseph C. Cabell on September 9, 1817, and enclosed his "draft of the Elementary School Act," which said: "Ministers of the Gospel are excluded [from serving as overseers of the county elementary schools] to avoid jealousy from the other sects, were the public education committed to the ministers of a particular one; and with more reason than in the case of their exclusion from the legislative and executive functions."[32] The rationale here is clearly not secularism but to have religious equality in the schools and it seemed impossible if they did not keep specific denominational ministers from holding the reins of leadership. Further evidence is seen when Jefferson scratched out the following from the draft of the Act before sending it to Cabell: "No religious reading, instruction or exercise, shall be prescribed or practiced (in the elementary schools) inconsistent with the tenets of any religious sect or denomination."[33] This phrase is often cited by modern secularists, who fail to mention that Jefferson scratched it out. But even if he did not, a careful reading of it shows that the intent was not to ban all religious reading, but only to prohibit religious reading that was "inconsistent" with what all denominations believed. Regardless, the legislature did not adopt this Act as written.

Dedicating and Launching the New College

The board met on October 6, 1817, and the *Minutes of Central College* show that they approved the program in advance for the laying of the cornerstone of

---

31   Letter to Thomas Cooper, September 1, 1817. The Thomas Jefferson Papers Series 1, General Correspondence, 1651-1827, Library of Congress Manuscript Division.

32   Letter to Joseph C. Cabell, September 9, 1817. The Thomas Jefferson Papers Series 1, General Correspondence, 1651-1827, Library of Congress Manuscript Division.

33   Draft of the Elementary School Act, 1817. The Thomas Jefferson Papers Series 1, General Correspondence, 1651-1827, Library of Congress Manuscript Division.

Central College and that it included prayer and Scripture reading.[34] Episcopal Rev. William King of Staunton led this religious portion of the ceremony in the presence of Jefferson, Madison, and Monroe who had approved it all.[35] One day after the cornerstone ceremony, the board learned that Rev. Knox could not accept a professorship…"[36] At the same time Thomas Cooper (an aggressive Unitarian) was offered the chemistry professorship. This set off a religious controversy that took Jefferson by surprise.

Meanwhile, sometime that year, Jefferson wrote the recent president and now fellow-board member James Madison about the Scottish Common Sense philosophy that they wanted the Professor of Moral Philosophy to teach. The most important intellectual influence at the College of William and Mary at the precise time when Jefferson was a student there was Scottish Common Sense philosophy.[37]

This Scottish Realism or Common Sense school of thought, founded by Presbyterian clergymen Thomas Reid and Francis Hutcheson, was primarily a rejection of the skeptical Enlightenment of David Hume and the subjective idealism of George Berkeley (1685-1753).[38] Hume famously denied that Jesus rose from the dead because dead men don't rise (usually). Presbyterian clergyman Reid was the founder of Common Sense or Realism philosophy. It was furthered by Rev. Hutcheson, a professor at Glasgow and later at King's College in Aberdeen, Scotland who wrote *A System of Moral Philosophy* in 1755. Common Sense or Realism philosophy was based on the idea that God revealed Himself to the "moral sense" of ordinary people through the threefold means of reason, nature, and Biblical revelation.

On August 4, 1818, the legislature was seriously considering a proposal to turn the private Central College into a state institution and formed a commission to research the idea and make a proposal. Jefferson and the Board of the Commissioners met at Rockfish Gap and then Jefferson drafts its *Report* of its preliminary plans

---

34   Outline of Cornerstone Ceremonies, October 6, 1817, Beliles, *The Selected Religious Letters and Papers of Thomas Jefferson*, 283.

35   Joseph A. Waddell, *Annals of Augusta County, Virginia, 1726-1871, 2d ed.* (Bridgewater, Va.: C. J. Carrier Co., 1958), 451.

36   Minutes of the Board of Visitors of Central College, October 7, 1817. The Thomas Jefferson Papers Series 1, General Correspondence, 1651-1827, Library of Congress Manuscript Division. Also see *Early History of Virginia as contained in the Letters of Thomas Jefferson and Joseph C. Cabell* (Richmond, Vir.: J.W. Randolph, 1856), 396.

37   *Autobiography*, January 6, 1821. The Thomas Jefferson Papers Series 1, General Correspondence, 1651-1827, Library of Congress Manuscript Division.

38   Hume was skeptical of the veracity of what the senses convey to the mind, and Berkeley believed that only what is internally perceived exists.

for the University that included "rooms for religious worship" but no professor of divinity. This was:

> ...in conformity with the principles of our Constitution, which places all sects of religion on an equal footing...and with the sentiments of the Legislature in favor of freedom of religion....Proceeding thus far without offence to the Constitution, we have thought it proper at this point to leave every sect to provide, as they think fittest, the means of further instruction in their own peculiar tenets.[39]

This report is significant in that it affirms the use of a state university and its buildings for worship and the teaching of the existence of God as being constitutional actions. At Jefferson's university, there was to be no naked public square—no God-free zone. Plus, this statement shows an encouragement of a great deal of Christian doctrine without getting into the issues on which denominations disagree. This reference to the "Constitution" refers to the Virginia state constitution, not the U.S. Constitution.

Interestingly, when the co-authors of this present volume toured Monticello, the tour guide made a strong point that at Jefferson's university there was to be no chapel. Thus, he was founding a secular university. But it is evident from the actual language of the above statement that, instead, a non-denominational—not a secular—vision for the school was being planned. Modern critics need to understand the definite difference between a non-denominational school and a secular non-religious one. There is no question that the college was not to be a denominational church-school per se. But that doesn't mean that biblical concepts, including belief in God, were to be banned in the classroom or on the campus.

In October 1818, nationally-prominent Presbyterian Rev John Holt Rice visited the site of the University in Charlottesville and wrote approvingly of it:[40] So Rice's support of Jefferson's school was no small endorsement.

On November 30, 1818, Presbyterian Rev. Samuel Knox wrote to Jefferson and expressed his interest in the offer to teach at the University, but being a year after the offer was made, the board had assumed he was not interested (although apparently he did not get the offer communicated to him in a timely fashion),

---

39   "Report of the Board of Commissioners for the University of Virginia to the Virginia General Assembly, August 4, 1818" (also known as the Rockfish Gap Report). Founders Online, National Archives (http://founders.archives.gov/documents/Madison/04-01-02-0289, ver. 2013-06-10).

40   Maxwell, *Memoir of the Rev. John H. Rice*, 151-153.

and therefore had extended an offer to another. Jefferson replied to Rev. Knox on December 11 and explained that it was too late.[41] (Six weeks later on January 25, 1819 the Central College was officially chartered as the state University of Virginia)

But when Presbyterian Knox did not get a professorship at Central College and aggressive Unitarian Thomas Cooper did, a major public relations problem emerged with the school's evangelical supporters. Some of Jefferson's private unorthodox views had been known through some of the state newspapers since 1814 but had not generated any overt attack upon him. But it created suspicion in the minds of some, and this turn of events with Knox and Cooper erupted into a perfect storm. Many evangelicals who had supported the establishment of the college, unaware that the offer to Rev. Knox had fallen through, felt betrayed.

In New England, colleges like Harvard had already been taken over by Unitarians, and Transylvania University in Kentucky had been struggling with it for years. Because the Presbyterian theological battles in America were intense at that very moment, Presbyterians in favor of the University of Virginia could not afford to be associated with unorthodoxy. As a result, Rev. Rice in his influential *Evangelical Magazine* began to publicly oppose the hiring of Cooper (without attacking Jefferson's faith).

At the same time that Jefferson was re-associating with the Trinitarian and the orthodox Episcopal Church in his hometown, Presbyterians in the state effectively rallied opposition to the university without ever questioning Jefferson's faith. Their complaints resulted in the Board of Visitors rescinding its professorship offer to Unitarian Thomas Cooper. The Board forced Jefferson to dismiss Professor Cooper in early 1820 before he ever began teaching a single class. Since Jefferson was the one who offered the position to Cooper, it fell to him to dismiss as well.

Jefferson did not grasp the depth and breadth of the criticism of the University due to the Cooper affair. He knew a form of Unitarianism had been acceptable among evangelicals (Restorationists) in Jefferson's Piedmont for years, so he began to attribute the criticism to a desire among Presbyterian clergymen to control the university for themselves. Jefferson was also embarrassed that he had to let Cooper go. He was also angry. In the heat of the moment Jefferson wrote to Cooper:

> ...I must explain to you the state of religious parties with us. About 1/3 of our state is Baptist, 1/3 Methodist, and of the remaining third two parts may be Presbyterian and one part Anglican. The Baptists are sound

---

41   Letter to Rev. Samuel Knox, December 11, 1818. Beliles, *The Selected Religious Letters and Papers of Thomas Jefferson*, 297.

republicans and zealous supporters of their government. The M'ethodists are republican mostly, satisfied with their governmt. Medling with nothing out the concerns of their own calling and opposing nothing, these two sects are entirely friendly to our university, the anglicans are the same, the Presbyterian clergy alone (not their followers) remain bitterly federal and malcontent with their government, they are violent, ambitious of power, and intolerant in politics as in religion and want nothing but license from the laws to kindle again the fires of their leader John Knox, and to give us a 2d blast from his trumpet. Having a little more monkish learning than the clergy of the other sects, they are jealous of the general diffusion of science, and therefore hostile to our Seminary lest it should qualify their antagonists of the other sects to meet them in equal combat.[42]

This private criticism by Jefferson was really unfounded and unfair, but thankfully his targets never learned of this. The 16th century Scotsman John Knox was a direct follower (and acquaintance of John Calvin, earlier in Geneva). Knox is credited with being the founder of the Presbyterian Church.

Jefferson's April 9, 1820, letter to the college board member John Hartwell Cocke shows that the board had officially let go of Cooper. Jefferson then wrote to Catholic friend Rev. José Correia da Serra on April 11 to explain the situation:

[in]…our University;…There exists indeed an opposition to it by the friends of William and Mary, which is not strong. The most restive is that of the priests of the different religious sects, who dread the advance of science as witches do the approach of day-light; and scowl on it the fatal harbinger announcing the subversion of the duperies on which they live. In this the Presbyterian clergy take the lead. The tocsin [i.e., alarm bell] is sounded in all their pulpits, and the first alarm denounced is against the particular creed of Doctr. Cooper; and as impudently denounced as if they really knew what it is.[43]

Although Jefferson primarily blamed Presbyterian clergy, he broadened his critique to include Episcopalians ("friends of William and Mary") and others.

---

42   Letter to Thomas Cooper, March 13, 1820. The Thomas Jefferson Papers Series 1, General Correspondence, 1651-1827, Library of Congress Manuscript Division.

43   Letter to Rev. Correa da Serra, April 11, 1820. Beliles, *The Selected Religious Letters and Papers of Thomas Jefferson*, 305.

But it is still private, and it's obvious that Jefferson's comment about clergy, did not include some clergymen such as Rev. Correia who received the letter. The charge against Christians opposing science is not directed at Christians in general, for it was Christians, building on a foundation from ancient Greece, who had created modern science.[44] As Jefferson himself had affirmed, "the Christian religion . . . is a religion of all others most friendly to liberty, science, and the freest expansion of the human mind."[45] Rather, his comment was directed at what he personally considered to be a narrow category of intolerant and unthinking Christians.

Jefferson wrote to a Jewish man named Joseph Marx about that time on the matter of higher education and its difficulties for those who were not Christians, saying:

> ... I have thought it a cruel addition to the wrongs...that [Jewish] youth should be excluded from...our public seminaries...; in the University lately established here, we have set the example of ceasing to violate the rights of conscience by any injunction on the different sects respecting their religion.[46]

Again, religious freedom for all (including Jews and of course Christians of all denominations) is the key to understanding Jefferson. When he uses the term "seminaries," he is not talking about theological institutions per se, but rather institutions of higher learning (e.g., colleges, universities). The word

---

44   D. James Kennedy and Jerry Newcombe, *What If Jesus Had Never Been Born?* (Nashville: Thomas Nelson Publishers, 1994 / 2001), Chapter 7 on Science, "Thinking God's Thoughts After Him."

45   Thomas Jefferson Randolph, ed., *Thomas Jefferson, Memoir, Correspondence, and Miscellanies*

46   Letter to Joseph Marx, July 8, 1820. The Thomas Jefferson Papers Series 1, General Correspondence, 1651-1827, Library of Congress Manuscript Division. Six years later Jefferson wrote to another Jewish man saying, "...I have thought it a cruel addition to the wrongs which that injured sect [i.e., the Jews] have suffered that their youths should be excluded from the instructions in science [i.e., knowledge] afforded to all others in our public seminaries by imposing on them a course of theological reading which their consciences do not permit them to pursue, and in the University lately established here we have set the example of ceasing to violate the rights of conscience by any injunctions on the different sects respecting their religion." Letter to Isaac Harby, January 6, 1826. Beliles, *The Selected Religious Letters and Papers of Thomas Jefferson*, 374.

seminaries used in this context points out to the Christian origin of institutions of higher learning.[47]

By rescinding of the offer for Cooper to teach at the University, peace was made between the school (including Jefferson) and the Presbyterians. By the end of this year on December 29, 1820, Jefferson's attitude was returning to the pre-Cooper incident, and he wrote to thank Rev. Rice for his support and then appealed for continuing support of the creation of the University of Virginia.

> …I return you thanks for the donation and also for the friendly interest you are pleased to express for its success. The want of such an establishment in our quarter of the Union has been long felt and regretted, and its consequences are but too sensibly seen. Parents especially have lamented it, who knows the efficacy of sound and useful education towards forming the morals, thro' character & habits of youth. Should the legislature know in the same light the importance of this instruction to the character and prosperity of our state, and aid it accordingly, I hope it will be recommended and conducted us to merit the continuation of your friendly dispositions toward it. Accept I pray you my thanks for the kind wishes you are so good to express towards myself and the assurance of my highest respect.[48]

In light of Jefferson's feelings, and knowing Rice's leadership in the criticism, this was a gracious effort on his part.

Yet the incident with Cooper had seemed to crystalize some Presbyterian opposition to the University. On August 5, 1821, Jefferson received a letter from college board member Joseph C. Cabell saying that the Presbyterian clergy "… believe that the Socinians [i.e., Unitarians] are to be installed at the University for the purpose of overthrowing the prevailing religious opinions of the country. They are therefore drawing off, and endeavoring to set up establishments of their own, subject to their own control. Hence the great efforts now making at Hampden Sidney, and the call on all the counties on the south side of James River to unite in support of that college."[49] The battle lines were being drawn,

---

47   Kennedy and Newcombe, *What If Jesus Had Never Been Born?*, Chapter 4, "Education for All."

48   Letter to Rev. John Holt Rice, December 29, 1820. Beliles, *The Selected Religious Letters and Papers of Thomas Jefferson*, 318.

49   Joseph C. Cabell to Jefferson, August 5, 1821. The Thomas Jefferson Papers Series 1, General Correspondence, 1651-1827, Library of Congress Manuscript Division.

and Jefferson's university—not even opened yet—was being lumped in with the Unitarians all because of Trinitarian Samuel Knox not being hired while Unitarian Cooper was.

But a few months later, Cabell writes Jefferson on January 7, 1822, informing him of his plan to try to smooth things over with clergy by meeting with Dr. John Holt Rice, the Presbyterian minister who led the attack on Thomas Cooper (and the school because of him), and Bishop Richard Channing Moore, who was attempting to reestablish an Episcopalian divinity school at the College of William and Mary. The divinity school had ended there long ago, in 1779, through Jefferson's cooperation with Episcopalian Bishop Madison. Then on January 14, Cabell reported: "Mr Rice assured me that he was a warm friend of the University; and that…the Presbyterians sought no peculiar advantages, and that they and the other sects would be well satisfied by the appointment of an Episcopalian. I stated that I…was sure no desire existed anywhere to give any preference to Unitarians."[50] (To put this controversy in context, the University had 10 teaching slots, and Cooper would have filled only one of those ten, yet that single hiring was sufficient to overshadow all the others.) Rice and the Presbyterians, however, wanted proof after the hiring of Cooper that orthodox believers were not going to be excluded from the university's faculty.

Meanwhile, the foremost leader of the Restoration movement at this time in Virginia was Alexander Campbell whose similar disdain for the denominational monopoly over learning led him to eventually found Bethany College in 1840, in what is now West Virginia. It was organized the same as Jefferson's University of Virginia—with no professorship of theology—to encourage any Christian regardless of creed to attend.

Presbyterians Withdraw Their Support

Despite efforts to mend relationships and rebuild trust with Presbyterians, the criticism of fellow Presbyterians toward Rev. Rice's support of Jefferson finally forced him to withdraw his support from the university. The Board of Visitors responded with an effort to rebuild trust with all evangelicals. Jefferson therefore wrote the Report to the President and Directors of the Literary Fund (a term for the legal body that directed the University's funding) on October 7, 1822, affirming that religion was important at the University:

---

50   Joseph C. Cabell to Jefferson, January 14, 1822. The Thomas Jefferson Papers Series 1, General Correspondence, 1651-1827, Library of Congress Manuscript Division.

…It was not…to be understood that instruction in religious opinion and duties was meant to be precluded by the public authorities, as indifferent to the interests of society. On the contrary, the relations which exist between man and his Maker, and the duties resulting from those relations, are the most interesting and important to every human being, and the most incumbent on his study and investigation.[51]

Jefferson is saying that while this was a school not catering to any one "sect" or denomination, it definitely would not preclude teaching about God.

Jefferson continues in this vein—that religion is important to learning:

The want of instruction in the various creeds of religious faith existing among our citizens presents, therefore, a chasm in a general institution of the useful sciences. But it was thought that this want, and the entrustment to each society of instruction in its own doctrine, were evils of less danger than a permission to the public authorities to dictate modes or principles of religious instruction, or than opportunities furnished them by giving countenance or ascendancy to any one sect over another.[52]

In a very real sense, here is Jefferson decrying the very thing that is happening *today* in his name—the establishment of a secular humanist, godless worldview in the public arena. He did not want any one denomination to lord it over the other denominations, but now, members of virtually all Christian denominations are treated as second class citizens. There is a huge difference between a non-denominational approach (which Jefferson advocated) and an exclusively secular one (which he did not).

Jefferson further reported to the college board:

A remedy, however, has been suggested of promising aspect, which, while it excludes the public authorities from the domain of religious freedom, will give to the sectarian schools of divinity…[an invitation] to establish their religious schools on the confines of the University, so as to give to

---

51   "Report to the President and Directors of the Literary Fund, October 7, 1822." Beliles, *The Selected Religious Letters and Papers of Thomas Jefferson*, 334.

52   Ibid.

their students ready and convenient access and attendance on the scientific lectures of the University.[53]

Jefferson continues, "Such establishments would offer the further and greater advantage of enabling the students of the University to attend religious exercises with the professor of their particular sect, either in the rooms of the building still to be erected, and destined to that purpose under impartial regulations, as proposed in the same report of the commissioners, or in the lecturing room of such professor."[54] Jefferson is not envisioning atheist professors, but rather professors of various denominations. Jefferson is clearly not picturing his school as one where God would be banished—rather it just would be a school that did not allow one one denomination ascendancy over any other.

Jefferson also writes,

...the regulations of the University should be so modified and accommodated as to give every facility of access and attendance to their students, with such regulated use also as may be permitted to the other students, of the library which may hereafter be acquired, either by public or private munificence. But always understanding that these schools shall be independent of the University and of each other. Such an arrangement would complete the circle of the useful sciences embraced by this institution, and would fill the chasm now existing, on principles which would leave inviolate the constitutional freedom of religion, the most inalienable and sacred of all human rights, over which the people and authorities of this state, individually and publicly, have ever manifested the most watchful jealousy...[55]

In short, for those who wanted it, theological education would be accommodated at the school. This is Jefferson's idea of constitutional church and state policy. Freedom of religion is encouraged—not freedom from religion. Thomas Jefferson does not envision the University of Virginia to be a godless place, but writers today wrongly claim that this was his intent.

On November 2, 1822, he wrote to Thomas Cooper:

---

53   Ibid.
54   Ibid.
55   Ibid.

In our university you know there is no Professorship of Divinity. A handle has been made of this, to disseminate an idea that this is an institution, not merely of no religion [i.e., no denominational divinity school], but against all religion [i.e., against general principles taught in other classes and against chapel services, etc.]. Occasion was taken at the last meeting of the Visitors [i.e., the board of directors] to bring forward an idea that might silence this calumny [i.e., false statement], which weighed on the minds of some honest friends to the institution. In our annual report to the legislature, after stating the constitutional reasons against a public establishment of any religious instruction [i.e., divinity school], we suggest the expediency of encouraging the different religious sects to establish, each for itself, a professorship of their own tenets, on the confines of the university, so near as that their students may attend the lectures there, and have the free use of our library, and every other accommodation we can give them; preserving, however, their independence of us and of each other. This fills the chasm objected to ours, as a defect in an institution professing to give instruction in *all* useful sciences.[56]

Jefferson sees the university allowing theological professors at the school and with students having access to the library and other services. Thus, the university would not be officially teaching the doctrines of any one denomination.

Although Rev. Knox was not obtained as a professor of ancient languages for the University of Virginia, an invitation went out from Jefferson to a new clergyman in 1824. On April 26 he wrote to Rev. Samuel Parr of England and asked for him to either take the position or suggest others. Parr declined due to his age and infirmities, but it offers again another proof that to not create a professor of divinity at the university was not to create a secular university, simply a non-denominational one.[57] A clergyman teaching languages, unlike teaching divinity, was perceived as not likely to cause the people or any denominations to think the university was favoring one theological tradition.

On March 24, 1824, Jefferson wrote federal judge Augustus Woodward saying: "…in my catalogue [for the University]…ethics, as well as religion, as supplements

---

56   Letter to Thomas Cooper, November 2, 1822. Beliles, *The Selected Religious Letters and Papers of Thomas Jefferson*, 337.

57   Letter to Rev. Samuel Parr, April 26, 1824. Beliles, *The Selected Religious Letters and Papers of Thomas Jefferson*, 365.

to law in the government of man…"[58] Thomas Jefferson and James Madison (i.e., the president), who was likewise interested in this new college, were seeking books for the new university library. Jefferson wrote to Madison the year before to ask him to identify the essential Christian books (since Madison had studied theology at Princeton). In September 1824, Madison sent his list to Jefferson of religious books for the university. In it he included: the works of the Alexandrian Church fathers; Latin authors such as Augustine; the writings of Thomas Aquinas and others from the Middle Ages; and the works of Desiderias Erasmus, Martin Luther, John Calvin, Faustus Socinius (father of the Unitarians), and Robert Bellarmine from the Reformation era. It also included more modern writers such as Hugo Grotius, John Tillotson, Richard Hooker, Blaise Pascal, John Locke, Isaac Newton, Joseph Butler, Adam Clarke, William Wollaston, Jonathan Edwards, Cotton Mather, William Penn, John Wesley, Joseph Priestley, Richard Price, Gottfried Leibnitz, and William Paley. In that list are mostly orthodox Christian writers, with a few Unitarian authors mixed in as well.

Despite these various assurances, many religious leaders continued to be reluctant to wholeheartedly support the university, so the board, including Jefferson, continued efforts to rebuild trust with their Christian constituents. Their *Regulations for the University* that Jefferson drafted on October 4, 1824, made it abundantly clear (about what was previously implied) for everyone to know that in the central building of the university, called the Rotunda,: "…one of large elliptical rooms on its middle floor shall be used for…religious worship [and]…the students of the University will be free, and expected to attend."[59] In other words, through classes and campus worship, this would not be a religion-free institution. (By the way, once time proved that the University would not be oriented to unorthodoxy and secularism, Presbyterians and all evangelical denominations fully backed the university.)

This was the general plan, but issues arose needing clarification when a couple of the local churches asked to use the Rotunda for their weekly worship services. In a letter to the University Proctor, Arthur Brockenbrough, Jefferson replies on April 21, 1825, to his questions about how to manage the buildings of the university in regards to such outside religious requests. Jefferson clarifies that the university buildings should not be used for worship by local churches [i.e., non-students], although religious services for students were permitted and expected.

---

58   Letter to Augustus Woodward, March 24, 1824. Beliles, *The Selected Religious Letters and Papers of Thomas Jefferson*, 364.

59   University of Virginia Board of Visitors Minutes (October 4–5, 1824). Beliles, *The Selected Religious Letters and Papers of Thomas Jefferson*, 368.

(Although the churches could not use it, five years later the local Presbyterian and Episcopalian pastor were secured by the college to conduct regular services for the students there.) But Jefferson explained this denial of outside churches to conduct their church meetings there as follows:

> In answer to your letter proposing to permit the lecturing room of the Pavilion No. 1. to be used regularly for prayers and preachings on Sundays, I have to observe that some 3. or 4. years ago, an application was made to permit a sermon to be preached in one of the pavilions on a particular occasion, not now recollected, it brought the subject into consideration with the Visitors [i.e., the university's board], and altho' they entered into no formal and written resolution on the occasion, the concurrent sentiment was that the buildings of the University belong to the state that they were erected for the purposes of an University, and that the Visitors, to whose care they are committed for those purposes have no right to permit their application to any other...[60]

By saying the buildings were "for the purposes of an University," he means for students, not the town. It was not a statement to exclude religion (as Jefferson had previously and would subsequently reaffirm), but rather it was to simply exclude non-students.

Jefferson continues in his letter to the proctor:

> In the Rockfish report [identified earlier as the Report of the Commissioners in 1818] it was stated as probable that a building larger than the Pavilions might be called for in time, in which might be rooms for a library, for public examinations, and for religious worship under such impartial regulations as the Visitors should prescribe, the legislature neither sanctioned nor rejected this proposition; and afterwards, in the Report of Oct 1822 the board suggested, as a substitute, that the different religious sects should be invited to establish their separate theological schools in the vicinity of the University, in which the Students might attend religious worship, each in the form of his respective sect, and thus avoid all jealousy of attempts on his religious tenets. Among the enactments of the board is one looking to this object, and superseding the first idea of permitting a room in the

---

60   Letter to the University Proctor Arthur Brockenbrough, April 21, 1825. Beliles, *The Selected Religious Letters and Papers of Thomas Jefferson*, 373.

Rotunda to be used for religious worship, and of undertaking to frame a set of regulations of equality and impartiality among the multiplied sects. I state these things as manifesting the caution which the board of Visitors thinks it a duty to observe on this delicate and jealous subject. Your proposition therefore leading to an application of the University buildings to other than University purposes, and to a partial regulation in favor of two particular sects, would be a deviation from the course which they think it their duty to observe…they are building, or about to build [in town], proper churches and meeting houses, much better adapted to the accomodation of a congregation than a scanty lecturing room…I think therefore that, independant of our declining to sanction this application, it will not, on further reflexion, be thought as advantageous to religious interests as their joint assembly at a single place…[61]

So although the university should not be used for non-student religious groups, every other religious accommodation was encouraged, but without coercion or favoritism of any one sect. The official *Centennial of the University of Virginia*, written in 1921, explains correctly that in organizing the university as he did, "*Thomas Jefferson…aimed no blow at any religious influence that might be fostered by it. The blow was at sectarianism only.*"[62]

Church and state historian Anson Phelps Stokes affirmed that "even in establishing a quasi-state university on broad lines, the greatest liberal who took part in founding America's government felt that instruction in the fundamentals of Christian theism and Christian worship were both important and proper."[63] That point is so important, it's worth repeating: at the University of Virginia Jefferson felt that Christian instruction and Christian worship "were both important and proper." Sadly, Jefferson today has wrongly been made into an apostle of secularism, when in reality he was actually an apostle of non-denominationalism in public institutions.

---

61   Ibid.

62   John Calvin Metcalf, et al., eds. *The Centennial of the University of Virginia 1819-1921* (New York: G. P. Putnam's Sons, 1921), 3-18. [Emphasis added]. Another historian of the university said that the "The motto of the University, selected by Jefferson is 'And ye shall know the truth and the truth shall make you free.'" And he said that these words of Jesus from John 8:32 were ordered by Jefferson to be "inscribed upon the frieze of the Rotunda of the auditorium." William E. Curtis, *The True Thomas Jefferson* (Philadelphia: J. B. Lippincott Co., 1901), 267, 331. After the Rotunda burned down the motto was not returned. Instead it was put on the portico of Cabell Hall.

63   Anson P. Stokes, *Church and State in the United States*, 3 vols. (New York: Harper and Brothers, 1950), I:338-339, 515-516.

To Jefferson, the right of conscience was sacrosanct. Allow for religious expression but never use government to coerce belief or participation.

Conclusion

In closing, it is clear that Jefferson early on consistently endorsed and aided different Christian educational institutions, including those run by Presbyterians, whom he later viewed as adversaries. When he finally became directly involved with starting a college during his retirement years, he used a model of non-denominational education that had been suggested by Presbyterian Rev. Samuel Knox about 20 years earlier.

He then tried to hire Trinitarian Knox for his college, but then that fell through, and people heard of the offer of a job to Unitarian Thomas Cooper, whom Presbyterians opposed, although they still supported the University. The University of Virginia has been wrongly characterized by modern biographers as being founded as a secular institution, but in reality it was a non-denominational one that encouraged worship by the students and had Christian subjects taught by the professor of moral philosophy and other professors. Divorcing education from non-denominational religion was not Jefferson's view, and his idea of what was constitutionally permissible is diametrically opposed to what the modern advocates of the separation of church and state argue for today.

Significantly, all three of the accomplishments Jefferson selected for his tombstone included religious language that he used to articulate important political, religious and educational advancements in freedom. All Americans and especially evangelical Christians should be thankful for Jefferson's true religious legacy secured in the Declaration of Independence, the Virginia Statute for Religious Freedom, and the founding of the University of Virginia.

Monticello Sep. 9. 21.

I thank you, dear Sir, ... volume of the LXX sent me. the Prolegomena is the only part wanting in my copy. the Psalterion shall therefore be returned. but as I shall send the former to Richmond to be bound, I will take the liberty of sending the latter part also, and will return it to you bound. this being but the 2d. vol. of the Prolegomena, I have still to seek for the 1st. The last time I had the pleasure of seeing you you mentioned that your future plan, as to your school, would be to take half a dozen boys, and board them. as it is more convenient for us to board ours at home, & their half year will be out on Thursday next, we will then withdraw them with our thanks for your past cares. their joining their elder brother at the same school will be a circumstance of some satisfaction to their parents.

I understand that mr Horsitz is with you in Charlottesville. you will do me an acceptable favor in bringing him to dine at Monticello, with the assurance of my respect and ... west. any day of the week which suits your convenience will be equal to me after that I shall be returning to Bedford for the rest of the autumn. ever & respectfully yours.

Revd. mr Hatch.   Th: Jefferson

Jefferson's 1821 letter to Rev. Frederick Hatch, pastor of Christ Episcopal Church in Charlottesville. Rev. Hatch was able to re-establish an Episcopal church in Charlottesville (after a hiatus of many years), and Jefferson rejoined the church at that time, c. 1820 until his death. Rev. Hatch was one of the many orthodox ministers with whom Jefferson had a positive relationship. (Courtesy of the Library of Congress).

PART III

THE DISTORTED
RELIGIOUS LEGACY OF
THOMAS JEFFERSON

whole a great deal of sound and practical morality. but the greatest
of all the Reformers of the depraved religion of his own country, was Jesus
of Nazareth. abstracting what is really his from the rubbish in which it
is buried, easily distinguished by it's lustre from the dross of his biographers, and as separable from that as the diamond from the dung hill,
we have the outlines of a system of the most sublime morality which
has ever fallen from the lips of man: outlines which it is lamentable
he did not live to fill up. Epictetus & Epicurus give us laws for
governing ourselves, Jesus a supplement of the duties & charities we
owe to others. the establishment of the innocent and genuine character of this benevolent moralist, and the rescuing it from the imputation of
imposture, which has resulted from artificial systems, invented by Ultra-christian sects, unauthorised by a single word ever uttered by him
is a most desirable object, and one to which Priestly
has successfully devoted his labors and learning, it would in fact, it
is to be hoped, effect a quiet euthanasia of the heresies of bigotry
and fanaticism which have so long triumphed over human reason
and so generally & deeply afflicted mankind. but this work is
to be begun by winnowing the grain from the chaff of the historians
of his life. I have sometimes thought of translating Epictetus (for
he has never been tolerably translated into English) of adding
the genuine doctrines of Epicurus from the Syntagma of Gassendi,
and an Abstract from the Evangelists of whatever has the stamp of
the eloquence and fine imagination of Jesus. the last I attemp-
-ted too hastily some 12 or 15. years ago. it was the work of 2. or 3
nights only at Washington, after getting thro' the evening task

* e.g. the immaculate conception of Jesus, his deification, the creation of the world by him, his miraculous powers, his resurrection & visible as-
-cension, his corporeal presence in the Eucharist, the trinity, original sin, atonement, predestination, orders of hierarchy &c.

Perhaps the most controversial letter Jefferson ever wrote on religion, yet he never
sent the most unorthodox parts. Yet the full letter, as if he had sent it, is often
reproduced to promote the notion of Jefferson the lifelong skeptic. This is his 1819
letter to William Short with the unsent footnote. See pp. 346-347. (Courtesy of
Library of Congress).

INTRODUCTION TO
THE DISTORTED
RELIGIOUS LEGACY

"[Some] indeed have heretofore thought proper to ascribe to me religious, or rather anti-religious sentiments, of their own fabric... They wished him [Jefferson] to be thought atheist, deist, or devil..."
—Thomas Jefferson, 1816 [1]

T he reality today is that Jefferson has a legacy far beyond what he suggested for his epitaph. The modern perception of the religious legacy that many today attribute to Jefferson is well known but not necessarily accurate. This is especially true in regards to what is believed to be his adversarial relationship with the clergy, his loathing of the Bible, his rejection of orthodoxy (i.e., the Trinity), and ardent support of complete and total separation of church and state. Is this modern view correct, or is it a distortion of reality?

As Gregg Frazer in *The Religious Beliefs of America's Founders* identifies it, the problem is that "The vast majority of those who have presented the religious beliefs of Adams, Jefferson, and Franklin in the past have done so selectively to advance

---

1   To Margaret Bayard Smith, August 6, 1816. Mark A. Beliles, ed., *The Selected Religious Letters and Papers of Thomas Jefferson* (Charlottesville, VA: America Publications, 2013), 272.

an agenda or have simply accepted the labels traditionally applied to them."[2] As a result, the story on Thomas Jefferson's religious life is often written incorrectly.

He has often been portrayed as an anti-church activist or a closet atheist, an infidel or Deist, or at best a Unitarian. One definition of a Deist is one who believes that a clockmaker god made the world, wound it all up, but then abandoned his creation. This kind of Deist would not believe in a prayer-answering God and would certainly not subscribe to the Christian understanding of the Triune God. But there are other definitions and nuances for Deism. Unfortunately, scholars, while often using the same terms do not consistently use the same definitions. Jefferson could fit some criteria of some definitions but not others. Frazer himself creates the term Theistic Rationalism to describe Jefferson's religion, which is still quite inadequate in light of the facts thus far presented.

Christian Writers Debate

Controversy surrounding the faith of Thomas Jefferson has occurred many times in history and recently can be seen in 2012 when the popular conservative Christian historian David Barton of WallBuilders wrote *The Jefferson Lies: Exposing the Myths You've Always Believed About Thomas Jefferson.*

Two teachers at Grove City College, also a conservative Christian institution, Warren Throckmorton (a psychology professor) and Michael Coulter (a history professor) wrote a book, *Getting Jefferson Right*, critiquing Barton's book and much of Barton's teaching in general.

And others joined in the debate, but the entire controversy surrounding these two dueling books well illustrates that this subject is potentially a minefield. Views of Jefferson, even by respected Christian scholars, are perhaps among the most passionately (and selectively) quoted of any American historical figure. Unfortunately, even the majority of Christian scholars seem to have embraced the view of Jefferson held by most secular biographers and commentators of Jefferson, who exclude or ignore much of what Jefferson actually said or did.

Secular Opinions of Jefferson's Faith

Here are a few examples of how many Jefferson scholars and writers of today and times past refer to him in ways that define him as an unorthodox believer or unbeliever:

---

2   Gregg Frazer, *The Religious Beliefs of America's Founders* (Lawrence, Kansas: University Press of Kansas, 2012), 162.

- Merrill Peterson, former head of the University of Virginia history department and noted Jefferson biographer, calls Thomas Jefferson a "secular liberal."[3]
- Dumas Malone, in his six-volume biography of Jefferson, said, "in theology he was a Unitarian, but he was no sectarian…"[4]
- R. B. Bernstein said, "he embraced deism, the view that God had created the universe to run according to fixed, unchanging laws and therefore was not involved in people's daily lives."[5]
- Charles Sanford, in *The Religious Life of Thomas Jefferson,* said, "He was not an atheist, he was a deist…"[6]

Similar terminology is repeated by general biographers Joseph Ellis, Adrienne Koch, Peter Onuf, Jon Meacham (among others), and those writers focusing on Jefferson's religion such as Dickinson Adams and Ruth Lester, Eugene Sheridan, and Edwin Gaustad.

One lesser-known author of Jefferson's religious beliefs, Stephen Vicchio, made a distinction, saying, "he was not an atheist, not a Deist, nor…a member of a Christian church… [and although] attracted to the theology of the Unitarians, nowhere…among their members."[7] Yet even this is not fully accurate, for throughout his long life, Jefferson was a member of a Christian church—whenever it was available to him, even in the last years of his life.

Charges of Atheism

For the past century and a half, virtually no scholars would make the assertion that Jefferson was an atheist. Author and scholar Virginius Dabney wrote: "As all informed historians know, Jefferson was far from being an atheist… This was among the libels spread against him by the Federalists."[8] Only recently has the canard of Jefferson as an atheist gained traction.

---

3   Merrill D. Peterson, *Thomas Jefferson and the New Nation: A Biography* (New York: Oxford University Press, 1970), 133. He says: "secular liberals like Jefferson."

4   Dumas Malone, *The Sage of Monticello* (Boston, Mass.: Little, Brown and Co., 1981), 492.

5   Robert Bernstein, *Thomas Jefferson* (Oxford: Oxford University Press, 2003), 42.

6   Charles Sanford, *The Religious Life of Thomas Jefferson* (Charlottesville, Va.: University Press of Virginia, 1984), 173.

7   Stephen J. Vicchio, *Jefferson's Religion* (Eugene, Oregon: WIPF and STOCK Publishers, 2007), 121.

8   Virginius Dabney, *The Jefferson Scandals: A Rebuttal* (New York: Dodd, Mead & Company, 1981), 71.

For example, the atheist claim was made by ABC News anchor Peter Jennings in a 2001 broadcast,[9] and others have said similar things:

- Militant and military atheist Michael Weinstein of the "Military Religious Freedom Foundation," said of Jefferson, "It's very likely he was an atheist."[10]
- Author Farrell Till, in an essay called, "The Christian Nation Myth," called Jefferson "fiercely anti-clerical"—meaning Jefferson hated Christian clergy.[11]
- Even in fiction sources, it's just assumed that Thomas Jefferson was not a believer in God even in a general sense. For example, in *Sally Hemings*, a 1980 novel supposedly based on historical fact by Barbara Chase-Riboud, a character says, "He was an atheist, like Jefferson."[12]

One of the aggressive atheists in recent times is the late Christopher Hitchens who wrote the best-selling atheist manifesto, *god Is Not Great*. (He purposefully chose not to capitalize the g in God out of disrespect.) Hitchens wrote a book about Thomas Jefferson and called him "The Author of America." He presents Jefferson as virtually a complete skeptic—that is, a disbeliever in God—who, on occasion, used theological language that didn't conform to his true skeptical self.

Hitchens claimed, in reference to Jefferson's "Virginia Statute for Religious Freedom": "There was a small element of hypocrisy in Jefferson's own position, since as a 'Deist' he did not believe that God intervened in human affairs at all, and was thus in a weak position to claim divine authority for a secular bill."[13]

And of Thomas Jefferson's *Philosophy of Jesus* (i.e., the so-called "Jefferson Bible") Hitchens writes that it was to be "unembarrassed with matters of fact or faith beyond the level of [the Indians'] comprehensions." He adds, "This certainly matched Jefferson's view that Indians should be protected from Christian

9   Stephen J. Vicchio, *Jefferson's Religion* (Eugene, Oregon: WIPF and STOCK Publishers, 2007), 121.

10   David Barton, *The Jefferson Lies* (Nashville, Tennessee: Thomas Nelson Publishers, 2012), 163.

11   Farrell Till, "The Christian Nation Myth," the Secular Web. Quoted in Barton, *The Jefferson Lies*, 141.

12   Quoted in Virginius Dabney, *The Jefferson Scandals: A Rebuttal* (New York: Dodd, Mead & Company, 1981), 71.

13   Christopher Hitchens, *Thomas Jefferson: Author of America* (New York: Atlas Books, a division of HarperCollins*Publishers*, 2005), 37.

missionaries."[14] Hitchens gets this completely wrong. Jefferson supported Christian missions to Indians and entitled his abridgement specifically for them.

Hitchens further states: "Toward the end of his life, in 1820, Jefferson published a more complete expurgation, in which he excised all mentions of angels, miracles, and the resurrection."[15] That is not an accurate assessment either. Jefferson created a list of 81 significant moral teachings of Jesus and arranged them in different columns. King James English, Greek (the original), Latin, and French. He studied these morals of Jesus, which he called on numerous occasions the best morality ever given to humanity. But to Hitchens, the "Jefferson Bible" was simply Jefferson taking another opportunity to essentially dethrone Jesus and rob him of His divinity.

So the modern portrayal is that Jefferson, the "author of America," was a closet infidel intent on making the rest of the nation in his image. Unfortunately, people such as Jennings, Hitchens, and so many more can get away with these statements without much accountability. But that's still not the full story. Even legitimate scholars and biographers of Jefferson have also contributed to the modern false portrayal of his religious beliefs and legacy.

Avoiding Extremes

One common extreme in prevailing biographical treatments of Jefferson is to claim he was a secular Deist or an approximate portrayal. A less common but growing extreme; akin to what is represented by the likes of Christopher Hitchens, is to identify Jefferson essentially as an atheist who wanted state-sanctioned atheism. But an equally errant extreme, although less common, is to claim that he was essentially an orthodox Christian. As already demonstrated, by his own admission, at least later in life, Jefferson believed that the original Christian faith—as given by Jesus—and the Scriptures, had been corrupted.

The real Thomas Jefferson is found by recognizing his time period and context as determinative. What historian Paul Johnson says of Winston Churchill seems to fit Jefferson too: "Churchill, then and always, was a mass of contradictions."[16]

Daniel Dreisbach, political science professor at American University and author of *Thomas Jefferson and the Wall of Separation of Church and State*, says about him: "Jefferson described himself as 'a real Christian,' although he was certainly aware that his beliefs were unconventional...[and] rejected key tenets of orthodox

---

14   Ibid., 181.

15   Ibid.

16   Paul Johnson, *Churchill* (New York et al.: Penguin Books, 2010), 19.

Christianity."[17] To be accurate, the words "late in life" should be added to the second half of that sentence. If so, it's probably the most accurate description possible.

Although late in life Jefferson did not hold to all the doctrines of orthodox, historic Christianity, yet he was still attending such churches and perhaps positively influenced by them. And he certainly made significant contributions to the cause of freedom, even the Christian cause.

Although it was late in his life that Jefferson seemed to reject some of the key doctrines of the Christian faith while maintaining an orthopraxic lifestyle, most commentators tend to ascribe these latter beliefs to him for all of his 65 adult years. Thus, the 33-year old who wrote of God-given rights in the Declaration was supposedly holding to a Unitarian or unorthodox idea of God as he did as a 73 year old. In reality, Jefferson was a constantly developing and changing person of faith, an historically indisputable fact that is flatly ignored by most modern commentators. Jefferson did not view himself as an atheist nor a Deist; but he rather saw himself as one trying to save Christianity, as he understood it, from centuries of corruptions. Get back to Jesus, cries Jefferson, unencumbered by all the artificial vestments put on His Church by charlatans who obfuscate simple truths that they might have a livelihood.

Jefferson is a man of contradictions. And it stretches all imagination to think of him as being in line with historic Christianity by the end of his life. But the real question is: Are the policies of today that are essentially fashioned in his name in line with what he himself would agree to?

In Jefferson's Name

Whatever doubts he personally may have had, they do not justify what is happening today: In Jefferson's name, any expression of Christianity is often driven from the public realm. In Jefferson's name, religious freedom is under direct attack. In Jefferson's name, all sorts of terrible threats to religious liberty continue. For example, a couple of years ago, the former mayor of New York City decreed that all the churches meeting in public schools must be evicted,[18] despite all the good they do for the community, and despite the fact that other groups were allowed to rent these facilities, Christian churches alone were targeted for discrimination. How is any of this related to Thomas Jefferson? Because of his letter on the separation

---

17   Daniel Dreisbach, *Christian History & Biography Magazine,* Issue #99 (Wall of Separation), 2008. http://www.christianhistorymagazine.org/index.php/past-pages/99separation/

18   This case continues in the courts. http://www.jerrynewcombe.com/resources/Evicting+Chur ches+from+Public+Schools.pdf

of church and state that came (incorrectly) to be the arbiter of what the founders meant when they gave us the First Amendment.

It seems that a misreading of Jefferson has altered the institutional separation of church and state as the founders would have understood and approved it to what now is a larger separation of God from the public square. The evidence as shown in this book suggests that Thomas Jefferson was not in favor of what has become state-sanctioned and state-enforced atheism. He was for removing all barriers to religious expression.

What kind of public policies did Jefferson advocate when it comes to religion? What were his views on the freedom of religion, God-given rights, freedom of conscience, and public education?

CHAPTER 9

JEFFERSON AND THE CLERGY: AN EXAGGERATED CONFLICT

"The clergy, by getting themselves established by law, & ingrafted into the machine of government, have been a very formidable engine against the civil and religious rights of man... [But] The clergy here [in Virginia] seem to have relinquished all pretension to privilege... They ought therefore to possess the same rights." —Thomas Jefferson, 1800 [1]

I n this chapter and the three that follow is an examination of the religious legacy of Jefferson that that has been distorted as it relates to clergy, the Bible, orthodoxy, and the separation of church and state. In discussing these topics, in all of them there are some things Jefferson truly said or did that are troublesome to evangelical Christians, while there is much with which they will agree with him. Although those are undeniable, most of the next chapters will be devoted to the distortion, selective use, or overemphasis of those things. The first deals with Jefferson and the clergy and the organized church they represented.

As already clearly established, and contrary to the modern understanding of Thomas Jefferson, he enjoyed many positive relations with various clergymen

---

1   "From Thomas Jefferson to Rev. Jeremiah Moore, August 14, 1800," www.founders. archives.gov.

and active laypeople, the majority of whom were believers in historic, traditional, orthodox Christianity. However, he was the recipient of a vicious attack by northern Federalist clergymen during the 1800 election—initially because of a misinterpretation of his work and motives to dis-establish the state church of Virginia. While this chapter will summarize data from previous chapters regarding his relations with the clergy, it will particularly look at the modern exaggeration of Jefferson's alleged antagonism and independence from orthodox churches and their leadership. Also included is a look at some of the exaggerated historical claims made against Jefferson by Federalist clergy and supporters in the ugly election of 1800.

Friendly Relationships With the Clergy

Contrary to the modern idea of Jefferson as a sort of minister-hater, there were over 300 ministers or ministries that Jefferson is proven to have interacted with over his 65 adult years. Of these about a third provide useful information on his religious life. Of that 100 or so about 80 percent were Protestant Trinitarians, eight percent Catholic Trinitarians, eight percent Unitarian/Universalist, three percent other, and one percent Jewish. Among the Protestant Trinitarians there were: 23 Presbyterians, 18 Anglicans-Episcopalians, 18 Baptists, four Methodists, four Congregationalists, and 17 other. The "other" category includes one or two Lutherans, un-identified missionaries, a Bible Society, and one or two each of the Swedenborgians, Quakers, Sandemanians and Restorationists. Additionally, the appendix shows a list of about 150 clergymen or religious groups who received letters from Jefferson.

Despite these indisputable numbers, almost all commentators of Jefferson today seem to focus primarily on the small eight percent of his correspondence with unorthodox associates, while ignoring the vast majority of letters exchanged with orthodox Christian ministers or ministries. Also in the appendix are listed about 50 recipients of his donations found in his account book but which never appear in his letters. About 130 times have been identified where he donated money or his time and assistance to religious purposes spread over 85 different religious leaders or groups—again, the vast majority of which supported the historic Christian faith (e.g., the redeeming death and resurrection of Jesus, the Son of God, the Trinity, etc.).

Jefferson's interaction with the unorthodox Unitarians and Universalists, both clergy and lay persons, was a much higher percentage in the last 15 or so years of Jefferson's life. About half of all of Jefferson's surviving letters are from that final period when he was also the most unorthodox. But to let that small portion of his life dominate the picture of his entire religious life creates an impression that is false.

Jefferson Both Praised and Criticized Clergy in Politics

From the chronological chapters at the first of the book, the many positive relationships Jefferson had with clergy up until the election of 1800 were evident. What follows are a few reminders of Jefferson's remarks and actions for the clergy.

In 1779, Jefferson praised Rev. Charles Clay's religious-based patriotism in a testimonial letter which said of him: "[H]is deportment has been exemplary…; In the earliest stage of the present contest with Great Britain, while the clergy of the established church in general took the adverse side, or kept aloof from the cause of their country, he took a decided and active part with his countrymen, and has continued to prove his Whiggism unequivocal, and his attachment to the American cause to be sincere and zealous."[2]

Jefferson also supported clergy in America getting involved in government— although there was a time when he felt that the state-established Anglican clergy had an unfair advantage in Virginia politics, so he agreed with what became a temporary measure to curb their political involvement. Meanwhile, he writes Rev. Clay on January 27, 1790: "I understand you are a candidate for…Congress;…I am sure I shall be contented with such a representative as you will make;…Wishing you every prosperity in this…undertaking;…your friend & servant."

Jefferson's friend Bishop James Madison, the first bishop of the Virginia Episcopal Church, was far from being an opponent of Jefferson. In fact, the bishop had managed to lead some from the Episcopal Church in Virginia into the same political party as their enemies, the evangelicals, who had long fought against the preferential legal status given that state-established church. Though not an evangelical, Bishop Madison, was a supporter of Jefferson and "coadjutor in… the development of the Democratic-Republican Party."[3] A letter from the bishop to Jefferson in 1800 criticized the Federalist clergy in New England and said: "…

---

2 Testimonial for Rev. Charles Clay, August 15, 1779, www.founders.archives.gov.

3 Thomas Thompson, *The Failure of Jeffersonian Reform: Religious Groups and the Politics of Morality in Early National Virginia* (Unpublished dissertation, University of California, Riverside, 1990), 346. See also David Holmes, *Up from Independence: The Episcopal Church in Virginia* (Orange, VA: Interdiocesan Bicentennial Committee of the Virginias, 1976), 6. See Morton H. Smith, *Studies in Southern Presbyterian Theology* (Phillipsburg, N.J.: Presbyterian and Reformed Publishing Co., 1962), 424.

The true Christian must be a good Democrat"[4] –that is, a person involved with the Democrat-Republican Party in opposition to the Federalists.

By this time, back in the Virginia Piedmont around Charlottesville, the religious leaders who had a good relationship with Jefferson—Baptist William Woods, Episcopal-Presbyterian Charles Wingfield, and Methodist Tandy Key— continued to dominate local politics and all held public office. These were joined by John Goss, who became pastor of Blue Run and Preddy's Creek Baptist churches around 1800, and served them for about forty years. He was elected Sheriff of Madison County from 1800 to 1803.[5]

When Jefferson expressed opposition to clergy in politics, it was first focused on state-established Catholics of medieval Europe or in France at that time. Although having praise for some Catholic clergy, he frequently mentioned in various letters in late 1788 and 1789 the "...priests and nobles [in France] combin[in]g together against the people ..." and that "...The [Catholic French] clergy and nobility, as clergy and nobility eternally will, are opposed to giving...representation [to the people] as may dismount them from their back."[6] These kinds of criticisms of European clergy continued throughout Jefferson's life of correspondence. Certainly his criticism would apply as well to state-established Protestant clergy in Europe or to early colonial clergy in America.

His Comments About Virginia Clergy in Politics

The criticism of European clergy in politics is consistent, but it was different in Virginia. At the very end of 1784, Jefferson sends a letter from France to lawyer James Madison who was pushing for religious freedom in the Virginia legislature. Madison informed Jefferson that the Episcopal clergy were pushing for preserving legal incorporation status for their historically state-established Church. Jefferson responded that "...the Episcopalians have again shewn their teeth and fangs..."[7] This was the first critical statement that Jefferson ever expressed about Episcopalians (and perhaps clergy) in America. All other

---

4   "To Thomas Jefferson from Bishop James Madison, February 11, 1800," www.founders. archives.gov . Also see Edwin Gaustad, *Sworn On the Altar of God: A Religious Biography of Thomas Jefferson* (Grand Rapids, Mich.: W. B. Eerdmans Publishers, 1996), 204.

5   Preddy's Creek's oral tradition says that Jefferson had also occasionally visited and worshiped at their church. Gayle Marshall, *Preddy's Creek Baptist Church, 1781-1981* (Albemarle County, Va: Published by the church, 1981).

6   Letter to W. Carmichael, December 25, 1788, www.founders.archives.gov.

7   Letter to James Madison, December 8, 1784 www.founders.archives.gov.

comments before then were about priests in European history or early America (as in his *Notes on the State of Virginia*).[8]

Jefferson cited in various letters sent home from France of his desire to see religious freedom succeed in Virginia and in a letter to Marquis de Chastellux on September 2, 1785, he defended (even though he was not responsible for) the Virginia Constitution's prohibition of clergy in public office: "The clergy are excluded, because, if admitted into the legislature at all, the probability is that they would form it's majority. For they are dispersed through every county in the state, they have influence with the people, and great opportunities of persuading them to elect them into the legislature. This body, tho shattered, is still formidable;...(and) merit a proscription from meddling with government."[9]

But Jefferson reversed this opinion a decade-and-a-half later. On August 14, 1800, Jefferson replied to a letter from Baptist Rev. Jeremiah Moore, saying: "...after 17 years more of experience and reflection, I do not approve [a clause in the Virginia constitution]. It is the incapacitation of a clergyman from being elected. The clergy, by getting themselves established by law, & ingrafted into the machine of government, have been a very formidable engine against the civil and religious rights of man. They are still so in many countries & even in some of these United States..."[10]

That place in the United States where clergy still posed problems was in the northeastern states where the Federalist Party was strong. His first criticism of northern clergymen took place in a letter to James Madison dated March 2, 1798, when he said that the New England states "are so priest-ridden, that nothing is to be expected from them, but the most bigoted passive obedience."[11] And Jefferson wrote his friend Bishop James Madison of Virginia on January 31, 1800, saying: "...[Jedidiah] Morse...& his ecclesiastical and monarchical associates [in Massachusetts] have been making such a hue and cry."[12] Rev. Morse led the Congregational alliance with the Federalist Party in New England in opposition to Jefferson's party.

---

8   Jefferson's *Notes On the State of Virginia*, 1782, www.founders.archives.gov.

9   Letter to Marquis de Chastellux, September 2, 1785, www.founders.archives.gov.

10   Letter to Rev. Jeremiah Moore, August 14, 1800, www.founders.archives.gov.

11   Letter to James Madison, March 2, 1798, www.founders.archives.gov.

12   Letter to Rev. James Madison, January 31, 1800, www.founders.archives.gov.

First Attack on Jefferson's Faith

1800 marks the first overt attack on Jefferson's faith ever. There had been a couple vague attacks a couple years earlier without naming Jefferson specifically or identifying a specific sign of heterodoxy. Many scholars note that this was for political reasons by northerners (whom he sometimes called Easterners) associated with the Federalist opposing party. Jefferson made a few critical comments on those northerners who did this, but his first critical statement against Presbyterian clergy in general was not until 1820. Throughout his entire life, research so far revealed only one clergyman south of New York that ever attacked Jefferson's faith. None were in Virginia. Not one. The evangelicals in Virginia loved Jefferson (and Madison) because they had championed disestablishing the state-church.

Despite the overwhelming number of positive relationships with clergy in politics in Jefferson's lifetime, an image of him as being anti-clerical developed especially during the mud-slinging of the 1800 election, America's first heated presidential campaign.

Jefferson was accused by Federalists of not being a Christian during that election. The irony is that his Federalist opponent, John Adams, was less of one (in terms of Trinitarian orthodoxy). Allegations against Jefferson were so prominent during that ugly campaign that the gist of them is still remembered to this day: that Jefferson was allegedly an infidel. This is a false but stubborn legacy.[13]

Jefferson biographer Merrill Peterson comments: "For nearly a decade the Federalists had been fashioning an ugly image of Jefferson. Little was added in 1800, but everything was raised to the *nth* dimension. The fear and distrust dedicated Federalists felt for Jefferson presumably had psychological validity in the Federalist political mind."[14]

In his book, *Separation of Church and State*, Phillip Hamburger states: "Many Federalist clergymen claimed that Jefferson was not a Christian, and they thereby introduced into a national political campaign the old issue of religion's civil importance."[15] For example, he was often accused of being secretly committed to French infidelism.

---

13   The only real reason Adams has not been lumped with Jefferson among founding father skeptics is because a majority of northerners supported his party, and southern Republicans did not respond with similar smears against him as had been thrown at Jefferson.

14   Merrill D. Peterson, *Thomas Jefferson and the New Nation: A Biography* (New York: Oxford University Press, 1970), 636-637.

15   Phillip Hamburger, *Separation of Church and State* (Cambridge, MA: Harvard University Press, 2002 / 2004), 112-113.

Daniel Dreisbach is a professor of justice, law, and society at American University and author of *Thomas Jefferson and the Wall of Separation of Church and State*. He wrote a lengthy article on the 1800 election and the religious controversy: "In few, if any, presidential contests has religion played a more divisive and decisive role than in the election of 1800. Jefferson's religion, or alleged lack thereof, emerged as a critical issue in the campaign."[16]

For example, Dreisbach points out: "In the days before the election, the *Gazette of the United States*, a leading [Philadelphia-based] Federalist newspaper, posed the 'grand question' of whether Americans should vote for 'GOD—AND A RELIGIOUS PRESIDENT [i.e., John Adams]; or impiously declare for JEFFERSON—AND NO GOD!!!'"[17] Even as early as 1798, the president of Yale, the normally-wise Rev. Timothy Dwight feared that if Jefferson became president, "we may see the Bible cast into a bonfire, the vessels of the sacramental supper borne by an ass in public procession, and our children...chanting mockeries against God...[to] the ruin of their religion, and the loss of their souls."[18] It must be noted that Dwight did not give specific criticism of Jefferson's religion, but he more broadly expressed worry over what he perceived as a party of leaders emerging who seemed too silent regarding the anti-Christian behavior of the French Revolution, and other cultural trends that seemed to threaten the Christian status-quo of America. It is true that Jefferson did not disavow the French, but neither did he affirm their excesses. And it must be noted that Dwight's predecessor at Yale, Rev. Stiles, held a view of the French more like Jefferson, and indeed supported Jefferson for President.

Rev. Linn and Rev. Mason

Although many of the ministers accusing Jefferson of unbelief hailed from New England, two of the most prominent names were ministers from New York. Hamburger notes, "The onslaught against Jefferson began in earnest when Federalist pamphlets charged that Jefferson was a deist and an infidel. William Linn and John Mitchell Mason—the one a Dutch Reformed pastor in New York City, the other a Presbyterian minister of the city's Associate Reformed Church—initiated the assault, and numerous other Federalists quickly joined the fray."[19] The

---

16   Daniel Dreisbach, "The Wall of Separation," *Christian History & Biography Magazine*, Issue #99, 2008. https://www.christianhistoryinstitute.org/uploaded/50b787762d bd67.76222839.pdf

17   Ibid.

18   Ibid.

19   Hamburger, *Separation of Church and State*, 113.

attack by Rev. William Linn was the most unexpected in light of previous friendly correspondence and cooperation with Jefferson. The content of Linn's earlier letters offer no explanation or hint of any discomfort with Jefferson's faith.

But in the 1800 election season Linn warned:

- "the election of any man avowing the principles of Mr. Jefferson" would "destroy religion, introduce immorality, and loosen all the bonds of society."[20]
- a vote for Jefferson "must be construed into no less than rebellion against God." Linn feared the "destruction of all social order and happiness."[21]

Second, there were similar dire predictions from Rev. John Mitchell Mason: "By giving your support to Mr. Jefferson, you are about to strip infidelity of its ignominy [i.e., public disgrace, dishonor]…By this act, you will proclaim to the whole world…that you do not believe it subversive of moral obligation and social purity."[22]

Rev. Mason saw a Jefferson victory as "a crime never to be forgiven," that the people would transfer the presidency "upon an open enemy to their religion, their Redeemer, and their hope, [and it] would be mischief to themselves and sin against God."[23] Jefferson's "favorite wish," according to Rev. Mason, is "to see a government administered without any religious principle among either rulers or ruled." He charged that Jefferson's perspective is: *Religion has nothing to do with politics.*[24]

Defending Jefferson

Not a single clergyman from the south joined in this attack on Jefferson's faith at this time nor for that matter at any time throughout Jefferson's lifetime. There was an Episcopal minister in Philadelphia, Rev. James Abercrombie, who on August 24, 1800, was reported in the *Philadelphia Aurora* newspaper to have preached: "Beware—Men, Brethren, and fellow Christians—Beware of ever placing at the Head of Civil Society a man who is not an avowed Christian and

---

20 William Linn, *Serious Considerations on the Election of a President: Addressed to the Citizens of the United States* (New York: 1800), 24.

21 Ibid.

22 John Mitchell Mason, *The Voice of Warning, to Christians, on the Ensuing Election of a President of the United States* (New York: 1800), 35.

23 Ibid.

24 Ibid.

an exemplary believer in our Holy Religion…"[25] He did not directly mention Jefferson, and his words could be applied to any election about any candidate. Although he gave no specific evidence about Jefferson, people knew who was implied. Furthermore, this minister earlier said a similar thing about George Washington. Abercrombie's superior, Bishop William White (a chaplain of the U. S. Senate when Thomas Jefferson was President of the Senate and Vice-President of the United States), did not support this view, and so this implied charge against Jefferson had little impact.

The refusal by any Virginia or Albemarle County clergyman to agree with these northern accusations was because those who knew Jefferson best viewed these as baseless and partisan charges. Meanwhile, evidence abounds of support and affection for Jefferson (and Madison) from the *evangelicals* of Virginia, because these two men had worked so closely with them to secure full religious freedom there. Although evangelicals were smaller in number and influence in the north, they strongly defended Jefferson during that contentious 1800 election. Hamburger writes of one notable defender in New York: "Tunis Wortman, pointed out that Jefferson's 'only object' in discussing religion was 'to discountenance political establishments in theology.'"[26]

Meanwhile, the Presbyterian Rev. Samuel Knox, Principal of Baltimore College, and an advocate of public education, wrote "A Vindication of the Religion of Mr. Jefferson" in 1800, and worked for the Republican cause in Maryland.[27] Over a decade later, on the National Day of Humiliation and Prayer proclaimed by President James Madison in 1812, Rev. Knox gave a sermon in which he asserted that "Our national cause is a religious cause."[28]

Certainly, there were a few clergy who publicly opposed Jefferson on religious grounds (including several northern Federalist Unitarians) but just as many defended him. Overall, the current portrayal that most clergy opposed Jefferson during that election is the result of the exaggeration of modern historians. Overall, it was merely one element of the political, partisan attack against Jefferson.

---

25   Richard Rosenfeld, *American Aurora* (New York: St. Martin's Press, 1997), 840.

26   Hamburger, *Separation of Church and State*, 118.

27   Samuel Knox, "A Vindication of the Religion of Thomas Jefferson" (Baltimore, Md.: W. Pechin, 1800).

28   Steven Watts, *The Republic Reborn: War and the Making of Liberal America, 1790-1820* (Baltimore, Md.: Johns Hopkins University Press, 1987), 156.

Jefferson's Response

Jefferson biographer Merrill Peterson comments on how Jefferson took all this criticism. Jefferson was "personally hurt by the smear campaign"[29] but thought it was reaction to his position of the disestablishment of state-established religions which northeasterners had yet to embrace as Virginia had done. Note how Jefferson dealt with this unjustified criticism; he trusted that God would eventually hold accountable those who had lied about him: "I know that I might have filled the courts of the United States with actions for these slanders, and have ruined perhaps many persons who are innocent. But this would be no equivalent for the loss of character. I leave them, therefore, to the reproof of their own consciences. If these do not condemn them, there yet come a day when the false witness will meet a judge who has not slept over his slanders."[30]

Dreisbach shows how Adams, as well as Jefferson, was hurt by the false accusations against their religious beliefs (or the reported lack thereof): "Both men were deeply wounded by the vicious attacks on their characters and the ruinous campaign tactics. An anguished Jefferson compared his persecution at the hands of critics—especially among the New England clergy—with the crucified Christ: 'from the clergy I expect no mercy. They crucified their Saviour, who preached that their kingdom was not of this world; and all who practice on that precept must expect the extreme of their wrath. The laws of the present day withhold their hands from blood; but lies and slander still remain to them.'"[31]

Despite all the dire predictions of what would happen should Jefferson win, the new nation still carried on. Writes Peterson: "Direct consequences were predicted from seating a visionary, a demagogue, and a 'howling atheist' at the head of the nation. But in the victory celebrations even church bells rang for Jefferson."[32]

After the Election of 1800

Having examined Jefferson's relations with clergy both before and at the beginning of his presidency, what were his relations with the clergy in America from that election to the end of his life? Significantly, Jefferson corresponded with and worked in alliance with just as many new clergy after this point in his life as before. And they were about 90 percent orthodox clergy and very friendly. So there did

---

29   Peterson, *Thomas Jefferson and the New Nation*, 639.

30   Ibid., 640.

31   Dreisbach, "The Wall of Separation," https://www.christianhistoryinstitute.org/uploaded/50 b787762dbd67.76222839.pdf

32   Peterson, *Thomas Jefferson and the New Nation*, 642.

not seem to be any significant change in that regard. But the most noticeable difference is that prior to that election, Jefferson's criticism of clergy in America had been almost non-existent. Most references had been aimed at European clergy connected to state churches. But now in the post 1800 election era, Jefferson began making more comments, although always private, about the attacks from the northeastern clergy.

Let us look at several of these comments in his private correspondence. A careful reading of the context of each letter shows that most of his focus is on the Federalist clergy in New York and the New England states. Sometimes Jefferson himself used the term "eastern" or "northern," but when neither is used we inserted "northeastern" in brackets.

To his evangelical friend Benjamin Rush on September 23, 1800, he said:

> …I promised you a letter on Christianity…; I do not know that it would reconcile…the genus irritable vatum who are all in arms against me. Their hostility is on too interesting ground to be softened;…the clause of the constitution, which…covered…the freedom of religion, had given to the clergy a very favorite hope of obtaining an establishment of a particular form of Christianity thro' the U.S.;…especially the Episcopalians & Congregationalists. The returning good sense of our country threatens abortion to their hopes, & they believe that any portion of power confided to me, will be exerted in opposition to their schemes. And they believe rightly; for I have sworn upon the altar of God, eternal hostility against every form of tyranny over the mind of man.[33]

Jefferson replied to Vermont Governor Moses Robinson on March 23, 1801: "…The eastern States will be the last to come over, on account of the dominion of the clergy, who had got a smell of union between Church and State…[34]

He said in a letter to William Short on March 17, 1801, "…in this transition the New England states are slowest because under the dominion of their priests who had begun to hope they could toll us on to an established church to be in union with the state. even there however they are getting to rights…"[35]

A few days later (March 1801), he said to Unitarian Rev. Priestley: "…What an effort, my dear sir, of bigotry in politics and religion have we gone through! The

33   "From Thomas Jefferson to Benjamin Rush, September 23, 1800," www.founders.archives.gov.

34   "From Thomas Jefferson to Moses Robinson, March 23, 1801," www.founders.archives.gov.

35   "From Thomas Jefferson to William Short, March 17, 1801," www.founders.archives.gov .

barbarians [i.e., northeastern opponents in the recent campaign] really flattered themselves they should be able to bring back the times..., when ignorance put everything into the hands of power and priestcraft..."[36]

And a few days later (March 1801), he said to Elbridge Gerry:

> ...[In] Your part of the Union [New England]...the temples of religion and justice, have all been prostituted there to toll us back to the times when we burnt witches...; the mild and simple principles of the Christian philosophy...[the] priesthood...twist it's texts till they cover the divine morality of it's author with mysteries, and require a priesthood to explain them. The Quakers...have no priests...; they judge of the text by the dictates of common sense & common morality.[37]

Jefferson informed his Attorney General Levi Lincoln on January 1, 1802, that "...I have long wished to find [an occasion] of saying why I do not proclaim fastings and thanksgivings, as my predecessors did;...I know it will give great offense to the New England clergy; but the advocate of religious freedom is to expect neither peace nor forgiveness from them."[38] Again, it is notable that he had no problem proclaiming days of fasting and thanksgiving as Governor of Virginia. What he felt was unconstitutional was doing that on the federal level.

Rev. Henry Fry, the chief Methodist organizer of camp meeting revivals in the Piedmont during the Second Great Awakening, maintained a close friendship with Jefferson. In 1804, Jefferson expressed his "affectionate salutations and respect" in a couple of letters to this preacher-politician that have been preserved. Jefferson was told by Fry that he (Jefferson) "deservedly [gets] the credit (also reproach)" for severing the connections "in church and state which deterred investigation and freedom." Jefferson responded to this with a letter saying that the doctrines of Jesus had been corrupted "by priestcraft and established by kingcraft constituting a conspiracy of church and state against the civil and religious liberties of mankind."[39] Since he was writing to a minister who was a political ally, Jefferson obviously did not mean *all* clergymen, but mainly the Federalist clergy of the

36   "From Thomas Jefferson to Joseph Priestley, March 21, 1801," www.founders.archives.gov .

37   "From Thomas Jefferson to Elbridge Gerry, March 29, 1801," www.founders.archives.gov .

38   III. To Levi Lincoln, 1 January 1802," www.founders.archives.gov.

39   Letter to Rev. Henry Fry, May 21, 1804, and June 17, 1804. Also Fry to Jefferson, June 9, 1804. Beliles, *The Selected Religious Letters and Papers of Thomas Jefferson*, 121 and 124.

northeastern states.[40] This is an important distinction that is almost always ignored by modern biographers.

On January 29, 1815, Jefferson replies to Rev. Charles Clay: "…I abuse the priests, indeed, who have so much abused the pure and holy doctrines of their Master…scourges of priest-craft."[41]

On August 6, 1816, Jefferson wrote Margaret Bayard Smith (also known as Mrs. Samuel Harrison Smith), saying: "…the priests indeed have heretofore thought proper to ascribe to me religious, or rather anti-religious sentiments, of their own fabric…"[42]

On May 5, 1817 he wrote to John Adams: "…I join you therefore in sincere congratulations that this den of the priesthood [i.e., an official state Congregational church in Connecticut] is at length broken up, and that a protestant popedom is no longer to disgrace the American history and character…"[43]

Clearly, a repeated pattern is seen of Jefferson's antipathy toward abuse of power by those priests and clergy who were leaders of a church-state system. But at the same time, Jefferson enjoyed relationships with Christian dissenters and evangelicals, and also had strong and positive relationships with clergy of his own life-long denomination, the Episcopal Church. Jefferson's antipathy was toward the abuse of power, (especially if it was) in the name of God.

While he maintained friendly relations with many clergy for the bulk of his life, there arose a conflict between him and Presbyterians in 1820. That was the exception in Virginia, not the norm, in his long life in the region.

Criticism of Presbyterians in Virginia in 1820

While Jefferson clearly condemned church-state clergy in Europe and in the northeastern parts of the United States, he had a completely different view of

---

40   Many modern scholars quote Jefferson's condemnations of clergy and make two incorrect conclusions: (1) They suppose that he was against all clergy and organized religion. This letter is often quoted without noticing that it was written to a local Methodist preacher and friend. (2) They assume the Federalist clergy were the equivalent of modern evangelicals. But Jefferson's anti-clerical comments almost always targeted non-evangelical leaders of the Established Church in New England or New York. The Unitarians and "rational Christians," along with the Congregationalist of New England, were virtually all Federalists and opposed Jefferson for President.

41   Letter to Rev. Charles Clay, January 29, 1815. Beliles, *The Selected Religious Letters and Papers of Thomas Jefferson*, 251.

42   Letter to Margaret Bayard Smith, August 6, 1816. Beliles, *The Selected Religious Letters and Papers of Thomas Jefferson*, 272.

43   Letter to John Adams, May 5, 1817. Beliles, *The Selected Religious Letters and Papers of Thomas Jefferson*, 280.

clergy in Virginia for most of his last several decades. In late 1813, he wrote John Adams saying that "...The law for religious freedom...[in Virginia has] put down the aristocracy of the clergy and restored to the citizen the freedom of the mind."[44]

But as already shown, a misunderstanding over hiring of professors at the University of Virginia brought forth criticism from him of clergy in that state for the first time. Recall that the Presbyterians who had been vocal in favor of the non-sectarian nature of the school, did not know of the first invitation to Rev. Samuel Knox, so they now felt betrayed by the job offer to Unitarian Thomas Cooper. The fuss they raised over this left Jefferson angered, for the first time, at the Presbyterians.[45]

He thus told Cooper on March 13, 1820, "...the Presbyterian clergy alone (not their followers) remain...violent, ambitious of power, and intolerant in politics as in religion and want...to kindle again the fires of their leader John Knox..."[46] Four weeks later, he told his Catholic friend Rev. José Correia da Serra that Presbyterian clergy "...dread the advance of science as witches do the approach of day-light..."[47]

Two days later, he told William Short:

> ...The Presbyterian clergy are loudest; the most intolerant of all sects, the
> most tyrannical and ambitious; ready at the word of the lawgiver, if such a
> word could be now obtained, to put the torch to the pile, and to rekindle in
> this virgin hemisphere, the flames in which their oracle Calvin consumed
> the poor Servetus..."[48] [Michael Servetus was a Unitarian who preached in
> Calvin's 16th century Geneva and was put to death for it in what is one of
> the most criticized events of the Protestant Reformation.]

Although clergy criticized the university's hiring of a Unitarian not once was Jefferson's faith itself attacked or questioned by these Virginian ministers. Nonetheless, Jefferson released some of his harshest criticisms against Presbyterians for the first time in his life. It was an unfortunate misunderstanding that was brief and did not last long.

---

44   Letter to John Adams, October 28, 1813. www.founders.archives.gov.

45   You can read more details about this conflict in chapter 11 on the University of Virginia.

46   Letter to Thomas Cooper, March 13, 1820. The Thomas Jefferson Papers Series 1, General
      Correspondence, 1651-1827, Library of Congress Manuscript Division.

47   Letter to Rev. Correa da Serra, April 11, 1820. Beliles, *The Selected Religious Letters and
      Papers of Thomas Jefferson*, 305.

48   Letter to William Short, April 13, 1820. Beliles, *The Selected Religious Letters and Papers of
      Thomas Jefferson*, 306.

It is certainly an error to interpret this conflict as a desire in Jefferson to have all clergy excluded from his state university. Besides offering a professorship to Rev. Knox, Jefferson sought advice for and perhaps even offered a professorship to Anglican Rev. Samuel Parr in 1824. There clearly was no general anti-clerical bias held by Jefferson.

Jefferson's Views on Political Preaching

Some insights on Jefferson's views on preaching politics from the pulpit are seen in his reply to Peter Wendover on March 13, 1815. The letter began with a comment on "...the Eastern clergy" and also mentioned "...the Robespierres of the priesthood..."[49] Robespierre, of course, was the notoriously anti-Christian French Revolutionary, who in the "reign of terror," imposed his views in the name of the Deist Supreme Being. This description does not support the image of Jefferson as a French-minded Deist. Rather he connects that with the clergy of New England.

This letter from Jefferson to Wendover was also one of those that had a longer unsent draft that it would be worth taking some time now for analysis. Wendover had written to Jefferson and enclosed a political sermon by a New York Presbyterian preacher who was a political supporter of Jefferson. In Jefferson's unsent reply he commended the sermon but added some observations as to when it is proper for a pastor to preach on politics. Jefferson wrote:

> I have to thank you for the volume of discourses [*A Scriptural View of the...Present War*, by Rev. Alexander McLeod, 1815 in New York] which you have been so kind as to send me. I have gone over them with great satisfaction, and concur with the able preacher in his estimate of the character of the belligerents in our late war, and lawfulness of defensive war. I consider the war, with him, as "made on good advice" that is, for just causes, and its dispensation as providential,...All this Mr. McLeod has well proved, and from these sources of argument particularly which belong to his profession.

So far Jefferson approves of McLeod's exegesis and thesis. But now, in this unsent portion of the letter, he also expresses disagreement:

---

49   Letter to Peter H. Wendover, March 13, 1815. Beliles, *The Selected Religious Letters and Papers of Thomas Jefferson*, 253.

On one question only I differ from him, and it is that which constitutes the subject of his first discourse, the right of discussing public affairs in the pulpit. I add the last words [i.e., "in the pulpit"], because I admit the right in general conversation and in writing; in which last form it has been exercised in the valuable book you have now favored me with.... Collections of men associate together, under the name of congregations, and employ a religious teacher of the particular sect of opinions of which they happen to be, and contribute to make up a stipend as a compensation for the trouble of delivering them, at such periods as they agree on, lessons in the religion they profess.

...In choosing our pastor we look to his religious qualifications, without inquiring into his physical or political dogmas, with which we mean to have nothing to do. I am aware that arguments may be found, which may twist a thread of politics into the cord of religious duties. So may they for every other branch of human art or science.[50]

Jefferson feels that one's views on non-religious subjects is not to be the primary basis for hiring a pastor, but that the pastor may certainly freely address such subjects if the congregation feels like he should and could do it. As he explains:

I do not deny that a congregation may, if they please, agree with their preacher that he shall instruct them in Medicine also, or Law, or Politics. Then, lectures in these, from the pulpit, become not only a matter of right, but of duty also. But this must be with the consent of every individual; because the association being voluntary, the mere majority has no right to apply the contributions of the minority to purposes unspecified in the agreement of the congregation. I agree, too, that on all other occasions, the preacher has the right, equally with every other citizen, to express his sentiments, in speaking or writing, on the subjects of Medicine, Law, Politics, etc., his leisure time being his own, and his congregation not obliged to listen to his conversation or to read his writings.[51]

All citizens, including the preacher, are entitled to their opinions (and to express those views). Jefferson happens to agree with this minister's reasoning on the subject. He goes on:

---

50   Ibid.

51   Ibid.

...I feel my portion of indebtment to the reverend author [McLeod] for the distinguished learning, the logic and the eloquence with which he has proved that religion, as well as reason, confirms the soundness of those principles on which our government has been founded and its rights asserted. These are my views on this question. They are in opposition to those of the highly respected and able preacher, and are, therefore, the more doubtingly offered. Difference of opinion leads to inquiry, and inquiry to truth; and that, I am sure, is the ultimate and sincere object of us both. We both value too much the freedom of opinion sanctioned by our Constitution, not to cherish its exercise even where in opposition to ourselves...While I know I am safe in the honor and charity of a McLeod, I do not wish to be cast forth to the Marats, the Dantons, and the Robespierres of the priesthood; I mean the [Elijah] Parishes, the Ogdens [i.e., David Osgood], and the [John] Gardiners of Massachusetts.[52]

The key phrase in this letter is a desire for such preaching by the congregation. It was based on a congregational view of church government (a view that the congregation itself is the final authority rather than any outside hierarchy or leader) that Jefferson seemed to hold. Clearly, this unsent letter was not a general anti-clerical statement and neither is it a categorical rejection of political preaching. Nevertheless, it is a letter distorted, by some modern commentators who interpret Jefferson as being against any political preaching. Of course, Jefferson explicitly praised such preaching by his pastor Rev. Charles Clay in the 1770s and personally donated to have such sermons delivered in the courthouse in Charlottesville.

Posthumous Misrepresentations of Jefferson

As noted, some Virginians criticized Thomas Cooper's hiring without questioning Jefferson's personal faith; and no clergyman in Virginia or anywhere south of New York ever criticized Jefferson's faith in his entire lifetime. However, after Jefferson's death, historical revisionism in this area began.

One of the more surprising of these was Rev. Samuel Miller, Presbyterian of New York. Miller had friendly correspondence with Jefferson and even supported Jefferson during his elections, unlike fellow-New Yorker Rev. Linn. However, several years after Jefferson's death, he expressed "regret and shame" after some posthumous evidence of heterodox views emerged in his published writings that made Miller "aware of the rottenness of [Jefferson's] moral and religious

---

52   Ibid.

opinions."[53] Eventually Miller wrote in 1830 that "after the publication of his [Jefferson's] posthumous writings, in 1829, my respect for him was exchanged for contempt and abhorrence…His own writings evince a hypocrisy…a blasphemous impiety, and a moral profligacy, which no fair, honest mind, to say nothing of piety, can contemplate without abhorrence."[54] Miller added that "It was wrong for a minister of the gospel to seek any intercourse with such a man." But Miller admits that he had been a "warm and zealous partisan in favor of Mr. Jefferson's administration," while also claiming that "I thought, even then, that he was an infidel; but I supposed that he was an honest, truly republican, patriotic infidel."[55] It was convenient for Miller to say it in 1830 after he read some of Jefferson's private letters, but there is no evidence for Miller's critical view at the earlier date.

Dr. Francis Lister Hawks was an Episcopal priest, and a politician in North Carolina who wrote in 1836, ten years after Jefferson's death, an *Ecclesiastical History of the Protestant Episcopal Church in Virginia* that portrayed Jefferson negatively in regards to his faith. Hawks, not a minister until after Jefferson's death, relied on some of Jefferson's posthumously published private writings and second-hand stories. It was strongly rebuffed by family and neighbors of Jefferson and in a biography of Jefferson by George Tucker the following year.[56] But it started a trend that was continued by Presbyterian minister Robert Baird in his 1844 *Religion in America*. Baird called Jefferson a Deist without the benefit of research or facts.[57] Episcopal Bishop William Meade made the same mistake two decades after Jefferson's death saying, without proof, that, "Even Mr. Jefferson and [George] Wythe, who did not conceal their disbelief in Christianity, took their parts in the

---

53   Samuel Miller, The Life of Samuel Miller, D.D., LL.D., (Philadelphia: Claxton, Remsen and Haffelfinger, 1869), 235, 131-132. Miller wrote in 1830 that when he wrote the letter to Jefferson in 1808, he wanted to assure Jefferson "that neither I, nor my associates in this plan, had any wish to embarrass him; and that, if it would give him pain to be thus addressed, I would endeavor to prevent the adoption of the proposed measure." When Jefferson replied and gave his reason not to make the proclamation, there was still no change in Miller's support of him, nor of the other clergy. They remained supporters during his lifetime even if they disagreed on this point.

54   Samuel Miller, *The Life of Samuel Miller, D.D., LL.D.*, (Philadelphia: Claxton, Remsen and Haffelfinger, 1869), 235, 131-132.

55   Ibid.

56   See Ellen W. Randolph Coolidge letter to (George Tucker?) written January 27, 1833 (or 1834).

57   Robert Baird, *Religion in America* (New York: Harper & Brothers, 1844), 286.

duties of vestrymen, the one at Williamsburg, the other at Albemarle; for they wished to be men of influence."[58]

Seven Decades After the Election of 1800

In July 1873, author James Parton wrote a lengthy essay in *Atlantic Magazine* about the 1800 campaign.[59] It is interesting for it provides an analysis by a writer somewhat closer to those events than scholars today, and it attempted to correct some of the inaccurate portrayal of Jefferson in the previous half-century. Parton was a popular American nineteenth century biographer. He notes that religion's role in the 1800 election apparently was unique (at least at the time he was writing this article in 1873):

> Religion, for the first and last time, was an important element in the political strife of 1800. There was not a pin to choose between the heterodoxy of the two candidates [neither Adams nor Jefferson were orthodox.]; and, indeed, Mr. Adams was sometimes, in his familiar letters, more pronounced in his dissent from established beliefs than Jefferson.[60]

Parton then continues, giving his own opinion on religion, and then explains the "Jefferson Bible," which, if nothing else, shows that the third president appreciated the teachings and morals, if nothing else, of Jesus Christ:

> But, in truth, the creed of Jefferson is, and long has been, the real creed of the people of the United States. They know, in their hearts, whatever form of words they may habitually use, that Christianity is a life, not a belief; a principle of conduct, not a theory of the universe. "I am a Christian," wrote Jefferson, "in the only sense in which Jesus wished any one to be; sincerely attached to his doctrines in preference to all others." One evening, in Washington, having, for a wonder, a little leisure, he took two cheap

---

58   William Meade, *Old Churches, Ministers and Families of Virginia*, 2 vols., (Philadelphia, 1857), I:191. Although Meade claims Jefferson's disbelief, nonetheless he confirms Jefferson's part in the Anglican vestry. Scholars who refuse to accept that Jefferson served on the vestry tend to also think Jefferson a skeptic, but they don't usually accept both as true. In reality, the vestry book proves the former, while nothing proves the latter. It seems more likely that Jefferson believed the doctrines of the church—even if perhaps he had some private doubts.

59   James Parton, "The Presidential Election of 1800," *Atlantic Magazine*, July 1873. http://www.theatlantic.com/magazine/archive/1873/07/the-presidential-election-of-1800/307019/?single_page=true.

60   Ibid.

copies of the New Testament, procured for the purpose, and cut from them the words of Jesus, and such other passages of the evangelists as are in closest accord with them. These he pasted in a little book, and entitled it, The Philosophy of Jesus extracted from the Text of the Evangelists. Two evenings were employed in this interesting work; and when it was done he contemplated it with rapturous satisfaction.[61]

This was the first time the so-called "Jefferson Bible" was mentioned other than in Randall's 1858 biography of Jefferson, but the title Parton used left out a reference to it being done for the use of the Indians.

Parton points out that some in New England feared terrible consequences for Christians in the Jefferson years to come: "Tradition reports, that when the news of his election reached New England, some old ladies, in wild consternation, hung their Bibles down the well in the butter-cooler."[62] These fears proved totally unfounded.

Conclusion

Most clergy in Jefferson's lifetime were not antagonistic to him, nor he to they. Only later did today's false portrayal begin to be popular in some historical works by clergy. Likewise Jefferson was not universally opposed to the clergy—but his anti-clericalism was clearly selective and focused (against state-church or abuse of power). Despite outrageous comments from the pulpit during the acrimonious 1800 election, any fear that the people of New England may have had that they should hide their Bibles in case Jefferson were elected president proved completely baseless. The accusations against Jefferson's faith in the 1800 election were not true. Disestablishing a state church is not the same thing as opposing a church or religion.

Likewise, modern biographers and commentators have misrepresented Jefferson by exaggerating the attacks of clergy against him (and his selective attacks against clergy) and ignoring the overwhelming number of favorable relationships. They have fabricated a dominant and simplistic image of anticlericalism that is misleading and false. Thus, according to the modern distortion, today if a person stands against conservative Christians being active in politics is to stand with Jefferson in upholding the Constitution against the danger of religious tyranny and

---

61   Ibid.
62   Ibid.

theocracy. But in reality, most clergy of that day stood side-by-side with Jefferson for full religious liberties and helped him against such dangers.

Modern distortions of Jefferson's relations with religious leaders tends to encourage and even approbate a new kind of discrimination against people of faith in the public arena. Jefferson wanted religion to be free and uncoerced, for religion to neither diminish nor enlarge one's political capacity, and for clergy to have the same rights in public life as any other citizen.

Indeed, those that fail to make the distinction put themselves on the side of Jefferson's political enemies. Significantly, Jefferson's understanding of religious freedom is today held by the vast majority of American evangelicals. They agree with him in opposition to coercive religion, whether by state or church.

CHAPTER 10

JEFFERSON AND THE BIBLE: A MISUNDERSTANDING OF HIS EXTRACTS OF THE GOSPELS

"I...enclose you cheerfully...fifty dollars, for the purposes of the [Virginia Bible] society, sincerely agreeing with you that there never was a more pure and sublime system of morality delivered to man than is to be found in the four evangelists." —Thomas Jefferson, 1814[1]

An honest evaluation of the faith of Thomas Jefferson would be remiss without a serious look at the so-called "Jefferson Bible." Jefferson never called it by that term, but that has become the popular moniker. Without doubt, Jefferson eventually came to believe that the Scriptures had been corrupted over time so that the true Word of God was only discoverable through analysis and filtering of texts.

In this chapter is an analysis of material related to the Bible that was only briefly presented earlier in the chronological chapters.

Sometime in the spring of 1800 during the presidential campaign, the Presbyterian of New York, Rev. William Linn, argued that Jefferson's *Notes on the*

---

1   Letter to Samuel Greenhow [of the Virginia Bible Society], January 31, 1814, www. founders.archives.gov

State of Virginia led him to conclude that Jefferson held a "disbelief of the Holy Scriptures."[2] This was the first time this was said about him, and it was based on flimsy evidence. Today many people think the same, in part because of his private abridgement that now has been repeatedly published, but especially because of the modern mischaracterizations made about it.

As seen in the previous chapter, Rev. Linn was prominent in leading the charge against the Virginian. During that election, many accusations against Jefferson's faith (or the lack thereof) arose. But Jefferson (and all clergymen south of New York for that matter) believed that it was because he had disestablished the Church in Virginia that he earned the wrath of some northeastern churchmen who did not understand the situation. (Ironically, somehow John Adams, Jefferson's opponent in that contentious election got off scot-free from anti-religious accusations, yet his views on religion were less orthodox than those of Jefferson.)

Did Jefferson have a "disbelief" of the Bible? To explore that question is the purpose of this chapter which begins with a chronological review of his actions regarding the Bible.

1762-1803—References to the Bible and Philosophy

When Jefferson was in college, he was exposed to Enlightenment writers that doubted the Scriptures.[3] Although Jefferson copied some of the writings of the skeptic Lord Bolingbroke in his Literary Commonplace Book around 1765, Douglas Wilson, modern scholar and expert on the Commonplace books, says it cannot be proven that Jefferson believed the same.

The same could be said of the orthodox "Notes on Religion" Jefferson compiled in 1776. In these notes, Jefferson wrote of the Bible that "...the writers were inspired" and that "If we are Protestants, we reject all tradition, and rely on the Scripture alone."[4] This statement cannot be used to prove his personal faith since he simply copied these quotes without comment (from John Locke and Anthony Ashley-Cooper). Yet, in a letter in 1816, he again made the statement that the Psalmist (one of the Bible writers) was writing with an "inspired pen."[5]

---

2   Jefferson's *Notes On the State of Virginia*, 1782, www.founders.archives.gov.

3   Douglas Wilson, *Jefferson's Literary Commonplace Book* (Princeton, N.J.: Princeton University Press, 1989), 40-50.

4   "Notes on Religion," 1776, www.founders.archives.gov (See document 7).

5   Letter to Mary Briggs, April 17, 1816. Beliles, *The Selected Religious Letters and Papers of Thomas Jefferson*, 267.

Meanwhile, it should be noted, that just a few months after Jefferson's orthodox "Notes on Religion," he drafted the founding subscription document and gave the most money to start the Calvinistical Reformed Church because they were "...desirous of...deriving to our selves, through the ministry of its teachers, the benefits of Gospel knowledge and...for explaining the holy scriptures..."[6] He may well have believed what he had written in his "Notes on Religion" just six months before about the writers of Scripture being inspired. The Bible is 66 books that were written by about 40 different writers, over a span of about 1400 years. Orthodox believers recognize it as one book with one overall writer, God, Who used human writers in the process.

Jefferson kept a family Bible and prayer book that today can be seen at the University of Virginia library. It has his signature on the front page and has his name printed publicly in it as one of the first investors for the printing of it. In 1786, Jefferson obtained a *Greek and English Lexicon to the New Testament* by John Parkhurst, which showed he had some interest in further biblical study at that time.[7]

In a variety of letters, Jefferson recommended the reading of the Bible and quoted the Bible, including both the Old and New Testaments. Jefferson wrote in 1787 to his nephew Peter Carr with advice on studying religion that Carr should "...Read the bible;...It is said that the writer of that book was inspired. Examine therefore candidly what evidence there is of his having been inspired. The pretension is entitled to your inquiry, because millions believe it;...Read the new testament. It is the history of a person called Jesus."[8]

Jefferson wrote to one of his lifelong ministers, Rev. Matthew Maury, on January 8, 1790, asking for information on a Bible and pledging to support Rev. Maury's school: 'I recollect you have...Grabe's septuagint in 10. vols. Not knowing where, when, and by whom it was printed, I have been unable to ask for it in Europe, which I had wished to do. I will thank you to inform me of these circumstances that I may be enabled to have the edition procured for me by the first occasion in Europe."[9] The Septuagint was the translation of the Old Testament into Greek for the use of those Jews living around Alexandria who spoke Greek but no longer Hebrew; it was produced about a century and a half before Jesus. It is used

6   Subscription to Support a Clergyman, February 1777, www.founders.archives.gov.
7   Account book, 1786. For Greek and English Lexicon to the New Testament. Beliles, *The Selected Religious Letters and Papers of Thomas Jefferson*, 46.
8   Letter to Peter Carr, August 10, 1787, www.founders.archives.gov.
9   Letter to Rev. Matthew Maury, January 8, 1790, www.founders.archives.gov.

by serious students of the Bible. It would seem that Jefferson was such a student—at least at this stage of his life.

On February 26, 1798, Jefferson "Paid...subscription for a hot press bible" published by Thompson and Small. This Holy Bible was printed using a new technology (i.e., heating the ink before applying to the paper in order to secure its deeper penetration), hence the term Jefferson uses for it. To subscribe meant to make a pledge ahead of time to the publishers so that the capital was there to accomplish the project. Of course, buying this orthodox Bible continued to show Jefferson's interest in Scripture study.[10] But more significant was the fact that he approved his name to be listed publicly in the volume as a subscriber or advance investor. He also subscribed and thus approved that his name be printed later in two other biblical works.[11]

In a letter to publisher Henry Remsen on December 31, 1800, he said: "I see advertised...Scatcherd's pocket bible, bound in Marocco, it is an edition which I have long been wishing to get, to make part of a portable library which the course of my life has rendered convenient. Will you be so good as to get a copy for me and forward by post."[12]

When Jefferson was sworn in as President on March 4, 1801, he laid his hand on the Bible as was standard practice. But then in 1801 for the first time Jefferson implies that the Scriptures had been corrupted when he said in a private letter to Massachusetts legislator, Elbridge Gerry: "...[In] Your part of the Union [New England]...[the] priesthood...twist it's texts [i.e., the Bible] till they cover the divine morality of it's author with mysteries..."[13] Jefferson derived this view apparently from reading a book titled the *Corruptions of Christianity* in the late 1790s that was authored by Unitarian Joseph Priestley.

Rev. William Pryce, of the Protestant Episcopal Church in Wilmington, Delaware, wrote to Jefferson on October 10, 1803, asking him if he would subscribe to *the History of our Blessed Lord and Saviour Jesus Christ*. Pryce and this book were orthodox theologically. And despite Jefferson's emerging perspective of alleged corruptions in the Bible and despite having one of the busiest offices in the world, the third president replied: "Your favor of the 10 is duly recieved, and I

---

10   Account book, February 1798. For hot press bible. Beliles, *The Selected Religious Letters and Papers of Thomas Jefferson*, 62.

11   In 1805 for *The History of our Blessed Lord and Saviour Jesus Christ*, and in 1807 for the Scott Bible.

12   Letter to Henry Remsen, December 31, 1800, www.founders.archives.gov.

13   Letter to Elbridge Gerry, March 29, 1801, www.founders.archives.gov.

subscribe with great pleasure to the work you propose. It comprehends exactly the most interesting period of Christian history, and it will be the more interesting if, as I presume it does, the plan embraces the object of giving the primitive & earlier opinions entertained, being persuaded that nothing would place Christianity on so firm a base as the reducing it simply to it's first & original principles."[14]

A year and a half later on March 9, 1805, Pryce sent the finished book with a letter to Jefferson: "You have no doubt learned the liberty I have taken, of publishing your kind favor to me; for which I feel bound to offer no apology, conscious that it would do honor to the Head and Heart, of any Man on Earth..." Jefferson wrote with "...his respects to the rev mr Pryce, acknoleges the reciept of his book..."[15] And on May 3, 1805 Jefferson's account book notes that he paid for it. The full title of the book was *The History of our Blessed Lord and Saviour Jesus Christ: with the Lives of the Holy Apostles, and their successors for three hundred years after the Crucifixion.*

Rather than a historical biography, this work was an orthodox devotional meditation on the life of Jesus and His apostles by Rev. John Fleetwood and published by Ebenezer Thompson and William Charles Price. Of most significance is the comment on this by Monticello historians that "Jefferson was one of the original subscribers to this work, and his name heads the list (vol. II, page 435)."[16] This endorsement by Jefferson with his name among the subscribers, saying, "I subscribe with great pleasure," with the financial pledge and follow-up to pay for it, is evidence of his continuing interest in learning from orthodox writers about Jesus and Christianity.

But at that same time he privately was inclining toward Priestley's heterodox views on the Bible. He sent on April 24, 1803, to Priestley a copy of his "Syllabus of the Doctrines of Jesus." In Jefferson's syllabus he asserted that scripture texts had been corrupted over time.

> ...Hence the doctrines which [Jesus] really delivered were defective
> as a whole, and fragments only of what he did deliver have come to us
> mutilated, misstated, & often unintelligible;...They have been still more

---

14   Letter to Rev. William Pryce, October 15, 1803. Beliles, *The Selected Religious Letters and Papers of Thomas Jefferson*, 117.

15   Letter to Rev. William Pryce, March 13, 1805. Beliles, *The Selected Religious Letters and Papers of Thomas Jefferson*, 143.

16   "Thomas Jefferson and the Bible Publications He Owned," Thomas Jefferson Foundation, January 2007. http://www.monticello.org/library/exhibits/images/biblepublications.pdf.

disfigured by the corruptions of schismatising followers, who have found an interest in sophisticating & perverting the simple doctrines he taught by engrafting on them the mysticisms of a Grecian sophist [i.e., Plato], frittering them into subtleties, & obscuring them with jargon, until they have caused good men to reject the whole in disgust, & to view Jesus himself as an impostor;...Notwithstanding these disadvantages, a system of morals is presented to us, which, if filled up in the true style and spirit of the rich fragments he left us, would be the most perfect and sublime that has ever been taught by man...[17]

At this point Jefferson had a high view of the teaching of Jesus. But he thought such teaching had been partially distorted—thus, he had bought into Priestley's notion that the Bible had been supposedly corrupted. He wanted just the pure teachings of Jesus to be brought forth because of their moral clarity—and to do it in a way that bypassed any disputed questions of theology (what he called "mysticisms").

1804—A Digest of the Moral Teachings of Jesus For "The Indians"

As explained in the earlier chronological narrative Jefferson began thinking of a digest of the words of Jesus in conjunction with his comparison of philosophy. This digest is mentioned for the first time in a letter to Priestley on January 29, 1804:

> ...I rejoice that you have undertaken the task of comparing the moral doctrines of Jesus with those of the ancient Philosophers. You are so much in possession of the whole subject, that you will do it easier & better than any other person living. I think you cannot avoid giving, as preliminary to the comparison, a digest of his moral doctrines, extracted in his own words from the Evangelists, and leaving out everything relative to his personal history and character. It would be short and precious. With a view to do this for my own satisfaction, I had sent to Philadelphia to get two testaments Greek of the same edition, & two English, with a design to cut out the morsels of morality, and paste them on the leaves of a book, in the

---

17   Letter to Rev. Joseph Priestley, April 24, 1803. Beliles, *The Selected Religious Letters and Papers of Thomas Jefferson*, 106.

manner you describe as having been pursued in forming your Harmony. But I shall now get the thing done by better hands.[18]

Jefferson saw Rev. Priestley as the most capable one around for what he saw as such an important task—certainly more capable than himself. But Priestley died shortly afterwards. Although that project stopped, Jefferson began to work on a digest for apparently a different reason that becomes evident by a title he gives to it in the winter of 1804. This was due to his simultaneous interest with Priestley on philosophy and also with various missions organizations that were seeking to serve Native Americans. The issue came to a head at that moment due to the Louisiana Purchase, America's largest single property acquisition, during Jefferson's administration that brought thousands of new tribal groups under American oversight. As seen previously Jefferson had been corresponding for several years with a number of individuals involved in Indian missions and even had made personal donations to some of them:

Bishop Madison, 1779 "instructing them [i.e., Indians] in the principles of Christianity,"

Account Book, 1792 "Paid…a subscription for missionaries,"

William Linn, 1798 "for the use of [your New York Missionary Society],"

John Heckewelder, 1798 "give me any information you can on this subject,"

Samuel Miller, 1802 "sermon [to New York Missionary Society]…read with pleasure,"

Edward Dowse, 1803 "[I] have perused [the sermon on morality & missions] with attention,"

Treaty with Kaskaskia tribes, 1803 "give annually…a priest…[&] erection of a church."

And there were similar letters to David Redick (1802), John Bacon (1803), John Sergeant (1803), and later to the Society of Friends (1807), and James Jay (1809). And he gave federal dollars to Rev. Blackburn's school for Cherokees in 1804. Furthermore, in 1814 Jefferson donated money to the Virginia Bible Society, whose mission was to distribute Bibles "to the poor of our country, and to the Heathen [i.e., the Indians]."[19]

---

18   Letter to Rev. Joseph Priestley, January 29, 1804. Beliles, *The Selected Religious Letters and Papers of Thomas Jefferson*, 119.

19   Letter to Samuel Greenhow [of the Virginia Bible Society], January 31, 1814, www.founders.archives.gov.

Missionaries urged the distribution of Bibles to the multitudes of new Indian tribal groups, but Jefferson thought it better to not use whole Bibles for that purpose. On January 20, 1816, he wrote to Peter Wilson (who apparently had urged Jefferson's support of Bible translations in languages of Indians) explaining why not:

> ...I think, therefore, the pious missionaries who shall go to the several tribes to instruct them in the Christian religion will have to learn a language for every tribe they go to; nay, more, that they will have to create a new language for every one, that is to say, to add to theirs new words for the new ideas they will have to communicate. Law, medicine, chemistry, mathematics, every science has a language of its own, and divinity not less than others. Their barren vocabularies cannot be vehicles for ideas of the fall of man, his redemption, the triune composition of the Godhead, and other mystical doctrines considered by most Christians of the present date as essential elements of faith. The enterprise is therefore arduous, but the more inviting perhaps to missionary zeal.[20]

This comment on the difficulty of communicating all of the doctrines of the Christian faith seems to be what induced him to take a couple of evenings in February or March 1804 to compile what he called *The Philosophy of Jesus of Nazareth Extracted From the Account of His Life and Doctrines as Given by Matthew, Mark, Luke and John; Being an Abridgement of the New Testament for the Use of the Indians Unembarrassed with Matters of Fact or Faith Beyond the Level of Their Comprehensions.*[21] This title is written in Jefferson's own hand. There is no evidence that it ever was published for the Indians (or at all) during his lifetime.

The only early comment on the 1804 abridgement was made by his early biographer Henry Randall, who wrote in 1858 that it was "...Mr. Jefferson's 'Collection for the Indians.'"[22] That is strong evidence that corroborates the title Jefferson gave to it in his own hand because Randall's biography of Jefferson, written when his family and friends were still alive, states confidently that he

---

20   Letter to Peter Wilson, January 20, 1816. Beliles, *The Selected Religious Letters and Papers of Thomas Jefferson*, 262.

21   *The Philosophy of Jesus, Abridgement of the Words of Jesus of Nazareth . . . for the Use of the Indians*, 1804. Beliles, *The Selected Religious Letters and Papers of Thomas Jefferson*, 397.

22   Henry S. Randall, *The Life of Thomas Jefferson*, 3 vols. (New York: Derby and Jackson, 1858), 3:654-658.

"conferred with friends on the expediency of having it published in the different Indian dialects as the most appropriate book for the Indians to be instructed to read in."[23] Despite this confirmation some modern commentators flatly deny this or pursue alternative explanations based on very flimsy evidence.[24]

At this point in Jefferson's life, the abridgement had little or nothing to do with asserting what are true and allegedly false passages of scripture or not. But it did connect the interest Jefferson had in both missions and in Jesus' philosophy. (For studying the philosophy of Jesus, Jefferson, also in early 1804, ordered from bookseller Nicholas Dufief two copies of a Greek and Latin New Testament and two copies of a New Testament in English.)

The multi-lingual edition of Jefferson's compilation of the teachings of Jesus did not get done until at least fifteen years later. Only his abridgement for the Indians appears at this early date. As Jefferson stated, the "digest of his moral doctrines" was to be a "preliminary to the comparison" of philosophy. In other words you have to assemble all His teachings before you can organize and compare it with anything else. So this abridgement was not to be a biography of Jesus and as such it left out most material found in the Gospels that did not fit the goal of compiling a "philosophy"—i.e., a summary of Jesus' ethics. If this 1804 work was based on a motive to delete all of the miracles or evidences of Jesus' divinity, as many critics today hold, then why, for instance, did it include such verses as these?

Heal the sick, cleanse the lepers, raise the dead, cast out devils: freely ye have received, freely give (Matthew 10:8).

And they held their peace. And he took him, and healed him, and let him go (Luke 14:4).

---

23   Ibid., 3:654-658.

24   Jefferson's Second Inaugural Address in 1805 included a reference to the "prejudice" of the Indians of which Jefferson noted in an unused draft of the speech that it "admits by inference a more general extension." [See draft of Second Inaugural Address, The Thomas Jefferson Papers Series 1, General Correspondence, 1651-1827, Library of Congress Manuscript Division] This note by Jefferson led editors Dickinson Adams and Ruth Leser to say the term "Indians" was really nothing more than a "code word" for referring to his New England Federalist religious critics. See Adams and Lester, *Jefferson's Extracts From the Gospels*, 28. That prejudice existed in more than the Indians is obvious, but to leap from that to say that Jefferson's title for his digest was therefore not intended for the Indians is wholly lacking in scholarly foundation, and was rejected by other Jefferson scholars such as Malone. See Dumas Malone, *Jefferson the President – First Term 1801-1805* (Boston, Mass.: Little, Brown and Co., 1970), 205.

But as touching the resurrection of the dead, have ye not read that which was spoken unto you by God…(Matthew 22:31).

When the Son of man shall come in his glory, and all the holy angels with him, then shall he sit upon the throne of his glory (Matthew 25:31).[25]

The important thing to realize is that many things were left out of both the 1804 and 1820 versions but this simple excision cannot be considered as a reliable basis for knowing Jefferson's beliefs. Whole chapters in John's Gospel that teach some of the most sublime of Christ's philosophy are left out. For example, John 3 on the new birth; chapter 4 on the woman at the well and fields for harvest; chapter 5, various precepts; chapter 6 on the bread of life; chapter 8 on the truth setting one free; chapter 11 on how Jesus is the resurrection and the life; chapter 13 on Jesus' washing of the disciples' feet and the commandment to love; chapter 14 on the promised Comforter (the Holy Spirit) and peace; chapter 15 on the vine; chapter 16 with more details on the Spirit; and chapter 17, the prayer for disciples.

A feasible explanation is that they do not fit in an obvious chronological place with the other three synoptic Gospels, so since he could not figure it out easily in the couple evenings he spent on it, he just avoided trying. And despite leaving some verses out, Jefferson quotes some of these Johanine verses elsewhere, such as the first three verses of the Gospel of John, which Jefferson discusses as God's Word (while interpreting it incorrectly) in a letter to John Adams in 1823. And some things were dropped when updating the 1804 version in 1820, such as Matthew 10:8 above, but the other three verses above were retained. Along with Matthew 10:8, the verse above on healing, Jefferson's 1820 update also deleted John 10:10: "I have come that they might have life, and that they might have it more abundantly." It does not seem likely to think that that was rubbish to Jefferson. Another passage cut out was John 4:24 which says "God is a Spirit." Though left out of the 1820 version, Jefferson nonetheless quotes that verse in that same 1823 letter to Adams, saying it was Jesus' words.

So just because something was cut, it is not a reliable basis to assume that Jefferson rejected it as inauthentic. The bottom line is that the extracts from the Gospels, both versions, must be put in a similar category as the Literary

---

25   The entire abridgement of 1804 can be found in Beliles, *The Selected Religious Letters and Papers of Thomas Jefferson* , 397-428. Note: All versions of the so-called Jefferson Bible use the later 1820 version. Beliles is the only one to publish the entire 1804 version (although a facsimile of a reconstruction of it is found in *Jefferson's Extracts of the Gospels* by Dickinson Adams and Ruth Lester).

Commonplace Notes (his schoolwork writings) and "Notes on Religion" (compiled in 1776) that he kept without comment. And like some letters he never sent, the 1804 and 1820 digests of the Gospels also were never sent nor shown to anyone in his entire life. Therefore, these digests must be considered by scholars as less reliable for determining his beliefs when examined apart from his other words and works. At best, they only supplement whatever conclusions the clear and direct sources tell us about Jefferson's faith. Meanwhile, there is eyewitness testimony to the effect that Jefferson was a regular reader and an avid follower of the teachings of Jesus. It would seem especially true with the 1820 digest (with its multiple columns of the same text in different languages).

Jefferson was a serious student of significant portions of the Bible. Imagine the president of the United States being so impressed with the sayings of Jesus Christ, that despite all of his pressing urgent business, he culls through the sayings to choose gems from His teaching. Jefferson said that he did the abridgement for his "own satisfaction" but this does not mean for his personal use only, yet also for his satisfaction that an effective tool was created for the Indians. (This last point is because of the exact title Jefferson himself gave the work when he produced it in 1804.)

1805-1812—Jefferson's Use and Distribution of the Whole Bible

In April 1804, following his younger daughter's death, his other daughter Martha said she "found him with the Bible in his hands [seeking]…consolation in the Sacred Volume."[26] In an 1804 letter to a boyhood friend, John Page, Jefferson quoted from a New Testament letter of the Apostle Paul (1 Thessalonians 4:13) saying, 'We sorrow not then as others who have no hope.'"[27]

Jefferson's in-depth study of Scripture continued. His letter to publisher Matthew Carey on March 7, 1805, referenced a purchase of a Bible, and his account book that day noted that he bought "books" (which the editors say included a "Greek Testament" and another Bible).[28] On April 27 the entry recorded

---

26   Sarah N. Randolph, *The Domestic Life of Thomas Jefferson* (Charlottesville: University Press of Virginia, 1978), 300.

27   Letter to John Page, June 25, 1804, Beliles, *The Selected Religious Letters and Papers of Thomas Jefferson*, 124. Also see Edwin Gaustad, *Sworn On the Altar of God: A Religious Biography of Thomas Jefferson* (Grand Rapids, Mich.: W. B. Eerdmans Publishers, 1996), 142.

28   Letter to Matthew Carey, March 7, 1805. The Thomas Jefferson Papers Series 1, General Correspondence, 1651-1827, Library of Congress Manuscript Division.

he "Inclosed...for books," which was for two copies of a New Testament.[29] And on May 3, he paid for the above-mentioned, *The History of our Lord and Saviour Jesus Christ*, by Thompson and Price.

Jefferson's account book on December 21, 1807, shows that he "Inclosed... [$20] for subscription to bible."[30] This was called Scott's Bible because it included commentary by the evangelical Anglican Rev. Thomas Scott. On March 30, 1808, William Woodward of Philadelphia wrote Jefferson with a question about his $20 order for a copy of Thomas Scott's *Holy Bible, containing the Old and New Testaments, 5 vols*. Jefferson replied two years later on April 18, 1810, that he would prefer the last portion be divided into two volumes. Then Woodward in turn wrote on April 27 that he had sent "as you requested the last part of Scott's Bible." Jefferson, as did most citizens, simply purchased books after they were printed, but unlike most people, he pre-pledged and invested ahead of time in 1798 to obtain the John Thompson Bible and then in 1807 for the Thomas Scott Bible. The Scott's Bible was the one Jefferson mainly used for the rest of his life and has his signature prominent on the front page.[31] If someone asked Jefferson what was his Bible, this is what he would have shown to them; and it included all 66 books that are in a typical Bible. That is the real "Jefferson Bible." This was yet two more occasions in which Jefferson's money and printed name were publicly associated with a Bible.

At about the same time, further indications as to Jefferson's growing unorthodoxy occur in a November 18, 1807 reply to Universalist minister Rev. Ralph Eddowes of Philadelphia. Jefferson gave his

> ...thanks for the two pamphlets he has been so kind as to send him. He has read them with so much satisfaction that he has desired mr. Dobson to forward him the successive discourses as they shall come out, and also the new translation of the New Testament announced in page 22. This latter work is particularly interesting as he has always been persuaded that the different translations of that book have been warped in particular passages to the tenets of the church of which the translator has been a member. He has received great pleasure from some of the writings of his venerable friend

---

29   Account book, April 27, 1805. For books (including two copies of New Testament). Beliles, *The Selected Religious Letters and Papers of Thomas Jefferson*, 142.

30   Account book, December 21, 1807. For subscription to bible. Scott's Bible. Beliles, *The Selected Religious Letters and Papers of Thomas Jefferson*, 165.

31   Today his Bible is housed at the University of Virginia library.

Doctr. Priestley, on these subjects, and is sensible, from the specimen sent, that he shall do the same as to the discourses, as promised.[32]

Jefferson ordering a Unitarian-oriented New Testament in the same year as the evangelical Scott Bible, makes it difficult to make definite and absolute generalizations of his faith at this time in his life. Publicly he was always orthodox, while privately obtaining and reading both orthodox and heterodox literature. On December 13, 1808, Charles Thomson sent Jefferson a copy of his translation of The Holy Bible translated from the Greek.

Also in this time period, Jefferson's personal overseer at Monticello, Edmund Bacon, who lived there for twenty years and began working in late 1806, spoke of often seeing Jefferson with his Bible. He wrote: "[There was] a large Bible which nearly always lay at the head of his sofa. Many and many a time I have gone into his room and found him reading that Bible."[33] Soon after this, in 1808, Jefferson obtained a copy of Dictionary of the Holy Bible by John Brown, as gift from publisher Zadok Cramer. He had this sent "to binding" on September 3, 1808.[34]

In letters on various topics, even nonreligious ones, Jefferson sometimes quotes the Bible, as in his letter to John Milledge on October 10, 1809: "...the scripture precept of 'prove all things & hold fast that which is good' is peculiarly wise in objects of agriculture..."[35] This was a passage written by the Apostle Paul (1 Thessalonians 5:21); so, of course, Jefferson is quoting from more than just the words of Jesus from the Bible. To an abolitionist neighbor, Edward Coles, Jefferson wrote on August 25, 1814, saying on "...the subject of slavery...you will be supported by the religious precept, 'be not weary in well-doing.'"[36] This is from a letter of Paul in the New Testament (Galatians 6:9).

A Congregational clergyman and teacher in Maine named Rev. Amos Jones Cook was also a missionary for the Bible Society of Massachusetts. He wrote Jefferson in December 1815, and Jefferson replied on January 21, 1816, in which he quoted from Ecclesiastes 2:3-13:

32   Letter to Rev. Ralph Eddowes, November 18, 1807. Beliles, The Selected Religious Letters and Papers of Thomas Jefferson, 162.

33   James A. Bear, Jr., ed., Jefferson At Monticello, (Charlottesville, Va.: University Press of Virginia, 1967), 109.

34   Account books, September 3, 1808. For binding Brown's Dictionary of the Holy Bible (according to reference in Papers of Jefferson for March 8, 1809).

35   Letter to John Milledge, October 10, 1809, www.founders.archives.gov.

36   Letter to Edward Coles, August 25, 1814, www.founders.archives.gov. Coles eventually moved to Illinois so he could free his slaves legally. There he worked with Rev. James Lemen in this cause.

"I sought in my heart to give myself unto wine; I made me great works; I builded me houses; I planted me vineyards; I made me gardens and orchards, and pools to water them; I got me servants and maidens, and great possessions of cattle; I gathered me also silver and gold, and men singers, and women singers, and the delights of the sons of men, and musical instruments of all sorts; and whatsoever mine eyes desired I kept not from them; I withheld not my heart from any joy. Then I looked on all the works that my hands had wrought, and behold! All was vanity and vexation of spirit! I saw that Wisdom excelleth folly, as far as light excelleth darkness." The Preacher, whom I abridge, has indulged in a much larger amplification of his subject.[37]

Jefferson closed his letter wishing Rev. Cook "the prosperity of your institution, accept the assurances of my great respect and esteem."[38] Jefferson obviously still read the Old Testament and quoted it approvingly.

Again, Jefferson would frequently quote the Bible in his letters, drawing from more than just the Gospels. Another example was in his letter to Mary Briggs on April 17, 1816. He encouraged her from Psalm 37:25 saying: "Be strong in the assurance given by an inspired pen, 'I have been young, and now I am old; and yet never saw I the righteous forsaken, or his seed begging their bread': and if the prayers of an old man can be of any avail, you shall ever have mine most ardently."[39] It is noteworthy also that Jefferson calls a passage from the Old Testament "inspired" which is a word he used for Scripture in his 1776 "Notes On Religion."

Jefferson did not limit his study to the Gospels, for in 1821 he asked his pastor Rev. Frederick Hatch for an additional copy of the Greek Old Testament (the Septuagint), and wrote him on September 9, "I thank you, dear sir, for the volume of the LXX [i.e., Greek Old Testament] sent me."[40]

Plus, Jefferson had invested financially and permitted his name publicly to endorse Thompson's "Hot Press" Bible in 1798, and likewise in 1803 *The History of our Blessed Lord and Saviour Jesus Christ,* and likewise again in 1807 Scott's Holy

---

37 Letter to Rev. Amos Jones Cook, January 21, 1816, Beliles, *The Selected Religious Letters and Papers of Thomas Jefferson,* 263.

38 Ibid.

39 Letter to Mary Briggs, April 17, 1816, Beliles, *The Selected Religious Letters and Papers of Thomas Jefferson,* 267.

40 Letter to Rev. Frederick Hatch, September 9, 1821, Beliles, *The Selected Religious Letters and Papers of Thomas Jefferson,* 322.

Bible; and he paid the amount to be a lifetime member of the Virginia Bible Society that distributed whole Bibles to those lacking it. In 1815 he also obtained Charles Thomson's *Synopsis of the Four Evangelists: or, a Regular History of the Conception, Birth, Doctrine, Miracles, Death, Resurrection, and Ascension of Jesus Christ, in the Words of the Evangelists.*

Plus, Jefferson quoted the Old Testament. For example, Jefferson:

1804 to Sister Therese Farjon—quotes Proverbs 22:6,
1811 to Thomas Law—quotes Joshua 10,
1813 to John Adams—quotes Psalm 148,
1813 to William Cocke—-quotes Psalm 90:10,
1813 to John Waldo——quotes Psalm 121:6,
1814 to Walter Jones—quotes 2 Samuel 3:38,
1816 to Mary Briggs—quotes Psalm 37:25,
1816 to Amos Cook—quotes Ecclesiastes 2:3-13,
1824 to Isaac Engelbrecht—quotes Psalm 15.[41]

Clearly Jefferson uses Old Testament scripture with enthusiasm even after making his digest of the words of Jesus. And he likewise quoted the New Testament and especially Paul (about whom he had expressed some serious doubt):

1804 to John Page—quotes 1 Thessalonians 4:13,
1809 to John Milledge—quotes 1 Thessalonians 5:21,
1814 to Edward Coles—quotes Galatians 6:9,
1814 to Edward Coles—quotes 2 Thessalonians 3:13,
1823 to John Adams—quotes John 4:24, (which was not in his abridgement)
1823 to John Adams—[wrongly] quotes "3 first verses of the 1ˢᵗ chapter of John."

Many other examples such as this are found in Jefferson's writings that will not be mentioned because they have been previously referenced in the chronological chapters. Overall, they show a man who had a high level of biblical literacy and used it for encouragement and guidance both for himself and others, regardless of how much he privately criticized its supposed corruptions.

---

41   Letter to Isaac Englebrecht, February 25, 1824, The Thomas Jefferson Papers Series 1, General Correspondence, 1651-1827, Library of Congress Manuscript Division.

1813, Sharing the Syllabus and
Ideas of "Corruptions" of Scripture

A definitive statement was finally made by Jefferson about the Bible in a letter to John Adams in August 1813. He sent to Adams a copy of the 1803 Syllabus comparing the moral teachings of Jesus with the ancient philosophers. That document originally avoided discussion of Jesus' deity, but now Jefferson overtly expresses unorthodox views.

Jefferson wrote of Priestley: "...I have read his *Corruptions of Christianity*, and *Early Opinions of Jesus*, over and over again; and I rest on them, and on Middleton's writings, especially his *Letters from Rome*, and *To Waterland*, as the basis of my own faith. These writings have never been answered, nor can be answered..."[42] Priestley claims that God's original revelation was correct, but was corrupted in the translation of the Scriptures themselves. Middleton questioned miracles and the literal inerrancy of the Bible.

Weeks later, on October 12, Jefferson wrote to John Adams:

> ...I now send you, according to your request a copy of the Syllabus...
> It was the reformation of this 'wretched depravity' of morals which Jesus
> undertook. In extracting the pure principles which he taught, we should
> have to strip off the artificial vestments in which they have been muffled
> by priests, who have travestied them into various forms, as instruments
> of riches and power to them...We must reduce our volume to the simple
> evangelists, [43] select, even from them, the very words only of Jesus,
> paring off the Amphibologisms [i.e., phrases that can be interpreted
> in different ways] into which they have been led by forgetting often,
> or not understanding, what had fallen from him, by giving their own
> misconceptions as his dicta, and expressing unintelligibly for others what
> they had not understood themselves. There will be found remaining the
> most sublime and benevolent code of morals which has ever been offered to
> man. I have performed this operation for my own use, by cutting verse by
> verse out of the printed book, and arranging, the matter which is evidently
> his, and which is as easily distinguishable as diamonds in a dunghill. The
> result is an 8 vo. [i.e., Octavo eight-leaves format] of 46. pages of pure
> and unsophisticated doctrines, such as were professed and acted on by the

---

42   Letter to John Adams, August 22, 1813, www.founders.archives.gov. Note: There are
      answers to these objections. We provide brief answers even in this book, in the Appendix.

43   Matthew, Mark, Luke, and John.

unlettered apostles, the Apostolic fathers, and the Christians of the 1st. century;...Turn to the 148th. psalm, in Brady and Tate's version. Have such conceptions been ever before expressed? Their version of the 18th. Psalm...expresses the majesty of God descending on the earth, in terms not unworthy of the subject. "The Lord descended from, And bowed the heav'ns most, above high; And underneath his feet he cast, The darkness of the sky. On Cherubim and Seraphim, Full royally he rode; And on the wings of mighty, Came flying all abroad."[Psalm 18:9-10][44]

Regardless of Jefferson's criticism of some Scripture, it is clear that he still read much of it and admired even passages from the Old Testament (among others).

Jefferson also says in this letter for the first time that his abridgement of the words of Jesus was something he personally used, ten years after first compiling it, as he explained—in his own words in the subtitle—for the use of the Indians. He also spoke of his belief that additions were made to the words of Jesus by Plato-influenced theologians in the early centuries of Christianity—including their promotion of the Trinity. This is what he called the "dunghill" that he hoped would die out. Despite all this, he still goes on to say that Jesus—despite the supposedly false additions—has the best content of all teachers. The modern scholars who want to trumpet the religious views of Jefferson the skeptic regularly ignore the bigger picture: he was a serious student of the Bible, although he came to believe the book had become flawed by layers and layers of "artificial vestments." Obviously, biblically minded Christians recognize that translations are not inerrant, but they do not believe that the original manuscripts of the Scriptures themselves are inherently corrupted. In this letter, Jefferson seems to suggest that the corruption of the words of Jesus started with the Gospel writers themselves who either forgot or misunderstood or poorly expressed what they heard.

This is more troubling than blaming it on the Plato-influenced theologians of later centuries. It seems to blame the Apostles themselves, whom biblically minded Christians believe were inspired by God in their writings. Thus, Christians cannot agree with Jefferson if he's stating that the Scriptures themselves are inherently corrupted. Another letter to Adams adds further light.

Jefferson wrote to him on January 24, 1814, and he again expressed, even more succinctly, his mistrust of scriptural texts passed down over time. "...Where get we the ten commandments? The book...itself tells us they were written by

---

44   Letter to John Adams, October 12, 1813, www.founders.archives.gov.

the finger of God on tables of stone…; But the whole history of these books is so defective and doubtful that it seems vain to attempt minute enquiry into it; and such tricks have plaid with their text, and with the texts of other books relating to them, that we have a right, from that cause, to entertain much doubt what parts of them are genuine. In the New Testament there is internal evidence that parts of it have proceeded from an extraordinary man; and that other parts are of the fabric of very inferior minds. It is as easy to separate those parts, as to pick diamonds from dunghills."[45]

Here Jefferson speaks of the Bible as not reliable, but it does not appear that he means the *original* manuscripts, for he talks of "tricks have plaid with their text." This implies his criticism is of later translations and additions to the original manuscripts by "inferior minds." If so, then his use of the term "dung" is not of what he believes is God's Word, but perversions of it. Clearly, though, he sets himself up as a judge of what is true versus what is false in the Scriptures themselves. A true Christian takes a humbler approach: the historic Councils of the ancient church were composed of scholar theologians and historians well-versed in these ancient texts and subsequent translations, in contrast to single individuals millennia later who think themselves wiser than all the historic scholars used by God to evaluate and determine the inspired content of the New Testament. Now, centuries later, those texts are still accepted as reliable by scholars, as they had by subsequent scholars across previous centuries.

Furthermore, scholars today are in a better position than Jefferson was to know how wrong he was on the problem with subsequent translations. Biblical scholars have what is sometimes called "an embarrassment of riches" when it comes to a plethora of biblical manuscripts, including thousands in the original Greek—plus manuscripts translated into Syriac, Latin, Coptic, and so on. Biblical scholars today can judge how trustworthy the New Testament was. Scholars maintain that only about 3-4 percent of the text of the New Testament is questionable, and even that 3-4 percent does not impact any major doctrines. The Bible is far and away the best attested book of antiquity because so many ancient contemporary copies now prove the reliability of the original. So even if one is not inclined to trust the historic church councils of the fourth and fifth centuries, the scholarship on this topic provides a reasonable basis to trust what has survived in the typical modern Bible to be authentic.

And it is also notable that although Jefferson spoke to John Adams of concentrating on the Gospels, yet he still quoted and used the Psalms and other

---

45   Letter to John Adams, January 24, 1814, www.founders.archives.gov.

writings of Paul. So although he certainly disbelieved and criticized some parts of the Scriptures, including the Book of Revelation, it would be incorrect to say he rejected everything else in the Bible; for indeed he read it and funded its printing and distribution.

Lifetime Membership in the Virginia Bible Society

Jefferson's general and public support for the Bible is illuminated further when Samuel Greenhow wrote Jefferson in November 1813. Greenhow was the treasurer of the new Virginia Bible Society. Greenhow wrote: "...without Enquiring whether you or I receive this Book as a work of Inspiration, I shall hope for your patronage of the Association—We should be much pleased to number you among the members of the Society; But, if you should prefer it, we will thankfully receive any donation that you may be pleased to aid us with..."[46] Enclosed was the *Address of the Managers of the Bible Society of Virginia, to the Public.* This society was started in 1813 mainly through the leadership of Presbyterian Rev. John Holt Rice to distribute Bibles "...to the poor of our country, and to the Heathen [i.e., the Indians]."[47]

Jefferson replied to Greenhow on January 31, 1814, saying:

...Your letter on the subject of the [Virginia] Bible Society arrived here while I was on a journey to Bedford,...I presume the views of the society are confined to our own country, for with the religion of other countries my own forbids intermeddling. I had not supposed there was a family in this State not possessing a Bible, and wishing without having the means to procure one. When, in earlier life, I was intimate with every class, I think I never was in a house where that was the case. However, circumstances may have changed, and the society, I presume, have evidence of the fact. I therefore enclose you cheerfully, an order on Messrs. Gibson & Jefferson for fifty dollars, for the purposes of the [Virginia Bible] society, sincerely agreeing with you that there never was a more pure and sublime system of morality delivered to man than is to be found in the four evangelists. Accept the assurance of my esteem and respect.[48]

---

46   Letter from Samuel Greenhow, November 11, 1813. Beliles, *The Selected Religious Letters and Papers of Thomas Jefferson*, 215.

47   Ibid.

48   Letter to Samuel Greenhow [of the Virginia Bible Society], January 31, 1814, www. founders.archives.gov.

His account book entry for January 31 says: "Inclosed to Samuel Greenhow an order...for 50 Dollars for the Bible society of Virginia."[49] Although Jefferson's reply especially praised the "evangelists," i.e., Matthew, Mark, Luke, John, yet he did not refrain from support for distributing whole Bibles.

Greenhow replied on February 4, saying: "I have this day recd. Your...$50... (for) the Bible Society...; I also am gratified, that my Application has been successful as to it's Object, because that Success assures me that you approve our Association, if the Bibles are wanted in our Country, by persons too poor to purchase them;... Bibles were school books thirty years ago, at present, they are out of use in most schools;...The great deficiency of Bibles in Louisiana has been satisfactorily shewn—...An Edition of 5000 Copies is now (I believe) in press—the translation in press, is that called the Geneva translation, which does not differ materially from that in use among Protestants here...—To this Edition our Society mean to subscribe—In this only, have we, as yet had a view, extending beyond this State."[50]

Samuel Greenhow clearly understood Jefferson's donation as making him a member in the Bible Society. (Madison and Monroe also joined). The founder of the Virginia Society, Presbyterian minister Rev. John Holt Rice, also confirmed Jefferson's membership in his memoir, saying that "Madison, Monroe, and Jefferson are all members of the Bible Society of Virginia."[51] The amount of $50 is the reason this was clear to Rice.

The rules Jefferson read before sending the donation were: "Persons of every religious creed or denomination may become Members of this Society upon paying five dollars subscription money, and binding themselves to pay four dollars annually so long as they choose to continue in the Society. The payment, however, of fifty dollars in advance, shall without any further contribution constitute a person *member for life*."[52] Jefferson gave $50 and that made him a "member for life" of the Virginia Bible Society.

However, a few years later, Jefferson declined membership in the *national* American Bible Society that Rice also helped establish; this stance would be consistent with Jefferson's emphasis on anti-centralization and on states' rights

---

49   Account book, January 1814. For the Bible Society of Virginia. Beliles, *The Selected Religious Letters and Papers of Thomas Jefferson*, 223.

50   Letter from Samuel Greenhow, November 11, 1813. Beliles, *The Selected Religious Letters and Papers of Thomas Jefferson*, 215.

51   Samuel Greenhow to Jefferson, February 4, 1814, www.founders.archives.gov. See also William Maxwell, *Memoir of the Rev. John H. Rice* (Philadelphia: J. Whetham, 1835), 127.

52   Letter from Samuel Greenhow, November 11, 1813. Beliles, *The Selected Religious Letters and Papers of Thomas Jefferson*, 215.

versus national authority.[53] Even though the American Bible Society was not a government organization, his refusing to join is consistent with the way Jefferson thinks. He does not support centralization of almost anything because of its inherent dangers of abuse when not accountable to people locally who can see what is happening through it.

Despite some private reservations about the reliability of the Scripture texts and references to parts of the alleged corruptions as the "dunghill," it is important to remember that at that very moment, Jefferson nonetheless believed in the benefit of knowing the whole Bible and supported its distribution. That was what the public knew of him, and the other speculations and opinions expressed to Adams and other friends were done in the confidence that they would stay private.

Jefferson received a request in February 1813 from Joseph Delaplaine and from Murray, Draper, Fairman & Company that said "we should derive peculiar gratification from receiving your name as a subscriber to our edition of Macklin's Bible. Permit us to express our hopes that you will honor us with your name on this occasion." This Bible published by Thomas Macklin in England was an expensive affair that included great artistic elements. These American publishers were proposing their own version of it to subscribers. This expensive Bible project was not going to be published for a number of years, even though subscribers would make financial pledges ahead of time. Jefferson replied on March 4, 1813, saying:

> ...I am duly sensible of the obliging motives you express for desiring my subscription to the very magnificent edition you propose to publish of Maclin's bible. But age and infirmity warn me from engaging in new undertakings which will require for their completion more years than I have to live, the prospectus supposes the work will be completed in six years, but this depending on many others besides the editors, the term cannot be within their control. Declining therefore the subscription to the work I tender every wish for it's success, with the assurance of my respect.[54]

---

53   Thomas Thompson, *The Failure of Jeffersonian Reform: Religious Groups and the Politics of Morality in Early National Virginia* (Unpublished dissertation, University of California, Riverside, 1990), 365. See Robert M. Healey, *Jefferson on Religion in Public Education* (New Haven, Conn.: Yale University Press, 1962), 243-244 and Alan Heimert, *Religion and The American Mind: From the Great Awakening to the Revolution* (Cambridge, Mass.: Harvard University Press, 1966).

54   Letter to Joseph Delaplaine and to Murray, Draper, Fairman & Company, March 4, 1813. www.founders.archives.gov.

Although supportive of the project, he wasn't sure if he would live long enough to see their publication.

Prophetic Warning From Rev. Charles Clay

Jefferson asked bookseller Nicolas Dufief on August 21, 1814, "...to procure and send him a copy of [Edward] Evanson's *Dissonance of the four Evangelists*."[55] Evanson, a Unitarian minister, rejected most of the books of the New Testament as forgeries, and of the four gospels he accepted only the Gospel of Luke. (It should be noted that if he accepted that book alone, he is still dealing with the virgin-born Son of God, Who died on behalf of sinners and rose again from the dead, as well as many other historically orthodox theological Christian teachings.)

Rev. Clay, in his letter to Jefferson on December 20, 1814, warned against making a public . . .

> ...expression of yours Relative to an idea Sometimes entertained by you of Compressing the Moral doctrines taught by Jesus of Nazareth in the Gospels, divested of all other Matters into a small and Regular system of the purest morality ever taught to Mankind, & meriting the highest praise, & most worthy the Strictest attention, etc., etc. However laudable may be your View & meritorious your intentions in Such a [new?] & Critical (delicate) undertaking, I cannot help entertaining doubts & fears for the final issue...[56]

Rev. Clay is warning his old friend that a public declaration or publication of his personal doubts might indeed damage his reputation. Clay continues:

> ...the public...might not sufficiently appreciate your good intentions, but ascribe it to Views as inimical to the christian Religion in particular, and eventually to all religion from divine Authority, which I am persuaded you Can have no intention of doing ...should the performance not exactly Coincide with their Ideas & meet their entire approbation, even in the minutiae of diction (which it is highly probable it would not) they would...be found barking at your heels![57]

---

55   Thompson, *The Failure of Jeffersonian Reform*, 365.

56   Charles Clay to Jefferson, December 20, 1814, Beliles, *The Selected Religious Letters and Papers of Thomas Jefferson*, 250-251.

57   Ibid.

Clay knew more of Jefferson's private speculations from private conversations than most, and Clay was concerned that Jefferson might now become more public with his views. Clay feared Jefferson would be misunderstood and accused of all manner of unbelief. Clay knew Jefferson personally over several decades; modern writers do not have that knowledge. Clay said to his friend that he was "persuaded you Can have no intention" of rejecting "the christian Religion." This should give pause to those modern writers who lump Jefferson in with Voltaire types. Clay went on to voice his fears that Jefferson would be (falsely) "rankled with the wild Sophisters of Jacobinism [i.e., unsound advocates of extreme politically radical ideas]," etc.[58]

About a month later on January 29, 1815, Jefferson replied to the warning of his evangelical friend, Rev. Clay:

> Your letter of December 20th was four weeks on its way to me. I thank you for it; for although founded on a misconception, it is evidence of that friendly concern for my peace and welfare, which I have ever believed you to feel. Of publishing a book on religion, my dear Sir, I never had an idea...Probably you have heard me say I had taken the four Evangelists, had cut out from them every text they had recorded of the moral precepts of Jesus, and arranged them in a certain order, and although they appeared but as fragments, yet fragments of the most sublime edifice of morality which had ever been exhibited to man. This I have probably mentioned to you, because it is true; and the idea of its publication may have suggested itself as an inference of your own mind.[59]

Recall that Jefferson had earlier acknowledged that he had probably spoken about religion more with Rev. Clay than anyone else, which underscores the significance of Clay's remarks highlighted above—that Clay knew Jefferson was not a disbeliever in the "christian religion," but that it would easily be misconstrued that he was should he publish his book.

Clay's letter to Jefferson on February 8 said:

> I am pleased to find you viewed my letter in the light it was intended,—A Real Concern for your present peace & future Reputation alone dictated

---

58   Ibid., 251. Jacobinism refers to the subversive secret French Revolutionaries.

59   Letter to Rev. Charles Clay, January 29, 1815, Beliles, *The Selected Religious Letters and Papers of Thomas Jefferson*, 251.

it, & Strongly impressed my mind to draw your attention to the probable Consequences Should your ultimate Views have seen publication; in the brokn form of fragments [in Jefferson's 1804 abridgement for the Indians] & which must have been connected perhaps by some observations, or explanations, to preserve a concatenation of Ideas, in these lay the difficulties & dangers I was apprehensive of;—& although every one may, & every one has an undoubted Right to amuse himself sometimes, & even be playful in his Closet on any Subject.[60]

Clay believed that Jefferson's abridgement, and any views he expressed to Clay, was nothing more than him being "playful in his Closet," and he agreed that anyone has the "Right to amuse himself sometimes" with speculations on religious topics. It is no small matter that the evangelical minister —whom Jefferson spoke with the most about his religious views and who knew him best for about five decades, viewed the third president as a believer.

Benjamin Rush was another evangelical friend of Jefferson, and likewise, after Jefferson told him about the extracts he made from the Gospels, he recommended it not to be published, lest its editor be misunderstood.[61] Jefferson took Rush's advice in 1804 and never sent his extracts to anyone, nor did he share his later version of it. Likewise, he listened to Clay's advice. He never deliberately expressed anything contradictory of Scripture in public. But unfortunately, it turns out in history that Clay's fears came true. In recent years publication of what some people call the "Jefferson Bible" has created an impression that Jefferson **publicly** rejected the Scriptures and the Trinity, and modern Christians thus feel alienated by him. But Jefferson heeded Clay's advice and never shared unorthodox thoughts publicly. Clay would be puzzled and dismayed that two centuries later the standard image of Thomas Jefferson is that he was a skeptic with no love for any portion of Scripture or any part of the Christian faith.

As he had done so often throughout his life, on March 28, 1815, Jefferson again purchased some orthodox religious literature. In a letter to bookseller Joseph Milligan, he ordered: "the Book of Common prayer, an 8vo edition; the power of religion on the mind by Lindlay Murray; [Lawrence] Sterne's sermons."[62] Milligan replied on May 6 to Jefferson and confirmed that Jefferson also bought "Thomsons

---

60 Charles Clay to Jefferson, February 8, 1815, Beliles, *The Selected Religious Letters and Papers of Thomas Jefferson*, 252.

61 To Thomas Jefferson from Benjamin Rush, August 29, 1804. The Thomas Jefferson Papers Series 1, General Correspondence, 1651-1827, Library of Congress Manuscript Division.

62 Letter to Joseph Milligan, March 28, 1815, The Thomas Jefferson Papers Series 1, General Correspondence, 1651-1827, Library of Congress Manuscript Division.

Four Gospels" which was the newly published book by Charles Thomson: "A Synopsis of the Four Evangelists: or, a Regular History of the Conception, Birth, Doctrine, Miracles, Death, Resurrection, and Ascension of Jesus Christ, in the Words of the Evangelists."[63] Note that Charles Thomson was not only a writer of Christian books and translator of the Bible, but he had served as the secretary for the Continental Congress, including that of 1776 which produced the Declaration of Independence. Thomson was a great Christian patriot.

On January 9, 1816, Jefferson wrote to Charles Thomson informing him of his own digest of the four Gospels (his "the Philosophy of Jesus" of 1804). Later, in 1820, he expanded his digest of the teachings of Jesus and place these teachings in columns—of English, Greek, Latin, and French texts.

1816—Mention of His Desire to Modify His Extracts of the Gospels

On April 25, 1816, Jefferson corresponds again with Francis A. Van der Kemp, another northern Unitarian:

> ...after writing the *Syllabus*, I made, for my own satisfaction, an *Extract from the Evangelists* of the texts of his morals, selecting those only whose style and spirit proved them genuine, and his own: and they are as distinguishable from the matter in which they are imbedded as diamonds in dunghills. A more precious morsel of ethics was never seen. It was too hastily done however, being the work of one or two evenings only, while I lived at Washington, overwhelmed with other business: and it is my intention to go over it again at more leisure.[64]

Again, biblical Christians cannot agree with this approach of picking and choosing. Once a person accepts the idea of a flawed text, where do they draw the line? Modern Unitarians today hardly accept anything from the Bible. There is often no logical end to the reductionist trend.

Jefferson continues to Van der Kemp about a plan to upgrade his digest of moral teachings,

---

63   Letter from Joseph Milligan, May 6, 1815. The Thomas Jefferson Papers Series 1, General Correspondence, 1651-1827, Library of Congress Manuscript Division.

64   Letter to Francis Van der Kemp, April 25, 1816, Beliles, *The Selected Religious Letters and Papers of Thomas Jefferson*, 267.

This shall be the work of the ensuing winter. I gave it the title of "The Philosophy of Jesus extracted from the texts of the Evangelists;"…the world, I say, will at length see the immortal merit of this first of human Sages. I rejoice that you think of undertaking this work…; If the Syllabus and Extract (which is short) either in substance, or at large, are worth a place under the same cover with your biography, they are at your service. I ask one only condition, that no possibility shall be admitted of my name being even intimated with the publication.[65]

Although the "ensuing winter" was his plan, it was at least 1819 before it was started. (For the sake of identification, we will assign 1820 as the date for the second version throughout the rest of this book.) Van der Kemp has asked for Jefferson's permission to print these writings of Jefferson in his forthcoming book. Jefferson permits it only if it not have Jefferson's name associated with it. That is completely understandable. He did not want to incur more wrath from religious critics, as Rev. Clay had advised, nor to ever disturb others. He was not a public reformer of religious doctrine.

On March 9, 1818, Jefferson's account book said he "Paid for a book."[66] The editors say it was a book by George Bethune English entitled *The Grounds of Christianity Examined by Comparing the New Testament with the Old.* It was not an orthodox work and had led to the excommunication of Mr. English. Jefferson wrote to his former aide and diplomat William Short two years later in 1820:

…Among the sayings and discourses imputed to Him [i.e., Jesus] by His biographers, I find many passages of fine imagination, correct morality, and of the most lovely benevolence; and others, again, of so much ignorance, so much absurdity, so much untruth, charlatanism and imposture, as to pronounce it impossible that such contradictions should have proceeded from the same Being. I separate, therefore, the gold from the dross…I found the work obvious and easy, …the most beautiful morsel of morality which has been given to us by man…[67]

65   Ibid.

66   Account book, March 1818. For a book. (editors say it was *The Grounds of Christianity* by George Bethune English). Beliles, *The Selected Religious Letters and Papers of Thomas Jefferson*, 289.

67   Letter to William Short, April 13, 1820, Beliles, *The Selected Religious Letters and Papers of Thomas Jefferson*, 306.

Jefferson's account book on July 4, 1824 shows him buying a book which the editors say was *A Greek and English Lexicon* by John Jones. About a year before he died, Jefferson wrote in very critical terms about the last book of the Bible. In a letter to General Alexander Smyth on January 17, 1825, Jefferson replied that he was glad to hear (as Smyth believed) that Saint John was not the author the book of Revelation in the Bible:

> ...It is between fifty and sixty years since I read it, and I then considered it as merely the ravings of a maniac...You will perceive, I hope, also, that I do not consider them as revelations of the Supreme Being, whom I would not so far blaspheme as to impute [its authorship] to Him...[68]

Jefferson shows again his belief that portions of the Bible have been corrupted. In criticizing the book of Revelation, he does not reject the Apostle John's work, but as he thought, the work of someone "a century after the death of the apostle," [69] by someone who used John's name. But, manuscript-wise, there is no evidence for this theory that this book was written any later than the end of the first century. Jefferson's personal distaste for apocalyptic literature along with bad historical data about its authorship led him to reject as rubbish a book which Christians today accept as the final portion of Holy Writ. It was among the last of the books of the New Testament to be accepted, but once the canon was determined in the mid-4th century, all major branches of Christendom have accepted the 27 books of the New Testament. (The issue of the canon is addressed in the Appendix.)

Before ending this chapter, two less reliable documents for making absolute conclusions about Jefferson's faith should be mentioned here. Jefferson began as early as age 15 under Rev. James Maury in preparation for college to keep his commonplace book that included extensive quotes from English political philosopher Lord Bolingbroke—a skeptic on matters of religion. Douglas Wilson, Monticello scholar and editor of *Jefferson's Literary Commonplace Book*, shows that it cannot be proven that Jefferson agreed (or disagreed) with Bolingbroke's quotes that he copied. With this in mind, here are a few of the quotes from the Commonplace Book around the year 1765 or so:

---

68   Letter to General Alexander Smyth, January 17, 1825, Beliles, *The Selected Religious Letters and Papers of Thomas Jefferson*, 371.

69   Ibid.

...[Scripture has] gross defects and palpable falsehoods;...[portraying God as] partial, unjust, and cruel;...[who] delights in blood, commands assassinations, massacres, and even exterminations of people,...[while in the New Testament he] elects some of his creatures to salvation, and predestinates others to damnation even in the womb of their mothers... [This God] sent his only begotten son, who had not offended him, to be sacrificed by men, who had offended him, that he might expiate their sins, and satisfy his own anger;...[The miracles Jesus supposedly worked] were equivocal at best, such as credulous superstitious persons, and none else, believed, such as were frequently and universally imposed by the first fathers of the Christian church, and are so still by their successors, wherever ignorance or superstition abound.[70]

If Jefferson wrote these thoughts himself or made any comment on them that he agreed with them, then this collection of quotes would certainly modify the view of him as consistently orthodox in the first phase of his religious life. It would suggest a Jefferson who was skeptical of Scripture, miracles and the basic redemption mission of Jesus to die on the cross for the sins of the world. But since he may not have had free choice during his college years with such note-taking, and he never made any comments on these particular passages, it is not valid to make such a conclusion.[71] It would be feasible to consider that such passages from that skeptic sowed seeds in Jefferson's mind, so that later he was more open to Joseph Priestley's more subtle skepticism of the Bible.

One's approach to such commonplace notes is important because another set of notes appears about a decade later that the *Papers of Thomas Jefferson* call his "Notes on Religion." It was during the final months of 1776 that Jefferson

---

70   Douglas L. Wilson, *Jefferson's Literary Commonplace Book* (Princeton, N.J.: Princeton University Press, 1989), 40-50.

71   Douglas L. Wilson, paper entitled: "Jefferson and Bolingbroke: Some Notes On the Question of Influence," which was presented at the symposium on Religious Culture in Jefferson's Virginia, in January 1996. See also Douglas Wilson, *Jefferson's Literary Commonplace Book*, 36-37. Although Jefferson's quotes from Bolingbroke far exceeds the word count of any other author represented, Douglas Wilson, Monticello's chief historian and editor of *Jefferson's Literary Commonplace Book*, admits that "Jefferson makes no comment on the material he copies into it, so we can only guess at or infer his reasons for commonplacing Bolingbroke's writings at such length." Wilson said he believed that Bolingbroke "is unlikely to have been the actual source for most of the Enlightenment ideas Jefferson espoused later in life." In this case no honest scholar can make an assertion that they represent Jefferson because he made no comments on them.

personally compiled these nine documents which expressed very orthodox beliefs.[72] Jefferson copied from John Locke's book, *A Vindication of the Reasonableness of Christianity* and concerning the Bible, he copied words saying that "...the writers were inspired."[73] Jefferson also quotes a phrase that references the Protestant principle of *Sola Scriptura*: "If we are Protestants, we reject all tradition, and rely on the Scripture alone."[74] And concerning the church, he quotes a Bible verse: "Christ has said 'wheresoever 2 or 3 are gathered together in his name he will be in the midst of them.'"[75]

Conclusions

Having looked at all the evidence of quotes by Jefferson regarding the Bible, it is apparent that Jefferson loved much of the content of Scripture, but seemed, especially late in life, to have a low view of the reliability of Scripture overall. In his Syllabus, he wrote, "the committing to writing [Jesus'] life & doctrines fell on the most unlettered & ignorant men; who wrote, too, from memory, & not till long after the transactions had passed."[76] There are strong Christian answers to what appears to be Jefferson's core assumptions, which will be addressed in the Appendix.

Any honest reading of the faith of Thomas Jefferson should take in all sides of the story. When examining Jefferson and the Bible, it is clear that he was overall a student of the Scriptures. At times in his life, he also had bought into the philosophy, prevalent in Unitarian circles (and even some of the Restoration circles, popular in his area of Virginia in that day), that the Bible is corrupted. One of the leaders of the Restoration church movement was Alexander Campbell, a major figure in the Second Great Awakening's famous religious revivals. He was anti-Trinitarian, anti-Calvinist, and said that he wanted to save "the Holy Scriptures from the perplexities of the commentators and system-makers of the dark ages."[77]

---

72   Scholars have used "Notes on Religion" as one way to identify these documents. But another way is "Notes and Proceedings on Discontinuing the Establishment of the Church of England," 1776, www.founders.archives.gov.

73   Document 6. Notes and Proceedings on Discontinuing the Establishment of the Church of England," 1776, www.founders.archives.gov.

74   Document 7. Notes and Proceedings on Discontinuing the Establishment of the Church of England," 1776, www.founders.archives.gov.

75   Document 5. Notes and Proceedings on Discontinuing the Establishment of the Church of England," 1776, www.founders.archives.gov.

76   Syllabus of an Estimate of the Merit of the Doctrines of Jesus Compared with Others, May 21, 1803, Beliles, *The Selected Religious Letters and Papers of Thomas Jefferson*, 110.

77   Nathan O. Hatch, *Democratization of American Christianity* (New Haven, Conn.: Yale University Press, 1989), 163.

He even therefore published his own edition of the New Testament in 1826 to correct the alleged flaws and perversions. Significantly, Campbell is still treated by the evangelical world today as a legitimate Christian in American history, but Jefferson has not been treated with the same deference. It seems fairer for scholars to treat them the same, and perhaps Jefferson be given even more slack since he was not formally trained in theology, as was Campbell.

Over the past century, the proponents of Jefferson the skeptic have wrongly concocted a purported "legacy" of Jefferson that he certainly never intended. Jefferson never once expressed his disbelief about portions of the Bible in public; not once. He privately speculated on the reliability of certain Scriptures in confidence to friends including evangelicals, who respectfully disagreed with him for it but not enough to consider him an outsider. And when he created his abridgement of Jesus' words, all the miracles of Jesus were definitely not deleted from that abridgement.[78] At first he thought his digest of Jesus' teachings could be used as a simple tool for missionaries among Indian tribes, until his friend Benjamin Rush pushed back saying he would not support it if Christ's death and resurrection were not in it. And later in 1815 when Pastor Charles Clay warned that publication of gospel extracts would be misunderstood, Jefferson continued to keep it from ever been seen by anyone.

He mentioned it in a couple letters but no one saw it, not even his family, until after his death. No one else ever saw it until the Smithsonian museum obtained it in 1895. Because of publication in the last century of what they wrongly call the "Jefferson Bible," modern generations have been presented with a false impression that Jefferson publicly rejected all the Scriptures and thus Christians feel alienated by him. This was the last thing he wanted to happen. The claim that Jefferson was generally anti-Bible is an exaggerated and false legacy, not supported by historical context. The true "Jefferson Bible" was never what you see in print today. Jefferson's real Bible is found in the library at the University of Virginia, and it contains all the books that are found in the Bibles, and that orthodox Christians today have in their own possession.

---

78   Almost all printed versions of the 1820 *Life and Morals* are filled with skewed editorial comments on Jefferson's faith. Of all the "Jefferson Bibles" in print today, the one edition that is faithful to the evidence is: *Jefferson's "Bible": The Life and Morals of Jesus of Nazareth*, edited by Judd W. Patton (Grove City, Pennsylvania: American Book Distributors, 2014). http://jpatton.bellevue.edu/jefferson_bible/.

CHAPTER 11

JEFFERSON AND ORTHODOXY: HIS MISUNDERSTANDING OF THE TRINITY AND OTHER DOCTRINES

"Jesus Himself, the Founder of our religion…teaches expressly that the body is to rise in substance. In the Apostles' Creed, we all declare that we believe in the 'resurrection of the body.'" —Thomas Jefferson, 1824 [1]

I n this chapter more time is allotted to discuss Jefferson's views of the Trinity and orthodox Christian doctrines that were mentioned in a brief way earlier.

Late in life, Jefferson believed in what he viewed as "rational Christianity," by which he meant a form of Unitarianism. Any analysis of what he believed needs to always be identified with his age. The younger Jefferson apparently believed in the historic Christian faith,[2] when he organized the Calvinistical Reformed Church and wrote the Virginia Statute for Religious Freedom. The later

---

1   Letter to Augustus Woodward, March 24, 1824. Mark A. Beliles, ed., *The Selected Religious Letters and Papers of Thomas Jefferson* (Charlottesville, VA: America Publications, 2013), 364.

2   As seen in chapter 2 the evidence of all reliable documents give no indication that suggest Jefferson to be anything other than an orthodox Christian in the first major phase of his life, through 1787.

post-presidential Thomas Jefferson, seemed to reject the Trinity and other key historic Christian beliefs. During the last phase of his life, his views were certainly not compatible with an orthodox, historic understanding of Christianity. But quotes from one particular phase cannot represent him completely.

The chronological chapters revealed that about the time Jefferson became president at the turn of the 19th century, there were two new influences in his life: the popular Restoration movement in his home area (with its emphasis on getting away from doctrinal creeds) and a new friendship with an English Unitarian newly settled in Philadelphia.

Rev. Joseph Priestley

Rev. Joseph Priestley (1733-1804) was a scientist, theologian, and prominent Unitarian minister, whom Jefferson respected. He had fled England because of persecution against him for his unorthodox views. He settled in Philadelphia and was a Unitarian minister there. When Jefferson was in Philadelphia in the late 1790s, he said he attended Priestley's church. Jefferson said in his presidential and post-presidential years that his religious views were shaped most by Joseph Priestley's writings. To fully grasp Jefferson's understanding, especially the later Jefferson, it's helpful to understand Priestley and his book, *The Corruptions of Christianity.*

Priestley believed that just as the worship of saints and of Mary, the Mother of Jesus, arose within the Church—comprising "corruptions" in the Church—so there were corruptions even earlier within Christianity. He puts in that category core Christian doctrines, such as the deity of Christ, the Trinity, and the atonement— Jesus' death for sinners. Priestley said that the cross of Christ was a "shocking degradation." This clearly puts Priestley outside orthodox belief.

Thus, Rev. Joseph Priestley thought the original Christianity, given to the world by Jesus, was good, but was later corrupted by the Church. After describing this process of chipping away at all the alleged corruptions of Christianity, Priestley wrote, "Hence we may safely conclude, that this natural process, now happily commenced, will proceed till every remaining corruption of Christianity be removed, and nothing will be found in it that any unbeliever, any Jew, or Mahometan, can reasonably object to."[3]

He looks for the day when true Christianity (as he sees it) will be restored, when what he sees as bogus claims added later to the faith are rejected and all that

---

3   Ira V. Brown, ed., *Joseph Priestley: Selections from His Writings* (University Park, PA: The Pennsylvania State University, 1962), 329.

remains is the pure, primitive faith. Again, those so-called bogus claims include the Trinity, the deity of Jesus, and His death on behalf of sinners. If those things are bogus, then the Christian faith is bogus because they were there from the beginning.

Priestley viewed himself as a Christian and lamented it when others did not believe in Jesus. He felt that way, for instance, about Ben Franklin. It is important to note that Priestley did not consider Jefferson an unbeliever like Franklin.

In reading Priestley, it is evident that he is a man convinced that Jesus was the Messiah, that He was sent by God the Father, but that the record about Him was corrupted in the transmission. Priestley believed in primitive Christianity, so he says, but not later versions of it. But how does a person regain that primitive Christianity? By stripping away the miraculous from the Gospels? Priestley himself embraced the biggest of all miracles in the Gospel—the historic, bodily resurrection from the dead of Jesus. If you accept that, then don't all the details that can't be proven tend to fall in line?

To critique Priestley from an orthodox perspective, consider his argument that the atonement was a "corruption" of the gospel—that it was not there from the very beginning. But Paul's letter to the Galatians was likely the first book of the New Testament to be penned. In that book, salvation by faith in Christ's death on the cross was central.

In the Gospels, the atonement is taught by Jesus—particularly in the Last Supper. He said that His blood was the blood of the New Covenant, shed for the remission of sins for many. He said in Mark that He was giving His life as a ransom for many. John's Gospel is filled with examples of Jesus speaking of His death on behalf of sinners. It should be noted that Jefferson included such passages as found in the Synoptics in his abridgements.

Priestley's Own Words Rejecting Fundamentals of the Faith

Priestley did affirm some aspects of Christianity, such as life after death. We need to be "be preparing for that world."[4] But Priestley rejects the deity of Jesus despite the fact that in the four Gospels, written in the first century, there is evidence of the claim that Jesus was divine. His claim to divinity is the reason He was delivered up to be crucified. The Temple authorities accused Him of blasphemy, which is why they arrested Jesus and had a "trial" among themselves as recorded in the Gospel of Mark 14:61-64 below:

---

4   Ibid.

Again, the high priest asked Him, "Are you the Christ, the Son of the Blessed?"

Jesus said, "I am. And you will see the Son of Man sitting at the right hand of the Power, and coming with the clouds of heaven."

Then the high priest tore his clothes and said, "What further need do we have of witnesses? You have heard the blasphemy! What do you think?"

And they all condemned Him to be deserving of death.

Nonetheless, Priestley writes, "Jesus Christ, whose history answers to the description given of the messiah by the prophets, made no other pretensions; referring all his extraordinary power to God, his Father, who, he expressly says, spoke and acted by him, and who raised him from the dead…"[5]

Priestley goes on to cite specific statements from the New Testament, from which he infers the idea that Jesus is just a man and not divine. For example:

- He is "a man approved by God, by wonders and signs which God did by him" (Acts 2.22).
- "There is one God, and one mediator between God and men, the man Christ Jesus" (1 Tim. 2:5).

If Priestley or Jefferson emphasized that Jesus was a man these verses indicate they would not be wrong per se. However, Christians believe Jesus wasn't *just* a man. He was both fully God and fully human.

Despite the biblical evidence, Priestley blames the teaching of Jesus' divinity on Christian theologians, such as the fourth century St. Augustine.[6] Priestley blames the Greek philosopher Plato for the misunderstanding of the Trinity. So also does Jefferson. Jefferson has multiple negative references to the influence of Plato on those Christians who accept the Trinity.

Priestley goes on to say that those who hold the divinity of Jesus were later imposters and not the original disciples: "it is now pretended that the apostles taught the doctrine of the proper divinity of Christ."[7] And Priestley claims that: "We find nothing like divinity ascribed to Christ before Justin Martyr" in the mid-second century.[8]

---

5   Ibid., 283.
6   Ibid., 285.
7   Ibid.
8   Ibid.

Yet the Gospels show that:

- Jesus could forgive sins, although only God can forgive sins (Mark 2:7);
- Jesus was the Word of God made flesh "and the Word was with God, and the Word was God" (John 1:14, 1);
- the Jews picked up stones to kill Him "for blasphemy, because you, a mere man, claim to be God" (John 10:33)—a claim Jesus did not dispute;
- Jesus said, "before Abraham was, "'I am,'" (John 8:58, a claim of deity, echoing back to God's claim before Moses in the burning bush);
- Jesus was Immanuel, which means "God with us" (Isaiah 7:14, Matthew 1:23).

And there are other verses that teach the divinity of Jesus. And clearly, Paul teaches in Philippians 2:6-11 the Deity of Christ, while quoting a Christian saying or hymn that must have already been in circulation in Christian circles. And to Titus, Paul spoke of the return of "our great God and Savior, Jesus Christ" (Titus 2:13). The Deity of Jesus was unquestionably an early doctrine.

The Trinity is also referred to at the end of Matthew's Gospel, where Jesus tells His followers to baptize disciples in the name (singular) of the Father, Son, and Holy Spirit (plural) (28:19). In all four Gospels the Trinity is at work. When Jesus (the Son) is baptized the Spirit comes upon Him as a dove, and the heavens open, and the voice of God the Father is heard, declaring, "This is my beloved Son. Listen to Him." In the lengthy upper room discourse in John's Gospel, Jesus explains the role of the Father, the Son, and the Holy Spirit, who is with them, but will soon (at Pentecost) be in them. The Trinity is not something later Church Fathers just made up.

So Priestley is just wrong about the New Testament witness regarding the Trinity.[9]

In a letter to Thomas Jefferson, Joseph Priestley showed that he not only rejected the doctrine of the Trinity, but also the atonement of Christ (i.e., that Jesus died for sinners). Priestley declares: "I conclude with sincerely thanking you, Sir, for giving me this opportunity of declaring my disbelief of the *great doctrines,* as you call them of the *trinity* and *atonement*; the former a manifest infringement of the truly great doctrine of the divine unity, and the latter a shocking degradation of

---

9   There are Christian answers to these charges against the Gospels. We provide some in the Appendix.

the character of the one God and Father of all. I, therefore, regard them as nothing less than idolatry and blasphemy."[10]

In the above statement, Priestley clearly defines himself out of the historic Christian faith. Paul points out that the core Christian doctrines for salvation (the make-it-or break it beliefs) are the atoning death of Christ and His resurrection (1 Corinthians 15:3-4).

The atonement was taught by Jesus himself. He said He gave His life as a ransom for many; He said at the Last Supper that His body would be broken and His blood shed for the forgiveness of sins: "Now as they were eating, Jesus took bread, and after blessing it broke it and gave it to the disciples, and said, 'Take, eat; this is my body.' And he took a cup, and when he had given thanks he gave it to them, saying, 'Drink of it, all of you, for this is my blood of the covenant, which is poured out for many for the forgiveness of sins'" (Matthew 26:26-28).

Surprisingly, Joseph Priestley believed in the resurrection of Jesus.

Said Priestley: "This doctrine of a resurrection was laughed at by the conceited Athenians, and will always be the subject of ridicule to persons of a similar turn of mind; but it is abundantly confirmed to us by the well-attested resurrection of Jesus Christ, and the promises of the gospel, established on all the miraculous events by which the promulgation of Christianity was attended."[11]

Usually, theological liberals do not affirm the historical, bodily resurrection of Jesus from the dead. But Priestley does. It's interesting to note too that, although Priestley apparently rejected the atonement, he calls Jesus "our Saviour."

But if Christ's death did not atone for sin then what exactly would Jesus as "Saviour" mean? "Christ crucified, for sinners died"[12] is as old as any teaching of the Christian faith. There is a wide variety of beliefs within the Christian tent. It is a very wide tent with much true diversity. However, rejection of the atonement and the resurrection are clear New Testament dividing lines between salvation and the lack thereof.

In the fourth century, two church leaders were at odds with each other over the deity of Christ. Both of these men were from Alexandria, Egypt. Arius was a Presbyter who believed Jesus was "a god," but not the God. He believed that "there

---

10   Warren Throckmorton and Michael Coulter, *Getting Jefferson Right: Fact Checking Claims about Our Third President* (Grove City, PA: Salem Grove Press, 2012), 127. [Emphasis in the original].

11   Brown, *Joseph Priestley*, 271-272.

12   This particular phrase comes from the New England Primer, 1692. (It was how Puritans and many early Americans learned the letter C in the alphabet.)

was a time when he was not." Athanasius, on the other hand, was the champion of the orthodox doctrine of the Trinity. He believed that just as the Father was eternal, so the Son was eternal.

The Council of Nicea (A.D. 325) was called to resolve the controversies brought on by Arius' views. At the Council, Arius and his doctrine were denounced. Athanasius was there in a background role, but later he worked indefatigably to get the Nicene Creed to be widely adopted. (He was banished five times from the empire for championing the truth.) The matter was finally resolved in 381 with the Council of Constantinople, which reaffirmed the Nicene Creed (with brief additions). Thus, during the fourth century, the Athanasian view was ultimately declared orthodox.

Rev. Joseph Priestley had great influence on the thinking of Thomas Jefferson. When one reads the later Jefferson on theology, Priestley's influence seems very clear.

Thomas Jefferson's Core Doctrines

There is no evidence that Jefferson expressed any agreement with Priestley or unorthodoxy for the first half of his adult years. However, later in life, Jefferson did say he had attended services sometimes at Priestley's church in Philadelphia and at about age 60 Jefferson said that Priestley formed the basis of his own views. However, no clear declarations about these basic doctrines occurred until he was in his 70s in retirement. Did Jefferson hold these same views as Priestley on the atonement and the resurrection? Perhaps. There are clear letters that show him rejecting the doctrine of the Trinity, but not one that he *sent* that ever expresses a rejection of the atonement or resurrection. There is one less reliable document (because he chose not to send it) that suggests as much, and it will be examined later in this chapter.

Jefferson's ideas on these doctrines first began to emerge as of April 21, 1803, when he wrote to his friend, the devout Presbyterian, Dr. Benjamin Rush, and enclosed his "Syllabus." Wrote Jefferson:

...My views...are very different from that Anti-Christian system imputed to me by those who know nothing of my opinions. To the corruptions of Christianity I am indeed opposed; but not to the genuine precepts of Jesus himself. I am a Christian, in the only sense he wished any one to be; sincerely attached to his doctrines, in preference to all others; ascribing to himself every human excellence; & believing he never claimed any other...[13]

Jefferson mentioned the issue of the divinity of Jesus without fully expressing a conclusion. But by saying he believed Jesus "never claimed" more than "human excellence," it revealed an affinity with Unitarian theology. He also said that "Dr. Priestley's *History of the Corruptions of Christianity*...establishes the groundwork of my view of this subject."[14]

Here's what Jefferson said in what is called his "Syllabus" (unessential portions not included):

Syllabus of an Estimate of the Merit of the Doctrines of Jesus

In a comparative view of the Ethics of the enlightened nations of antiquity, of the Jews and of Jesus, no notice should be taken of the corruptions of Christianity by the learned among its professors. Let a just view be taken of the moral principles inculcated by the most esteemed of the sects of ancient philosophy, or of their individuals; particularly Pythagoras, Socrates, Epicurus, Cicero, Epictetus, Seneca, Antoninus.

II. Jews. 1. Their system was Deism; that is, the belief of one only God.[15] But their ideas of him & of his attributes were degrading & injurious. 2. Their Ethics were...repulsive & anti-social, as respecting other nations. They needed reformation, therefore, in an eminent degree.

I. Philosophers. 1. Their precepts related chiefly to ourselves, and the government of those passions which, unrestrained, would disturb our tranquillity of mind.

III. Jesus. In this state of things among the Jews Jesus appeared. His parentage was obscure; his condition poor; his education null; his natural

---

13 Letter to Benjamin Rush, April 21, 1803, Beliles, *The Selected Religious Letters and Papers of Thomas Jefferson*, 109.

14 Letter to Martha Jefferson Randolph, April 23, 1803. *The Family Letters of Thomas Jefferson*, Edwin Morris Betts and James Adam Bear, Jr., eds. (Columbia, Missouri: University of Missouri Press, 1966), 243-244. Jefferson also sent at this time two letters to Priestley: Letter to Rev. Joseph Priestley, April 9, 1803, and Letter to Rev. Joseph Priestley, April 24, 1803, Beliles, *The Selected Religious Letters and Papers of Thomas Jefferson*, 106. Jefferson while living in Philadelphia came to know Priestley and Quakers who emphasized the moral teachings of Jesus above doctrinal formulations. Jefferson's approach to the Bible was similar. Also see Letter to Elbridge Gerry, March 29, 1801, www.founders.archives.gov.

15 It is worth noting that Jefferson defined Deism as "the belief of one only God." Although Jefferson never called himself a Deist, modern scholars do. If so, his own definition should be used for him.

endowments great; his life correct and innocent: he was meek, benevolent, patient, firm, disinterested, & of the sublimest eloquence.

The disadvantages under which his doctrines appear are remarkable.

1. Like Socrates & Epictetus, he wrote nothing himself.
2. But the committing to writing his life & doctrines fell on the most unlettered & ignorant men; who wrote, too, from memory, & not till long after the transactions had passed.
3. ...he fell an early victim to the jealousy & combination of the altar and the throne.
4. Hence the doctrines which he really delivered were defective as a whole, and fragments only of what he did deliver have come to us mutilated, misstated, & often unintelligible.
5. They have been still more disfigured by the corruptions of schismatising followers, who have found an interest in sophisticating & perverting the simple doctrines he taught by engrafting on them the mysticisms of a Grecian sophist [i.e., Plato], frittering them into subtleties, & obscuring them with jargon, until they have caused good men to reject the whole in disgust, & to view Jesus himself as an impostor.

Notwithstanding these disadvantages, a system of morals is presented to us, which, if filled up in the true style and spirit of the rich fragments he left us, would be the most perfect and sublime that has ever been taught by man. The question of his being a member of the Godhead, or in direct communication with it, claimed for him by some of his followers, and denied by others is foreign to the present view, which is merely an estimate of the intrinsic merit of his doctrines.

Jefferson was trying to avoid any controversy on the divinity of Jesus or lack thereof, but rather to put the spotlight on the excellency of Christ's moral teachings. The Syllabus continued:

1. He corrected the Deism of the Jews, confirming them in their belief of one only God, and giving them juster notions of his attributes and government.

2. His moral doctrines, relating to kindred & friends, were more pure & perfect than those of the most correct of the philosophers, and greatly more so than those of the Jews; and they went far beyond both in inculcating universal philanthropy, not only to kindred and friends, to neighbors and countrymen, but to all mankind, gathering all into one family, under the bonds of love, charity, peace, common wants and common aids. A development of this head will evince the peculiar superiority of the system of Jesus over all others.

3. The precepts of philosophy, & of the Hebrew code, laid hold of actions only. He pushed his scrutinies into the heart of man; erected his tribunal in the region of his thoughts, and purified the waters at the fountain head.

4. He taught, emphatically, the doctrines of a future state, which was either doubted, or disbelieved by the Jews; and wielded it with efficacy, as an important incentive, supplementary to the other motives to moral conduct...[16]

Benjamin Rush wrote back to Jefferson on May 5, 1803 that he did not agree on what Jefferson had said about Jesus: "I do not think with you on your account of the character and mission of the author of our Religion." But Rush also said to Jefferson that you are "by no means so heterodox as you have been supposed by your enemies."[17] In the *Autobiography of Benjamin Rush,* he said Jefferson believed in "the divine mission of the Saviour of the World, but he did not believe he was the Son of God in the way in which many Christians believed it."[18] And Rush said that Jefferson also believed in "the resurrection and a future state of rewards and punishments."[19] Indeed in several of Jefferson's letters he uses the term "Savior" and "Christ" to refer to Jesus and affirms his belief in the teaching of Jesus about resurrection. Although these references are minimal, they seem to corroborate Rush's statement.

Jefferson also sent this syllabus to Priestley on April 24, 1803, saying that "there is a point or two in which you and I probably differ." And on May 7, Joseph Priestly wrote to Jefferson: "...you will allow me to express some surprise...that you should

---

16   Syllabus of an Estimate of the Merit of the Doctrines of Jesus Compared with Others, May 21, 1803, Beliles, *The Selected Religious Letters and Papers of Thomas Jefferson,* 110.

17   Letter from Benjamin Rush, May 5, 1803. Beliles, *The Selected Religious Letters and Papers of Thomas Jefferson,* 114.

18   George W. Corner, ed., *The Autobiography of Benjamin Rush* (Princeton: American Philosophical Society, 1948), 152.

19   Ibid.

be of the opinion, that Jesus never laid claim to a divine mission. It is an opinion that I do not remember ever to have heard before."[20] Although Jefferson's words are a bit vague in that regard, in a later letter Jefferson changed slightly to say Jesus having a divine mission was "possible."[21]

It is also important to note that although Jefferson generally says Priestley's writings were the basis of his views on Christianity, it cannot precisely be known what points of difference Jefferson had in mind since he did not elaborate, but it seems likely that if the resurrection of Jesus from the dead was a disagreement, then it would have been noted by Priestley as well. Since Priestley did not, it seems unlikely that Jefferson expressed disbelief in it.

Jefferson said later in a letter to Francis Van der Kemp on March 16, 1817 that someone had obtained a copy of the Syllabus and was planning to use it against Jefferson. Jefferson said: "...I shall really be glad to see on what point they will begin their attack. For it expressly excludes all questions of supernatural character or endowment."[22] Jefferson here said that his Syllabus left out all "questions [i.e., inquiries] of supernatural character or endowment," but some modern writers wrongly interpret that to mean Jefferson left out all evidence of it. Indeed, in the Syllabus, he did not deny Jesus' deity per se, he simply avoided taking any position on the subject in his goal of compiling Jesus' moral doctrines. This is an important comment by Jefferson on his own Syllabus because some modern commentators try to claim Jefferson was clearly expressing a denial of Jesus' divinity in the document. One could argue that by not taking a position, he was implicitly taking a position against it; but that is speculative. Other statements would be needed to make a stronger case.

Jefferson's reliable writings never denied the resurrection of Jesus. Some might infer denial of it due to his Gospels abridgement that closes with Christ being buried and the stone rolled in front of the grave (but no resurrection mentioned). But that is not a reliable assertion because the purpose of his digest was focusing on the moral teachings of Jesus and not dealing with a full biographical presentation. "Godhead" topics were also "foreign" to the Syllabus because Jefferson said it was "merely an estimate of the intrinsic merit of his doctrines." Furthermore,

---

20   Letter from Rev. Joseph Priestley, May 7, 1803. Beliles, *The Selected Religious Letters and Papers of Thomas Jefferson*, 115.

21   Letter to William Short, August 4, 1820. Beliles, *The Selected Religious Letters and Papers of Thomas Jefferson*, 311.

22   Letter to Francis Van der Kemp, March 16, 1817. Beliles, *The Selected Religious Letters and Papers of Thomas Jefferson*, 278.

Jefferson much later (in 1824) wrote that he believed the creed of his church that acknowledged the "resurrection of the body."[23]

Meanwhile, it's interesting that Jefferson uses the term "Christ" or the word "Savior" a handful of times in his writings. It could be that these terms were mere rhetorical defaults to the name by which Jesus is known, rather than a meaningful indicator of Jefferson's view that Christ is more than human. But on the other hand in such a deeply theological letter on the nature of the Godhead, is it plausible that the use of this word was given no thought by Jefferson?

One of the evangelical Restoration leaders popular at that time also spoke in similar ways. Rev. Elias Smith, who became the movement's national spokesman at a meeting in adjacent Orange County, traveled throughout the Central Virginia Piedmont preaching in 1811. He said: "In all the glorious things said of Christ, there is no mention of his divinity, his being God-man, his incarnation, the human and divine nature, the human soul of Christ, his being God the Creator, and yet the Son of the Creator; these things are the inventions of men, and ought to be rejected."[24] It is illogical to deny Jesus as part of the Trinity but speak of him as the Christ if a person studies theology seriously, but these untrained frontier preachers were the most popular in Charlottesville, and Jefferson sometimes worshiped in the local broadly-Christian "union" services. It's easy to understand him freely articulating the same views.

1813 - Jefferson Sends First Letters Clearly Rejecting the Trinity

If the 1803 Syllabus subtly revealed some budding unorthodox beliefs, ten years after the Syllabus Jefferson for the first time sent a letter that privately, but clearly, rejected orthodox Christian views. When Jefferson sent this new letter on August 22, 1813, to John Adams, who had already rejected Trinitarian doctrine for half a century, Jefferson felt free to more boldly express unorthodox beliefs (but he still wishes it to remain private). He wrote:

> …It is too late in the day for men of sincerity to pretend they believe in the Platonic mysticism that three are one and one is three, and yet, that the one is not three, and the three not one…[25]

---

23   Letter to Augustus Woodward, March 24, 1824. Beliles, *The Selected Religious Letters and Papers of Thomas Jefferson*, 364.

24   Michael G. Kenny, *The Perfect Law of Liberty: Elias Smith and the Providential History of America* (Washington, D.C.: Smithsonian Institution Press, 1994).93.

25   Letter to John Adams, August 22, 1813, www.founders.archives.gov.

This is the very first time Jefferson overtly said he rejected the Trinity. Twenty-five years earlier in 1788, he had said he did not understand the Trinity, and therefore could not personally in good conscience be a godfather for a friend's child. But now he clearly says it is an error based on pagan Greek thought through Plato.

A Quaker from Delaware named William Canby wrote to Jefferson on August 27, 1813. They had corresponded in 1802, 1803, and 1808 on religion. Jefferson, confident in Canby's Quaker rejection of creeds and even professional clergy, replied on September 18, saying:

> …An eloquent preacher of your religious society…[said] that in heaven, God knew no distinctions, but considered all good men as his children, and as brethren of the same family. I believe, with the Quaker preacher, that he who steadily observes those moral precepts in which all religions concur, will never be questioned at the gates of heaven, as to the dogmas in which they all differ. That on entering there, all these are left behind us, and the Aristides and Catos, the Penns and Tillotsons, Presbyterians and Baptists, will find themselves united in all principles which are in concert with the reason of the supreme mind.[26]

In this last point Jefferson includes pagans with Christians as being in heaven, and thus strays into the error of Universalism which rejected the need of Christ's atoning death for men to be restored to fellowship with God (or that the atonement applied to all, including those who did not believe in Jesus). Jefferson continued, observing that Jesus condemned religious leaders who:

> …denounce as his enemies all who cannot perceive the Geometrical logic of Euclid in the demonstrations of St. Athanasius, that three are one, and one is three; and yet that the one is not three nor the three one.[27]

Euclid was an ancient Greek mathematician. But, argues Jefferson, fourth century St. Athanasius was ignoring plain mathematical facts Euclid taught the world when he promoted the doctrine of the Trinity.

There were multiple letters expressing the same critique of the Trinity over the last decade of Jefferson's life. Here are some more examples:

---

26   Letter to William Canby, August 27, 1813, www.founders.archives.gov.
27   Ibid.

- of the mountebanks [i.e., charlatans] calling themselves the priests of Jesus.[28]

- …When we shall have done away the incomprehensible jargon of the Trinitarian arithmetic, that three are one, and one is three; when we shall have knocked down the artificial scaffolding, reared to mask from view the simple structure of Jesus, when, in short, we shall have unlearned every thing which has been taught since his day, and got back to the pure and simple doctrines he inculcated, we shall then be truly and worthily his disciples…[29]

- …the doctrine of one God, pure and uncompounded, was that of the early ages of Christianity; and was…ousted from the Christian creed [not] by the force of reason, but by the sword of civil government, wielded at the will of the fanatic Athanasius. The hocus-pocus phantasm of a God like another Cerberus, with one body and three heads…[30]

His Attack on "Artificial" Systems, Especially Calvinism

On August 6, 1816, Jefferson wrote a Washington author Margaret Bayard Smith (also known as Mrs. Samuel Harrison Smith), saying: "The artificial structures they [i.e., priests] have built on the purest of all moral systems, for the purpose of deriving from it pence and power, revolts those who think for themselves…"[31]

On May 5, 1817, Jefferson wrote to John Adams to compare the religion of Jesus to religious systems added to it:

> …If by religion we are to understand sectarian dogmas, in which no two of them agree, then your exclamation on that hypothesis is just, "that this would be the best of all possible worlds, if there were no religion in it." But if the moral precepts, innate in man, and made a part of his physical constitution, as necessary for a social being, if the sublime doctrines of philanthropism [i.e., love of man] and deism [i.e., one God] taught us by Jesus of Nazareth, in which all agree, constitute true religion, then,

28   Letter to Francis Van der Kemp, April 25, 1816. Beliles, *The Selected Religious Letters and Papers of Thomas Jefferson*, 267.

29   Letter to Timothy Pickering, February 27, 1821. Beliles, *The Selected Religious Letters and Papers of Thomas Jefferson*, 319.

30   Letter to Rev. James Smith, December 8, 1822. Beliles, *The Selected Religious Letters and Papers of Thomas Jefferson*, 340.

31   Letter to Margaret Bayard Smith, August 6, 1816. Beliles, *The Selected Religious Letters and Papers of Thomas Jefferson*, 272.

without it, this would be, as you again say, "something not fit to be named even, indeed, a hell."[32]

This shows Jefferson agreeing with Adams that sectarian religion is undesirable, but that a completely secular society, one devoid of the religion of Jesus and its moral teachings, would be far worse. Notable also here is the word "deism" used by Jefferson interchangeably with theism as taught by Jesus himself, in contrast to atheism. In this sense Jefferson might think of himself as a Deist (but he never said so). In his 1803 Syllabus, he used the term somewhat similarly in reference to theistic Jewish belief, in contrast to polytheism.

But the first time Jefferson spoke of Deism was in 1800 when he said some of his views would please the Deists—a group he seemed to indicate he was not one of. Jefferson wrote of Deism another time saying:

I have observed, indeed, generally, that while in Protestant countries the defections from the Platonic Christianity of the priests is to Deism, in Catholic countries they are to Atheism.[33]

Jefferson here in this mention seems to portray Deism as something he is critical of and the destination of the apostate Platonic (i.e., Trinitarian) Christians he strongly criticized, and not likely to identify with himself. He is making the point that fallen away Catholics usually end up as atheists; fallen away Protestants as Deists, but he certainly does not seem to portray himself as one of these.

Arminianism was the theology of the Restoration movement that was dominant in Central Virginia at this time. Their leaders were vocal against Calvinism. Jefferson's theological views were in line with that perspective as is apparent when he began to comment on Calvinism for the first time in his life. In a July 26, 1818, letter to New Hampshire Republican Congressman Salma Hale, Jefferson describes John Calvin along with Martin Luther as reformers but:

...The truth is that Calvinism has introduced into the Christian religion more new absurdities than it's leader had purged it of old ones. Our saviour did not come into this world to save metaphysicians only. His doctrines are leveled to the simplest understandings and it is only by banishing

---

32   Letter to John Adams, May 5, 1817. Beliles, *The Selected Religious Letters and Papers of Thomas Jefferson*, 280.

33   Letter to Thomas Law, June 13, 1814, www.founders.archives.gov.

Hierophantic [i.e., priestly] mysteries and Scholastic subtleties, which they have nick-named Christianity, and getting back to the plain and unsophisticated precepts of Christ, that we become real Christians. The half reformation of Luther and Calvin did something towards a restoration of his genuine doctrines; the present contest will, I hope, compleat what they begun, and place us where the evangelists left us.[34]

This letter is also interesting because it again includes the usage of "our saviour" and "Christ" to refer to Jesus. Jefferson may have rejected the Trinity and yet still held a view of Jesus that was more than mere human.

On May 15, 1819, Jefferson replied to Unitarian clergyman Thomas B. Parker saying:

...I thank you, Sir, for the pamphlet you have been so kind as to send me on the reveries, not to say insanities of [John] Calvin and [Samuel] Hopkins; ...Were I to be the founder of a new sect, I would call them Apiarians [i.e. beekeepers], and, after the example of the bee, advise them to extract the honey of every sect. My fundamental principle would be the reverse of Calvin's, that we are to be saved by our good works which are within our power, and not by our faith which is not within our power.[35]

Hopkins was a Connecticut Congregational minister who especially built on the works of Jonathan Edwards to develop what became known as the New Divinity or New Haven Theology that tried to merge some Arminian[36] views with Calvinism. Jefferson's disdain was for any attempt to argue over fine points of theology that are used to define who is a true believer and who is not. Hopkins was the latest to do this. Jefferson preferred to be connected to many varieties of Christianity, like a bee landing on many flowers and receiving good from all.

Meanwhile, a Presbyterian minister named Rev. Ezra Stiles Ely wrote to Jefferson on June 14. Jefferson replied on June 25, saying:

---

34   Letter to Salma Hale, July 26, 1818. Beliles, *The Selected Religious Letters and Papers of Thomas Jefferson*, 292.

35   Letter to Rev. Thomas B. Parker, May 15, 1819. Beliles, *The Selected Religious Letters and Papers of Thomas Jefferson*, 298.

36   Arminianism is a school of Christian theology (in contrast with Calvinism), which tends to focus on man's free will as opposed to God's sovereign grace.

… We probably differ on the dogmas of theology, the foundation of all sectarianism, and on which no two sects dream alike; for if they did they would then be of the same. You say you are a Calvinist. I am not….[W]e should all be of one sect, doers of good, and eschewers of evil. No doctrines of his [i.e. Jesus] lead to schism.[37]

On August 24, 1819, Jefferson wrote to Unitarian Rev. John Brazier of Salem, Massachusetts, saying: "…this most benign and pure of all systems of morality became frittered into subtleties and mysteries, and hidden under jargons incomprehensible to the human mind. To these original sources he must now, therefore, return, to recover the virgin purity of his religion."[38]

And on November 4, 1820, Jefferson wrote to Unitarian Rev. Jared Sparks, saying: "…I adhere to the principles of the first age; and consider all subsequent innovations as corruptions of his religion, having no foundation in what came from him. The metaphysical insanities of Athanasius, of Loyola, and of Calvin, are, to my understanding, mere relapses into polytheism, differing from paganism only by being more unintelligible."[39]

Across the Line – and Back?

To William Short Jefferson continued to criticize the "…artificial systems, invented by ultra-Christian sects, unauthorized by a single word ever uttered by Him [i.e., Jesus]…"[40] In this letter, Jefferson also explains for the first time that he made his first attempt to make an abridgement of the Gospels over a few days in 1804 while he was president. And a few months later Jefferson wrote again to William Short, saying in response to a request for a copy of the syllabus [not the abridgement]:

…it is not to be understood that I am with Him [i.e., Jesus] in all His doctrines. I am a Materialist; he takes the side of Spiritualism; he preaches the efficacy of repentance towards forgiveness of sin; I require a counterpoise of good works to redeem it, etc., etc. …Of this band of dupes

37   Letter to Rev. Ezra Stiles Ely, June 25, 1819. Beliles, *The Selected Religious Letters and Papers of Thomas Jefferson*, 298.

38   Letter to Rev. John Brazier, August 24, 1819. The Thomas Jefferson Papers Series 1, General Correspondence, 1651-1827, Library of Congress Manuscript Division.

39   Letter to Rev. Jared Sparks, November 4, 1820. Beliles, *The Selected Religious Letters and Papers of Thomas Jefferson*, 317.

40   Letter to William Short, October 31, 1819. Beliles, *The Selected Religious Letters and Papers of Thomas Jefferson*, 300.

and impostors, Paul was the great Coryphaeus [i.e., leader of the chorus], and first corruptor of the doctrines of Jesus...The syllabus is therefore of *his* doctrines, not *all* of *mine*...[41]

Of course, it is a stretch to say Paul was the first corrupter of the doctrines of Jesus when Paul was the first to write down anything of early Christianity! In this 1820 letter was the first very obvious declaration by Jefferson that the writings of Paul himself were corruptions and that Jefferson actually disagreed with some of Jesus' teachings. Little needs to be said about the arrogance of Jefferson to contrast his own opinions with Jesus' teachings. In reality, Jefferson was no longer a true Christian by his <u>own</u> earlier definition as one who accepted all that Jesus taught. But a follow-up letter to Short softened his earlier letter, saying:

> ...My aim in that was, to justify the character of Jesus against the fictions of his pseudo-followers, which have exposed him to the inference of being an impostor...That Jesus did not mean to impose himself on mankind as the son of God, physically speaking, I have been convinced by the writings of men more learned than myself in that lore. But that he might conscientiously believe himself inspired from above, is very possible.[42]

Jefferson recognized that his previous letter had been a bit extreme and easily misunderstood as rejecting Jesus' inspiration and divine mission completely, so he softens his stance a little here by speaking of what was "possible." And his reference to Jesus "physically speaking" is hard to grasp its meaning as part of a discussion of materialism.

In many ways, this was the furthest point in Jefferson's unorthodoxy trend. He rejoined a Trinitarian church about one year before this, and its influence perhaps gradually and modestly modified his views until his death. It must be remembered that for over 30 years the Episcopal Church in Virginia had stopped requiring use of the Athanasian Creed and mainly only used the Apostles' Creed, which Jefferson could recite at the Trinitarian church he had just rejoined, apparently with no problem. The congregation would recite the Apostles' Creed, which included:

---

41   Letter to William Short, April 13, 1820, Beliles, *The Selected Religious Letters and Papers of Thomas Jefferson*, 306.

42   Letter to William Short, August 4, 1820, Beliles, *The Selected Religious Letters and Papers of Thomas Jefferson*, 311.

I believe in God the Father, Almighty, Maker of heaven and earth: And in Jesus Christ, his only begotten Son, our Lord: Who was conceived by the Holy Ghost, born of the Virgin Mary: Suffered under Pontius Pilate; was crucified, dead and buried: He descended into hell: The third day he rose again from the dead: He ascended into heaven, and sits at the right hand of God the Father Almighty.

It also included a reference to "the resurrection of the body" at the end. A little over a year after worshiping regularly again at the Trinitarian Episcopal Church (i.e., Christ Episcopal) that restarted in his town, he replies to a letter from Rev. Thomas Whittemore, the minister of the First Universalist Society in Cambridge, Massachusetts. On June 5, 1822, Jefferson wrote to him saying:

…You ask my opinion on the items of doctrine in your catechism. I have never permitted myself to meditate a specified creed. These formulas have been the bane and ruin of the Christian church…[43]

Jefferson continues:

The religions of antiquity had no particular formulas of creed. Those of the modern world none, except those of the religionists calling themselves Christians, and even among these the Quakers have none. And hence, alone, the harmony, the quiet, the brotherly affections, the exemplary and unschismatizing Society of the Friends, and I hope the Unitarians will follow their happy example. With these sentiments of the mischiefs of creeds and confessions of faith, I am sure you will excuse my not giving opinions on the items of any particular one…[44]

Jefferson declines even to affirm a Unitarian creed as Whittemore wished and recommends that Unitarians in the north stay more non-creedal like the Quakers (or he could also have mentioned the Restoration Christians in his home area). Jefferson here contrasts it with "the religionists calling themselves Christians," such as the Catholic, Episcopal, Lutheran, Presbyterian, and Methodist groups, all of which used creeds. Jefferson has a serious problem with the fighting of one

---

43   Letter to Rev. Thomas Whittemore, June 5, 1822. Beliles, *The Selected Religious Letters and Papers of Thomas Jefferson*, 327.

44   Ibid.

denomination against another. Of course, so do many Christians. Creeds have their place in articulating the overall teaching of the Bible.[45]

Clearly he preferred to not go on record about either Trinitarian or Unitarian creeds at this point, but when Jefferson says here that he never did meditate on a specified creed, there is plenty of evidence to show this is not true. His earliest involvement as an Anglican vestryman required it of him and his name in the vestry book stated his agreement. As in other cases, Jefferson is exaggerating or not being honest here. And it's likely that, now that he recommitted to the Episcopal church in his home town, he was weekly reciting the Apostles' Creed in those worship services.

On June 26, 1822, Jefferson wrote a letter to Unitarian Rev. Benjamin Waterhouse. This letter—along with his 1803 letter to Dr. Benjamin Rush, with the so-called "Syllabus"—contains an important distillation of Jefferson's understanding of "the doctrines of Jesus" versus the "dogmas of Calvin."

Writes Jefferson:

...The doctrines of Jesus are simple, and tend all to the happiness of man.
1. That there is one only God, and he all perfect.
2. That there is a future state of rewards and punishments.
3. That to love God with all thy heart and thy neighbor as thyself; is the sum of religion.

These are the great points on which he endeavored to reform the religion of the Jews. But compare with these the demoralizing dogmas of Calvin.
1. That there are three Gods.
2. That good works, or the love of our neighbor, are nothing.
3. That faith is every thing, and the more incomprehensible the proposition, the more merit in its faith.

45　In 1 Corinthians 15:3-4, the Apostle Paul repeats a kind of creed—a creed that apparently was already circulating in Christian circles. The creed said that Christ died for sinners according to the Scriptures, and that He was buried, and rose again from the dead on the third day. Without formulations of doctrine to help root a church in truth, groups such as today's Unitarians cut themselves off from historic Christianity and then drift from there away from the Bible almost completely. In fact, a 2006 study found that less than 20 percent of Unitarians in the United States even label themselves as Christians. It is a big historical mistake to think of Jefferson (or Priestley) as being like today's Unitarians. Jefferson identified himself as a Christian and was, like other non-creedal persons in his day who rejected the Trinity, at least focusing on the Bible and reason as the basis of his faith, even if he felt the former was inaccurate on some points. Christians historically believe in what the Bible says about the Godhead. Here are seven basic beliefs that are the essence of the Trinity in the Bible: the Father is God, the Son is God, the Spirit is God, the Father is not the Son, the Father is not the Spirit, the Son is not the Spirit, there is only one God.

4. That reason in religion is of unlawful use.
5. That God, from the beginning, elected certain individuals to be saved, and certain others to be damned; and that no crimes of the former can damn them; no virtues of the latter save.[46]

Jefferson continued:

Now, which of these is the true and charitable Christian? He who believes and acts on the simple doctrines of Jesus? Or the impious dogmatists as Athanasius and Calvin? Verily I say these are the false shepherds foretold as to enter not by the door into the sheepfold, but to climb up some other way. They are mere usurpers of the Christian name, teaching a counter-religion made up of the deliria of crazy imaginations, as foreign from Christianity as is that of Mahomet.

Their blasphemies have driven thinking men into infidelity, who have too hastily rejected the supposed author himself, with the horrors so falsely imputed to him. Had the doctrines of Jesus been preached always as pure as they came from his lips, the whole civilized world would now have been Christian. I rejoice that in this blessed country of free inquiry and belief, which has surrendered its creed and conscience to neither kings nor priests, the genuine doctrine of one only God is reviving, and I trust that there is not a young man now living in the United States who will not die an Unitarian. But much I fear, that when this great truth shall be re-established, its votaries will fall into the fatal error of fabricating formulas of creed and confessions of faith, the engines which so soon destroyed the religion of Jesus, and made of Christendom a mere Aceldama [i.e., the field bought with the blood money Judas received for betraying Jesus]; that they will give up morals for mysteries, and Jesus for Plato. How much wiser are the Quakers, who, agreeing in the fundamental doctrines of the gospel, schismatize about no mysteries, and, keeping within the pale of common sense, suffer no speculative differences of opinion, any more than of feature, to impair the love of their brethren. Be this the wisdom of Unitarians; this the holy mantle which shall cover within it's charitable circumference all who believe in one God, and who love their neighbor.[47]

---

46   Letter to Rev. Benjamin Waterhouse, June 26, 1822. Beliles, *The Selected Religious Letters and Papers of Thomas Jefferson*, 329.

47   Ibid.

Jefferson's main worry in his letter was that Unitarians will make the same "fatal error" and develop their own "formulas of creed and confessions." It should be noted also that Jefferson's statement of "the dogmas of Calvin" shows such a poor understanding of the work of the sixteenth century Reformer of Geneva. Jefferson obviously relied on writings or conversational characterizations of the Calvinist position from people who were critics—not evaluating the points fairly at all. And associating Calvin with Athanasius is something new in Jefferson's argument. He created a straw man and then tears it down.

Unfortunately, it is true that once the fourth century church decided for the Athanasian view of the Trinity, the Roman Empire enforced this view with the coercive arm of the state. And one of Thomas Jefferson's greatest accomplishments was in fighting the notion of a state church in which doctrine was enforced "by the sword of civil government." Jefferson is right to say that never should blood be spilled over differences in doctrine; however, the problem lays not with creeds. If church and state had remained separate, then creeds alone would likely have led to no bloodshed.

Jefferson also said in the 1822 letter to Waterhouse:

> ...I write with freedom, because, while I claim a right to believe in one God, if so my reason tells me, I yield as freely to others that of believing in three. Both religions, I find, make honest men, and that is the only point society has any right to look to....And with the assurance of all my good will to Unitarian and Trinitarian, to Whig and Tory, accept for yourself that of my entire respect.[48]

Although Jefferson still thinks Unitarianism is the dominant trend, he shows a higher desire to be part of and friends with others, including those in Trinitarian churches, and that is his reason for his views to remain private. It's not just that he wants to avoid criticism. He wants unity. And although he held Unitarian views, he did so privately and was never a public advocate of it. He simply felt it should not divide believers in Jesus.

In his desire for unity, Jefferson seems to have saved most of his venom for people he perceives as most responsible for corruption and disunity—mainly, Plato (of course, the pre-Christian philosopher), Athanasius, and John Calvin. For instance, on April 11, 1823, Jefferson replied to John Adams, who somehow admired Calvinism and Unitarianism at the same time:

---

48   Ibid.

…The wishes expressed, in your last favor, that I may continue in life and health until I become a Calvinist, at least in his exclamation of "*mon Dieu!* jusque à quand!" [translated: "My God! How long?"] would make me immortal. I can never join Calvin in addressing *his God.* He was indeed an Atheist, which I can never be; or rather his religion was Daemonism. If ever man worshipped a false god, he did. The being described in his 5. points is not the God whom you and I acknolege and adore, the Creator and benevolent governor of the world; but a daemon of malignant spirit. It would be more pardonable to believe in no God at all, than to blaspheme him by the atrocious attributes of Calvin…[49]

Jefferson then boldly claims that

…the day will come when the mystical generation of Jesus, by the supreme being as his father in the womb of a virgin will be classed with the fable of the generation of Minerva in the brain of Jupiter. But we may hope that the dawn of reason and freedom of thought in these United States will do away with all this artificial scaffolding, and restore to us the primitive and genuine doctrines of this the most venerated reformer of human errors…[50]

Here Jefferson clearly denies the virgin birth—which he puts on the level of Greek mythology. Of course, Jefferson never studied theology systematically, and although brilliant in many other fields, he was sorely lacking in this area (although he thought himself more learned in it than was the reality). These are the things over which evangelical friends of Jefferson like Rev. Charles Clay and Dr. Benjamin Rush were concerned. He liked to speculate on such things in private, but his friends warned against expressing them since they recognized he did not really understand them well.

1824 - Does Jefferson Reaffirm the Apostles' Creed?

When Jefferson recommitted to the Episcopal Church by 1820 (or earlier) his attendance at worship meant he participated in the reciting of the Apostles Creed. In this light it is interesting to see his comments on the creed on March 24, 1824 when Jefferson wrote Federal Judge Augustus Woodward:

---

49   Letter to John Adams, April 11, 1823. Beliles, *The Selected Religious Letters and Papers of Thomas Jefferson*, 343.

50   Ibid.

...Indeed, Jesus Himself, the Founder of our religion, was unquestionably a Materialist as to man. In all His doctrines of the resurrection, He teaches expressly that the body is to rise in substance. In the Apostles' Creed, we all declare that we believe in the 'resurrection of the body.'[51]

Here Jefferson seems to affirm the teachings of Jesus on resurrection and references the Apostles' Creed that his church used each week; and when he says "we all declare," it appears he includes himself. If he did not participate in the liturgy, he would have written that "they all declare." At the very least, in this letter he declines to disassociate himself from the creed which also clearly states belief in God the Father, Son, and Holy Ghost. (And his annual donations made it possible for this liturgy to be observed on a weekly basis.) Perhaps his views were moderating slightly now that he was worshiping in an orthodox congregation again—perhaps.

Despite worshiping in the Trinitarian Episcopal church, Jefferson wrote in 1825 to Unitarian Rev. Benjamin Waterhouse expressing his regret that there seems to be no place in his native town for a Unitarian preacher at present: "I am anxious to see the doctrine of one God commenced in our state...I must therefore be contented to be an Unitarian by myself, altho I know there are many around me who would become so, if once they could hear the questions fairly stated...[52]

This is the first and only time Jefferson identified himself as a Unitarian (but still in a private letter). In saying "by myself" he obviously did not refer to church, but to a theological persuasion on some points. Again, modern commentators completely misjudge this statement without the context. These two letters to Woodward and Waterhouse in the last year or so of his life tell us where he stood at the end: as a professing Christian who privately held to Unitarianism but who publicly worshiped regularly at a Trinitarian church and likely recited the Apostles' Creed. That reality leaves both unorthodox and orthodox groups today uncomfortable with Jefferson if they are honest with the evidence. Unfortunately, many modern commentators are not aware of the full evidence, and so have embraced a popular but skewed perspective of Jefferson's faith.

There is ample evidence of Jefferson's heterodox views but keep in mind that he never expressed them publicly. Keeping with the advice of both evangelical friends Benjamin Rush and Rev. Charles Clay, whether settled views or being "playful in

---

51   Letter to Augustus Woodward, March 24, 1824. Beliles, *The Selected Religious Letters and Papers of Thomas Jefferson*, 364.

52   Letter to Rev. Benjamin Waterhouse, January 8, 1825. Beliles, *The Selected Religious Letters and Papers of Thomas Jefferson*, 370.

the closet," Jefferson only shared his dispute with orthodoxy with a limited number of people in strict confidence. As a result, his image to the public to the end of his life was that of an orthodox and orthopraxic believer.

Less Reliable Sources for Understanding Jefferson

It is worth noting that there were several other documents that were never seen by anyone in Jefferson's lifetime. Some were letters *he never sent*. Because Jefferson is so famous, the editors of his papers have made known in their published editions of his writings these unfinished and unused draft documents. Some only became known in recent decades.

If a person today had their unsent letters found in a draft folder in their computer files or in other places, they might truly disagree with their own words. Sometimes this is the reason a person does not send something, because they recognize their emotions involved perhaps may have clouded their own judgment; and after much more time, they would disavow some of what they wrote. If they were alive, they could explain that is the reason it was not sent; but when it is published after one's death, that is not possible. An unused draft is even less reliable than a diary for a diary at least is considered a person's true thoughts, but a rejected draft is fundamentally an <u>unacceptable</u> work of the writer.

In any event, Jefferson's unsent letters and unacceptable drafts are obviously less reliable than Jefferson's other papers for making definitive conclusions about his beliefs. But unfortunately the letters that follow next are often the very quotes that are the most often repeated in almost any reference to Jefferson's religion. The same references are recycled over and over in books and websites and articles as the most featured representations of Jefferson's beliefs. This is unfair and certainly unscholarly without at least making a clear qualification. Scholars can honestly and intellectually disagree on the conclusions from these letters, but these quotes no longer should be exaggerated so as to definitively represent him.

Having read everything so far that Jefferson sent, it is time to look at these unsent letters and see if they redefine Jefferson in any important way from what the main narrative revealed.

A letter on September 27, 1809 to Presbyterian layman James Fishback (who later became a Baptist minister) spoke of religion as follows:

> ...Every religion consists of moral precepts, and of dogmas. In the first they all agree. All forbid us to murder, steal, plunder, bear false witness &ca. and these are the articles necessary for the preservation of order,

justice, and happiness in society. In their particular dogmas all differ; no two professing the same. These respect vestments, ceremonies, physical opinions, and metaphysical speculations, totally unconnected with morality, and unimportant to the legitimate objects of society. Yet these are the questions on which have hung the bitter schisms of Nazarenes, Socinians, Arians, Athanasians in former times, and now of Trinitarians, Unitarians, Catholics, Lutherans, Calvinists, Methodists, Baptists, Quakers &c.[53]

Sadly, divisive factionalism is a part of the Christian tradition, even to this day. Jefferson continues—in this unsent letter:

Among the Mahometans we are told that thousands fell victims to the dispute whether the first or second toe of Mahomet was longest; and what blood, how many human lives have the words "this do in remembrance of me" cost the Christian world! [That is, debates over communion have led to deaths.] We all agree in the obligation of the moral precepts of Jesus; but we schismatize and lose ourselves in subtleties about his nature, his conception maculate or immaculate, whether he was a God or not a God, whether his votaries are to be initiated by simple aspersion, by immersion, or without water; whether his priests must be robed in white, in black, or not robed at all; whether we are to use our own reason, or the reason of others, in the opinions we form, or as to the evidence we are to believe. It is on questions of this, and still less importance, that such oceans of human blood have been spilt, and whole regions of the earth have been desolated by wars and persecutions, in which human ingenuity has been exhausted in inventing new tortures for their brethren.[54]

Tragically, wars of religion—over nuances of Christian doctrine, such as modes of baptism—have led to the slaughter of many people. Many Christians would agree with the criticism. Then he says it is: "…enough to hold fast to those moral precepts which are of the essence of Christianity, and of all other religions. No where are these to be found in greater purity than in the discourses of the great

---

53   Letter to Rev. James Fishback, September 27, 1809. Beliles, *The Selected Religious Letters and Papers of Thomas Jefferson*, 392.

54   Ibid.

reformer of religion whom we follow."[55] It is true that there are moral principles in all religions but that is definitely not "enough" for being in right standing with God. Note too that Jefferson still counts himself among those following Jesus. The content of this letter does not seem to add any new insights into Jefferson's beliefs than the main narrative that relied on more reliable documents.

Another unsent letter was on January 7, 1810 to Pennsylvania botanist and Quaker William Baldwin, who wrote to Jefferson and enclosed for him some essays for the Society of Friends, i.e., Quakers, in Pennsylvania that were entitled: *Observations on Infidelity, and the Religious and Political Systems of Europe, compared with those of the United States of America: showing the incompatibility of religion with the despotism of national churches.* Clearly, this book was in line with Jefferson's views that church and state both did better when they were separate institutions. Jefferson responded with a letter to Baldwin on January 19. The one he sent had nothing religious per se in it, but an *unsent* draft of it was found in Jefferson's papers that again shows some of his religious thoughts which he did not choose to communicate. It follows below:

> ...Nothing can be more exactly and seriously true than what is there stated; that but a short time elapsed after the death of the great reformer of the Jewish religion [i.e., Jesus], before his principles were departed from by those who professed to be his special servants, and perverted into an engine for enslaving mankind, and aggrandising their oppressors in Church and State; that the purest system of morals ever before preached to man, has been adulterated and sophisticated by artificial constructions, into a mere contrivance to filch wealth and power to themselves; that rational men not being able to swallow their impious heresies, in order to force them down their throats, they raise the hue and cry of infidelity, while themselves are the greatest obstacles to the advancement of the real doctrines of Jesus, and do in fact constitute the real Anti-Christ.[56]

When Jefferson says "a short time" before Jesus' principles were perverted, it seems to be associated with the joining of church and state which did not occur until the fourth century (beginning in subtle ways under Emperor Constantine in the 300s, but in earnest under Emperor Theodosius in 380 A.D., when he

---

55   Ibid.

56   Letter to William Baldwin, January 19, 1810 (sometimes erroneously identified as a letter to Samuel Kercheval). Beliles, *The Selected Religious Letters and Papers of Thomas Jefferson*, 393.

declared the empire "Christian"), so it appears Jefferson does not refer to the first century disciples here. Jefferson continued later in the letter with criticism of the political hypocrisy of the Quakers. It was in contrast to many letters commending them, but once again, the content of this letter does not seem to add any significant insights into Jefferson's beliefs than the main narrative that relied on more reliable documents.

In all the private letters discussed so far, sent or unsent, there never was a clear statement by Jefferson that rejected the resurrection and the atonement. But the most troubling passage of all in Jefferson's unsent versions of his letters was one to William Short, dated October 31, 1819. Short was one of his most trusted confidantes with whom he had shared many strong opinions many times. It does not make sense that Jefferson would withhold the following thoughts for a motive that he did not want to get in trouble or be persecuted. The motive to not send this version would seem to be something else.

In this unsent and unacceptable draft Jefferson added a footnote at the bottom of the letter with an asterisk after the words "artificial systems," as in supposed artificial systems within Christianity—i.e., made up things that can easily be jettisoned because they simply cause division. That footnote said: "*e.g. The immaculate conception of Jesus, his deification, the creation of the world by him, his miraculous powers, his resurrection and visible ascension, his corporeal presence in the Eucharist, the Trinity; original sin, atonement, regeneration, election, orders of Hierarchy, etc.*" Obviously some things in this list are indeed found in the New Testament and from an orthodox perspective would hardly comprise "artificial systems." Jesus' deification, miraculous powers, resurrection and visible ascension are all clearly found in the Bible, but it is hard to find in Scripture other items in Jefferson's list such as "orders of Hierarchy." And there is great disagreement, even today, over how to define "his corporeal presence in the Eucharist." So it is a list that itself may on some points be truly "artificial systems," but without elaboration or explanation from Jefferson, leaves us unable to know his precise thinking. It is unfortunate that modern commentators often prominently pick this footnote in an unacceptable draft letter to portray Jefferson as absolutely rejecting these things, when in fact no one ever in his entire life had heard him ever express it.

If this represented how he really felt, then biblically Jefferson defined himself out of the bounds of the Christian faith. The resurrection and the atonement are certainly found in Scripture and are truly central to orthodox Christian beliefs. But this is the only time Jefferson ever made any doubtful reference to these in his whole life of letters. The only time. Ever. This unacceptable draft seems to imply that he thought the atonement and the resurrection were something that was "artificial," yet since he did not send this letter, and footnote was added even later to the unacceptable draft, it should give the reader pause. The list could simply be something Jefferson pondered as a *potential* list without making up his mind. Perhaps with more thought and time, he might add or delete some items from this list of "artificial systems."

It is also worth mentioned here something Jefferson said just two months before this footnote. In a letter to Unitarian Rev. John Brazier of Salem, Massachusetts in response to Brazier's [sic] request to publish Jefferson's earlier letter to him, Jefferson made a firm refusal because letters:

> …which are written when in the carelessness and confidence of private correspondence, may have blots to be hit, which could have been filled up if meant to meet public criticism….[and] when the body is sensibly decayed, we may well suspect that the mind is in some sympathies with it, when the coat is well-worn we ought to expect that the lining also is becoming thread bare. We are the last too ourselves in perceiving this wane of the understanding…[57]

This appeal is important for the modern reader, for it encourages us not to scrutinize Jefferson's private letters too much especially at this stage of his life. He did not intend for them to meet public criticism which if he did, he would have worked on them more. Even if he did, his mind at this advanced age might not have caught everything needing correcting. The letter to Short with the footnote should certainly be read in this light. Of course it could reflect his real views yet at the very least it may be considered one of those "playful in the closet" moments that Rev. Clay spoke about.

The bottom line is that, although the footnote would significantly add to the main narrative if it was reliable, it seems improper to give it any weight because it was a subsequently-added footnote to an already-unacceptable draft. It is an unreliable source on which to reach significant interpretations or conclusions. Most people would ask posterity to not use their own unacceptable draft documents to make judgments about them. It is the fair thing to do.

---

57   Letter to Rev. John Brazer, August 24, 1819. The Thomas Jefferson Papers Series 1, General Correspondence, 1651-1827, Library of Congress Manuscript Division. Also Letter to Rev. John Brazer, November 22, 1819. Beliles, *The Selected Religious Letters and Papers of Thomas Jefferson*, 304.

Other material of Jefferson that is less reliable would include notes he took in his Literary Commonplace Book as a college student. He copied down some skeptical thoughts but it is not clear if he believed them or not. Perhaps it was part of his college research. It is impossible to know for sure. These quotes have already been cited.

About a dozen years later he compiled his "Notes on Religion" just several months after writing the Declaration of Independence. In these "Notes on Religion," Jefferson recorded the following concerning salvation that he copied from John Locke's book, *A Vindication of the Reasonableness of Christianity*:

…to those who believed, their faith was to be counted for righteousness;
…`There is no other name under heaven by which a man may be saved' (i.e., the defects in good works shall not be supplied by a faith in…any other except Christ).[58]

Jefferson also wrote in his *Notes* that "…The fundamentals of Christianity were to be found in the preaching of our Savior;…The fundamentals of Christianity… are: Faith [and] Repentance;…Faith is…a belief that Jesus was the Messiah."[59] And Jefferson also quotes a phrase concerning the church:

"Christ has said `wheresoever 2 or 3 are gathered together in his name he will be in the midst of them.' This is his [Christ's] definition of a society. [It is] a voluntary society of men, joining themselves together of their own accord…It is voluntary because no man is by nature bound to any church. The hope of salvation is the cause of his entering into it."[60]

His statement that the "hope of salvation" was the reason a person joins a church is important because of Jefferson's own activity in helping to start the new independent Calvinistical Reformed Church within just a few months of recording these words. This gives more credibility to the possibility that the religious notes above were *genuinely* believed by Jefferson at the first phase of his adult life, but still

58   Document 6. Notes and Proceedings on Discontinuing the Establishment of the Church of England," 1776, www.founders.archives.gov. (The statement following the "i.e." is Jefferson's own words.)

59   Document 6. Notes and Proceedings on Discontinuing the Establishment of the Church of England," 1776, www.founders.archives.gov.

60   Document 5. Notes and Proceedings on Discontinuing the Establishment of the Church of England," 1776, www.founders.archives.gov.

since they are quotes without comment, it should not modify the main narrative (and that first stage of Jefferson's religious life suggested him to be an orthodox believer anyway).

Conclusion

It would be safe to say that Jefferson appeared to hold to orthodox beliefs for the first several decades of his adult years; but by the end of his life, Jefferson did not appear to subscribe to all points of the historic Christian faith. Nonetheless, he had a great interest in the moral teachings of Christ. Jefferson became convinced, certainly in the later phases of his life, that the doctrine of the Trinity was a false construct imposed on true "primitive" Christianity. He believed the day would come that just as the Reformation helped strip away false corruptions from the faith, so also one day the supposedly false doctrine of the Trinity would be stripped away. He predicted that everyone would one day become a Unitarian because of its popularity at the time, but the 19th century instead saw great growth in the United States of the evangelical movement and the decline of Unitarianism. And for the most part subsequent scholarship proved greater reliability of the Scripture text rather than vice-versa.

Jefferson was a person who sincerely called himself a Christian and seemed to be faithful to worship in church virtually all his life, albeit sparingly only when it was not possible in France (1784-1788) and when Charlottesville churches lacked pastors in his early retirement years (1809-1819).

Yes, he held heterodox views later in life, but he only let those doubts be known to others privately. He was never a propagandist of heterodoxy, but so many modern biographies and republications of the modern-named "Jefferson Bible" have created a false image that offends traditional Christians. The reality is that Jefferson was always respectful of orthodox views in public and both at the beginning and end of his adult years was involved in Trinitarian churches that likely included confessing the Apostles' Creed every week. And that was what he funded as well. And with his letter to Augustus Woodward in 1824, he mentioned reciting this creed; so perhaps he was moderating his beliefs in small ways just before his death.

There was not a single person who knew him personally, nor any clergyman among the dozens south of New York who he interacted with regularly, who ever thought or spoke of Jefferson as anything but a Christian. Benjamin Rush and Rev. Charles Clay discussed his private beliefs with him as much or more than anyone, but still vouched for him, while recognizing he privately and "playfully in the closet" questioned and challenged many orthodox beliefs.

Jefferson defies all simplistic explanations and yet people want to create labels that can be used for his whole life. On the one hand, he certainly wasn't (by the end of his life) a Trinitarian Christian, but nor was he an opponent of general Christianity and its expression in the public square. But readers should not miss the big picture here. The father of the Declaration of Independence, the Virginia Statute for Religious Freedom, the University of Virginia, and our nation's third President, was fascinated with the teachings of Jesus and studied them often, called himself a Christian, and was a member of orthodox churches. As good as that is, a person does not obtain eternal life that way.

The New Testament makes it clear that the purpose of the death of Jesus was so that sins might be forgiven. Christians believe that faith in Jesus involves believing in who He is and what He accomplished for sinners in His death and resurrection—not just the morals He taught. Those who knowingly and explicitly reject the cross do so at their eternal peril. Whether Jefferson made such a mistake is not provable. Jefferson said things like the essence of religion is to do good. If he thought he could work his way to heaven, as many do, he was badly mistaken.

But it is not for us to judge the state of Jefferson's soul because ultimately God alone knows the heart, and He alone will be the judge of Thomas Jefferson and each one of us.

CHAPTER 12

CHURCH AND STATE: THE MISAPPLICATION OF JEFFERSON'S "WALL OF SEPARATION"

"…I consider the government of the U S. as interdicted by the Constitution from intermeddling with religious institutions… This results not only from the provision that no law shall be made respecting the establishment, or free exercise, of religion, but from that also which reserves to the states the powers not delegated to the U.S. …It must then rest with the states, as far as it can be in any human authority." —Thomas Jefferson, 1808 [1]

Virtually every day, there are stories throughout this country of some new conflict related to "the separation of church and state." Ultimately, each of these conflicts gets back, to some degree, to misunderstanding the views of Thomas Jefferson and James Madison in this regard.

Jefferson's original policies were an enormously positive development for religious liberty and for civil government too. But what has happened today is

---

1   Letter to Samuel Miller, January 23, 1808. Mark A. Beliles, ed., *The Selected Religious Letters and Papers of Thomas Jefferson* (Charlottesville, VA: America Publications, 2013), 167.

the converting of the founders' quest to protect both church and state from past abuses to a scorched-earth policy against any and all vestiges of religion in the public square.

In this chapter Jefferson's original idea will be summarized and then evidence of its distortion will be discussed in-depth.

The First Amendment

As previously noted, Jefferson's famous letter to the Danbury Baptists in 1802 spoke of a "wall of separation between church and state." This phrase has dramatically shaped how people interpret the First Amendment today.

Today the words are repeated so often that one would think that the phrase was in the Constitution. It is not. Instead what the Constitution actually says, in the First Amendment, is, "Congress shall make no law respecting an establishment of religion or prohibiting the free exercise thereof…" The first section there is known as the establishment clause.

James Madison's original wording of the Establishment of Religion Clause was as follows: "The Civil rights of none shall be abridged on account of religious belief of worship, *nor shall any national religion be established*, nor shall the full and equal rights of Conscience be in any manner, or on any pretext, infringed."[2] Thus, it is seen that the establishment clause originally meant no national religion shall be established as existed at that time in most European countries. Even when the First Amendment was written and adopted in 1791, it only prohibited the national government from having an established church. A handful of the thirteen states still had state-established denominations. These were never declared unconstitutional but they were gradually abolished over time. The last state to end the practice in 1833 was Massachusetts.

The founding fathers recognized there were many different Christian sects in America. Part of the whole reason for statutes like those advocated by Jefferson and Madison was to make sure that no one group could lord it over another. Madison said this on June 12, 1788, at the Virginia Convention:

Fortunately for this Commonwealth, a majority of the people are decidedly against any exclusive establishment—I believe it to be so in other states. There is not a shadow of right in the general government to intermeddle with religion…The United States abound in such a variety of sects, that

2   Robert L. Cord, *Separation of Church and State: Historical Fact and Current Fiction* (Grand Rapids, MI: Baker Book House, 1988), 7.

it is a strong security against religious persecution, and it is sufficient to authorize a conclusion, that no one sect will ever be able to outnumber or depress the rest.[3]

The government has not even the "shadow of a right" to interfere with religion, says Madison.

Former Northeastern University professor of political science, Robert Cord, explains that there were three purposes to the First Amendment, according to the Congressional record of those who drafted, debated and adopted it. The first purpose was already discussed—no National Church was to be established. Cord enumerates the other two aims:

Second, it was designed to safeguard the right of freedom of conscience in religious beliefs against invasion solely by the national Government. Third, it was so constructed in order to allow the States, unimpeded, to deal with religious establishments and aid to religious institutions as they saw fit. There appears to be no historical evidence that the First Amendment was intended to preclude Federal governmental aid to religion when it was provided on a nondiscriminatory basis. Nor does there appear to be any historical evidence that the First Amendment was intended to provide an absolute separation or independence of religion and the national state. The actions of the early Congresses and Presidents, in fact, suggest quite the opposite.[4]

An example of a contemporary action supportive of religion in Congress was the establishment of the Congressional Chaplains paid with federal funds. Madison was part of the committee that recommended it.[5]

Years later when Jefferson was President and Madison was Secretary of State, Jefferson planned to give a message to Congress that mentioned the federal funding for religion in a treaty with Indian tribes. Jefferson would often ask for feedback before making a speech. He apparently was not thinking about how government funding of religion for the Indians might upset some people, but Madison

---

3   Saul K. Padover, *The Complete Madison* (New York: Harper and Brothers, 1953), 306.

4   Ibid., 15.

5   Ibid., 23. Madison did claim later, as an old man, retired from office, that if he could do it over again, he would not have done that. But his actions while he was active in office are far more important than his later musings.

replied with the following advice: "May it not be as well to omit the detail of the stipulated considerations, and particularly, that of the Roman Catholic Pastor? The jealousy of some may see in it a principle, not according with the exemption of Religion from Civil power &c. In the Indian Treaty it will be less noticed than in a President's Speech."[6]

This advice was heeded by Jefferson. He submitted the treaty to Congress but did not draw attention to the religion provision. It shows that Jefferson and Madison were more pragmatic in their principles of the relations between church and state than other strict separationist allies. Indeed Jefferson and Madison seemed more driven by federalism than secularism. To them the Constitution's wall of separation was to keep religion out of the jurisdiction of *national* power, but others (some religious constituents in Jefferson and Madison's political coalition) thought it was to keep all "religion from civil power." They believed the First Amendment mainly was to protect the rights of the states to decide on religion, but others believed it was mainly to exempt churches from all government involvement (neither to promote nor to prohibit).

It seems that Jefferson and Madison held a much more nuanced position on the relation of church and state than most people realize.

In 1790 Jefferson wrote to educator Noah Webster, that "…there are also certain fences which experience has proved peculiarly efficacious against wrong…; Of the first kind, for instance, is freedom of religion."[7] Here Jefferson refers to religious freedom itself being a fence against tyranny. His later use of the "wall" metaphor was consistent with this.

The Origins of the Phrase "Separation of Church and State"

Thomas Jefferson's 1800 campaign for president was heavily supported by religious dissidents. These were committed Christians who were opposed to state churches, including those few states that still approved a state church. One such state was Connecticut, where the Congregationalist Church was officially established. After Jefferson's victory, a group of Baptists from Danbury in that state wrote to the new president on October 7, 1801 "…to express our great satisfaction in your appointment to the Chief Magistracy in the Unite[d] States."[8]

---

6   Memoranda from James Madison, October 1, 1803. www.founders.archives.gov.

7   Letter to Noah Webster, December 4, 1790, www.founders.archives.gov.

8   Letter of October 7, 1801 from Danbury Baptist Association (Connecticut) to Thomas Jefferson, www.founders.archives.gov.

The idea that Christians opposed Jefferson's presidency is proven false in this passage and so many others already presented in earlier chapters. There were many evangelicals who were grateful for Jefferson's leadership and his election. They continued:

> Our sentiments are uniformly on the side of religious liberty: that Religion is at all times and places a matter between God and individuals, that no man ought to suffer in name, person, or effects on account of his religious opinions, [and] that the legitimate power of civil government extends no further than to punish the man who works ill to his neighbor. But sir, our constitution of government is not specific. Our ancient charter, together with the laws made coincident therewith, were adapted as the basis of our government at the time of our revolution. And such has been our laws and usages, and such still are, [so] that Religion is considered as the first object of Legislation, and therefore what religious privileges we enjoy (as a minor part of the State) we enjoy as favors granted, and not as inalienable rights. And these favors we receive at the expense of such degrading acknowledgments, as are inconsistent with the rights of freemen.[9]

Their view is that the government has no business interfering with the church. Religion is first and foremost "a matter between God and individuals." Implied in their letter is this notion: Since rights come from the Creator (and not the state), free men shouldn't feel like second-class citizens for not being members of the state church. These Baptists align themselves with the president—in that both he and they could be reproached as supposedly being "enem[ies] of religion" for not agreeing with the state interfering with religious practices.

Their hope is that the principle of the federal government against making any law establishing religion will one day apply to the states. This would imply a separation of the institution of the church from the institution of the state. But not a separation of God and state. Even in this very letter, they call on "America's God" to grant the president the strength he needs to do the right things: "And may the Lord preserve you safe from every evil and bring you at last to his Heavenly Kingdom through Jesus Christ our Glorious Mediator."[10]

In Thomas Jefferson's response to the Danbury Baptist Association, he writes one of the most important paragraphs ever written by any founding father:

9   Ibid.
10   Ibid.

Believing with you that religion is a matter which lies solely between man and his God, that he owes account to none other for faith or his worship, that the legitimate powers of government reach actions only, and not opinions, I contemplate with solemn reverence that act of the whole American people which declared that their legislature should "make no law respecting an establishment of religion, or prohibiting the free exercise thereof," thus building a wall of separation between Church and State.[11]

Jefferson extols the virtues of the American system, where religion is between a "man and his God" and not a matter of the state. He interprets the religion clauses of the First Amendment as meaning the separation of church and state. As indicated in an earlier chapter, Jefferson originally wrote another sentence at this point that mentioned that he "refrained from prescribing" days of prayer because, unlike in Europe, he was not the "head of a national church." But Jefferson deleted that sentence before sending it because he noted that he did not want to "give uneasiness to some of our republican friends in the eastern states where the proclamation of thanksgivings &c by their Executive is an antient habit, & is respected."[12]

Jefferson then concluded the final sent draft saying: "I reciprocate your kind prayers for the protection and blessing of the common Father and Creator of man, and tender you for yourselves and your religious association, assurances of my high respect and esteem."[13] Appealing to prayer in this presidential reply while also citing a wall of separation between church and state does not seem to be a contradiction to him.

Indeed Jefferson set a life-long unwavering example of a public official expressing faith in God in his correspondence and official events. Many examples of him doing so have already been documented. An example was his letter to the Citizens of Albemarle on February 12, 1790: "In the holy cause of freedom... heaven has rewarded us...; that it may flow through all times...is my fervent prayer to heaven."[14] Similarly, in a letter to William Hunter, the Mayor of Alexandria, on

---

11   Thomas Jefferson, Letter to the Danbury Baptists, January 1, 1802, www.founders.archives.gov.
12   Ibid. [but see the unsent draft]
13   Ibid.
14   Letter to the Citizens of Albemarle, February 12, 1790, www.founders.archives.gov.

March 11, he refers to "…my prayers" and prays: "…Heaven help their struggles, and lead them, as it has done us, triumphantly through them."[15]

So what did Jefferson intend by the phrase in the Danbury Baptist letter?

Daniel Dreisbach's Remarks

Co-author Jerry Newcombe once interviewed American University professor Daniel Dreisbach on his book, *Thomas Jefferson and the Wall of Separation Between Church and State*.[16] One of the things he said was that we are misreading the whole church and state separation debate because we misunderstand federalism. The founders did not want a *national* state-church. Says Dreisbach:

> Federalism is a political system that separates the powers of a centralized authority and the powers of regional authorities. That, of course, describes these United States, where we have a national government. But we, also, have governments at the state level. This is a fundamental feature of the church/state arrangement worked out by the American founders. What they wanted to accomplish was: they wanted to deny the national government the authority to establish churches, to interfere with existing religious arrangements at the state and local level.[17]

Furthermore, Dreisbach points out that Jefferson's goal in the letter was to protect religion, in this case, as represented by the dissenters—a Baptist minority in a state (Connecticut) with a state-church (Congregationalist). Says Dr. Dreisbach:

> Now, what's interesting is that one can very easily interpret Jefferson's language here to suggest that the point, the purpose of this wall is to protect the Baptists from restrictions, perhaps, even persecutions of the state, because, keep in mind, the Baptists that he was writing to were a persecuted minority. They were religious dissenters in Connecticut, a state that had an established church. And so, I think Jefferson, we don't know for sure what's in his mind, but I think Jefferson saw this wall as a

---

15   Letter to William Hunter, March 11, 1790, www.founders.archives.gov.

16   Daniel Dreisbach, *Thomas Jefferson and the Wall of Separation Between Church and State* (New York University Press, 2002).

17   Transcript of a television interview of Dr. Daniel Dreisbach by Jerry Newcombe (Ft. Lauderdale: Coral Ridge Ministries-TV, 2005).

way of protecting the religious liberties of this religious minority group, the Baptists.[18]

How ironic also that he spent much of his time—while as president of the United States (and beyond)—poring through the words of Jesus. We miss the big picture if we think Jefferson wanted the words of Jesus to be censored in public debate.

Let's look at the wider context of Jefferson and church and state relations.

Separation of Church and State Meant Religious Freedom

For many years before his famous letter to the Danbury Baptists, Jefferson often spoke of a need for "a bill of rights providing clearly...for freedom of religion."[19] Jefferson's letters never use the phrase "separation of church and state" or phrases advocating complete secularism in public life. The phrase he used dozens of times was simply "freedom of religion." This did not mean exclusion or diminishing of religion, but simply equal opportunity of exercising one's preferences without legal hindrance. Indeed Jefferson's Virginia Statute for Religious Freedom had said that one's beliefs should neither enlarge nor diminish one's civil rights. The goal was freedom, not secularism. Separation of church and state was not the goal; it was a means to the reach the goal of religious freedom.

In November 1798, while Jefferson was back home, he anonymously drafted the Kentucky Resolutions. It was a response by the Virginia legislature to the Alien and Sedition Acts that they deemed unconstitutional infringements on the rights of the people:

> ...Resolved...that no power over the freedom of religion...being delegated to the United States by the Constitution, nor prohibited by it to the States, all lawful powers respecting the same did of right remain, and were reserved to the States or the people;...And thus also they guarded against all abridgement by the United States of the freedom of religious opinions and exercises, and retained to themselves the right of protecting the same...; One of the amendments to the Constitution... expressly declares that "Congress shall make no law respecting an

---

18   Ibid.

19   "From Thomas Jefferson to James Madison, 20 December 1787," www.founders.archives. gov.

establishment of religion, or prohibiting the free exercise thereof, or abridging the freedom of speech, or of the press," thereby guarding in the same sentence and under the same words, the freedom of religion, of speech, and of the press; insomuch that whatever violates either throws down the sanctuary which covers the others;…heresy and false religion, are withheld from the cognizance of federal tribunals;…let no more be said of confidence in man, but bind him down from mischief by the chains of the Constitution.[20]

This effectively expressed his views on church and state being based on the premise that men are sinful and cannot be trusted with centralized power and therefore the need for decentralized (i.e., state and local) authority over religious policy. This seemed to argue that the security for religious freedom was the Constitutional principle of federalism rather than of secularism.

How does Jefferson here define the first two phrases of the First Amendment (no establishment of religion and free exercise of it)? He summarizes it as freedom of religion. Freedom of religion—freedom from what? From potential "mischief" by the government. In short, Jefferson's "separation of church and state" is there to protect the church from an encroaching state. He clearly wants to protect people from religious controversies being settled by the state. It's not up to the government to punish "heresy and false religion." In short, it's not up to the government to decide what is theologically correct or incorrect.

Along this line of reasoning, Jefferson also wrote to Elbridge Gerry, a Massachusetts politician who was on the verge of joining the Republicans and becoming a candidate for Governor. On January 26, 1799, Jefferson wrote him saying: "I am for freedom of religion, and against all maneuvers to bring about a legal ascendency of one sect over another."[21] Gerry had recently switched parties to join Jefferson's Democratic-Republicans and was an Episcopalian in the Congregational stronghold of New England who supported religious freedom.

Jefferson's hostility was against one church denomination having the coercive powers and funding of the state. Most of the political leaders at the time thought it was acceptable on the state level, but a few like Jefferson thought any coercion to be wrong. But the separation of church and state to the founders, including Jefferson, had nothing to do with hostility to non-coercive religion.

---

20   "II. Jefferson's Fair Copy, [before 4 October 1798]," www.founders.archives.gov.
21   "From Thomas Jefferson to Elbridge Gerry, 26 January 1799," www.founders.archives.gov.

Jefferson's Actions Did Not Show Hostility to Public Religion

Evidence that Jefferson never intended complete secularism through the separation of God and state is abundant. Modern commentators often take this one Danbury letter and reinterpret it to mean something else simply because it is detached from the body of Jefferson's work and actions through many years of public service. (They also ignore the letter itself, when he asks them to pray for him and he commits to pray for them.)

Here is a review of Jefferson's promotion of nondenominational non-coercive religion in public institutions. As a public official (governor, secretary of state, president, etc.), Thomas Jefferson:

- Promoted legislative and military chaplains,
- Proposed establishing a national seal using a biblical image (reverse had pagan theme),
- Proclaimed official days of fasting and prayer on the state level,
- Proposed a law in Virginia to punish Sabbath breakers,
- Punished irreverent soldiers (while president),
- Proposed a law in Virginia to protect the property of churches,
- Granted aid to Christian churches and schools to reach the Indians,
- Allowed government property and facilities to be used for worship,
- Exempted churches from taxation.

In short, as Chief Executive of the nation, Jefferson saw no problem supporting religion where it did not infringe on a state government, such as with federal territories. The District of Columbia was under the control of the national government; and therefore, in 1802, Jefferson signed "An Act Concerning the District of Columbia" which approved tax exemption for churches.

Dr. James Hutson of the Library of Congress summed up Jefferson's view that "the government could not be a party to any attempt to impose upon the country a uniform religious exercise or observance; it could, on the other hand, support, as being in the public interest, voluntary, non-discriminatory religious activity, including church services, by putting at its disposal public property, public facilities, and public personnel, including the president himself."[22]

The use of the U. S. Capitol building for worship began while Jefferson was president. These services were held first in the old Supreme Court chamber and

---

22   James H. Hutson, *Religion and the Founding of the American Republic* (Washington, D.C.: Library of Congress, 1998), 93.

later, in 1807, in the new House wing of the building (now called Statuary Hall). As noted before, when he became president,

> Jefferson permitted executive branch employees under his direct control, members of the Marine Band, to participate in House church services…on Sundays, as they tried to help the congregation by providing instrumental accompaniment to its psalm singing;…[He also decided] to let executive branch buildings, the War Office and the Treasury, be used for church services. Episcopal services [associated with Christ Church, were held on Sunday afternoons] in the War Office [adjacent to the White House, and in]…the Treasury…a Baptist service.[23]

Jefferson's support of local churches lends plausibility to an anecdote from someone who was surprised when he met Jefferson on his way to church. Jefferson was said to have responded to this skeptic by saying, "No nation has ever yet existed or been governed without religion; nor can be. The Christian religion is the best religion that has been given to man and I as chief Magistrate of this nation am bound to give it the sanction of my example."[24]

Jefferson's idea of separation of church and state did not mean a completely secular public life. Church and state historian Thomas Buckley points out that Jefferson, in an 1807 letter to DeWitt Clinton, clarified that he did not want to have "a government…without religion."[25]

---

23 Hutson, *Religion and the Founding*, 89. On Sunday mornings, Christ Church also used a former tobacco warehouse on New Jersey Avenue (near D. Street S. E.), but the War Office was where Jefferson apparently worshipped most.

24 Hutson, *Religion and the Founding*, 96. This anecdote is found originally in a history of Christ Episcopal Church, Washington, D.C. written by Rev. Ethan Allen, the pastor that came after Rev. McCormick in 1823. See Ethan Allen, *Historical Sketch: Washington Parish, Washington City, 1794-1857* (Washington, D.C.: Protestant Episcopal Church, [1857]), 156. (It is also interesting to note that the pastor of Christ Church who replaced Allen in 1830 was Frederick Hatch, Jefferson's pastor in Charlottesville in the 1820s.) What Hutson says about this anecdote can also be applied to other anecdotes. These quotes sound very Jeffersonian in that they place value in religion based on its ability to shape public morals and principles.

25 Jefferson to DeWitt Clinton, May 27, 1807. Beliles, *The Selected Religious Letters and Papers of Thomas Jefferson*, 154. Thomas Buckley is one of the few to cite these letters. See Merrill Peterson and Robert Vaughan, eds., *The Virginia Statute for Religious Freedom* (Cambridge, England: Cambridge University Press, 1988), 93. Clinton was leader of the Republicans in New York. He helped in 1806 to abolish his state's bar against Catholics holding public office, yet he also worked to "disassociate republicanism from deism." See A. James Reichley, *Religion in American Public Life* (Washington, D.C.: The Brookings Institution, 1985), 172, 184. Jefferson said in another letter that he wanted government to "strengthen . . . religious

There are many examples of President Jefferson's personal introduction of religion into official public proceedings. In his First Inaugural Address, he reminded Americans of God's necessary aid and included references to God often in his Annual Messages to Congress and in other official letters and speeches. In Jefferson's Second Inaugural Address in 1805, he claimed that God had led America, like Israel in the Old Testament, and asked for God to enlighten them all. In his 1808 Reply to an Address from the North Carolina Legislature, he said: "I supplicate the Being in whose hands we all are, to preserve our country in freedom and independence, and to bestow on yourselves the blessings of His favor."[26]

In his 1809 Reply to an Address from Republicans at New London, he wrote: "I join in supplications to that Almighty Being, Who has heretofore guarded our councils, still to continue His gracious benedictions towards our country."[27] As president he saw no problem in personally asking for Americans to pray in his public speeches (as long as the call for prayer did not originate from the Congress).

Jefferson's correspondence while president frequently included church groups and religious leaders to whom he expressed his support.[28] In one of these letters he said to the Methodists: "To me no information could be more welcome than that… several religious societies [have experienced]…larger additions than have been usual, to their several associations." Jefferson wrote also to a Society of Friends (Quakers) praising their efforts to civilize and give "religious instruction" to the Indians in cooperation with the Federal Government.[29]

While holding government office in Virginia and on the national level, Thomas Jefferson consistently encouraged religion in public life and only refrained from

---

freedom." Jefferson to John Bacon, April 30, 1803. The Thomas Jefferson Papers Series 1, General Correspondence, 1651-1827, Library of Congress Manuscript Division.

26   Letter to North Carolina Legislature, January 10, 1808. Lipscomb and Bergh, eds. *The Writings of Thomas Jefferson*, Vol. 11, 299.

27   Letter to the Republican Young Men of New London [Connecticut], February 24, 1809. Ibid. 339.

28   Jefferson to Captain Thomas of the Baptist Church of New Hope, November 18, 1807. Jefferson to Baltimore Baptist Association, October 17, 1808. Jefferson to Ketoctin Baptist Association, October 18, 1808. Jefferson to Associations at Chesterfield, November 21, 1808. Jefferson to Albemarle Buckmountain Baptist Church, April 13, 1809. Jefferson to Methodist Episcopal Church of Pittsburg, December 9, 1808. Jefferson to Methodist Episcopal Church of New London, February 4, 1809. Beliles, *The Selected Religious Letters and Papers of Thomas Jefferson*, 183. Also see Jefferson to Abner Watkins and Bernard Todd of the Appomattox Baptist Association, December 21, 1807, Beliles, *The Selected Religious Letters and Papers of Thomas Jefferson*, 164.

29   Jefferson to Thomas, Ellicot and the Society of Friends, November 13, 1807. Beliles, *The Selected Religious Letters and Papers of Thomas Jefferson*, 161.

doing so if it violated federalism (i.e., the right of states or of the people to decide on religious matters). As James Hutson showed, even Jefferson saw "the value of the faith in civil affairs…"[30]

The Supreme Court in 1947

In 1947, the U.S. Supreme Court made use of Jefferson's above-quoted letter to the Danbury Baptists. They wrote a decision which changed everything when it comes to church/state relations. After this decision there began a systematic discrimination against things Christian in the public arena, no longer just focused on state-coerced religion.

The Court's 1947 ruling, *Everson v. the Board of Education*, involved the use of state-funded buses to be used to shuttle Catholic students in the public schools for some after-hours teaching on their faith. For the first time in about 150 years, the Supreme Court took the words "Congress shall make no law respecting an establishment of religion …" to now mean "the separation of church and state."

The *Everson* decision was written by Justice Hugo Black who was a Unitarian with an anti-Catholic, anti-orthodox Christian bias. Black donated money to Unitarian causes, and author Paul Fisher writes that he was interested in "advancing liberal religion."[31] Several years ago, Hugo Black's anti-Catholic prejudice and its significance in the *Everson* decision were brought to light. "What we have today is not really Jefferson's wall, but Supreme Court Justice Hugo Black's wall," said Dreisbach. "You can't understand the period when Justice Black was on the court without understanding the fear American elites had of Catholic influence and power," said Mr. Dreisbach, who is not a Catholic. Supreme Court Justice Clarence Thomas wrote in a concurring opinion some years ago. "This doctrine, born of bigotry, should be buried now."[32]

The Supreme Court wrote that Jefferson (and implied: the other founders) thought that the establishment clause built a Berlin-wall type barrier between church and state. In his decision, Justice Black wrote: "The First Amendment

---

30   Hutson, *Religion and the Founding*, viii and xii. James H. Billington, The Librarian of
      Congress, welcomed Hutson's "fresh interpretations" which show a surprising "enthusiasm
      with which Thomas Jefferson supported" the use of "federal facilities [for] . . . religion."
      Jaroslav Pelikan of Yale commented that Hutson's book shows "that, both in theory and
      especially in practice, the separation [of church and state] was, from the beginning, anything
      but 'absolute.'"

31   Paul A. Fisher, *Behind the Lodge Door* (Rockford, IL: Tan Books and Publishers, 1988 /
      1994), 11.

32   Larry Witham, "Church, state 'wall' not idea of Jefferson," *Washington Times*, August 5, 2002.

has erected a wall between Church and State. That wall must be kept high and impregnable. We could not approve the slightest breach."[33]

Journalist Robert Knight adds more about the context of the *Everson* case, and how it was born of a certain prejudice: "Catholic schools had taken children out of the increasingly secular public school system. And a lot of activist judges, like Hugo Black, didn't like that. And so, in the name of Separation of Church and State, they started using this misinterpretation of religious liberty to actually bash Catholics and Catholic schools. And in turn, they began bashing Protestant-based schools. It became an anti-religious sentiment overall in the law."[34]

After The *Everson* Decision

Time Magazine points out about the *Everson* decision: "That ruling marked a sharp separationist turn in court thinking. It unleashed a torrent of litigation that continues to flood courtrooms…years later. And in a succession of cases, the court drew the line ever more strictly."[35]

Over time, this interpretation of the First Amendment as requiring a high wall between church and state came to gain wide circulation, so much so that, again, the average person today most likely thinks that the Constitution even states the words, "the separation of Church and State." What this misinterpretation of the First Amendment has done is to effectively turn the First Amendment against religion, instead of protecting religion as it was designed to do.

As the effect of the *Everson* decision began to be felt, it achieved its zenith in the Supreme Court's rulings when led by Chief Justice Earl Warren. In 1962 and 1963, official school prayer and Bible reading (in devotion) was outlawed.

The June 25, 1962 ruling by the Supreme Court was *Engel v. Vitale*, the first in a string of decisions that seemed to rule God and the Bible out of the public schools. Justice Hugo Black wrote the Engel decision, saying, "a union of government and religion tends to destroy government and to degrade religion."[36] Although his statement was right, his decision was not.

---

33   Hugo Black, *Everson v. Board of Education,* U.S. Supreme Court, February 10, 1947, http://caselaw.lp.findlaw.com/cgi-bin/getcase.pl?court=US&vol=330&invol=1.

34   Robert Knight in D. James Kennedy, "The First Amendment on Trial" (Ft. Lauderdale: Coral Ridge Ministries, 2004), a video.

35   Nancy Gibbs, "America's Holy War," *Time* Magazine, December 9, 1991, 64.

36   Hugo Black, *Engel v. Vitale,* U.S. Supreme Court, June 25, 1962, http://supreme.justia.com/cases/federal/us/370/421/case.html

"I think this decision is wrong,"[37] said the lone dissenter, Justice Potter Stewart. At that time, *Newsweek* quoted Stewart as saying he couldn't see how "'an official religion' is established by letting those who want to say a prayer to say it. Citing several examples of U.S. institutions that invoke prayer (including the Supreme Court itself, which opens with the words, 'God save the United States and this honorable Court'), the Ohio jurist summed up his attitude with a line from a ten-year-old Court decision [*Zorach v. Clauson*, 1952]: 'We are a religious people whose institutions presuppose a Supreme Being.'"[38]

Part of the problem with the case in question was that the New York State Board of Regents—a government body—had written a bland prayer that they hoped would offend no one: "Almighty God, we acknowledge our dependence upon Thee, and we beg Thy blessing upon us, our parents, our teachers and our country."[39]

Well, bad cases can end up causing bad precedents. Those who objected to the prayer could, and did, point out that the state had no business getting into the prayer-writing business. But the bigger issue is the symbolic one. The Supreme Court seemed to begin a process of the censorship of God in the public schools that continues to this day. And it all gets back to applying Jefferson's phrase, "wall of separation of church and state," to the First Amendment.

In 1963, the next year, the high court said you can't read the Bible in the schools—for devotional purposes—but they explicitly said that objective "study of the Bible or of religion" is to be allowed in schools. But many schools eventually threw the Bible out entirely.

There are many well-intentioned people who oppose any form of school prayer, but the foundation of much of the opposition is quite questionable—that is, that the founders of America intended any reference to God in the public arena to be strictly forbidden.

When he was sworn in, George Washington said "it would be peculiarly improper to omit in this first official act my fervent supplications to that Almighty Being who rules over the universe."[40] The Constitution, signed "in the year of our

---

37   "While Most Believe in God. . . ." *Newsweek*, July 9, 1962, 44.

38   *Newsweek*, July 9, 1962, 44.

39   Hugo Black, *Engel v. Vitale*, US Supreme Court, June 25, 1962, http://supreme.justia.com/cases/federal/us/370/421/case.html

40   George Washington, "First Inaugural Address," April 30, 1789, in John Rhodehamel, ed., *George Washington: Writings* (New York: The Library of America, 1997), 731-732.

Lord" (referring to Jesus), is predicated on the Declaration of Independence, which says that rights come from the Creator.

The founders who gave us the First Amendment also passed the Northwest Ordinance, which states, "Religion, morality, and knowledge, being necessary for good government and the happiness of mankind, schools and the means of education shall forever be encouraged."[41]

As was previously shown, in Jefferson's state University of Virginia he affirmed that teaching about God was to take place in the curriculum, and space given for religious worship by its students. Secularism was never the purpose of the "wall of separation of church and state." The goal was freedom of religion.

Rehnquist's Argument With the "Wall of Separation"

A later Chief Justice of the Supreme Court had a problem with the whole misapplication of the separation of church and state in American jurisprudence. The late William Rehnquist dissented in a 1985 decision, *Wallace v. Jaffree,* where the majority ruled a *moment of silence* in school was unconstitutional (lest the children pray). Here's what Rehnquist wrote:

> It is impossible to build sound constitutional doctrine upon a mistaken understanding of constitutional history, but unfortunately the Establishment Clause has been expressly freighted with Jefferson's misleading metaphor for nearly 40 years. Thomas Jefferson was of course in France at the time the constitutional Amendments known as the Bill of Rights were passed by Congress and ratified by the States. His letter to the Danbury Baptist Association was a short note of courtesy, written 14 years after the Amendments were passed by Congress. He would seem to any detached observer as a less than ideal source of contemporary history as to the meaning of the Religion Clauses of the First Amendment...[42]

Since Jefferson wasn't at the heart of helping to write the Constitution or the First Amendment, why then he should be viewed as the arbiter of its meaning? Rehnquist continued:

---

41   Article III of "The Northwest Ordinance," the United States Congress, adopted 1787 and re-adopted 1789, in *The Annals of America* (Chicago et al.: Encyclopaedia Britannica, 1976), 3:194-195.

42   William Rehnquist, dissenting, *Wallace v. Jaffree,* U.S. Supreme Court, June 5, 1985, http://supreme.justia.com/cases/federal/us/472/38/case.html.

The "wall of separation between church and State" is a metaphor based on bad history, a metaphor which has proved useless as a guide to judging. It should be frankly and explicitly abandoned…The true meaning of the Establishment Clause can only be seen in its history…The Framers intended the Establishment Clause to prohibit the designation of any church as a "national" one. The Clause was also designed to stop the Federal Government from asserting a preference for one religious denomination or sect over others. Given the "incorporation" of the Establishment Clause as against the States via the Fourteenth Amendment in *Everson*, States are prohibited as well from establishing a religion or discriminating between sects. As its history abundantly shows, however, nothing in the Establishment Clause requires government to be strictly neutral between religion and irreligion, nor does that Clause prohibit Congress or the States from pursuing legitimate secular ends through nondiscriminatory sectarian means…[43]

This dissent is superb. Here one of America's great legal minds is saying that the current interpretation of religion in public is a wrong one that continues to wreak legal havoc on the Constitution and havoc on society. What Rehnquist said bears repeating: "The 'wall of separation between church and State' is a metaphor based on bad history, a metaphor which has proved useless as a guide to judging. It should be frankly and explicitly abandoned." Would that more judges, law professors, teachers, and principals would follow his advice.

Conclusion

By misreading Jefferson and misapplying his words, the courts have inflicted serious damage on the republic. In his Farewell Address, Washington said we can't maintain morality without religion. George Washington wrote in a letter dated May 10, 1789, to the United Baptist Churches in Virginia, that if he thought the Constitution would "possibly endanger the religious rights of any ecclesiastical Society,"[44] then he absolutely would not have signed the document.

Here's the man who presided over the convention and all its proceedings, objecting to the idea that the Constitution could be used against churches. But isn't

---

43   Ibid.

44   To the United Baptist Churches of Virginia, George Washington, "First Inaugural Address," April 30, 1789, in John Rhodehamel, ed., *George Washington: Writings* (New York: The Library of America, 1997), 738-739.

that what is happening today in the misapplied understanding of the separation of church and state? Our first president said, in another letter to a religious body (the Synod of the Dutch Reformed Church in North America): "true religion affords to government its surest support."[45]

Thomas Jefferson and James Madison expressed similar views yet were architects of freedom of religion. But their words have been twisted today to mean freedom *from* religion. Jefferson's approach, based on a Christian worldview, was neither theocracy nor secularism. The dominant modern image of Jefferson (and other founders) is as an Enlightenment Deist secularist who championed the separation of church and state against religion-oriented leaders who wanted to use government to coerce others. But in this book is seen a much more religiously-connected Jefferson (at least at the time of writing the Virginia Statute and Danbury letter). And he, along with so many religious friends, secured freedom for everyone.

Freedom is the legacy of a religious nation, not a secular one. The modern advocates of secularism use Jefferson out of context as they suggest too much religion today is harmful and dangerous to American pluralistic society, or that those who are motivated by religion and express it in public life are going against Jefferson and the founder's intent. In European history and colonial America there was some basis for that view, but there is no historical basis since Jefferson's time to support it.

The only way that the modern secularist can come to the conclusion that the founders of this country intended a purely secular state, where the state is "neutral" toward religion, is by selective history. They base their decisions on a few selected passages from history and ignore a mountain of evidence to the contrary.

Jefferson's idea was that the state should neither coerce belief nor unbelief. It should get out of the way and not help either way. But today government is getting in the way all too often. Instead of creating an inclusive environment open to any expression of faith, government now works to create an exclusive environment where religious voices are prohibited. As the Virginia Statute for Religious Freedom said: religion should neither enlarge nor reduce one's civil capacity.

---

45   George Washington, to the Synod of Dutch Reformed Church in North America, October 9, 1789, in Jared Sparks, ed., *The Writings of George Washington* (Boston: Ferdinand Andrews, 1838), Vol. XII, 166-167.

The Serious Situation Today...

Because of this misunderstanding and misapplication of "the separation of church and state" all sorts of terrible things are happening against people of faith today.[46] Jefferson believed in a level playing field when it comes to religion. But today's secularists are trying (and often succeeding) in imposing state-sanctioned atheism. Ironically, much of that is done in Jefferson's name.

The founders (including Thomas Jefferson) believed that belief in religion—by which they meant Christianity (for the most part)—should not be coerced by government, but be voluntary. But at the same time, its free exercise and expression should not be hindered by government; it should be allowed to flourish in the public arena. If some religious views were unhealthy or wrong, the free marketplace of ideas would provide the means to limit those views.

An anti-Christian crusade is taking place lately—using the courts to scrub the public arena of any vestige of Christian expression in the public arena. Even Jefferson, when he heard of plans by the New England brand of faith to evangelize Virginia, did not go to court; he fought it with ideas. (He sent a letter to be published anonymously in a Richmond newspaper). That was the Jefferson way. He did not try to bring the state back into a role of deciding matters of religion and of being a barrier to anyone.

The modern restriction of religious expression in America has not come through the free market of ideas as Jefferson imagined but through the coercive power of the courts. Case after case is brought against some sort of Christian expression in the public arena. Just look at some recent stories:

- A church in Arkansas cancels a matinee presentation of "A Charlie Brown Christmas," which would have been attended by grade-schoolers, should their parents allow them to attend. But the Arkansas Society of Freethinkers complained to the school that this would have been an alleged violation of the First Amendment.[47]

---

46 Of course, one could argue that the separation of the institution of the church and of the state can be found in the Bible itself. For example, there was a distinct separation of the king from the temple and religious duties. See Exodus 30:1-10. 2 Chronicles 26:16-20 describes a situation where the king was punished severely by God for overstepping his regal authority and taking on priestly duties.

47 Peter Blair, "Church's 'Charlie Brown' Christmas play a casualty of culture wars," WashingtonTimes.com, Dec. 6, 2012. http://www.washingtontimes.com/news/2012/dec/6/charlie-brown-christmas-play-casualty-culture-wars/

- A Christmas tree had to come down at the Willows, a retirement home in Newhall, California, for being a "religious symbol" and, therefore, a supposed violation of the separation of church and state. (Thankfully, enough complaints caused the center to allow a new tree.)[48]
- An eight-year-old girl, Olivia Turton, was not allowed to sing "Awesome God" during a talent show after school hours at a Frenchtown, New Jersey school. Authorities claimed it was the "musical equivalent of a spoken prayer." (Later, a court ruled in Turton's favor—long after she had lost the opportunity to perform at the contest.)[49]

These are no longer isolated, rare incidents. Along the same lines, here are more recent headlines, going beyond just the war on Christmas:

- "ACLU wants veterans' group removed from cross case." The ACLU is aggressively suing for the removal of a 29-foot-high veteran's memorial cross on top of a mountain in San Diego.[50]
- "ACLU demands Miss. school stop prayers." The ACLU sent a cease and desist letter to a southern Mississippi school district to halt prayers. The letter alleges that "West Lincoln students, faculty, and staff are routinely subjected to official prayer at numerous school events, including student awards ceremonies and banquets, school-day assemblies, teacher meetings, holiday celebrations, sporting events and graduation ceremonies."[51]
- "Holy Photoshop! LSU erased Christian football fans' crosses." Some Christian college students were shocked to see that their university engaged in a petty type of censorship. Fox News notes: "A group of Louisiana State University football fans whose admiration for the Tigers is second only to their love for Jesus is outraged after the school digitally erased the tiny crosses they painted on their bare upper chests at a recent football game." In the heyday of the Soviet Union, when politicians fell out of favor with

---

48   Susan Abram and Mariecar Mendoza, "Seniors save Christmas tree at apartment complex in Newhall," *The Daily News* (Los Angeles), December 6, 2012. http://www.dailynews.com/santaclarita/ci_22140598/seniors-save-christmas-tree-at-senior-apartment-complex

49   *The Limbaugh Letter* (New York, February 2013), 15.

50   "ACLU wants veterans' group removed from cross case," Associated Press, April 19, 2012. http://bigstory.ap.org/article/aclu-wants-veterans-group-removed-cross-case

51   "ACLU pushes Mississippi district to cease religious activity," *Commercial Appeal,* October 17, 2012. http://www.commercialappeal.com/news/2012/oct/17/aclu-pushes-mississippi-district-to-cease/?print=1

Stalin, their image was often erased in photographs. Now you see them, now you don't. Now you see the cross, now you don't.[52]

- "From Jailing Evangelists to Church Bomb Plot, Christian Persecution on the Rise in America." Writing for the *Christian News*, author Heather Clark opines: "Throughout 2012, numerous incidents have been making headlines pertaining to the persecution of Christians in America. Some believe that persecution is on the rise, and that matters will only continue to get worse across the country on both the federal and local levels."[53]

And on and on it goes in an increasingly secular America. All of these can be traced back to the U.S. Supreme Court's misreading of Thomas Jefferson. And it never stops. Soon the point may come where state-sanctioned atheism becomes state-mandated atheism. Christian believers are definitely becoming second class citizens in many contexts for their faith.

In Jefferson's name, today, Americans are being robbed of their religious freedom—much less their heritage. It's going beyond reason—as in the example John Whitehead of the Rutherford Institute described in his book, *Religious Apartheid*. He tells there of a five-year-old girl who wrote "I love God" on the palm of her hand, and her teacher rebuked her since God is supposedly not allowed at school.[54]

It seems that every week brings news of a new assault on religious liberty in America. As of this writing, football helmets that contain a picture of a bishop's hat are being removed because of the separation of church and state. Recently, the U.S. House of Representatives has a new rule that a Member of Congress cannot say Merry Christmas if they send out an official mailing to their constituents. Why? Because of the "separation of church and state." Just another day in an increasingly secular America.

With each passing year, it seems that the only principle getting stronger in popular culture is the ABC principle—Anything But Christ. The misunderstanding

---

52   "Holy Photoshop! LSU erased Christian football fans' crosses," FoxNews.com, October 22, 2012. http://www.foxnews.com/sports/2012/10/22/holy-photoshop-lsu-erased-christian-football-fans-crosses/#ixzz2XFfgqpuc.

53   Heather Clark, "From Jailing Evangelists to Church Bomb Plot, Christian Persecution on the Rise in America," ChristianNews.com, October 27, 2012. http://christiannews.net/2012/10/17/jailing-of-evangelists-to-plot-to-bomb-churches-christian-persecution-on-the-rise-in-america/.

54   John W. Whitehead, *Religious Apartheid* (Chicago: Moody Press, 1994) 155.

of Jefferson's words to the Danbury Baptists continues to fuel the fire to strip away America's religious freedoms.

CONCLUSION

The Courthouse in Charlottesville where Jefferson often attended Christian worship services, 1803-1826. He worshiped in the previous structure on the site for his first 25 adult years also. (Photo by Jerry Newcombe).

CHAPTER 13

CONCLUSIONS AND IMPLICATIONS FOR TODAY

"...[if you publish your Gospel abridgement] the public...might not Sufficiently appreciate your good intentions, but ascribe it to views as inimical to the Christian religion...which I am persuaded you Can have no intention of doing...My fears are, that...future Historians will most assuredly denominate [you] by some opprobrious epithet... —Rev. Charles Clay to Jefferson, 1814 [1]

Thomas Jefferson was a complicated man.

He was an outspoken champion of freedom and opponent of slavery, yet he owned slaves virtually all his life and never freed them, not even upon death. Around the time of the American Revolution, Dr. Samuel Johnson in England asked a penetrating question. "How is it that the loudest YELPS for LIBERTY come from the drivers of Negroes?"[2]

---

1 Rev. Charles Clay to Jefferson, December 20, 1814. Mark A. Beliles, Ed., *The Selected Religious Letters and Papers of Thomas Jefferson* (Charlottesville, VA: America Publications, 2013), 250.

2 Paul Johnson, *A History of the American People* (New York: HarperCollins Publishers, 1997), 72. Note: For the purposes of this book, we have decided to not focus on the slavery issue. When Jefferson wrote his first draft of the Declaration of Independence, it contained a strong denunciation of slavery. But the committee struck it down as too extreme. It certainly

Thomas Jefferson was also complex when it comes to religion. Prevailing perceptions today think he was a skeptic and opposed to organized religion. But the evidence in this book has shown much voluntary involvement in orthodox churches. Was there something genuine in his interest or was he basically a hypocrite involved in church to gain political points, while inwardly a closet unbeliever? It is clear that Jefferson was not an atheist, and he did not fit the paradigm of a Deist as neatly as many believe. But neither did he fit the orthodox Christian mold late in life.

Most people have no awareness of the Christian milieu that was so prevalent in Jefferson's home area. Now that more of the facts about Jefferson are fully examined, it is clear that he changed over time and wasn't always consistent. But there are some definite traceable patterns. The purpose of this final chapter is to review the overall thrust of what has been seen and then to make recommendations based on the conclusions of this study.

Trinitarian Church Membership and Worship All His Life

Despite Jefferson's late unorthodoxy, he maintained his support and attendance with orthodox Trinitarian churches (when available) his entire life. (He once described himself as a lifelong Episcopalian; but for two periods that type of church was unavailable to him—when he was in France (1784-1789) and after he retired back to Charlottesville (1809-1819).

The evidence in this book from his own writings and actions shows Thomas Jefferson to be much more involved in Christian activity than most people realize. Documents prove about 70 times that Jefferson worshiped or attended services, and over 400 incidents of him supporting religion or religious persons in one way or another. And it was proven that Jefferson worshiped other times, which he mentions in letters, but which simply do not show up in any documents.

Some may argue that just showing Jefferson financially supporting his local church does not mean he attended its services, but the overwhelming testimony of so many diverse observers clearly testify that he did so. For instance, Margaret B. Smith describes his eight years in Washington by saying: "Jefferson during his whole administration was a most regular attendant [at church in the Capitol]."[3]

---

reflects a Christian view of justice. Jefferson's other writings seem to indicate a repugnance with "the perculiar institution" yet he was a life-long slave-owner. Therefore, Jefferson's legacy on slavery certainly came short of what we would expect of a consistent practicing Christian.

3   Margaret Bayard Smith, *First Forty Years of Washington Society* (London: T. Fisher Unwin, 1906), 13.

His political opponent Manasseh Cutler confirmed the same during those years—and even use the phrase "ardent zeal" in reference to Jefferson attending Christian services there. And Jefferson's overseer at Monticello said of Jefferson's retirement years that he never missed a chance to hear any preacher that came along. (This was even during the period before the Episcopal Church started back up in Charlottesville.) His family members and neighbors confirmed the same for his retirement years. And never once did any of his local pastors nor any other person in Williamsburg, Richmond, Philadelphia or Washington mention that Jefferson refrained from attending church or taking communion and participating in the weekly recitation of the Apostles' Creed. On the positive side are many comments from the same, noting his attendance. In short, Thomas Jefferson was a committed, life long churchman.

Let's review some of the other highlights of his personal pro-faith religious life:

- He received his education at the hands of Christians, and he paid for his children and grandchildren to receive such an education. He also was a financial supporter of many Christian schools and colleges.
- He was a member in good standing at Episcopalian Trinitarian congregations and a frequent worshiper at services organized by many other denominations that were predominantly orthodox.
- On occasion, he even recommended a preacher to the Congressional chaplains, whose responsibility it was to fill that pulpit.
- He was a very active giver to Christian causes. This was a pattern throughout his life, even in the last phase, which was the least orthodox of his earthly sojourn. Per capita, Jefferson probably gave more than today's average Christian. He kept meticulous record of his expenditures, and it shows repeated donations to Christian churches and causes.
- As a young man, Jefferson served as a vestryman (like an elder and a deacon rolled into one) for the Anglican Church. Also, around this same time, in 1777, he wrote up the charter for the Calvinistical Reformed Church in his town with an evangelical preacher, the Rev. Charles Clay—with whom he had a lifelong friendship. Jefferson was the biggest single contributor to this fledgling congregation.
- Between 1821 and 1826 dozens of letters between Jefferson and Rev. Hatch, along with donations, show a renewed orthopraxic faith. At that last stage he was publicly a Christian member of a Trinitarian Episcopal

church and he was accepted as a member by his pastor, while privately holding to Unitarian views.

Yet there was also evidence of doubts beginning with the 1788 letter, where he declined being a godparent because he did not understand the Trinity. But there was no subsequent evidence of a separation or withdrawal from Trinitarian churches. Despite the influence of Rev. Joseph Priestley and Unitarian friends, Jefferson claimed he did not turn away from the Christian faith. On April 21, 1803, to Rush he said unapologetically: "…I am a Christian…"

But after ten years more, in private—never public—he began to clearly express more unorthodoxy in his views. From about 1813 onward, Jefferson's own words show a desire to promote a "restored" Christianity (that jettisoned the doctrine of the Trinity). In these later years there are several letters clearly identifying himself as an Episcopalian and a Christian (but in a non-creedal way). He said he could never be an atheist, and never once called himself a Deist. In his last year he called himself a Unitarian for the first time. Like many of the Restorationist believers in his area and like Unitarian Rev. Joseph Priestley, he believed the Scriptures had been corrupted over time, but his long-time pastors thought it was intellectual playfulness in the closet. Their perspective hopefully has been introduced through this book as a legitimate way of interpreting Jefferson's personal faith.

Jefferson's Distorted Legacy

After looking at the information in-depth in this book, it is useful to now summarize the four areas that people most often view Jefferson through a distorted lens.

His Relations With the Clergy

The image of Jefferson being attacked by clergy and of Jefferson condemning them is one of the most flawed modern conceptions surrounding his religion. Criticisms against Jefferson by ministers were largely politically based. They came from Federalist clergy up north—including Unitarians—primarily from New England. One in Philadelphia obliquely opposed him, but no others in all of the states south of New York did whatsoever.

In his writings, there are often very strong condemnations of some clergy, but the vast majority of those condemnations are against state-church leaders— those who used the power of the state to coerce belief or at least state funding and privileges for their denomination. But such criticism was commonly expressed by Dissenting orthodox clergy (i.e., Baptists, Presbyterians, etc) as well.

It's clear that Jefferson saw his motive as pro-Christian, as did many clergy friends. Jefferson was a folk hero to the evangelicals of Virginia, many of whom came from denominations that had been persecuted before Jefferson's Virginia Statute for Religious Freedom.

The evidence in this book identified about 300 clergy or church groups that Jefferson interacted with. About half of those received letters from him that have survived, and the other half were identified in his account book or in other letters and primary sources. Only about ten of the 300 religious persons or groups were Unitarian in theology, but correspondence with those few dominate the quotes in virtually all biographies of Jefferson.

The four long-term Episcopal pastors that he financially supported and attended their services were Charles Clay, Matthew Maury, Andrew McCormick and Frederick Hatch. But the Presbyterian John Glendy was his favorite preacher whom he went out of his way to arrange preaching opportunities in the Capitol and in the Charlottesville courthouse.

People need to learn about these religious friends of Jefferson. There is a great neglect of this other 95 percent of clergy and churches and other religious activity in his life.

His Treatment of the Bible

Jefferson was a lifelong reader of the Bible but came to believe that the Scriptures had been corrupted over time. He had come under the influence of Unitarian Rev. Joseph Priestley who believed that the original Christian revelation had become corrupted very early in church history. Jefferson eventually adopted a pick-and-choose approach to the Holy Scriptures. No true Christian can agree with this approach. Jefferson mistakenly thought he (and Priestley) were correct in this approach.

But more importantly, Jefferson was a major fan of major portions of the Bible. For his own edification, Jefferson arrayed major portions of the teachings of Jesus, which he studied in English, in the original Greek and in other languages. Yet these are words that Jefferson pored over repeatedly.

He had nothing but the highest praise for Jesus' moral teaching, which he thought was the best in the whole world. He even studied the sayings of Jesus in the original Greek. He said it was "the most sublime and benevolent code of morals which has ever been offered to man."[4]

His View of the Trinity and Other Key Doctrines

Jefferson also had the notion— which biblical Christians would say mistaken notion—that one is saved through works, not faith. Evangelical Protestants would say that the Bible teaches that one is saved through faith in Christ, which if it is true faith will result in good works.

It was evident how some influences turned Jefferson toward Unitarian views. In 1786, Jefferson attended John Adams' Unitarian church in London led by Rev. Richard Price. In 1788, Jefferson declined being a godfather in a baptism because he confessed lack of comprehension of the Trinity. In 1789, Jefferson asked Rev. Price for works on Socinian [proto-Unitarian] doctrines. Then in the late 1790s, Jefferson read Unitarian Rev. Joseph Priestley's book on the *Corruptions of Christianity* and this soon became the basis for his view of the godhead.

In 1803 Jefferson's Syllabus and his letter to Benjamin Rush suggested a view of Jesus that was less than fully orthodox, but he did not elaborate. By 1813 he began to clearly reject the Trinity in his letters to John Adams and others. This is undeniable in that last period of his life.

Jefferson also expressed views leaning toward universalism. If he rejected the resurrection and several other fundamentals of the faith it was never explicitly expressed unless one accepts an added footnote to an unsent draft document. In that theological area, claims of his unorthodoxy would be distortions.

His View of the Separation Of Church And State

In the vast number of letters written by Jefferson, he used the phrase "religious freedom" or "freedom of religion" many, many times, but only once did he ever use the phrase "separation of church and state." Yet this one phrase is repeated and distorted and defined today completely out of context. This phrase is not found in the Constitution, but it comes from Thomas Jefferson's 1802 letter to a religious group (the Baptists of Danbury, Connecticut).

In the Danbury letter where the wall of separation phrase actually comes from, President Jefferson asks the Danbury Baptists to pray for him, as he promises to pray for them. Here is this government leader asking for prayer—he's violating the separation of church and state (as popularly expressed today)—in the very

---

4   Letter to John Adams, October 13, 1813. Beliles, *The Selected Religious Letters and Papers of Thomas Jefferson*, 212.

document used to give us the doctrine of the separation of church and state. This shows how absurd and distorted today's understanding has become.

In his role as Governor he proclaimed a public day of thanksgiving and prayer. In Washington and in Charlottesville he supported the use of government buildings for religious uses. As President Jefferson gave federal aid to religious groups working in federal territories. He was going to proudly announce this aid in a message to Congress but Madison advised him to simply let it go unnoticed in a treaty because of other's sensibilities. Likewise he sought "every accommodation we can give them" when referring to religious groups at his state University of Virginia.[5]

These are just a few examples of his aid to religion in public life. As long as it did not violate the rights of state authorities and of individual rights of conscience, Jefferson sought to be more nuanced and accommodating of religion in public life than most people think.

In short, even if Thomas Jefferson was not a true Christian in the sense that he fell short of trusting in Jesus' atoning death and resurrection for his salvation, the third president was far from the caricature often made of him as one who wanted to banish all religion from the public arena. He was sensible and balanced in his church and state policies.

Jefferson's True Legacy

America needs to recover this Jeffersonian way of thinking as expressed in the three things he wanted to be remembered on his tombstone. They were embodied in three works of his life: The authorship of the Declaration of Independence and of the Virginia Statute for Religious Freedom, and the founding of the University of Virginia.

From these three acts and his other public policy actions, it is evident that he advocated three things that he believed would best serve America:

- Non-secular government. God-given rights and freedom of faith expression in politics.
- Non-coercive religion. Freedom to be right (or wrong) without state interference.
- Non-denominational education. Learning that includes general Christian principles.

---

5   Letter to Thomas Cooper, November 2, 1822. Beliles, *The Selected Religious Letters and Papers of Thomas Jefferson*, 337.

This is the essence of Americanism. These things, in their genuine context, are truly worth fighting for today. It is the heart of what has made us great. Remove the foundation of God, and you remove the basis of all rights. As Jefferson himself said: "God who gave us life gave us liberty. And can the liberties of a nation be thought secure when we have removed their only firm basis, a conviction in the minds of the people that these liberties are of the Gift of God? That they are not to be violated but with His wrath?"[6] His implied answer is no, they cannot.

Repeatedly, he used language in his other documents and public speeches and actions that freely expressed his faith and showed support for others of faith to have freedom to operate in the public sphere. Jefferson had no problem linking God with government his entire career. Modern states that adopt an atheistic secular approach have produced very different results. Jefferson's legacy of non-secular government has blessed America.

Jefferson (and Madison) gave the world religious freedom based on the premise that Almighty God has created the mind free and to restrict that freedom is a departure from true Christianity. Who is the state (any state—no matter how "Christian" it may imagine itself to be) to interfere with the consciences of citizens? God is the Judge—and He will judge—and Jefferson trembles when he remembers that. To God we all shall surely give an account for our beliefs, but not to the state. Christianity flourishes best when it is not allied with the state. When it is allied with the state, it becomes corrupted (and often ends up propagating unjust conditions).

Jefferson was a firm believer in the rights of conscience. This would include the rights of dissenters. The seventeenth century Westminster Confession of Faith says, "God alone is Lord of the conscience." While Jefferson would apparently disagree with many particulars of that lengthy creed, he certainly would agree with that statement. Jefferson consistently sought to protect the rights of conscience, even if he happened to personally disagree with the views of those whose consciences he sought to protect.

Jefferson consistently condemns any sort of religious tribunal or inquisition when it is a part of the government. He was committed to end government aid of one particular denomination and the coercion of others to support it and to hold to certain beliefs.

Jefferson's idea for public education was expressed in his founding of the University of Virginia. It was not to be a religion-free zone. But the various

6   Thomas Jefferson, *Notes on the State of Virginia*, 1781, http://etext.virginia.edu/toc/modeng/public/JefVirg.html

denominations were to be on an equal footing—none of them would be shown preference.

Jefferson wrote the *Report to the President and Directors of the Literary Fund* on October 7, 1822, that said:

> ...It was not, however, to be understood that instruction in religious opinion and duties was meant to be precluded by the public authorities, as indifferent to the interests of society. On the contrary, the relations which exist between man and his Maker, and the duties resulting from those relations, are the most interesting and important to every human being, and the most incumbent on his study and investigation.[7]

Jefferson is saying that while this would not be a denominational school, it would not preclude teaching about God, which he said is "the most interesting and important." This school would theoretically also allow other religions to play by the same rules. Public education for Jefferson was most certainly not to be religion-free, just non-denominational.

These are principles and policies that virtually all Christians, and likely most Americans can agree with.

The Failure of Most Jefferson Biographers

After reviewing the facts presented in this book, the chronological analysis of over 1000 documents, and the topical study of those facts that form Jefferson's true and distorted legacy, it is time to compare this history with those that have gone before.

From all the things attributed to Jefferson by many modern commentators, you would think he was not a Christian, even in a loose definition of one. The late atheistic journalist, Christopher Hitchens, makes these claims with little uproar. But even the more respected modern biographers and historians rarely seem to fully examine the religious history of the Central Virginia Piedmont and thus make conclusions about Jefferson without the context of his religious community.[8]

Unfortunately, the lack of contextualization has led to many modern scholars citing Jefferson and Madison as leaders of a "secular" Enlightenment tradition in

---

7   "Report to the President and Directors of the Literary Fund, October 7, 1822." Beliles, *The Selected Religious Letters and Papers of Thomas Jefferson*, 334.

8   Gilbert Chinard, *Thomas Jefferson: The Apostle of Americanism* (Mich.: University of Michigan Press, 1964), 103-105. Chinard is the only biographer to quote Jefferson's *Subscription* document to support Rev. Clay, but then he misses its significance.

a coalition with religious groups.[9] By doing this they maintain what Christian historian Nathan Hatch describes as "a sharply defined intellectual cleavage between rationalists and evangelicals;...between forces of the revival and those of the Enlightenment." Most modern historians who believe in a secular coalition then argue that "after flirting briefly with the rationalism of the Enlightenment, Americans embraced revivalism with a vengeance...[and thus brought an end to] the American Enlightenment."[10]

The discoverable facts of this study suggest that this view is wrong. Jefferson was *not* a leader of a secular group distinct from his religious culture; rather, he was part and parcel of it. Jefferson's consistent involvement of time, money, and words supportive of his Anglican parish, of his evangelical neighbors, and of his own independent church and so many other evangelical clergyman (especially Rev. Charles Clay) provide a context that is essential when also analyzing his private beliefs. But even more important is the fact that the religious community and ideas that Jefferson overtly identified with at the time that he wrote *public* documents such as the Virginia Statute for Religious Freedom and the Declaration of Independence, were of an evangelical, Calvinistic, dissenting nature.

The late Harvard Professor Alan Heimert has said that the evidence of co-author Mark Beliles' 1999 doctoral thesis—the content of which forms the basis for this new book—provides "truly new and original insight into the religious atmosphere

---

9   James H. Hutson, *Religion and the Founding of the American Republic* (Washington, D.C.: Library of Congress, 1998), 70. James Hutson said at least one "recent scholar has made the provocative claim that they [i.e., Jefferson and Madison] actually shared the agenda of their evangelical allies...'"

10   Nathan O. Hatch, *Democratization of American Christianity* (New Haven, Conn.: Yale University Press, 1989), 35. For example, Merrill D. Peterson argues that the coalition for religious freedom in Virginia had two parts: "one secular in the Enlightenment mold, one theological in the Evangelical Protestant mold." He then argues that "... *philosophes,* like Jefferson and Madison," were leaders of a "secular religion of the left . . . in the Enlightenment mold." See Richard A. Rutyna, ed., *Conceived in Conscience* (Norfolk, Va.: Donning Co. Publishers, 1983), 34-42. Peterson creates an artificial cleavage between Jefferson and Madison and their religious communities in the Piedmont: "The achievement was made possible by an unusual alliance: on the one side, liberals and rationalists like Jefferson, his young colleague James Madison, George Mason, and others; on the other side, the various dissenting sects, led by the evangelical Baptists. They shared the same goal, though for different reasons. And so by the unique logic of American history, the seekers after enlightenment and the seekers after salvation were allies in liberty." Merrill Peterson and Robert Vaughan, eds., *The Virginia Statute for Religious Freedom* (Cambridge, N.Y.: Cambridge University Press, 1988), viii. Such separation is really artificial and groundless; it was one movement.

of pre-Revolutionary Virginia, adding immeasurably to...Thomas Jefferson's own intellectual biography."[11]

If a historian today only mentions Jefferson attending Unitarian services, but none of these other orthodox churches, it creates a false impression. Or if they give only his late-in-life unorthodox quotes, and none of his other expressions of traditional faith, or they make his unsent letters and notes the predominant way of interpreting him, then they do a disservice to Jeffersonian scholarship. An honest biographer of Jefferson must mention Glendy (or even more so, Rev. Clay) at least as much as Priestley, or the Calvinistical Reformed Church as much as the French philosophes.

The source of much of Jefferson's unorthodoxy was the American revivalism and Restoration movements of the early nineteenth century, along with the writings of Joseph Priestley. Jefferson's waywardness more closely parallels the theologically-confused evangelical church in the Virginia Piedmont than the rationalist Unitarianism of New England.

Without yet seeing the new evidence in this book, Gregg Frazer says in *The Religious Beliefs of America's Founders* that, "The vast majority of those who have presented the religious beliefs of Adams, Jefferson, and Franklin in the past have done so selectively to advance an agenda or have simply accepted the labels traditionally applied to them."[12] He then asserts that they "were not deists" and says:

> Ultimately, they have been categorized as deists because of a false dichotomy. They clearly were not Christians, and the only other option that has been recognized by scholars has been deism. "Deist" has been a catchall designation for anyone at that time who was not a Christian or atheist, so Jefferson and Franklin have been put in that category.[13]

Frazer adds: "...Jefferson never claimed to be a deist" and then proposes that his "theology may best be termed theistic rationalism."[14] Although Frazer makes

---

11   Letter to Mark Beliles, April 8, 1996, after the symposium on Religious Culture in Jefferson's Virginia, held at the University of Virginia.

12   Ibid, 162.

13   Gregg L. Frazer, *The Religious Beliefs of America's Founders: Reason, Revelation, Revolution* (Lawrence, Kan.: University Press of Kansas, 2012), 162.

14   Ibid, 162.

an effort to be accurate it seems best to us to only use the terms Jefferson used for himself.

Jefferson never used Deist as a term for himself. He made it clear that Deist, atheist, and infidel were terms that his enemies used as labels for himself which he denied. He did call himself a "Christian" (1803, 1816) and very late in his life a "Unitarian" (1825). He also called himself in 1822 "a lifelong member of the Episcopalian church" (although he was a member of a "Calvinistical Reformed" church in the Revolutionary period).

So even to use Jefferson's own terminology depends on the time. It would not necessarily be accurate to call him a Unitarian all of his life when he never called himself that until the last year before his death. (However, he could still have held that position even while not using the label.) Neither would it be very accurate to call him simply a Christian at the end of his life, although it would be fair up to at least 1812.

Was Thomas Jefferson A Christian?

In addition to this historical analysis we have provided, many Christians today often want a simple answer to their question if Jefferson was a believer in Jesus Christ.[15] Ultimately, only God can answer that question, but Christian leaders do have an obligation to help people know how to become a true Christian.

The authors of this book, being evangelical Christian pastors, will not offer a simple answer directly to the question. A true Christian is one who at minimum, believes that Jesus died for him—in his place, for his sins—and rose again bodily from the dead. Based on the writings of Jefferson, there is no definitive proof that he did not believe these things, but neither is there a clear statement that he did. Often when researching figures in history, such personal private statements are not often recorded. This absence of direct statements does not prove anything.

Late in life Jefferson clearly but privately expressed disagreement with some basic Christian beliefs such as the Triune nature of God, yet remained an active and enthusiastic supporter of a church that held to orthodox truths. His pastor

---

15   To some degree this question would be answered a little differently by Christian leaders in the Eastern Orthodox Church, the Roman Catholic Church, or a Protestant church. It would also be answered a little differently by various Protestants—even Jefferson's Anglican/ Episcopal church leaders would have different criteria than the non-denominational revivalist Lorenzo Dow or the Virginia Baptists. (Note that Jefferson's life-long friend, Rev. Charles Clay, would have answered that in a way closer to the Baptists than to the average Anglican minister of his day.)

Rev. Clay thought his private dissent was being "playful in the closet." In fact, all of Jefferson's pastors seem to have considered him a true believer. They had the advantage of knowing him personally and conversing with him and worshiping with him. Modern historians do not have their first-hand access to Jefferson.

All these pastors of Jefferson accepted him as a Christian. Perhaps they are correct.

Even if so, some of Jefferson's private religious perspectives were views that are not commendable from a biblical perspective. Who is anyone to subtract from the Word of God and declare this is inspired and that is not? The true Christian can't approach his faith cafeteria style.

The Fruit of Bad History

The overwhelming prevalence of literature about Jefferson tells an incomplete story and the result is that less credible commentators take things to extremes today with impunity. Assertions of Jefferson as an atheist occur with little pushback when such a claim has absolutely no factual basis. And commentators reframe even overt religious actions of Jefferson routinely. An example is when Jefferson himself noted that he drew on a Puritan document as his model for calling for the day of fasting and prayer in 1774, but Christopher Hitchens completely reframes it by saying Jefferson called for "a day of solidarity with the people of Massachusetts."[16] Through relentless retelling of Jefferson's life, as seen in this typical example, no wonder the majority of us today think of Thomas Jefferson as basically a skeptic.

But even worse is what the modern "civil libertarians" have done to turn Jefferson on his head. They have made a mockery of the religious freedom bequeathed to us by America's founders. They have replaced the goal of non-denominationalism with secularism and expression with exclusion. The founders didn't want any one sect in charge of the other sects using the coercive powers of the state. But they certainly were supportive of religion operating freely on a voluntary basis. The Virginia Statute said religion should neither enlarge nor diminish one's civil capacity. Indeed, Jefferson wanted to remove the barrier of a state church so as to give freedom to all religious groups, but today the secular state establishment has been imposed in his name and now forms a new barrier to religious persons in public life.

Today when people talk about the separation of church and state, they often really mean the separation of God and state. Some modern lawyers and elitists

---

16   Christopher Hitchens, *Thomas Jefferson: Author of America* (New York: Atlas Books, a division of HarperCollins *Publishers,* 2005), 17.

today have perverted the separation of church and state (not a bad doctrine, if understood as the separation of the institution or sphere of the church from the institution or sphere of the state) into state-sanctioned atheism. It has become a reverse of the discrimination Jefferson loathed. Now anything religious cannot be expressed in public life and any religious group cannot have the same government benefits that secular organizations receive.

Co-author Jerry Newcombe's daughter taught English as a second-language in rural Thailand a few years ago. On Christmas day, the school where she was teaching hundreds of mostly Buddhist children had a general assembly. They asked her if she would explain to the entire student body and faculty what Christmas was all about, including Santa Claus. She was able to share from the Gospel of Luke and to present a directly Christian message, and tie the tradition of Santa Claus (based on the Christian fourth century hero, St. Nicholas), to this group of more than 2,000 people. Could you picture such a speech in an American public school? Today there seems to be more freedom to read the Bible in the public schools of Russia than in those of America.

It is a major misreading of history to say that Jefferson would have us censor things by the government because they promote religious ideas. The crusade of the ACLU (American Civil Liberties Union) and others has no grounding in American history.

Based on the research in this book it is evident that Jefferson had a much more accommodating and nuanced policy regarding religion and public life than is commonly thought. In this light, a few common sense measures are recommended. Return to Jeffersonian common sense and stop the witch-hunt against anything Christian in the public arena.

Ideas Have Consequences

There has been significant fallout from the misreading of Jefferson's letter to the Danbury Baptist Association and of making that interpretation the key arbiter of church-state relations. It has not only brought new intrusion of the power of government to discriminate against the Christian religion that gave us religious freedom in the first place, but it has actually caused blood to spill.

In recent years there have been dozens of school shootings, with hundreds of people (mostly fellow students) killed in this country. These shootings began in the 1990s and continue on and off to this day. This nation has had guns for four centuries but secularized schools for only half a century or so.[17] After a few generations of this rejection of Christian morals, of the removal of the Ten Commandments from school rooms, the lack of inward restraint is finally bearing bitter fruit. As John Adams famously said, "Our constitution was made only for a moral and religious people. It is wholly inadequate to the government of any other."[18]

After the Columbine school massacre in Colorado, Darryl Scott, father of a slain student, testified to Congress:

> Your laws ignore our deepest needs, your words are empty air.
> You've stripped away our heritage, you've outlawed simple prayer.
> Now gunshots fill our classrooms and precious children die.
> You seek for answers everywhere, and ask the question "why?"
> You regulate restrictive laws through legislative creed.
> And yet you fail to understand that God is what we need.[19]

More lives may yet be at stake if we do not look deeper beyond the immediate tragedy we read in the news. We reap what we sow. It is ironic that the founding father who fought so hard for religious freedom, for the expansion of its expression, should be the one in whose name religious speech is being taken away. It's time to discover a more complete and nuanced Jefferson toward religion both personally and in public life. The real Jefferson is much more accommodating and supportive of the spiritual side of culture than has been typically understood. That model of free expression is what America needs again.

---

17 It should not be assumed that the authors of this book both necessarily advocate for a return of prayer and bible reading in government schools. The Founders, in the Northwest Ordinance, said that "religion, morality, and knowledge" must "forever be encouraged." But that was at a time when government had no control of education. Addressing the decline of morals in the culture will require a discussion of how "encouragement" can take place today in light of changes that have occurred in the last two centuries.

18 John Adams, October 11, 1798, in a letter to the officers of the First Brigade of the Third Division of the Militia of Massachusetts, in Charles Francis Adams (son of John Quincy Adams and grandson of John Adams), ed., *The Works of John Adams - Second President of the United States: with a Life of the Author, Notes, and Illustration* (Boston: Little, Brown, & Co., 1854), Vol. IX, 228-229.

19 Darryl Scott, "Hearing Before the Subcommittee on Crime," U.S. Congress, May 27, 1999 in D. James Kennedy, *Violence in the Schoolyard* (Ft. Lauderdale: Coral Ridge Ministries, 1999), a video.

ABOUT THE AUTHORS

Dr. Mark A. Beliles is an historian and teacher of American religious culture. He is editor of The Selected Religious Letters and Papers of Thomas Jefferson (America Publications, 2013) that included over 50 Jefferson letters never before seen in print. Beliles earned his Ph.D. from Whitefield Theological Seminary and his dissertation was *"Free As the Air"—Churches and Politics in Jefferson's Virginia, 1736-1836*. The dissertation and another book in 2014 entitled *"Playful in His Closet"—The Complete Religious History of Thomas Jefferson* are both available at www.AmericaPublications.com. Beliles has organized, with sponsorship of the Virginia Foundation for the Humanities, several scholarly symposiums held at the University of Virginia on Jefferson and religion that each featured dozens of nationally-known Jefferson scholars and church and state historians. He has contributed to volumes of collected essays such as *Religion and Political Culture in Jefferson's Virginia* (Rowman and Littlefield Publishers, 2000). He resides in Jefferson's hometown where he has served for many years as Chairman of the Charlottesville Historic Resources Committee and co-chairman of the city's 250th Anniversary observed in 2012.

As president of the Global Transformation Network (www.NationalTransformation.com) and the America Company (www.AmericaCompany.org) Beliles is a popular speaker and cultural leadership coach who has traveled to over 50 countries and addressed parliaments and high-level leaders of nations on the topic of faith and freedom. He founded an educational ministry called the Providence Foundation in 1983 and co-authored other books for popular audiences such as *America's Providential History* and *Contending for the Constitution: Recalling the Christian Influence on the Writing of the Constitution and the Biblical Basis of American Law and Liberty* (Providence Foundation Press).

Rev. Beliles is an ordained minister who has served as pastor over various non-denominational churches in the United States and stills serves as overseeing bishop of Grace Covenant Church in Charlottesville which he founded in 1981. He and his wife Nancy have three children and five grandchildren.

Dr. Jerry Newcombe serves as the senior producer, co-host, columnist, and as a spokesperson for "Kennedy Classics," the television outreach of the late Dr. D. James Kennedy, the senior pastor of the Coral Ridge Presbyterian Church for 48 years, until his death in 2007.

Newcombe earned his B.A. in history with honors at Tulane University (1978) and his M.A. with honors in communications at Wheaton Graduate School (1983) and his D.Min. (Doctorate of Ministry) from Knox Theological Seminary (2008). Dr. Newcombe wrote his thesis on the importance of America's Christian heritage and how pastors and laypeople can pass on that heritage, and a variation of that thesis became one of his most recent books (*The Book That Made America*, Nordskog Publishing, 2009).

He has produced or co-produced more than 60 one-hour television specials, mostly with Dr. Kennedy as the host. These programs have aired nationwide and have dealt with such subjects as the Person of Jesus and questions dealing with the reliability of the Gospels, church and state issues, creation/evolution, indecency on the airwaves, gambling, the ACLU, socialism, the health care debate, the rise of radical Islam, and so on.

Newcombe is the author or co-author of twenty-four books, at least two of which have been bestsellers, *George Washington's Sacred Fire* (with Dr. Peter Lillback) and *What If Jesus Had Never Been Born?* (with Dr. D. James Kennedy). Other books have included *The Moral of the Story, Coming Again, A Way of Escape* (with Kirsti Newcombe), and (with David Gibbs, Jr.) *One Nation Under God: Ten Things Every Christian Should Know About the Founding of America*. Some of these books have been translated into Chinese, Korean, Russian, Indonesian, Norwegian, Spanish, and Portuguese.

Jerry has appeared on numerous talk shows as a guest, including *Politically Incorrect with Bill Maher* (4x), Janet Parshall's America, Point of View, the Moody radio network, TBN, the Fox News Channel, the Fox Business Channel, Glenn

Beck's television program, C-Span2's "Book Notes," etc. Jerry hosts a weekly radio program on Christian radio, "GraceFM," www.gracenetradio.com, Thursdays, 12-1 PM Eastern time.

Rev. Newcombe serves as an associate minister at New Presbyterian Church (Wilton Manors, Florida). Jerry is happily married to Kirsti Newcombe with two children and a grandchild. The Newcombes reside in South Florida.

APPENDICES

The Philosophy

of Jesus of Nazareth—
extracted from the account of
his life and doctrines as given by
Mathew, Mark, Luke, & John.

being an abridgement of
the New Testament
for the use of the Indians
unembarrassed with matters of fact
or faith beyond the level of their
comprehensions.

This is the title page in Jefferson's own handwriting of the first of two digests he wrote up, excerpting statements of Jesus from the Gospels---popularly known as "the Jefferson Bible." This 1804 version was clearly geared to begin to introduce the teachings of Jesus to the Indians, bypassing theological controversy as to the person of Jesus.

APPENDIX 1

CHRONOLOGY OF KEY RELIGIOUS WRITINGS AND ACTIONS OF JEFFERSON

Phase One:

1767 Joins vestry of Fredericksville Parish Anglican Church and takes oath agreeing with orthodox beliefs; serves as church warden; also worships at Bruton Parish when serving as legislator in Williamsburg;

1774 Recommends and attends special Public Fast Day service in Albemarle with Rev. Clay;

1776 In Congress; drafts Declaration of Independence and proposes a national seal with religious phrases;

1777 Leads effort to start independent "Calvinistical Reformed Church" in Charlottesville courthouse led by Rev. Charles Clay. Then in VA Assembly oversees drafting of five bills on religion;_

1779 As VA Governor, proclaims Public Day of Thanksgiving & Prayer;

1782 Begins annual donations to Rev. Matthew Maury to preach & lead services in Charlottesville;

1784 Goes to France and becomes friends with many Catholic clergy; criticizes others.

1785 Letter defends the Virginia Constitution's prohibition of clergy in public office;

1786 VA passes two of Jefferson's religious bills: for Religious Freedom & to Punish Sabbath Breakers;

1787 Private letter advises nephew Peter Carr to consider views of both pro and con about religion; English printing of *Notes on the State of Virginia* mentioning God, criticizes state church, intolerance, etc.;

Phase Two:

1788 Private letter to J. P. Derieux expresses difficulty since early in life in comprehending the Trinity;

1789 Private letter asks Unitarian Rev. Richard Price for literature on Socinian (i.e., Unitarian) doctrine;

1790 Returns to America; Private letter endorses Rev. Charles Clay's candidacy in Bedford for Congress;

1792 Seeks advice/tutors from Presbyterian Rev. John Witherspoon; Donates to unidentified missionaries

1797 in Philadelphia attends both Joseph Priestley's First Unitarian Society and Christ Episcopal Church;

1798 Publicly Subscribes for a hot press Bible; Letters with Presbyterian Rev. William Linn and Moravian Rev. John Heckewelder on Indian missions; gives help to Linn's New York Missionary Society

1800 First attacks by Federalist clergy (including Rev. Linn) on Jefferson's personal religion; Private letters criticize northeastern Federalist clergy but tells Baptist Rev. Jeremiah Moore that he now disagrees with VA constitution that prohibits clergy to hold official positions in state;

1801 Moves to D.C.; Appeals to God's aid in First Inaugural Address as President; Worships regularly in Capitol building & joins Christ Episcopal Church; Replies to many friends such as Delaware Baptists;

1802 Hosts Dorothy Ripley, Bishop Madison and Baptist Rev. John Leland in President's house; arranges for Leland to preach in Capitol and sends reply to Danbury Baptists agreeing with their belief in separation of church and state; Donates to 10 different ministers; Corresponds about Indian missions

Phase Three:

1803 Writes Syllabus comparing the philosophy of Jesus with others; Says he is a Christian.

1804 Meets Methodist campmeeting leader Rev. Henry Fry; Replies to New Orleans Ursuline nuns and promises patronage to Catholic school; Gets his favorite Presbyterian Rev. Glendy to preach at Capitol;

1807 Shifts worship from Christ Church henceforth to Capitol; Commends Rev. McCormick & sends last annual donations to Christ Church (cites membership); Publicly subscribes for Scott's Bible; Replies to Universalist Rev. Eddowes with private agreement on corruption of Scripture texts;

1808 Private Letter to Presbyterian Rev. Samuel Miller declining prayer proclamations because it violates states rights; Replies to many groups of Baptists, Methodists and Quakers

1809 Retires to Charlottesville; there are no resident pastors of main denominational churches for 10 yrs

Phase Four:

1813 Expresses unorthodox views for first time in private letters to John Adams and William Canby;

1814 Privately doubts reliability of Scripture, yet donates to and joins VA Bible Society to spread Bibles; Rev. Charles Clay advises against publishing Gospel extracts because people will misunderstand intent;

1815 Assures Rev. Clay that he would never share extracts publicly; also says he discussed religion with Clay more than anyone; Organizes service in courthouse for Presbyterian Rev. John Glendy;

1816 Letter to Charles Thomson tells of his Gospel extracts (today a.k.a. as "the Jefferson Bible") and that he is a "real Christian;" other private letters show agreement with unorthodox northerners (Unitarians).

1817 In Central College he approves Presbyterian Rev. Samuel Knox to be first professor along with Unitarian Thomas Cooper as chemistry professor. Approves for clergy, prayer & scripture at dedication;

1818 Private letter criticizes Calvinism for first time; Asks for letters not to be ever published.

Phase Five:

1820 Starts donating annually to Episcopal Rev. Frederick Hatch; Cooper is forced out as professor at UVa; Private letter makes first condemnation of Presbyterian clergy; Letter to Rev. John Holt Rice asks for Presbyterian support; Private letter to Short says that the Apostle Paul supposedly corrupted scripture;

1821 Gives to Rev. Hatch extra donation for "our pastor's" house;

1822 Encourages churches to provide professors & use facilities at UVa; Praises union courthouse services

1824 Donates to building of Episcopal, Presbyterian and Baptist churches; Speaks of resurrection doctrine in Apostles' Creed that "we all declare"; Approves Rotunda for worship; says students expected to attend

1825 Private letter to Rev. Benjamin Waterhouse says he is Unitarian.

Chronology of Less Reliable Documents

1760s While a student he compiles Literary Commonplace Book that includes unorthodox quotes;

1776 Compiles "Notes on Religion" that affirms orthodox beliefs and criticizes state-established churches;

1801 Unsent letter to Danbury Baptists;

1804 Compiles private "Philosophy of Jesus...an Abridgement of the Gospels for the use of the Indians"

1809 Unsent letter to Presbyterian/Baptist Rev. James Fishback shows unorthodox leanings;

1810 Unsent letter to Quaker William Baldwin;

1815 Unsent letter to Peter Wendover praises Rev. Alexander McLeod sermon that affirms pastors' right to teach on politics but only if congregation requests it;

1819 Unsent footnote to William Short rejects most fundamentals of orthodox Christianity;

1820 Compiles private document: "The Life and Morals of Jesus;" (today called the "Jefferson Bible").

APPENDIX 2

SOME RELIGIOUS LETTERS FROM JEFFERSON'S PAPERS

[About a thousand letters to and from Jefferson plus account book entries have been studied and cited in this book. A few of these are included below because they mark the transitions in Jefferson's beliefs over his life. About a dozen other letters are included simply because they have never been seen in print before. Over 50 other Jefferson letters never printed before, along with about 400 others, are found in *The Selected Religious Letters and Papers of Thomas Jefferson* [2013], edited by Mark Beliles. An exhaustive list of almost 1200 religious-oriented papers of Jefferson is found in Beliles' other work: *Playful in the Closet: A Complete Religious History of Thomas Jefferson* published simultaneously as a companion to this volume. See links to these in the back.]

[Letters below are used courtesy of the Library of Congress (DLC), the Massachusetts Historical Society (MHi), the Missouri History Museum Archives (MoSHi), the College of William and Mary-Swem Library (ViW), and the New York Public Library (NYPL).]

Subscription to Support a Clergyman
of the Calvinistical Reformed Church

[Charlottesville, February 1777] [MHi]

Whereas by a late act of General assembly freedom of Religious opinion and worship is restored to all, and it is left to the members of each religious society to employ such teachers as they think fit for their own spiritual comfort and instruction, and to maintain the same by their free and voluntary contributions: We the subscribers, professing the most Catholic affection for other religious sectaries who happen to differ from us in points of conscience, yet desirous of encouraging and supporting the Calvinistical Reformed church, and of deriving to our selves, through the ministry of it's teachers, the benefits of Gospel knolege and religious improvement; and at the same time of supporting those, who, having been at considerable expence in qualifying themselves by regular education for explaining the holy scriptures, have dedicated their time and labour to the service of the said church; and moreover approving highly the political conduct of the Revd. Charles Clay, who, early rejecting the tyrant and tyranny of Britain, proved his religion genuine by it's harmony with the liberties of mankind, and, conforming his public prayers to the spirit and the injured rights of his country, ever addressed the God of battles for victory to our arms, while others impiously prayed that our enemies might vanquish and overcome us: do hereby oblige ourselves our heirs executors and administrators to pay to the said Charles Clay of Albemarle his executors or administrators the several sums affixed to our respective names on the 25th day of December next, and also to make the like annual paiment on the 25th. day of December in every year following until we shall withdraw the same or until the legislature shall make other provision for the support of the said Clergy. In Consideration whereof we expect that the said Charles Clay shall perform divine service and preach a sermon in the town of Charlottesville on every 4th. Saturday till the end of the next session of general Assembly and after that on every 4th. Sunday or oftener if a regular rotation with the other churches which shall have put themselves under his cure will admit a more frequent attendance.

And we further mutually agree with each other that we will meet at Charlottesville on the 1st. day of March in the present year and on in every year following so long as we continue our subscriptions and there make choice by ballot of three Wardens to collect our said subscriptions to take care of such books and vestments as shall be provided for the use of our church to call meetings of our Congregation when necessary and to transmit such other business relating to our said Congregation as we shall hereafter confide to them.

February. 1777.

- Th: Jefferson, six pounds.
- Philip Mazzei sixteen shillings & eight pence
- Randolph Jefferson two pounds ten shillings
- Nicholas Lewis three Pounds ten Shillings
- [plus 15 others]

Proclamation Appointing a Day of Publick and Solemn Thanksgiving and Prayer

November 11, 1779 [DLC]

By his Excellency Thomas Jefferson, Esq. Governour or Chief Magistrate of the commonwealth of Virginia.

PROCLAMATION

Whereas the Honourable the General Congress, impressed with a grateful sense of the goodness of Almighty God, in blessing the greater part of this extensive continent with plentiful harvests, crowning our arms with repeated successes, conducting us hitherto safely through the perils with which we have been encompassed and manifesting in multiplied instances his divine care of these infant states, hath thought proper by their act of the 20th day of October last, to recommend to the several states that Thursday the 9th of December next be appointed a day of publick and solemn thanksgiving and prayer, which act is in these words, to wit.

"Whereas it becomes us humbly to approach the throne of Almighty God, with gratitude and praise, for the wonders which his goodness has wrought in conducting our forefathers to this western world; for his protection to them and to their posterity, amidst difficulties and dangers; for raising us their children from deep distress, to be numbered among the nations of the earth; and for arming the hands of just and mighty Princes in our deliverance; and especially for that he hath been pleased to grant us the enjoyment of health and so to order the revolving seasons, that the earth hath produced her increase in abundance, blessing the labours of the husbandman, and spreading plenty through the land; that he hath prospered our arms and those of our ally, been a shield to our troops in the hour of danger, pointed their swords to victory, and led them in triumph over the bulwarks of the foe; that he hath gone with those who went out into the wilderness against the savage tribes; that he hath stayed the hand of the spoiler, and turned back his meditated destruction; that he hath prospered our commerce, and given success to those who sought the enemy on the face of the deep; and above all, that he hath diffused the glorious light of the gospel, whereby, through the merits of our gracious Redeemer, we may become the heirs of his eternal glory. Therefore,

"Resolved, that it be recommended to the several states to appoint THURSDAY the 9th of December next, to be a day of publick and solemn THANKSGIVING to Almighty God, for his mercies, and of PRAYER, for the continuance of his favour and protection to these United States; to beseech him that he would be graciously pleased to influence our publick Councils, and bless them with wisdom from on high, with unanimity, firmness and success; that he would go forth with our hosts and crown our arms with victory; that he would grant to his church, the plentiful effusions of divine grace, and pour out his holy spirit on all Ministers of the gospel; that he would bless and prosper the means of education, and spread the light of christian knowledge through the remotest corners of the earth; that he would smile upon the labours of his people, and cause the earth to bring forth her fruits in abundance, that we may with gratitude and gladness enjoy them; that he would take into his holy protection, our illustrious ally, give him victory over his enemies, and render him finally great, as the father of his people, and the protector of the rights of mankind; that he would graciously be pleased to turn the hearts of our enemies, and to dispence the blessings of peace to contending nations.

"That he would in mercy look down upon us, pardon all our sins, and receive us into his favour; and finally, that he would establish the independance of these United States upon the basis of religion and virtue, and support and protect them in the enjoyment of peace, liberty and safety."

I do therefore by authority from the General Assembly issue this my proclamation, hereby appointing Thursday the 9th of December next, a day of publick and solemn thanksgiving and prayer to Almighty God, earnestly recommending to all the good people of this commonwealth, to set apart the said day for those purposes, and to the several Ministers of religion to meet their respective societies thereon, to assist them in their prayers, edify them with their discourses, and generally to perform the sacred duties of their function, proper for the occasion.

Given under my hand and the seal of the commonwealth, at Williamsburg, this 11th day of November, in the year of our Lord, 1779, and in the fourth of the commonwealth.

Th: Jefferson

To Justin P. P. Derieux

Paris, July 25, 1788 [DLC]

Sir

[note: initial paragraph not included due to no religious content]

I am truly sensible, Sir, of the honour you do me in proposing to me that of becoming one of the Sponsors of your child, and return you my sincere thanks for it. At the same time I am not a little mortified that scruples, perhaps not well founded, forbid my undertaking this honourable office. The person who becomes sponsor for a child, according to the ritual of the church in which I was educated, makes a solemn profession, before god and the world, of faith in articles, which I had never sense enough to comprehend, and it has always appeared to me that comprehension must precede assent. The difficulty of reconciling the ideas of Unity and Trinity, have, from a very early part of my life, excluded me from the office of sponsorship, often proposed to me by my friends, who would have trusted, for the faithful discharge of it, to morality alone instead of which the church requires faith. Accept therefore Sir this conscientious excuse which I make with regret…

Th: Jefferson

To the Danbury Baptist Association in Connecticut

January 1, 1802. [DLC]

To messers. Nehemiah Dodge, Ephraim Robbins, & Stephen S. Nelson, a committee of the Danbury Baptist association in the state of Connecticut.

GENTLEMEN

The affectionate sentiments of esteem and approbation which you are so good as to express towards me, on behalf of the Danbury Baptist association, give me the highest satisfaction. my duties dictate a faithful & zealous pursuit of the interests of my constituents, & in proportion as they are persuaded of my fidelity to those duties, the discharge of them becomes more and more pleasing.

Believing with you that religion is a matter which lies solely between Man & his God, that he owes account to none other for his faith or his worship, that the legitimate powers of government reach actions only, & not opinions, I contemplate with sovereign reverence that act of the whole American people which declared that *their* legislature should "make no law respecting an establishment of religion, or prohibiting the free exercise thereof," thus building a wall of separation between Church & State. adhering to this expression of the supreme will of the nation in behalf of the rights of conscience, I shall see with sincere satisfaction the progress of those sentiments which tend to restore to man all his natural rights, convinced he has no natural right in opposition to his social duties.

I reciprocate your kind prayers for the protection & blessing of the common father and creator of man, and tender you for yourselves & your religious association, assurances of my high respect & esteem.

Th: Jefferson

To Benjamin Rush
Washington, April 21, 1803. [DLC]
DEAR SIR,

In some of the delightful conversations with you in the evenings of 1798-99, and which served as an anodyne to the afflictions of the crisis through which our country was then laboring, the Christian religion was sometimes our topic; and I then promised you that one day or other I would give you my views of it. They are the result of a life of inquiry and reflection, and very different from that anti-Christian system imputed to me by those who know nothing of my opinions. To the corruptions of Christianity I am indeed opposed, but not to the genuine precepts of Jesus himself. I am a Christian, in the only sense in which he wished anyone to be: sincerely attached to his doctrines in preference to all others, ascribing to himself every *human* excellence, and believing he never claimed any other.

At the short interval since these conversations, when I could justifiably abstract my mind from public affairs, the subject has been under my contemplation. But the more I considered it, the more it expanded beyond the measure of either my time or information. In the moment of my late departure from Monticello, I received from Dr. Priestley his little treatise of "Socrates and Jesus Compared." This being a section of the general view I had taken of the field, it became a subject of reflection while on the road and unoccupied otherwise. The result was, to arrange in my mind a syllabus or outline of such an estimate of the comparative merits of Christianity as I wished to see executed by someone of more leisure and information for the task than myself.

This I now send you as the only discharge of my promise I can probably ever execute. And in confiding it to you, I know it will not be exposed to the malignant perversions of those who make every word from me a text for new misrepresentations and calumnies. I am moreover averse to the communication of my religious tenets to the public, because it would countenance the presumption of those who have endeavored to draw them before that tribunal, and to seduce public opinion to erect itself into that inquisition over the rights of conscience which the laws have so justly proscribed. It behooves every man who values liberty of conscience for himself, to resist invasions of it in the case of others; or their case may, by change of circumstances, become his own. It behooves him, too, in his own case, to give no example of concession, betraying the common right of independent opinion, by answering questions of faith which the laws have left between God and himself. Accept my affectionate salutations.

Th: Jefferson

To Revd. Joseph Priestley, Unitarian in Pennsylvania
Washington, January 29, 1804 [DLC]
DEAR SIR,
[note: paragraph here not included due to no religious content]

I rejoice that you have undertaken the task of comparing the moral doctrines of Jesus with those of the ancient Philosophers. You are so much in possession of the whole subject, that you will do it easier & better than any other person living. I think you cannot avoid giving, as preliminary to the comparison, a digest of his moral doctrines, extracted in his own words from the Evangelists, and leaving out everything relative to his personal history and character. It would be short and precious. With a view to do this for my own satisfaction, I had sent to Philadelphia to get two testaments Greek of the same edition, & two English, with a design to cut out the morsels of morality, and paste them on the leaves of a book, in the manner you describe as having been pursued in forming your Harmony. But I shall now get the thing done by better hands.

[note: paragraph here not included due to no religious content]
Th: Jefferson

To Henry Dearborn
Monticello, August 3, 1804 [DLC]
Dear Sir

I inclose you a letter from mr Boudinot to whom an answer is promised as soon as I shall hear from you on the subject. I think this mr [Rev. Gideon] Blackburn called on us, and recieved such assurances as then gave him satisfaction. as we have in other instances encouraged the cooperation of the Quakers in Indian civilization, it is to be considered whether we may with advantage do the same with other sects. the spirit of that which now applies is materially different from that of the Quakers, and in all cases we must keep in our own hands the essential direction of the application of our funds. not knowing whether you have left Washington, I direct this to that place, presuming, if you have, it will be forwarded to you. I hope your health is perfectly re-established, as well as mrs Dearborne's. Accept affectionate salutations & assurances of respect.

Th: Jefferson

To John Hollins
Washington, December 12, 1804 [DLC]
Dear Sir

I recieved last night your favor of the day before & this morning I obtained the Speaker's order for reserving the desk [i.e. podium] of the H[ouse] of R[epresentatives] for [Rev] mr [John] Glendy on Sunday next, where many of us will be glad to see him. should he arrive here before half after three on Saturday I will expect him to dine with me, as well as yourself if you accompany him. Govr. Bowdoin accepts his appointment, but is too unwell to come on here for some time. mr Irving his nephew is appointed his secretary of legation. as he has been the agent at London on all the business before that board of Commrs. detailed communications from you to him would probably be better understood by him than by his principal. as he has been much in the large cities of the middle states I presume you know him. accept my friendly salutations for yourself & mr Glendy & assurances of great esteem.

Th: Jefferson

To Revd. Andrew McCormick, Senate Chaplain, Episcopal in Washington
Washington, December 12, 1804 [ViW]
Dear Sir,

The liberality which I have seen practiced by the gentlemen, chaplains of Congress, in admitting others of their profession who happen here occasionally to perform the Sabbath-day functions in the chamber of the H. of Representatives, induces me to ask that indulgence for the revd. Mr [John] Glendye a Presbyterian clergyman from Baltimore who will be in this place next Sunday forenoon. Being acquainted with mr Glendye, I can assure you that no person to whom that permission could be transferred, will be heard with more satisfaction than he would. If the desk be at your disposal for the next Sunday forenoon I will ask that favor on his behalf if [Senate Chaplain Presbyterian Revd.] mr [James] Lowry [Laurie] be the person to whom that day belongs, as my acquaintance with him would hardly justify the liberty of a direct application, could I be allowed so far to profit of your friendship as to ask your requesting this favor from mr Lowry. Accept my friendly salutations and assurances of great esteem & respect.

Th: Jefferson

To John George Jackson

Washington, February 22, 1806 [DLC]

Sir

I recieved in Nov. a petition from some Wiandot Indians praying for a grant of the reservation of 2. miles square at the lower rapids of Sandusky, part to themselves, & part to some missionaries; and lately I have recieved a counterpetition from other Indians: but neither coming through our agent, we have no proper means of knowing that they are genuine, or have been fairly obtained. they will be properly referred for enquiry.

I recieved at the same time a memorial & representation of the Western missionary society, addressed to the President & Congress, praying that half the reserve might be granted to the General assembly of the Presbyterian church in America. Congress alone being competent to determine on the merits of this paper & all persons having a right to address them immediately, I presumed they would have sent a copy to them. it is not proper for me to become the channel of individual applications to Congress: and as individuals we must consider them, the incorporation of religious societies in the states being out of the constitutional notice of the general government. should the society have sent no other copy of their memorial, you shall be furnished with the one sent to me, on application to the War–office, where it is deposited. Accept my salutations & respects.

Th: Jefferson

To Joseph Stanton, Jr.

Washington, March 28, 1806 [MoSHi]

Sir

I return you inclosed the papers solliciting a contribution for a meeting house. the number of applications to me from the different parts of the Union for contributing to the building of churches & Meeting houses is so great that no resources I can command could answer to them. I have therefore been obliged to prescribe to myself as a rule to contribute to those only in the district where I live, & the state in which my property lies. the rule, I think, is a reasonable one and it should be observed with all or none. I must therefore ask to be excused from departing from it in the case under your patronage. Accept my salutations & assurances of respect.

Th: Jefferson

To William W. Woodward

Washington, December 21, 1806 [MoSHi]

Sir

Your favour of the 18th. has come to hand, and three volumes of Scott's family bible had been before recieved at different times. it has been so usual for some person to apply here for the subscriptions for books by those who reside here, that I have not attended to the case of this particular one, nor do I know whether any one has ever called for the subscription. but presuming it has not been paid I now inclose you 20. D. as near the fractional sum for either the three or the four volumes as I can come in paper. I shall be glad to recieve the 4th. vol. when ready. with my thanks for the kind sentiments expressed in your letter, I pray you to accept my salutations & best wishes.

Th: Jefferson

To Revd. Andrew McCormick, Episcopal in Washington

Washington, November 6, 1807 [ViW]

Dear Sir,

On recurring to my books, I find I have been a very unpunctual debtor to you. I beg you to be assured that it has been merely owing to the want of my attention being called to it, a circumstance often rendered necessary by other occupations & always received with thankfulness. Inclosing you now a check on the bank for my arrearages, I take this occasion of testifying the pleasure with which I have received in attending the performance of the functions of your office whenever I have been able to attend and the satisfaction with which I have continued a member of your congregation from my first residence here till the removal of the church to it's present distance. This circumstance solely occasioning my discontinuance of attendance I cannot refuse myself the gratification of declaring to you the high estimation in which I hold your character & conduct, and the pleasure it will give me at all times to avail myself of occasions of manifesting it. I pray you to accept my friendly salutation & assurances of my high respect & esteem.

Th: Jefferson

To John Adams
Monticello, August 22, 1813 [DLC]
Dear Sir,

Since my letter of June the 27th, I am in your debt for many; all of which I have read with infinite delight. They open a wide field for reflection, and offer subjects enough to occupy the mind and the pen indefinitely. I must follow the good example you have set, and when I have not time to take up every subject, take up a single one.

Your approbation of my outline to [Unitarian Revd.] Dr. [Joseph] Priestley is a great gratification to me; and I very much suspect that if thinking men would have the courage to think for themselves, and to speak what they think, it would be found they do not differ in religious opinions as much as is supposed. I remember to have heard Dr. Priestley say, that if all England would candidly examine themselves, and confess, they would find that Unitarianism was really the religion of all; and I observe a bill is now depending in parliament for the relief of Anti-Trinitarians. It is too late in the day for men of sincerity to pretend they believe in the Platonic mysticisms that three are one, and one is three; and yet that the one is not three, and the three are not one; to divide mankind by a single letter into ομο _____ σιανς and ὀμοι _____ σιανς. But this constitutes the craft, the power and the profit of the priests. Sweep away their gossamer fabrics of factitious religion, and they would catch no more flies. We should all then, like the Quakers, live without an order of priests, moralize for ourselves, follow the oracle of conscience, and say nothing about what no man can understand, nor therefore believe; for I suppose belief to be the assent of the mind to an intelligible proposition.

It is with great pleasure I can inform you, that Priestley finished the comparative view of the doctrines of the philosophers of antiquity, and of Jesus, before his death; and that it was printed soon after.

[note: paragraph here not included due to insignificant content]

Very soon after my letter to Doctor Priestley, the subject being still in my mind I had leisure during an abstraction from business for a day or two, while on the road, to think a little more on it, and to sketch more fully than I had done to him, a syllabus [Comparative Merits of the Doctrines of Jesus to Others] of the matter which I thought should enter into the work. I wrote it to Doctor Rush, and there ended all my labor on the subject; himself and Doctor Priestley being the only two depositories of my secret.

[note: paragraph here not included due to insignificant content]

But I have read his *Corruptions of Christianity,* and *Early Opinions of Jesus,* over and over again; and I rest on them, and on Middleton's writings, especially his letters from Rome, and to Waterland, as the basis of my own faith. These writings have never been answered, nor can be answered by quoting historical proofs, as they have done. For these facts, therefore, I cling to their learning, so much superior to my own.

[note: paragraph here not included due to no religious content]

Th: Jefferson

To Revd. Charles Clay, Episcopal/Independent in Bedford, Virginia

Monticello, January 29, 1815 [DLC]

Dear Sir

Your letter of Dec. 20. Was 4. Weeks on it's way to me. I thank you for it; for altho founded on a misconception, it is evidence of that friendly concern for my peace and welfare which I have ever believed you to feel.

Of publishing a book on religion, my dear Sir, I never had an idea. I should as soon think of writing for the reformation of Bedlam, as of the world of religious sects. Of these there must be at least ten thousand, every individual of every one of which believes all are wrong but his own. To undertake to bring them all right, would be like undertaking, single handed, to fell the forests of America. Probably you have heard me say I had taken the four evangelists, had cut out from them every text they had recorded of the moral precepts of Jesus, and arranged them in a certain order, and altho' they appeared but as fragments, yet fragments of the most sublime edifice of morality which had ever been exhibited to man. This I have probably mentioned to you, because it is true; and the ideas of it's publication may have suggested itself as an inference of your own mind. I not only write nothing on religion, but rarely permit myself to speak on it, and never but in a reasonable society.

I have probably said more to you than to any other person, because we have had more hours of conversation in *duetto* in our meetings at the Forest. I abuse the priests, indeed, who have so much abused the pure and holy doctrines of their Master, and who have laid me under no obligations of reticence as to the tricks of their trade. The genuine system of Jesus, and the artificial structures they have erected, to make him the instruments of wealth, power, and preeminence to themselves, are as distinct things in my view as light and darkness; and while I have classed them with soothsayers and necromancers, I place Him among the greatest reformers of morals, and scourges of priest-craft that have ever existed. They felt Him as such, and never rested until they had silenced Him by death. But his heresies against Judaism prevailing in the long run, the priests have tacked about, and rebuilt upon them the temple which he destroyed, as splendid, as profitable, and as imposing as that.

Government, as well as religion, has furnished it's schisms, it's presecutions, and it's devices for fattening idleness on the earnings of the people. It has it's hierarchy of emperors, kings, princes and nobles, as that has of popes, cardinals, archbishops, bishops, and priests. In short, Cannibals are not to be found in the wilds of America only, but are reveling on the blood of every living people. Turning, then, from this loathsome combination of Church and State, and weeping over the follies of our fellow men who yield themselves the willing dupes and drudges of these Mountebanks, I consider reformation and redress as desperate, and abandon them to the Quixotism of more enthusiastic minds.

[note: paragraph here not included due to no religious content]

Th: Jefferson

To Revd. John Glendy, Presbyterian in Baltimore

Monticello, October 22, 1815 [DLC]

Dear Sir,

I was absent on a journey at the date of your favor of Sep. 28. And arrived here a day or two only before that on which you gave us to hope we might attend you [i.e., hear Glendy preach] at Charlottesville. I should have much regretted the want of time to give notice; but that my family assured me that your intentions had been known and notified generally, the change in the weather was a great disappointment; and the morning itself so threatening as to deter all distant persons from coming. I set out from home myself at 11. aclock in expectation momently of rain; but before I reached Charlottesville, it cleared away. You had left the place about an hour. About twelve aclock many came, all indeed who were near enough to get there in time after the weather cleared up. The loss of the pleasure of hearing you is the more regretted, as it can rarely if ever be expected to be renewed. Yet we will not despair of it. I hope you enjoy good health, and I know you have the happiness of being amidst the affections & respect of those around you, and of none more than of Your friend & servant,

Th: Jefferson

To Rev. John Brazer, Unitarian in Massachusetts
Poplar Forest, August 24, 1819 [DLC]
Sir

....among the values of classical learning I estimate the Luxury of reading the Greek & Roman authors in all the beauties of their originals,

....to the Moralist they are valuable, because they furnish ethical writings highly & justly esteemed: altho', in my own opinion the moderns are far advanced beyond them in this line of science, the Divine finds in the Greek language a translation of his primary code of more importance to him than the original, because better understood: and in the same language, the newer code, with the doctrines of the earliest fathers, who lived and wrote before the simple precepts of the founder of this most benign and pure of all systems of morality became frittered into subtleties & mysteries & hidden under jargons incomprehensible to the human mind. to these original sources he must now therefore return to recover the virgin purity of his religion....

Th: Jefferson

To John D. Wolf
Monticello, October 30, 1821 [MHi]

Th:J. returns his thanks to mr De Wolf for his excellent oration on the 4th of July sent him either by mr De Wolf or some friend who has not named himself, he is happy to see an example set of something solid substituted for the usual froth of that day. our citizens have much need of being reminded of the doctrines of this oration, for altho' we are entitled to religious freedom by law, we are denied it by public opinion fanaticism being in fact stronger than law. Th:J. is one of those who fondly believes in the improvability of the condition of man, and anxiously prays for it.

he salutes mr De Wolf with respect.

Th: Jefferson

To Revd. Frederick Hatch, Episcopal in Charlottesville

Monticello, December 8, 1821 [MHi]

Dear Sir,

In the antient Feudal times of our good old forefathers when the Seigneur married his daughter, or knighted his son, it was the usage for his vassals to give him a year's rent extra in the name of an *Aid*. I think it as reasonable when our Pastor builds a house, that each of his flock should give him an *Aid* of a year's contribution. I inclose mine as a tribute of Justice, which of itself indeed is nothing, but as an example, if followed, may become something. In any event be pleased to accept it as an offering of duty, & a testimony of my friendly attachment and high respect.

Th: Jefferson

To Richard Bruce

Monticello, February 19, 1823 [DLC]

Dear Sir

The use of my hand is so much impaired that I must be brief in acknoleging your favor of the 17th we have lived in times as remarkable as the history of the world has presented. we have had our full share in the events which have passed and have all acted with zeal in the posts assigned to us severally. as Providence intended that such events should take place, we should be thankful they were destined for our times and we chosen as instrunts for effecting them. I salute you with wishes for your better health, & a continuance of life as long as you think it worth enduring.

Th: Jefferson

To Revd. Frederick Hatch, Episcopal in Charlottesville

March 13, 1823 [DLC]

Dear Sir

I observe that a meeting of the inhabitants of Charlottesville is called on Saturday on the subject of our proposn. for [_____] a circulating library by annual subscription. I shall not be able to attend it but sollicit to become a member of the society on any scale they may chuse to adopt, great or small, as our stock will be small it should be confined to the purchase of books of general instruction, in the English language, excluding professional & sectarian books, that is to say those of Law Physics & divinity and excluding Novels also. this may be an instrn to the Commie who may be seen to act as the Exve of the society. accept my wishes for the success of the proposition and the assurance of my high esteem and respect.

Th:J

To Thomas Cooper
Monticello, April 12, 1823 [DLC]
Dear Sir

....I very much rejoiced at the report you sent me of the legislative commee so honorably acknoleging their obligns for your services. it holds up a hope that priestcraft has not in that body the baleful ascendancy it has else where. here their effort has been to represent ours as an anti-religious institution. we disarmed them of this calumny, however in our last report by inviting the different sects to establish their respective divinity schools on the margin of the grounds of the University, so that their students might attend it's schools & have the benefit of it's library, to be entirely independent of it at the same time, and no ways incorporated with it. one sect, I think, may do it, but another, disdaining equality, ambitioning nothing less than a soaring ascendancy, will despise our invitation. they are hostile to all educn of which they have not the direction, and foresee that this instn, by enlightening the minds of the people and encouraging them to appeal to their own common sense is to dispel the fanaticism on which their power is built...

Th:J.

To Revd. Benjamin H. Rice, Presbyterian in Albemarle
Monticello, August 10, 1823 [ViW]
Revd Sir,

The principle that every religious sect ought to maintain its own teachers & inst[itutions] is too reasonable & too well established in our country to need justification. I have been from my infancy a member of the Episcopalian church and to that I owe and make my contributions. Were I to go beyond that limit in favor of any other sectarian institution I should be equally bound to do so for every other and their number is beyond the faculties of any individual. I believe therefore that in this, as in every other case, every thing will be better conducted if left to those immediately interested. On these grounds I trust that your candor will excuse my returning the inclosed paper without my subscription, and that you will accept the assurance of my great personal esteem & respect.

Th: Jefferson

To Adamantios Coray
Monticello, October 31, 1823 [DLC]
Dear Sir

Your favor of July 10. is lately recieved. I recollect with pleasure the short opportunity of acquaintance with you afforded me in Paris by the kindness of mr Paradise….No people sympathise more feelingly than ours with the sufferings of your countrymen [i.e., Greeks], none offer more sincere and ardent prayers to heaven for their success: and nothing indeed but the fundamental principle of our government, never to entangle us with the broils of Europe, could restrain our generous youth from taking some part in this holy cause. possessing ourselves the combined blessings of liberty and order, we wish the same to other countries, and to none more than yours, which, the first of civilised nations, presented examples of what man should be. ....

I have stated that the constitutions of our several states vary more or less in some particulars. but there are certain principles in which all agree, and which all cherish as vitally essential to the protection of the life, liberty, property and safety of the citizen.

1. Freedom of religion, restricted only from acts of trespass on that of others.
2. Freedom of person, securing every one from imprisonment, or other bodily restraint, but by the laws of the land. this is effected by the well-known law of Habeas Corpus.
3. Trial by jury, the best of all safeguards for the person, the property and the fame of every individual.
4. the Exclusive right of legislation and taxation in the Representatives of the people.
5. Freedom of the Press, subject only to liability for personal injuries. this formidable Censor of the public functionaries, by arraigning them at the tribunal of public opinion, produces reform peaceably, which must otherwise be done by revolution. it is also the best instrument for enlightening the mind of men, and improving him as a rational, moral, and social being

....while we offer to heaven the warmest supplications for the restoration of your countrymen to the freedom and science of their ancestors, permit me to assure yourself of the cordial esteem and high respect which I bear and cherish towards yourself personally.

Th: Jefferson

To William Carver
Monticello, December 4, 1823 [MHi]

I thank you, Sir, for the inedited letter of Thos Paine which you have been so kind as to send me. I recognise in it the strong pen & dauntless mind of Common sense, which, among the numerous pamphlets written on the same occasion, so preeminently united us in our revolutionary opposition.

I return the two numbers of the periodical paper, as they appear to make part of a regular file. the language of these is too harsh, more calculated to irritate than to convince or persuade. a devoted friend myself to freedom of religious enquiry and opinion, I am pleased to see others exercise the right without reproach or censure; and I respect their conclusions, however different from my own. it is their own reason, not mine, nor that of any other, which has been given them by their Creator for the investigation of truth, and of the evidences even of those truths which are presented to us as revealed by himself. fanaticism, it is true, is not sparing of her invectives against those who refuse blindly to follow her dictates in abandonment of their own reason. For the use of this reason however every one is responsible to the God who has planted it in his breast, as a light for his guidance, and that, by which alone, he will be judged. yet why retort invectives? it is better always to set a good example than to follow a bad one....

Th: Jefferson

To P. B. Tindall
Monticello, April 20, 1824 [MHi]

Sir

I duly recieved your favor of the 13th and with it the pamphlet you were so kind as to send me. but your request to give my opin on it I must pray your permission to decline from this office I have universally excused myself. I have neither the time, the talents nor the taste to become a Reviewer of books. my inclinations lead me to a very different choice of Occupation. I have ceased also to subscribe for books yet to be published. At the age of 81. it would be an act of presumption to expect to live to see them. yet I should wish you to proceed in that which you propose, as I am pleased with every effort to restore the primitive and genuine doctrines of Jesus, and to overturn the corruptions which have been introduced solely to answer the worldly purposes of those who preach them. with these my excuses I pray you to accept the assurance of my esteem & respect

Th: J

To Revd. Federick Hatch, Episcopal in Charlottesville

November 11, 1824 Thursday [NYPL]

The weather having disappointed Th: Jefferson of the pleasure of mr Hatch's company on Tuesday he will be happy to recieve him to dinner to-day, or any day during Genl LaFayette's stay at Monticello which may suit the convenience of mr Hatch.

Th: J

To Revd. Benjamin Hale

Monticello, December 6, 1824 [DLC]

Th: Jefferson returns his thanks to the revd mr Hale for the pamphlets accompanying his kind letter of Nov. 19. and explaining the character of the Lyceum newly established at Gardiner very much weaned by age and debility from all attention to public things he still sees with pleasure every effort for the advcemt of science,_____ the applicn of it to the useful arts of life is especially desirable and has been too much neglected. with his best wishes for the prosperity of the Lyceum he prays mr Hale to accept the assurance of his respectful considn.

Th: J

Thoughts on Lotteries

ca. January 20, 1826 [DLC]

....Since then the permission to exercise the right has been taken into the hands of the legislre let us examine the purposes for which they have permitted it in practice. [Here Jefferson lists legitimate purposes for it and includes one...] ... for religious Congregns. [Then Jefferson lists 8 church buildings aided by lottery between 1785 and 1790 and later reiterates good reasons for lotteries including:] …to enable religious congregations to build or repair their churches, ….

….the leading and most important laws of that day [i.e. the Revolutionary Period] were prepared by myself and carried chiefly by my effort….The attack on the establishment of a dominant religion was first made by myself; it could be carried at first only by suspending salaries for one year by battling again at the next session for another year and so from year to year until the public mind was ripened for the bill for religious freedom which I had prepared for the revised code. This was at length established permanently by the efforts of mr Madison, being myself in Europe at the time that work was brought forward.

Th: J

Less Reliable Documents (Never Sent By Jefferson):

1801 [12-31], Sentence in a Letter to the Danbury Baptists
[After the words "separation of Church and state" Jefferson originally had this sentence:] Congress thus inhibited from acts respecting religion and the Executive authorised only to execute their acts, I have refrained from prescribing even occasional performances of devotion prescribed indeed legally where an Executive is the legal head of a national church, but subject here, as religious exercises only to the voluntary regulations and discipline of each respective sect.

1819 [10-31], Footnote in a Letter to William Short
[After the words "artificial systems" Jefferson put this footnote:] The immaculate conception of Jesus, his deification, the creation of the world by him, his miraculous powers, his resurrection and visible ascension, his corporeal presence in the Eucharist, the Trinity; original sin, atonement, regeneration, election, orders of Hierarchy, &c

---

1804, The Philosophy of Jesus of Nazareth extracted from the account of his life and doctrines as given by Matthew, Mark, Luke, and John; being an abridgment of the New Testament for the use of the Indians unembarrassed with matters of fact or faith beyond the level of their comprehensions. [Note: A few notable verses found in this digest are below:]

Luke 14:4, "And they held their peace. And he took *him*, and healed him, and let him go.

Matthew 10:8 And as ye go, preach, saying, The kingdom of heaven is at hand. Heal the sick, cleanse the lepers, raise the dead, cast out devils: freely ye have received, freely give.

Matthew 22:29-32 Jesus answered and said unto them, Ye do err, not knowing the scriptures, nor the power of God. For in the resurrection they neither marry, nor are given in marriage, but are as the angels of God in heaven. But as touching the resurrection of the dead, have ye not read that which was spoken unto you by God, saying, I am the God of Abraham, and the God of Isaac, and the God of Jacob? God is not the God of the dead, but of the living.

Matthew 25:31-34 When the Son of man shall come in his glory, and all the holy angels with him, then shall he sit upon the throne of his glory: And before him shall be gathered all nations: and he shall separate them one from another, as a shepherd divideth *his* sheep from the goats: And he shall set the sheep on his right hand, but the goats on the left. Then shall the King say unto them on his right hand, Come, ye blessed of my Father, inherit the kingdom prepared for you from the foundation of the world.

1819, The Life and Morals of Jesus of Nazareth Extracted Textually from the Gospels in Greek, Latin, French & English

[Note: Jefferson added about 1/3 more verses to the 1804 version. It is readily available in print today.]

APPENDIX 3

LIST OF CLERGY
TO WHOM JEFFERSON
SENT LETTERS OR GAVE MONEY

Jefferson wrote letters to about 100 Clergymen, churches or groups (about 150 if counting all clergy listed on some letters). He also made donations to about 50 more. These are listed below. Over 150 more clergy interacted with Jefferson either in personal meetings or in other ways and full commentary on all of these is found in Beliles' *Playful in the Closet: A Complete Religious History of Thomas Jefferson*. A link to it is found in the back of this book.

Period One, 1767-1787:
Letters Jefferson sent:
Anglicans: James Ogilvie, Samuel Henley, Peter Muhlenberg, James Madison, Robert Andrews
Presbyterians: Samuel S. Smith, John Todd,
Congregationalists: Ezra Stiles, Hugh Williamson

Catholics: Abbe Morellet, Abbe Gibelin, Abbe Gaubert, Abbe d'Arnal, Abbe Arnoux, Abbe Chalut
Independent Calvinist: Charles Clay (previously Anglican)
Unitarians: Richard Price

In this period he also donated to many of the above plus the additional ones below:
Anglicans: William Coutts, William Davis
Anglican parishes: Fredericksville, St. Anne's, Bruton, Henrico
Catholics: monk at Calais; Panthemont School; Mont Calvaire monastery
Liberty Hall Academy (Timber Ridge, Presbyterian, William Graham)
German church in Philadelphia
Independent Calvninistical church in Charlottesville
Other unknown church in Philadelphia
Yale college (Congregational)

Period Two, 1788-1802:

Letters Jefferson sent:
Catholics: Abbes Dugnani, Chauvier, Cice, Sieyes, John Carroll
Congregationalist: Joseph Willard, Joel Barlow, Abraham Baldwin, Isaac Story, Nathaniel Niles, Manasseh Cutler
Presbyterian: John Steele, William Linn, John Witherspoon, Samuel Miller, Stephen Balch, David Austin
Episcopal: Matthew Maury, William Smith, Jr., Needler Robinson, Samuel Magaw, Uzal Ogden, Mason Weems, Edward Gantt
Lutheran: Frederick Muhlenberg, Nicholas Collin
Moravian: John Heckewelder
Unitarian: Joseph Priestley
Baptist: Jeremiah Moore, James Garrard, Association of Delaware (Joseph Flood, John Boggs), Association of Cheshire, CT (John Leland, Darius Brown, Mason, Richardson, Waterman, Wells), Association of Danbury, CT (Nehemiah Dodge, Ephraim Robbins, Stephen Nelson)
Sandemanian: Joseph M. White
Swedenborgian: John Hargrove and New Jerusalem Church
Unknown: John Smith
Muslim: Mawlay Sulayman
In this period he also donated to many of the above plus the additional ones below:
Catholics: Foreign mendicant friars, John Debois, Rev. Lora

Fredericksville Episcopal parish
Maury's independent church and school in Charlottesville
Unknown "missionaries"
Chapel for David Austin (Lady Washington's chapel)
Unknown church in Albemarle
Rev. Eaden (or Eden)
Meeting house for blacks (Thomas Lucas, Methodist)
Baptist meeting house (William Parkinson)
Princeton College (Presbyterian)

Period Three: 1803-1812
Letters Jefferson sent:
Episcopal: James Wilmer, William Pryce, Andrew McCormick, George C. Jenner, John Bracken, Joseph Pilmore

Baptist: William Woods, James Lemen, Charles Polk, Robert Semple, James Fishback, William Plumer, William Rogers, William Staughton, William White, Albemarle Buckmountain Church

Baptist Associations of: Portsmouth, VA (Rev. Davis Biggs, John Foster), Chowan, NC (Rev. George Outlaw, Lemuel Burkitt), New Hope/Friends of Humanity, KY/OH (Rev. John Thomas, John Winn, David Barrow, and 28+), Appomattox, VA (Rev. Abner Warkins, Bernard Todd), Baltimore, MD (Rev. Obadiah Brown, John Welch), Ketocton, VA (Rev. William Tristoe, Thomas Buck, Jeremiah Moore), Chesterfield, VA (Rev. Robert Semple, +5)

Methodist: Henry Fry, John Magruder, William Martin, John Ravenscroft, William Colbert

Methodist Societies of: Pittsburg, PA (Robert McElhenny, John Wrenshall, Thomas Cooper) and New London, CT (Richard Douglas, Isaiah Bolles)

Catholic: Ursuline Nuns (Farjon, +10), Henri Gregoire, Abbe Salemankis, Pierre Paganel

Congregational: John Bacon Abiel Holmes, Thomas Allen, Thomas Birch

Unitarian: William Bentley

Universalist: Ralph Eddowes

Presbyterian: John Glendy, Samuel Knox, Robert Elliott, Charles Wingfield, Ashbel Green, James Gray, George Potts, Jacob Janeway

Swedenborgian: Hugh White

Society of Friends: Baltimore (Evan Thomas, George Ellicott, Gerard Hopkins)

Mennonite: Francis Adrian Van der Kemp

German Lutheran: J. Henry C. Helmuth
Independent: John Hey
Associate: Joseph Shaw
German Reformed: Samuel Helfenstein
Unknown: Donald Fraser

<u>In this period he also donated to many of the above plus the additional ones below:</u>
Presbyterian: building in Washington, church in Washington (Rev. Laurie's F. St. church), Washington Academy in Lexington, VA (George Baxter), Gideon Blackburn's Cherokee school
Methodist: church in Alexandria and church in Georgetown, and meetinghouse [place unknown]
Meeting house in Charlottesville area
Church in Louisiana for building
Thomas S. Cavender [Christian/Restorationist Unitarian]
Jacob Eyerman [Lutheran-Reformed]
Charles Coffin [Presbyterian Greeneville College]
Unknown Church in Washington
Baptist church in Alexandria
Academy in Washington [Rev. Elliot]
Rev. Osgood

Period Four, 1813-1819
<u>Letters Jefferson sent:</u>
Baptist: Burgess Allison, John Waldo, Egerton Leigh, David Leonard, David Barrow
Catholic: Jose Correa da Serra, Alexis Rochon, Ambrose Marechal
Episcopal: Rodolphus Dickinson
Lutheran: Henry Muhlenberg
Methodist: Miles King
Congregationalist: Amos J. Cook
Unitarian Benjamin Waterhouse, Noah Worcester, John Brazier, Thomas Parker
Presbyterian: Ezra S. Ely
Bible Society: Samuel Greenhow
<u>In this period he also donated to many of the above plus an additional unknown person</u>

Period Five, 1820-1826

Letters Jefferson sent:

Jewish: Jacob De la Motta

Unitarian: Jared Sparks, James Smith, Edward Everett

Universalist: Thomas Whittemore

Presbyterian: John H. Rice, Benjamin Rice, Francis Bowman

Episcopal: Frederick Hatch, Frederick Beasley (and Anglican: Samuel Parr)

Congregationalist: Jedidiah Morse, Benjamin Hale

Lutheran: Frederick C. Schaeffer

Catholic: William Matthews

Unknown: John Davis

Rational Brethren: William Ludlow & Church of God in Ohio

In this period he also donated to many of the above plus the additional ones below:

Hatch's house and school

Episcopal building in Charlottesville

Presbyterian building in Charlottesville

Baptist building in Charlottesville

Others: David Warden, Edward Tiffen, James Wallace, James Freeman, Jason Chamberlain

Below are others Jefferson interacted with in his life (although not sending letters or donations):

James Maury, William Douglass, James Fontaine, William Irvin, Devereaux Jarratt, Rev. Kohle, Miles Selden, Bishop William White, Dorothy Ripley, Thomas Claggett, John Sayrs, James Laurie, Lyell Green, John Hurt, David Kerr, Gabriel Richard, Lorenzo Dow, James Chambers, William Walters, Charles Crawford, William Hiter, William King, John Goss, Joseph P. Bertrum, other French abbesses & New Orleans nuns.

APPENDIX 4

A 1775 SERMON BY JEFFERSON'S PASTOR CHARLES CLAY

For the first time in print, we present in this book two of the sermons of Rev. Charles Clay. We have already shown how this minister was an evangelical who was ordained as an Anglican pastor. Then he led the new independent Calvinistical Reformed Church started and funded most by Jefferson. A life-long friend and neighbor, Jefferson said in 1815 that he had discussed religion with Clay more than any other human being. Here are two samples of the types of sermons Rev. Clay delivered, printed with permission of Virginia Historical Society. ( ) indicates a word that is unclear in the original.

God, The Adversary of the Sinner
Matthew 5:25,26

Agree with thine adversary quickly whiles thou art in the way with him, lest at any time the Adversary deliver thee to the Judge, and the Judge deliver thee to the Officer, and thou be cast into prison. Verily I say unto thee, thou shalt by no means come out thence till thou hast paid the utmost farthing.

The words which I have just rehearsed, are part of the most Divine Sermon, that ever was delivered. They were spoken by the Greatest preacher that ever appeared upon earth. They are the words of Our blessed Redeemer himself; which when rightly understood, he has elsewhere told us, and Spirit and ( ) life. God grant they may be Spirit and life both to you and me.

In this sermon he opens and explains the spirituality of the Law; assures us that a Just God will by no means accept of a partial obedience and that nothing short of a perfect obedience will be pleasing to a perfect God.

If we attend to the strictness and spirituality of the Law (as explained by Our Lord) we cannot but see how grossly we have violated it; and that no man living (the man Christ Jesus excepted) was ever able to perform it. For according to this explanation, the most High God requires truth in the inward parts. His law extends to our inmost parts and justly condemns the least irregularity of them. This being the case we cannot but own the necessity of our being cloathed with a better righteousness than our own if ever we would be partakers of the Kingdom of Heaven. To induce us to apply for this royal robe is Our Lord's design, in the words of the text. For after having proved us all guilty before God (which he did by giving us the Spiritual meaning of it, and proposing it with such rigor, and requiring an observance of it to such a degree of exactness, as I am sure no man ever arrived at.) I say having proved us all guilty before God of a violation of his law, he then advises us what we are to do in the words of the text, agree with thine Adversary quickly whiles thou art in the way with him, lest at any time the Adversary deliver thee to the Judge, and the Judge deliver thee to the Officer, and thou be cast into prison. Verily I say unto thee thou shalt by no means come out thence till thou hast paid the utmost farthing.

In discoursing further on which words, I propose (God willing) to observe the following method:

First, I shall endeavour to show you who is meant by the adversary here spoken of,
  "...*agree with thine adversary.*"
Secondly, in what manner, and at what time we are to agree with him, "*Agree...
  quickly whiles thou art in the way with him.*"
Three, Who is meant by the Judge, "...*lest at any time the Adversary...Judge.*"
Four, I shall inform you who the Officer is here spoken of, and the consequence of
  being given into his power, "...*and the Judge...Officer...prison. Verily I say...*"

And each of which I shall endeavour to apply as I go along. And may the good Spirit of God breathe into all our souls the true breath of life, and enable you to look up to him for a blessing while I endeavour, in the first place to show you who is meant by the Adversary here spoken of, "Agree with…Adversary."

Now this Adversary is the Almighty God. Every man by nature is an enemy to him. We read in Scripture that God is of purer eyes than to behold evil, that no evil dwills with him, and that without holiness no man shall see him. Now we are evil from the womb, God himself hath declared, that the thoughts of man's hearts are only evil continually. The sacred writings inform us, that we are all gone out of the way; that we are altogether become abominable; that there is none righteous, no not one. Consequently without agreeing with this Adversary we shall never enjoy his heavenly bliss. We brought this enmity to God into the world with us: for we are all by nature born in sin. Our natures are corrupted, and we have no power of ourselves to serve and please God. As the Scriptures assure us of this, our hearts (if we examine them) will convince us of it. We may have indeed some specious qualities in our dispositions, that may appear amiable in the eyes of men like ourselves, but in the sight of infinite Purity, we sink into nothing and are corrupt before him. Every one of us in this situation by nature, and nothing but an Almighty Arm can raise us out of it. The first man indeed was created in the image of God; but that image was defaced by his fall. In the day he ate of the forbidden fruit he died unto God; he died to the Divine life; he died to all Spiritual grace and power. This spiritual death he entailed upon his posterity. We partake of his evil nature and are dead to God.

We have no natural ability to turn to him. We are all by nature the children of wrath. We are dead in trespasses and sins. To what but original corruption can we possibly ascribe that coldness and inattention to Spiritual things, that aversion to God and goodness which every one of us must percieve to be more or less in all our hearts? Hence the diseased persons we read of in the Gospels are emblems of the Spiritual malodies of our souls. In the man that was born blind, we have an image of our spiritual blindness. By nature the eyes of our minds are ( ) against the light of the Gospel. The situation of such is represented by the ( ) that of men having their understanding darkened. The lepers full of spots and blemishes, was an exact picture of the leprosy of sin, with which our souls by nature are infected, and all our bodily defects are so many images of our depravity and corruption. Now against all this sinful corruption polution, the Almighty God is the declared Enemy. It cannot consist with the Purity of the divine essence to have any communion with persons in this state; and in this state is every man by nature, and if so every man, by nature

God in Jesus Christ is a consuming Fire. As we are enemies to God by our natural defilement, we have also made him our adversary by actual transgression. We have been ungrateful to this Our best benefactor; we provoke him every day; we have ( ) iniquity with greediness; We have rushed into sin; like the horse into the battle. The bold defiance of his law, the open breach of his commands, the contempt of his Gospel, the profaning his holy name, in short, the many acts of impiety, intemperance, laciviousness, and injustice, now prevailing, loudly proclaim this awful truth; and although some persons may have been preserved from enormous and grievous sins, yet we have all of us the seeds of them in our hearts; and nothing but the Divine interposition prevents their sprouting into action; a sense of this made an eminent Christian say (when he heard of a criminal who was carrying to execution for some flagrant act) there goes my wicked self. I have the same root of bitterness in my deceitful heart and it has been owing to the restraining grace of God alone, that I have been preserved from falling into the same sin. But in many things the best of us offend often; nor till our natures are renewed by the Spirit of God can it possibly be otherwise! While the fountain is defiled the streams that flow from it cannot be clear and untainted.

Some think that God is not their Adversary because they perform some outward ceremonies; but alas all outward duties, unless they proceed from an inward principle of love to God, are only so many glittering vices, which can never abide the test of Infinite Justice. Men may skin over the would sine has made in their soulls, by these outward duties but the blood of Jesus Christ alone applies by faith can effectually heal it.

Such as imagine God is not their Adversary because they pay a regard to certain moral duties, and perform some religious ceremonies, I would ask do you render an entire obedience to the law of God? The law of God is holy just and good; and he requires an exact conformity to it thought word and deed. A perfect God will have perfect service. This you must allow. The thing speaks for itself. If you have done this indeed God is not your adversary. You have no need for a Redeemer. But if you have differed ever so little from the path of God's commands (even in thought) your works will profit you nothing; and then every one of us are become guilty before God.

Thus the Apostle argues; I had not known sin but by the Law. Before his conversion he thought himself a very good man because he was strict in the observance of the outward part of it, and little thought he was a lost sinner. But when he saw the spiritual meaning of it the law, when he saw that nothing short of an universal obedience to it would be admitted by infinite Justice, he then saw that he had by no means performed it. He then knew that sine reigned in his members. Again he saith, when the commandments came, sin revived and I died. When I percieved how rigorous the commandment was, the consciousness of sin revived in my soul, and I found myself to be dead in trespasses and sins; and in ( ) spiritual deadness he must have remained, had not the Lord Jesus proclaimed a ( ) to his soul.

The substance of the first head is this - the eternal God is made our Adversary by original sin and active transgression. Every man by nature is at enmity with God. I would then ask every sould in this congregation (and may the eternal God enable you to answer aright) are you yet in your natural state or are you not? Have you felt the weight of sin, and are you sincerely desirous to be freed from it by the (blood?) of Jesus Christ? If so the Spirit of God is at work on your hearts. The lord is bringing you out of your natural darkness into his marvellous light. If not, if you have never yet seen the evil of sin, if you have never mourned ove the corruption of your hearts, but on the contrary are thoughtless of eternity, indifferent about salvation and unconverned about your souls, you are in a state of nature.

Nay though you may perform the outward duties of religion and appear very exemplary in the sight of men, yet if your hearts are unrenewed by the Spirit of God you are still in a state of nature; you are no better than painted sepulchers, awhich appear beautiful outward, but within are full of corruption and uncleanness. Your inward man is corrupted and defiled with sin, however specious your outward deportment may be. Hear this (you?) natural men and tremble; for whover you are the eternal God is your Adversary ( ). My brethren how powerful an enemy you have to deal with. No wealth can bribe no subtlety can deceive, no strenth can overcome him. Remember while you are at enmity with God, that all nature is at enmity with you. You are under the curse of God. Your wealth is often a curse, since it is too frequently the means of hardening you in your sins, and drawing you from God. And unless you are reconciled to him the sorest of his vengeance will light upon you. And if he should be pleased to make bare his arm upon this guilty land (as he has done on other countries) to whom, to whom, my brethren can you apply for shelter? What must be your grief! How great your horror of soul when you recollect that these judgments are the instruments of that Being whom you have wantonly made your foe? That they are sent to hurry you into the regions of despair? I fear too many of you my brethren however you may flatter yourselves I fear too many of you are in this dreadful situation, viz. in a state of enmity with the Lord of Hosts. Good God, how can you be easy! How can you enjoy one moment's peace while this tremendous being is unappeased? How can you venture to close your eyes to sleep when you know not but with the rich man, ou may open them in everlasting burnings? My dear unhappy man you are nder the curse of almighty God. And can you then be safe? Can you evade his anger? Can you resist omnipotence? O no! The nations of the world compared to him, are no more than a drop of the bucket. This may be an unpleasing truth, but truth it is; and unless your hearts are renewed by God's holy Spirit (if God be true) he is to you a consuming fire.

You would judge that sentinel to be deserving of the severest punishment who should neglect to give notice of the enemy's approach! The same fault should I be guilty of was I to neglect to tell you of your danger.

And what means so likely to cause you to humble yourselves as by convincing you of the danger you are in? What season so prosperous as the present, when we have all the reason in the world to expect some signal instances of the Divine displeasure? However all I can say is but a dead letter unless the Spirit of God be pleased to animate it, and to carry it home to your hearts. May he therefore open the eyes of your minds, athat you may see your danger. May he dispose your hearts to apply to the means of reconciliation with your almighty for, while I endeavor in the second place

to show in what manner and at what time we are to agree with him. "Agree with thine Adversary quickly whiles thou art in the way with him."

Now some think to agree with this adversary by the practice of morality; which however useful and amiable in its proper place; can by no means answer the end designed. For as I observed before as long as the heart is a polluted fountain, the streams that flow from it must necessarily be impure also. If we believe the Scriptures there is only one method of reconciliation with God. There is no other name under Heaven given among men - [but the] name of the Lord Jesus Christ. Repentance and faith in the Lord Jesus Christ are the means of the sinner's reconciliation with God. By bidding us agree with our adversary then, our Lord exhorts us to repent of our sins, and to believe in him. By nature we are sinful and polluted, and have made the eternal God our adversary.

And this is the method the Son of God observes in reconciling the sinner to the adversary - he first convinces him of sin, by the preaching of the word, or some other way that his infinite wisdom is pleased to direct. The sinner is by this means awakened from the lethargy in which he had been so long lulled; he sees his wretchedness, he mourns over his guilt and cries mightily to God for pardon and deliverance; the now sees his utter inability to help himself, and desires to rely on the merits of the Lord Jesus Christ alone. He is thus wounded in order that he may be healed. The same good Spirit that has awakened him to a sense of his danger enables him to see his help laid on one is who willing and mighty to save. He is led to the throne of Jesus where he finds rest and peace ( ) to his soul. He has the comfortable sense that his sins are pardoned witnessed to his soul by the Spirit of God. The Spirit itself beareth witness with his spirit that he is the child of God. You then who desire to be reconciled or to agree with your adversary have a way opened for you. You indeed have forfeited all little to the favor of God, by the violation of his law, but the blessed Jesus has made full satisfaction to his Father's wrath. He has obeyed the law of God in every the most miniscule particular; and by virtue of his perfect obedience, shall you be accepted. I now invite you to agree with your Adversary, by turning from sin and believing in the name of Jesus Christ; or rather beg of God to give you his Holy Spirit, that you may be made acquainted with your own hearts, and desire to be experimentally aquainted with the Lord Jesus Christ by faith. It is not enough that you look on him as a redeemer in general, unless you can know him to be indeed your Savior; that he died to expiate your sins, and to bring pardon and peace to your souls. But this is the gift of God, it is not in man to turn himself unto God. Implore then his Holy Spirit to lead you into all truth, [that] you may know what the will of the Lord is if you turn to God with your whole hearts, you shall be justified from all you sins by faith which is in him. His death shall be thy sacrifice Oh sinner, and his obedience shall be thy righteousness. Thou shalt be looked upon as perfect in Jesus Christ thy head. Believe on the Lord Jesus Christ and thou shalt be saved. If you ask how you shall be able to know when you have true saving faith in your Redeemer, I answer your faith is then genuine when it (enables you to see your sins pardoned, and is with all) a vital principal of holiness within you, reforming your life and teaching you to practice the duties of the Gospel. Defer not then Oh sinner! this important work. Set about it today; for the night cometh when no man can work.

And this leads us to examine at what time we are to agree with our adversary. "Agree with thine Adversary quickly; whiles thou art in the way with him."

There is no time to be lost; this moment you can ( ) call your own; let me exhort you therefore quickly to be reconciled to our offended God. Sinner whoever thou art (and by the term sinner I mean all those that have experienced nothing of the grace of God upon their hearts). Sinner, whoever thou art, the Almighty God is thy Adversary. Agree with him therefore quickly. Lose no time but embrace the opportunity whiles thou art in the way with him. Now thou art in the way with him, because thou art on this side eternity. Now is thy time to call upon him. Thou hast seen numbers fall beside thee, but as yet thou art spared. Remember a few days will put a period to thy life, and then thou art fixed forever. When once the curtain of life shall be dropped, then thy doom shall be unalterably fixed. Now mercy may be had. Now the Lord Jesus Christ waits to be gracious unto thee; he invites thee to be reconciled unto him here that thou mayest reign with him for ever. When you come to lie on your death bed, you will see the truth of what I am now advancing; but then perhaps it may be too late. Behold now is the accepted time, now is the day of salvation. Again thou art at present in the way with God in the course of his judgements; Thousands have fallen victims to his wrath, but thou art spared. But who knowest thou Oh man! but his judgments are hasting towards thee? And art thou ready supposing God should call upon thee by some alarming judgment? If thou art not, resolve to give no sleep to thine eyes, nor suffer the temples of thy head to take any rest till thou hast made a friend of this incensed God. I hope it is with this desire we are all assembled here this day! O wrestle with him then by prayer, entreat him to cast thy sins behind his back, and to wash thy polluted soul in the blood of Jesus.

Again thou art in the way with tine adversary Oh sinner, at this present time; thou art in the way with him in his word. The eternal Lord of Angels and men is now in the midst of this congregation; he now sees the inmost thoughts of every heart before him. He sees whether you have offered up your prayers unto him with sincerity or not. He sees whether you are only formal in your devotional duties, or whether your hearts are truly humbled. The Great God of Heaven and Eternity sees whether you are attending on this word with an humble desire for instruction and information, or whether you are secretly opposing and rejecting it. Be humbled then my brethren in the presence of that being, before whom the angels are not pure in his sight. This God is now inviting you by me to turn and live. The Lord Jesus Christ invites you by the worm that now addresses you to com to him that you may have life. The dying Jesus calls to you from his cross, not to make his wounds wider by your ingratitude and impiety. Thrust not thy unhallowed hands into his precious side. He has suffered enough already. Behold the purpole ( ) streaming from his side, but do not trample upon it, do not join the chief priests in deriding him, but be reconciled unto him. Pity thy agonizing bleeding God. Hear him calling unto you, is it nothing unto you all thee that pass by? Behold and see if there be any sorrow like unto my sorrow. Now this Savior waits to be gracious, he pities thee O Sinner; he feels more for thee than for himself he wants to embrace thee. Return then, whoever thou art that hast been ungrateful unto him. Serve his enemies no longer. I call thee in behalf of God; my blessed Master wants to cleanse thy polluted soul, and to cloathe thee with the robe of own righteousness. I have spoken to your ears; may the Lord Jesus Christ speak unto all your hearts; for unless you obey the call of mercy now, you must expect to hear the voice of judgment hereafter; for unless you agree with thine Adversary my brother, you will be assigned over to a just Judge.

And this brings me to show in the third place, who is meant by the Judge, "… lest at any time the Adversary deliver thee to the Judge."

This Judge is the Lord Jesus Christ himself. He is appointed to be the judge of quick and dead. God hath appointed a day in which he will judge the world by that man whom he hath ordained the man Christ Jesus. Before his tribunal we must all appear. The Father hath committed all judgment to the Son. the same Jesus who came into the world attended by a few poor fishermen will then appear with legions of angels and archangels and all the celestial hosts. He who had no where to lay his head, will then have the Kingdom of heaven at his disposal, to give to whomsoever he will. He who came meek and lowly into Jerusalem riding on an ass, will then apear in tremendous majesty riding on the clouds of Heaven. His crown of thorns will be exchanged for a crown of glory; and he will display all the majesty and fulness of the Godhead.

That Redeemer whom you now reject with scorn, will then Oh Sinner be thine angry judge. Be not therefore secure and easy; for although you may escape a temporal punishment; die you must. Die you must and appear at the judgement seat of heaven. Then every thought of thy heart will be disclosed: all the pains you have taken to hide your wickedness and deceit from man will then be too slender a covering. Offended Justice will then throw it open, and you shall be exposed and confounded before men and angels. Now you are invited to come to Jesus Christ. As a merciful Savior but if you will not hear; if you are still resolved to harden your heart, remember God will most assuredly bring thee into judgment. Thy Redeemer then may justly say, ungrateful wretch, what can you plead in excuse for thyself? Thou hast crucified me afresh. Thou has acted my sufferings over again; thou hast refused the offer of mercy; now thou hast nothing to expect but the fiery indignation of God; Now thou shalt find the wrath of an Almighty God not so trifling as thou hast thought it. Then will that same Jesus, who now pleads with his Father for mercy for returning sinners, then will he plead for justice to his adversaries. Then will he deliver them to a most cruel officer. This leads us

to consider, in the last place who the Officer is, what is here spoken of, and the consequence of being delivered into his power. "And the Judge deliver thee to the Officer, and thou be cast into prison, verily I say unto thee, thou shalt by no means come out thence till thou hast paid the uttermost farthing."

This officer is the devil the grand enemy of souls; with whom hardened and impenitent sinners shall be tormented for ever. He will be the minister of God's eternal vengeance. At the awful tribunal of Heaven all those whose name shall not be found written in the book of life, will then be delivered to this infernal Officer, who will cast them out into the prison of damnation and hell. Verily I say unto thee (saith Our Redeemer) thou shalt by no means come out thence till thou hast paid utmost farthing; i.e. never. The sinner shall never be freed from the torments of hell till he has satisfied the whole law of God in every particular which will be impossible. If it cannot be done here, hell is a very improper place to begin it. the torments of the damned in hell will last as long as eternity itself. Some people indeed will not believe the eternity of hell torments; but then they must not believe the Bible. If God be true hell torments will endure forever. Go ye accursed into everlasting fire, saith our Savior where the worm dieth not and the fire is not quenched. I allow it is the interst of many to disbelieve this truth; but they oughts to remember that the decrees of God are not to be altered as their fancies shall suggest. Men will not believe this, because they cannot reconcile it to themselves. I would ask them how they can reconcile any one of the attributes of God? They may remember that a God of all mercy is a God unjust. But supposing they may not be mistaken that the torments of the damned may have an end; act they not very absurdly in hazarding their souls upon this issue, because there is a bare possibility that their torments may have an end after an 1,000,000 years? Do not imagine my brethren that it is in your power to alter the decrees of God. He has denounced eternal torments against all impenitent sinners.

Let this then prevail with you to make the Lord Jesus Christ your Friend; for although you may escape here, yet if you die in your present state, eternal vengeance will be sure to overtake you. And if you would avoid the horid company of the damned in hell; if you would avoid the company of the devil and his angels; if you would not be blaspheming the name of Jesus with the internal crew; if you would not be banished the presence of God, and be tormented for ever in seas of liquid fire, come humbly to the Lord Jesus Christ and entreat him to be merciful unto you.

The sum of what has been said is this, the eternal God is an Adversary to every man in a state of nature; and every man that is not born again of the Spirit of God, is in a state of nature consequently in a state of enmity with God. To this Adversary it is every man's interest to be reconciled, as he would avoid eternal misery The only way to be thus reconciled, is to turn from sin, and be united to the Lord Jesus Christ by faith. This is the work of the Spirit of God whos assistance I would entreat you to implore. Let me beseech you to call on the Lord Jesus while he may yet be found. For ( ) upon if you refuse and rebel, and die without the knowledge of Jesus Christ in your hearts, nothing can save you from the damnation of hell at the day of judgment. God will not pity you, I will not spare you, hell and satan will have full dominion over you. This is what you must expect. Remember eternal misery is the consequence of refusing God's gracious call; and if that consideration will not move you nothing will.

My brethren your souls, your precious souls are at stake; you hang by a very slender thread over the bottomless pit. O call upon God while it is time; Harden not your hearts against him. Let what I have said have its due weight. Do not steel your breath against what I have offered. Do not refuse a blessing at my hands, but come to the Lord Jesus Christ and be at peace with him. Remember it is not I, but the Lord Jesus Christ himself that speaks, and says unto thee, agree with thine Adversary quickly whiles thou are in the way with him.

APPENDIX 5

A 1775 SERMON BY JEFFERSON'S PASTOR CHARLES CLAY

The Necessity of National Humility and Repentance[1]
James 4:9,10

Be afflicted and mourn, and weep, and let your laughter be turned to mourning and your joy to heaviness. Humble yourselves in the sight of the Lord and he shall lift you up.

This is the advice the Apostle gives those to whom he wrote this Epistle in order to deprecate the judgments of God that were hanging over their heads. As the cause of all signal and national punishments is the iniquity of mankind, we are advised to humble ourselves under a sense of that iniquity, that the anger of the Lord may

---

1   Title added. Clay simply began with the Scripture text. Two dates recorded by Clay on the cover of the sermon are 1775 and 1780, and the text of the sermon itself refers to the approaching lenten season which would indicate a late February delivery for one of those years (probably 1780). An earthquake is mentioned as a recent occurrence in the sermon. Jefferson records that this happened on February 21-22, 1774. See *Memorandum Books*, Vol. I, p. 369.

be turned away from us. He tells us in the first verse of this chapter that wars and fightings, as well as all other grievious calamities proceed from those lusts that war in our members, and it certainly follows, that if we would be freed from the effect we must remove the cause.

Therefore we are told in the text, that the only way to remove both the cause and effect is to humble ourselves before God, by way of repentance for the cause, and by way of deprecation of the effect. In consequence of this humiliation we shall be lifted up from that deplorable state into which we have fallen, and shall be exalted to the love and favor of God. This is the substance of the text "Be afflicted, and mourn and weep; and let your laughter be turned to mourning, and your joy into heaviness. Humble yourselves in the sight of the Lord and he shall lift you up". In my following discourse I purpose by divine assistance to show,

1st, the great reason we all have to humble ourselves before Almighty God; "be aflicted and mourn and weep".

2ly, where in this humiliation may be said to consist. "let your laughter be turned to mourning and your joy into heaviness".

3ly, the happy effects of this turning to God. "humble yourselves in the sight of God and he shall lift you up".

And may the good Spirit of God dispense his gracious influences to every one here present, and give you the hearing ear and the understanding heart, while I am endeavouring to show the great reason we all have thus to humble ourselves before Almighty God.

"Be afflicted and mourn and weep".

Under the first head that we may the more easily percieve the reason we have to repent and turn to the lord, we may consider ourselves as members of society, or as individuals. And first as members of society or parts of one whole, and as interested and connected in one frame or Body politic. If we survey the infidelity in principle and the dissoluteness in practice, of the people of this land, we cannot but own that we have abundant reason to implore the Divine mercy and forgiveness.

Our guilt as a people rises in proportion to the blessings we recieve at the hand of Heaven. That british America has been peculiarly favoured with the blessings of Providence is a real fact; the temperature of our climate, and the remarkable plenty which distinguish this and our neighbouring colonies in particular are too notorious to be denied, for we have always been able to export grain even in years of the greatest scarcity.[2]

---

2   This reference to "british America" and to "colonies" is here because of the first
     date on this sermon - 1775. It was before independence. However, it was probably

Add to all this that remarkable instance of God's goodness in indulging us with so great a plenty of the gospel of Christ. We enjoy the Christian Religion in its primitive purity, and can call upon our Redeemer in those ways we see laid down in his holy word. And this is another very eminent advantage we enjoy while many other nations are obliged to depend upon the traditions of men, while they are debared the use of the Scriptures, or at least have them put into their hands, mangled and defaced by their crafty designing teachers, it is our privilege and happiness to have free access to the fountain of knowledge, the lively oracles of God, which by the Grace of his Holy Spirit are able to make us wise unto salvation; while our persecuted brethren abroad are obliged to retire into holes and corners that they may have an opportunity of hearing the word of God and joining in religious worship, we are not only permitted the free use and exercise of religious duties but are invited to call upon God and attend upon his Holy worship.

What would the poor Protestants in France give for that liberty and indulgence which we are born to? Many of them you know at the peril of their own fortunes and lives have left their native country and friends, and came and settled in this colony, committed themselves to us their national enemies, and exposed themselves to the inhuman savages of the wilderness. You will readily understand that I mean the refugees who settled the Manikin Town.[3] Again while they are the slaves of tyrants and Dukes of arbitrary power, it is our happiness to breath the freer and a purer air in the more mild regions of liberty and plenty. Liberty is the inheritance of British subjects, and the government inculcated[?or instituted] to support, not to undermine and destroy it. Unless by our rebellion against God we should provoke him to strengthen the hands of our domestic enemies to liberty, and so increase the ill impression already made upon the mind of our gracious Sovereign, and in the hearts of our brethren and fellow subjects in Britain by malicious evil and designing men.[4] But humble yourselves in the sight of the Lord, and he will debase the enemies of your liberty and peace, and will lift you up, and give you a name among the nations.

---

after hostilities had commenced with Britain in April because of its reference in the first paragraph to "wars and fightings".

3 The history of the French Huguenots and their struggle for freedom in France was well-known to people of the Piedmont where many of their descendants had come to live. Jefferson's own tutor, Rev. James Maury, was born of Huguenot parents.

4 The acknowledgement of the authority of the King of England and reference to still being subjects of Britain again apply only to the 1775 delivery of this sermon. See also the closing prayer.

From all these and many more particulars that might be mentioned we may will conclude, that we are held under the strictest ties of gratitude to Almighty God (as a People) for the many spiritual privileges and temporal blessings he has showered down upon our heads. Let us now recollect what return we have made our wise and good[?] benefactor for these great and signal advantages which we enjoy.

And *first* with regard to the climate and the plenty of every necessary and even many luxuries our country produces. So far from being thankful for these gifts of Providence, that we are constantly murmuring and repining. The Commodities of our own country are despised and nothing but what is foreign will please. Our own manufactures and people concerned in them have been disregarded as useless and insignificant, while the most beggarly trash, provided it comes from a foreign land, has been eagerly purchased at any rate. And this erronious taste has been an effectual bar to people in setting up and improving the several different manufactures among us and has confined us solely to the culture of Tobacco in this colony to the destruction of our lands and has with all rendered us totally dependent upon other countries.[5] But as this is an evil of a political nature it does not come under my inspection. I only mention it and pass on to those general instances of ingratitude whereon it is more immediately my province to discover and enlarge.

What returns have we made to our Gracious God for that free use of his Holy word he has indulged us with? We have the lively oracles of God in our hands; many prophets and kings have desired to see the things which we see, and have not seen them. And to hear those things which ye hear and have not heard them. Now do we (I mean as a People) prize this inestimable jewel, these valuable records? Do we esteem this book of God as a pearl of Great Price? And do we implore the Spirit of God to remove the veil from our hearts that we may understand what we read? I fear that generally speaking we do not. To what but to a neglect of God's revealed will, and a contemplation of the offers of Grace which are daily made us, to what causes but these can we possibly ascribe that general infidelity, which is the characteristic of this age? The Word of God is treated by numbers with the greatest contempt.[6] That word of truth which, when understood is able to make men wise

---

5   This reference to the evil of Tobacco was uncommon among clergy of Virginia. It was undoubtedly unpopular, but so was much of what the Evangelicals would denounce.

6   This attack on infidelity and skepticism of the Bible is noteworthy in that Jefferson specifically praised Clay's ministry and paid to have him as his minister in a purely voluntary church in 1777.

to salvation, is looked upon by many as an old wife's fable. I am far from charging this up on the generality of mankind. No my brethren we hope better things of you and things that accompany salvation, but that it is a prevailing custom with many, is too plain to need a proof.

Fashion takes the lead in high life particularly our men of wit and spirit and scorn to be lied down to the same rules with the mean and vulgar. They must gratify every sensual appetite that rises in them; and they think it the most effectual method to remove the Bible (that bar to their pleasures) by pronouncing it spurious, ridiculous and the contrivance of priests. Thus they reject the word of God against themselves and go on indulging every filthy lust despising the commandments of Jehovah, and needing none of his reproofs. As this is the character of many so the practical part of it will suit too many of those who profess a mighty respect and veneration for the Scriptures; for among the numbers that join in professing those writings to be of Divine inspiration, how few are there that are really thankful for this precious gift, and shew that thankfulness by a diligent and constant use of them? The generality of you enhance your guilt by owning the Scriptures to be of Divine authority, when at the same time you pay no regard to the loud and solemn calls to repentance given you therein; when you despise that Redeemer of whom they treat, and count his blood where with alone you can be sanctified an unholy or common thing. We are as dissolute in our lives, as indulgent in our lusts, and as much keep under by their power, as if there was no restraint for them in the Bible. Wherefore my brethren it appears that you are practical infidels certainly for you are regardless of religion as if there were no Scriptures, as indifferent about their happiness, as if there was neither heaven nor Hell, and as hardened in sin as if there was no God. While our foreign Brethren mourn their loss of the fountain of all knowledge, we spurn it from us. And like disobedient Jews we loath the manna and are surfieted with it. We hew to ourselves broken cisterns; We have a fountain of living water to go to, and prefer the bread of falleness, of wickedness, debauchery, and impiety to that bread which came down from Heaven.

Again, are we truly thankful for the glorious privilege we and this nation enjoy? I mean the full and free use of our Religion? How do our suffering Brethren abroad long for the oppurtunities which we are so happy as to enjoy? How would they flock to hear the word of this life, and wait and hang upon the Preacher's lips, where as we are cold and indifferent, lifeless and inactive. Many of you are negligent in assembling yourselves together not withstanding you are expressly commanded to the contrary. For the Apostle Paul says in his Epistle to Hebrews: "Forsake not the assembling yourselves together as is the manner of some". And others when they repair to the temple of God, are so remiss, so unconcerned while there; sauntering out and in, as if their Salvation was a matter of indifference. Others again make a merit of their attendance, and of their weak performances; and a great part reject the merits of a crucified Savior with scorn.

This is but a faint sketch of the infidelity and profaness now prevailing. You will all I believe readily allow, that this age and nation are now wicked to a proverb. Infidelity has tainted the principles, vice and wickedness are become the practice of the generality of the people of this land. This then surely calls upon us to humble ourselves before God; Since practices of this nature will most assuredly draw down the divine vengence.

Nations and Kingdoms as such must be punished in this world, because hereafter all those relations and dependences, whereby one member of society is connected with the rest, will then cease, and be no more. Rewards or punishments will hereafter be dispensed to men, as individuals, according as they have embraced or rejected the Gospel of Jesus Christ, but all bodies or societies of men must be punished considered in a collective capacity in this world as this is necessary from the nature of things, so this has been the constant method of God's dealings with mankind. Whenever a people or nation have filled up the measure of their iniquity God fails not to vindicate his injured honor upon them, and to warn others by their example. These have been his dealings with the great empires and monarchies we read of in history; which are now no more.

This was the method he took with his own peculiar people of old, and this is what we of this land should expect and dread, unless we should repent and weep and mourn, and humble ourselves before the Lord who will then pardon our sins and iniquities and raise us up. From the tokens of God's wrath which were sent out against us last year (in the last four years) I need make no scruple to assert, that we have well nigh filled up the measure of our iniquities, and we have all the reason in the world to humble ourselves before God, in order to avert those heavy judgments our manifold sins have deserved. Especially when we recollect we have had warning given us, and that the judgments of the great and terrible God have been manifested among us. And the calamities that have happened to other sinful nations, call to us in more than the loudness of thunder, "Awake O sleeping land and call upon thy God, that thy whole people perish not!"

And this points out another advantage we enjoy, and another instance of our ingratitude. The advantage is God's mercifully sparing us hitherto notwithstanding our iniquities. Our sins have cried aloud for vengeance, but God has hitherto waited to be gracious.

He have, it is true, experienced some slight shocks of earthquakes but we have hitherto remained in safety, none of us have been swallowed up by them as others have been before us; the Lord has sent forth an untimely frost, and an unseasonable year whereby in a great measure the earth has denied us its fruits in its usual abundance, but yet by the mercy of God there was sufficient in the colony for its support, and not only so, but some for exportation, from hence our ingratitude is very evident since we are not (or at least do not show that we are) thankful for the goodness and further forbearance of God. How are we affected by the late earthquakes? Have they awakened any of us? Have they induced any of us to turn unto God? Or are we a whit the more serious than before? General observation confirms that we are not.[7] Those who may have called them judgments of God have been ridiculed. Natural causes have been sought out to account for them, but there can no better natural cause be given for them, than that great natural cause: sin and wickedness. Sin is the cause of earthquakes and therefore we of this land have great cause to tremble.

It is not yet a year since the late dreadful events and they are almost forgotten and out of mind. The Most High hath uttered his voice, yet none considereth it nor layeth it to heart. Some may think it quite foreign and ill timed to mention the Earthquake now, and say that I am on a barren subject, or only want to work upon your minds by insisting upon terrifying objects. Far from that My brethren, it is to put you in mind of the dealings of providence towards you in the course of the last year to convince you of your sinfulness as a people and that you might be afflicted and mourn and weep and humble yourselves before the Lord; for in the earthquake you were threatened, in the frost you felt a small chastening, and now my brethren finally the hand of arbitrary power is stretched out over you, which is more alarming than either of the others.

Let us therefore my Brethren, in the approaching season of lent, which is a time particularly set apart by the Church for Fasting and abstinence and acts of humiliation, humble ourselves before the Lord and confess our sins our iniquities and backslidings to him and say with David, let us now fall into the hand of the Lord, for his mercies are great and let us not fall into the hand of man and peradventure he may avert the impending danger and raise us up, and speak comfortably to us.[8]

---

7   Clay describes his congregation and perhaps the whole area as not being "awakened" at the moment. This perhaps was true around 1775, but Jarratt's description of the "Methodist phase" of the Great Awakening takes place in 1776 and 1777 in Virginia which probably included the Albemarle area.

8   This sermon being just before lent, must have been preached in late February. In the 1780 delivery of the sermon, it would have been preached in February

For not withstanding all our chastisements, few awakenings have been heard of among us in consequence of them. It would seem that we are quite hardened in sin, even to a degree of stupidity. Public diversions are frequented, and the worship of God almost slighted and neglected. And shall I not visit for these things saith the Lord? But as we are yet unmoved we have all the reason in the world to believe that our destruction lingereth not, but that some heavy punishment hangeth over our heads. In what way or manner God may be pleased to chastise this guilty land he only knows. (unintelligable) If we were not swallowed up by an earthquake, yet we may remember that the Lord's hand is not shortened; that he has various judgments whereby to execute his vengeance upon a guilty land. It is probable that We are now on the eve of (in) a bloody War![9] Who knows but we may fall by the sword, or be driven forth into the wilderness to perish among the wild beasts; or laying down our arms and liberties, submit to live as ignoble slaves, upon the nods and smiles of the arbitrary designing sycophants of a corrupt Court; or be delivered up into the hands of Popish enemies?[10] And in such a case the consequences are well known. However, in what manner soever the Lord shall be pleased to avenge himself upon us; some punishment we have reason to expect. Certainly then it will become us to humble ourselves before God, to confess our sins and provocations against him, and to implore his mercy for his dear Son's sake Jesus Christ our Lord.

As it is thus necessary for us to deprecate the divine displeasure (as a people) it is equally so as individuals. Every one of us, in our private capacity has abundant reason to humble himself before God; for besides those many tokens of God's displeasure against us which we have already experienced; there is one judgment seat where we must all appear, and unless we are reconciled to God by faith in Jesus Christ, while we live, nothing can save us from everlasting destruction. This is certain and therefore every soul here present that has never seen its corruption by nature, its enmity to God, and its state of pollution, and guilt; every soul that

---

but when preached in 1775 the Continental Congress was in session only in the summer and fall and the closing prayer refers to it. Perhaps this paragraph referring to lent only was used in the 1780 delivery. In Jefferson's *Memorandum Books* he records an earthquake occurred on February 21 and 22 in 1774. "The Church" refers here to the Anglican denomination as a whole.

9   In 1780, Clay inserts "in" where he preached earlier in 1775 that they were "on the eve of" war.

10   Corrupt Court refers to the Royal Court of King George III. This reference to the Pope probably stems from the fact that Britain had recently promised Canada they could enjoy their Roman Catholic faith unhindered, in order to keep them on the Crown's side.

is not brought home to God by the blood of Jesus Christ, is in danger of eternal destruction. And surely every one that is in danger of eternal misery, has abundant reason to humble himself before God, and implore his mercy.

I shall not enlarge further upon this subject now, but shall only observe at present, that the best of us must own ourselves to be vile and miserable sinners; that we are under the power of sin, and are held captives by our lusts and evil inclinations. And whoever thou art O man, whoever thou art O woman that art in thy natural state; who ever thou art that are not prepared if God should call thee this moment; humble thy self now before him, and beg of him to be reconciled unto thee for the sake of thy blessed Redeemer. Indeed thou hast abundant reason, for while thou art in a state of nature, thou art in a state of enmity against God; and how dreadful must his situation be who has the eternal Jehovah for his foe.[11] I hope my brethren that by this time you are all convinced what abundant reason you all have to humble yourselves before God; "Be afflicted and mourn and weep".

I shall now endeavour to show wherein this humiliation consists:

"Let your laughter be turned into heaviness, and your joy into mourning"

Now this humiliation consists in a real and unfeigned sorrow for our sins and offences, and in earnest prayer and supplication to God for mercy; if we are really convinced of our misery by nature, if we are really sensible how grossly we have offended our holy God by actual transgression, we shall be afflicted for so doing; we shall mourn over our unhappy state, we shall weep before him and entreat his forgiveness. This humility consists in real self abasement, in being divested of every proud thought, of every arrogant conceit of ourselves. In laying low before the throne of God owning our vileness, acknowledging ourselves to be less than the least of all his mercies. If we are truly humbled, we shall not rest till peace is spoken to us from God. We shall be alarmed at our danger, and groan earnestly for deliverance. Our laughter will be turned into mourning; all that profane wit and ridicule of holy things we before allowed ourselves in, will now cut us to the heart. And we shall mourn over our ingratitude and rebellion to our blessed Redeemer; all that mirth and gaity we before delighted in, will now appear flat and insiped; none but the (crucified Jesus?) can now speak comfort unto us, and the language of

---

11   Clay again reveals a Lockean mindset. The use here refers to sinful man in rebellion
       to God instead of an Enlightenment view that man is good. This kind of reasoning
       goes back to Scripture and long-standing Christian legal reasoning even before the
       Enlightenment.

our souls will be: *none but Jesus Christ to me be given, none but Jesus Christ in earth and heaven.*[12]

The fast of lent which is of ancient date, was instituted in or near the Apostolic Age; and was set apart by the Church as a proper season for mortification, and the exercise of self denial to humble and afflict ourselves for our sins by frequent fastings, and to punish our too often abuse of God's creatures by abstinence, to form and settle firm purposes of holy obedience, to pray frequently to God both in private and public for pardon, and his Holy Spirit. To put us in mind of that sore temptation and trial which Jesus Christ then endured for our sakes; particularly to perpetuate the memory of our Savior's sufferings, and to make as it were a public confession or belief, that he died for our salvation, and consequently for fitting ourselves to recieve in the Holy Sacraments, the tokens and pledges of his love with greater joy and gladness; because with fuller assurance that God is reconciled to us through the death and passion and Jesus Christ.

And the fast which the Lord will choose is a real sorrow of the heart, expressing itself in the outward acts of mortification and self denial and indeed, that soul that is in anguish for sin, will of course mortify the body, and bring it into subjection. Again true sorrow for sin will be attended with a desire, at least to forsake it, if we fall it will be really grievous and a matter of affliction to us. It is not outward form and ceremony; it is not praying with our lips will reconcile us to God, unless our hearts accompany our tongues, and cry for mercy. You will then do well to remember that your joining in the outward form of fasting as well as any other ordinance, and making a mere shew of humility will only increase your guilt, unless ye desire your hearts should be afflicted. Beg of God to prepare you to humble yourselves before him, by setting home the Law on your consciences, by convincing you of your sinfulness and danger, and by giving you a true humility of sorow of heart. Then shall ye cry and the Lord shall answer. Then shall ye call unto him, and he will say, "Behold, here am I".

And this brings us into the last place to consider, the happy effects of thus turning unto God.

"Humble yourselves in the sight of the Lord and he shall lift you up".

---

12   The style of the writing in the handwritten sermon seems to indicate that this was the end of the original sermon of 1775 except for the prayer. The remaining text following this paragraph is an apparent addition to the original sermon made for the 1780 version which was given probably in the Calvinistical Reformed Church of which then Governor Thomas Jefferson was a member.

Humility is the gate of honor. Whosoever humbleth himself shall be exalted. He that is convinced of his own weakness and inability, and cries to the Lord Jehovah for mercy, shall certainly find acceptance. He is thus wounded in order to healed. The Lord delighteth to help and save the humble soul, and to relieve those that are of a contrite heart. Those that are humbled under a sense of sin, the Lord will lift up to grace here, and glory hereafter. Beg of God my brethren to give you a true and hearty repentance. Beseech him to prepare your hearts, I can promise you in my Master's name, that if you are really afflicted, and call upon him from the bottom of your hearts, ye shall find rest and peace to your souls. Beseech him at the same time to enlarge your hearts and affections, that ye may remember your countrymen and brethren as well as yourselves and beg of him to be merciful, and spare this guilty land. I invite you in the name of God to humble yourselves. Be afflicted and mourn and weep, and the Lord graciously grant your requests, to whom with the Son and Holy Spirit be ascribed all glory. Finis.

[Prayer]: Most gracious God we humbly beseech thee that these Colonies may ever by under the care and protection of a kind Providence, and be prospered in all their interests both spiritual and temporal;[13] and that the Divine blessing may descend and rest upon all our rulers, and upon the Representatives of the People in their several Assemblies and Convention now or here after to be assembled; especially on the general Congress now convened by divine permission at Philadelphia,[14] that thou wouldst be pleased to direct and prosper all their consultations for the advancement of thy Glory, the good of the Church, the safety honour and welfare of our gracious Sovereign; and that they may be directed to wise and effectual measures for preserving the union and securing the just rights and privileges of the Colonies; the America may be redressed of her many grievances with the restoration of her invaded rights, and a reconciliation with the Parent State, on terms constitutional and honourable to both, and that her civil and religious privileges may be secured to the latest posterity; That (So…) peace and happiness, truth and justice, religion and piety, may be established among us for all generations. These and all other necessaries for them, for us, and thy whole Church we humbly beg in the name and mediation of Jesus Christ Our most blessed Lord and Saviour.

---

13   This prayer was made in the 1775 pre-independence sermon only. Note that not only are they still "colonies" but the reference to a "Sovereign" a few lines later, and the desire for "union" with the "parent state."

14   The Continental Congress was deliberating in both the summer and fall of 1775.

APPENDIX 6

CHRISTIAN ANSWERS TO JEFFERSON'S OBJECTIONS TO THE NEW TESTAMENT

In the last couple decades of his life Thomas Jefferson held the notion that the Bible he had in his day was not trustworthy. At the beginning of the 21st century, after thousands of copies of manuscripts of the New Testament have been found and translated since Jefferson's day, after archaeology has confirmed major portions of the Bible, we are in a much stronger position to assess the reliability of the Scriptures than he was. The writers that he believed credible in their skepticism were proved in fact to be wrong.

We have already seen how Jefferson appears to have bought into the Unitarian notion articulated in Rev. Joseph Priestley's book, *The Corruptions of Christianity.* The essence of this idea is that the original revelation of Jesus was correct. But early on the message was corrupted. Very early on.

The alleged corruption—according to this theory—was so early that it's hard to see how anyone could trust any parts of the Bible. Priestley's book helped promote the idea that the canon of the Bible (the New Testament in particular) was flawed. It isn't necessarily that the canon was flawed, but those portions of the New

Testament essentially involving miracles. (But even in that point, Priestley is not consistent, because he embraces the miracle of miracles—the resurrection of Jesus Christ from the dead.[1] This seems to defy logic. If you believe in the resurrection, then wouldn't other smaller miracles be easier to accept?)

The Canon of the New Testament

The canon refers to the choice of the books that comprise the New Testament. All major Christian groups accept the 27 books, from Matthew to Revelation. However, the Unitarians of Jefferson's day placed themselves out of the mainstream of historic Christian thought and belief. (That is even more true today with Unitarians—who have completely cut themselves off from any biblical standards.)

We believe that God inspired certain books that were written by men in a special way as to actually be a part of His Word. These inspired writings are known as the Scriptures. As Paul says in 2 Timothy 3:16: "All Scripture is God-breathed and is useful for teaching, rebuking, correcting and training in righteousness." The Greek word for "measuring rod" is canon. The canon of the Bible refers to the list of those books recognized as being divinely inspired. The canon of the New Testament specifically refers to 27 books, recognized by Orthodox, Catholic, and Protestant Christian groups, as the Word of God—from Matthew through Revelation.

The process of determining what was canonical and what was not took centuries. However, the bulk of the New Testament was recognized early on as being authoritative. The writing had to be by an apostle or by someone associated with an apostle. The great Church Father Tertullian, writing about AD 200, sheds light on what was accepted and what was not: "We Christians are forbidden to introduce anything on our own authority, or to choose what someone else introduces on his own authority. Our authorities are the Lord's apostles, and they in their turn choose to introduce nothing on their own authority. They faithfully passed on to the nations the teaching which they had received from Christ."[2]

Matthew, Mark, Luke, and John, and the book of Acts were recognized early on as Scripture, as were the writings of Paul. There was a functional "canon" of the New Testament as early as about 100 AD, which consisted of these Gospels and Paul's writings, James' letter, 1 Peter, and 1 John. About 80% of the New Testament was already part of what we could call a de facto canon.

---

1   Ira V. Brown, ed., *JOSEPH PRIESTLEY: Selections from His Writings* (University Park, PA: The Pennsylvania State University, 1962), 281-282.

2   John R. W. Stott, *The Authority of the Bible* (Downers Grove, Ill: IVP, 1974), 27.

Dr. Paul L. Maier said this on the canon: "The four Gospels were universally recognized from the start, the book of Acts (the earliest church history by Luke), the whole Pauline corpus (that is the body of all those letters that Saint Paul wrote and comprise almost half of our New Testament), the letter of James, and the letter of Peter (the first letter of Peter) and that is the core of the canon. The other writings were one by one coming in a little bit late."[3]

The first complete canonical list of all 27 books of the New Testament appeared in 367 A.D. in the Festal letter of Athanasius of Alexandria. At that time, there was no correct order for the arrangement of the New Testament books. The order we have today was borrowed from the Latin Vulgate, the official publication of the Roman Catholic Church.

The late Dr. F. F. Bruce, a first-rate New Testament scholar and author of the book, *The New Testament Documents: Are They Reliable?*, underscored the point that the canon was more *discovered* to be divine than merely *decreed* as such:

> One thing must be emphatically stated. The New Testament books did not become authoritative for the Church because they were formally included in a canonical list; on the contrary, the Church included them in her canon because she already regarded them as divinely inspired, recognizing their innate worth and generally apostolic authority, direct or indirectly. The first ecclesiastical councils to classify the canonical books were both held in North Africa—at Hippo Regius in 393 and at Carthage in 397—but what these councils did was not to impose something new upon the Christian communities but to codify what was already the general practice of these communities.[4]

This is reminiscent of the doctrine of the Trinity. Christian worship and belief from the beginning was in the triune God—Father, Son, and Holy Spirit. Although the word "trinity" is not in the Bible, it was part of the theology of the early Christians from the start of the Church. Not until the 4th century were the theological specifics nailed down. Again, belief in the Trinity was present from the start of the Church.

---

3   Transcript of an interview with Dr. Paul L. Maier by Jerry Newcombe on location in Sarasota, Florida (Ft. Lauderdale: Truth in Action Ministries-TV, 2013).

4   F. F. Bruce, *The New Testament Documents: Are They Reliable?* (Downers Grove, Ill.: IVP, 1943, 1974), 27.

When Were The Gospels Written?

A credible case can be made that the Gospels were not written "long after" the events described therein. This is an important issue because it bears directly on the New Testament's reliability. If liberal Bible scholarship was bad in Jefferson's day, perhaps it is worse in our day—even though we have "an embarrassment of riches" when it comes to ancient manuscripts.

Were all the Gospel writers "unlettered" men? That would be quite surprising to authors such as Matthew, Mark, Luke, and John. For example, here is what author Dr. Erwin Lutzer says about Dr. Luke:

> Luke tells us in the first chapter what his methodology was. He says, you know, many others have made careful investigation as to what has happened, but he says that I am investigating this, and he was in a position to be able to talk to people. There may have been other documents in existence that he used, but he carefully outlined his views of history and how history should be done. And he was very specific regarding the fact that what he was writing was credible and had witnesses that could be checked out.[5]

Dr. Paul L. Maier, professor of ancient history at Western Michigan University, is a first rate scholar. He can't seem to say enough positive things about the accuracy of Luke (and Acts, written by Luke):

> Unlike Matthew who wants to address a Hebrew audience, a Jewish audience, Luke wants to address a Gentile audience. And this is the reason why he's always throwing out anchors into the mainstream of Greco-Roman history to show how these things compare with the outside evidence for the ancient world. In a sense, I've been trying to copy Luke's method of comparing sacred with secular; the internal with the external. And he give us a wonderful account, it's very reliable. We can see how absolutely accurate Luke is, for example, when we take the book of Acts and trace Saint Paul's journeys; and really the second half of the book of Acts you might call the Gospel of Saint Paul, written by Luke, because he's a travel companion of Paul. He's an eyewitness of many of the details; and you can use the book of Acts as a travel guide to this day yet when you visit

---

5   Transcript of an interview with Dr. Erwin Lutzer by Jerry Newcombe on location in Dallas (Ft. Lauderdale: Coral Ridge Ministries-TV, 2004).

Turkey or Greece or Rome, and you find that Luke is absolutely deadly accurate. Every last place name that Luke mentions is authentic; some of the places have been excavated archeologically, he doesn't make any errors in terms of getting the cities out of line—they're absolutely in line.[6]

In the nineteenth century, Sir William Ramsay, a skeptical scholar who is regarded, Christian apologist Josh McDowell observes, "as one of the greatest archaeologists ever to have lived,"[7] doubted the historical reliability of Luke in his later work, the book of Acts. But Ramsay came to see that Luke was right after all. As Ramsay traveled to Asia Minor, following Luke's time and place descriptions in the book of Acts, he notes: "It was gradually borne upon me that in various details the narrative showed marvelous truth. In fact, beginning with a fixed idea that the work [Acts] was essentially a second century composition, and never relying on its evidence as trustworthy for first century conditions, I gradually came to find it a useful ally in some obscure and difficult investigations."[8] Ramsay came to see that Luke was very reliable after all.

In the first half of the 19th century, Simon Greenleaf, a life-long Episcopalian, taught at Harvard Law School. He helped expand the school and wrote a treatise on the laws of evidence that was important in the courts of America for the rest of the century. In 1847, he wrote a book on the four Gospel writers as if they were put on trial—*The Testimony of the Evangelists: The Gospel Examined by the Rules of Evidence*. He found them absolutely reliable guides. For example, he writes of the third Gospel writer: "If, therefore, Luke's Gospel were to be regarded only as the work of a contemporary historian, it would be entitled to our confidence. But it is more than this. It is the result of careful science, intelligence and education, concerning subjects which he was perfectly competent to peculiarly skilled, they being cases of the cure of maladies."[9]

So it would seem that Jefferson is wrong when he talks about "unlettered" men writing about Jesus, at least with respect to Luke. Matthew and John were direct eyewitness of Jesus, and Mark's Gospel relies heavily on Peter's memory. Again, we

---

6   Transcript of interview with Dr. Paul Maier.

7   Josh McDowell, *The New Evidence That Demands a Verdict* (Nashville: Thomas Nelson Publishers, 1999), 62.

8   William Ramsay, *St. Paul, the Traveler and Roman Citizen* (London: Angus Hudson, Ltd., 2001, edited reprint from 15th edition published by Hodder and Stoughton, London, 1925), 19. Quoted in McDowell, *The New Evidence That Demands a Verdict*, 62.

9   Simon Greenleaf, *The Testimony of the Evangelists: The Gospels Examined by the Rules of Evidence* (Grand Rapids: Kregel Classics, 1995), 25-26.

are at a better vantage point to see these things because of more than a hundred years of archaeology and manuscript discoveries. That was obviously not true in Jefferson's time. Nonetheless, there was plenty of evidence favoring the reliability of the New Testament even in Jefferson's day.

Greenleaf notes this about Matthew, the former tax-collector, as well as Luke the doctor: "Matthew was trained, by his calling, to habits of severe investigation and suspicious scrutiny; Luke's profession demanded an exactness of observation equally close and searching. The other two evangelists, it has been well remarked, were as much too unlearned to forge the story of their master's life, as these were too learned and acute to be deceived by any imposture."[10] Greenleaf wrote these words about twenty years after Jefferson's death.

"An Embarrassment of Riches"

Jefferson (and Priestley) seems to have held the view that major portions of the New Testament were corrupt.[11] But scholars have since learned from the manuscript evidence that that is not the case. Dr. D. A. Carson, professor at Trinity Evangelical Divinity School north of Chicago, notes: "Almost all text critics will acknowledge that 96—even 97 percent—of the text of the Greek New Testament is morally certain; it's just not in dispute."[12] The 3-4 percent "in dispute" cast no doubt on the major doctrines of the faith, all of which are established by multiple verses in the New Testament. Most of the 3-4 percent "in dispute" is minor word or spelling discrepancies or word order rearrangements (which doesn't change the meaning in Greek). That 96-97 percent text certainty is an extremely high number for any book of antiquity. The only thing coming close would be the Old Testament.

In a sense Jefferson (and Priestley) was rating the New Testament as having a much higher percentage rate of corrupt material. He was wrong. There is no textual base by which to come to this conclusion. Again, we are in a much stronger position to see that than he was.

---

10   Ibid., 24.

11   Of course there are errors in copies over the years but as Dr. Timothy Paul Jones of Southern Baptist Theological Seminary says: "The Scriptures are inerrant in their inspiration, they are sufficient in their preservation...[but] it seems that [some people demand] for God somehow, not only to have dictated the Scriptures, but then to have overseen the copying, such that copying was perfect, generation after generation after generation." Transcript of a television interview of Timothy Paul Jones by Jerry Newcombe (Ft. Lauderdale: Coral Ridge Ministries, 2008).

12   D. A. Carson, quoted in D. James Kennedy with Jerry Newcombe, *Who Is This Jesus: Is He Risen?* (Ft. Lauderdale: Coral Ridge Ministries, 2002), 74.

Furthermore, there are more than 5,000 whole or partial copies of the Greek New Testament. Scholars translate our modern English Bibles from these Greek New Testament texts. There are also thousands of early manuscript copies in other languages, such as Latin, Syriac, Coptic, Armenian, and so on, that are all based on the original Greek manuscripts. Because of the sheer number of the ancient manuscripts, the New Testament is unequaled among the writings of antiquity. This puts the New Testament in a completely different category than other writings of the ancient world.

We don't have the original manuscripts because they were originally written on materials that eventually disintegrated. When a document was believed to be inspired, for example, an epistle of Paul's, monks would copy it down. The copies we have are copies of copies. But we have enough of them to verify that they are good copies. When some modern critics sneer at the idea that the originals disintegrated, we should remember that many of the original prints of silent movies, less than a hundred years old, have already started to disintegrate. We must not let our modern technology allow us to sit in judgment on those who lived in bygone eras.

The late Dr. Bruce Metzger, long time professor at Princeton Theological Seminary and a top-notch Bible scholar, said, "The very fact that there are so many [manuscript] copies still available from ancient times means that the degree of reliability of what has been transmitted to us in the New Testament is at a high level."[13]

Dr. Sam Lamerson of Knox Theological Seminary observes, "It seems to me that if you throw out the reliability of the New Testament documents, one must become an historical agnostic. If you're not going to accept that as basically historically reliable, you cannot accept any writings as historically reliable, because we do not have of them the same amount of backing that we do for the New Testament."[14]

British scholar N. T. Wright notes that the New Testament is in a league of its own among ancient books, including the Gnostic gospels, from antiquity: "The New Testament is simply on a different scale entirely in terms of the depth and range of the manuscript evidence."[15]

---

13   Bruce Metzger, quoted in D. James Kennedy, *Who Is This Jesus* (Ft. Lauderdale: Coral Ridge Ministries-TV, 2000), a video.

14   Sam Lamerson, quoted in Kennedy, *Who Is This Jesus*, a video.

15   N. T. Wright, quoted in Kennedy, *Who Is This Jesus*, a video.

The Best Attested Book of Antiquity

Dr. Dana Harris of Trinity Evangelical Divinity School says, "Beyond the shadow of a doubt, the New Testament is better attested than any other manuscript coming out of antiquity. There is no reason to doubt the reliability of the Gospels, I would say even more strongly. The burden of proof is on those who say without basis that the Gospels are unreliable."[16]

Despite all the evidence we have available today, there's a terrible injustice that's being done to *the* best attested book of antiquity, the New Testament. If the same principles of scrutiny were applied to the writings of Cicero, Caesar, and Marcus Aurelius, we would reject virtually all of them as hopelessly unreliable.

The critical thing to understand is that the New Testament is not viewed as unreliable because of some factual data, but rather unproven assumptions. Namely, that it was allegedly written later than it likely was and that miracles are not possible; therefore, since the book (or 27 books) contains an abundance of miracles, it cannot be accurate. Again, these charges are unproven assumptions—not actual facts or manuscript or archaeological evidence.

In reality, the accusers—for example, liberal Bible scholars who teach at major universities and appear on network television specials—begin with the premise that miracles are not possible. Based on that unproven construct, they then theorize to debunk major portions of the New Testament. By the way, there are many well-qualified conservative Bible scholars and historians who don't buy these theories. They know the same facts, but they come to different conclusions than the liberals because they don't reject the supernatural *a priori* before they study the facts.

Much of the conflict centers around *when* the New Testament was written. Most of the liberal scholars assert as *fact* that the Gospels we have in the Bible were written so late that they do not reflect personal memory. We saw earlier Jefferson's assumption that these sources were written late.

Very liberal scholars reject the idea that the Gospels retain personal memory because they assume they were written a long time after the events they describe. For example, Dr. Helmut Koester of Harvard holds this position. He said: "None of the Gospels is written before the year 70; that is forty years after the death of Jesus. All the disciples were most likely dead at that time. So it's not personal memory that goes from Jesus' preaching and ministry to the Gospels."[17]

---

16   Transcript of an interview with Dr. Dana Harris by Jerry Newcombe on location in Deerfield, IL (Ft. Lauderdale: Truth in Action Ministries, 2013).

17   Dr. Helmut Koester, in D. James Kennedy with Jerry Newcombe, *Who Is This Jesus: Is He Risen?* (Ft. Lauderdale: Coral Ridge Ministries, 2002), 60.

Why do these liberal scholars, like Dr. Koester, hold this theory? Because the fall of Jerusalem was predicted so accurately in the first three Gospels by Jesus that these liberal scholars assume these documents had to have been written after that event in A.D. 70, which is 40 years removed from the time of Jesus, in their opinion. By then, many of the disciples would have already died.

But wait. What if there is a God (the New Testament surely assumes there is), and what if that God and His Son, Jesus Christ (clearly the central figure of the New Testament), could do miracles and did know the future? Then Jesus could perform the miracle of predicting what would happen in the future, i.e., the fall of Jerusalem and the destruction of the temple. Predictions so stunningly accurate that to the modern miracle-denying Bible scholar, these writings *had to have been written after* A.D. 70. (See Matthew 24, Mark 13, and Luke 21.)

The first great historian of the Christian Church was Eusebius of the fourth century, who wrote the first complete history of the Church. He marveled at how Jesus was able to predict the fall of Jerusalem with such stunning accuracy. He said, "If any one compares the words of our Saviour with the other accounts of the historian [Josephus] concerning the whole war [between Rome and the Jews], how can one fail to wonder, and to admit that the foreknowledge and the prophecy of our Saviour were truly divine and marvelously strange?"[18]

Here we see an important ancient source recognizing the miraculous nature of Christ, who could predict the future. The modern scholar doesn't buy it because he *knows* miracles (including predictive prophecy) cannot happen.

But even if a modern scholar thinks there is no such thing as a miracle, it's interesting to note that in the first century, the temple authorities indirectly acknowledged that Jesus was doing miracles—only they said He was doing them by the power of the devil.

In his book, *In the Fullness of Time,* Dr. Paul L. Maier has reproduced from the Talmud what was essentially an arrest warrant for Jesus of Nazareth (listed here as Yeshu Hannozri) while He was on earth:

---

18   Eusebius, *Church History,* Book III, Chapter 7, "The Predictions of Christ." Reproduced in *A Select Library of Nicene and Post-Nicene Fathers of the Christian Church,* Second series, translated into English with Prolegomena and Explanatory Notes under the editorial supervision of Philip Schaff and Henry Wace, Volume I. *Eusebius: Church History, Life of Constantine the Great, and Oration in Praise of Constantine.* Eusebius notes by Arthur Cushman McGiffert (Grand Rapids: Wm. B. Eerdmans Publishing Company, 1890, 1986), 142.

Wanted: Yeshu Hannozri

He shall be stoned because he has practiced sorcery and enticed Israel to apostasy…Anyone who knows where he is, let him declare it to the Great Sanhedrin in Jerusalem.[19]

So here we have a source traced back to the first century providing attestation from a hostile source that Jesus Christ did supernatural works (attributed to demonic, not divine, power). Would it be so hard to picture Jesus predicting the future—something only God can do (with accuracy)?

Because of the late-dating of the Gospels, as held by these liberal scholars, virtually everything else in the New Testament becomes suspect—including the writing of James, Peter, John, and half of Paul's letters. Sadly, the assumption that Jefferson and today's modern liberal scholars seem to buy into is one of approaching the Scriptures with skepticism until they can be proven reliable.

A Reasonable Dating of the Gospels

But what if we approach the dating issue like historians—not treating the New Testament as guilty until proven innocent?

Scholars tell us that Mark's Gospel was written first. Matthew and Luke clearly had access to and incorporated major portions of Mark's Gospel in theirs. An early Church Father, Pappias, tells us that Mark was based on Peter's remembrances.

As noted earlier, Luke is the physician who accompanied Paul on some of his missionary travels. He wrote at least two books in the New Testament, the Gospel According to Luke and Acts. They are Part I and Part II of his writings. Acts (Part II) ends with Paul under house arrest in Rome.

The great fire of Rome has not yet happened. Paul has not yet been executed. By the time Acts (Part II of Luke) ends, Paul is still alive. He died around 65 or 66 AD. Certainly no later than 68, when Nero was deposed. That would be true of Peter also, since tradition holds that these two pillars of the first century Church were both executed in Rome under Nero. (Paul, a Roman citizen was beheaded; Peter was crucified—upside down, by his choice).

In 1 Timothy 5:18, Paul quotes Luke's Gospel as "Scripture." That means that already Luke's Gospel (and, therefore, Mark's and likely Matthew's) was circulating before Paul's death.

---

19   Wanted: Yeshu Hannozri, *Sanhedrin* 43a of the Babylonian Talmud, quoted in Paul L. Maier, *In the Fullness of Time: A Historian Looks at Christmas, Easter, and the Early Church* (Grand Rapids, MI: Kregel Publications, 1997), 114.

As to Matthew's Gospel, Paul Maier notes that the evangelist repeatedly refers to prophecies Jesus fulfilled. Over and over, Matthew will say how a certain event happened, thus fulfilling what the prophets had foretold.

Dr. Maier once said, "Can you imagine that if Matthew had been written after the fall of Jerusalem? Wild horses couldn't have prevented Matthew from saying, 'And Jesus' prediction was fulfilled when Jerusalem was destroyed.' He doesn't say that, and that's very unlike Matthew."[20] Implied in this is that Matthew was written before A.D. 70.

That leaves John's Gospel. Early Church Father Polycarp was John's direct disciple, and he says that John probably wrote his Gospel in the last decade of the first century.

Even though John was old by then, he recalls the incredible events he personally witnessed—events that changed everyone's life. (Events that have changed the whole world.) He had spent three and a half years as a young man in the public ministry together with Jesus. This was not something easily forgotten.

Testimony Sealed In Blood

With the exception of John—who tradition tells us was boiled in hot oil for not denying Christ, yet it didn't kill him—all the eleven remaining apostles (twelve minus Judas Iscariot) died a martyr's death. Early Christian writings tell us that everyone who wrote any portion of the New Testament, except for John, died at the hands of the authorities (usually Roman), unwilling to deny the risen Jesus whom they had seen.

They could have saved their skin if they denied Christ. But how could they deny what they themselves saw and heard? They chose faithfulness to Christ, even though it meant a horrible death. In many cases, those deaths were in the arena, with cheering and jeering crowds. Dr. Sam Lamerson, professor at Knox Theological Seminary, put it all in perspective:

> Those people who died did so knowing that it was going to be painful, knowing that it was going to be embarrassing, knowing that it was going to be terror-filled, and yet they did it anyway as a direct result of the fact that they believed that Jesus Christ was God. And they lived in the first century, and we live in the twenty-first century. And it seems to me that it is the height of arrogance for us to say in the twenty-first century, "You,

---

20   Transcript of an interview of Dr. Paul L. Maier by Jerry Newcombe on location in Kalamazoo, Michigan (Ft. Lauderdale: Coral Ridge Ministries-TV, 2000).

all you people who died, you were just foolish, you just didn't know any better. And, we scholars, we know a lot better than you do."…It seems to me, almost absurd to think, that we, in the twenty-first century, can sit in judgment on eyewitnesses who actually saw what it was that Jesus did and said and say, "Well, sorry Matthew, you may have been there, but I'm from the twenty-first century. I know that didn't happen."[21]

The apostles' testimony is sealed in blood. People can be fooled into believing something is wrong and even giving their life for that which is wrong. But if the apostles just made up the story, e.g., that Jesus had risen from the dead, then they would have folded when they were being persecuted and about to be killed. That's just human nature.

Dr. Maier points out: "Myths do not make martyrs. And if this story had been invented, they would not have gone to death for it. If Peter had invented the account as he's ready to be hoisted up on a cross in Rome, he would've blown the whistle and said, 'Hold it! I'll plea bargain with you. I'll tell you how we did it if I can come off with my life.'"[22]

Dr. N. T. Wright, former Canon Theologian of Westminster Abbey, once said this about the disciples giving their lives based on what they themselves saw—Jesus risen from the dead after His crucifixion: "The interesting thing about the early Christians is not just that they were transformed from being a dejected and a despairing, frightened little group into being a dynamic and lively and outgoing group and brave group, though that's true too, [it]is that they didn't get another Messiah, they said Jesus was the Messiah."[23]

In the nineteenth century, Dr. Principal Hill, who wrote "Lectures in Divinity," wrote so clearly about how significant it is that the disciples sealed their testimony in their own blood:

You must suppose that twelve men of mean [i.e., average] birth, of no education, living in that humble station which placed ambitious views out of their reach and far from their thoughts, without any aid from the state, formed the noblest scheme which ever entered into the mind of man, adopted the most daring means of executing that scheme, conducted it with

21   Dr. Samuel Lamerson in D. James Kennedy, *Who Is This Jesus: Is He Risen?* (Ft. Lauderdale: Coral Ridge Ministries-TV, 2001). A video.

22   Dr. N. T. Wright in Kennedy, *Who Is This Jesus: Is He Risen?*

23   Dr. Paul L. Maier in Kennedy, *Who Is This Jesus: Is He Risen?*

such address as to conceal the imposture under the semblance of simplicity and virtue. You must suppose, also, that men guilty of blasphemy and falsehood, united in an attempt the best contrived, and which has in fact proved the most successful for making the world virtuous; that they formed this single enterprise without seeking any advantage to themselves, with an avowed contempt of loss and profit, and with the certain expectation of scorn and persecution; that although conscious of one another's villainy, none of them ever thought of providing for his own security by disclosing the fraud, but that amidst sufferings the most grievous to flesh and blood they persevered in their conspiracy to *cheat* the world into *piety, honesty and benevolence*. Truly, they who can swallow such suppositions have no title to object to miracles.[24]

How could Jefferson and so many modern critics be so spiritually blind? We find it fascinating that when Jesus said to His disciples, "You shall be My witnesses" in Acts 1:8, the Greek word for witnesses there is the word from which we get the English word martyr. He said you shall be My martyrs—witnesses for Christ unto death.

Because so many of the early Christians witnessed for Christ—unto death—the word came to mean one who witnesses for Christ unto death. But initially it only meant to testify. Implied in the word's development over time is yet another witness to the truth of the resurrection. These kinds of things convinced Priestley that the resurrection was an historical fact. Since Jefferson said Priestley's views were the basis of his views as well and there is no evidence that Jefferson differed on this point, then perhaps Jefferson accepted it as fact as well.

The Apostle Paul
The first writer of the New Testament was the Apostle Paul. He wrote about half of what comprises the New Testament. Early on, his books were accepted as Scripture. Even though he and Peter had a falling out at one point, described in Galatians 2, near the end of Peter's life, he described some people who distort the writings of Paul and other Scriptures (2 Peter 3:16). Implied in this remark is that Paul's writings (mostly letters to churches) were already recognized as divinely inspired. They were already circulating in the early Church.

---

24   *Hill's Lectures in Divinity*, I:47-48. Quoted in William Taylor, *The Miracles of Our Saviour* (New York: Hodder and Stoughton, 1890), 2122.

If Paul didn't write inspired Scripture, then what in the New Testament is inspired? Jefferson is inconsistent with Paul as he was with the Gospels. On one occasion Jefferson essentially described Paul as one of the early corrupters of the doctrines of Jesus, yet he quoted Paul's writings for spiritual purposes multiple times in his letters. And he also described a writer of the Old Testament as "inspired" about the same time, so Jefferson's inconsistency is apparent. Two hundred years removed from Jefferson, we have stronger reasons for believing the Bible to be God's inspired Word and the New Testament as the most reliable book (or sets of books) of antiquity.

Conclusion

In short, we are in much better shape than was Thomas Jefferson to see how little the New Testament was corrupted. Jefferson had feared that priests through the ages had corrupted the pages of the Bible. So, for example, he sorted through the Gospels, looking for the statements of the true Jesus. Jefferson was free to hold his unorthodox opinions about the reliability of the Gospels and the rest of the New Testament. But he was not entitled to his own facts about them. Jefferson may have been an excellent statesman, but as a theologian he fell far short.

Yet despite all his misgivings of the New Testament, Jefferson still saw shining there the character and teaching of Jesus. As he noted in a letter to William Short on April 13, 1820, "It is the innocence of his character, the purity & sublimity of his moral precepts, the eloquence of his inculcations, the beauty of the apologias in which he conveys them, that I so much admire; sometimes indeed needing indulgence to Eastern hyperbolism."[25] He also said, "Of all the systems of morality, ancient or modern, which have come under my observation, none appear to me so pure as that of Jesus."[26]

---

25   Thomas Jefferson, Letter to William Short, April 13, 1820, http://memory.loc.gov/cgi-bin/query/r?ammem/mtj:@field(DOCID+@lit(ws03101)).

26   Thomas Jefferson to William Canby, Sept. 18, 1813, *Writings*, XIII, p. 377, in Caroline Thomas Harnsberger, ed., *Treasury of Presidential Quotations* (Chicago: Follett Publishing Company, 1964), 194.

APPENDIX 7

THE GOSPEL MESSAGE FUNDED BY THOMAS JEFFERSON

Although he was not orthodox late in life, one can still see that Jefferson was a member who attended and funded an orthodox church. And when a young man we can also learn a lot from the pastor, Rev. Charles Clay, whom Thomas Jefferson personally supported from his own money. We have portions here from Clay's sermons not publicly seen since the 1770s.

Jefferson believed that Jesus' moral teaching was the best among men. What do we find in Jesus' teaching? We see that He told His followers they must be perfect as their Father in Heaven is perfect (Matthew 5:48). But no one is perfect. Jesus said, "If you, being evil, know how to give good gifts to your children…" (Matthew 7:11).

So if no one can get to Heaven unless they're perfect, and if no one is perfect, then how can anyone get to Heaven? It may be impossible with man, but with God all things are possible. The solution is found when Jesus said, "For even the Son of Man came not to be served but to serve, and to give his life as a ransom for many" (Mark 10:45).

On the night He was betrayed, Jesus took the bread and said, This is my body, which is broken for you. Eat from it all of you. Do this in remembrance of Me (Luke 22:19). "In the same manner, after supper, He also took the cup and said, 'This cup is the new covenant in my blood, which is shed for many for the remission of sins. Drink from it all of you'" (Luke 22:20).

The blood of Jesus shed for us is the only key by which people can be saved. This is the clear teaching of Jesus Christ and the New Testament. Rev. Charles Clay said of Jesus that you must "count his blood where with alone you can be sanctified."

Jesus didn't come to condemn the world. The world is already condemned. He came that those who believe might be saved. He said, "For God so loved the world that He gave His only begotten Son that whoever believes in Him shall not perish but have everlasting life. For God did not send His Son into the world to condemn the world, but that the world might be saved through Him" (John 3:16-17).

As we pointed out earlier, for a while, Thomas Jefferson sat under Rev. Charles Clay and Jefferson was the largest single contributor to Clay's church, the Calvinistical Reformed Church of Charlottesville. What did Rev. Clay preach about salvation—about the Gospel?

In his 1776 sermon, "The Government of God," Rev. Charles Clay points out that as human beings, we must obey and revere God:

And *first*, we may hence see how much it is the duty of all the people of the earth to fear before God, and to render him our religious homage and obedience as their Supreme universal king and Lord…All kings should fall down before him, and all nations should serve him, "*for as much as there is none like unto thee, O Lord and Thy name is great in might, who would not fear thee, O King of nations? For unto thee doth it appertain*" [Jeremiah 10:6,7].

Rev. Clay also says that all good things come from God:

All the *blessings and advantages* that are bestowed upon societies must be thankfully ascribed to Divine Providence. If arts and sciences flourish among a people, if they are furnished with valuable means of improving useful knowledge, if they have peace and plenty, and are free from foreign invasions and domestic conspiracies and tumults, or have success in just and necessary wars, if they are blessed with a good constitution of government and have the advantage of wise and honest governors to rule over them, if they are preserved in the enjoyment of their liberties and privileges civil and religious, if they have healthy and fruitful seasons, and other instances of public prosperity, in all these and the like cases, the goodness of Divine Providence is to be acknowledged, not excluding secondary causes but overruling and directing them. And devout and pious minds will find abundant matter of thankfulness to these.

Yet it's often easy for men to not thank God for all these blessings; it's easy to neglect to see His providential hand in these things. Clay observes that it's very easy for us to not recognize God's providence and His providential acts:

In all events of a public nature whether prosperous or adverse, we should fix our views not merely or principally upon secondary causes, but should look above them to God, and endeavor to comply with the designs of infinite wisdom and righteousness. With regard to national affairs, men are very apt to confine their whole attention to second causes, and overlook or neglect the agency of Divine Providence. When they observe that prudence and ability in counsel, and courage and skill in war, are generally crowned with success, that great and well disciplined armies under able generals prove victorious; they are apt to look no farther, as if men had the whole management of affairs in their command. But this is a very wrong way of judging. It is no argument at all, that, because these events are usually conducted according to the ordinary course of second causes, that they are not under the direction of superintendency of Divine Providence. For it is Providence that hath appointed that this shall be the general course of things and that events shall ordinarily happen in this way…

Rev. Clay also says that God wants and waits for our repentance—turning away from our sins. The Lord is patient in waiting for his:

God may indeed in his great wisdom and patience, long bear with a sinful degenerate people. He may suffer them to enjoy great prosperity for a while, and may pour forth many blessings upon them, even when they are in a corrupt state. For the methods of Providence towards societies are generally slow though sure…

Not only do we need to confess our sins and humble ourselves before the Lord, we need to find the real key to God's forgiveness of our sins—through the shed blood of Jesus Christ. He spoke of the "Redeemer," as in Jesus, and that we need to "count his blood where with alone you can be sanctified." Because of our sin, and because God will punish sin, we need to embrace Jesus Christ:

> Nations and Kingdoms as such must be punished in this world, because hereafter all those relations and dependences, whereby one member of society is connected with the rest, will then cease, and be no more. Rewards or punishments will hereafter be dispensed to men, as individuals, according as they have embraced or rejected the Gospel of Jesus Christ...[1]

These evangelical and evangelistic sermons by Rev. Charles Clay are typical of him. And, again, this is the man that Thomas Jefferson invested money in, in order to support his new church.

Another of those sermons was preached in 1775, a sermon called "God, The Adversary of the Sinner." Rev. Clay's text was Matthew 5:25,26, which states: "Agree with thine adversary quickly whiles thou art in the way with him, lest at any time the Adversary deliver thee to the Judge, and the Judge deliver thee to the Officer, and thou be cast into prison. Verily I say unto thee, thou shalt by no means come out thence till thou hast paid the utmost farthing."

Rev. Clay said that since we are all sinners, we should see that God is our Adversary. God loves sinners, but hates sin. Therefore, in our natural state, God will punish sin. Rev. Clay preached: "The sinner shall never be freed from the torments of hell till he has satisfied the whole law of God in every particular which will be impossible. If it cannot be done here, hell is a very improper place to begin it. The torments of the damned in hell will last as long as eternity itself." These were not the rants of a backwoods obscurantist; they were part of the sermon ministry supported financially by Mr. Jefferson.

After elaborating on the very real threat of hell, Rev. Clay warns his hearers to not go there by embracing Jesus before it's too late: "Let this then prevail with you to make the Lord Jesus Christ your Friend; for although you may escape here, yet if you die in your present state, eternal vengeance will be sure to overtake you... come humbly to the Lord Jesus Christ and entreat him to be merciful unto you."

---

1   Rev. Charles Clay, "The Necessity of National Humility and Repentance," 1775.

If this has possibly been unclear to anyone, Jefferson's one time pastor sums up his sermon: "The sum of what has been said is this, the eternal God is an Adversary to every man in a state of nature; and every man that is not born again of the Spirit of God, is in a state of nature consequently in a state of enmity with God. To this Adversary it is every man's interest to be reconciled…The only way to be thus reconciled, is to turn from sin, and be united to the Lord Jesus Christ by faith. This is the work of the Spirit of God whose assistance I would entreat you to implore. Let me beseech you to call on the Lord Jesus while he may yet be found."

To paraphrase, Jesus went to hell for us on the cross so we don't have to go there. But anyone who knowingly rejects Jesus and His once and for all sacrifice for sinners will find that he will be punished for his sins. Thus, everyone's sins merit judgment. Either we allow Jesus to take our judgment upon Himself or we will be punished for those sins.

Rev. Clay calls on his hearers (and this is our paraphrase): Respond now, believe now, before it's too late. He declared, "My brethren your souls, your precious souls are at stake; you hang by a very slender thread over the bottomless pit. O call upon God while it is time; Harden not your hearts against him. Let what I have said have its due weight. Do not steel your breath against what I have offered. Do not refuse a blessing at my hands, but come to the Lord Jesus Christ and be at peace with him. Remember it is not I, but the Lord Jesus Christ himself that speaks, and says unto thee, agree with thine Adversary quickly whiles thou are in the way with him."

Rev. Clay's words are just as relevant today as they were in the time of Jefferson. As Clay points out, from a biblical perspective, embracing Jesus is the key to avoiding hell. Above all, we must remember that Rev. Clay points to Jesus, the "Redeemer," and that we need to "count his blood where with alone you can be sanctified."

BIBLIOGRAPHY

Adams, Dickinson and Ruth W. Lester, eds., *Jefferson's Extracts From the Gospels* (Princeton, N.J.: Princeton University Press, 1983).

Adams. Charles Francis, ed., *The Works of John Adams - Second President of the United States: with a Life of the Author, Notes, and Illustration* (Boston: Little, Brown, & Co., 1854).

Ahlstrom, Sydney, *A Religious History of the American People* (New Haven, Conn.: Yale University Press, 1972).

Allen, Carlos, "The Great Revival in Virginia, 1783-1812" (Unpublished master's thesis, University of Virginia, 1948).

Allen, Ethan, *Historical Sketch: Washington Parish, Washington City, 1794-1857* (Washington, D.C.: Protestant Episcopal Church, [1857]).

Amos, Gary, *Defending the Declaration: How the Bible and Christianity Influenced the Writing of the Declaration of Independence* (Charlottesville, Va.: Providence Press, The Providence Foundation, 1994).

Bailey, James Henry, "John Wayles Eppes, Planter and Politician," (Unpublished dissertation, University of Virginia, 1948).

Baird, Robert, *Religion in America* (New York: Harper & Brothers, 1844).

Baldwin, Alice M., *The New England Clergy and the American Revolution* (New York: F. Ungar Publishing Co., 1965).

————, "Sowers of Sedition: The Political Theories of Some of the New Light Presbyterian Clergy in Virginia and North Carolina," *The William and Mary Quarterly*, 3rd ser., 5 (1948).

468

Bancroft, George, *History of the United States of America, From the Discovery of the Continent,* Six Volumes (New York: D. Appleton and Company, 1890).

Barrett, John P., *The Centennial of Religious Journalism* (Dayton, Ohio: Christian Publishing Association, 1908).

————, ed., *Herald of Gospel Liberty* (Dayton, Ohio: Christian Publishing Association, 1908).

Barton, David, *Original Intent: The Courts, the Constitution, and Religion* (Aledo, Tx.: Wallbuilder Press, 1996).

————, *The Jefferson Lies* (Nashville: Thomas Nelson Publishers, 2012).

Bear, James A., Jr., ed., *Jefferson At Monticello,* (Charlottesville, Va.: University Press of Virginia, 1967).

————, and Lucia C. Stanton, eds., *Jefferson's Memorandum Books: Accounts, with Legal Records and Miscellany, 1767-1826* (Princeton: Princeton University Press, 1997).

Beliles, Mark, ed., *Thomas Jefferson's Abridgement of the Words of Jesus of Nazareth* (Charlottesville, Va.: self-published, 1993).

————, ed., *The Selected Religious Letters and Papers of Thomas Jefferson* (Charlottesville, VA: America Publications, 2013).

————, *Free As the Air: Churches and Politics in Jefferson's Virginia* (PhD. Dissertation published in electronic format by America Publications, 2000).

————, *Playful in the Closet: A Complete Religious History of Thomas Jefferson* (Charlottesville, VA: America Publications, 2014).

Bennett, William, *Memorials of Methodism in Virginia* (Richmond, Va.: self-published, 1871).

Bernstein, Robert, *Thomas Jefferson* (Oxford: Oxford University Press, 2003).

Blackstone, Sir William, *Commentaries on the Laws of England,* 4 Volumes (Philadelphia: J. B. Lippincott and Co., 1879).

Boles, John B., *A Bicentennial History of Chestnut Grove Baptist Church, 1773-1973* (Richmond, Va.: Lewis Printing Co., 1973).

————, *The Great Revival, 1787-1805* (Lexington, KY.: University Press of Kentucky, 1972).

Bonomi, Patricia U., *Under the Cope of Heaven: Religion, Society, and Politics in Colonial America* (New York: Oxford University Press, 1986).

Bowers, Claude G., *Jefferson in Power* (Boston, Mass.: Houghton Mifflin Co., 1936).

————, *The Young Jefferson, 1743-1789* (Boston, Mass.: Houghton Mifflin Co., 1945).

Boyd, Julian B., *The Papers of Thomas Jefferson*, 28 vols. to date (Princeton, N.J.: Princeton University Press, 1950-present).

Brown, Ira V., ed., *Joseph Priestley: Selections from His Writings* (University Park, PA: The Pennsylvania State University, 1962).

Brown, Katharine L., *Hills of the Lord: Background of the Episcopal Church in Southwestern Virginia 1738-1938* (Roanoke, Va.: Diocese of Southwestern Virginia, 1979).

Bruce, Philip, *History of the University of Virginia* (New York: The MacMillan Co., 1920).

Brydon, George, "A Sketch of the Early History of St. Anne's Parish" in *A History of Christ Church, Glendower* by Elizabeth C. Langhorne (Albemarle County, Va.: Christ Church, 1957).

————, *Virginia's Mother Church* (Richmond, VA: Virginia Historical Society, 1947-1952)

Buckley, Thomas, *Church and State in Revolutionary Virginia, 1776-1787* (Charlottesville, Va.: University Press of Virginia, 1977).

————, "Establishing an Evangelical Culture: Religion and Politics in Jeffersonian Virginia" (paper presented at a symposium at the University of Virginia, 19-20, January 1996).

Butler, Jon, *Awash in a Sea of Faith: Christianizing the American People* (Cambridge, Mass.: Harvard University Press, 1990).

Butterfield, Lyman H., "Elder John Leland, Jeffersonian Itinerant," *Proceedings of the American Antiquarian Society*, 62 (Worcester, Mass.: 1952).

"Calendar of the Correspondence of Thomas Jefferson," *Bulletin of the Bureau of Rolls and Library of the Department of State,*(Washington, D.C.: Department of State, 1903), ser. 6, vol. 10 and 12.

Cappon, Lester J., ed., *The Adams-Jefferson Letters: The Complete Correspondence Between Thomas Jefferson and Abigail and John Adams* (Chapel Hill, NC: the University of North Carolina Press, 1988).

Carter, Stephen L., *The Culture of Disbelief* (New York: Doubleday, 1993).

Catalogue of the University of Virginia (Charlottesville, Va.: 1866).

Chinard, Gilbert, *Thomas Jefferson: The Apostle of Americanism*, 2d ed. (Ann Arbor, Mich.: University of Michigan Press, 1957).

The Christian Watchman, 14 July 1826 (microfilm, University of Virginia Library).

"Clay Family Papers," Mss 1c5795a in the Virginia Historical Society, Richmond, Virginia.

Cleaveland, George J., "The Church of Virginia Established and Disestablished," in *Up From Independence: The Episcopal Church in Virginia* (Orange, Va.: Interdiocesan Bicentennial Committee of the Virginias, 1976).

Cord, Robert L., *Separation of Church and State: Historical Fact and Current Fiction* (Grand Rapids, MI: Baker Book House, 1988).

Corner, George, ed., *The Autobiography of Benjamin Rush* (Princeton: American Philosophical Society, 1948).

Cox, F. A., *Baptists in America* (New York: Leavitt, Lord, 1837). (Transcripts of pages found in files of Monticello research library).

Cullen, Charles T., ed., The Papers of Thomas Jefferson, second series (Princeton: Princeton University Press, 1997).

Curtis, William E., *The True Thomas Jefferson* (Philadelphia: J. B. Lippincott Co., 1901).

Cutler, Manasseh, *Life, Journal, and Correspondence,* 2 vols.(Cincinnati, Ohio: Robert Clarke and Co., 1888).

Dabney, Virginius, *The Jefferson Scandals: A Rebuttal* (New York: Dodd, Mead & Company, 1981)

Dawson, Joseph Martin, *Baptists and the American Republic* (Nashville, Tenn.: Broadman Press, 1956).

Davis, Robert P. et al, *Virginia Presbyterians in American Life: Hanover Presbytery 1755-1980*, (Richmond, Va.: Hanover Presbytery, 1982).

"Diary of Col. Francis Taylor 1786-1799" (microfilm, University of Virginia Library).

"Diary of John Goss" (University of Virginia Library).

"Diary of John Early," *Virginia Magazine of History and Biography,* 33-39(Richmond, Va.: Virginia Historical Society).

The Diary of Robert Rose, 1746-1751, ed. Ralph Fall (Verona, Va.: McLure Press, 1977).

Dow, Lorenzo, *The History of the Cosmopolite, or the four volumes of Lorenzo Dow's Journal* (Wheeling, Va.: Joshua Martin, 1848).

Dow, Peggy, *The Dealings of God, Man, and the Devil; as Exemplified in the Life, Experience, and Travels of Lorenzo Dow* (New York: Cornish, Lamport and Co., 1852).

Dreisbach, Daniel L., "A New Perspective on Jefferson's Views on Church/State Relations," *The American Journal of Legal History*, 35 (Philadelphia: Temple University School of Law, 1991).

———, *Real Threat and Mere Shadow* (Westchester, Ill.: Crossway Books, 1987).

———, *Religion and Politics in the Early Republic: Jasper Adams and the Church-State Debate* (Lexington, Ky.: The University Press of Kentucky, 1996).

———, *Thomas Jefferson and the Wall of Separation Between Church and State* (New York University Press, 2002).

———, "The Wall of Separation," *Christian History & Biography Magazine,* Issue #99, 2008. https://www.christianhistoryinstitute.org/uploaded/50b78776 2dbd67.76222839.pdf

Earnest, Joseph B., Jr., *The Religious Development of the Negro in Virginia* (Charlottesville, Va.: Michie Co., Printers, 1914).

Eaton, Clement, *The Freedom of Thought Struggle in the Old South* (New York: Harper Torchbooks, 1940).

Eckenrode, Hamilton James, *Separation of Church and State in Virginia: A Study in the Development of the Revolution* (Richmond, Va.: Davis Bottom, 1910).

Editors of Newsweek Books, The, *Thomas Jefferson: A Biography in His Own Words,* Volume 2 (New York: Newsweek, 1974).

Eidsmoe, John, *Christianity and the Constitution* (Grand Rapids: Baker Book House, 1987).

Eliot, Charles W., LL.D., ed., *American Historical Documents 1000-1904* (New York: P.F. Collier & Son Company, The Harvard Classics, 1910),

"Excerpt from the Schueler von Senden Journal [1778-1780]," *Magazine of Albemarle County History* 41 (Charlottesville, Va.: Albemarle County Historical Society, 1983).

Federer, William J., *America's God and Country: Encyclopedia of Quotations* (St. Louis, MO: Amerisearch, 2000).

———-, *Library of Classics* (St. Louis, MO: Amerisearch, Inc., 2002), a CD-ROM.

Fischer, David Hackett, *Albion's Seed: Four British Folkways in America* (New York: Oxford University Press, 1989).

Foote, Henry Wilder, *The Religion of Thomas Jefferson* (Boston, Mass.: Beacon Press, 1963).

Foote, William Henry, *Sketches of Virginia, Historical and Biographical* (Philadelphia: William S. Martien, 1850).

Ford, Paul Leicester, ed., *The Writings of Thomas Jefferson*, 12 vols. (New York: G. P. Putnam's Sons, 1892).

Ford, Worthington C., ed. *Thomas Jefferson Correspondence Printed From the Originals in the Collection of William K. Bixby* (Boston, Mass.: 1916).

Fossett, Peter, "Recollections of Peter Fossett" (found in Monticello research library).

Frazer, Gregg, *The Religious Beliefs of America's Founders* (Lawrence, Kansas: University Press of Kansas, 2012).

Fredericksville Parish Vestry Book 1742-1787,ed. Rosalie Davis (Manchester, Mo.: self-published, 1978).

Frohnen, Bruce, ed., *The American Republic: Primary Sources* (Indianapolis: Liberty Fund, 2002).

Garrett, Leroy, *Alexander Campbell and Thomas Jefferson: A Comparative Study of Two Old Virginians* (Dallas, Tx.: Wilkinson Publishing Co., 1963).

Gaustad, Edwin, *Sworn On the Altar of God: A Religious Biography of Thomas Jefferson* (Grand Rapids, Mich.: W. B. Eerdmans Publishers, 1996).

Gewehr, Wesley M., *The Great Awakening in Virginia 1740-1790* (Durham, N.C.: Duke University Press, 1930).

Goetz, David L., "The Gallery: Zealous, Eccentric Leaders," in *Christian History Magazine* (Carol Stream, Ill.: Christianity Today, 1995).

Gould, William D., "Religious Opinions of Thomas Jefferson," *Mississippi Valley Historical Review*, 20 (Cedar Rapids, Iowa: 1933).

Grayson, Jennie, "Old Christ Church," in *Magazine of Albemarle County History*, 8 (Charlottesville, Va.: Albemarle County Historical Society, 1947-48). Originally printed in *The Parish Register* 1918-1923.

Greene, L. F., ed., *The Writings of the Late Elder John Leland,* (New York: G. W. Wood, 1845).

Grigsby, Hugh Blair, *The History of the Virginia Federal Convention of 1788, 2 vols.* (Richmond, Va.: Virginia Historical Society, 1891).

Gundersen, Joan, *The Anglican Ministry in Virginia, 1723-1776: A Study of a Social Class* (New York: Garland Publishing, 1989).

———, "The Myth of the Independent Virginia Vestry," *Historical Magazine of the Protestant Episcopal Church*, 44 (Austin, Tx.: The Church Historical Society, 1975).

Hamburger, Phillip, *Separation of Church and State* (Cambridge, MA: Harvard University Press, 2002 / 2004).

Harris, James F., *The Serpentine Wall: The Winding Boundary between Church and State in the United States (New Brunswick, NJ: Transaction Publishers, 2013).*

Hatch, Nathan O., *Democratization of American Christianity* (New Haven, Conn.: Yale University Press, 1989).

Healey, Robert M., *Jefferson on Religion in Public Education* (New Haven, Conn.: Yale University Press, 1962).

Heimert, Alan. *Religion and The American Mind: From the Great Awakening to the Revolution* (Cambridge, Mass.: Harvard University Press, 1966).

Hennesey, James, S.J., *American Catholics: A History of the Roman Catholic Community in the United States* (New York: Oxford University Press, 1981).

"Henry Fry's Account Book 1759-1795," *The Papers of the Fry, Maury and Barksdale Families*, (Accession #10659-a, University of Virginia Library).

Hitchens, Christopher, *Thomas Jefferson: Author of America* (New York: Atlas Books, a division of HarperCollins*Publishers*, 2005)

Hodge, Frederick A., *The Plea and the Pioneers in Virginia: A History of the Rise and Early Progress of the Disciples of Christ in Virginia* (Richmond, Va.: Everett Waddey Co., 1905).

Holmes, David, "Devereux Jarratt" (unpublished paper presented at a symposium at the University of Virginia, 19-20 January, 1996).

————, et al., *Up From Independence: The Episcopal Church in Virginia* (Interdiocesan Bicentennal Committee of the Virginias, Orange, VA, 1976)

Hood, Fred, *Reformed America: The Middle and Southern States, 1783-1837* (University: University of Alabama Press, 1980).

Honeywell, Roy, *The Educational Work of Thomas Jefferson* (Cambridge: Harvard University Press, 1931).

Hooper, William, "Diary" (photocopy found in Monticello research library).

Howell, Robert B., *The Early Baptists of Virginia*, (Philadelphia: The Bible and Publication Society, 1857).

Humphrey, Edward Frank, *Nationalism and Religion in America, 1774-1789* (Boston: Chipman Law Publishing Co., 1924).

Hutchinson, William T., ed., *The Papers of James Madison*, 14 vols. (Chicago: The University of Chicago Press, 1962).

Hutson, James H., *Religion and the Founding of the American Republic* (Washington, D.C.: Library of Congress, 1998).

Isaac, Rhys, *The Transformation of Virginia, 1740-1790* (Chapel Hill, N.C.: Institute of Early American History and Culture; University of North Carolina Press, 1982).

————, "'The Rage of Malice of the Old Serpent Devil': The Dissenters and the Making and Remaking of the Virginia Statute for Religious Freedom," in Merrill Peterson and Robert Vaughan, eds. *The Virginia Statute for Religious Freedom* (Cambridge, NY: Cambridge University Press, 1988).

James, Charles F., *Documentary History of the Struggle for Religious Liberty in Virginia* (Lynchburg, Va.: J. P. Bell Co., 1900).

Jarratt, Devereux, *The Life of the Reverend Devereux Jarratt* (Baltimore: Warner and Hanna, 1806).

Jefferson, Thomas, *Notes on the State of Virginia* (Boston: David Carlisle, 1801, Eighth American Edition).

Johnson, Paul, *A History of the American People* (New York: HarperCollins Publishers, 1997).

————, *The Quest for God: A Personal Pilgrimmage* (New York: HarperCollinsPublishers, 1996).

Joyner, Ulysses P., Jr., *The First Settlers of Orange County, Virginia* (Baltimore, Md.: Gateway Press, Inc., 1987).

Justus, Judith P., *Down From the Mountain* (Perrysburg, Ohio: Jeskurtara, Inc., 1991).

Kennedy, D. James and Jerry Newcombe, *What If Jesus Had Never Been Born?* (Nashville: Thomas Nelson, Publishers, 1994 /2001).

————, *What If The Bible Had Never Been Written?* (Nashville: Thomas Nelson, Publishers, 1998).

————, *Who Is This Jesus: Is He Risen?* (Ft. Lauderdale: Coral Ridge Ministries, 2002).

Kenny, Michael G., *The Perfect Law of Liberty: Elias Smith and the Providential History of America* (Washington, D.C.: Smithsonian Institution Press, 1994).

Ketcham, Ralph, *James Madison: A Biography* (New York: The MacMillan Co., 1971).

————, "James Madison and Religion: A New Hypothesis," in Merrill Peterson and Robert Vaughan, eds. *The Virginia Statute for Religious Freedom* (Cambridge, NY: Cambridge University Press, 1988).

Knox, Samuel, *An Essay On the Best System of Liberal Education* (Baltimore, Md.: Warner and Hanna, 1799).

————, *A Vindication of the Religion of Thomas Jefferson* (Baltimore, Md.: W. Pechin, 1800).

Koch, Adrienne and William Peden, eds, *The Life and Selected Writings of Thomas Jefferson* (New York: Random House, Inc., 1944).

Langhorne, Elizabeth C., *A History of Christ Church, Glendower* (Albemarle County, Va.: Christ Church, 1957).

Lednum, John, *A History of the Rise of Methodism in America* (Philadelphia: self-published, 1859).

Lee, Jesse, *A Short History of the Methodists* (Baltimore, Md.: Magill and Clime, 1810).

Legislative Petitions from Albemarle County, 8 December 1815, 14 December 1818 (Richmond, Va.: Library of Virginia).

Lewis, C.S., *Mere Christianity* (New York: Collier Books, MacMillan Publishing Company, 1952, 1984).

Lewis, Jan, *The Pursuit of Happiness: Family and Values in Jefferson's Virginia* (Cambridge, England: Cambridge University Press, 1983).

Linn, William, *Serious Considerations on the Election of a President: Addressed to the Citizens of the United States* (New York: 1800).

Lipscomb, Andrew A. and Albert Ellery Bergh, eds., *The Writings of Thomas Jefferson*, 20 vols. (Washington, D.C.: The Thomas Jefferson Memorial Association, 1904-05).

Little, Lewis P., *Imprisoned Preachers and Religious Liberty in Virginia* (Lynchburg, VA: J.P. Bell Co., 1938).

Locke, John, *The Second Treatise of Government: And, A Letter Concerning Toleration* (Courier Dover Publications, 1956).

Lumpkin, William L., *Baptist Foundations in the South: Tracing through the Separates the Influence of the Great Awakening, 1754-1787* (Nashville, Tenn.: Broadman Press, 1961).

Lupold, Dorothy M., "Methodism in Virginia From 1772-1784" (Unpublished masters thesis, Accession #1625, University of Virginia library, 1949).

Lutz, Donald S., *The Origins of American Constitutionalism* (Baton Rouge: Louisiana State University Press, 1988).

MacClenny, W. E., *The Life of Rev. James O'Kelly and the Early History of the Christian Church in the South* (Raleigh, N.C.: Edwards and Broughton Printing Co., 1910).

McCleskey, Jo, *St. Anne's Parish, Albemarle County, Virginia.* (Albemarle County, Va.: self-published, 1996).

Maier, Paul L., *In the Fullness of Time: A Historian Looks at Christmas, Easter, and the Early Church* (Grand Rapids, MI: Kregel Publications, 1997).

Malone, Dumas, *Jefferson the Virginian* (Boston, Mass.: Little, Brown and Co., 1948).

——Malone, Dumas, *Jefferson and the Ordeal of Liberty* (Boston, Mass.: Little, Brown and Co., 1962).

——Malone, Dumas, *Jefferson the President – First Term 1801-1805* (Boston, Mass.: Little, Brown and Co., 1970).

——Malone, Dumas, *The Sage of Monticello* (Boston, Mass.: Little, Brown and Co., 1981).

Mapp, Alf J., Jr., *Thomas Jefferson: A Strange Case of Mistaken Identity* (New York: Madison Books, 1987).

Marini, Stephen A., "Religion, Politics, and Ratification," in *Religion in a Revolutionary Age*, ed. Ronald Hoffman and Peter J. Albert (Charlottesville, Va.: United States Capitol Historical Society; University Press of Virginia, 1994).

Marraro, Howard, *Memoirs of the Life and Peregrinations of the Florentine Philip Mazzei, 1730-1816* (New York: Columbia University Press, 1942).

Marsden, George M., *The Soul of the American University: From Protestant Establishment to Established Nonbelief* (New York: Oxford University Press, 1994).

Marshall, Gayle, *Preddys Creek Baptist Church, 1781-1981* (Albemarle County, Va.: Published by the church, 1981).

Mason, John Mitchell, *The Voice of Warning, to Christians, on the Ensuing Election of a President of the United States* (New York: 1800).

Matthews, Donald G., *Religion in the Old South* (Chicago: The University of Chicago Press, 1977).

Mattern, David B., J. C. A. Stagg, Mary Parke Johnson, and Anne Mandeville Colony, eds., *The Papers of James Madison*, Retirement Series, vol. 1, *4 March 1817–31 January 1820* (Charlottesville: University of Virginia Press, 2009).

Maxwell, William, *Memoir of the Rev. John H. Rice* (Philadelphia: J. Whetham, 1835).

May, Henry, *The Enlightenment in America* (New York: Oxford, 1976).

Mead, Edward. *Historic Homes of the South-West Mountains Virginia* (C. J. Carrier Company, Harrisonburg, Virginia, 1978)

Meade, William, *Old Churches, Ministers and Families of Virginia*, 2 vols. (Philadelphia: Lippincott Co., 1857).

Metcalf, John Calvin, et al., eds. *The Centennial of the University of Virginia 1819-1921* (New York: G. P. Putnam's Sons, 1921).

Miller, Perry, *Nature's Nation* (Cambridge, Mass.: Harvard-Belknap, 1967).

Miller, Samuel, *The Life of Samuel Miller, D.D., LL.D.*, (Philadelphia: Claxton, Remsen and Haffelfinger, 1869).

Miller, William Lee, *The Business of May Next: James Madison and the Founding* (Charlottesville, Va.: University Press of Virginia, 1992).

Miller, William lee, The First Liberty: Religion and the American Republic (Charlottesville, Va.: University Press of Virginia, 1986).

Minute Book, 1773-1811, Chestnut Grove Baptist Church (microfilm, Accession # 7403-a, University of Virginia Library).

Minutes of the University of Virginia, including minutes of Central College, Rockfish Gap Reports, 1822 and 1823 and other Regulations for the University of Virginia, 1824 (University of Virginia Library).

Minutes of the Presbytery of Hanover, 1755-1769 (Richmond,Va.: found at Union Theological Seminary).

Moore, Jeremiah, *An Enquiry into the Nature and Propriety of Ecclesiastical Establishments* (1808).

Moore, Chief Justice Roy S., *Our Legal Heritage* (Montgomery, AL: The Administrative Office of Courts, June 2001).

Moore, John Hammond, *Albemarle: Jefferson's County, 1727-1976* (Charlottesville, Va.: Albemarle County Historical Society and University Press of Virginia, 1976).

Moore, William Cabell, "Jeremiah Moore, 1746-1815," *William and Mary College Quarterly Historical Magazine* (January 1933).

Moran, Charles E., Jr., ed., *The Magazine of Albemarle County History*, Vol. 9, 35, 40, 41, (Albemarle County Historical Society: Charlottesville, VA, 1983)

Mundy, W. L., *A Brief Historical Sketch* (Charlottesville, Va.: Albemarle Baptist Association, 1921).

Noll, Mark, et al., eds., *Eerdman's Handbook to Christianity in America* (Grand Rapids, Mich.: William B. Eerdmans Publishing Co., 1983).

Oberg, Barbara B., ed., *The Papers of Thomas Jefferson*, (Princeton: Princeton University Press, 2013).

Onuf, Peter, ed., *Jeffersonian Legacies* (Charlottesville, Va.: University Press of Virginia, 1993).

"Papers, Military and Political, 1775-1778, of George Gilmer, M. D., of Pen Park, Albemarle County, Virginia," *Miscellaneous Papers 1672-1865…in the collections of the Virginia Historical Society* (Richmond, Va.: Virginia Historical Society, 1887).

Padover, Saul, *The Complete Jefferson* (New York: Harcourt, Brace, Cotet and Co., 1942).

Parton, James, "The Presidential Election of 1800," *Atlantic Magazine,* July 1873.

Patton, John and Sallie Doswell, *The University of Virginia* (Lynchburg, Va.: J. P. Bell Co., 1900).

Perdue, Charles L., Jr., ed., *The Negro in Virginia* (New York: Hastings House, 1940).

Peterson, Merrill, *Thomas Jefferson and the New Nation* (New York: Oxford University Press, 1970).

————, and Robert Vaughan, eds., *The Virginia Statute for Religious Freedom* (New York, NY: Cambridge University Press, 1988).

Pfeffer, Leo, "Madison's 'Detached Memoranda': Then and Now," in Merrill Peterson and Robert Vaughan, eds. *The Virginia Statute for Religious Freedom* (Cambridge, NY: Cambridge University Press, 1988).

Pocock, J. G. A., "Religious Freedom and the Desacralization of Politics: From the English Civil Wars to the Virginia Statute," in Merrill Peterson and Robert Vaughan, eds., *The Virginia Statute for Religious Freedom* (Cambridge, N.Y.: Cambridge University Press, 1988).

The Portuguese American, 1992 (article in the files of Monticello research library).

Proctor, John C., *Washington Past and Present* (New York: Lewis Historical Publishing Co., 1930).

Ragosta, John, *Wellspring of Liberty: How Virginia's Religious Dissenters Helped Win the American Revolution and Secured Religious Liberty* (Oxford University Press, 2010).

Rahe, Paul A., *Republics Ancient and Modern: Classical Republicanism and the American Revolution* (Chapel Hill, N.C.: University of North Carolina Press, 1992).

Randall, Henry S, *The Life of Thomas Jefferson*, 3 vols. (New York: Derby and Jackson, 1858).

Randolph, Sarah N., *The Domestic Life of Thomas Jefferson* (Charlottesville: University Press of Virginia, 1978).

Rawlings, Mary, *The Albemarle of Other Days* (Charlottesville, Va.: Michie Co., 1925).

————, *Antebellum Albemarle* (Charlottesville, Va.: Michie Co., 1935).

Rayner, B. L., *Life of Thomas Jefferson* (Boston, Mass.: Lilly, Wait, Colman and Holden, 1834).

Reichley, A. James, *Religion in American Public Life* (Washington, D.C.: The Brookings Institution, 1985).

Reid, Daniel G., Robert Linder, Bruce Shelley, and Harry Stout, eds. *Dictionary of Christianity in America* (Downers Grove, Ill.: InterVarsity Press, 1990).

The Religious Herald, 23 October 1829 (microfilm, University of Virginia Library).

Rhodehamel, John, ed., *George Washington: Writings* (New York: The Library of America, 1997).

Richardson, James D, *A Compilation of the Messages and Papers of the Presidents, 1789-1897* (New York: Published by Authority of Congress, 1899).

Rivera de Simpkins, Ana Esther, *"James Madison and Education 1751-1796"* (Unpublished doctoral dissertation, University of Virginia, 1998).

Rives, William C., *History of the Life and Times of James Madison*, 4 vols. (Boston: Little, Brown and Co., 1868).

Rosenfeld, Richard, *American Aurora* (New York: St. Martin's Press, 1997).

Rutherford, Samuel, *Lex Rex, or The Law and the Prince* (Harrisonburg, Va.: Sprinkle Publications, 1982).

Rutyna, Richard A., ed., *Conceived in Conscience* (Norfolk, Va.: Donning Co. Publishers, 1983).

Ryland, Garnett, *The Baptists of Virginia 1699-1926* (Richmond, Va.: The Virginia Baptist Board of Missions and Education, 1955).

Sandoz, Ellis, *A Government of Laws: Political Theory, Religion, and the American Founding* (Baton Rouge: Louisiana State University Press, 1985).

————, *Political Sermons of the American Founding Era, 1730-1805,* (Indianapolis, Ind.: Liberty Press, 1991).

Sanford, Charles. *The Religious Life of Thomas Jefferson* (Charlottesville, Va.: University Press of Virginia, 1984).

Schultz, Roger, "A Celebration of Infidels: The American Enlightenment in the Revolutionary Era," in *Contra Mundum* (Moscow, Idaho: 1991).

Seaman, Catherine, *Tuckahoes and Cohees: The Settlers and Cultures of Amherst and and Nelson Counties 1607-1807* (Sweet Briar, Va.: Sweet Briar College Press, 1992).

Semple, Robert B., *A History of the Rise and Progress of the Baptists in Virginia* (Richmond, Va.: Pitt and Dickinson Publishers, 1894).

Shade, William G., *Democratizing the Old Dominion: Virginia and the Second Party System 1824-1861* (Charlottesville, Va.: University Press of Virginia, 1996).

Sheldon, Garrett Ward, *The Political Philosophy of Thomas Jefferson* (Baltimore: The Johns Hopkins University Press, 1991).

———, and Daniel Dreisbach, eds, *Religion and Political Culture in Jefferson's Virginia* (Lanham, MD: Rowman and Littlefield, Publishers, 1996).

Simpson, Robert E., *History of First Presbyterian Church, Charlottesville, Virginia, 1839-1989* (Charlottesville, Va.: 1990).

Slaughter, Philip, *Memoir of Col. Joshua Fry…with an Autobiography of his Son, Rev. Henry Fry* (Richmond,Va.: Randolph and English, 1880).

Smith, Elias, *The Life, Conversion, Preaching, Travels, and Sufferings of Elias Smith* (Portsmouth, N.H.: Beck and Foster, 1816).

———, *The Whole World Governed By A Jew: A Discourse On the Government of Christ as King and Priest* (Exeter, N.H.: Henry Ranlet, 1805).

Smith, Glenn Curtis, "Our City's History," in the *Daily Progress*, 21 March 1940 (Charlottesville, Va.: Charlottesville Newspapers, Inc., 1940).

Smith, H. Shelton, Robert T. Handy, and Lefferts A. Loetscher, eds., *American Christianity: An Historical Interpretation With Representative Documents*, 2 vols (New York: Charles Scribner's Sons, 1960).

Smith, Morton H. Smith, *Studies in Southern Presbyterian Theology* (Phillipsburg, N.J.: Presbyterian and Reformed Publishing Co., 1962).

Smith, Samuel Stanhope, *Lectures on the Subjects of Moral and Political Philosophy* (New York: Whiting and Watson, 1812).

Sobel, Mechal, *The World They Made Together: Black and White Values in Eighteenth-Century Virginia* (Princeton, N.J.: Princeton University Press, 1987).

Sonne, Niels H., *Liberal Kentucky, 1780-1828* (Lexington, Ky.: University of Kentucky Press, 1968).

Sparks, Jared, ed., *The Writings of George Washington* (Boston: Ferdinand Andrews, 1838).

Sprague, William B., *Annals of the American Pulpit* (New York: Robert Carter and Brothers, 1858).

Stokes, Anson P., *Church and State in the United States*, 3 vols. (New York: Harper and Brothers, 1950).

Stout, Harry S., *The New England Soul: Preaching and Religious Culture in Colonial New England* (New York: Oxford University Press, 1986).

Strout, Cushing, "Jeffersonian Religious Liberty and American Pluralism," in Merrill Peterson and Robert Vaughan, eds., *The Virginia Statute for Religious Freedom* (Cambridge, N.Y.: Cambridge University Press, 1988).

Swanson, Mary Elaine, *The Education of James Madison: A Model For Today* (Montgomery, AL.: The Hoffman Education Center for the Family, 1992).

Sweet, William Warren. *Religion on the American Frontier: The Baptists 1783-1830*, (New York: Henry Holt and Co., 1931).

————, *Virginia Methodism: A History* (Richmond, Va.: Whittet and Shepperson, 1955).

Taylor, James B., *Virginia Baptist Ministers*, (Richmond, Va.: Yale and Wyatt, 1837).

Temple, Oliver Perry, *The Covenanter, The Cavalier, and the Puritan* (Cincinnati, Oh.: Robert Clarke Co., 1897).

Thomas, William H. B., *"Faith of Our Fathers!;" Religion and the Churches in Colonial Orange County* (Orange, Va.: Orange County Bicentennial Commission, Bicentennial Series No. 2, 1975).

Thompson, Thomas, *The Failure of Jeffersonian Reform: Religious Groups and the Politics of Morality in Early National Virginia* (Unpublished dissertation, University of California, Riverside, 1990).

"Three Grand and Interesting Objects - An 1828 Visit to Monticello, the University, and Montpelier," in *The Magazine of Albemarle County History*, 51 (Charlottesville, Va.: Albemarle County Historical Society, 1993).

Throckmorton, Warren and Michael Coulter, *Getting Jefferson Right: Fact Checking Claims about Our Third President* (Grove City, PA: Salem Grove Press, 2012).

Thweatt, Henry C., "Diary" (transcripts in files of Monticello research library).

Turpin, John B., *A Brief History of the Albemarle Baptist Association* (Richmond, Va.: Virginia Baptist Historical Society, 1891).

Tyler, Alice Felt, *Freedom's Ferment: Phases of American Social History from the Colonial Period to the Outbreak of the Civil War* (New York: Harper and Row, Publishers, 1944).

Tyree, Garland, *Old Blue Run Baptist Church* (Orange, Va.: Self-published, 1994).

Vestrybook of Saint Anne's Parish, 1772-1785, (copy in the Scottsville Museum in Albemarle County, Va.) The original is in the Huntington Library in California.

Vicchio, Stephen J., *Jefferson's Religion* (Eugene, Oregon: WIPF and STOCK Publishers, 2007).

Waddell, Joseph A., *Annals of Augusta County, Virginia, 1726-1871, 2d ed.* (Bridgewater, Va.: C. J. Carrier Co., 1958).

Walker, Frances M., *The Early Episcopal Church in the Amherst-Nelson Area* (Lynchburg, Va.: J. P. Bell Co. Inc., 1964).

Washington, H.A., *The Writings of Thomas Jefferson,* 9 vol.s (New York: H. W. Derby, 1861).

Watts, Steven, *The Republic Reborn: War and the Making of Liberal America, 1790-1820* (Baltimore, Md.: Johns Hopkins University Press, 1987).

Weaver, Bettie Woodson, *Thomas Jefferson and the Virginia Baptists* (Richmond, Va.: Virginia Baptist Historical Society, 1993).

Whitehead, John, *An American Dream* (Westchester, Ill.: Crossway Books, 1987).

————-, *Religious Apartheid* (Chicago: Moody Press, 1994).

Wilson, Douglas, ed., Jefferson's Literary Commonplace Book (Princeton, N.J: Princeton University Press, 1989).

Wilson, Douglas L., "Jefferson and Bolingbroke: Some Notes On the Question of Influence" (an unpublished paper presented at a symposium, January 1996, at the University of Virginia).

Wilson, Howard McKnight, *The Tinkling Spring: Headwater of Freedom* (Fishersville, Va.: Tinkling Spring and Hermitage Presbyterian Churches, 1954).

Wiltse, Charles M., ed., *The Papers of Daniel Webster* (Hanover, N.H.: University Press of New England, 1974).

Woods, Edgar, *Albemarle County in Virginia* (Charlottesville, Va.: Michie Co., 1901).

Wranek, William, "Charlottesville and the University: A Jeffersonian View", in *Magazine of Albemarle County History*, 21 (Charlottesville, Va.: Albemarle County Historical Society, 1962-63).

www.founders.archives.gov/documents/Jefferson/01-01-02-0001, ver. 2014-02-12

ACKNOWLEDGMENTS

We are most grateful to the Max B. Tharpe Foundation for providing the funding to make the research and writing possible for this book. Barb Morin of the Foundation was extremely generous and encouraging. We are truly in the debt of this great organization. There are many people to thank for this book, including Greg and Susie Beaty, homeschool leaders who introduced the authors to each other. Also we must thank our wives, who patiently endured as we worked on this material.

We received feedback from several friends who read the manuscript and made important suggestions. But special notice is due for the invaluable advice and assistance from the editors of the *Papers of Thomas Jefferson* at Princeton and at Monticello. Access to transcripts yet to be completed and published was very helpful. The authors acknowledge the use of these transcripts courtesy of Princeton University Press, but chiefly for comparison. Any transcript here from the unpublished years that has errors, should in no way be attributed to Princeton or Monticello, but are solely the responsibility of the authors.

Papers of Jefferson

Founders Online, a service of the National Archives, is the source of text for all letters except for the years 1803-1808 and 1815-1826 (although a few letters in those years were also used from the Early Access documents). This invaluable online source became available for the first time in 2013. The documents are from the printed collection of *The Papers of Thomas Jefferson* in several series, that began under editor Julian Boyd in 1950 and now being done by Barbara B. Oberg. Beginning in 2004 the Retirement Series began under editor J. Jefferson Looney with ten volumes to date. To help identify unpublished letters and the repositories of the originals, Barbara Oberg and her staff (especially Bland Whitley) at Princeton and Jefferson Looney and his staff (especially Lisa Francavilla) at Monticello were extremely helpful.

Jefferson's most complete writings are found in the sources below:

The Papers of Thomas Jefferson, vols. 1-40, ed. Julian Boyd and Barbara B. Oberg, (Princeton: Princeton University Press, 1950-).

The Papers of Thomas Jefferson, Retirement Series, vols. 1-10, ed. J. Jefferson Looney, (Princeton: Princeton University Press, 2004-).

Jefferson's Memorandum Books: Accounts, with Legal Records and Miscellany, 1767-1826, 2 vols, edited by James A. Bear Jr., & Lucia C. Stanton (Princeton: Princeton University Press, 1997).

Jefferson's Literary Commonplace Book, edited by Douglas L. Wilson, (Princeton: Princeton University Press, 1989).

Jefferson's Extracts From the Gospels, edited by Dickinson W. Adams and Ruth Lester, (Princeton: Princeton University Press, 1983).

These published volumes are considered the definitive editions of Jefferson's papers, and are by far the most comprehensive. The papers in the most recent printed volumes however are not yet available on any website. And furthermore, *The Papers of Thomas Jefferson* have yet to publish many of Jefferson's papers from over fifteen years of his life in his latter years as President and in his retirement years. In this book, some Jefferson letters from these years (1803-1808 and 1816-1826) are drawn from older published editions of Jefferson's writings a century or more ago. These collections are listed below:

1. Washington, H. A. (ed.). *The Writings of Thomas Jefferson*. Washington, D.C.: Taylor & Maury, 1853-54. 9 vols.
2. Ford, Paul Leicester (ed.). *The Writings of Thomas Jefferson*. New York, London: G.P. Putnam's Sons, 1892-99. 10 vols. A commemorative edition of Ford's compilation, titled *The Works of Thomas Jefferson* (also called the "Federal Edition,") was published in 1904 and consisted of 12 volumes.
3. Lipscomb, Andrew A. and Bergh, Albert E. (ed.). *The Writings of Thomas Jefferson*. Washington, D.C.: Issued under the auspices of the Thomas Jefferson Memorial Association, 1905. There are several versions of this edition which do not differ significantly in content.

The Washington, Ford, and Lipscomb-Bergh editions, as well as most volumes of the Princeton edition are available online and collectively searchable in the Hathi Trust Digital Library.

Of most significance to the reader of this volume is over one hundred letters that were never before seen in print anywhere before Mark Beliles compiled them in 2013. That work entitled *The Selected Religious Letters and Papers of Thomas Jefferson* (Charlottesville, VA: America Publications, 2013) was invaluable for this study.

The repositories of the originals of Jefferson's papers were generous in the help and permission granted to use these documents. The repositories are listed below:

The Coolidge Collection of Thomas Jefferson Manuscripts, microfilm edition, 16 reels; Boston: Massachusetts Historical Society, 1977. (MHi)

The Thomas Jefferson Collection, Missouri History Museum Archives, St. Louis, Missouri. (MoSHi)

The Library of Virginia. (Vi)

Thomas Jefferson Papers, Special Collections Research Center, Swem Library, College of William and Mary, Williamsburg, Virginia. (ViW)

The Thomas Jefferson Papers, Manuscript Department, The Huntington Library, San Marino, California. (CSmH)

The Thomas Jefferson papers, Manuscripts and Archives Division, The New York Public Library (NN).

The Papers of Thomas Jefferson, University of Virginia, Charlottesville, Virginia. (ViU)

The two sermons by Charles Clay in the appendix is printed here by permission from the Virginia Historical Society: The Clay Family Papers (Mss 1c5795a).

INDEX

COMPANION BOOKS FOR THIS STUDY
BY MARK BELILES

The Selected Religious Letters and Papers of Thomas Jefferson

For the first time, most of Jefferson's religious correspondence and documented religious actions have been collected into one volume. *The Papers of Thomas Jefferson*, published by Princeton University, have yet to print many of Jefferson's correspondence from over fifteen years of his life. But Beliles has brought over 50 of those letters into print here for the first time ever along with many previously unpublished letters written to Jefferson from religious leaders and communities of faith. Furthermore, entries from his Memorandum Books and other documents are included. The result: over 400 religious documents valuable for scholars but also interesting to many readers in the field of Jefferson and America's founding era.

Playful in His Closet — A Complete Religious History of Thomas Jefferson

This book takes the chronological analysis in the first five chapters of *Doubting Thomas?* And presents it in far more detail with more complete letters and references to virtually every religious word and event in Jefferson's life. The result is a religious history of Jefferson that is four times the length of those five chapters and is truly the most complete religious history of Jefferson that has ever been done. Beliles analyzes over 300 clergymen and churches that Jefferson interacted with in his lifetime and includes a list of about 1100 of Jefferson's religious papers.

Free as the Air — Churches and Politics in Jefferson's Virginia, 1736-1836

This Ph.D. dissertation goes in-depth into the history of the religious communities and culture of the central Virginia piedmont in the time of Jefferson and Madison. The analysis of many local records and historical resources not readily available to the typical historian of Jefferson helps to create a clearer picture of the trends not only in religion but also in political thought and social movements of the period. Special attention is given to how Jefferson and Madison interacted and influenced these communities and vice-versa. [Originally published electronically, year 2000]

www.AmericaPublications.com

CPSIA information can be obtained at www.ICGtesting.com
Printed in the USA
LVOW11s1816301014

411261LV00002B/118/P